SECOND E

The Leadership Experience

Richard L. Daft

Owen Graduate School of Management
Vanderbilt University

With the assistance
of Pat Lane

THOMSON

SOUTH-WESTERN

Australia · Canada · Mexico · Singapore · Spain · United Kingdom · United States

To the spiritual leaders who shaped my growth and development as a leader and as a human being.

THOMSON
™
SOUTH-WESTERN

The Leadership Experience, Second Edition

Richard L. Daft

With the assistance of Pat Lane

Publisher:
Mike Roche

Acquisitions Editor:
Tracy Morse

Developmental Editor:
CJ Jasieniecki

Marketing Strategist:
Beverly Dunn

Project Manager:
Angela Williams Urquhart

Library of Congress Catalog
Card Number: 00-102500

ISBN: 0-03-033572-8

Preface

My vision for the second edition is to give students an exciting and comprehensive view of the leadership experience in today's world. The book integrates recent ideas and practices with established scholarly research in a way that makes the topic of leadership come alive. The world of leadership and organizations is undergoing a revolution, and this textbook addresses the qualities and skills leaders need in this rapidly changing world.

The emergence of e-commerce, learning organizations, virtual teams, globalization, knowledge work, and other ongoing transformations place new demands on leaders that go well beyond the ideas traditionally taught in courses on management or organizational behavior. My experiences teaching leadership to students and managers, and working with leaders to change their organizations, have affirmed for me the value of traditional leadership concepts, while highlighting the importance of including new ideas and approaches. *The Leadership Experience* thoroughly covers the history of leadership studies and the traditional theories, but goes beyond that to incorporate valuable ideas such as leadership vision, leading a learning organization, and shaping culture and values. The book expands the treatment of leadership to capture the excitement of the subject in a way that motivates students and challenges them to develop their leadership potential.

New to the Second Edition

The second edition of *The Leadership Experience* has been thoroughly revised and updated. A new chapter on The Leader as an Individual provides an in-depth look at some individual differences that can affect leadership abilities and effectiveness, including leader-related personality dimensions, values and attitudes, and cognitive differences. An exciting aspect of this chapter is an exploration of the concept of brain dominance and how leaders can develop their "whole brains" to strengthen their influence and effectiveness. The chapter on Leadership Power and Influence had been extensively revised to place more emphasis on this important topic. The chapter expands the student's understanding of how leadership differs from power, the role of dependency in power relationships, how leaders gain and use power, and the political processes leaders may use to influence others. The chapter also briefly addresses some of the ethical issues of using power.

Another important addition to the book is a consideration of e-commerce as a driving force for change in organizations and leadership. The chapter on the learning organization takes a close look at some unique challenges associated with leadership and e-commerce. The significant impact of e-commerce and information technology is also addressed throughout the text. Other concepts that have been added or expanded in this edition include self-management leadership, virtual and global teams, an expanded discussion of mental models and how leaders can broaden their thinking to be successful in a changing world, an amplified and clarified discussion of basic motivational theories, and a consideration of the negative side of change, including the difficult issue of downsizing.

The organization of the book is based on first understanding basic ways in which leaders differ from managers, and the ways leaders set direction, seek alignment between organizations and followers, build relationships, and create change. Thus the organization of this book is in five parts:

1. Introduction to leadership
2. Research perspectives on leadership
3. The personal side of leadership
4. The leader as relationship builder
5. The leader as social architect

The book integrates materials from both micro and macro approaches to leadership, from both academia and the real world, and from traditional ideas and recent thinking. This book has a number of special features that are designed to make the material accessible and valuable to students.

IN THE LEAD   This book is loaded with new examples of leaders in traditional, learning, and e-commerce organizations. Several of these examples are highlighted within each chapter, including the chapter opening examples. Opening and In the Lead spotlights include Carly Fiorina of Hewlett Packard, Herb Kelleher of Southwest Airlines, Martin Luther King, Jr., Phil Jackson of the Los Angeles Lakers, Deborah S. Kent of Ford Motor Co., John Chambers of Cisco Systems, David Pottruck of Charles Schwab & Co., Frances Hesselbein of the Drucker Foundation, Lloyd Ward of Maytag, Rear Admiral Albert H. Konetzni of the U.S. Navy, William Pollard of Service Master and Lorraine Monroe, who transformed two troubled New York city schools. The spotlights also describe leaders in new, learning organizations such as Cementos Mexicanos, Techies.com, IDEO Product Development, St. Luke's Advertising, and the virtual ad agency Host Universal. Other companies highlighted include Born Information Services, Oracle Corporation, Duval County Schools, and the U.S. Army. These spotlight examples are drawn from a wide variety of organizations including education, the military, government agencies, businesses, and not-for-profit organizations.

LIVING LEADERSHIP   Each chapter contains a Living Leadership box that is personal, compelling, real, and inspiring. This box may be a saying from a famous leader, or wisdom from the ages. Examples include "A Lesson for Leaders" (from General Colin Powell), excerpts from Nelson Mandela's inaugural speech, "Developing Character," "The Ripple Effect," "Lessons from Geese," "Discerning Feelings," "Vision's Offspring," and "Flexible or Rigid." These Living Leadership boxes provide novel and interesting material to expand the reader's thinking about the leadership experience.

LEADER'S BOOKSHELF   Each chapter also includes a review of a recent book relevant to the chapter's content. The Leader's Bookshelf connects students to issues and topics being read and discussed in the worlds of academia, business, military, education, and not-for-profit. Examples of these books include *Culture.com, The Magic of Dialogue, Mastering Virtual Teams, When Sparks Fly: Igniting Creativity in Groups, Corps Business: 30 Management Principles of the U.S. Marines, Managing with the Wisdom of Love, Maximum Leadership, PeopleSmart: Developing Your Interpersonal Intelligence,* and *The Cluetrain Manifesto.*

STUDENT DEVELOPMENT   Each chapter ends with two activities for student development. The first is a personal feedback questionnaire that assesses the student's personal standing with respect to the leadership qualities described in the chapter. These questionnaires were chosen to give students feedback on their personal progress toward leadership. Two short, problem-oriented cases for analysis are also provided at the end of each chapter. These cases test the student's ability to apply concepts when dealing with real-life leadership issues. The cases challenge the student's cognitive understanding of leadership ideas while the feedback questionnaire assesses the student's progress as a leader.

Acknowledgments

Textbook writing is a team enterprise. The book has integrated ideas and support from many people whom I want to acknowledge. I especially thank Bob Lengel, at the University of Texas at San Antonio. Bob's enthusiasm for leadership many years ago stimulated me to begin reading, teaching, and training in the area of leadership development. His enthusiasm also led to our collaboration on the book, *Fusion Leadership: Unlocking the Subtle Forces that Change People and Organizations.* I thank Bob for keeping our shared leadership dream alive, which in time enabled me to pursue my dream of writing this leadership textbook.

Here at Vanderbilt, in my new leadership role as Associate Dean at the Owen School, I want to thank my assistant, May Woods, for the tremendous volume and quality of work she accomplishes on my behalf that gives me time to write. Bill Christie, the Dean at Owen, has maintained a positive scholarly atmosphere and supported me with the time and resources needed to complete this book. I also appreciate the intellectual stimulation and support from friends and colleagues at the Owen School—Bruce Barry, Ray Friedman, Neta Moye, Rich Oliver, David Owens, and Bart Victor.

I want to acknowledge the reviewers who provided feedback and a very short turnaround. Their ideas helped me improve the book in many areas. Thanks to Shane Spiller—University of Montevallo; Dan Sherman—University of Alabama at Huntsville; Ahmad Tootonchi—Frostburg State University; Bill Service—Samford University; and Ranjna Patel—Bethune Cookman College. Also, thanks to the reviewers from the first edition: Bill Bommer—Georgia State University; Nell Hartley—Robert Morris College; and Gregory Manora—Auburn University-Montgomery.

I want to extend special thanks to my editorial associate, Pat Lane. I could not have undertaken this revision without Pat's help. She skillfully drafted materials on a variety of chapters and boxes, found sources, and did an outstanding job with last-minute changes, the copy-edited manuscript, art, and galley proofs. Pat's talent and personal enthusiasm for this text added greatly to its excellence.

The editors also deserve special mention. Tracy Morse, acquisitions editor, supported the concept for this book and obtained the resources necessary for its completion. CJ Jasieniecki, developmental editor, provided terrific support for the book's writing, reviews, copyediting, and production. Cliff Kallemeyn and the team at Clarinda Publication Services smoothly took the book through the production process.

Finally, I want to acknowledge my loving family. I received much love and support from my wife, Dorothy Marcic, and daughters, Solange and Elizabeth, here at home, and appreciate the good feelings and connections with daughters who live elsewhere. On occasion, we have been able to travel, ski, watch a play, or just be together—all of which reconnect me to things that really count.

Contents

PART THREE

The Personal Side of Leadership   115

CHAPTER 4

The Leader as an Individual   116

CHAPTER 5

Leadership Mind and Heart   164

PART ONE

Introduction to Leadership

1

What Does It Mean to Be a Leader?

CHAPTER OUTLINE

YOUR LEADERSHIP CHALLENGE

After reading this chapter, you should be able to:

- Understand the full meaning of leadership and see the leadership potential in yourself and others.

- Recognize and facilitate the five fundamental transformations in today's organizations and leaders.

- Identify the primary reasons for leadership derailment and the new paradigm skills that can help you avoid it.

- Recognize the traditional functions of management and the fundamental differences between leadership and management.

- Appreciate the crucial importance of providing direction, alignment, relationships, personal qualities, and outcomes.

What Does It Mean to Be a Leader?

When Lorraine Monroe became principal of Harlem's Frederick Douglass School (which she renamed Frederick Douglass Academy), the school was known for excessive violence, poor attendance, and low achievement. Only five years later, test scores of Frederick Douglass students ranked among the best in New York City, and 96 percent of the school's graduates went on to college.

Monroe believed in a dream and inspired others to help make it come true. She came to Frederick Douglass with a vision of turning the troubled school into one of New York City's finest. She inspired teachers and students to imagine greater possibilities for themselves and believe they could achieve them. Her Twelve Non-Negotiable Rules and Regulations, based on respect for oneself, for one's associates, and for the school, formed a code by which everyone lived. "People want to be about good things," Monroe says. "They want to believe that the work they do has meaning, some purpose beyond making a salary."

As a leader, Monroe turns a workplace into a community by making sure people are nurtured and respected. She demands the best from people and helps them achieve it. She takes every opportunity to convey new ideas, hammer home the need for change, and give people the freedom to be "creatively crazy." Monroe stresses that good businesses demand the same leadership abilities—taking risks, freeing people from the mundane, giving work meaning and purpose, and treating people with respect. It's easy for busy leaders, she says, to get further and further away from "where the magic happens," where the real work of the organization goes on.

In 1997, Monroe founded the School Leadership Academy at the Center for Educational Innovation, a business-sponsored group designed to foster creative educational leadership. In addition, she's written two books that distill the leadership lessons she has learned from more than 30 years as a teacher and principal. "I like to invent the future, to dream the next thing," she says. "That's the juice. And organizations suffer when a leader's juice is gone."[1]

What does it mean to be a leader? For Lorraine Monroe, it means being "the drum major, the person who keeps a vision in front of people."[2] It means loving the work you do and infusing others with energy and enthusiasm. Most importantly, it means building a community where people have the ability, the freedom, and the will to accomplish amazing results. Leadership makes a difference—in our schools, athletic teams, and student organizations, as well as in the business world. You may never have heard of Lorraine Monroe, but her leadership has transformed two troubled New York City schools and changed the lives of thousands of students and teachers.

When we think of leaders in today's world, we often think first of the "big names" we hear in the news—Colin Powell or Yasser Arafat in politics, Jack Welch or Bill Gates in business, Oprah Winfrey in entertainment, former president Jimmy Carter in charitable and social causes. Yet there are leaders working in every organization, large and small. In fact leadership is all around us every day, in all facets of our lives—our families, schools, communities, churches, social clubs, and volunteer organizations, as well as in the world of business and sports. The qualities that make Lorraine Monroe a good leader can be effective whether one is leading a school, a basketball team, a business, or a family.

THE NATURE OF LEADERSHIP

Before we can examine what makes an effective leader, we need to know what leadership means. Leadership has been a topic of interest to historians and philosophers since ancient times, but scientific studies began only in the twentieth century. Scholars and other writers have offered more than 350 definitions of the term "leadership," and one authority on the subject has concluded that leadership "is one of the most observed and least understood phenomena on earth."[3] Defining leadership has been a complex and elusive problem largely because the nature of leadership itself is complex. Some have even suggested that leadership is nothing more than a romantic myth, perhaps based on the false hope that someone will come along and solve our problems by force.[4] In recent years, however, much progress has been made in understanding the essential nature of leadership as a real and powerful influence in organizations and societies.

Definition of Leadership

Leadership studies are an emerging discipline and the concept of leadership will continue to evolve. For the purpose of this book, we will focus on a single definition that delineates the essential elements of the leadership process: **Leadership** is an influence relationship among leaders and followers who intend real changes and outcomes that reflect their shared purposes.[5]

The key elements in this definition are summarized in Exhibit 1.1. Leadership involves influence, it occurs among people, those people intentionally desire significant changes, and the changes reflect purposes shared by leaders and followers. *Influence* means that the relationship among people is not passive; however, also inherent in this definition is the concept that influence is multidirectional and noncoercive. The basic cultural values in North America make it easiest to think of leadership as something a leader does to a follower.[6] However, leadership is reciprocal. In most organizations, superiors influence subordinates, but subordinates also influence superiors. The people involved in the relationship want substantive *changes*—leadership involves creating change,

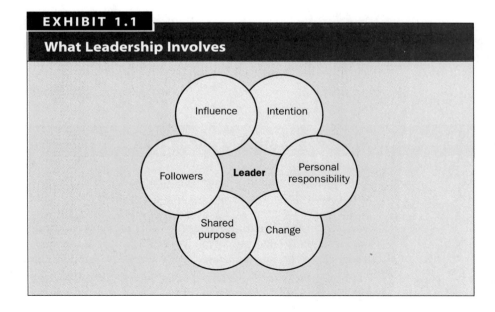

EXHIBIT 1.1

What Leadership Involves

not maintaining the status quo. In addition, the changes sought are not dictated by leaders but reflect *purposes* that leaders and followers share. Moreover, change is toward an outcome that leader and followers both want, a desired future or shared purpose that motivates them toward this more preferable outcome. An important aspect of leadership is influencing others to come together around a common vision, as Lorraine Monroe did at Frederick Douglass Academy. Thus leadership involves the influence of people to bring about change toward a desirable future.

Also, leadership is a *people* activity and is distinct from administrative paperwork or planning activities. Leadership occurs *among* people; it is not something done *to* people. Since leadership involves people, there must be *followers*. An individual performer who achieves excellence as a scientist, musician, or woodcarver may be a leader in her field of expertise, but is not a leader as it is defined in this book unless followers are involved. Followers are an important part of the leadership process, and leaders are sometimes followers. Good leaders know how to follow, and they set an example for others. The issue of *intention* or will means that people—leader and followers—are actively involved in the pursuit of change toward a desired future. Each person takes *personal responsibility* to achieve the desired future.

One stereotype is that leaders are somehow different, that they are above others; however, in reality, the qualities needed for effective leadership are the same as those needed to be an effective follower.[7] Effective followers think for themselves and carry out assignments with energy and enthusiasm. They are committed to something outside their own self-interest, and they have the courage to stand up for what they believe. Good followers are not "yes people" who blindly follow a leader. Effective leaders and effective followers may sometimes be the same people, playing different roles at different times. At its best, leadership is shared among leaders and followers, with everyone fully engaged and accepting higher levels of responsibility.

LEADERSHIP AND THE BUSINESS OF LIVING

Think for a moment about someone you personally have known that you would consider a leader—a grandparent, a supervisor, a coach, or even a fellow student. Perhaps you consider yourself a leader, or know that you want to be one. If we stop equating leadership with greatness and public visibility, it becomes easier to see our own opportunities for leadership and recognize the leadership of people we interact with every day. Leaders come in all shapes and sizes, and many true leaders are working behind the scenes. Leadership that has big outcomes often starts small.

- Thirty-three years ago, Eleanor Josaitis and her parish priest, the late Father William Cunningham, co-founded a small program to feed malnourished babies in Detroit. Staffed by volunteers and run out of a basement, the organization's goal was to make a substantive difference in the lives of disenfranchised people. Today, Focus: Hope has grown into a large, powerful organization with 850 employees and more than 50,000 volunteers. It not only feeds the hungry (48,000 people), but also runs a training program in precision machining and metalworking, sponsors a day-care center, and runs several for-profit manufacturing companies, whose plants and equipment are worth over $100 million.[8]

- Several years ago, hundreds of unarmed residents of an Argentinean farming village stormed the local police station after officials had refused to search for a missing child who was later found by villagers, raped and strangled. The siege ended only when the provincial government agreed to replace the entire police department, with the villagers allowed to name the new chief.[9] This could not have happened without leadership, and yet no one stepped forward to claim the title of "leader," and no one was able to specifically state who had provided the leadership for this initiative.

- When Jeff Davis moved to Tennessee and offered to volunteer at the Nashville Humane Association, no one ever called him for help—the organization was so understaffed and overwhelmed that it didn't know how to take advantage of the many people wanting to donate their time. Davis decided to organize a truly useful volunteer program. He created a database of people willing to volunteer, redesigned forms, computerized the mailing list, developed volunteer training, and even designed a Web page. The Association now regularly uses volunteers to do everything from cleaning smelly cages to taking puppies into nursing homes for pet therapy.[10]

- In the early 1990s, a small but determined group of political outsiders met in Washington, D.C., and began a campaign to ban land mines. The grassroots movement, spurred by Robert Muller, a Marine veteran who lost the use of his legs during the Vietnam War, seemed to have little chance of influencing anyone at all. Yet six years later, nearly 100 governments signed a treaty that outlaws land mines and requires countries to clean up those already sown. In 1997, the Nobel Peace Prize was awarded to the International Campaign to Ban Landmines, a coalition of organizations from about 60 countries.[11]

There are opportunities for leadership all around us that involve influence and change toward a desired goal or outcome. Without leadership, our families and communities, as well as our organizations, would fall apart. The leaders of to-morrow's organizations will come from anywhere and everywhere, just as they always have. You can start now, wherever you are, to practice leadership in your own life. Leadership is an everyday way of acting and thinking that has little to do with a title or formal position in an organization. As we will discuss in the following section, business leaders need to understand this tenet more than ever in the world of the twenty-first century.

THE NEW REALITY FOR TODAY'S ORGANIZATIONS

The world of organizations is changing rapidly. Globalization. Deregulation. E-commerce. Telecommuting. Virtual teams. Outsourcing. People throughout the business world are feeling the impact of these and other trends, forced to adapt to new ways of working. It takes strong leaders to effect the changes needed for survival and to guide people and organizations through the uncertainty and confusion of rapid change. Consider companies in the publishing and bookselling industry. Barnes & Noble and other bricks-and-mortar bookstores are struggling to adapt in the world of e-commerce and compete online. In addition, the emerging e-publishing industry brings even greater challenges to traditional booksellers and publishers. Stephen King's e-book, *Riding the Bullet,* sold 30,000 copies, and panels on e-publishing drew standing-room-only crowds at the 2000 BookExpo America. Ken Brooks, vice president of digital content for Barnes & Noble, says leaders are striving to position the company to compete as the industry shifts "from 'p-books' to e-books over the next five years."[12] The environment for all organizations is changing fast and leaders are responsible for positioning their organizations for a new reality.

The world today is undergoing a change more profound and far-reaching than any experienced since the dawn of the modern age and the scientific revolution about 500 years ago. Rapid environmental changes are causing fundamental transformations that have a dramatic impact on organizations and present new challenges for leadership.[13] The transformations represent a shift from a traditional to a new paradigm, as outlined in Exhibit 1.2. A **paradigm** is a shared mind-set that represents a fundamental way of thinking about, perceiving, and understanding our world.

Although many leaders are still operating from an old-paradigm mind-set, as outlined in the left-hand column of Exhibit 1.2, they are increasingly ineffective in today's world. As more and more work becomes knowledge- and information-based, leaders have to take a new approach. Effective and successful leaders in the twenty-first century will respond to the new reality outlined in the right-hand column of the exhibit.

EXHIBIT 1.2

The New Reality for Leadership

OLD Paradigm	NEW Paradigm
Industrial Age	Information Age
Stability	Change
Control	Empowerment
Competition	Collaboration
Things	People and relationships
Uniformity	Diversity

From Cherishing Stability to Valuing Change

Today's world is in constant motion, and organizations suffer when their leaders cherish stability. In the past, many leaders assumed that if they could just keep things running on a steady, even keel, the organization would be successful. Maintaining stability was considered a cost-saving and energy-efficient way of doing business, and change was perceived to disrupt operations and exhaust resources.[14] However, as the pace of change has accelerated in recent years, leaders have recognized that trying to maintain stability is a losing battle. It actually takes tremendous energy and resources to try to keep things stable. The new paradigm recognizes that, as suggested by the science of chaos theory, we live in a complex world characterized by randomness and uncertainty and small events often have massive and far-reaching consequences. For example, a seemingly insignificant lawsuit against AT&T some years ago had far-reaching effects, resulting in the emergence of MCI, Sprint, and other long-distance carriers and ultimately creating a whole new world of telecommunications.

Technological advances and globalization have significantly increased the rate and the impact of change for today's companies. Communications around the world are instant, products can be shipped anywhere within a matter of days, and consumer tastes are converging in everything from clothing to cellular phones. Worldwide events that may change rapidly and unpredictably can cause dramatic effects for every organization, large and small.[15]

The system of life—and organizations—is fluid, dynamic, and potentially self-renewing. Today's best leaders are learning to "go with the flow," to accept the inevitability of constant change and recognize change itself as a potential source of energy. They see change as an opportunity for something better, and they cherish the ongoing development of individual workers and of the organization itself. Beyond accepting change, they embrace and create it, realizing that the benefits associated with stability are a myth; that when things do not change, they die.

From Control to Empowerment

Leaders in powerful positions once thought workers should be told what to do, how to do it, when to do it, and who to do it with. They believed strict control was needed for the organization to function efficiently and effectively. Rigid organizational hierarchies, structured jobs and work processes, and detailed, inviolate procedures let everyone know that those at the top had power and those at the bottom had none. Today, the old assumptions about the distribution of power are no longer valid.

People are demanding empowerment and participation in their lives, including their work, and the emphasis on control and rigidity serves to squelch motivation and morale rather than produce desired results. Today's leaders need to share power rather than hoard it and find ways to increase an organization's brain power by getting everyone in the organization involved and committed.

One reason for this is that the financial basis of today's economy is rapidly becoming *information* rather than the tangible assets of land, buildings, and machines. This means that the primary factor of production is human knowledge, which increases the power of employees. The educational and skill level of employees in the United States and other developed countries has steadily increased over the past several decades, and many people are no longer satisfied working in an organization that doesn't give them opportunities to participate and learn. For example, today's highly educated, computer-literate knowledge workers (often called gold-collar workers) are demanding not only good salaries but also interesting and challenging jobs, training and development opportunities, and the chance to fully use their minds and abilities without being hampered by strict rules and tight top-down control.[16]

When all the organization needed was workers to run machines eight hours a day, traditional command-and-control systems generally worked quite well, but the organization received no benefit from employees' minds. Frank Ostroff, who took a summer job at a tire-making factory as a college student, recalled: "We'd spend eight hours a day doing something completely mindless. . . . And then these same people would go home and spend their evenings and weekends rebuilding entire cars from scratch or running volunteer organizations."[17] No longer can organizations afford to have workers check their minds at the door. Success depends on the intellectual capacity of all employees, and leaders have to face a hard fact: Buildings and machines can be owned; people cannot. One of the leader's most challenging jobs is to guide workers in using their own power effectively and responsibly by creating and developing a climate of respect and development for all employees.[18] Power lies more in the strength and quality of relationships rather than in titles, policies, and procedures.

From Competition to Collaboration

The move to empowerment also ties directly into new ways of working that emphasize collaboration over competition and conflict. Although some companies still encourage internal competition and aggressiveness, most of today's organizations are stressing teamwork and cooperation. Self-directed teams and other forms of horizontal collaboration are breaking down boundaries between departments and helping to spread knowledge and information throughout the organization. Compromise and sharing are recognized as signs of strength, not weakness. The concept of *knowledge management,* which relies on a culture of sharing rather than hoarding information, has taken firm hold in many companies.[19]

Some competition can be healthy for an organization, but many leaders are resisting the idea of competition as a struggle to win while someone else loses. Instead, they direct everyone's competitive energy toward being the best that they can be. There is a growing trend toward reducing boundaries and increasing collaboration with other organizations, so that companies think of themselves as teams that create value jointly rather than as autonomous entities in competition with all others.[20] A new form of global business, the "relationship enterprise," is made up of networks of independent companies that share financial risks and leadership talents and provide access to one another's technologies and markets.[21]

The move to collaboration presents greater challenges to business leaders than did the old concept of competition. Within the organization, leaders will need to create an environment of teamwork and community that fosters collaboration and mutual support. The call for empowerment, combined with an understanding of organizations as part of a fluid, dynamic, interacting system, makes the use of intimidation and manipulation obsolete as a means of driving the competitive spirit.

From Things to Relationships

The increase in collaboration both within and among organizations reflects another fundamental transformation—a shift from an emphasis on things to an emphasis on relationships. Most of our existing ideas about organizations and leadership are based on an industrial-age paradigm that treats the world as a machine that can be taken apart and examined piece by piece—every object can be identified, described, and measured. Broken parts can be fixed or replaced and everything keeps running smoothly. This paradigm has translated into a view of organizations as a conglomeration of "things." The new paradigm, however, takes its cue from quantum physics and ecology, which tell us that some phenomena can be understood only in relation to other phenomena, and that everything is connected to everything else.[22] In this view, the world is perceived as a complex, dynamic system where reality lies not in discrete parts, but in the relationships among them. Thus, leaders will look at their "reality" in a whole new light. Rather than operating on a yes-or-no, black-or-white basis, they will learn to deal with the gray areas—the nuances, subtleties, and possibilities inherent in relationships. Rather than focusing on segments, they will focus on the whole. The dominant image of the organization will be not as a machine, but as a living system or a web of interaction. The Leader's Bookshelf box describes how the new sciences are transforming the view of leadership.

When we think about our personal lives, we have little difficulty understanding that we act and feel differently depending on the situation—who we are with, what we are doing. Yet transferring this understanding to the organization may be one of the greatest challenges for leaders of tomorrow. Whereas objects are concrete and unchanging, relationships are intangible and ever-shifting. It is somehow comforting to conceptualize the organization as a machine that leaders only have to keep oiled. The reality for today is much more challenging, and much more interesting.

From Uniformity to Diversity

Many of today's organizations were built on assumptions of uniformity, separation, and specialization. People who think alike, act alike, and have similar job skills are grouped into a department, such as accounting or manufacturing, separate from other departments. Homogenous groups find it easy to get along, communicate, and understand one another. The uniform thinking that arises, however, can be a disaster in a world becoming more multinational and diverse.

Robert Swan, a modern-day explorer and the first person ever to walk to both the North and South Poles, stresses the importance of team diversity when facing extreme conditions: "If everybody is the same, you won't have the diversity that you need to survive. You need to have different attitudes, different ways of thinking and doing things."[23] You'll hear more about Swan's leadership in the next chapter.

Although they weren't facing life-or-death situations, two business school graduates in their twenties also discovered the importance of diversity when they started a specialized advertising firm. They worked hard, and as the

Leadership and the New Science

Margaret J. Wheatley

In searching for a better understanding of organizations and leadership, Margaret Wheatley looked to science for answers. In the world of Newtonian physics, every atom moves in a unique predictable trajectory determined by the forces exerted on it. Prediction and control are accomplished by reducing wholes into discrete parts and carefully regulating the forces that act on those parts. Applied to organizations, this view of the world led to rigid vertical hierarchies, division of labor, task descriptions, and strict operating procedures designed to obtain predictable, controlled results.

Just as Newton's laws broke down as physics explored ever-smaller elements of matter and ever-wider expanses of the universe, rigid, control-oriented organizations don't work well in a world of instant information, constant change, and global competition. The physical sciences responded to the failure of Newtonian physics with a new paradigm called quantum mechanics. In *Leadership and the New Science,* Wheatley explores how leaders are redesigning organizations to survive in a quantum world.

Chaos, Relationships, and Fields

From quantum mechanics and chaos theory emerge new understandings of order, disorder, and change. Individual actions, whether by atoms or people, cannot be easily predicted and controlled. Here's why:

- Nothing exists except in relationship to everything else. It is not things, but the relationships among them that are the key determinants of a well-ordered system we perceive. Order emerges through a web of relationships that make up the whole, not as a result of controls on individual parts.

- The empty space between things is filled with fields, invisible material that connects elements together. In organizations, the fields that bind people include vision, shared values, culture, and information.

- Organizations, like all open systems, grow and change in reaction to disequilibrium, and disorder can be a source of new order.

Implications for Leadership

These new understandings provide a new way to see, understand, and lead today's organizations. The new sciences can influence leaders to:

- Nurture relationships and the fields between people with a clear vision, statements of values, expressions of caring, the sharing of information, and freedom from strict rules and controls.

- Focus on the whole, not on the parts in isolation.

- Reduce boundaries between departments and organizations to allow new patterns of relationships.

- Become comfortable with uncertainty and recognize that any solutions are only temporary, specific to the immediate context, and developed through the relationship of people and circumstances.

- Recognize that healthy growth of people and organizations is found in disequilibrium, not in stability.

Wheatley believes leaders can learn from the new sciences how to lead in today's fast-paced, chaotic world, suggesting that "we can forego the despair created by such common organization events as change, chaos, information overload, and cyclical behaviors if we recognize that organizations are conscious entities, possessing many of the properties of living systems."

Leadership and the New Science, by Margaret J. Wheatley, is published by Berrett-Koehler Publishers.

firm grew, they hired more people just like themselves—bright, young, intense college graduates, committed and hard-working. The firm grew to about 20 employees over two and a half years, but the expected profits never materialized. The two entrepreneurs could never get a handle on what was wrong, and the firm slid into bankruptcy. Convinced the idea was still valid, they started over, but with a new philosophy. They sought employees with different ages, ethnic backgrounds, and work experience. People had different styles, yet the organization seemed to work better. People played different roles, and the diverse experiences of the group enabled the firm to respond to unique situations and handle a variety of organizational and personal needs. The advertising firm is growing again, and this time it is also making a profit.

The world is rapidly moving toward diversity at both national and international levels. In the United States, roughly 45 percent of all net additions to the labor force for the next few years will be non-white—half of these will be first-generation immigrants, mostly from Asian and Latin countries. Almost two-thirds will be female. Bringing diversity into the organization is the way to attract the best human talent and to develop an organizational mind-set broad enough to thrive in a multinational world. Organizations suffer when their leaders don't respond to today's diverse environment. For example, the reputations of well-known companies such as Coca-Cola, Texaco, and Jenny Craig have been tarnished by charges of racial or sexual discrimination.

COMPARING MANAGEMENT AND LEADERSHIP

The shift from an old to a new paradigm, outlined in Exhibit 1.2 and discussed in the previous section, also reflects a shift from a traditional, rational management approach that emphasizes stability and control to a leadership approach that values change, empowerment, and relationships. In the old paradigm, a traditional management approach worked well, but the new paradigm requires that managers also become effective leaders. Managers can make the transition to a new paradigm, as David Pottruck learned at Charles Schwab & Co.

IN THE LEAD   David Pottruck, Charles Schwab & Co.

David Pottruck, now co-CEO of Charles Schwab & Co., spent years thinking the only thing that mattered was bottom-line results. He rose quickly through the ranks in the financial services industry by getting things done and keeping companies on a steady course. The only problem was that Pottruck paid little attention to what effect his strict, demanding approach had on his staff. He issued orders and expected them to be carried out—no questions, no excuses. "I emitted a vibe of 'Don't come to me with your problems,'" Pottruck now says. His intense, hard-charging style worked just fine for years, but an interesting thing happened after Pottruck joined Charles Schwab & Co.—he learned that being a hard-nosed, competitive manager was actually hurting his company. As the nature of the financial services industry changed, Pottruck found that he needed to put more emphasis on people than on profits.

Pottruck's transformation began when founder and chairman Chuck Schwab confronted him and told him he was a "divisive executive." Schwab & Co. has always been a company based on putting customers and employees first and worrying about profits later. An executive trying to ram decisions down people's throats and pushing his staff until they dropped just didn't fly at Schwab. In addition, Schwab wanted to put the emerging Internet at the very heart of its business, and doing so required leaders who were collaborative rather than competitive, who could inspire and energize rather than divide people.

Pottruck took the message to heart, even hiring a consultant to help him shift to a softer, collaborative approach that valued the input and ideas of others. He began to direct his competitive drive outward toward Schwab's competitors rather than inward toward his staff and colleagues. He learned to listen and began preaching the message that there's more to life than work and more to work than making money. He embraced the importance of corporate culture and began looking for ways to instill a sense of passion and meaning and commitment in employees' work lives. By the time Pottruck's transformation was complete, employees throughout the company were talking about his inspiring leadership, how he kept them fired up about working for Schwab.[24]

Importantly, Pottruck was evolving as a leader at just the right time to help lead Charles Schwab & Co. into the world of e-commerce. By changing *himself*, Pottruck also helped transform his company into the dominant player in online financial services. Executives like David Pottruck have embraced the new reality and combined leadership qualities with rational management skills.

Let's begin our adventure into the study of leadership by considering what distinguishes the process of leadership from that of management. **Management** can be defined as the attainment of organizational goals in an effective and efficient manner through planning, organizing, staffing, directing, and controlling organizational resources. Much has been written in recent years about the difference between management and leadership. Unfortunately, with the current emphasis on the need for leadership, managers have gotten a bad name.[25] Managers and leaders are not inherently different types of people, and many managers already possess the abilities and qualities needed to be effective leaders in today's world. Leadership cannot replace management; it should be *in addition* to management. General Electric's Jack Welch (set to retire at the end of 2001) is one of the best-known examples of a business executive who combines good management and effective leadership.[26] Welch clearly understands and practices good management, such as controlling costs, establishing goals and plans, providing coordination, and monitoring company activities and performance. Yet he is also a master leader, actively promoting change, communicating a vision, providing a clear sense of direction, and energizing and inspiring employees. There are many other less-celebrated managers in today's organizations who are also good leaders, and most people can develop the qualities needed for effective leadership.

Exhibit 1.3 compares management to leadership in five areas crucial to organizational performance—providing direction, aligning employees, building relationships, personal qualities, and leader outcomes.[27]

EXHIBIT 1.3

Comparing Management and Leadership

	Management	Leadership
Direction:	Planning and budgeting Keeping eye on bottom line	Creating vision and strategy Keeping eye on horizon
Alignment:	Organizing and staffing Directing and controlling Create boundaries	Creating shared culture and values Helping others grow Reduce boundaries

Relationships:	Focusing on objects—producing/
	  selling goods and services
	Based on position power
	Acting as boss
		Focusing on people—inspiring
		  and motivating followers
		Based on personal power
		Acting as coach, facilitator, servant

Personal Qualities:	Emotional distance Expert mind Talking Conformity Insight into organization	Emotional connections (Heart) Open mind (Mindfulness) Listening (Communication) Nonconformity (Courage) Insight into self (Integrity)
Outcomes:	Maintains stability	Creates change, often radical change

SOURCES: John P. Kotter, *Leading Change* (Boston, MA: Harvard Business School Press, 1996), 26; Joseph C. Rost, *Leadership for the Twenty-first Century*, (Westport, CT: Praeger, 1993), 149; and Brian Dumaine, "The New Non-Manager Managers," *Fortune*, February 22, 1993, 80–84.

Providing Direction

Both leadership and management are concerned with providing direction for the organization, but there are differences. Management focuses on establishing detailed plans and schedules for achieving specific results, then allocating resources to accomplish the plan. Leadership calls for creating a compelling vision of the future and developing farsighted strategies for producing the changes needed to achieve that vision. Whereas management calls for keeping an eye on the bottom line and short-term results, leadership means keeping an eye on the horizon and the long-term future.

A **vision** is a picture of an ambitious, desirable future for the organization or team.[28] It can be as lofty as Motorola's aim to "become the premier company in the world" or as down-to-earth as the Swedish company IKEA's simple vision "to provide affordable furniture for people with limited budgets." Recall that Lorraine Monroe had a vision of transforming Frederick Douglass School from one of New York City's worst to one of its best.

To be compelling for followers, the vision has to be one they can relate to and share. In *Fortune* magazine's study of the "100 Best Companies to Work for in America," two of the recurring traits of great companies were a powerful, visionary leader and a sense of purpose beyond increasing shareholder value. At Medtronic, for example, which makes pacemakers and other medical devices, company leaders stress the vision of "restoring patients to full life." Rather than concentrating on shareholders or doctors, workers at Medtronic are told to focus on the people who will actually have the company's devices implanted inside them. Workers who are inspired and motivated to help sick people get well have made the company's total return to shareholders great too.[29]

Alignment

Management entails organizing a structure to accomplish the plan; staffing the structure with employees; and developing policies, procedures, and systems to direct employees and monitor implementation of the plan. Managers are thinkers and workers are doers. Leadership is concerned instead with communicating the vision and developing a shared culture and set of core values that can lead to the desired future state. This involves others as thinkers, doers, and leaders themselves, fostering a sense of ownership in everyone.[30] Whereas the vision describes the destination, the culture and values help define the journey toward it. Leadership focuses on getting everyone lined up in the same direction. Gertrude Boyle, a housewife and mother who took charge of Columbia Sportswear after her husband's early death, created a comfortable, down-to-earth corporate culture that propelled the outdoor clothing manufacturer from sales of $800,000 to just under $300 million. She came into the company with no business experience, but says: "Running a company is like raising kids. You all have to be in the same line of thinking."[31]

Managers often organize by separating people into specialties and functions, with boundaries separating them by department and hierarchical level. Leaders break down boundaries so people know what others are doing, can coordinate easily, and feel a sense of teamwork and equalness for achieving outcomes.

Rather than simply directing and controlling employees to achieve specific results, leaders "align [people] with broader ideas of what the company should be and why."[32] Leaders encourage people to expand their minds and abilities and to assume responsibility for their own actions. Think about classes you have taken at your college or university. In some college classes, the professor tells students exactly what to do and how to do it, and many students expect this kind of direction and control. Have you ever had a class where the instructor instead inspired and encouraged you and your classmates to find innovative ways to meet goals? The difference reflects a rational management versus a leadership approach. Whereas the management communication process generally involves providing answers and solving problems, leadership entails asking questions, listening, and involving others.[33]

Relationships

In terms of relationships, management focuses on objects such as machines and reports, on taking the steps needed to produce the organization's goods and services. Leadership, on the other hand, focuses on motivating and inspiring people.

Whereas the management relationship is based on formal authority, leadership is a relationship based on personal influence. Formal **position power** means that there is a written, spoken, or implied contract wherein people accept either a superior or subordinate role and see the use of coercive as well as noncoercive behavior as an acceptable way to achieve desired results.[34] For example, in an authority relationship, both people accept that a manager can tell a subordinate to be at work at 7:30 A.M. or her pay will be docked. Leadership, on the other hand, relies on influence, which is less likely to use coercion. Followers are empowered to make many decisions on their own. Leadership strives to make work stimulating and challenging and involves pulling rather than pushing people toward goals. The role of leadership is to attract and energize people, motivating them through identification rather than rewards or punishments.[35] The formal position of authority in the organization is the source of management power, but leadership power comes from the personal characteristics of the leader. Leadership does not require that one hold a formal position of authority, and many people holding positions of authority do not provide leadership. The differing source of power is one of the key distinctions between management and leadership. Take away a manager's formal position and will people choose to follow him? Leadership truly depends on who you are rather than on your position or title.

Personal Leadership Qualities

Leadership is more than a set of skills; it relies on a number of subtle personal qualities that are hard to see but are very powerful. These include things like enthusiasm, integrity, courage, and humility. First of all, good leadership springs from a genuine passion for the work and a genuine concern for other people. Great leaders are people who love what they do and want to share that love with others. The process of management generally encourages emotional distance, but leadership means being emotionally connected to others. Where there is leadership, people become part of a community and feel that they are contributing to something worthwhile.[36] This chapter's Living Leadership emphasizes the importance of being emotionally connected to followers.

Whereas management means providing answers and solving problems, leadership requires the courage to admit mistakes and doubts, to take risks, to listen, and to trust and learn from others. Emotional connections are risky but necessary for true leadership to happen. George Sparks, a graduate of the Air Force Academy and general manager of Hewlett-Packard's measuring-equipment business, says he learned this from a Girl Scout leader.

LIVING LEADERSHIP

A Lesson for Leaders

Lesson # 2 from General Colin Powell: "The day soldiers stop bringing you their problems is the day you have stopped leading them. They have either lost confidence that you can help them or concluded that you do not care. Either case is a failure of leadership."

If this were a litmus test, the majority of CEOs would fail. One, they build so many barriers to upward communication that the very idea of someone lower in the hierarchy looking up to the leader for help is ludicrous. Two, the corporate culture they foster often defines asking for help as weakness or failure, so people cover up their gaps, and the organization suffers accordingly. Real leaders make themselves accessible and available. They show concern for the efforts and challenges faced by [followers], even as they demand high standards. Accordingly, they are more likely to create an environment where problem analysis replaces blame.

SOURCE: General Colin Powell, Chairman (Ret.), Joint Chiefs of Staff, "A Leadership Primer."

IN THE LEAD   Frances Hesselbein and the Girl Scout Way

"The best two days of my career" is how George Sparks describes the time he spent following Frances Hesselbein around. Hesselbein is currently Chairman of the Board of the Drucker Foundation, a small organization dedicated to sharing the leadership thinking of Peter Drucker with other nonprofits. She began her career more than 41 years ago as a volunteer Scout leader. She eventually rose to CEO of the Girl Scouts, inheriting a troubled organization of 680,000 people, only 1 percent of whom were paid employees. By the time she retired in 1990, Hesselbein had turned around declining membership, dramatically increased participation by minorities, and replaced a brittle hierarchy with one of the most vibrant organizations in the nonprofit or business world.

Hesselbein describes how she works with others as a circle in which everyone is included. As Sparks observed her in action, the most compelling quality he noted was her ability to sense people's needs on an emotional level. He explains, "Time and again, I have seen people face two possible solutions. One is 20 percent better, but the other meets their personal needs—and that is the one they inevitably choose." He noticed that Hesselbein would listen carefully and then link people in such a way that their personal needs were met at the same time they were serving the needs of the organization. Hesselbein recognizes that the only way to achieve high performance is through the work of others, and she consistently treats people with care and respect.

Her definition of leadership, she says, was "very hard to arrive at, very painful. . . . [It] is not a basket of tricks or skills. It is the quality and character and courage of the person who is the leader. It's a matter of ethics and moral compass, the willingness to remain highly vulnerable."[37]

As Frances Hesselbein noted, developing leadership qualities can be painful. Abraham Zaleznik has referred to leaders as "twice-born personalities," who struggle to develop their sense of self through psychological and social change.[38] For leadership to happen, leaders have to know who they are and what they stand for. And they remain constant so followers know what to expect. A recent study revealed that people would much rather follow individuals they can count on, even when they disagree with their viewpoint, than people they agree with but who frequently shift their viewpoints or positions.[39] One employee described the kind of person she would follow as this: ". . . it's like they have a stick down through the center of them that's rooted in the ground. I can tell when someone has that. When they're not defensive, not egotistical. They're open-minded, able to joke and laugh at themselves. They can take a volatile situation and stay focused. They bring out the best in me by making me want to handle myself in the same way. I want to be part of their world."[40]

True leaders draw on a number of subtle but powerful forces within themselves. For example, leaders tend to have an open mind that welcomes new ideas rather than a closed mind that criticizes new ideas. Leaders tend to care about others and build personal connections rather than maintain emotional distance. Leaders listen and discern what people want and need more than they talk to give advice and orders. Leaders are willing to be nonconformists, to disagree and say no when it serves the larger good, and to accept nonconformity from others rather than try to squeeze everyone into the same mind-set. They and others step outside the traditional boundary and comfort zone, take risks, and make mistakes to learn and grow. Moreover, leaders are honest with themselves and others to the point of inspiring trust. They set high moral standards by doing the right thing, rather than just going along with standards set by others. Leadership causes wear and tear on the individual, because leaders are vulnerable, take risks, and initiate change, which typically encounters resistance.

Outcomes

The differences between management and leadership create two differing outcomes, as illustrated at the bottom of Exhibit 1.3. Management produces a degree of stability, predictability, order, and efficiency. Thus, good management helps the organization consistently achieve short-term results and meet the expectations of various stakeholders. Leadership, on the other hand, creates change, often to a dramatic degree. For example, Hans Becherer, CEO of Deere & Co., is inspiring employees with his vision of transforming Deere from an equipment maker into an information-age company. Deere is building an information network that gives farmers real-time information on weather and soil conditions in different parts of their fields, enabling them to treat each part as needed for maximum productivity. Becherer's leadership is not only expanding Deere's customer base, but could also remake the entire agricultural industry.[41]

Leadership means questioning and challenging the status quo so that outdated or unproductive norms can be replaced to meet new challenges. Good leadership can lead to extremely valuable change, such as new products or services that gain new customers or expand markets. Thus, although good management is needed to help organizations meet current commitments, good leadership is needed to move the organization into the future.

WHERE HAVE ALL THE LEADERS GONE?

As the world changes, organizations and leaders are beginning to change in response. Yet we are still in a transition period between the old and the new, which partly explains why we often hear talk about a current "leadership crisis." Many business schools still teach a rational management approach, but executives working in real-life organizations know that today's companies need people who can unite rational management skills with the ability to provide effective leadership. In a survey of executives with the United States' 1,000 largest corporations, nearly half of respondents listed leadership ability as the most important attribute of a manager today, with an additional 37 percent ranking communication and interpersonal skills at the top of their list.[42]

Just a few decades ago, the business world seemed full of powerful leaders who were capable of taking their organizations to prosperity. When the world was more stable, the rational control model was productive. Today, it is increasingly counterproductive, and the world is searching for leaders of a new kind.[43] Management and leadership are both important to organizations. Traditional management is needed to help meet current obligations to customers, stockholders, employees, and others. But organizations also need strong leadership to visualize the future, motivate and inspire employees, and adapt to changing needs. The problem for today's organizations is that there are too many people doing management, too few providing leadership, and fewer still who have integrated the skills and qualities needed for meeting both leadership and management challenges.

EXHIBIT 1.4

Today's Management-Leadership Mix

		LEADERSHIP	
		Weak	Strong
MANAGEMENT	Strong	Too many	Almost none
	Weak	Too many	Too few

SOURCE: Based on John P. Kotter, *A Force for Change: How Leadership Differs from Management* (New York: The Free Press, 1990)

Nearly two-thirds of respondents in one survey reported that their organizations had too many people who were strong in management but weak in leadership, prompting researcher Warren Bennis to suggest that many of today's corporations are "over-managed and under-led."[44] As illustrated in Exhibit 1.4, today's organizations have insufficient leadership and are particularly bereft of people who can provide both good management and good leadership.

LEADERSHIP IS NOT AUTOMATIC

Many leaders are caught in the transition between the practices and principles that defined the industrial era and the new reality of the twenty-first century. Attempts to achieve collaboration, empowerment, and diversity in organizations may fail because the beliefs and thought processes of leaders as well as employees are stuck in an old paradigm that values control, stability, and homogeneity. It is difficult for many leaders to let go of the methods and practices that have made them and their organizations successful in the past. For example, at W. W. Grainger Inc., leaders recognized that they were still operating from their old command-and-control mind-set even though they espoused empowerment and collaboration.

IN THE LEAD   W. W. Grainger Inc.

"If, as leaders, we put ourselves on a pedestal above it all, that sends a dangerous message to employees," says Wes Clark, a member of W. W. Grainger's top leadership team. However, even though Grainger's leaders talked about equality, empowerment, and participation, they were still relying on the command-and-control habits their training and careers had taught them. Clark and others knew that needed to change if Grainger, a large distributor of maintenance, repair, and operating supplies based in Lincolnshire, Illinois, was to have the flexibility and employee commitment to fend off new competition.

The leadership team decided to use a symbolic event to kick off a change campaign. Called "Painting Our Future," the companywide meeting was designed as a set resembling an artist's studio, with drop cloths, paint cans, and a giant, blank canvas on which employees would help to "paint" the company's new cultural values. Every aspect of the meeting was aimed at breaking long-held habits and preconceptions. One important session had the top leadership team answering questions from employees. Sounds like pretty standard stuff, but the kicker was that the session was moderated by John Callaway, a respected journalist and host of a PBS public affairs show. After hearing the CEO's answer to the first audience question, Callaway turned to him and said, "That sounds like management-speak to me." Although he was momentarily stunned, the CEO realized that he had slipped into using habitual jargon rather than answering the question openly and honestly. Because top leaders were willing to question their own beliefs and habits and put themselves on the firing line, employees responded more easily when managers asked them to question everything about how Grainger does business and find new and better ways of working.

One meeting can't change a leader, or a company culture, but "Painting Our Future" set W. W. Grainger on a new course. It has revived employees' sense of initiative, trust, imagination, and commitment. And that, in turn, has helped Grainger compete with smaller, more aggressive companies in the industry.[45]

Leaders at W. W. Grainger continue to look for ways to encourage collaboration, the sharing of information and knowledge, and continuous change. Although leaders may sometimes slip into old habits, employees now feel free to point out when leaders aren't living up to their espoused ideals and values.

A few clues about the importance of acquiring new leadership skills were brought to light by the Center for Creative Leadership in Greensboro, North Carolina.[46] The study compared twenty-one derailed executives with twenty executives who successfully arrived at the top of a company. The derailed managers were successful people who were expected to go far, but they reached a plateau, were fired, or were forced to retire early. They were all bright, worked hard, and excelled in a technical area such as accounting or engineering.

The striking difference between the two groups was the ability to use human skills, the essence of the new leadership paradigm. Only 25 percent of the derailed group were described as being good with people, whereas 75 percent of those who arrived at the top had people skills. The top seven reasons for failure are listed in Exhibit 1.5. Unsuccessful managers were insensitive to others, abrasive, cold, arrogant, untrustworthy, overly ambitious and selfish, unable to delegate or build teams, and unable to acquire appropriate staff to work for them. These managers did not thrive in rapidly changing organizations moving into the new paradigm. For example, one derailed manager was a superb engineer who bogged down in details and tended to lose composure under stress.

Bill Prince says his fast-track career at Bell South ground to a halt because of his lack of human skills. He admits that he was a "brusque and unfeeling" manager who praised people infrequently, treated subordinates coldly, and publicly demeaned employees for their mistakes. Today, however, thanks to

EXHIBIT 1.5

Top 7 Reasons for Executive Derailment

1. Insensitive, abrasive, intimidating, bullying style
2. Cold, aloof, arrogant
3. Betrayal of personal trust
4. Overly ambitious, self-centered, thinking of next job, playing politics
5. Specific performance problems with the business
6. Overmanaging: unable to delegate or build a team
7. Unable to select good subordinates

the advice of a former colleague and an intensive leadership development program, Prince has made the shift to a new kind of leader. As CEO of his own company, he focuses on building and maintaining good relationships with employees as well as clients. Rather than looking at people as instruments to get things done through, Prince considers their feelings and needs, which is helping him build a stronger company.[47]

Human skills are increasingly important for leaders in today's economy. Organizations frequently lose good employees because of front-line bosses who fail to show respect and concern for workers. As one engineering manager who walked away from a generous pay package and several thousand stock options because of an overbearing supervisor put it, "There are too many great jobs available in the market today to put up with this sort of crap."[48]

Interestingly, even people who do make it to the top of organizations sometimes fail in the role of CEO because of poor human skills, particularly the inability to select good people and help them learn and contribute. The best leaders are those who are deeply interested in others and can bring out the best in them.[49] In the new paradigm, leaders put people first. In addition, today's successful leaders value change over stability, empowerment over control, collaboration over competition, relationships over things, and diversity over uniformity, as discussed earlier.

A study by Korn/Ferry International of changes in the business environment forecasts that the all-powerful, controlling boss—or "controllasaurus"—will be extinct within the next decade.[50] The old ways no longer work and the new ways are just emerging. Everywhere, we hear the cry for leadership.

LEARNING THE ART AND SCIENCE OF LEADERSHIP

Leadership is both an art and a science. It is an art because many leadership skills and qualities cannot be learned from a textbook. Leadership takes practice and hands-on experience. However, knowing about leadership research helps people analyze situations from a variety of perspectives and learn how to be more effective as leaders. Leadership is considered a science as well as an art because a growing body of knowledge and objective facts describes the leadership process and how to use leadership skills to attain organizational goals.

How can a book or a course on leadership help you be a leader? By exploring leadership in both business and society, students gain an understanding of the importance of leadership to an organization's success, as well as the difficulties and challenges involved in being a leader. Studying leadership can also lead to the discovery of abilities you never knew you had. When students in a leadership seminar at Wharton were asked to pick one leader to represent the class, one woman was surprised when she outpolled all other students. Her leadership was drawn out not in the practice of leadership in student government, volunteer activities, or athletics, but in a classroom setting.[51]

Studying leadership gives you skills you can apply in the practice of leadership in your everyday life. Many people have never tried to be a leader because they have no understanding of what leaders actually do. The chapters in this book are designed to help you gain a firm knowledge of what leadership means and some of the skills and qualities that make a good leader. You can build competence in both the art and science of leadership by working on the exercises and cases at the end of each chapter, and by applying the concepts you learn in class, in your relationships with others, in student groups, at work, and in voluntary organizations. Although this book and your instructors can guide you in your development, only you can apply the concepts and principles of leadership in your daily life. Learning to be a leader starts now, with you. Are you up to the challenge?

Rest of the Book

The plan for this book reflects the shift to a new paradigm summarized in Exhibit 1.2 and the discussion of management versus leadership summarized in Exhibit 1.3. The framework in Exhibit 1.6 illustrates the organization of the book. Part One introduces leadership, its importance, and the transition to a new leadership paradigm. Part Two explores basic research perspectives that evolved during a more stable time when rational management approaches were effective. These basic perspectives, including the Great Man and trait theories, behavior theories, and contingency theories, are relevant to dealing with spe-

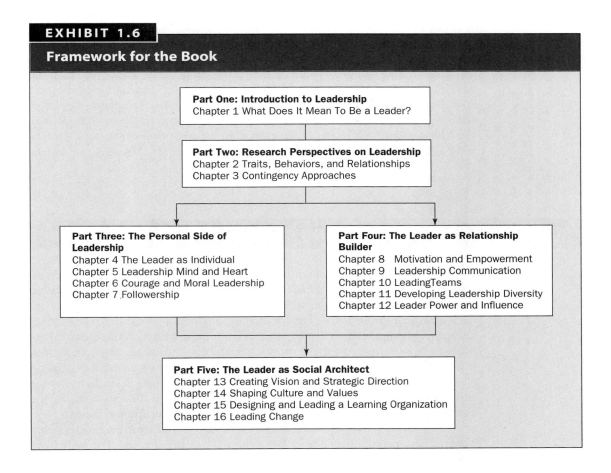

EXHIBIT 1.6

Framework for the Book

Part One: Introduction to Leadership
Chapter 1 What Does It Mean To Be a Leader?

Part Two: Research Perspectives on Leadership
Chapter 2 Traits, Behaviors, and Relationships
Chapter 3 Contingency Approaches

Part Three: The Personal Side of Leadership
Chapter 4 The Leader as Individual
Chapter 5 Leadership Mind and Heart
Chapter 6 Courage and Moral Leadership
Chapter 7 Followership

Part Four: The Leader as Relationship Builder
Chapter 8   Motivation and Empowerment
Chapter 9   Leadership Communication
Chapter 10 LeadingTeams
Chapter 11 Developing Leadership Diversity
Chapter 12 Leader Power and Influence

Part Five: The Leader as Social Architect
Chapter 13 Creating Vision and Strategic Direction
Chapter 14 Shaping Culture and Values
Chapter 15 Designing and Leading a Learning Organization
Chapter 16 Leading Change

cific tasks and individuals and are based on a premise that leaders can predict and control various aspects of the environment to keep the organization running smoothly.

Parts Three, Four, and Five switch to leadership perspectives that reflect the paradigm shift to the chaotic, unpredictable nature of the environment and the need for fresh leader approaches. Part Three focuses on the personal side of leadership and looks at some of the qualities and forces that are required to be effective in the new reality. These chapters emphasize the importance of self-awareness and self-understanding, the development of one's own leadership mind and heart, moral leadership and courage, and appreciating the role of followership. Part Four is about building effective relationships, including motivating and empowering others, communicating as a leader, leading teams, embracing the diversity of today's world, and using power and influence.

Part Five brings together all of these ideas to examine the leader as builder of a social architecture that can help an organization create a brighter future. These chapters deal with creating vision and strategic direction, aligning culture and values to achieve the vision, and using leadership to build today's learning organizations. A final chapter focuses on leading change.

Taken together, the sections and chapters paint a complete portrait of the leadership experience as it has evolved to the present day and emphasize the new paradigm skills and qualities that are relevant from today and into the future. This book blends systematic research evidence with real-world experiences and impact.

SUMMARY AND INTERPRETATION

This chapter introduced the concept of leadership and explained how individuals can grow as leaders. Leadership is defined as an influence relationship among leaders and followers who intend real changes and outcomes that reflect their shared purposes. Thus leadership involves people in a relationship, influence, change, a shared purpose of achieving a desired future, and taking personal responsibility to make things happen. Most of us are aware of famous leaders, but most leadership that changes the world starts small and may begin with personal frustrations about events that prompt people to initiate change and inspire others to follow them. Your leadership may be expressed in the classroom, your neighborhood, community, or volunteer organizations.

The major challenge facing leaders today is the changing world that wants a new paradigm of leadership. The new reality involves the shift from stability to change, from control to empowerment, from competition to collaboration, from focusing on things to building relationships, from uniformity to diversity. These dramatic changes suggest that a control philosophy of leadership based on industrial-age thinking will probably fail. The challenge for leaders is to grow into an information-age mind-set that involves the development of "soft" leadership skills that supplement the "hard" skills of management.

Although leadership is often equated with good management, leadership and management are different processes. Management strives to maintain stability and improve efficiency. Leadership, on the other hand, is about creating a vision for the future, designing social architecture that shapes culture and values, inspiring and motivating followers, developing personal qualities, and creating change, often dramatic change, to improve organizational effectiveness. Leadership can be combined with management to achieve the greatest possible outcomes. Organizations need to be both managed and led, particularly in today's chaotic environment. Many managers already have the qualities needed to be effective leaders, but they may not have gone through the process needed to bring these qualities to life. It is important to remember that most people are not born with natural leadership skills and qualities, but leadership can be learned and developed.

KEY TERMS

leadership   position power
management   vision
paradigm

DISCUSSION QUESTIONS

1. What do you consider your own strengths and weaknesses for leadership? Discuss your answer with another student.

2. How do you feel about changing yourself first in order to become a leader who can change an organization?

3. Of the elements in the leadership definition as illustrated in Exhibit 1.1, which is the easiest for you? Which is hardest? Explain.

4. What does the paradigm shift from control to empowerment mean for you? Discuss.

5. Describe the best leader you have known. How did this leader acquire his or her capability?

6. Why do you think there are so few people who succeed at both management and leadership? Is it reasonable to believe someone can be good at both? Discuss.

7. "Leadership is more concerned with people than is management." Do you agree? Discuss.

8. What personal capacities should a person develop to be a good leader versus those developed to be a good manager?

9. Why is leadership considered both an art and a science?

LEADERSHIP DEVELOPMENT: Personal Feedback

Your Leadership Potential

Questions 1–6 below are about you right now. Questions 7–22 are about how you would like to be if you were the head of a major department at a corporation. Answer yes or no to indicate whether the item describes you accurately, or whether you would strive to perform each activity.

Now

1. When I have a number of tasks or homework assignments to do, I set priorities and organize the work to meet the deadlines.
2. When I am involved in a serious disagreement, I hang in there and talk it out until it is completely resolved.
3. I would rather sit in front of my computer than spend a lot of time with people.
4. I reach out to include other people in activities or when there are discussions.
5. I know my long-term vision for career, family, and other activities.
6. When solving problems, I prefer analyzing things to working through them with a group of people.

Head of Major Department

7. I would help subordinates clarify goals and how to reach them.
8. I would give people a sense of mission and higher purpose.
9. I would make sure jobs get out on time.
10. I would scout for new product or service opportunities.
11. I would use policies and procedures as guides for problem solving.
12. I would promote unconventional beliefs and values.
13. I would give monetary rewards in exchange for high performance from subordinates.
14. I would inspire trust from everyone in the department.
15. I would work alone to accomplish important tasks.
16. I would suggest new and unique ways of doing things.
17. I would give credit to people who do their jobs well.
18. I would verbalize the higher values that I and the organization stand for.
19. I would establish procedures to help the department operate smoothly.

20. I would question the "why" of things to motivate others.

21. I would set reasonable limits on new approaches.

22. I would demonstrate social nonconformity as a way to facilitate change.

Scoring

Count the number of yes answers to even-numbered questions. Count the number of yes answers to odd-numbered questions. Compare the two scores.

Interpretation

The even-numbered items represent behaviors and activities typical of leadership. Leaders are personally involved in shaping ideas, values, vision, and change. They often use an intuitive approach to develop fresh ideas and seek new directions for the department or organization. The odd-numbered items are considered more traditional management activities. Managers respond to organizational problems in an impersonal way, make rational decisions, and work for stability and efficiency.

If you answered yes to more even-numbered than odd-numbered items, you may have potential leadership qualities. If you answered yes to more odd-numbered items, you may have management qualities. Leadership qualities can be developed or improved with awareness and experience.

LEADERSHIP DEVELOPMENT: Cases for Analysis

Sales Engineering Division

When DGL International, a manufacturer of refinery equipment, brought in John Terrill to manage its Sales Engineering division, company executives informed him of the urgent situation. Sales Engineering, with twenty engineers, was the highest-paid, best-educated, and least-productive division in the company. The instructions to Terrill were: Turn it around. Terrill called a meeting of the engineers. He showed great concern for their personal welfare and asked point blank: "What's the problem? Why can't we produce? Why does this division have such turnover?"

Without hesitation, employees launched a hail of complaints. "I was hired as an engineer, not a pencil pusher." "We spend over half of our time writing asinine reports in triplicate for top management, and no one reads the reports." "We have to account for every penny, which doesn't give us time to work with customers or new developments."

After a two-hour discussion, Terrill began to envision a future in which engineers were free to work with customers and join self-directed teams for product improvement. Terrill concluded he had to get top management off the engineers' backs. He promised the engineers, "My job is to stay out of your way so you can do your work, and I'll try to keep top management off your backs too." He called for the day's reports and issued an order effective immediately that the originals be turned in daily to his office rather than mailed to headquarters. For three weeks, technical reports piled up on his desk. By month's end, the stack was nearly three feet high. During that time no one called for the reports. When other managers entered his office and saw the stack, they usually asked, "What's all this?" Terrill answered, "Technical reports." No one asked to read them.

Finally, at month's end, a secretary from finance called and asked for the monthly travel and expense report. Terrill responded, "Meet me in the president's office tomorrow morning."

The next morning the engineers cheered as Terrill walked through the department pushing a cart loaded with the enormous stack of reports. They knew the showdown had come.

Terrill entered the president's office and placed the stack of reports on his desk. The president and the other senior executives looked bewildered.

"This," Terrill announced, "is the reason for the lack of productivity in the Sales Engineering division. These are the reports your people require every month. The fact that they sat on my desk all month shows that no one reads this material. I suggest that the engineers' time could be used in a more productive manner, and that one brief monthly report from my office will satisfy the needs of the other departments."

Questions

1. Does John Terrill's leadership style fit the definition of leadership in Exhibit 1.1? Explain.
2. With respect to Exhibit 1.2, in what paradigm is Terrill? In what paradigm is headquarters?
3. What approach would you have taken in this situation?

Airstar, Inc.

Airstar, Inc. manufactures, repairs, and overhauls pistons and jet engines for smaller, often privately owned aircraft. The company had a solid niche, and most managers had been with the founder for over twenty years. With the founder's death five years ago, Roy Morgan took over as president at Airstar. Mr. Morgan has called you in as a consultant.

Your research indicates that this industry is changing rapidly. Airstar is feeling encroachment of huge conglomerates like General Electric and Pratt & Whitney, and its backlog of orders is the lowest in several years. The company has always been known for its superior quality, safety, and customer service. However, it has never been under threat before, and senior managers are not sure which direction to take. They have considered potential acquisitions, imports and exports, more research, and additional repair lines. The organization is becoming more chaotic, which is frustrating Morgan and his vice presidents.

Before a meeting with his team, he confides to you, "Organizing is supposed to be easy. For maximum efficiency, work should be divided into simple, logical, routine tasks. These business tasks can be grouped by similar kinds of work characteristics and arranged within an organization under a particularly suited executive. So why are we having so many problems with our executives?"

Morgan met with several of his trusted corporate officers in the executive dining room to discuss what was happening to corporate leadership at Airstar. Morgan went on to explain that he was really becoming concerned with the situation. There have been outright conflicts between the vice president of marketing and the controller over merger and acquisition opportunities. There have been many instances of duplication of work, with corporate officers trying to outmaneuver each other.

"Communications are atrocious," Morgan said to the others. "Why, I didn't even get a copy of the export finance report until my secretary made an effort to find one for me. My basis for evaluation and appraisal of corporate executive performance is fast becoming obsolete. Everyone has been working up their own job descriptions, and they all include overlapping responsibilities. Changes and decisions are being made on the basis of expediency and are perpetuating too many mistakes. We must take a good look at these organizational realities and correct the situation immediately."

Jim Robinson, vice president of manufacturing, pointed out to Morgan that Airstar is not really following the "principles of good organization." "For instance," explained Robinson, "let's review what we should be practicing as administrators." Some of the principles Robinson believed they should be following are:

1. Determine the objectives, policies, programs, and plans that will best achieve the desired results for our company.
2. Determine the various business tasks to be done.
3. Divide the business tasks into a logical and understandable organizational structure.

4. Determine the suitable personnel to occupy positions within the organizational structure.

5. Define the responsibility and authority of each supervisor clearly in writing.

6. Keep the number of kinds and levels of authority at a minimum.

Robinson proposed that the group study the corporate organizational chart, as well as the various corporate business tasks. After reviewing the corporate organizational chart, Robinson, Morgan, and the others agreed that the number and kinds of formal corporate authority were logical and not much different from other corporations. The group then listed the various corporate business tasks that went on within Airstar.

Robinson continued, "How did we ever decide who should handle mergers or acquisitions?" Morgan answered, "I guess it just occurred over time that the vice president of marketing should have the responsibility." "But," Robinson queried, "where is it written down? How would the controller know it?" "Aha!" Morgan exclaimed. "It looks like I'm part of the problem. There isn't anything in writing. Tasks were assigned superficially, as they became problems. This has all been rather informal. I'll establish a group to decide who should have responsibility for what so things can return to our previous level of efficiency."

SOURCE: Adapted from Bernard A. Deitzer and Karl A. Shilliff, *Contemporary Management Incidents* (Columbus, OH: Grid, Inc., 1977), 43–46. Reprinted by permission of John Wiley & Sons, Inc.

Questions

1. What is your reaction to this conversation? What would you say to Morgan to help him lead the organization?

2. To what extent do you rate both Morgan and Robinson as a good manager versus a good leader according to the dimensions in Exhibit 1.3?

3. If you were to take over as president of Airstar, what would you do first? Second? Third?

REFERENCES

1. Keith H. Hammonds, "The Monroe Doctrine," *Fast Company,* October 1999, 230–236; and Lorraine Monroe, *Nothing's Impossible: Leadership Lessons from Inside and Outside the Classroom* (New York: Times Books, 1997).
2. Hammonds, "The Monroe Doctrine."
3. Warren Bennis and Burt Nanus, Leaders: *The Strategies for Taking Charge* (New York: Harper & Row, 1985), 4; James MacGregor Burns, *Leadership* (New York: Harper & Row, 1978), 2.

4. J. Meindl, S. Ehrlich, and J. Dukerich, "The Romance of Leadership," *Administrative Science Quarterly* 30 (1985): 78–102.

5. Joseph C. Rost, *Leadership for the Twenty-First Century* (Westport, CT: Praeger, 1993), 102.

6. Peter B. Smith and Mark F. Peterson, *Leadership, Organizations, and Culture: An Event Management Model* (London: Sage Publications, 1988), 14.

7. Robert E. Kelley, "In Praise of Followers," *Harvard Business Review*, November–December 1988, 142–148.

8. Curtis Sittenfeld, "Hope is a Weapon," *Fast Company*, February–March 1999, 179–184.

9. Robin Wright and Doyle McManus, *Flashpoints: Promise and Peril in a New World* (New York: Alfred A. Knopf, 1991), 107–110.

10. Gregg Stuart, "One Person Can Make a Difference," *The Critter Chronicle: The Quarterly News Magazine of the Nashville Humane Association*, Spring 1997, 1.

11. Raymond Bonner, "Small Band Took on Land Mines-And Won," *The Tennessean*, September 21, 1997, 3D, and "Peace Prize Targets U.S. Mine Policy," *The Tennessean*, October 11, 1997, 1A.

12. Warren St. John, "Barnes & Noble's Epiphany," *Wired*, June 1999, 132–144, and Jim Milliot, "E-Publishing Panel a Sell-Out," *PublishersWeekly.com*, June 5, 2000, *http://www.publishersweekly.com/articles/20000605_87105.asp* accessed on June 7, 2000.

13. The discussion of these transformations is based on Daniel C. Kielson, "Leadership: Creating a New Reality," *The Journal of Leadership Studies* 3, No. 4 (1996): 104–116; and Mark A. Abramson, "Leadership for the Future: New Behaviors, New Roles, and New Attitudes," *The Public Manager,* Spring 1997. See also Frances Hesselbein, Marshall Goldsmith, and Richard Beckhard, eds. *The Leader of the Future: New Visions, Strategies, and Practices for the Next Era* (San Francisco: Jossey-Bass, 1996).

14. Kielson, "Leadership: Creating a New Reality."

15. R. Duane Ireland and Michael A. Hitt, "Achieving and Maintaining Strategic Competitiveness in the 21st Century: The Role of Strategic Leadership," *Academy of Management Executive* 13, No. 1 (February 1999): 43–57.

16. Nina Munk, "The New Organization Man," *Fortune*, March 16, 1998, 63–74.

17. Thomas A. Stewart, "Brain Power: Who Owns It . . . How They Profit From It," *Fortune*, March 17, 1997, 105–110.

18. Charles Handy, *The Age of Paradox* (Boston: Harvard Business School Press, 1994), 146–147.

19. Andrew Mayo, "Memory Bankers," *People Management*, January 22, 1998, 34–38; William Miller, "Building the Ultimate Resource," *Management Review*, January 1999, 42–45; Todd Datz, "How to Speak Geek," *CIO Enterprise,* Section 2, April 15, 1999, 46–52; and Richard McDermott, "Why Information Technology Inspired But Cannot Deliver Knowledge Management," *California Management Review* 41, No. 4 (Summer 1999): 103–117.

20. Richard L. Daft, *Organization Theory and Design*, 6th ed. (Cincinnati, OH: South-Western College Publishing, 1998), 523.

21. Cyrus F. Friedheim Jr., *The Trillion-Dollar Enterprise: How the Alliance Revolution Will Transform Global Business* (Reading, MA: Perseus Books, 1999).

22. James R. Carlopio, "Holism: A Philosophy of Organizational Leadership for the Future," *Leadership Quarterly* 5, no. 3/4 (1994): 297–307, and Daniel C. Kielson, "Leadership: Creating a New Reality," *The Journal of Leadership Studies* 3, No. 4 (1996): 104–116.
23. Curtis Sittenfeld, "Leader on the Edge," *Fast Company,* October 1999, 212–226.
24. Joseph Nocera, "A Mug Only 20,000 Employees Could Love," *eCompany Now,* June 2000, 159–166.
25. Martha H. Peak, "Anti-Manager Named Manager of the Year," *Management Review,* October 1991, 7.
26. Geoffrey Colvin, "The Ultimate Manager," *Fortune,* November 22, 1999, 185–187.
27. This section is based largely on John P. Kotter, *A Force for Change: How Leadership Differs from Management* (New York: The Free Press, 1990), 3–18.
28. *Leadership, A Forum Issues Special Report* (Boston, MA: The Forum Corporation, 1990), 13.
29. Ronald B. Lieber, "Why Employees Love These Companies," *Fortune,* January 12, 1998, 72–74.
30. *Leadership: A Forum Issues Special Report* (Boston, MA: The Forum Corporation, 1990), 15.
31. James Kaplan, "Amateur's Hour," *Working Woman,* October 1997, 28–33.
32. John P. Kotter, quoted in Thomas A. Stewart, "Why Leadership Matters," *Fortune,* March 2, 1998, 71–82.
33. John P. Kotter, *Leading Change* (Boston, MA: Harvard Business School Press, 1996), 26.
34. Joseph C. Rost, *Leadership for the Twenty-First Century* (Westport, CT: Praeger, 1993), 145–146.
35. Warren Bennis, *Why Leaders Can't Lead* (San Francisco: Jossey-Bass, 1989).
36. Bennis, *Why Leaders Can't Lead;* and Stewart, "Why Leadership Matters."
37. Stratford Sherman, "How Tomorrow's Best Leaders Are Learning Their Stuff," *Fortune,* November 27, 1995, 90–102.
38. Abraham Zaleznik, "Managers and Leaders: Are They Different?" *Harvard Business Review,* March–April 1992, 126–135.
39. Bennis, *Why Leaders Can't Lead.*
40. Sherman, "How Tomorrow's Best Leaders Are Learning Their Stuff."
41. Jennifer Reingold, "In Search of Leadership" (an interview with Thomas J. Neff and James M. Citrin, authors of *Lessons from the Top: The Search for America's Best Leaders*), *Business Week,* November 15, 1999, 172, 176.
42. Reported in "By the Numbers: Director's Set," *Success,* August 1998, 14.
43. Genevieve Capowski, "Anatomy of a Leader: Where Are the Leaders of Tomorrow?" *Management Review,* March 1994, 10–17.
44. Cited in John P. Kotter, *A Force for Change: How Leadership Differs from Management* (New York: The Free Press, 1990), 3–18. See also Warren Bennis and Burt Nanus, *Leaders: The Strategies for Taking Charge* (New York: Harper & Row, 1985).
45. Susan A. Tynan, "BEST Behaviors," *Management Review,* November 1999, 58–61.
46. Morgan W. McCall, Jr., and Michael M. Lombardo, "Off the Track: Why and How Successful Executives Get Derailed" (Technical Report No. 21, Center for

Creative Leadership, Greensboro, NC, January 1983); Carol Hymowitz, "Five Main Reasons Why Managers Fail," *The Wall Street Journal,* May 2, 1988.

47. Hal Lancaster, "Given a Second Chance, A Boss Learns to Favor Carrots Over Sticks," *The Wall Street Journal,* November 30, 1999, B4.

48. Sue Shellenberger, "From Our Readers: The Bosses That Drove Me to Quit My Job," *The Wall Street Journal,* February 7, 2000, B1.

49. Ram Charan and Geoffrey Colvin, "Why CEOs Fail," *Fortune,* June 21, 1999, 68–78.

50. Sharon Nelton, "Leadership for the New Age," *Nation's Business,* May 1997, 18–27.

51. Russell Palmer, "Can Leadership Be Learned?" *Business Today,* Fall, 1989, 100–102.

Research Perspectives on Leadership

2
Traits, Behaviors, and Relationships

3
Contingency Approaches

CHAPTER OUTLINE

YOUR LEADERSHIP CHALLENGE

After reading this chapter, you should be able to:

- Identify personal traits and characteristics that are associated with effective leaders.

- Recognize autocratic versus democratic leadership behavior and the impact of each.

- Know the distinction between people-oriented and task-oriented leadership behavior and when each should be used.

- Understand how dyadic theories of leadership have broadened the understanding of relationships between leaders and followers, and recognize how to build partnerships for greater effectiveness.

Traits, Behaviors, and Relationships

Imagine slogging through near-freezing water up to your waist, or walking for miles and then discovering you're only a hundred yards closer to your destination. That's what happened when Robert Swan led a team to the North Pole and the ice cap began to melt beneath their feet. Swan's carefully planned expedition, made up of eight people from seven countries, became a nightmare when the ice cap began to melt in April—four months earlier than usual.

The group survived—barely—because of teamwork and Swan's extraordinary leadership. "What I learned as a leader is that you don't bullshit people under hostile circumstances," Swan now says. "You tell them the truth." Swan's honesty, as well as his ability to maintain his poise, self-confidence, and sense of purpose amid life-threatening and constantly changing conditions, helped to nourish the spirit and motivation of the team. With the completion of the journey, Swan became the first person ever to walk to both the North and the South Poles. Today, he recounts his adventures to groups around the world, including businesspeople hungry to learn what it means to be a leader in a dangerous and hostile environment.

Swan had dreamed of walking to the South Pole, tracing the route taken by Robert Falcon Scott in 1912, since he was a child. As a young adult, he spent seven years working as a taxi driver, a tree cutter, a gardener, and a hotel dishwasher to earn money, all the while selling the dream to others to help raise funds. His first expedition to Antarctica in 1986 changed his life completely. Motivated by first-hand experience with the destruction of the ozone layer and by the waste and pollution he encountered on his journey, Swan became deeply committed to environmental issues. He took on the difficult challenge of raising money for his second expedition, to the North Pole, inspired primarily by the dream of helping to save the polar regions from human destruction. Again, the difficulties of the journey left him even more determined to draw worldwide attention to environmental problems.

As one of today's top motivational speakers, Swan is inspiring people around the world to become involved in saving the environment. He leads young people from many countries on expeditions that focus on research and education. He offers employees of his corporate sponsors the opportunity to sail to Antarctica and participate in cleaning up the region. From the business viewpoint, Swan's stories of courage, adventure, determination, and risk-taking are good metaphors for what many leaders are feeling in today's shifting business world. And those who participate in his clean-up missions get a first-hand lesson in leadership.[1]

Robert Swan is a world-renowned explorer who is influencing young people, world leaders, businesspeople, and organizations around the globe. He works tirelessly for what he believes in and has inspired others to become more actively involved. Those who participate in his expeditions take what they learn back to their organizations, further extending Swan's influence. Several personal attributes contribute to Swan's leadership. He had the courage, self-confidence, and determination to try something that everyone told him couldn't be done. He had the drive and the commitment to work for years in menial jobs to make his dream a reality, and he continues to raise money for the causes he believes in. His poise and ability to maintain a positive attitude have helped team members survive harrowing conditions.

In considering Swan's influence, it seems evident that characteristics such as courage, self-confidence, drive, determination, and a willingness to take risks are part of the personality that make him a good leader. Indeed, personal traits are what captured the imagination of the earliest leadership researchers. Many leaders possess traits that researchers believe affect their leadership impact. For example, President Andres Pastrana of Colombia has been recognized for his courage, will, and determination in his efforts to end political corruption. Isabel Maxwell, president of the Israeli-founded Commtouch, the world's leading provider of branded e-mail, is known in the industry for her high energy, forthrightness, and integrity.[2]

Moreover, successful leaders display traits through patterns in their behavior. Consequently, many researchers have examined the behavior of leaders to determine what behavioral features comprise leadership style and how particular behaviors relate to effective leadership. Later research specified behavior between a leader and each distinct follower, differentiating one-on-one behavior from leader-to-group behavior.

This chapter provides an overview of the initial leadership research in the twentieth century. We will examine the evolution of the trait approach and the behavior approach, and introduce the dyadic theory of leadership. The path illuminated by the research into leader traits and behaviors is a foundation for the field of leadership studies and still enjoys remarkable dynamism for explaining leader success or failure.

THE TRAIT APPROACH

Early efforts to understand leadership success focused on the leader's personal traits. **Traits** are the distinguishing personal characteristics of a leader, such as intelligence, honesty, self-confidence, and appearance. Research early in this century examined leaders who had achieved a level of greatness, and hence became known as the Great Man approach. Fundamental to this theory was the idea that some people are born with traits that make them natural leaders. The **Great Man approach** sought to identify the traits leaders possessed that distinguished them from people who were not leaders. Generally, research found only a weak relationship between personal traits and leader success.[3] For example, college football coaches Phil Fulmer at Tennessee and Steve Spurrier at Florida have very different personality traits, but both are successful leaders of their football teams. Indeed, the diversity of traits that effective leaders possess indicates that leadership ability is not necessarily a genetic endowment.

Nevertheless, with the advancement of the field of psychology during the 1940s and 1950s, trait approach researchers began to use aptitude and psychological tests to examine a broad range of personal attributes. Initially, researchers focused on isolating the characteristics that leaders possessed and that nonleaders did not possess. By measuring the traits of successful leaders in correlation to effective leadership, it might be possible to compile a checklist of leadership attributes.

Researchers began by examining personality traits such as creativity and self-confidence, physical traits such as age and energy level, abilities such as knowledge and fluency of speech, social characteristics such as popularity and sociability, and work-related characteristics such as the desire to excel and persistence against obstacles. Effective leaders were often identified by exceptional follower performance, or by a high status position within an organization and a salary that exceeded that of one's peers.[4]

In a 1948 literature review[5] Stogdill examined over 100 studies based on the trait approach. He uncovered several traits that appeared consistent with effective leadership, including general intelligence, initiative, interpersonal skills, self-confidence, drive for responsibility, and personal integrity. Stogdill's findings also indicated, however, that the importance of a particular trait was often relative to the situation. Initiative, for example, may contribute to the success of a leader in one situation, but it may be irrelevant to a leader in another situation. Thus, possessing certain personal characteristics is no guarantee of success.

Many researchers desisted their efforts to identify leadership traits in light of Stogdill's 1948 findings and turned their attention to examining leader behavior and leadership situations. However, others continued with expanded trait lists and research projects. Stogdill's subsequent review of 163 trait studies conducted between 1948 and 1970 concluded that some personal traits do indeed seem to contribute to effective leadership.[6] The study identified many of the same traits found in the 1948 survey, along with several additional characteristics, including aggressiveness, independence, and tolerance for stress. However, Stogdill again cautioned that the value of a particular trait or set of traits varies with the organizational situation.

In recent years, there has been a resurgence of interest in examining leadership traits. A 1991 review by Kirkpatrick and Locke identified a number of personal traits that distinguish leaders from nonleaders, including some pinpointed by Stogdill.[7] Other studies have focused on followers' perceptions and indicate that certain traits are associated with individuals' perceptions of who is a leader. For example, one study found that the traits of intelligence, masculinity, and dominance were strongly related to how individuals perceived leaders.[8] More recently, the management consulting firm Andersen Consulting, with the assistance of leadership scholars, interviewed dozens of leaders and hundreds of emerging leaders around the world and asked them to rank the importance of various characteristics. Based on these interviews and surveys, the research team developed a list of fourteen characteristics believed to be important for successful leadership in today's world.[9] Similarly, star headhunters Thomas J. Neff and James N. Citrin believe there are some traits that are shared by today's best leaders, as described in this chapter's Leader's Bookshelf. A concern with traits is also evidenced by the recent interest in emotional intelligence, which includes characteristics such as self-awareness, the ability to manage one's emotions, the capacity to be hopeful and optimistic despite obstacles, the ability to empathize with others, and strong social and interpersonal skills.[10] Emotional intelligence will be discussed in greater detail in Chapter 5.

In summary, trait research has been an important part of leadership studies throughout the twentieth century and continues into the twenty-first. Many researchers still contend that some traits are essential to effective leadership, but only in combination with other factors.[11] Exhibit 2.1 presents some of the traits and their respective categories that have been identified through trait research over the years. Some of the traits considered essential are self-confidence, honesty and integrity, and drive.

SELF-CONFIDENCE   The trait of **self-confidence** refers to the degree to which one is self-assured in his or her own judgments, decision making, ideas, and capabilities. A leader with a positive self-image who displays certainty about his or her own ability fosters confidence among followers, gains respect and admiration, and meets challenges. The confidence a leader displays and develops creates motivation and commitment among followers for the mission at hand.

EXHIBIT 2.1

Personal Characteristics of Leaders

Physical characteristics

Energy

Physical Stamina

Intelligence and ability

Intelligence, cognitive ability

Knowledge

Judgment, decisiveness

Personality

Self-confidence

Honesty and integrity

Enthusiasm

Desire to lead

Independence

Social characteristics

Sociability, interpersonal skills

Cooperativeness

Ability to enlist cooperation

Tact, diplomacy

Work-related characteristics

Achievement drive, desire to excel

Responsibility in pursuit of goals

Persistence against obstacles, tenacity

Social Background

Education

Mobility

SOURCE: *Bass & Stogdill's Handbook of Leadership: Theory, Research, and Management Applications*, 3rd ed. (New York: The Free Press, 1990), 80-81; and S.A. Kirkpatrick and E. A. Locke, "Leadership: Do Traits Matter?" *Academy of Management Executive* 5, No. 2 (1991), 48-60.

LEADER'S BOOKSHELF

Lessons From the Top: The Search for America's Best Business Leaders

by Thomas J. Neff and James M. Citrin

What makes a great leader? Thomas J. Neff and James M. Citrin attempt to answer that question through profiles of fifty leaders in some of America's most successful organizations, including well-known CEOs such as Steve Case of America Online, Jack Welch of General Electric, and the American Red Cross's Elizabeth Dole, as well as lesser-known leaders such as Autodesk's Carol Bartz, Martha Ingram of Ingram Industries, and Fannie Mae's Frank Raines. In their book, *Lessons from the Top,* Neff and Citrin (chairman and managing director respectively of Spencer Stuart, a top executive search firm) describe what they believe are the qualities and principles that define effective leadership in today's world.

The Traits and Principles of a Leader

Even though the authors found vast differences in personality among the leaders they interviewed, they also determined that there are some traits and philosophies shared by most of them. After evaluating the profiles, Neff and Citrin synthesize the qualities of effective leaders into 10 common traits: passion, intelligence, communication skill, high energy, controlled ego, inner peace, a defining background, a strong family life, a positive attitude, and a focus on "doing the right things right."

In addition, the authors distinguish six core principles that successful leaders live by:

- **Live with integrity; lead by example.** Integrity builds trust and confidence among followers that is necessary for high-performing organizations.

- **Develop a winning strategy.** Neff and Citrin point out that a successful leader has to be able to understand what the company does best and build on it.

- **Build a great management team.** Great leaders hire people "whose skills and experiences [complement] their own, but whose passion, attitudes, and values [are] one and the same."

- **Inspire employees.** To be effective, leaders communicate constantly and listen carefully. In addition they encourage risk-taking, and even failure, as a learning experience.

- **Create a flexible organization.** The best leaders get rid of practices and policies that stand in the way of flexibility and customer responsiveness.

- **Implement relevant systems.** "Compensation . . . must be consistent with and reinforce the values and strategy of the organization."

Applying the Lessons

One excellent aspect of *Lessons from the Top* is that it allows readers to spend some time getting to know fifty of today's most successful leaders. The authors also summarize the lessons from these leaders in two clear and concise chapters, "Doing the Right Things Right: A New Definition of Business Success," and "Common Traits: A Prescription for Success in Business." By taking the experiences of these fifty real-life leaders and distilling them into a framework of effective leadership, the book helps readers see how individual experiences fit into a larger picture and how to apply these lessons from the top to their own lives and leadership.

Lessons from the Top: The Search for America's Best Leaders, by Thomas J. Neff and James M. Citrin, is published by Doubleday.

Active leaders need self-confidence. Leaders initiate changes and they often make decisions without adequate information. Problems are solved continuously. Without the confidence to move forward and believe things will be okay, even if an occasional decision is wrong, leaders could be paralyzed into inaction. Setbacks have to be overcome. Risks have to be taken. Competing points of view have to be managed, with some people left unsatisfied. Self-confidence is the one trait that enables a leader to face all these challenges.[12]

Leaders in today's Internet-based companies know the value of self-confidence because they frequently have to make major decisions based on limited information. According to Yahoo Chairman Tim Koogle, "You have to be able to say no to $10 million."[13] Leaders in e-corporations need the self-confidence to make difficult decisions incredibly fast and inspire others to support those decisions. However, leaders in all types of organizations need self-confidence because of the important role it plays in decision making and gaining others' respect and commitment.

HONESTY/INTEGRITY   Honesty refers to truthfulness and nondeception. It implies an openness that subordinates welcome. Integrity means that one is whole, so one's actions are in keeping with one's words. Robert Swan, described in the opening case for this chapter, provides a good illustration of personal integrity. During one sailing trip to Antarctica when the ship sank, cleaning up all the garbage proved to be a tremendous inconvenience. However, Swan was determined to do it, showing that his commitment to environmental causes was not all talk and no action. When leaders model their convictions through their daily actions, they command admiration, respect, and loyalty. These virtues are the foundation of trust between leaders and followers. Today people tend to be highly informed and wary of authority and the deceptive use of power. Possessing the traits of honesty and integrity is essential to minimize skepticism and to build productive relationships.

Successful leaders have been found to be highly consistent, doing exactly what they say they will do when they say they will do it. Successful leaders are easy to trust. They have basic principles and consistently apply them. One survey of 1,500 managers asked the values most desired in leaders. Integrity was the most important characteristic. The authors concluded:

> Honesty is absolutely essential to leadership. After all, if we are willing to follow someone, whether it be into battle or into the boardroom, we first want to assure ourselves that the person is worthy of our trust. We want to know that he or she is being truthful, ethical, and principled. We want to be fully confident in the integrity of our leaders.[14]

Consider the example of Roy Vagelos of Merck and Co., who seemingly broke all the rules of business to remain true to his own beliefs and to the company's mission.

IN THE LEAD   ## Roy Vagelos, Merck & Co.

"We are in the business of preserving and improving human life," Merck's mission statement reads. However, when in the late 1970s Roy Vagelos (then Merck's senior vice president of research) and his colleagues found a potential cure for river blindness, they faced a dilemma. The drug would cost more than $200 million to develop, and it was needed only by people who couldn't afford to pay for it—poor villagers in West Africa and other developing countries. One of the world's most dreaded diseases, river blindness had long frustrated public health agencies trying to control its spread. When a scientist in Merck's laboratories hit upon a possible solution, many people in the company argued that proceeding with the drug's development was a costly mistake. However, Vagelos (who was promoted to CEO during this period) held firmly to the company's stated axiom that "health precedes wealth" and authorized the continuation.

His decision to authorize a drug that would likely never make money and would cost more than $3 a tablet to produce and distribute was not an easy one, but Vagelos stood by his beliefs and those espoused by his organization. When Merck couldn't get the governments of developing nations to buy the new drug, Mectizan, the company announced that they would give the drug away. Some people argued that the decision was irresponsible and violated the fiduciary trust placed in Vagelos by Merck's stockholders. But Vagelos believed that focusing on the company's guiding mission was the best way to create shareholder value in the long run, and he stuck by these principles. According to Vagelos, "I thought that the company couldn't have done otherwise." By showing the entire world the integrity and consistency of Merck's organizational leadership, the decision ultimately served the company well. The development of Mectizan is considered one of the twentieth century's greatest medical triumphs, and river blindness has nearly been eradicated as a public health threat in many areas. Merck's reputation soared, helping the company attract some of the best scientific researchers in the world. However, even without this benefit, Roy Vagelos says he would still make the same decision, indicating that he really had no choice. "My whole life has been dedicated to helping people."[15]

Vagelos believes his effectiveness as a leader, as well as the leadership position of his company, would have been threatened had he not held to the principles on which Merck was founded. Most of Merck's employees approved of the decision because it was consistent with the company's values. Even though Vagelos emphasizes that he was guided by the company's mission and culture, his decision still required tremendous self-confidence as well as personal integrity.

DRIVE   A third characteristic considered essential for effective leadership is drive. **Drive** refers to high motivation that creates a high effort level by a leader. Leaders with drive seek achievement, have energy and tenacity, and are frequently seen to have ambition and initiative to achieve their goals. Leaders rise to the top often because they actively pursue goals. Ambition enables them to set challenging goals and take initiative to achieve those goals.[16]

A strong drive is associated with high energy. Leaders work long hours over many years. They have stamina and are vigorous and full of life in order to handle the pace, the demands, and the challenges of leadership. Leaders often are responsible for initiating new projects as well as guiding projects to successful completion. The following sketch illustrates the kind of drive that predicts successful leadership.

"I want to be able to demonstrate the things I learned in college and get to the top," said Al, "maybe even be president. I expect to work hard and be at the third level within five years, and to rise to much higher levels in the years beyond. I am specifically working on my MBA to aid in my advancement. If I am thwarted on advancement, or find the challenges lacking, I'll leave the company."[17]

Traits such as drive, self-confidence, and integrity have great value for leaders. The Living Leadership box considers the notion that personal charac-

LIVING LEADERSHIP

Leader Qualities

The quality of the leader determines the quality of the organization.

A leader who lacks intelligence, virtue, and experience
Cannot hope for success.

In any conflict
the circumstances affect the outcome.

Good leaders can succeed in adverse conditions.

Bad leaders can lose in favorable conditions.

Therefore, good leaders constantly strive to perfect themselves,
Lest their shortcomings mar their endeavors.

When all other factors are equal,

It is the character of the leader that determines the outcome.

Source: Deng Ming-Dao, *Everyday Tao: Living with Balance and Harmony* (New York: HarperCollins, 1996), 66. Used with permission.

teristics of the leader are ultimately responsible for leadership outcomes. In Chapter 4, we will further consider individual characteristics and qualities that play a role in leadership effectiveness.

However, as indicated earlier, traits alone cannot define effective leadership. A great deal of research has also explored how leader behavior contributes to the success or failure of leadership.

BEHAVIOR APPROACHES

The behavior approach says that anyone who adopts the appropriate behavior can be a good leader. Diverse research programs on leadership behavior have sought to uncover the behaviors that leaders engage in rather than what traits a leader possesses. Behaviors can be learned more readily than traits, enabling leadership to be accessible to all.

Autocratic versus Democratic Leadership

One study that served as a precursor to the behavior approach recognized autocratic and democratic leadership styles. An **autocratic** leader is one who tends to centralize authority and derive power from position, control of rewards, and coercion. A **democratic** leader delegates authority to others, encourages participation, relies on subordinates' knowledge for completion of tasks, and depends on subordinate respect for influence.

The first studies on these leadership behaviors were conducted at the University of Iowa by Kurt Lewin and his associates.[18] The research included groups of children, each with its own designated adult leader who was instructed to act in either an autocratic or democratic style. These experiments produced some interesting findings. The groups with autocratic leaders performed highly so long as the leader was present to supervise them. However, group members were displeased with the close, autocratic style of leadership, and feelings of hostility frequently arose. The performance of groups who were assigned democratic leaders was almost as good, and these groups were characterized by positive feelings rather than hostility. In addition, under the democratic style of leadership, group members performed well even when the leader was absent. The participative techniques and majority-rule decision making used by the democratic leader trained and involved the group members so that they performed well with or without the leader present. These characteristics of democratic leadership may partly explain why the empowerment of employees is a popular trend in companies today.

This early work implied that leaders were either autocratic or democratic in their approach. However, further work by Tannenbaum and Schmidt indicated that leadership behavior could exist on a continuum reflecting different amounts of employee participation.[19] Thus, one leader might be autocratic (boss-centered), another democratic (subordinate-centered), and a third a mix of the two styles. The leadership continuum is illustrated in Exhibit 2.2.

Tannenbaum and Schmidt also suggested that the extent to which leaders should be boss-centered or subordinate-centered depended on organizational circumstances, and that leaders might adjust their behaviors to fit the circumstances. For example, if there is time pressure on a leader or if it takes too long for subordinates to learn how to make decisions, the leader will tend to use an autocratic style. When subordinates are able to learn decision-making skills readily, a participative style can be used. Also, the greater the skill difference, the more autocratic the leader approach, because it is difficult to bring subordinates up to the leader's expertise level.[20] But followers may not be as independent when the leader is autocratic.

For example, Stephen Fleming used an autocratic style as a marketing manager in an oil products company. He was being groomed for a higher position because his department performed so well. However, this meant time spent at meetings away from his group, and performance declined because the subordinates had not learned to function independently. In contrast, Dorothy

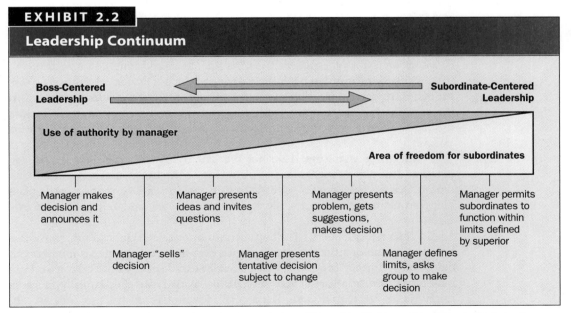

EXHIBIT 2.2

Leadership Continuum

SOURCE: *Harvard Business Review.* An exhibit from Robert Tannenbaum and Warren Schmidt, "How to Choose a Leadership Pattern" (May–June 1973). Copyright 1973 by the president and Fellows of Harvard College.

Roberts, CEO of Echo Scarves, behaves toward people by showing respect and courtesy. Decision making is shared by representatives of design, sales, marketing, and operations. In the traditionally tough fashion industry, her nice-guy leadership behavior permeates the entire company, creating a unique corporate culture that is open, honest, and supportive of employees. Company prosperity is centered on treating people well. Roberts' leadership behavior creates satisfied employees who in turn create satisfied customers, which is certainly correct in her company situation.[21]

The findings of the original University of Iowa studies indicated that leadership behavior had a definite effect on outcomes such as follower performance and satisfaction. Equally important was the recognition that effective leadership was reflected in behavior, not simply by what personality traits a leader possessed. This recognition provided a focus for subsequent studies based on the behavior approach.

Ohio State Studies

An early series of studies on leadership behavior was conducted at Ohio State University. Researchers conducted surveys to identify specific dimensions of leader behavior. Narrowing a list of nearly 2,000 leader behaviors into a questionnaire containing 150 examples of definitive leader behaviors, they developed the Leader Behavior Description Questionnaire (LBDQ) and administered it to employees.[22] Hundreds of employees responded to behavior examples according to the degree to which their leaders engaged in the various behaviors. The analysis of ratings resulted in two wide-ranging categories of leader behavior types, later called consideration and initiating structure.

Consideration describes the extent to which a leader is sensitive to subordinates, respects their ideas and feelings, and establishes mutual trust. Showing appreciation, listening carefully to problems, and seeking input from subordinates regarding important decisions are all examples of consideration behaviors.

Initiating structure describes the extent to which a leader is task oriented and directs subordinates' work activities toward goal achievement. This type of leader behavior includes directing tasks, working people hard, planning, providing explicit schedules for work activities, and ruling with an iron hand.

While many leaders fall along a continuum that includes both consideration and initiating structure behaviors, these behavior categories are independent of one another. In other words, a leader can display a high degree of both behavior types, or a low degree of both behavior types. Additionally, a leader might demonstrate high consideration and low initiating structure, or low consideration and high initiating structure behavior. Research indicates that all four of these leader style combinations can be effective.[23] As superintendent of

Florida's Duval County school system, John Fryer demonstrates both high consideration and high initiating structure.

IN THE LEAD   John Fryer, Duval County Schools

As a major general in the U. S. Air Force, John Fryer learned all about setting goals and establishing high performance standards. Many people believe he's just what is needed to turn Duval County's schools around. Students in Duval County score well below the state average on standardized tests, and five of the county's schools got Fs from the Florida Department of Education. When Fryer first took the job as superintendent, he approached things as a general might, setting a strategic plan that included rigorous goals for academics and discipline that are the same from class to class and school to school. He established high performance standards for teachers as well as students. To encourage students to raise their reading skills, he challenged them to read 25 books each. Even though parents complained that the goal was too high, an auditorium full of students recently received awards for reading 100 books each during the last school year.

Although many teachers were at first skeptical about meeting Fryer's high goals, they have been won over to his motto of "Aim High," which he adopted from the Air Force. One reason Fryer gained the commitment of teachers was that he involved them in the process. "We finally got a superintendent who will listen," said Terrie Brady, president of the teachers' union. Fryer holds monthly dinners for ten to fifteen teachers at a time, and he is working hard to give them the training they told him they need to meet the new standards. Teachers also appreciate that they have definite goals to work toward. Sylvia Johnson, principal of West Jacksonville Elementary, one of the poorest schools in the county, says her staff likes knowing that the standards won't keep changing, as they have in the past. At Johnson's school, where only 10 percent of students passed the "Florida Writes!" test five years ago, 83 percent passed last year.

It isn't clear yet whether Fryer's leadership can completely turn things around for Duval County Schools, but there is a definite shift in motivation and commitment. "I found there are a lot of good people in school systems," Fryer says. "You just need to learn how to tap into them."[24]

John Fryer used initiating structure behavior to clarify goals and set performance standards to be achieved. The high degree of initiating structure behavior was necessary to get everyone focused in the same direction—moving Duval County schools toward higher standards. He also demonstrated consideration by anticipating possible resistance among teachers and involving them in the process. He asks questions, and listens to the answers, recognizing that the teachers on the front lines often understand a problem better than he does. Thus, Fryer can be considered a "high-high" leader by exhibiting high levels of both types of leader behavior.

Additional studies that correlated the two leader behavior types and impact on subordinates initially demonstrated that "considerate" supervisors had a more positive impact on subordinate satisfaction than did "structuring" supervisors.[25] For example, when leader effectiveness was defined by voluntary turnover or amount of grievances filed by subordinates, considerate leaders generated less turnover and grievances. But research that utilized performance criteria, such as group output and productivity, showed initiating structure behavior was rated more effective. Other studies involving aircraft commanders and university department heads revealed that leaders rated effective by subordinates exhibited a high level of both consideration and initiating structure behaviors, while leaders rated less effective displayed low levels of both behavior styles.[26]

University of Michigan Studies

Studies at the University of Michigan took a different approach by directly comparing the behavior of effective and ineffective supervisors.[27] The effectiveness of leaders was determined by productivity of the subordinate group. Initial field studies and interviews at various job sites gave way to a questionnaire not unlike the LBDQ, called the Survey of Organizations.[28]

Over time, the Michigan researchers established two types of leadership behavior, each type consisting of two dimensions.[29] First, **employee-centered** leaders display a focus on the human needs of their subordinates. Leader support and interaction facilitation are the two underlying dimensions of employee-centered behavior. This means that in addition to demonstrating support for their subordinates, employee-centered leaders facilitate positive interaction among followers and seek to minimize conflict. The employee-centered style of leadership roughly corresponds to the Ohio State concept of consideration. Because relationships are so important in today's work environment, many organizations are looking for leaders who can facilitate positive interaction among others. Damark International, a general merchandise catalogue company, even has a position designed to help people get along better. Although his official title is director of leadership and team development, Mark Johansson calls himself a "relationship manager." Johansson works with managers throughout the organization to help them improve their relationship and interpersonal skills and become more employee-centered.[30]

In contrast to the employee-centered leader, the **job-centered** leader directs activities toward efficiency, cost-cutting, and scheduling. Goal emphasis and work facilitation are dimensions of this leadership behavior. By focusing on reaching task goals and facilitating the structure of tasks, job-centered behavior approximates that of initiating structure.

However, unlike the consideration and initiating structure defined by the Ohio State studies, Michigan researchers considered employee-centered leadership and job-centered leadership to be distinct styles in opposition to one another. A leader is identifiable by behavior characteristic of one or the other style, but not both. Another hallmark of later Michigan studies is the acknowledgment that often the behaviors of goal emphasis, work facilitation, support, and interaction facilitation can be meaningfully performed by a subordinate's peers, rather than only by the designated leader. Other people in the group could supply these behaviors, which enhanced performance.[31]

In addition, while leadership behavior was demonstrated to affect the performance and satisfaction of subordinates, performance was also influenced by other factors related to the situation within which leaders and subordinates worked. The situation will be explored in the next chapter.

The Leadership Grid

Blake and Mouton of the University of Texas proposed a two-dimensional leadership theory called **The Leadership Grid** that builds on the work of the Ohio State and Michigan studies.[32] Based on a week-long seminar, researchers rated leaders on a scale of one to nine according to two criteria: the concern for people and the concern for production. The scores for these criteria are plotted on a grid with an axis corresponding to each concern. The two-dimensional model and seven major leadership styles are depicted in Exhibit 2.3.

Team management (9,9) often is considered the most effective style and is recommended because organization members work together to accomplish tasks. *Country club management* (1,9) occurs when primary emphasis is given to people rather than to work outputs. *Authority-compliance management* (9,1) occurs when efficiency in operations is the dominant orientation. *Middle-of-the-road management* (5,5) reflects a moderate amount of concern for both people and production. *Impoverished management* (1,1) means the absence of a leadership philosophy; leaders exert little effort toward interpersonal relationships or work accomplishment. Consider these examples:

Dick Notebaert, CEO of Ameritech Corporation, replaced 60 percent of top executives in a three-year period. In addition, the goals he set challenged people to reach double-digit growth, increase profit percentages, and claim a share of the long-distance telephone services market—high standards for a regional operating service.[33] Conversely, Principal Rob McPhee gave priority to people in devising a school plan for W. P. Wagner High School in Edmonton, Alberta, Canada. Students, teachers, parents, and community members all contributed to the development of educational goals. McPhee even made special efforts to include those parents and citizens typically uninvolved in

EXHIBIT 2.3

The Leadership Grid® Figure

High

9 **1,9**
   Country Club Management
   Thoughtful attention to the
8 needs of people for satisfying
   relationships leads to a comfortable, friendly organization
7 atmosphere and work tempo.

9,9
Team Management
Work accomplishment is
from committed people;
interdependence through
a "common stake" in
organization purpose
leads to relationships of
trust and respect.

6

5,5
5 **Middle-of-the-Road Management**
   Adequate organization performance is
   possible through balancing the necessity
4 to get out work with maintaining morale of
   people at a satisfactory level.

Authority-Compliance
Management
3 Efficiency in operations
   results from arranging
   Impoverished Management conditions of work in
2 Exertion of minimum effort such a way that human
   to get required work done elements interfere to a
   is appropriate to sustain minimum degree.
   organization membership.
1 **1,1**   **9,1**

Concern for People (y-axis, High to Low, 1–9)

Low

   1   2   3   4   5   6   7   8   9
Low   **Concern for Results**   **High**

Opportunism

1,9   9,9
        9+9
              9,1

5,5

1,1   9,1

People adapt and shift to any grid style needed to gain the
maximum advantage. Performance occurs according to
selfish gain. Effort is given for advantage or personal gain.

9+9 Paternalism/
Maternalism
Reward and approval gain
loyalty and obedience to work
requirement. Failure leads
to punishment.

1,9
     9+9
          9,1

SOURCE: The Leadership Grid (figure, Paternalism figure and Opportunism figure from *Leadership Dilemma—Grid Solutions* by Robert R. Blake and Anne Adams McCanse (formerly the Managerial Grid by Robert R. Blake and Jane S. Mouton). Houston: Gulf Publishing Company (Grid figure: p. 29, Paternalism figure: p. 30, Opportunism figure: p. 31). Copyright 1991 by Scientific Methods, Inc. Reproduced by permission of the owners.

school policy making. Having their input recognized, McPhee reasoned, would inspire people to have a stake in the future of education.[34]

Both styles reflect an integration of the two concerns presented in the grid. Notebaert's leadership style represents a high concern for results working simultaneously with a low concern for others. The reverse is true for McPhee. In each case, both concerns are present, but integrated at different levels.

How Grid Styles Emerge

Grid styles emerge in a relationship when the two concerns meet at the point of interaction with others. This includes any time when more than one person is involved in an activity. This involvement doesn't necessarily mean face-to-face meetings or discussions. Grid styles come into play, for example, when a leader considers who to recommend for a promotion, or who to include (or exclude) in a new opportunity. This interaction of concerns where Grid styles emerge is called *interdependence*. Interdependence is important because if you only think of Grid styles in terms of the independent levels of concerns (people or results), you risk misinterpreting the overall style. For example, in Grid terms, you cannot consider a person's level of concern for people without also considering their related concern for results. The style depends not on the individual levels of concern, but on the levels of concern *interacting*. To illustrate, the high 9 level of concern for people is present in two different Grid styles and the expression of that concern is extremely different in each style. The difference lies in how the person expresses the high concern for others in relation to the interdependent concern for results.

Two styles with the same level of concern for people are described below:

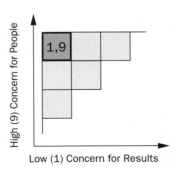

This joining of high concern for people with low concern for results leads to a 1,9 Country Club leader who puts people first in the workplace, even at the expense of achieving sound results. Every action this leader takes is compared against a standard of keeping people happy. This leader is more concerned with maintaining a pleasant environment, even if it means results must suffer. He or she is constantly influenced by the questions, "What will people think? Will this make people angry and disrupt the pleasant environment we enjoy now?"

Even though the concern for people is high in the 1,9 style, it takes on a characteristic of hiding and protecting people from unpleasantness. This leader may, for example, decline and hide an opportunity posed to the team because he or she thinks that the mere mentioning may generate conflict, resentment, fears, too much pressure, etc. Instead of posing the opportunity to the team, he or she hides it from members, or presents it in a way that they will accept. "I told them we weren't interested. We would have lost all of the momentum we've made on our current project, and it would be impossible to complete it in time. They weren't in the least upset about it."

Another aspect of this style it that the quest for happiness makes it very difficult for this leader to confront problems because he or she doesn't want to generate conflict. For example, if a team member is abusing policies or taking advantage of other team members, the 1,9 Country Club leader will ignore, make excuses, and dismiss the problem for as long as possible.

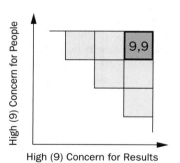

High (9) Concern for People

High (9) Concern for Results

In the 9,9 Team Management style, the same level of concern for people takes on completely different characteristics as it joins with a high level of concern for results. The emerging style is a leader who encourages and motivates himself and others to achieve excellence. Every action this leader takes is compared against a standard of excellence rather than a standard of making people happy.

The concern for people is the same level for the 9,9 Team Management style as in the 1,9 Country Club style, but the difference is the interacting concern for results. When the two high concerns join, the overall style becomes one where happiness and comfort are important, but in relation to also achieving sound results. Happiness is not the overruling priority in this leader. If a person is abusing policies or taking advantage of other team members, the leader will confront the issue for resolution so that it doesn't distract from the team achieving sound results.

Theories of a "High-High" Leader

The leadership styles described by the researchers at Ohio State, University of Michigan, and University of Texas pertain to variables that roughly correspond to one another: consideration and initiating structure; employee-centered and job-centered; concern for people and concern for production, as illustrated in Exhibit 2.4. The research into the behavior approach culminated in two predominate types of leadership behaviors—people-oriented and task-oriented.

The findings about two underlying dimensions and the possibility of leaders rated high on both dimensions raise four questions to think about. The first is whether these two dimensions are the most important behaviors of leadership. Certainly, these two behaviors are important. They capture fundamental, underlying aspects of human behavior that must be considered for organizations to succeed. One reason why these two dimensions are compelling is that the findings are based on empirical research, which means that researchers went into the field to study real leaders across a variety of settings. When independent streams of field research reach similar conclusions, they probably represent a fundamental theme in leadership behavior. Concern for task and concern for people must be shown toward followers at some reasonable level, either by the leader or by other people in the system. While these are not the only important behaviors, as we will see throughout this book, they certainly require attention.

EXHIBIT 2.4

Themes of Leader Behavior Research

	People-Oriented	Task-Oriented
Ohio State University	Consideration	Initiating Structure
University of Michigan	Employee-Centered	Job-Centered
University of Texas	Concern for People	Concern for Production

The second question is whether people orientation and task orientation exist together in the same leader, and how. The Grid theory argues that yes, both are present when people work with or through others to accomplish an activity. Although leaders may be high on either style, there is considerable belief that the best leaders are high on both behaviors. Superintendent John Fryer, described earlier, is an example of a leader who succeeds on both dimensions. How does a leader achieve both behaviors? Some researchers argue that "high-high" leaders alternate the type of behavior from one to the other, showing concern one time and task initiation another time.[35] Another approach says that effective "high-high" leaders encompass both behaviors simultaneously in a fundamentally different way than people who behave in one way or the other. For example, Fryer sets challenging goals for student performance and also works closely with teachers to provide the tools and training they feel they need to achieve those goals. A task-oriented leader might set difficult goals and simply pressure subordinates to improve quality. On the other hand, a person-oriented leader might ignore student achievement scores and goal attainment and simply seek to improve schools by consulting with teachers and building positive relationships with them. The "high-high" leaders seem to have a knack for displaying concern for both people and production in the majority of their behaviors.[36]

The third question is whether a "high-high" leadership style is universal or situational. Universal means that the behavior will tend to be effective in every situation, while situational means the behavior succeeds only in certain settings. Research has indicated some degree of universality with respect to people-oriented and task-oriented behavior. In other words, the leader behavior of concern for people tended to be related to higher employee satisfaction and fewer personnel problems across a wide variety of situations. Likewise, task-oriented behavior was associated with higher productivity across a large number of situations.

The fourth question concerns whether people can actually change themselves into leaders high on people and/or task-orientation. In the 1950s and 1960s, when the Ohio State and Michigan studies were underway, the assumption of researchers was that the behaviors of effective leaders could be emulated by anyone wishing to become an effective leader. In general it seems that people can learn new leader behaviors, as described in Chapter 1. There is a general belief that "high-high" leadership is a desirable quality, because the leader will meet both needs simultaneously. Despite the research indicating that "high-high" leadership is not the only effective style, researchers have looked to this kind of leader as a candidate for success in a wide number of situations. However, as we will see in the next chapter, the next generation of leadership studies refined the understanding of situations to pinpoint more precisely when each type of leadership behavior is most effective.

DYADIC APPROACHES

Dyadic theorists believe that trait and behavior theories oversimplify the relationship between leaders and subordinates. Dyadic theorists focus on the concept of exchange between a leader and a follower, a relationship known as a dyad. **Dyadic theory** involves a perspective that examines why leaders have more influence over and greater impact on some followers than on other followers. Dyadic theorists argue that leaders do not uniformly broadcast a trait such as self-confidence or a behavior such as people-orientation that is received equally by each subordinate. The dyadic view suggests that a single leader will form different relationships with different followers. For example, interviewing subordinates of a single leader will reveal different descriptions of the same person, with some descriptions being positive and some negative. To understand leadership in this perspective, a closer look at the specific relationship in each leader-subordinate dyad is necessary.[37]

The first dyadic theory was introduced more than twenty-five years ago and has been steadily revised ever since. The development of this viewpoint is illustrated in Exhibit 2.5. The first stage was the awareness of a relationship between a leader and each subordinate, rather than between a leader and a group of subordinates. The second stage examined specific attributes of the exchange between leader and subordinate. The third stage explored whether leaders could intentionally develop partnerships with each subordinate, and the fourth stage expanded the view of dyads to include larger systems and networks.

Vertical Dyad Linkage Model

The **Vertical Dyad Linkage (VDL) model** argues for the importance of the dyad formed by a leader with each member of the subordinate group. Initial findings indicated that subordinates provided very different descriptions of the same leader. For example, some subordinates reported a leader, and their relationship with the leader, as having a high degree of mutual trust, respect, and obligation. These high-quality relationships might be characterized as high on both people and task orientation. Other subordinates reported a low-quality relationship with the same leader, such as having a low degree of trust, respect, and obligation. These subordinates perceived the leader as being low on important leadership behaviors.

Based on these two extreme exchange patterns, subordinates were found to exist in either an in-group or an out-group in relation to the leader. Most of us who have had experience with any kind of group, whether it be a college class, an athletic team, or a work group, recognize that some leaders may spend a disproportionate amount of time with certain people, and that these

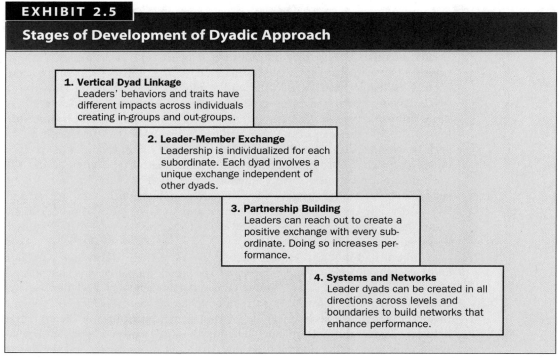

EXHIBIT 2.5

Stages of Development of Dyadic Approach

1. Vertical Dyad Linkage
Leaders' behaviors and traits have different impacts across individuals creating in-groups and out-groups.

2. Leader-Member Exchange
Leadership is individualized for each subordinate. Each dyad involves a unique exchange independent of other dyads.

3. Partnership Building
Leaders can reach out to create a positive exchange with every subordinate. Doing so increases performance.

4. Systems and Networks
Leader dyads can be created in all directions across levels and boundaries to build networks that enhance performance.

SOURCES: Based on Fred Danereau, "A Dyadic Approach to Leadership: Creating and Nurturing This Approach Under Fire," *Leadership Quarterly* 6, No. 4 (1995), 479–490, and George B. Graen and Mary Uhl-Bien, "Relationship-Based Approach to Leadership: Development of Leader-Member Exchange (LMX) Theory of Leadership Over 25 Years: Applying a Multi-level, Multi-domain Approach," *Leadership Quarterly* 6, No. 2 (1995), 219–247.

"insiders" are often highly trusted and may obtain special privileges. In the terminology of the VDL model, these people would be considered to participate in an *in-group exchange* relationship with the leader, while other members of the group who did not experience a sense of trust and extra consideration would participate in an *out-group exchange*.

In-group members, those who rated the leader highly, had developed close relationships with the leader and often became assistants who played key roles in the functioning of the work unit. Out-group members were not key players in the work unit. Because of these differences, individuals often fell into subgroups, which might be considered supporters and opponents of the leader. Some subordinates were getting their needs met, while others were not. These differences were based on the dyad between the leader and each subordinate. The in-group had high access to the leader, while the out-group members tended to be passive and did not have positions of influence or access to the leader. In-group members expressed greater mutual influence and collaborative effort with the leader, and they had opportunities to receive greater rewards and perform additional duties. Out-group members tended not to experience positive leader relationships and influence, and the leader was more likely to use formal authority and coercive behavior with these subordinates. In-group members typically received more attention, more approval, and probably more status, but they were also expected to be loyal, committed, and productive.

Thus, by focusing on the relationship between a leader and each subordinate, the Vertical Dyad Linkage research found great variance of leader style and impact within a group of subordinates.

Leader-Member Exchange

Stage two in the development of the dyad theory explored the **leader-member exchange (LMX)** in more detail, discovering that the impact on outcomes depends on how the leader-member exchange process develops over time. Studies evaluating characteristics of the LMX relationship explored such things as communication frequency, value agreement, characteristics of followers, job satisfaction, performance, job climate, and commitment. Leaders typically tend to establish in-group exchange relationships with individuals who have characteristics similar to those of the leader, such as similarity in background, interests, and values, and with those who demonstrate a high level of competence and interest in the job. Overall, studies have found that the quality of the leader-member exchange relationship is substantially higher for in-group members. LMX theory proposes that this higher-quality relationship will lead to higher performance and greater job satisfaction for in-group members, and research in general supports this idea.[38] High-quality LMX relationships have been found to lead to very positive outcomes for leaders, followers, work units, and the organization. For followers, a high-quality exchange relationship may mean more interesting assignments, greater responsibility and authority, and tangible rewards such as pay increases and promotions. Leaders and organizations clearly benefit from the increased effort and initiative of in-group participants to carry out assignments and tasks successfully.

LMX theorists identified three stages dyad members go through in their working relationship. In the initial stage, the leader and follower, as strangers, test each other to identify what kinds of behaviors are comfortable. The relationship is negotiated informally between each follower and the leader. The definition of each group member's role defines what the member and leader expect the member to do. Next, as the leader and member become acquainted, they engage in shaping and refining the roles they will play together. Finally, in the third stage, as the roles reach maturity, the relationship attains a steady pattern of behavior. Leader-member exchanges are difficult to change at this point. The exchange tends to determine in-group and out-group status.

Partnership Building

In this third phase of research, the focus was on whether leaders could develop positive relationships with a large number of subordinates. Critics of early LMX theory pointed out the dangers of leaders establishing sharply differentiated in-group and out-group members, in that this may lead to feelings of resentment or even hostility among out-group participants.[39] If leaders are perceived to be granting excessive benefits and advantages to in-group members, members of the out-group may rebel, which can damage the entire organization.

Thus, the third phase of research in this area focused on whether leaders could develop positive relationships with all subordinates, not just a few "favorites." The emphasis was not on how or why discrimination among subordinates occurred, but rather on how a leader might work with each subordinate on a one-on-one basis to develop a partnership. The idea was that leaders could develop a unique, beneficial relationship with each individual and provide all employees with access to high-quality leader-member exchanges, thereby providing a more equitable environment and greater benefits to leaders, followers, and the organization.

In this approach, the leader views each person independently, and may treat each individual in a different but positive way. Sometimes called individualized leadership, leaders strive to actively develop a positive relationship with each subordinate, although the positive relationship will have a different form for each person. For example, one person might be treated with "consideration," another with "initiating structure," depending on what followers need to feel involved and to succeed.

In cases where leaders were trained to offer the opportunity for a high-quality relationship to all of their subordinates, the followers who accepted the offer improved their performance dramatically. As these relationships matured, the entire work group became more productive, and the payoffs were tremendous. Leaders could count on followers to provide the assistance needed for high performance, and followers participated in and influenced decisions. Leaders provided support, encouragement, and training, and followers responded with high performance. In some sense, leaders were meeting both the personal and work-related needs of each subordinate, one at a time. The implications of this finding are that true performance and productivity gains can be achieved by having the leader develop positive relationships one-on-one with each subordinate.

Systems and Networks

The final stage of this work suggests that leader dyads can be expanded to larger systems. Rather than focusing on leaders and subordinates, a systems-level perspective examines how dyadic relationships can be created across traditional boundaries to embrace a larger system. This larger network for the leader may cut across work unit, functional, divisional, and even organizational boundaries. In this view, leader relationships are not limited to subordinates, but include peers, teammates, and other stakeholders relevant to the work unit. To this point, there has been little systematic research on a broader systemic view of dyadic relationships. But the theory suggests the need for leaders to build networks of one-on-one relationships and to use their traits and behaviors selectively to create positive relationships with as many people as possible. A large number of people thereby can be influenced by the leader, and these stakeholders will contribute to the success of the work unit.

After GE Plastics merged with Borg-Warner Chemicals, leaders saw a need to create partnerships among employees who were accustomed to viewing one another as rivals.

IN THE LEAD   ## GE Plastics/Borg Warner

GE Plastics, with headquarters in Pittsfield, Massachusetts, has recognized the importance of partnership for a long time, but it took on new urgency after the company purchased a long-time rival, Borg-Warner Chemicals, based in Parkersville, West Virginia. Many Borg-Warner employees still considered GE "the competition" and didn't feel like a part of the company—and what's more, they weren't sure they wanted to.

Company leaders wanted a way to get employees throughout the organization acting like partners, without regard to department or hierarchical levels. They considered the former types of team-building activities they had used—rowing events, donkey races, wilderness experiences—and realized what they really needed was an event that would make a lasting impression on employees while serving a larger purpose and creating something of enduring value. The decision was made that employees would renovate five nonprofit facilities, using many of GE's materials, borrowing equipment when possible, and purchasing other supplies and tools in the local community. Teams were carefully formed to give employees a chance to meet and work with new people, combine executives with lower-level workers, and, above all, mix former Borg-Warner employees with GE workers. In one 12-hour day, thirty teams completely renovated the run-down Copley Family YMCA, located in a low-income San Diego neighborhood riddled with gangs and drugs. They scraped and painted walls, cleaned graffiti, laid tile, replaced windows, landscaped the grounds, and even restored a 20-year-old mural covering a two-story outer wall. In the process, people had a chance to begin developing one-on-one relationships with fellow workers from different areas and levels of the company.

The final effect on the community was impressive, but what was most phenomenal was the impact on employees. The feelings of accomplishment and camaraderie were more than executives had ever hoped for, and the event proved to be the turning point in the integration of GE Plastics and Borg-Warner employees. After a day of pounding nails and painting walls, they shed their rivalries to become partners working toward a common cause they all felt proud of.[40]

SUMMARY AND INTERPRETATION

The point of this chapter is to understand the importance of traits and behaviors in the development of leadership theory and research. Traits include self-confidence, honesty, and drive. A large number of personal traits and abilities distinguish successful leaders from nonleaders, but traits themselves are not sufficient to guarantee effective leadership. The behavior approach explored autocratic versus democratic leadership, consideration versus initiating structure, employee-centered versus job-centered leadership, and concern for people versus concern for production. The theme of people versus tasks runs through this research, suggesting these are fundamental behaviors through which leaders meet followers' needs. There has been some disagreement in the research about whether a specific leader is either people- or task-oriented or whether they can be both. Today, the consensus is that leaders can achieve a "high-high" leadership style.

Another approach is the dyad between a leader and each follower. Followers have different relationships with the leader, and the ability of the leader to develop a positive relationship with each subordinate contributes to team performance. The leader-member exchange theory says that high-quality relationships have a positive outcome for leaders, followers, work units, and the organization. Leaders can attempt to build individualized relationships with each subordinate as a way to meet needs for both consideration and structure.

The historical development of leadership theory presented in this chapter introduces some important ideas about leadership. While certain personal traits and abilities constitute a greater likelihood for success in a leadership role, they are not in themselves sufficient to guarantee effective leadership. Rather, behaviors are equally significant, as outlined by the research at several universities. Therefore, the style of leadership demonstrated by an individual greatly determines the outcome of the leadership endeavor. Often, a combination of styles is most effective. To understand the effects of leadership upon outcomes, the specific relationship behavior between a leader and each follower is also an important consideration.

KEY TERMS

traits	democratic	dyadic theory
Great Man approach	consideration	vertical-dyad linkage
self-confidence	initiating structure	model
honesty	employee-centered	leader-member
drive	job-centered	exchange (LMX)
autocratic	The Leadership Grid	

DISCUSSION QUESTIONS

1. Is the "Great Man" perspective on leadership still alive today? Think about some recent popular movies that stress a lone individual as hero or savior. Discuss.

2. Suggest some personal traits of leaders you have known. Which traits do you believe are most valuable? Why?

3. What is the difference between trait theories and behavioral theories of leadership?

4. Would you prefer working for a leader who has a "consideration" or an "initiating-structure" leadership style? Discuss the reasons for your answer.

5. The Vertical Dyad Linkage model suggests that followers respond individually to the leader. If this is so, what advice would you give leaders about displaying people-oriented versus task-oriented behavior?

6. Does it make sense to you that a leader should develop an individualized relationship with each follower? Explain advantages and disadvantages to this approach.

7. Why would subordinates under a democratic leader perform better in the leader's absence than would subordinates under an autocratic leader?

8. Which type of leader—task-oriented or people-oriented—do you think would have an easier time becoming a "high-high" leader? Why?

LEADERSHIP DEVELOPMENT: Personal Feedback

Rate Your Self-Confidence

For each statement below, indicate the degree to which you agree or disagree with the statement. Place the number of your answer in the space to the left of the statement, based on the following scale: 1 = Strongly disagree; 2 = Disagree;

3 = Slightly disagree; 4 = Neither agree nor disagree; 5 = Slightly Agree; 6 = Agree; 7 = Strongly Agree

_____   1. When I make plans, I am certain I can make them work.

_____   2. One of my problems is that I cannot get down to work when I should.

_____   3. If I can't do a job the first time, I keep trying until I can.

_____   4. When I set important goals for myself, I rarely achieve them.

_____   5. I give up on things before completing them.

_____   6. I avoid facing difficulties.

_____   7. If something looks too complicated, I will not even bother to try it.

_____   8. When I have something unpleasant to do, I stick to it until I finish it.

_____   9. When I decide to do something, I go right to work on it.

_____   10. When trying to learn something new, I soon give up if I am not initially successful.

_____   11. When unexpected problems occur, I don't handle them well.

_____   12. I avoid trying to learn new things when they look too difficult for me.

_____   13. Failure just makes me try harder.

_____   14. I feel insecure about my ability to do things.

_____   15. I am a self-reliant person.

_____   16. I give up easily.

_____   17. I do not seem capable of dealing with most problems that come up in life.

SOURCE: M. Sherer, J. E. Maddux, B. Mercadante, S. Prentice-Dunn, B. Jacobs, and R. W. Rogers, "The Self-Efficacy Scale: Construction and Validity," _Psychological Reports_ 53 (1982): 899–902. Used with permission.

Scoring

Subtract each of your scores for questions 2, 4, 5, 6, 7, 10, 11, 12, 14, 16, and 17 from the number 8. Next, using your adjusted scores, sum your score for the 17 questions and then divide by 17. Enter your score here: _____

Interpretation

These questions are designed to assess your level of self-confidence as reflected in a belief in your ability to accomplish an outcome. Scores may range from 1 to 7; the higher your score, the greater your level of general self-confidence. Many researchers have noted that self-confidence is a precursor to strong and effective leadership, as described in this chapter. Self-confidence enables leaders to gain the confidence and respect of followers, make difficult decisions, and enact change. Do you believe you have the self-confidence to be a strong leader? If your score on this questionnaire is low, what can you do to increase your level of self-confidence?

LEADERSHIP DEVELOPMENT: Cases for Analysis

Consolidated Products

Consolidated Products is a medium-sized manufacturer of consumer products with nonunionized production workers. Ben Samuels was a plant manager for Consolidated Products for ten years, and he was very well liked by the employees there. They were grateful for the fitness center he built for employees, and they enjoyed the social activities sponsored by the plant several times a year, including company picnics and holiday parties. He knew most of the workers by name, and he spent part of each day walking around the plant to visit with them and ask about their families or hobbies.

Ben believed that it was important to treat employees properly so they would have a sense of loyalty to the company. He tried to avoid any layoffs when production demand was slack, figuring that the company could not afford to lose skilled workers that are so difficult to replace. The workers knew that if they had a special problem, Ben would try to help them. For example, when someone was injured but wanted to continue working, Ben found another job in the plant that the person could do despite having a disability. Ben believed that if you treat people right, they will do a good job for you without close supervision or prodding. Ben applied the same principle to his supervisors, and he mostly left them alone to run their departments as they saw fit. He did not set objectives and standards for the plant, and he never asked the supervisors to develop plans for improving productivity and product quality.

Under Ben, the plant had the lowest turnover among the company's five plants, but the second worst record for costs and production levels. When the company was acquired by another firm, Ben was asked to take early retirement, and Phil Jones was brought in to replace him.

Phil had a growing reputation as a manager who could get things done, and he quickly began making changes. Costs were cut by trimming a number of activities such as the fitness center at the plant, company picnics and parties, and the human relations training programs for supervisors. Phil believed that human relations training was a waste of time; if employees don't want to do the work, get rid of them and find somebody else who does.

Supervisors were instructed to establish high performance standards for their departments and insist that people achieve them. A computer monitoring system was introduced so that the output of each worker could be checked closely against the standards. Phil told his supervisors to give any worker who had substandard performance one warning, and then if performance did not improve within two weeks, to fire the person. Phil believed that workers don't respect a supervisor who is weak and passive. When Phil observed a worker wasting time or making a mistake, he would reprimand the person right on the spot to set an example. Phil also checked closely on the performance of his supervisors. Demanding objectives were set for each department, and weekly meetings were held with each supervisor to review department performance. Finally, Phil insisted that supervisors check with him first before taking any significant actions that deviated from established plans and policies.

As another cost-cutting move, Phil reduced the frequency of equipment maintenance, which required machines to be idled when they could be productive. Since the machines had a good record of reliable operation, Phil believed that the current maintenance schedule was excessive and was cutting into production. Finally, when business was slow for one of the product lines, Phil laid off workers rather than finding something else for them to do.

By the end of Phil's first year as plant manager, production costs were reduced by 20 percent and production output was up by 10 percent. However, three of his seven supervisors left to take other jobs, and turnover was also high among the machine operators. Some of the turnover was due to workers who were fired, but competent machine operators were also quitting, and it was becoming increasingly difficult to find any replacements for them. Finally, there was increasing talk of unionizing among the workers.

SOURCE: Reprinted with permission from Gary Yukl, *Leadership in Organizations,* 4th ed. Englewood Cliffs, NJ: Prentice Hall, 1998, 66–67.

Questions

1. Compare the leadership traits and behaviors of Ben Samuels and Phil Jones.

2. Which leader do you think is more effective? Why? Which leader would you prefer to work for?

3. If you were Phil Jones' boss, what would you do now?

D. L. Woodside, Sunshine Snacks

D. L. Woodside has recently accepted the position of research and development director for Sunshine Snacks, a large snack food company. Woodside has been assistant director of research at Skid's, a competing company, for several years, but it became clear to him that his chances of moving higher were slim. So, when Sunshine was looking for a new director, Woodside jumped at the chance.

At Skid's, Woodside had worked his way up from the mail room, going to school at night to obtain first a bachelor's degree and eventually a Ph.D. Management admired his drive and determination, as well as his ability to get along with just about anyone he came in contact with, and they gave him opportunities to work in various positions around the company over the years. That's when he discovered he had a love for developing new products. He had been almost single-handedly responsible for introducing four new successful product lines at Skid's. Woodside's technical knowledge and understanding of the needs of the research and development department were excellent. In addition, he was a tireless worker—when he started a project he rarely rested until it was finished, and finished well.

Despite his ambition and his hard-charging approach to work, Woodside was considered an easy-going fellow. He liked to talk and joke around, and whenever anyone had a problem they'd come to Woodside rather than go to the director. Woodside was always willing to listen to a research assistant's personal problems. Besides that, he would often stay late or come in on weekends to finish an assistant's work if the employee was having problems at home or difficulty with a particular project. Woodside knew the director was a hard taskmaster, and he didn't want anyone getting into trouble over things they couldn't help. In fact, he'd been covering the mistakes of George, an employee who had a drinking problem, ever since he'd been appointed assistant director. Well, George was on his own now. Woodside had his own career to think about, and the position at Sunshine was his chance to finally lead a department rather than play second-fiddle.

At Sunshine, Woodside is replacing Henry Meade, who has been the director for almost thirty years. However, it seems clear that Meade has been slowing down over the past few years, turning more and more of his work over to his assistant, Harmon Davis. When Woodside was first introduced to the people in the research department at Sunshine, he sensed not only a loyalty to Davis, who'd been passed over for the top job because of his lack of technical knowledge, but also an undercurrent of resistance to his own selection as the new director.

Woodside knows he needs to build good relationships with the team, and especially with Davis, quickly. The company has made it clear that it wants the department to initiate several new projects as soon as possible. One reason they selected Woodside for the job was his successful track record with new product development at Skid's.

SOURCE: Based in part on "The Take Over," Incident 52 in Bernard A. Deitzer and Karl A. Shilliff, *Contemporary Management Incidents* (Columbus, OH: Grid, Inc., 1977), 161–162, and "Choosing a New Director of Research," Case 2.1 in Peter G. Northouse, *Leadership Theory and Practice*, 2nd ed. (Thousand Oaks, CA: Sage Publications, 2001), 25–26.

Questions

1. What traits does Woodside possess that might be helpful to him as he assumes his new position? What traits might be detrimental?

2. Would you consider Woodside a people-oriented or a task-oriented leader? Discuss which you think would be best for the new research director at Sunshine.

3. How might an understanding of dyadic theory be useful to Woodside in this circumstance? Discuss.

REFERENCES

1. Curtis Sittenfeld, "Leader on the Edge," *Fast Company*, October 1999, 212–226.
2. Caley Ben-David, "The Next Big e-Thing," *Working Woman*, May 2000, 72–76.
3. G. A. Yukl, *Leadership in Organizations* (Englewood Cliffs, NJ: Prentice-Hall, 1981); and S. C. Kohs and K. W. Irle, "Prophesying Army Promotion," *Journal of Applied Psychology* 4 (1920), 73–87.
4. Yukl, *Leadership in Organizations*, 254.
5. R. M. Stogdill, "Personal Factors Associated with Leadership: A Survey of the Literature," *Journal of Psychology* 25 (1948), 35–71.
6. R. M. Stogdill, *Handbook of Leadership: A Survey of the Literature* (New York: Free Press, 1974); and Bernard M. Bass, *Bass & Stogdill's Handbook of Leadership: Theory, Research, and Managerial Applications*, 3rd ed. (New York: The Free Press, 1990).
7. S. A. Kirkpatrick and E. A. Locke, "Leadership: Do Traits Matter?" *The Academy of Management Executive* 5, No. 2 (1991): 48-60.

8. R. G. Lord, C. L. DeVader, and G. M. Alliger, "A Meta-Analysis of the Relation Between Personality Traits and Leadership Perceptions: An Application of Validity Generalization Procedures," *Journal of Applied Psychology* 71 (1986): 402–410.

9. Thomas A. Stewart, "Have You Got What It Takes?" *Fortune,* October 11, 1999, 318–322.

10. Daniel Goleman, *Emotional Intelligence: Why It Can Matter More Than IQ* (New York: Bantam Books, 1995), 289–290; Sharon Nelton, "Emotions in the Workplace," *Nation's Business,* February 1996, 25–30; and Lara E. Megerian and John J. Sosik, "An Affair of the Heart: Emotional Intelligence and Transformational Leadership," *The Journal of Leadership Studies* 3, No. 3 (1996), 31–48.

11. Edwin Locke and Associates, *The Essence of Leadership* (New York: Lexington Books, 1991).

12. Shelley A. Kirkpatrick and Edwin A. Locke, "Leadership: Do Traits Matter?" *Academy of Management Executive* 5, No. 2(1991): 48–60.

13. Geoffrey Colvin, "How to Be a Great eCEO," *Fortune,* May 24, 1999, 104–110.

14. James M. Kouzes and Barry Z. Posner, *Credibility: How Leaders Gain and Lose It, Why People Demand It* (San Francisco: Jossey-Bass Publishers, 1993), 14.

15. "Roy Vagelos Attacks River Blindness," in Michael Useem, *The Leadership Moment: Nine Stories of Triumph and Disaster and Their Lessons for Us All* (New York: Times Business, 1998), 10–42.

16. This discussion is based on Kirkpatrick and Locke, "Leadership: Do Traits Matter?"

17. A. Howard and D. W. Bray, *Managerial Lives in Transition: Advancing Age and Changing Times* (New York: Guilford Press, 1988).

18. K. Lewin, "Field Theory and Experiment in Social Psychology: Concepts and Methods," *American Journal of Sociology* 44 (1939): 868–896; K. Lewin and R. Lippet, "An Experimental Approach to the Study of Autocracy and Democracy: A Preliminary Note," *Sociometry* 1 (1938): 292–300; and K. Lewin, R. Lippett, and R. K. White, "Patterns of Aggressive Behavior in Experimentally Created Social Climates," *Journal of Social Psychology* 10 (1939): 271–301.

19. R. Tannenbaum and W. H. Schmidt, "How to Choose a Leadership Pattern," *Harvard Business Review* 36 (1958), 95–101.

20. F. A. Heller and G. A. Yukl, "Participation, Managerial Decision-Making and Situational Variables," *Organizational Behavior and Human Performance* 4 (1969), 227–241.

21. Patricia O'Toole, "How Do You Build a $44 Million Company? By Saying Please," *Working Woman,* April 1990, 88–92.

22. J. K. Hemphill and A. E. Coons, "Development of the Leader Behavior Description Questionnaire," in *Leader Behavior: Its Description and Measurement,* Eds. R. M. Stogdill and A. E. Coons (Columbus, OH: Ohio State University, Bureau of Business Research, 1957).

23. P. C. Nystrom, "Managers and the High-High Leader Myth," *Academy of Management Journal* 21 (1978), 325–331; and L. L. Larson, J. G. Hunt and Richard N. Osborn, "The Great High-High Leader Behavior Myth: A Lesson from Occam's Razor," *Academy of Management Journal* 19 (1976), 628–641.

24. Stephanie Desmon, "Schools Chief an Executive, Not an Educator," *The Palm Beach Post,* December 26, 1999, 1A, 22A.

25. E. W. Skinner, "Relationships Between Leadership Behavior Patterns and Organizational-Situational Variables," *Personnel Psychology* 22 (1969), 489–494; and E. A. Fleishman and E. F. Harris, "Patterns of Leadership Behavior Related to Employee Grievances and Turnover," *Personnel Psychology* 15 (1962), 43–56.

26. A. W. Halpin and B. J. Winer, "A Factorial Study of the Leader Behavior Descriptions," in *Leader Behavior: Its Descriptions and Measurement,* Eds. R. M. Stogdill and A. E. Coons, (Columbus, OH: Ohio State University, Bureau of Business Research, 1957); and J. K. Hemphill, "Leadership Behavior Associated with the Administrative Reputations of College Departments," *Journal of Educational Psychology* 46 (1955): 385–401.

27. R. Likert, "From Production- and Employee-Centeredness to Systems 1–4," *Journal of Management* 5 (1979), 147–156.

28. J. Taylor and D. Bowers, *The Survey of Organizations: A Machine Scored Standardized Questionnaire Instrument* (Ann Arbor, MI: Institute for Social Research, University of Michigan, 1972).

29. D. G. Bowers and S. E. Seashore, "Predicting Organizational Effectiveness with a Four-Factor Theory of Leadership," *Administrative Science Quarterly* 11 (1966), 238–263.

30. Carol Hymowitz, "Damark's Unique Post: A Manager Who Helps Work on Relationships," (In the Lead column), *The Wall Street Journal,* September 7, 1999, B1.

31. Bowers and Seashore, "Predicting Organizational Effectiveness with a Four-Factor Theory of Leadership."

32. Robert Blake and Jane S. Mouton, *The Managerial Grid III* (Houston: Gulf, 1985).

33. Peter Elstrom, "Telecom's Pit Bull," *Business Week,* July 1, 1996.

34. Rob McPhee, "Orchestrating Community Involvement," *Educational Leadership* 53 (December/January 1996), 71–76.

35. J. Misumi, "The Behavioral Science of Leadership: An Interdisciplinary Japanese Research Program" (Ann Arbor, MI: University of Michigan Press, 1985).

36. Fleishman and Harris, "Patterns of Leadership Behavior Related to Employee Grievances and Turnover"; and Misumi, "The Behavioral Science of Leadership: An Interdisciplinary Japanese Research Program."

37. This discussion is based on Fred Danereau, "A Dyadic Approach to Leadership: Creating and Nurturing This Approach Under Fire," *Leadership Quarterly* 6, No. 4 (1995), 479–490, and George B. Graen and Mary Uhl-Bien, "Relationship-Based Approach to Leadership: Development of Leader Member Exchange (LMX) Theory of Leadership Over 25 Years: Applying a Multi-Level Multi-Domain Approach," *Leadership Quarterly* 6, No. 2 (1995), 219–247.

38. See A. J. Kinicki and R. P. Vecchio, "Influences on the Quality of Supervisor-Subordinate Relations: The Role of Time Pressure, Organizational Commitment, and Locus of Control," *Journal of Organizational Behavior,* January 1994, 75–82; and R. C. Liden, S. J. Wayne, and D. Stilwell, "A Longitudinal Study on the Early

Development of Leader-Member Exchanges," *Journal of Applied Psychology,* August 1993, 662–674.

39. W. E. McClane, "Implications of Member Role Differentiation: Analysis of a Key Concept in the LMX Model of Leadership," *Group and Organization Studies* 16 (1991): 102–113; and Gary Yukl, *Leadership in Organizations,* Second Edition (New York: Prentice-Hall, 1989).

40. David Bollier, "Building Corporate Loyalty While Rebuilding the Community," *Management Review,* October 1996, 17–22.

CHAPTER OUTLINE

YOUR LEADERSHIP CHALLENGE

After reading this chapter, you should be able to:

- Understand how leadership is often contingent on people and situations.

- Apply Fiedler's contingency model to key relationships among leader style, situational favorability, and group task performance.

- Apply Hersey and Blanchard's situational theory of leader style to the level of follower readiness.

- Explain the path-goal theory of leadership.

- Use the Vroom-Jago model to identify the correct amount of follower participation in specific decision situations.

- Know how to use the power of situational variables to substitute for or neutralize the need for leadership.

Contingency Approaches

Tom Golisano turned an obscure business into a gold mine by giving small businesses a place where they can outsource the routine tasks associated with turning out paychecks. Paychex, Inc. has made Golisano and his partners millionaires. Golisano holds his managers' noses to the grindstone. He insists that they keep the client base growing at 10 percent a year—to do so, every salesperson is required to make fifty calls per week, eight personal presentations, and at least three sales. If they don't, they don't last long at Paychex. Golisano uses a boot-camp discipline, requiring employees to observe a strict dress code and a clean desk policy. He prides himself on running a tight operation—no company cars or country club memberships at this company, even for top executives. Despite the grueling pace Golisano sets for managers, those who can meet the standards are handsomely rewarded with stock options, helping to keep turnover low.

Compare Golisano's style to that of Tom Gegax, who calls himself head coach of Team Tires Plus, a fast-growing firm with 150 retail tire stores in ten states. Gegax believes that you can't manage people the same way you manage fixed assets. His emphasis is on treating employees just as well as they are expected to treat their customers, or "guests," as they are called. Gegax personally leads classes at Tires Plus University, where employees learn not just about changing tires but about how to make their whole lives better. The company's wellness center offers monthly classes in health and nutrition. In addition, a course called "Balancing Your Personal Tire" is a favorite among workers seeking work-life balance. Gegax also makes sure stores are clean, bright, and airy, so that employees have a pleasant work environment. He believes all this translates into better service. Employees, as well as customers, like the approach. Team Tires Plus welcomes more than 1.7 million guests a year and boasts an annual growth rate of 23 percent. "The last thing the world needs is another chain of stores," Gegax says. "What it does need is a company with a new business model—one that embraces customers and employees as whole people."[1]

Referring back to the previous chapter, the leadership behavior of Golisano is task-oriented, that is, characterized by high concern for tasks and production and low-to-moderate concern for people. Tom Gegax, in contrast, is a people-oriented leader, high on concern for people and moderate on concern for production. Both leaders are successful, although they display very different leadership styles. This difference points to what researchers of leader traits and behaviors eventually discovered: Many different leadership styles can be effective. What, then, determines the success of a leadership style?

In the above example, the *situation* of each organization is very different. Golisano is operating in a fast-paced business where competition is cutthroat and growing by the day. After starting the business with $30,000 borrowed from his sister (her late husband's life insurance), Golisano set his employees on a grueling march for growth in order to stand out in a growing industry. Gegax has to attract and retain top-notch service workers in a tight labor market, as well as provide customers with a unique experience compared to what they would get at a traditional tire retailer. The differences in the organizational situations faced by these leaders influence their leadership styles, and both styles have achieved success.

This chapter explores the relationship between leadership effectiveness and the situation in which leadership activities occur. Over the years, researchers have observed that leaders behave situationally—that is, they adjust their leadership style depending on a variety of factors in the situations they face. In this chapter, we will discuss the elements of leader, follower, and the situation, and the impact each has upon the others. We will examine several theories that define how leadership styles, follower attributes, and organizational characteristics fit together to enable successful leadership. The important point of this chapter is that the most effective leadership approach depends on many factors. Understanding the contingency approaches can help a leader adapt his or her approach, although it is important to recognize that leaders also develop their ability to adapt through experience and practice.

THE CONTINGENCY APPROACH

The failure to find universal leader traits or behaviors that would always determine effective leadership led researchers in a new direction. While leader behavior was still examined, the central focus of the new research was the situation in which leadership occurred. The basic tenet of this focus was that behavior effective in some circumstances may be ineffective under different conditions. Thus, the effectiveness of leader behavior is *contingent* upon organizational situations. Aptly called contingency approaches, these theories explain the relationship between leadership styles and effectiveness in specific situations.

The universalistic approach as described in Chapter 2 is compared to the contingency approach used in this chapter in Exhibit 3.1. In the previous chapter, researchers were investigating traits or behaviors that could improve performance and satisfaction in any or all situations. They sought universal leadership traits and behaviors. **Contingency** means that one thing depends on other things, and for a leader to be effective there must be an appropriate fit

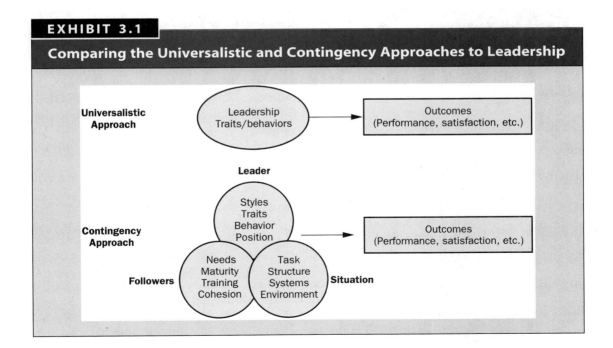

EXHIBIT 3.1

Comparing the Universalistic and Contingency Approaches to Leadership

between the leader's behavior and style and the conditions in the situation. A leadership style that works in one situation may not work in another situation. There is no one best way of leadership. Contingency means "it depends."

The contingencies most important to leadership as shown in Exhibit 3.1 are the situation and followers. Research implies that situational variables such as task, structure, context, and environment are important to leadership style, just as we saw in the opening examples with Golisano compared to Gegax. The nature of followers has also been identified as a key contingency. Thus the needs, maturity, and cohesiveness of followers make a significant difference to the best style of leadership.

Several models of situational leadership have been developed. The contingency model developed by Fiedler and his associates, the situational theory of Hersey and Blanchard, path-goal theory, the Vroom-Jago model of decision participation, and the substitutes for leadership concept will all be described in this chapter. The **contingency approaches** seek to delineate the characteristics of situations and followers and examine the leadership styles that can be used effectively. Assuming that a leader can properly diagnose a situation and muster the flexibility to behave according to the appropriate style, successful outcomes are highly likely.

FIEDLER'S CONTINGENCY MODEL

An early extensive effort to link leadership style with organizational situation was made by Fiedler and his associates.[2] The basic idea is simple: Match the leader's style with the situation most favorable for his or her success. **Fiedler's contingency model** was designed to enable leaders to diagnose both leadership style and organizational situation.

Leadership Style

The cornerstone of Fiedler's theory is the extent to which the leader's style is relationship-oriented or task-oriented. A *relationship-oriented leader* is concerned with people. As with the consideration style described in Chapter 2, a relationship-oriented leader establishes mutual trust and respect, and listens to employees' needs. A *task-oriented leader* is primarily motivated by task accomplishment. Similar to the initiating structure style described earlier, a task-oriented leader provides clear directions and sets performance standards.

Leadership style was measured with a questionnaire known as the least preferred coworker (LPC) scale. The LPC scale has a set of sixteen bipolar adjectives along an 8-point scale. Examples of the bipolar adjectives used by Fiedler on the LPC scale follow:

open	— — — — — — — —	guarded
quarrelsome	— — — — — — — —	harmonious
efficient	— — — — — — — —	inefficient
self-assured	— — — — — — — —	hesitant
gloomy	— — — — — — — —	cheerful

If the leader describes the least preferred coworker using positive concepts, he or she is considered relationship-oriented; that is, a leader who cares about and is sensitive to other people's feelings. Conversely, if a leader uses negative concepts to describe the least preferred coworker, he or she is considered task-oriented; that is, a leader who sees other people in negative terms and places greater value on task activities than on people.

Situation

Fiedler's model presents the leadership situation in terms of three key elements that can be either favorable or unfavorable to a leader: the quality of leader-member relations, task structure, and position power.

Leader-member relations refers to group atmosphere and members' attitudes toward and acceptance of the leader. When subordinates trust, respect, and have confidence in the leader, leader-member relations are considered good. When subordinates distrust, do not respect, and have little confidence in the leader, leader-member relations are poor.

Task structure refers to the extent to which tasks performed by the group are defined, involve specific procedures, and have clear, explicit goals. Routine, well-defined tasks, such as those of assembly-line workers, have a high degree of structure. Creative, ill-defined tasks, such as research and development or strategic planning, have a low degree of task structure. When task structure is high, the situation is considered favorable to the leader; when low, the situation is less favorable.

Position power is the extent to which the leader has formal authority over subordinates. Position power is high when the leader has the power to plan and direct the work of subordinates, evaluate it, and reward or punish them. Position power is low when the leader has little authority over subordinates and cannot evaluate their work or reward them. When position power is high, the situation is considered favorable for the leader; when low, the situation is unfavorable.

Combining the three situational characteristics yields a list of eight leadership situations, which are illustrated in Exhibit 3.2. Situation I is most favorable to the leader because leader-member relations are good, task structure is high, and leader position power is strong. Situation VIII is most unfavorable

---

EXHIBIT 3.2

Fiedler's Classification of Situation Favorableness

	Very Favorable			Intermediate			Very Unfavorable	
Leader-Member Relations	Good	Good	Good	Good	Poor	Poor	Poor	Poor
Task Structure	High		Low		High		Low	
Leader Position Power	Strong	Weak	Strong	Weak	Strong	Weak	Strong	Weak
Situations	I	II	III	IV	V	VI	VII	VIII

SOURCE: Fred E. Fiedler, "The Effects of Leadership Training and Experience: A Contingency Model Interpretation," *Administrative Science Quarterly* 17 (1972), 455. Reprinted by permission of *Administrative Science Quarterly*.

---

to the leader because leader-member relations are poor, task structure is low, and leader position power is weak. Other octants represent intermediate degrees of favorableness for the leader.

Contingency Theory

When Fiedler examined the relationships among leadership style, situational favorability, and group task performance, he found the pattern shown in Exhibit 3.3. Task-oriented leaders are more effective when the situation is either highly favorable or highly unfavorable. Relationship-oriented leaders are more effective in situations of moderate favorability.

The task-oriented leader excels in the favorable situation because everyone gets along, the task is clear, and the leader has power; all that is needed is for someone to take charge and provide direction. Similarly, if the situation is highly unfavorable to the leader, a great deal of structure and task direction is needed. A strong leader defines task structure and can establish authority over subordinates. Because leader-member relations are poor anyway, a strong task orientation will make no difference to the leader's popularity.

The relationship-oriented leader performs better in situations of intermediate favorability because human relations skills are important in achieving high group performance. In these situations, the leader may be moderately well liked, have some power, and supervise jobs that contain some ambiguity. A leader with good interpersonal skills can create a positive group atmosphere that will improve relationships, clarify task structure, and establish position power.

EXHIBIT 3.3

How Leader Style Fits the Situation

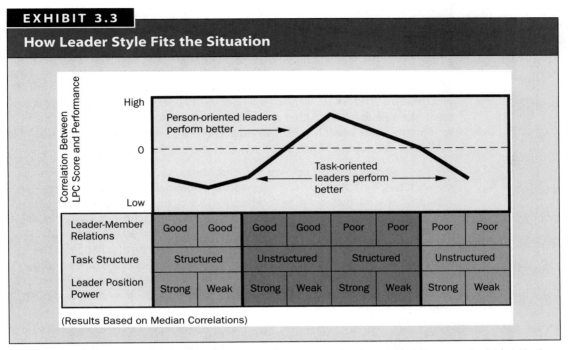

Leader-Member Relations	Good	Good	Good	Good	Poor	Poor	Poor	Poor
Task Structure	Structured		Unstructured		Structured		Unstructured	
Leader Position Power	Strong	Weak	Strong	Weak	Strong	Weak	Strong	Weak

(Results Based on Median Correlations)

SOURCE: Fred E. Fiedler, "The Effects of Leadership Training and Experience: A Contingency Model Interpretation," *Administrative Science Quarterly* 17 (1972), 455. Reprinted by permission of *Administrative Science Quarterly*.

A leader, then, needs to know two things in order to use Fiedler's contingency theory. First, the leader should know whether he or she has a relationship- or task-oriented style. Second, the leader should diagnose the situation and determine whether leader-member relations, task structure, and position power are favorable or unfavorable.

An incorrect style for the situation may be partly to blame for the problems Janet Reno experienced as U.S. Attorney General.

IN THE LEAD   Janet Reno, U.S. Attorney General

Janet Reno began her job as Attorney General in 1993 with much acclaim and was highly praised for some of her early efforts. Seven years later, even though she was recognized as the longest-serving attorney general of the twentieth century, Reno found herself almost constantly maligned by Congress and in the media.

Reno presided over a series of complicated and controversial investigations, and her supporters often blamed her battered reputation on politics. However, some think her leadership style was part of the problem. Reno has been called courteous and trusting to a fault. She values people and relationships, thus she would strive for consensus in important decisions. However, her desire for consensus often meant that thorny problems festered and turned into political time bombs. In addition, some people believed her emphasis on relationships meant that Reno failed to hold subordinates accountable for mistakes. "There were many times when I was surprised at the lack of consequences for poor performance," says her former deputy chief of staff, Kent Marcus.

Reno's flaws may be most evident in her interaction with the Federal Bureau of Investigation (FBI). Although FBI directors are nominally subordinate to the Attorney General, they are appointed to 10-year terms by the U. S. President and can be removed only by the President or through impeachment. Therefore, Reno had little formal power over the FBI. Even though she talked regularly with FBI director Louis Freeh, she rarely tried to assert her will or further her aims. Her main concern seemed to be making sure the Attorney General's office and the FBI got along and worked well together. Reno sometimes supported FBI actions over the interests of employees in her own department, which damaged trust from subordinates.[3]

Reno may be characterized as using a relationship-oriented style in an unfavorable situation. Leader-member relations were poor—Reno got little respect from Congress, members of her own department, other organizations, or the American public. She lost the trust of some employees because she failed to discipline performance problems and supported the FBI over her own department. In addition, the task structure was highly ambiguous and ill-defined. There were no clear-cut procedures to tell Reno and her staff how to conduct an investigation or handle problems. Position power was also low. Reno had little formal authority over many of the people she had to lead and had to lead by influence and persuasion rather than by position power. According to Fiedler's model, a task-oriented leader would be more successful in Reno's situation.

An important contribution of Fiedler's research is that it goes beyond the notion of leadership styles to try to show how styles fit the situation. Many studies have been conducted to test Fiedler's model, and the research in general seems to provide some support for the model.[4] However, Fiedler's model has also been criticized.[5] Using the LPC score as a measure of relationship- or task-oriented behavior seems simplistic to some researchers, and the weights used to determine situation favorability seem to have been determined in an arbitrary manner. In addition, some observers argue that the empirical support for the model is weak because it is based on correlational results that fail to achieve statistical significance in the majority of cases. How the model works over time is also unclear.

For instance, if a task-oriented leader is matched with an unfavorable situation and is successful, the organizational situation is likely to improve and become a situation more appropriate for a relationship-oriented leader. For example, after turning around a troubled Giddings & Lewis and spawning a steady climb in earnings and sales over a six-year period, William J. Fife, Jr. was asked to resign as director of the machine company. At Giddings, the situation improved, and the leadership needs of the organization changed. With an improved business climate, Fife's direct, quick-fix aggression became abrasive. Because the company was out of jeopardy, positive leader-member relations were more important to the organization. Creating enemies among subordinates and micromanaging every detail no longer made sense after the turnaround succeeded. Fife's extreme task-oriented leadership no longer suited the situation.[6] The Living Leadership box underscores the disadvantages of persisting in a behavior style despite the processes of change.

Finally, Fiedler's model and much of the subsequent research fails to consider *medium* LPC leaders, who some studies indicate are more effective than either high or low LPC leaders in a majority of situations.[7] Leaders who score in the mid-range on the LPC scale presumably balance the concern for relationships with a concern for task achievement more effectively than high or low LPC leaders, making them more adaptable to a variety of situations.

LIVING LEADERSHIP

The following points out that behavior that persists can be a disadvantage by ultimately resulting in the opposite of what the individual is striving for:

Polarities

All behavior consists of opposites or polarities. If I do anything more and more, over and over, its polarity will appear. For example, striving to be beautiful makes a person ugly, and trying too hard to be kind is a form of selfishness.

Any over-determined behavior produces its opposite:

- An obsession with living suggests worry about dying.

- True simplicity is not easy.

- Is it a long time or a short time since we last met?

- The braggart probably feels small and insecure.

- Who would be first ends up last.

Knowing how polarities work, the wise leader does not push to make things happen, but allows process to unfold on its own.

SOURCE: John Heider, *The Tao of Leadership: Leadership Strategies for a New Age* (New York: Bantam Books, 1986), 3. Copyright 1985 Humanic Ltd., Atlanta, GA. Used with permission.

New research has continued to improve Fiedler's model,[8] and it is still considered an important contribution to leadership studies. However, its major impact may have been to stir other researchers to consider situational factors more seriously. A number of other situational theories have been developed in the years since Fiedler's original research.

HERSEY AND BLANCHARD'S SITUATIONAL THEORY

The **situational theory** developed by Hersey and Blanchard is an interesting extension of the leadership grid outlined in Chapter 2. This approach focuses on the characteristics of followers as the important element of the situation, and consequently of determining effective leader behavior. The point of Hersey and Blanchard's theory is that subordinates vary in readiness level. People low in task readiness, because of little ability or training, or insecurity, need a different leadership style than those who are high in readiness and have good ability, skills, confidence, and willingness to work.[9]

The relationship between leader style and follower readiness is summarized in Exhibit 3.4. The upper part of the exhibit indicates the style of the leader, which is based on a combination of relationship behavior and task behavior. The bell-shaped curve is called a prescriptive curve because it indicates when each leader style should be used. The four styles are telling (S1), selling (S2), participating (S3), and delegating (S4).

Telling (S1) is a very directive style. It involves giving explicit direction about how tasks should be accomplished. Mickey Drexler, president of The Gap clothing stores, provides his employees with specific guidelines for how all merchandise is to be displayed, and he monitors stores to ensure consistency.

Selling (S2) involves providing direction, but also includes seeking input from others before making decisions. Cynthia Danaher, general manager of Hewlett-Packard's Medical Products Group, provides an example of a selling leadership style. She seeks input from managers throughout the division, asking them to think "like a board of directors," then uses their input and suggestions to make decisions and set direction.[10]

Participating (S3) is a style that focuses on supporting the growth and improvement of others by guiding skill development and acting as a resource for advice and information. Eric Brevig, a visual-effects supervisor with Industrial Light and Magic, maximizes the creativity of his artists and animators by encouraging everyone to participate. Rather than telling people how to do their jobs, Brevig presents them with a challenge and works with them to figure out the best way to meet it. Brevig serves primarily as a resource for guidance and advice, helping employees expand their knowledge and experience.[11]

EXHIBIT 3.4

The Situational Theory of Leadership

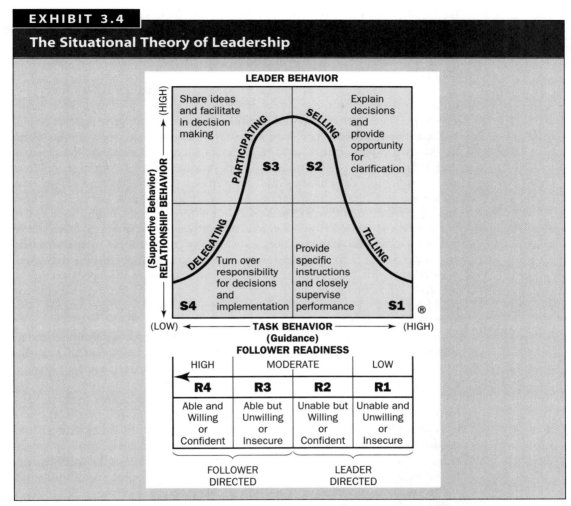

Delegating (S4) is a style that affords little direction and little support. Under such conditions, employees assume responsibility for their work—and for the success of their organization. Ted Turner gives free reign to employees of Cable Network News (CNN) because their experience and vested interest keeps them on the competitive edge.[12]

The appropriate style depends on the development or readiness of followers, indicated in the lower part of Exhibit 3.4. R1 is low readiness and R4 represents high readiness. The telling style is for low-readiness subordinates because people are unable or unwilling to take responsibility for their own task behavior. The selling and participating styles work for followers with moderate readiness, and delegating is appropriate for employees with high readiness.

This contingency model is easier to understand than Fiedler's model because it focuses only on the characteristics of followers, not those of the larger situation. The leader should evaluate subordinates and adopt whichever style is needed. For example, when Jack Johnson became manager of a forklift plant, he assumed a participative style of leadership with the idea that the foreman under him was able to continue the high production levels of the past. However, production decreased, while the number of errors increased. Jack was forced to re-examine the situation and decide upon a new course of action. First, he determined the readiness level of the foreman. Since the foreman had not solved the problem, nor sought Jack's assistance in doing so, Jack determined a lack of commitment, thus a low level of readiness. He focused his next encounter with the foreman exclusively upon the task of decreasing errors, delineated what the foreman must do, and closely monitored the progress of the foreman. Though the transition was difficult, Jack went from a participating (S3) leadership style appropriate for a higher level of readiness, to one for a low level of readiness, telling (S1).[13]

In this example the performance of the subordinate determined leadership style. Since the level of readiness for the foreman was low, Jack was able to gain control of the task and ensure a more effective outcome by assuming the style necessary to lead a low-readiness subordinate.

The style can be tailored to individual subordinates similar to the leader-member exchange theory described in Chapter 2. If one follower is at a low level of readiness, the leader must be very specific, telling them exactly what to do, how to do it, and when. For a follower high in readiness, the leader provides a general goal and sufficient authority to do the task as the follower sees fit. Leaders can carefully diagnose the readiness level of followers and then tell, sell, participate, or delegate. Classroom teachers face one of the toughest leadership challenges around because they usually deal with students who are at widely different levels of readiness. Consider how Carole McGraw of the Detroit, Michigan, school system met the challenge.

IN THE LEAD   ## Carole McGraw, Detroit Public Schools

Carole McGraw describes what she sees when she walks into a classroom for the first time: "A ubiquitous sea of easily recognizable faces. There's Jamie, whose eyes glow with enthusiasm for learning. And Terrell, who just came from the crib after having no breakfast, no supervision of his inadequate homework, and a chip on his shoulder because he needed to flip hamburgers 'til 10 o'clock at night. . . . And Matt, who slumps over his desk, fast asleep from the Ritalin he took for a learning disorder that was probably misdiagnosed to correct a behavior problem. . . ." And on and on.

McGraw diagnosed what teenagers have in common to find the best way to help students of such varying degrees of readiness learn. She realized that all teenagers are exposed to countless hours of MTV, television programs, CDs, and disc jockeys. They spend a lot of time playing sports, eating junk food, talking on the phone, playing computer games, going to the movies, reading pop magazines, hanging out with peers, and avoiding adults. After considering this, McGraw developed her teaching method focused on three concepts: painless, interesting, and enjoyable. Students in McGraw's biology class now do almost all of their work in labs or teamwork sessions. During the labs, a captain is selected to act as team leader. In teams, students select a viable problem to investigate and then split up the work and conduct research in books, on computers, and in laboratory experiments. Teams also spend a lot of time engaged in dialogue and brainstorming. McGraw will throw out an idea and let the students take off with it.

McGraw's teaching method combines telling and participating. Students are provided with direction about certain concepts, vocabulary words, and so forth that they must master, along with guidelines for doing so. This provides the structure and discipline some of her low-readiness level students need to succeed. However, most of her leadership focuses on supporting students as they learn and grow on their own. Does McGraw's innovative approach work? Sixty percent of the students get a grade of A and all score fairly well on objective tests McGraw gives after the teamwork is complete. Students from her classes score great on standardized tests like the SAT because they not only accumulate a lot of knowledge but also gain self-confidence and learn how to think on their feet. "All the stress my kids lived with for years disappears," McGraw says. "My classroom buzzes with new ideas and individual approaches."[14]

Kierstin Higgins, founder of Accommodations by Apple, a small company that handles corporate relocations, also understands how follower readiness determines leadership style. "Our employees are very young and energetic, but they're also very emotional, with major ups and major downs." She works closely with new employees and gives them more and more leeway as they mature in their readiness level. Higgins believes effective leadership in her organization means helping her young, relatively inexperienced workers "learn from the challenges they've experienced, as opposed to burning out."[15]

PATH-GOAL THEORY

Another contingency approach to leadership is called the path-goal theory.[16] According to the **path-goal theory,** the leader's responsibility is to increase subordinates' motivation to attain personal and organizational goals. As illustrated in Exhibit 3.5, the leader increases follower motivation by either (1) clarifying the follower's path to the rewards that are available or (2) increasing the rewards that the follower values and desires. Path clarification means that the leader works with subordinates to help them identify and learn the behaviors that will lead to successful task accomplishment and organizational rewards. Increasing rewards means that the leader talks with subordinates to learn which rewards are important to them—that is, whether they desire intrinsic rewards from the work itself or extrinsic rewards such as raises or promotions. The leader's job is to increase personal payoffs to subordinates for goal attainment and to make the paths to these payoffs clear and easy to travel.[17] This model is called a contingency theory because it consists of three sets of contingencies—leader style, followers and situation, and the rewards to meet followers' needs.[18] Whereas the Fiedler theory described earlier made the assumption that new leaders could take over as situations change, in the path-goal theory leaders change their behaviors to match the situation.

Leader Behavior

The path-goal theory suggests a fourfold classification of leader behaviors.[19] These classifications are the types of behavior the leader can adopt and include supportive, directive, achievement-oriented, and participative styles.

Supportive leadership shows concern for subordinates' well-being and personal needs. Leadership behavior is open, friendly, and approachable, and the leader creates a team climate and treats subordinates as equals. Supportive leadership is similar to the consideration or people-oriented leadership described earlier.

Directive leadership tells subordinates exactly what they are supposed to do. Leader behavior includes planning, making schedules, setting performance goals and behavior standards, and stressing adherence to rules and regulations. Directive leadership behavior is similar to the initiating structure or task-oriented leadership style described earlier.

Participative leadership consults with subordinates about decisions. Leader behavior includes asking for opinions and suggestions, encouraging participation in decision making, and meeting with subordinates in their workplaces. The participative leader encourages group discussion and written suggestions, similar to the S3 style in the Hersey and Blanchard model.

Achievement-oriented leadership sets clear and challenging goals for subordinates. Leader behavior stresses high-quality performance and improvement

EXHIBIT 3.5

Leader Roles in the Path-Goal Model

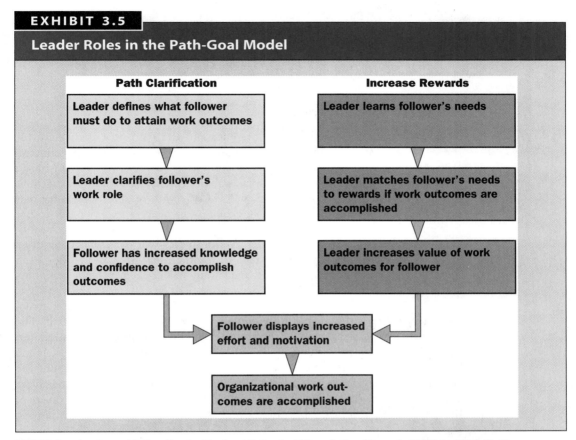

SOURCE: Based on Bernard M. Bass, "Leadership: Good, Better, Best," *Organizational Dynamics* 13 (Winter 1985), 26–40.

over current performance. Achievement-oriented leaders also show confidence in subordinates and assist them in learning how to achieve high goals.

To illustrate achievement-oriented leadership, consider the training of army officers in the ROTC. This training goes far beyond how to command a platoon. It involves the concepts of motivation, responsibility, and the creation of a team in which decision making is expected of everyone. Fundamentally, this training will enable officers to respond to any situation, not just those outlined in the manual. Thus achievement-oriented leadership is demonstrated: The set goals are challenging, require improvement, and demonstrate confidence in the abilities of subordinates—on the part of the future officers and the army that trains them.[20]

The four types of leader behavior are not considered ingrained personality traits as in the earlier trait theories; rather, they reflect types of behavior that every leader is able to adopt, depending on the situation. The Leader's Bookshelf also suggests that leaders consciously choose a leadership style that is suitable for their organization's circumstances.

Situational Contingencies

The two important situational contingencies in the path-goal theory are (1) the personal characteristics of group members and (2) the work environment. Personal characteristics of subordinates are similar to Hersey and Blanchard's readiness level and include such factors as ability, skills, needs, and motivations. For example, if an employee has a low level of ability or skill, the leader may need to provide additional training or coaching in order for the worker to improve performance. If a subordinate is self-centered, the leader may use monetary rewards to motivate him or her. Subordinates who want clear direction and authority require a directive leader to tell them exactly what to do. Craft workers and professionals, however, may want more freedom and autonomy and work best under a participative leadership style.

The work environment contingencies include the degree of task structure, the nature of the formal authority system, and the work group itself. The task structure is similar to the same concept described in Fiedler's contingency theory; it includes the extent to which tasks are defined and have explicit job descriptions and work procedures. The formal authority system includes the amount of legitimate power used by leaders and the extent to which policies and rules constrain employees' behavior. Work-group characteristics consist of the educational level of subordinates and the quality of relationships among them.

Use of Rewards

Recall that the leader's responsibility is to clarify *the path to rewards* for subordinates or to increase *the amount of rewards* to enhance satisfaction and job performance. In some situations, the leader works with subordinates to help them acquire the skills and confidence needed to perform tasks and achieve rewards already available. In others, the leader may develop new rewards to meet the specific needs of a subordinate.

Exhibit 3.6 illustrates four examples of how leadership behavior is tailored to the situation. In the first situation, the subordinate lacks confidence; thus, the supportive leadership style provides the social support with which to encourage the subordinate to undertake the behavior needed to do the work and receive the rewards. In the second situation, the job is ambiguous, and the employee is not performing effectively. Directive leadership behavior is used to give instructions and clarify the task so that the follower will know how to

Maximum Leadership: The World's Leading CEOs Share Their Five Strategies for Success

Charles M. Farkas and Philippe De Backer

According to Charles M. Farkas and Philippe De Backer, successful leaders around the world adopt leadership approaches that reflect the needs of the organization, not the personality of the leader. From interviews with 161 top leaders on six continents, including those from such companies as Nestlé, Gillette, Tenneco, and Dell Computer, Farkas and De Backer concluded that leaders can use five distinct leadership approaches to add value to their organizations. Although styles may overlap, most leaders focus on only one or two. Thus, regardless of personality, successful leaders demonstrate a knack for determining the style that is suitable for their particular organizational circumstances.

Five Strategies for Success

The five distinct approaches adopted by successful leaders are:

1. **The Strategic Approach:** The leader focuses on a vision of the organization's future and systematically maps out how to get there. A leader using this approach tries to see the big picture and may spend up to 80 percent of his or her time on external matters such as customers, competitors, technological advances, and market trends.

2. **The Human Assets Approach:** The leader cultivates empowered people through organizational policies and programs; rewards those who act; builds relationships; and focuses on shared values. These leaders spend most of their time in personnel-related activities because they consider the growth and development of employees their primary responsibility.

3. **The Expertise Approach:** The leader focuses the organization on a specific expertise that identifies the company's competitive edge. Most of this leader's time is spent cultivating and continually improving this expertise throughout the organization, such as studying new technological research, analyzing competitors' products, and meeting with engineers and customers.

4. **The Box Approach:** The leader who uses this approach concentrates on building a set of rules, systems, and procedures to control behavior and outcomes within well-defined boundaries. These leaders spend a lot of time looking at and correcting deviations from organizational controls, such as a project behind deadline or quarterly results below expectations.

5. **The Change Approach:** The leader who uses this approach sees his or her most critical role as creating an organizational environment of continual reinvention, even if it causes mistakes and temporarily hurts financial performance. These leaders encourage risk taking, and they spend most of their time communicating directly with a wide range of stakeholders—customers, investors, suppliers, and employees at all organizational levels.

A Leadership Framework

The authors emphasize that leadership style is a matter of informed choice, often requiring leaders to inhibit their personalities or develop traits they don't already have. By answering questions about an organization's maturity, competitive advantage, technology, and employees, a leader can determine which style will most effectively add value. Although the five leadership approaches are not recipes for success, they provide structure for the leader's role, and each can be powerful when used in the right circumstances.

Maximum Leadership: The World's Leading CEOs Share Their Five Strategies for Success, by Charles M. Farkas and Philippe De Backer, is published by Henry Holt & Company.

EXHIBIT 3.6

Path-Goal Situations and Preferred Leader Behaviors

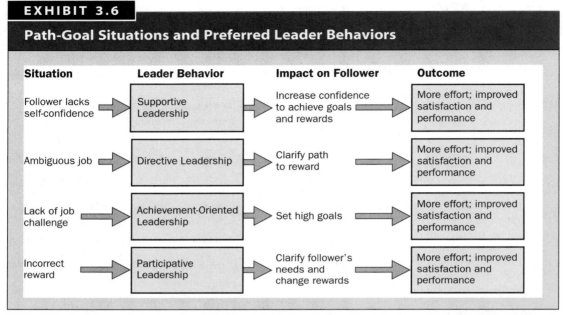

Situation	Leader Behavior	Impact on Follower	Outcome
Follower lacks self-confidence	Supportive Leadership	Increase confidence to achieve goals and rewards	More effort; improved satisfaction and performance
Ambiguous job	Directive Leadership	Clarify path to reward	More effort; improved satisfaction and performance
Lack of job challenge	Achievement-Oriented Leadership	Set high goals	More effort; improved satisfaction and performance
Incorrect reward	Participative Leadership	Clarify follower's needs and change rewards	More effort; improved satisfaction and performance

SOURCE: Adapted with permission from Gary A. Yukl, *Leadership in Organizations* 4th ed. (Englewood Cliffs, NJ: Prentice-Hall, 1998).

accomplish it and receive rewards. In the third situation, the subordinate is un-challenged by the task; thus, an achievement-oriented behavior is used to set higher goals. This clarifies the path to rewards for the employee. In the fourth situation, an incorrect reward is given to a subordinate, and the participative leadership style is used to change this. By discussing the subordinate's needs, the leader is able to identify the correct reward for task accomplishment. In all four cases, the outcome of fitting the leadership behavior to the situation produces greater employee effort by either clarifying how subordinates can receive rewards or changing the rewards to fit their needs.

At Katzinger's Delicatessen, co-owners Steve and Diane Warren used achievement-oriented leadership and saw a sharp performance improvement.

IN THE LEAD   Steve and Diane Warren, Katzinger's Delicatessen

Steve and Diane Warren instituted open-book management at Katzinger's Delicatessen in Columbus, Ohio, to help cut costs and save money. They trained workers in how to read the financials and told them Katzinger's would share the rewards with employees if financial performance improved. The Warrens felt confident that their well-trained, hard-working employees had the knowledge to cut costs significantly. They were surprised when nothing happened, but soon realized that workers didn't feel challenged by the vague goal of improving financial performance. Most of Katzinger's employees were young and mobile and they felt that they could do little to improve overall company performance.

To challenge workers and help them see how they could earn rewards, the Warrens proposed a specific ambitious goal: if workers could reduce food costs to below 35 percent of sales without sacrificing food quality or service, they would be rewarded with half the savings. With this goal before them, employees immediately began proposing ideas to reduce waste, such as matching the delicatessen's perishable food orders more closely to expected sales. At the end of the first month, costs had fallen nearly 2 percent and employees took home about $40 each from the savings. Later monthly payouts were as high as $95. By the end of the year, food consistency and service had actually *increased,* even though Katzinger's had met its goal of reducing food costs to below 35 percent of total sales. The Warrens distributed a total of $15,000 to workers for helping to meet the goal and have continued to set other ambitious goals to keep workers motivated and challenged.[21]

An achievement-oriented style proved to be just right for leading the workers at Katzinger's Deli. By setting a specific, ambitious goal, the Warrens clarified the path to rewards for their employees. Path-goal theorizing can be complex, but much of the research on it has been encouraging.[22] Using the model to specify relationships and make exact predictions about employee outcomes may seem difficult at first, but the four types of leader behavior and the ideas for fitting them to situational contingencies provide a useful way for leaders to think about motivating subordinates.

THE VROOM-JAGO CONTINGENCY MODEL

The **Vroom-Jago contingency model** shares some basic principles with the previous models, yet it differs in significant ways as well. This model focuses specifically on varying degrees of participative leadership, and how each level of participation influences quality and accountability of decisions. A number of situational factors shape the likelihood that either a participative or autocratic approach will produce the best outcome.

This model starts with the idea that a leader faces a problem that requires a solution. Decisions to solve the problem may be made by a leader alone, or through inclusion of a number of followers.

The Vroom-Jago model is very applied, which means that it tells the leader precisely the correct amount of participation by subordinates to use in making a particular decision.[23] The model has three major components: leader participation styles, a set of diagnostic questions with which to analyze a decision situation, and a series of decision rules.

Leader Participation Styles

The model employs five levels of subordinate participation in decision making ranging from highly autocratic (leader decides alone) to highly democratic (leader delegates to group), as illustrated in Exhibit 3.7.[24] The exhibit shows five decision styles, starting with the leader making the decision alone (Decide), presenting the problem to subordinates individually for their suggestions

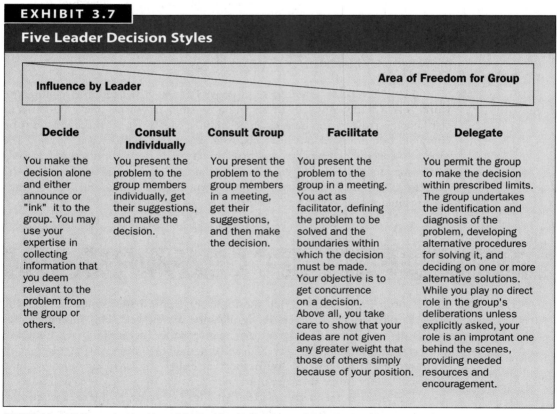

EXHIBIT 3.7

Five Leader Decision Styles

Influence by Leader   **Area of Freedom for Group**

Decide	Consult Individually	Consult Group	Facilitate	Delegate
You make the decision alone and either announce or "ink" it to the group. You may use your expertise in collecting information that you deem relevant to the problem from the group or others.	You present the problem to the group members individually, get their suggestions, and make the decision.	You present the problem to the group members in a meeting, get their suggestions, and then make the decision.	You present the problem to the group in a meeting. You act as facilitator, defining the problem to be solved and the boundaries within which the decision must be made. Your objective is to get concurrence on a decision. Above all, you take care to show that your ideas are not given any greater weight that those of others simply because of your position.	You permit the group to make the decision within prescribed limits. The group undertakes the identification and diagnosis of the problem, developing alternative procedures for solving it, and deciding on one or more alternative solutions. While you play no direct role in the group's deliberations unless explicitly asked, your role is an improtant one behind the scenes, providing needed resources and encouragement.

SOURCE: Victor H. Vroom, Leadership and the Decision Making Process," Organizational Dynamics 28, No. 4 (Spring 2000) :82-94. This is Vroom's adaptation of Tannenbaum and Schmidt's Taxonomy..

and then making the decision (Consult Individually), presenting the problem to subordinates as a group, collectively obtaining their ideas and suggestions, then making the decision (Consult Group), sharing the problem with subordinates as a group and acting as a facilitator to help the group arrive at a decision (Facilitate), or delegating the problem and permitting the group to make the decision within prescribed limits (Delegate). The five styles fall along a continuum, and the leader should select one depending on the situation.

Diagnostic Questions

How does a leader decide which of the five decision styles to use? The appropriate degree of the decision style to use? The appropriate degree of decision participation depends on a number of situational factors, such as the required level of decision quality, the level of leader or subordinate expertise, and the importance of having subordinates commit to the decision. Leaders can analyze the appropriate degree of participation by answering seven diagnostic questions.

1. **Decision Significance:** *How significaant is this decision for the project or organization?* If the decision is highly important and a high-quality decision is needed for the success of the project or organization, the leader has to be actively involved.

2. **Importance of Commitment:** *How important is subordinate commitment to carrying out the decision?* If implementation requires a high level of commitment to the decision, leaders should involve subordinates in the decision process.

3. **Leader Expertise:** *What is the level of the leader's expertise in relation to the problem?* If the leader does not have a high amount of information, knowledge, or expertise, the leader should involve subordinates to obtain it.

4. **Likelihood of commitment:** *If the leader were to make the decision alone, would subordinates have high or low commitment to the decision?* If subordinates typically go along with whatever the leader decides, their involvement in the decision making process will be less important.

5. **Group support for Goals:** *What is the degree of subordinate support for the team's or organization's objectives at stake in this decision?* If subordinates have low support for the goals of the organization, the leader should not allow the group to make the decision alone.

6. **Goal Expertise:** *What is the level of group members' knowledge and expertise in relation to the problem?* If subordinates have a high level of expertise in relation to the problem, more responsibility for the decision can be delegated to them.

7. **Team Competence:** *How skilled and commited are group members to working together as a team to solve problems?* When subordinates have high skills and high desire to work together cooperatively to solve problems, more responsibility for the decision making can be delegated to them.

These questions seem detailed, but considering these seven situational factors can quickly narrow the options and point to the appropriate level of group participation in decision making.

Selecting a Decision Style

Further development of the Vroom-Jago model added concern for time constraints and concern for follower development as explicit criteria for determining the level of participation. That is, a leader considers the relative importance of time versus follower development in selecting a decision style. This led to the development of two decision matrixes, a *time-based model*, to be used if time is critical, for example, if the organization is facing a crisis and a decision must be made immediately, and a *development-based model*, to be used if time and effiency are less important criteria than the opportunity to develop the thinking and decision-making skills of followers.

Consider the example of a small auto parts manufacturer, which owns only one machine for performing welds on mufflers. If the machine has broken down and production has come to a stand-still, a decision concerning the purchase of a new machine is critical and has to be made immediately to get the production line moving again. In this case, a leader would follow the time-based model for selecting the decision style. However, if the machine is scheduled for routine replacement in three months, time is not a critical factor. The leader is then free to consider the importance of involving production workers in the decision-making to develop their skills. Thus, the leader may follow the development-based model because time is not a critical concern.

Exhibits 3.8 and 3.9 illustrate the two decision matrixes—a time-based model and a development-based model—that enables leaders to adopt a participation style by answering the diagnostic questions in sequence. Returning to the example of the welding machine, if the machine has broken down and must be replaced immediately, the leader would follow the time-based model in Exhibit 3.8. The leader enters the matrix at the left hand side, at Problem Statement, and considers the seven situational questions in sequence from left to right, answering high (H) or low (L) to each one and avoiding crossing any horizontal lines. The first question would be: *How significant is this decision for the project or organization?* If the answer is High, the leader proceeds to importance of commitment: *How important is subordinate commitment to carrying out the decision?* If the answer is High, the next question pertains to leader expertise: *What is the level of the leader's expertise in relation to the problem?* If the leader's knowledge and expertise is High, the leader next considers

EXHIBIT 3.8

Time-Driven Model for Determining an Appropriate Decision-Making Style—Group Problems

Instuctions: The matrix operates like a funnel. You start at the left with a specific decision problem in mind. The column headings denote situational factors which may or may not be present in that problem. You progress by selecting High or Low (H or L) for each relevant situational factor. Proceed down from the funnel, judging only those situational factors for which a judgement is called for, until you reach the recommended process.

The left-hand margin of the matrix is labeled **PROBLEM STATEMENT** (read vertically). An arrow across the top indicates left-to-right progression.

Decision Significance?	Importance of Commitment?	Leader Expertise?	Likelihood Commitment?	Group Supports?	Group Expertise?	Team Competence?	
H	H	H	H	−	−	−	Decide
			L	H	H	H	Delegate
						L	Consult (Group)
					L	−	
				L	−	−	
		L	H	H	H	H	Facilitate
						L	Consult (Individually)
					L	−	
				L	−	−	
			L	L	H	H	Facilitate
						L	Consult(Group)
					L	−	
				L	−	−	
	L	H	−	−	−	−	Decide
		L	−	H	H	H	Facilitate
						L	Consult (Individually)
					L	−	
				L	−	−	
L	H	−	H		−	−	Decide
			L	−	−	H	Delegate
						L	Facilitate
	L	−		−		−	Decide

SOURCE: Victor H. Vroom "Leadership and the Decision-Making Process," Organizational Dynamics 28, No. 4 (Spring 2000):82-94. This is Vroom's adaptation of Tannenbaum and Schmidt's Taxonomy.

likelihood of commitment: *If the leader were to make the decision alone, how likely is it that subordinates would be commited to the decision?* If there is a high likelihood that subordinates would be commited, the decision matrix leads directly to the Decide style of decision making, in which the leader makes the decision alone and presents it to the group.

EXHIBIT 3.9

Development-Driven Model for Determining an Appropriate Decision-Making Style—Group Problems

Decision Significance?	Importance of Commitment?	Leader Expertise?	Likelihood of Commitment?	Group Support?	Group Expertise?	Team Competence?	PROBLEM STATEMENT
H	H	–	H	H	H	H	Delegate
H	H	–	H	H	H	L	Facilitate
H	H	–	H	H	L	–	Facilitate
H	H	–	H	L	–	–	Consult (Group)
H	H	–	L	H	H	H	Delegate
H	H	–	L	H	H	L	Facilitate
H	H	–	L	H	L	–	Facilitate
H	H	–	L	L	–	–	Consult (Group)
H	L	–	–	H	H	H	Delegate
H	L	–	–	H	H	L	Facilitate
H	L	–	–	H	L	–	Facilitate
H	L	–	–	L	–	–	Consult (Group)
L	H	–	H	–	–	–	Decide
L	H	–	L	–	–	–	Delegate
L	L	–	–	–	–	–	Decide

SOURCE: Victor H. Vroom "Leadership and the Decision-Making Process," Organizational Dynamics 28, No. 4 (Spring 2000):82-94. This is Vroom's adaptation of Tannenbaum and Schmidt's Taxonomy.

As noted earlier, this matrix assumes that time and efficiency are the most important criteria. However, consider how the selection of a decision style would differ if the leader had several months to replace the welding machine and considered follower development of high importance and time of little concern. In this case, the leader would follow the development-driven decision matrix in Exhibit 3.9. Beginning again at the left hand side of the matrix: *How significant is this decision for the project or organization?* If the answer is High, proceed to importance of commitment: *How important is subordinate commitment?* If high, the next question concerns likelihood of commitment (leader expertise is not considered since the development model is focused on involving subordinates even if the leader has knowledge and expertise): *If the leader were to make the decision alone, how likely is it that subordinates would be com-mited to the decision?* If there is a high likelihood, the leader next considers group support: *What is the degree of subordinate support for the team's or orga-nization's objectives at stake in this decision?* If the degree of support for goals is low, the leader would proceed directly to the Group Consult decision style. However, if the degree of support for goals is high, the leader would then ask: *What is the level of group members' knowledge and expertise in relation to the problem?* An answer of High would take the leader to the question: *How skilled and commited are group members to working together as a team to solve prob-lems?* An answer of High would lead to the delegate style, in which the leader allows the group to make the decision within certain limits.

Note that the time-driven model takes the leader to the first decision style that preserves decision quality and follower acceptance, whereas the de-velopment-driven model takes other considerations into account. It takes less time to make an autocratic decision (Decide) than to involve subordinates by using a Facilitate or Delegate style. However in many cases, time and efficiency are less important than the opportunity to further subordinate development. In many of today's organizations, where knowledge sharing and widespread participation are considered critical to organizational success, leaders are plac-ing greater emphasis on follower development when time is not a critical issue.

Leaders can quickly learn to use the model to adapt their styles to fit the situation. However, researchers have also developed a computer-based pro-gram that allows for greater complexity and precision in the Vroom-Jago model and incorporates the value of time and value of follower development as situational factors rather than portraying them in separate decision matrixes.

The Vroom-Jago model has been criticized as being less than perfect,[25] but it is useful to decision makers, and the body of supportive research is grow-ing.[26] Leaders can learn to use the model to make timely, high-quality deci-sions. Let's try applying the model to the following problem.

IN THE LEAD   Dave Robbins, Whitlock Manufacturing

When Whitlock Manufacturing won a contract from a large auto manufacturer to produce an engine to power their flagship sports car, Dave Robbins was thrilled to be selected as a project manager. The engine, of Japanese design and extremely complex, has gotten rave reviews in the automotive press. This project has dramatically enhanced the reputation of Whitlock Manufacturing, which was previously known primarily as a producer of outboard engines for marine use.

Robbins and his team of engineers have taken great pride in their work on the project, but their excitement was dashed by a recent report of serious engine problems in cars delivered to customers. Fourteen owners of cars produced during the first month have experienced engine seizures. Taking quick action, the auto manufacturer suspended sales of the sports car, halted current production, and notified owners of the current model not to drive the car. Everyone involved knows this is a disaster. Unless the engine problem is solved quickly, Whitlock Manufacturing could be exposed to extended litigation. In addition, Whitlock's valued relationship with one of the world's largest auto manufacturers would probably be lost forever.

As the person most knowledgeable about the engine, Robbins has spent two weeks in the field inspecting the seized engines and the auto plant where they were installed. In addition, he has carefully examined the operations and practices in Whitlock's plant where the engine is manufactured. Based on this extensive research, Robbins is convinced that he knows what the problem is and the best way to solve it. However, his natural inclination is to involve other team members as much as possible in making decisions and solving problems. He not only values their input, but thinks that by encouraging greater participation he strengthens the thinking skills of team members, helping them grow and contribute more to the team and the organization. Therefore, Robbins chooses to consult with his team before making his final decision. The group meets for several hours that afternoon, discussing the problem in detail and sharing their varied perspectives, including the information Robbins has gathered during his research. Following the group session, Robbins makes his decision. He will present the decision at the team meeting the following morning, after which testing and correction of the engine problem will begin.[27]

In the Whitlock Manufacturing case, either a time-driven or a development-driven decision tree can be used to select a decision style. Although time is of importance, a leader's desire to involve subordinates can be considered equally important. Do you think Robbins used the correct leader decision style? Let's examine the problem using the development-based decision tree, since Robbins is concerned about involving other team members. Moving from left to right in Exhibit 3.9, the questions and answers are as follows: *How sigificant is this decision for the organization?* Definitely high. Quality of the decision is of critical importance. The company's future may be at stake. *How important is subordinate commitment to carrying out the decision?* Also high. The team members must support and implement Robbins' solution. *If Robbins makes the decision on his own, will team members have high or low commitment to it?* The answer to this question is probably also high. Team members respect Robbins and they are likely to accept his analysis of the problem. This leads to the question, *What is the degree of subordinate support for the team's or oranization's objectives at stake in this decision?* Definitely high. This leads to the question, *What is the level of group members' knowledge and expertise in relation to the problem?* The answer to this question is probably Low, which leads to the Consult Group decision style. Thus, Robbins used the style that would be recommended by the Vroom-Jago model.

Now, assume that Robbins chose to place more emphasis on time than on participant involvement and development. Using the time-based decision matrix in Exhibit 3.8, trace the questions and answers based on the information just provided and rating Robbins' level of expertise as high. Remember to avoid crossing any horizontal lines. What decision style is recommended? Is it the same or different from that recommended by the development-based tree?

SUBSTITUTES FOR LEADERSHIP

The contingency leadership approaches considered so far have focused on the leader's style, the follower's nature, and the situation's characteristics. The final contingency approach suggests that situational variables can be so powerful that they actually substitute for or neutralize the need for leadership.[28] This approach outlines those organizational settings in which task-oriented and people-oriented leadership styles are unimportant or unnecessary.

Exhibit 3.10 shows the situational variables that tend to substitute for or neutralize leadership characteristics. A **substitute** for leadership makes the leadership style unnecessary or redundant. For example, highly educated,

EXHIBIT 3.10

Substitutes and Neutralizers for Leadership

Variable		Task-Oriented Leadership	People-Oriented Leadership
Organizational variables:	Group cohesiveness	Substitutes for	Substitutes for
	Formalization	Substitutes for	No effect on
	Inflexibility	Neutralizes	No effect on
	Low positional power	Neutralizes	Neutralizes
	Physical separation	Neutralizes	Neutralizes
Task characteristics:	Highly structured task	Substitutes for	No effect on
	Automatic feedback	Substitutes for	No effect on
	Intrinsic satisfaction	No effect on	Substitutes for
Follower characteristics:	Professionalism	Substitutes for	Substitutes for
	Training/experience	Substitutes for	No effect on
	Low value of rewards	Neutralizes	Neutralizes

professional subordinates who know how to do their tasks do not need a leader who initiates structure for them and tells them what to do. In addition, long-term education often develops autonomous, self-motivated individuals. Thus, task-oriented and people-oriented leadership is substituted by professional education and socialization.[29]

A **neutralizer** counteracts the leadership style and prevents the leader from displaying certain behaviors. For example, if a leader is physically removed from subordinates, the leader's ability to give directions to subordinates is greatly reduced. Kinko's, a nationwide copy center, includes numerous locations widely scattered across regions. Managers enjoy very limited personal interaction due to the distances between stores. Thus, their ability to both support and direct is neutralized.

Situational variables in Exhibit 3.10 include characteristics of the followers, the task, and the organization itself. For example, when subordinates are highly professional, such as research scientists in companies like Merck or Monsanto, both leadership styles are less important. The employees do not need either direction or support. With respect to task characteristics, highly structured tasks substitute for a task-oriented style, and a satisfying task substitutes for a people-oriented style. In other words, when a task is highly structured and routine, like auditing cash, the leader should provide personal consideration and support that is not provided by the task. Satisfied people don't need as much consideration. Likewise, with respect to the organization itself, group cohesiveness substitutes for both leader styles. For example, the relationship that develops among air traffic controllers and jet fighter pilots is characterized by high-stress interactions and continuous peer training. This cohesiveness provides support and direction that substitutes for formal leadership.[30] Formalized rules and procedures substitute for leader task orientation because the rules tell people what to do. Physical separation of leader and subordinate neutralizes both leadership styles.

The value of the situations described in Exhibit 3.10 is that they help leaders avoid leadership overkill. Leaders should adopt a style with which to complement the organizational situation. For example, the work situation for bank tellers provides a high level of formalization, little flexibility, and a highly structured task. The head teller should not adopt a task-oriented style because the organization already provides structure and direction. The head teller should concentrate on a people-oriented style. In other organizations, if group cohesiveness or previous training meets employee social needs, the leader is free to concentrate on task-oriented behaviors. The leader can adopt a style complementary to the organizational situation to ensure that both task needs and people needs of followers are met.

Recent studies examined how substitutes (the situation) can be designed to have more impact than leader behaviors on such outcomes as subordinate satisfaction.[31] The impetus behind this research is the idea that substitutes for leadership can be designed in organizations in ways to complement existing leadership, act in the absence of leadership, and otherwise provide more comprehensive leadership alternatives. For example, Paul Reeves, a foreman at Harmon Auto Parts, shared half-days with his subordinates during which they helped him perform his leader tasks. After Reeves' promotion to middle management, his group no longer required a foreman. Followers were trained to act on their own.[32] Thus, a situation in which follower ability and training were highly developed created a substitute for leadership.

The ability to utilize substitutes to fill leadership "gaps" is often advantageous to organizations. Indeed, the fundamental assumption of substitutes-for-leadership researchers is that effective leadership is the ability to recognize and provide the support and direction not already provided by task, group, and organization.

SUMMARY AND INTERPRETATION

The most important point in this chapter is that situational variables affect leadership outcomes. The contingency approaches were developed to systematically address the relationship between a leader and the organization. The contingency approaches focus on how the components of leadership style, subordinate characteristics, and situational elements impact one another. Fiedler's contingency model, Hersey and Blanchard's situational theory, the path-goal theory, the Vroom-Jago model, and the substitutes-for-leadership concept each examine how different situations call for different styles of leadership behavior.

According to Fiedler, leaders can determine whether the situation is favorable to their leadership style. Task-oriented leaders tend to do better in very easy or very difficult situations, while person-oriented leaders do best in situations of intermediate favorability. Hersey and Blanchard contend that leaders can adjust their task or relationship style to accommodate the readiness level of their subordinates. The path-goal theory states that leaders can use a style that appropriately clarifies the path to desired rewards. The Vroom-Jago model indicates that leaders can choose a participative decision style based on contingencies such as quality requirement, commitment requirement, or the leader's information. In addition, concern for time (the need for a fast decision) versus concern for follower development are taken into account. Leaders can analyze each situation and answer a series of questions that help determine the appropriate level of follower participation. Finally, the substitutes-for-leadership concept recommends that leaders adjust their style to provide resources not otherwise provided in the organizational situation.

By discerning the characteristics of tasks, subordinates, and organizations, leaders can determine the style that increases the likelihood of successful leadership outcomes. Therefore, effective leadership is about developing diagnostic skills and being flexible in your leadership behavior.

KEY TERMS

contingency
contingency approaches
Fiedler's contingency model

situational theory
path-goal theory
Vroom-Jago model

substitute
neutralizer

DISCUSSION QUESTIONS

1. Consider Fiedler's theory as illustrated in Exhibit 3.2. How often do you think very favorable, intermediate, or very unfavorable situations occur to leaders in real life? Discuss.

2. Do you think leadership style is fixed and unchangeable or flexible and adaptable? Why?

3. Consider the leadership position of the managing partner in a law firm. What task, subordinate, and organizational factors might serve as substitutes for leadership in this situation?

4. Compare Fiedler's contingency model with the path-goal theory. What are the similarities and differences? Which do you prefer?

5. Think of a situation in which you worked. At what level of readiness (R1 to R4) would you rate yourself and coworkers? Did your leader use the correct style according to the Hersey and Blanchard model?

6. Think back to teachers you have had, and identify one each who fits a supportive style, directive style, participative style, and achievement-oriented style according to the path-goal theory. Which style did you find most effective? Why?

7. Do you think leaders should decide on a participative style based on the most "efficient" way to reach the decision? Should leaders sometimes let people participate for other reasons?

8. Consider the situational characteristics of group cohesiveness, organizational formalization, and physical separation. How might each of these substitute for or neutralize task-oriented or people-oriented leadership? Explain.

LEADERSHIP DEVELOPMENT: PERSONAL FEEDBACK

T-P Leadership Questionnaire: An Assessment of Style

The following items describe aspects of leadership behavior. Respond to each item according to the way you would most likely act if you were a leader of a work group. Circle whether you would most likely behave in the described way: always (A), frequently (F), occasionally (O), seldom (S), or never (N).

1. I would most likely act as the spokesperson of the group.   A F O S N
2. I would encourage overtime work.   A F O S N
3. I would allow members complete freedom in their work.   A F O S N
4. I would encourage the use of uniform procedures.   A F O S N
5. I would permit members to use their own judgment in solving problems.   A F O S N
6. I would stress being ahead of competing groups.   A F O S N
7. I would speak as a representative of the group.   A F O S N
8. I would needle members for greater effort.   A F O S N
9. I would try out my ideas in the group.   A F O S N
10. I would let members do their work the way they think best.   A F O S N
11. I would be working hard for a promotion.   A F O S N
12. I would tolerate postponement and uncertainty.   A F O S N
13. I would speak for the group if there were visitors present.   A F O S N
14. I would keep the work moving at a rapid pace.   A F O S N
15. I would turn the members loose on a job and let them go for it.   A F O S N
16. I would settle conflicts when they occurred in the group.   A F O S N
17. I would get swamped by details.   A F O S N
18. I would represent the group at outside meetings.   A F O S N
19. I would be reluctant to allow the members any freedom of action.   A F O S N
20. I would decide what should be done and how it should be done.   A F O S N
21. I would push for increased production.   A F O S N
22. I would let some members have authority that I could keep.   A F O S N
23. Things would usually turn out as I had predicted.   A F O S N
24. I would allow the group a high degree of initiative.   A F O S N
25. I would assign group members to particular tasks.   A F O S N
26. I would be willing to make changes.   A F O S N
27. I would ask the members to work harder.   A F O S N
28. I would trust the group members to exercise good judgment.   A F O S N

29. I would schedule the work to be done.   A F O S N

30. I would refuse to explain my actions.   A F O S N

31. I would persuade others that my ideas are to their   A F O S N
advantage.

32. I would permit the group to set its own pace.   A F O S N

33. I would urge the group to beat its previous record.   A F O S N

34. I would act without consulting the group.   A F O S N

35. I would ask that group members follow standard rules   A F O S N
and regulations.

T _____   P _____

Scoring

The T-P Leadership Questionnaire is scored as follows:
a. Circle the item number for items 8, 12, 17, 18, 19, and 35.
b. Write the number 1 in front of circled item numbers to which you responded S (seldom) or N (never).
c. Also write a number 1 in front of item numbers not circled if you responded A (always) or F (frequently).
d. Circle the number 1s that you have written in front of the following items: 3, 5, 8, 10, 15, 18, 19, 22, 24, 26, 28, 30, 32, 34, and 35.
e. Count the circled number 1s. This is your score for concern for people. Record the score in the blank following the letter P at the end of the questionnaire.
f. Count uncircled number 1s. This is your score for concern for task. Record this number in the blank following the letter T.

Interpretation

Some leaders deal with people needs, leaving task details to subordinates. Other leaders focus on specific details with the expectation that subordinates will carry out orders. Depending on the situation, both approaches may be effective. The important issue is the ability to identify relevant dimensions of the situation and behave accordingly. Through this questionnaire, you can identify your relative emphasis on two dimensions of leadership: task orientation (T)

SOURCE: The T-P Leadership Questionnaire was adapted by J. B. Ritchie and P. Thompson in *Organization and People* (New York: West, 1984). Copyright 1969 by the American Educational Research Association. Adapted by permission of the publisher from "Toward a Particularistic Approach to Leadership Style: Some Findings" by T. J. Sergiovanni, AERA 6 (1), 62–79, 1969.

and people orientation (P). These are not opposite approaches, and an individual can rate high or low on either or both.

What is your leadership orientation? What would you consider an ideal leader situation for your style?

LEADERSHIP DEVELOPMENT: Cases for Analysis

Alvis Corporation

Kevin McCarthy is the manager of a production department in Alvis Corporation, a firm that manufactures office equipment. After reading an article that stressed the benefits of participative management, Kevin believes that these benefits could be realized in his department if the workers are allowed to participate in making some decisions that affect them. The workers are not unionized. Kevin selected two decisions for his experiment in participative management.

The first decision involved vacation schedules. Each summer the workers were given two weeks vacation, but no more than two workers can go on vacation at the same time. In prior years, Kevin made this decision himself. He would first ask the workers to indicate their preferred dates, and he considered how the work would be affected if different people were out at the same time. It was important to plan a vacation schedule that would ensure adequate staffing for all of the essential operations performed by the department. When more than two workers wanted the same time period, and they had similar skills, he usually gave preference to the workers with the highest productivity.

The second decision involved production standards. Sales had been increasing steadily over the past few years, and the company recently installed some new equipment to increase productivity. The new equipment would allow Kevin's department to produce more with the same number of workers. The company had a pay incentive system in which workers received a piece rate for each unit produced above a standard amount. Separate standards existed for each type of product, based on an industrial engineering study conducted a few years earlier. Top management wanted to readjust the production standards to reflect the fact that the new equipment made it possible for the workers to earn more without working any harder. The savings from higher productivity were needed to help pay for the new equipment.

Kevin called a meeting of his fifteen workers an hour before the end of the workday. He explained that he wanted them to discuss the two issues and make recommendations. Kevin figured that the workers might be inhibited about participating in the discussion if he were present, so he left them alone to discuss the issues. Besides, Kevin had an appointment to meet with the quality control manager. Quality problems had increased after the new equipment was installed, and the industrial engineers were studying the problem in an attempt to determine why quality had gotten worse rather than better.

When Kevin returned to his department just at quitting time, he was surprised to learn that the workers recommended keeping the standards the same. He had assumed they knew the pay incentives were no longer fair and would set a higher standard. The spokesman for the group explained that their base pay had not kept up with inflation and the higher incentive pay restored their real income to its prior level.

On the vacation issue, the group was deadlocked. Several of the workers wanted to take their vacations during the same two-week period and could not agree on who should go. Some workers argued that they should have priority because they had more seniority, while others argued that priority should be based on productivity, as in the past. Since it was quitting time, the group concluded that Kevin would have to resolve the dispute himself. After all, wasn't that what he was being paid for?

SOURCE: Reprinted with permission from Gary Yukl, *Leadership in Organizations,* Fourth Edition (Englewood Cliffs, NJ: Prentice Hall, 1998), 147–148.

Questions

1. Analyze this situation using the Hersey-Blanchard model and the Vroom-Jago model. What do these models suggest as the appropriate leadership or decision style? Explain.

2. Evaluate Kevin McCarthy's leadership style before and during his experiment in participative management.

3. If you were Kevin McCarthy, what would you do now? Why?

Finance Department

Ken Osborne stared out the window, wondering what he could do to get things back on track. When he became head of the finance department of a state government agency, Osborne inherited a group of highly trained professionals who pursued their jobs with energy and enthusiasm. Everyone seemed to genuinely love coming to work every day. The tasks were sometimes mundane, but most employees liked the structured, routine nature of the work. In addition, the lively camaraderie of the group provided an element of fun and excitement that the work itself sometimes lacked.

Ken knew he'd had an easy time of things over the last couple of years—he had been able to focus his energies on maintaining relationships with other departments and agencies and completing the complex reports he had to turn in each month. The department practically ran itself. Until now. The problem was Larry Gibson, one of the department's best employees. Well-liked by everyone in the department, Gibson had been a key contributor to developing a new online accounting system, and Ken was counting on him to help with the implementation. But everything had changed after Gibson attended a professional development seminar at a prestigious university. Ken had expected him to come back even more fired up about work, but lately Larry was spending more time on his outside professional activities than he was on his job. "If only I'd paid more attention when all this began," Ken thought, as he recalled the day Larry asked him to sign his revised individual development plan. As he'd done in the past, Ken had simply chatted with Larry for a few minutes, glanced at the changes, and initialed the modification. Larry's revised plan included taking a more active role in the state accountants society, which he argued would enhance his value to the agency as well as improve his own skills and professional contacts.

Within a month, Ken noticed that most of Gibson's energy and enthusiasm seemed to be focused on the society rather than the finance department. On "first Thursday," the society's luncheon meeting day, Larry spent most of the morning on the phone notifying people about the monthly meeting and finalizing details with the speaker. He left around 11 A.M. to make sure things were set up for the meeting and usually didn't return until close to quitting time. Ken could live with the loss of Gibson for one day a month, but the preoccupation with society business seemed to be turning his former star employee into a part-time worker. Larry shows up late for meetings, usually doesn't participate very much, and seems to have little interest in what is going on in the department. The new accounting system is floundering because Larry isn't spending the time to train people in its effective use, so Ken is starting to get complaints from other departments. Moreover, his previously harmonious group of employees is starting to whine and bicker over minor issues and decisions. Ken has also noticed that people who used to be hard at work when he arrived in the mornings seem to be coming in later and later every day.

"Everything's gone haywire since Larry attended that damn seminar," Ken brooded. "I thought I was one of the best department heads in the agency. Now, I realize I haven't had to provide much leadership until now. Maybe I've had things too easy."

SOURCE: Based on David Hornestay, "Double Vision," *Government Executive,* April 2000, 41–44.

Questions

1. Why has Ken Osborne's department been so successful even though he has provided little leadership over the past two years?

2. How would you describe Osborne's current leadership style? Based on the path-goal theory, which style do you think he might most effectively use to turn things around with Larry Gibson?

3. If you were in Osborne's position, describe how you would evaluate the situation and handle the problem.

REFERENCES

1. William C. Symonds, "The Power of the Paycheck," *Business Week,* May 24, 1999, 71–72; and Katharine Mieszkowski, "Changing Tires, Changing the World," *Fast Company,* October 1999, 58–60.

2. Fred E. Fiedler, "Assumed Similarity Measures as Predictors of Team Effectiveness," *Journal of Abnormal and Social Psychology* 49 (1954), 381–388; F. E. Fiedler, *Leader Attitudes and Group Effectiveness* (Urbana, IL: University of Illinois Press, 1958); and F. E. Fiedler, *A Theory of Leadership Effectiveness* (New York: McGraw-Hill, 1967).

3. David S. Cloud, "The Attorney General Gets Little Respect; What's Her Problem?" *The Wall Street Journal,* January 27, 2000, A1, A10.

4. M. J. Strube and J. E. Garcia, "A Meta-Analytic Investigation of Fiedler's Contingency Model of Leadership Effectiveness," *Psychological Bulletin* 90 (1981): 307–321; and L. H. Peters, D. D. Hartke, and J. T. Pohlmann, "Fiedler's Contingency Theory of Leadership: An Application of the Meta-Analysis Procedures of Schmidt and Hunter," *Psychological Bulletin* 97 (1985): 274–285.

5. R. Singh, "Leadership Style and Reward Allocation: Does Least Preferred Coworker Scale Measure Tasks and Relation Orientation?" *Organizational Behavior and Human Performance* 27 (1983), 178–197; D. Hosking, "A Critical Evaluation of Fiedler's Contingency Hypotheses," *Progress in Applied Psychology* 1 (1981), 103–154; Gary Yukl, "Leader LPC Scores: Attitude Dimensions and Behavioral Correlates," *Journal of Social Psychology* 80 (1970): 207–212; G. Graen, K. M. Alvares, J. B. Orris, and J. A. Martella, "Contingency Model of Leadership Effectiveness: Antecedent and Evidential Results," *Psychological Bulletin* 74 (1970): 285–296; R. P. Vecchio, "Assessing the Validity of Fiedler's Contingency Model of Leadership Effectiveness: A Closer Look at Strube and Garcia," *Psychological Bulletin* 93 (1983): 404–408.

6. Robert L. Rose, "Sour Note," *The Wall Street Journal,* June 22, 1993.

7. J. K. Kennedy, Jr., "Middle LPC Leaders and the Contingency Model of Leadership Effectiveness," *Organizational Behavior and Human Performance* 30 (1982): 1–14; and S. C. Shiflett, "The Contingency Model of Leadership Effectiveness: Some Implications of Its Statistical and Methodological Properties," *Behavioral Science* 18, No. 6 (1973): 429–440.

8. Roya Ayman, M. M. Chemers, and F. Fiedler, "The Contingency Model of Leadership Effectiveness: Its Levels of Analysis," *Leadership Quarterly* 6, No. 2 (1995):147–167.

9. Paul Hersey and Kenneth H. Blanchard, *Management of Organizational Behavior: Utilizing Human Resources,* 4th ed. (Englewood Cliffs, NJ: Prentice-Hall, 1982).

10. Carol Hymowitz, "How Cynthia Danaher Learned to Stop Sharing and Start Leading," (In the Lead column), *The Wall Street Journal,* March 16, 1999, B1.

11. Cheryl Dahle, "Xtreme Teams," *Fast Company,* November 1999, 310–326.

12. This example comes from *Soundview: Executive Book Summaries,* 16, No. 7 (July 1994): 3-4.

13. Adapted from Oliver Niehouse, "The Strategic Nature of Leadership," *Management Solutions,* July 1987, 27–34.

14. Carole McGraw, "Teaching Teenagers? Think, Do, Learn," *Education Digest,* February 1998, 44–47.

15. Michael Barrier, "Leadership Skills Employees Respect," *Nation's Business,* January 1999.

16. M. G. Evans, "The Effects of Supervisory Behavior on the Path-Goal Relationship," *Organizational Behavior and Human Performance* 5 (1970), 277–298; M. G. Evans, "Leadership and Motivation: A Core Concept," *Academy of Management Journal* 13 (1970), 91–102; and B. S. Georgopoulos, G. M. Mahoney, and N. W. Jones, "A Path-Goal Approach to Productivity," *Journal of Applied Psychology* 41 (1957), 345–353.

17. Robert J. House, "A Path-Goal Theory of Leadership Effectiveness," *Administrative Science Quarterly* 16 (1971), 321–338.

18. M. G. Evans, "Leadership," in *Organizational Behavior,* ed. S. Kerr (Columbus, OH: Grid, 1974), 230–233.

19. Robert J. House and Terrence R. Mitchell, "Path Goal Theory of Leadership," *Journal of Contemporary Business* (Autumn 1974), 81–97.

20. Dyan Machan, "We're Not Authoritarian Goons," *Forbes,* October 24, 1994, 264–268.

21. Mike Hofman, "Everyone's a Cost-Cutter," *Inc.,* July 1998, 117; and Abby Livingston, "Gain-Sharing Encourages Productivity," *Nation's Business,* January 1998, 21–22.

22. Charles Greene, "Questions of Causation in the Path-Goal Theory of Leadership," *Academy of Management Journal* 22 (March 1979), 22–41; and C. A. Schriesheim and Mary Ann von Glinow, "The Path-Goal Theory of Leadership: A Theoretical and Empirical Analysis," *Academy of Management Journal* 20 (1977), 398–405.

23. V. H. Vroom and Arthur G. Jago, *The New Leadership: Managing Participation in Organizations* (Englewood Cliffs, NJ: Prentice-Hall, 1988).

24. The following discussion is based heavily on Victor H. Vroom, "Leadership and the Decision-Making Process," *Organizational Dynamics* 28, No. 4 (Spring 2000): 82–94.

25. R. H. G. Field, "A Test of the Vroom-Yetton Normative Model of Leadership," *Journal of Applied Psychology* (October 1982), 523–532; and R. H. G. Field, "A

Critique of the Vroom-Yetton Contingency Model of Leadership Behavior," *Academy of Management Review* 4 (1979), 249–251.

26. Vroom, "Leadership and the Decision-Making Process"; Jennifer T. Ettling and Arthur G. Jago, "Participation Under Conditions of Conflict: More on the Validity of the Vroom-Yetton Model," *Journal of Management Studies* 25 (1988), 73–83; Madeline E. Heilman, Harvey A. Hornstein, Jack H. Cage, and Judith K. Herschlag, "Reactions to Prescribed Leader Behavior as a Function of Role Perspective: The Case of the Vroom-Yetton Model," *Journal of Applied Psychology* (February 1984), 50–60; and Arthur G. Jago and Victor H. Vroom, "Some Differences in the Incidence and Evaluation of Participative Leader Behavior," *Journal of Applied Psychology* (December 1982), 776–783.

27. Based on a decision problem presented in Victor H. Vroom, "Leadership and the Decision-Making Process," *Organizational Dynamics* 28, No. 4 (Spring, 2000): 82–94.

28. S. Kerr and J. M. Jermier, "Substitutes for Leadership: Their Meaning and Measurement," *Organizational Behavior and Human Performance* 22 (1978), 375–403; and Jon P. Howell and Peter W. Dorfman, "Leadership and Substitutes for Leadership Among Professional and Nonprofessional Workers," *Journal of Applied Behavioral Science* 22 (1986), 29–46.

29. J. P. Howell, D. E. Bowen, P. W. Doreman, S. Kerr, and P. M. Podsakoff, "Substitutes for Leadership: Effective Alternatives to Ineffective Leadership," *Organizational Dynamics* (Summer 1990), 21–38.

30. Howell, et al., "Substitutes for Leadership: Effective Alternatives to Ineffective Leadership."

31. P. M. Podsakoff, S. B. MacKenzie, and W. H. Bommer, "Transformational Leader Behaviors and Substitutes for Leadership as Determinants of Employee Satisfaction, Commitment, Trust, and Organizational Behaviors," *Journal of Management* 22, No. 2 (1996), 259–298.

32. Howell, et al., "Substitutes for Leadership."

The Personal Side of Leadership

CHAPTER OUTLINE

YOUR LEADERSHIP CHALLENGE

After reading this chapter, you should be able to:

- Identify major personality dimensions and understand how personality influences leadership and relationships within organizations.

- Clarify your instrumental and end values, and recognize how values guide thoughts and behavior.

- Define *attitudes* and explain their relationship to leader behavior.

- Recognize individual differences in cognitive style and broaden your own thinking style to expand leadership potential.

- Practice aspects of charismatic leadership by pursuing a vision or idea that you care deeply about and want to share with others.

- Apply the concepts that distinguish transformational from transactional leadership.

The Leader as an Individual

"**L**eadership is a performance," says Carly Fiorina, the first outsider ever appointed to run Hewlett-Packard. "You have to be conscious about your behavior, because everyone else is." As HP's new CEO, Fiorina is using her outgoing, forceful personality to shake things up at the venerable Silicon Valley company. She wants to bring the same focus, energy, and enthusiasm she's known for to the company she leads.

Fiorina grabbed as much media coverage as she could soon after her appointment to the top position at HP, with interviews appearing in well-respected business magazines as well as in *Cosmopolitan* and on television shows in the U.S., Britain, Japan, and France. Then she virtually disappeared from the public arena to focus all her time and effort on rooting out the complacency she sees as a threat to her organization. In the $30 million Gulfstream jet she recently bought, Fiorina has traveled to company sites from Germany to Korea, talking directly to HP workers, stressing the need for change, and listening to employees' concerns. Even though Fiorina believes employees need to be heard, she also thinks they need to know who gets to make the big decisions. At one coffee talk, when an employee challenged her brand strategy, Fiorina listened to his side and then responded, "You have some valid points, but this isn't one everybody gets to decide. I get to decide this one—and I've decided."

Fiorina respects Hewlett-Packard's culture and history of management through trust and openness, but she fears that "the HP Way" has degenerated into a situation "where everyone gets to say no, and no one gets to say yes." She is pushing managers throughout the company to make decisions and act quickly. A month after she arrived, she called together the four division heads and asked them to develop a major reorganization plan. Told it would take several months to do a review, Fiorina made clear that she expected it done in the three days of the retreat—no whining, just get it done. Fiorina thinks Hewlett-Packard has some of the smartest people in the industry, but she knows they need to move faster to keep up with the urgency of the Internet age. She has revised pay plans to reward top-notch performers and aggressive sellers and to punish laggards. In a company that has never had major layoffs for all six decades of its existence, Fiorina has publicly stated that "if one quarter of the people in HP don't want to make the journey, or can't take the pace, that's the way it has to be."[1]

Carly Fiorina has deliberately tied HP's makeover to her own energetic, somewhat aggressive personality and focused decision-making style, a strategy that seems to be working. In today's fast-paced business world, more attention is often given to the personalities of star leaders such as Jeff Bezos of Amazon.com, Scott McNealy of Sun Microsystems, and Steve Case of AOL than to the technology their companies are based on. Many of today's organizations are using personality tests as part of the process of hiring top executives. At Hewlett-Packard, Fiorina and the other top candidates took a 900-question test that included true-false questions such as "I don't ever go walking where there are poisonous snakes," "Employers should have a say in how employees behave when they are not at work," and "I try to avoid situations that have uncertain outcomes." According to psychologist Richard Hagberg, who designed the test, answers to these questions can help determine whether someone has the "right stuff" to lead the company.

In Chapter 2, we examined studies of some personality traits, individual qualities, and behaviors that are thought to be consistent with effective leadership. Chapter 3 examined contingency theories of leadership, which consider the relationship between leader activities and the situation in which they occur, including followers and the environment. Clearly, organizational leadership is both an individual and an organizational phenomenon. This chapter explores the individual in more depth, looking at some individual differences that can affect leadership abilities and success. Individuals differ in many ways, and these differences can profoundly affect leadership. We begin by looking at personality and some leader-related personality dimensions. Then, the chapter considers how values affect leadership and the ways in which a leader's attitudes toward self and others influence behavior. We will also explore cognitive differences, including a discussion of thinking and decision-making styles and the concept of brain dominance. Finally, the chapter explores charismatic and transformational leadership, two leadership styles that are based on the personal characteristics of the leader.

PERSONALITY AND LEADERSHIP

We all recognize that people are different in many ways. Some are consistently pleasant in a variety of situations while others may be moody or aggressive. To explain this behavior, we may say, "He has a pleasant personality," or "She has an aggressive personality." This is the most common usage of the term *personality*, and it refers to an individual's behavior patterns as well as how the person is viewed by others. However, there is also a deeper meaning to the term. **Personality** is the set of unseen characteristics and processes that underlie a relatively stable pattern of behavior in response to ideas, objects, or people in the environment. Leaders who have an understanding of how individuals' personalities differ can use this understanding to improve their leadership effectiveness.

A Model of Personality

Most people think of personality in terms of traits. As we discussed in Chapter 2, researchers have investigated whether any traits stand up to scientific scrutiny, and we looked at some traits associated with effective leadership. Although investigators have examined thousands of traits over the years, their findings have been distilled into five general dimensions that describe personality. These often are called the **Big Five personality dimensions,** as illustrated in Exhibit 4.1.[2] Each contains a wide range of specific traits—for example, all of the personality traits that you would use to describe a teacher, friend, or boss could be categorized as falling into one of the Big Five dimensions: extroversion, agreeableness, conscientiousness, emotional stability, and openness to experience. As illustrated in Exhibit 4.1, a person may have a low, moderate, or high degree of each of these general dimensions.

Extroversion is made up of traits and characteristics that influence behavior in group settings. Extroversion refers to the degree to which a person is outgoing, sociable, talkative, and comfortable meeting and talking to new people. This dimension also includes the characteristic of *dominance*. A person with a high degree of dominance likes to be in control and have influence over others. These people often are quite self-confident, seek out positions of

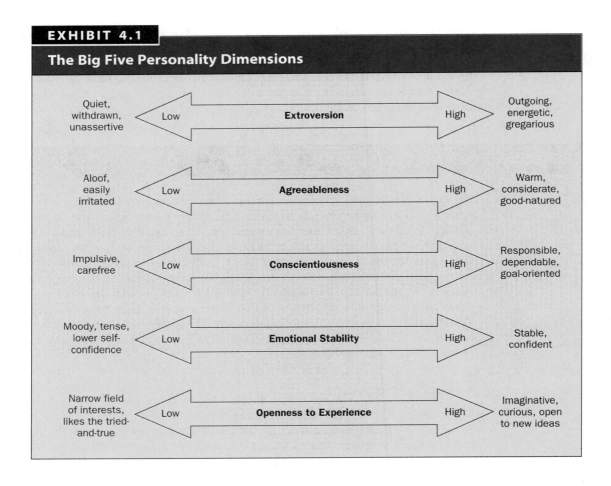

EXHIBIT 4.1

The Big Five Personality Dimensions

Quiet, withdrawn, unassertive	Low	**Extroversion**	High	Outgoing, energetic, gregarious
Aloof, easily irritated	Low	**Agreeableness**	High	Warm, considerate, good-natured
Impulsive, carefree	Low	**Conscientiousness**	High	Responsible, dependable, goal-oriented
Moody, tense, lower self-confidence	Low	**Emotional Stability**	High	Stable, confident
Narrow field of interests, likes the tried-and-true	Low	**Openness to Experience**	High	Imaginative, curious, open to new ideas

authority, and are competitive and assertive. They like to be in charge of others or have responsibility for others. Carly Fiorina at Hewlett-Packard appears to have a high degree of both dominance and extroversion. She enjoys being "on stage," speaking before a crowd, meeting new people in HP plants around the world. Fiorina also clearly enjoys being in a position of authority and influence. In contrast, Doug Ivester, who served as CEO of Coca-Cola for a short time following the death of Roberto Goizueta, seems to have a low degree of both dominance and extroversion. Ivester was known to be very reserved in many situations. In addition, he did not appear to have a great desire to influence others, preferring to focus on details and strategy rather than the subtlety of interpersonal relationships. Indeed, he sometimes came off as high-handed because he made and implemented decisions without trying to persuade others to his viewpoint. Some believe Ivester's lack of self-assurance about leading others and the fact that he made little attempt to exert influence were the biggest drawbacks to his success as CEO of a major corporation.[3]

It is obvious that both dominance and extroversion could be valuable for a leader. However, not all effective leaders necessarily have a high degree of these characteristics. In addition, a high degree of dominance and extroversion could even be detrimental to effective leadership if not tempered by other qualities, such as agreeableness or emotional stability.

Agreeableness is the degree to which a person is able to get along with others by being good-natured, co-operative, forgiving, compassionate, understanding, and trusting. A leader who scores high on agreeableness seems warm and approachable, whereas one who is low on this dimension may seem cold, distant, and insensitive. People high on agreeableness tend to make friends easily and often have a large number of friends, whereas those low on agreeableness generally establish fewer close relationships. Patricia Gallup, CEO of PC Connection, is a warm, approachable leader who's always willing to listen. She knows most of her employees by name and encourages them to talk with her about their problems or concerns.[4]

The third personality dimension, **conscientiousness,** refers to the degree to which a person is responsible, dependable, persistent, and achievement-oriented. A conscientious person is focused on a few goals, which he or she pursues in a purposeful way, whereas a less conscientious person tends to be easily distracted and impulsive. This dimension of personality relates to the work itself rather than to relationships with other people. Many entrepreneurs show a high level of conscientiousness. For example, Jari Ovaskainen gave up a high-paying consultant job and sold his beloved Mercedes 300CE coupe to pursue his dream of starting a business. Ovaskainen's conscientiousness and hard work have helped Iobox, the Helsinki-based company he co-founded, jump to an early lead in the market for wireless Internet service. Ovaskainen's high degree of conscientiousness is also reflected in the workplace. Unlike many Internet companies, Iobox doesn't have foosball tables or other diversions for employees: "We don't believe in mixing work life with play time," Ovaskainen says. He wants people focused on the goal of making Iobox the "next Yahoo."[5]

The dimension of **emotional stability** refers to the degree to which a person is well-adjusted, calm, and secure. A leader who is emotionally stable handles stress well, is able to handle criticism, and generally doesn't take mistakes and failures personally. In contrast, leaders who have a low degree of emotional stability are likely to become tense, anxious, or depressed. They generally have lower self-confidence and may explode in emotional outbursts when stressed or criticized. The related topic of *emotional intelligence* will be discussed in detail in the next chapter.

The final Big Five dimension, **openness to experience,** is the degree to which a person has a broad range of interests and is imaginative, creative, and willing to consider new ideas. These people are intellectually curious and often seek out new experiences through travel, the arts, movies, reading widely, or other activities. People lower in this dimension tend to have narrower interests and stick to the tried-and-true ways of doing things. Open-mindedness is important to leaders because, as we learned in Chapter 1, leadership is about change rather than stability. In a study of three nineteenth-century leaders— John Quincy Adams, Frederick Douglass, and Jane Addams—one researcher found that early travel experiences and exposure to different ideas and cultures were critical elements in developing leadership skills and qualities in these leaders.[6] Travel during the formative years helped these leaders develop a greater degree of openness to experience because it put them in situations that required adaptability.

Despite the logic of the Big Five personality dimensions, they can be difficult to measure precisely. In addition, since each dimension is made up of numerous traits, a person can be high on some of the specific traits but low on others. For example, considering the dimension of conscientiousness, it might be possible for a person to be highly responsible and dependable and yet also have a low degree of achievement-orientation. Furthermore, research has been mostly limited to subjects in the United States, so the theory is difficult to apply cross-culturally.

Although it seems logical that a high degree of each of the dimensions would generally be beneficial to leaders, few studies have carefully examined the connection between the Big Five and leadership success. One recent summary of more than seventy years of personality and leadership research did find evidence that four of the five dimensions were consistently related to successful leadership.[7] The researchers found considerable evidence that people who score high on the dimensions of extroversion, agreeableness, conscientiousness, and emotional stability are more successful leaders. Results for openness to experience were less consistent; that is, in some cases, higher scores on this dimension related to better performance, but they did not seem to make a difference in other cases. Yet, in a recent study by a team of psychologists of the personality traits of the greatest U.S. presidents (as determined by historians), openness to experience produced the highest correlation with historians' ratings of greatness. The study noted that presidents such as Abraham Lincoln and Thomas Jefferson were high on this personality dimension. Other personality dimensions the team found to be associated with great presidents were extroversion and conscientiousness, including traits such as aggressiveness, setting ambitious goals, and striving for achievement. Although agreeableness did not correlate with greatness, the ability to empathize with others and being concerned for others, which could be considered elements of emotional stability, did.[8]

It is important to note that few leaders have consistently high scores across all of the Big Five dimensions, yet there are many successful leaders.

Higher scores on the Big Five dimensions are not necessarily predictive of leadership effectiveness, and persons who score toward the lower end of the scale can also be good leaders. As we discussed in the previous two chapters, situational factors play a role in determining which traits may be most important. In addition, a leader's intelligence, knowledge of the business, values and attitudes, and problem-solving styles, which are not measured by the Big Five, also play a role in leadership effectiveness. Later in this chapter, we will discuss values and attitudes, as well as examine some cognitive differences that affect leadership. First, let's look more closely at two personality attributes that have significant implications for leaders.

Personality Traits and Leader Behavior

Two specific personality attributes that have a significant impact on behavior and are thus of particular interest for leadership studies are locus of control and authoritarianism.

LOCUS OF CONTROL Some people believe that their actions can strongly affect what happens to them. In other words, they believe they are "masters of their own fate." Others feel that whatever happens to them in life is a result of luck, chance, or outside people and events; they believe they have little control over their fate. A person's **locus of control** defines whether they place the primary responsibility within themselves or on outside forces.[9] People who believe their actions determine what happens to them have a high *internal* locus of control (internals), while those who believe outside forces determine what happens to them have a high *external* locus of control (externals).

Research on locus of control has shown real differences in behavior between internals and externals across a wide range of settings.[10] Internals in general are more self-motivated, are in better control of their own behavior, participate more in social and political activities, and more actively seek information. There is also evidence that internals are better able to handle complex information and problem solving, and that they are more achievement-oriented than externals. In addition, people with a high internal locus of control are more likely than externals to try to influence others, and thus more likely to assume or seek leadership opportunities. People with a high external locus of control typically prefer to have a structured, directed work situation. They are better able than internals to handle work that requires compliance and conformity, but they are generally not as effective in situations that require initiative, creativity, and independent action. Therefore, since externals do best in situations where success depends on complying with the direction or guidance of others, they are less likely to enjoy or succeed in leadership positions.

Leaders in today's Internet businesses often exhibit a high internal locus of control, as illustrated by Cisco CEO John Chambers.

IN THE LEAD   John Chambers, Cisco Systems

Cisco Systems, the leading maker of routers, switches, and other gear that keeps the Internet running, has defeated every challenge it has faced, thanks largely to the abilities of the company's CEO, John Chambers. During his first five years with Cisco, which has been called "The Corporation of the Future," the company's market capitalization grew from $9 billion to fifty-four times that amount. General Electric, often considered the best-managed company in the world, now regularly sends its managers to study Cisco.

Chambers battled a learning disability as a child and was made fun of by kids at school, but he always believed he could overcome anything with hard work and determination. He worked in sales at both IBM and Wang before heading to Cisco, but his goal was always to be a top leader at a successful company. Hired at Cisco in 1991, Chambers again faced discrimination—the Stanford University graduates who formed the core of the company at that time didn't think his business degree from West Virginia University was worth much, and they questioned whether his background in sales was what the company needed to move forward into the twenty-first century. Again, Chambers' high internal locus of control helped him believe that he alone was in control of his fate. In discussing his management style, Chambers points out his belief in the power of tenacity: "When it comes to customers, we will do whatever it takes to win them. 'No' to us just means we have to come back. That's in our genes."

Today, Cisco faces a host of new competitors, a declining stock price, and a tough economy, but Chambers believes he and his employees can again come out on top. He makes statements such as "We want to create the greatest company in history," and "We want to change the world," without a touch of irony or modesty. He actually believes it can be done.[11]

E-commerce leaders like John Chambers need a high internal locus of control to cope with the rapid change and uncertainty associated with Internet business. A person with a high external locus of control would likely feel overwhelmed trying to make the rapid decisions and changes needed to keep pace with the industry, assuming that little could be done to help the company counter the impact of outside forces and events.

Do you believe luck, chance, or the actions of other people play a major role in your life, or do you feel in control of your own fate? To learn more about your locus of control, complete the questionnaire in Exhibit 4.2.

AUTHORITARIANISM   The belief that power and status differences *should* exist in an organization is called **authoritarianism**.[12] Individuals who have a high

EXHIBIT 4.2

Measuring Locus of Control

The questionnaire below is designed to measure locus-of-control beliefs. Researchers using this questionnaire in a study of college students found a mean of 51.8 for men and 52.2 for women, with a standard deviation of 6 for each. The higher your score on this questionnaire, the more you tend to believe that you are generally responsible for what happens to you; in other words, higher scores are associated with internal locus of control. Low scores are associated with external locus of control. Scoring low indicates that you tend to believe that forces beyond your control, such as powerful other people, fate, or chance, are responsible for what happens to you.

For each of these ten questions, indicate the extent to which you agree or disagree using the following scale:

1. = strongly disagree   5. = slightly agree
2. = disagree   6. = agree
3. = slightly disagree   7. = strongly agree
4. = neither disagree nor agree

_____   1. When I get what I want, it's usually because I worked hard for it.
_____   2. When I make plans, I am almost certain to make them work.
_____   3. I prefer games involving some luck over games requiring pure skill.
_____   4. I can learn almost anything if I set my mind to it.
_____   5. My major accomplishments are entirely due to my hard work and ability.
_____   6. I usually don't set goals, because I have a hard time following through on them.
_____   7. Competition discourages excellence.
_____   8. Often people get ahead just by being lucky.
_____   9. On any sort of exam or competition, I like to know how well I do relative to everyone else.
_____ 10. It's pointless to keep working on something that's too difficult for me.

To determine your score, reverse the values you selected for questions 3, 6, 7, 8, and 10 (1 = 7, 2 = 6, 3 = 5, 4 = 4, 5 = 3, 6 = 2, 7 = 1). For example, if you strongly disagreed with the statement in question 3, you would have given it a value of 1. Change this value to a 7. Reverse the scores in a similar manner for questions 6, 7, 8, and 10. Now add the point values from all ten questions together.

Your score: _____

SOURCE: Adapted from J. M. Burger, *Personality: Theory and Research* (Belmont, Calif.: Wadsworth, 1986), 400-401, cited in D. Hellriegel, J. W. Slocum, Jr., and R. W. Woodman, *Organizational Behavior,* 6th ed. (St. Paul, Minn.: West Publishing Co., 1992), 97-100. Original Source: "Sphere-Specific Measures of Perceived Control" by D. L. Paul, *Journal of Personality and Social Psychology* 44, 1253–1265.

degree of this personality trait tend to adhere to conventional rules and values, obey established authority, respect power and toughness, judge others critically, and disapprove of the expression of personal feelings. A leader's degree of authoritarianism will affect how the leader wields and shares power. A highly authoritarian leader is likely to rely heavily on formal authority and unlikely to want to share power with subordinates. High authoritarianism is associated with the traditional, rational approach to management described in Chapter 1. The new leadership paradigm requires that leaders be less authoritarian, although people who rate high on this personality trait can also be effective leaders. Leaders should also understand that the degree to which followers possess authoritarianism influences how they react to the leader's use of power and authority. When leaders and followers differ in their degree of authoritarianism, effective leadership may be more difficult to achieve.

A trait that is closely related to authoritarianism is *dogmatism*, which refers to a person's receptiveness to others' ideas and opinions. A highly dogmatic person is closed-minded and not receptive to others' ideas. When in a leadership position, dogmatic individuals often make decisions quickly based on limited information, and they are unreceptive to ideas that conflict with their opinions and decisions. Effective leaders, on the other hand, generally have a lower degree of dogmatism, which means they are open-minded and receptive to others' ideas.

Understanding how personality traits and dimensions affect behavior can be a valuable ability for leaders. Knowledge of individual differences gives leaders valuable insights into their own behavior as well as that of followers. It also offers a framework leaders can use to diagnose situations and make changes to benefit the organization. For example, when Reed Breland became a team facilitator at Hewlett-Packard's financial services center in Colorado, he noticed immediately that one team was in constant turmoil. Breland's understanding of individual differences helped him recognize that two members of the team had a severe personality clash and could not see eye-to-eye on any issue. Although Breland tried to help work things out within the team, after several months he simply dissolved the group and reassigned members to other areas. The team members all did fine in other assignments; the personality conflict between the two members was just too strong to overcome and it affected the team's productivity and effectiveness.[13]

VALUES AND ATTITUDES

In addition to personality differences, people differ in the values and attitudes they hold. These differences also affect the behavior of leaders and followers.

Instrumental and End Values

Values are fundamental beliefs that an individual considers to be important, that are relatively stable over time, and that have an impact on attitudes and behavior.[14] Values are what cause a person to prefer that things be done one way rather than another way. Whether we recognize it or not, we are constantly valuing things, people, or ideas as good or bad, pleasant or unpleasant, ethical or unethical, and so forth.[15] When a person has strong values in certain areas, these can have a powerful influence on behavior. For example, a person who highly values honesty and integrity might resign from a company that routinely engages in unethical practices. The issue of moral leadership and leaders' ethical values will be considered in detail in Chapter 6.

One way to think about values is in terms of instrumental and end values, as illustrated in Exhibit 4.3.[16] Social scientist Milton Rokeach developed a list of eighteen instrumental values and eighteen end values that have been found to be more or less universal across cultures. **End values,** sometimes called terminal values, are beliefs about the kind of goals or outcomes that are worth trying to pursue. For example, some people value security, a comfortable life, and good health above everything else as the important goals to strive for in life. Others may place greater value on social recognition, pleasure, and an exciting life. **Instrumental values** are beliefs about the types of behavior that are appropriate for reaching goals. Instrumental values include such things as being helpful to others, being honest, or exhibiting courage.

Although everyone has both instrumental and end values, individuals differ in how they order the values into priorities, which accounts for tremendous variation among people. Part of this difference relates to culture. For example, in the United States, independence is highly valued and is reinforced by many institutions, including schools, religious organizations, and businesses. Other cultures place less value on independence and more value on being part of a tightly knit community. A person's family background also influences his or her values. Values are learned, not inherited, but some values become incorporated into a person's thinking very early in life. For example, some executives cite their mothers as a primary source of their leadership abilities because they helped to shape their values.[17] Jack Welch's mother was determined that he be successful and consistently encouraged him to do better in school. This helped him to acquire a value for achievement and ambition. William Monroe, CEO of Bertolli North America, developed values of risk-taking, responsibility, and courage very early in life. His father died when he was five years old, leaving Monroe's mother to raise two sons alone. "She picked herself up and went to work in a knitting factory," he says. In addition, she bought a house, despite warnings from relatives that she wouldn't be able to make the payments. "She took the risk and never looked back," Monroe says. "She knew how to make a decision and then not worry about it."[18]

EXHIBIT 4.3

Rokeach's Instrumental and End Values

End Values		Instrumental Values	
A comfortable life	_____	Ambition	_____
Equality	_____	Broad-mindedness	_____
An exciting life	_____	Capability	_____
Family security	_____	Cheerfulness	_____
Freedom	_____	Cleanliness	_____
Health	_____	Courage	_____
Inner harmony	_____	Forgiveness	_____
Mature love	_____	Helpfulness	_____
National security	_____	Honesty	_____
Pleasure	_____	Imagination	_____
Salvation	_____	Intellectualism	_____
Self-respect	_____	Logic	_____
A sense of accomplishment	_____	Ability to love	_____
Social recognition	_____	Loyalty	_____
True friendship	_____	Obedience	_____
Wisdom	_____	Politeness	_____
A world at peace	_____	Responsibility	_____
A world of beauty	_____	Self-control	_____

NOTE: The values are listed in alphabetical order and there is no one-to-one relationship between the end and instrumental values.

SOURCE: Robert C. Benfari, *Understanding and Changing Your Management Style* (San Francisco: Jossey-Bass, 1999), 178–183; and M. Rokeach, *Understanding Human Values* (New York: The Free Press, 1979).

Values are generally fairly well established by early adulthood, but a person's values can also change throughout life. This chapter's Living Leadership reflects on how the values that shape a leader's actions in a moment of crisis have been developed over time. Values may affect leaders and leadership in a number of ways.[19] For one thing, a leader's personal values affect his or her perception of situations and problems. By **perception,** we mean the process people use to make sense out of the environment by selecting, organizing, and interpreting information. A leader who greatly values ambition and career success may view a problem or a subordinate's mistake as an impediment to her own success, whereas a leader who values helpfulness and obedience might see it as a chance to help a subordinate improve or grow. Values also affect how leaders relate to others. A leader who values obedience, conformity, and politeness may have a

LIVING LEADERSHIP

Developing Character

"The character that takes command in moments of critical choices has already been determined. It has been determined by a thousand other choices made earlier in seemingly unimportant moments. It has been determined by all those 'little' choices of years past—by all those times when the voice of conscience was at war with the voice of temptation—whispering a lie that 'it doesn't really matter.' It has been determined by all the day-to-day decisions made when life seemed easy and crises seemed far away, the decisions that piece by piece, bit by bit, developed habits of discipline or of laziness; habits of self-sacrifice, or self-indulgence; habits of duty and honor and integrity—or dishonor and shame."

President Ronald Reagan, quoted in Norman R. Augustine, "Seven Fundamentals of Effective Leadership," an original essay written for the Center for the Study of American Business, Washington University in St. Louis, *CEO Series* Issue No. 27, October 1998.

---

difficult time understanding and appreciating a follower who is self-reliant, independent, creative, and a bit rebellious. Recognizing these value differences can help leaders better understand and work with varied followers.

A third way in which values affect leadership is that they guide a leader's choices and actions. A leader who places high value on being courageous and standing up for what you believe in, for example, is much more likely to make decisions that may not be popular but which he believes are right. Values determine how leaders acquire and use power, how they handle conflict, and how they make decisions. A leader who values competitiveness and ambition will behave differently from one who places a high value on co-operativeness and forgiveness. Ethical values help guide choices concerning what is morally right or wrong. Values concerning end goals also help determine a leader's actions and choices in the workplace.

For many organizations today, clarifying and stating their corporate values has become an important part of defining how the organization operates. Often, a company's values are an outgrowth of the values held by a founder or top leader, as at The Body Shop.

IN THE LEAD   Anita Roddick, The Body Shop

The Body Shop develops, manufactures, and sells more than 400 personal care products in 600 retail outlets worldwide and does over $200 million in sales. Founder and CEO Anita Roddick calls her organization a "benevolent anarchy," in which there is a strong link between organizational values and success.

The Body Shop's values include having fun, putting labor where love is, and going in the opposite direction of other companies in the personal care products industry. Employees are encouraged to constantly question what they are doing in order to find better working methods. The company even has a Department of Damned Good Ideas. Roddick values creativity, so all franchisees and store managers receive intensive training and attend seminars on how to encourage creativity in others. The values of personal responsibility and recognition are also important. Each store has a "who's who" system to identify each employee's responsibility and performance so that individual commitment and accomplishment can be recognized. Roddick has also instilled ethical and socially responsible values into the organization. She travels the world looking for new ingredients for the company's "natural products," as well as searching for ways the company can contribute to a better world. As a result, The Body Shop has been actively involved with Amnesty International, creating voter registration centers, and collecting toys for hospitals. Roddick takes the company's values so seriously that The Body Shop publishes an annual values report, and contributions to social and environmental issues are verified by external auditors.[20]

Leaders can become more effective by clarifying their values and understanding how they guide their actions. To begin clarifying your own values, go back to Exhibit 4.3 and rank the values from your most preferred (what you consider most important) to your least preferred. Were you surprised by any of your instrumental or end values?

How Attitudes Affect Leadership

Values help determine the attitudes leaders have about themselves and about their followers. An **attitude** is an evaluation—either positive or negative—about people, events, or things. Behavioral scientists consider attitudes to have three components: cognitions (thoughts), affect (feelings), and behavior.[21] The cognitive component includes the ideas and knowledge a person has about the object of an attitude, such as a leader's knowledge and ideas about a specific employee's performance and abilities. The affective component concerns how an individual feels about the object of an attitude. Perhaps the leader resents having to routinely answer questions or help the employee perform certain tasks. The behavioral component of an attitude predisposes a person to act in a certain way. For example, the leader might avoid the employee or fail to include him or her in certain activities of the group. Although attitudes change more easily than values, they typically reflect a person's fundamental values as well as a person's background and life experiences. A leader who highly values forgiveness, compassion toward others, and helping others would have different attitudes and behave very differently toward the above-mentioned subordinate than one who highly values personal ambition and capability.

LEADER'S BOOKSHELF

Maximum Success: Changing the 12 Behavior Patterns That Keep You From Getting Ahead

James Waldroop and Timothy Butler

We have all known talented people who aren't as effective as they should or could be. In their book, *Maximum Success*, James Waldroop and Timothy Butler, who are directors of the MBA career development program at Harvard Business School, identify twelve behavior patterns they believe are the most common reasons some people never live up to their abilities.

Nobody's Perfect

Everyone has some habits, behaviors, or attitudes that can limit their effectiveness. By understanding their own individual "Achilles' heel," leaders can learn to change their behaviors to improve leadership effectiveness and career success. Here are a few of the weaknesses Waldroop and Butler identify—do you recognize any of these in your own attitudes and behaviors?

- **INever feeling quite "good enough."** The authors refer to this as career-related acrophobia, or fear of falling from one's position in the organization. Many people who seem quite self-confident in a lower-level position become frightened and insecure when promoted to a position of leadership because they feel they don't deserve it. These leaders hurt themselves and others. They become self-conscious and awkward, have trouble gaining respect, and don't provide the leadership strength that followers want and need. People want a leader who exudes self-assurance and certainty, not worry and fear.

- **Pushing too hard.** Setting high goals and working hard to achieve them isn't a bad thing for a leader. Unfortunately, some people take this too far—they relentlessly drive themselves, and others, to achieve more and more. These people work compulsively and without joy, and they cause stress and unhappiness for anyone who has to work with or for them.

- **Being emotionally tone-deaf.** The authors refer to a leader with this characteristic as Mr. or Ms. Spock, after the character played by Leonard Nimoy in the television series *Star Trek*. A native of the planet Vulcan, Spock is unable to feel emotions himself or understand them in others. "Spocks" don't intend to be cold or hard-hearted; they simply don't recognize the role of human feelings and motivations in the organization. These leaders are usually highly rational, perceiving problems merely as objective issues to be resolved, devoid of a complex human component.

Change Is Possible

These patterns, and the other patterns Waldroop and Butler describe, are potentially fatal flaws for leaders. However, the authors emphasize that people can learn to manage their weaknesses and change their behaviors. In the first part of the book, each chapter describes one of the patterns and gives tips for how to break it. The second part of the book describes four psychological patterns that, in varying combinations, underlie these weaknesses, along with exercises and tips for change.

Maximum Success: Changing the 12 Behavior Patterns That Keep You From Getting Ahead, by James Waldroop and Timothy Butler, is published by Currency/Doubleday.

One consideration is a leader's attitudes about himself or herself. **Self-concept** refers to the collection of attitudes we have about ourselves and includes the element of self-esteem, whether a person generally has positive or negative feelings about himself. A person with an overall positive self-concept has high self-esteem, whereas one with a negative self-concept has low self-esteem. In general, leaders with positive self-concepts are more effective in all situations. Leaders who have a negative self-concept, who are insecure and have low self-esteem, often create environments that limit other people's growth and development.[22] They may also sabotage their own careers. This chapter's Leader's Bookshelf describes how certain attitudes and behavior patterns limit a leader's effectiveness and career development.

The way in which the leader relates to followers also depends significantly on his or her attitudes about others.[23] A leader's style is based largely on attitudes about human nature in general—ideas and feelings about what motivates people, whether people are basically honest and trustworthy, and about the extent to which people can grow and change. One theory developed to explain differences in style was developed by Douglas McGregor, based on his experiences as a manager and consultant and his training as a psychologist.[24] McGregor identified two sets of assumptions about human nature, called **Theory X** and **Theory Y,** which represent two very different sets of attitudes about how to interact with and influence subordinates. The fundamental assumptions of Theory X and Theory Y are explained in Exhibit 4.4.

In general, Theory X reflects the assumption that people are basically lazy and not motivated to work and that they have a natural tendency to avoid responsibility. Thus, a supervisor who subscribes to the assumptions of Theory X believes people must be coerced, controlled, directed, or threatened to get them to put forth their best effort. In some circumstances, the supervisor may come across as bossy or overbearing, impatient with others, and unconcerned with people's feelings and problems. Referring back to Chapter 3, the Theory X leader would likely be task-oriented and highly concerned with production rather than people. Theory Y, on the other hand, is based on assumptions that people do not inherently dislike work and will commit themselves willingly to work that they care about. Theory Y also assumes that, under the right conditions, people will seek out greater responsibility and will exercise imagination and creativity in the pursuit of solutions to organizational problems. A leader who subscribes to the assumptions of Theory Y does not believe people have to be coerced and controlled in order to perform effectively. These leaders are more often people-oriented and concerned with relationships, although some Theory Y leaders can also be task- or production-oriented. For example, consider how Mark Schmink blended a concern for tasks with a Theory Y approach to leadership when he was a plant manager at Dana Corp.

EXHIBIT 4.4

Attitudes and Assumptions of Theory X and Theory Y

Assumptions of Theory X

- The average human being has an inherent dislike of work and will avoid it if possible. . . .
- Because of the human characteristic of dislike for work, most people must be coerced, controlled, directed, or threatened with punishment to get them to put forth adequate effort toward the achievement of organizational objectives. . . .
- The average human being prefers to be directed, wishes to avoid responsibility, has relatively little ambition, wants security above all.

Assumptions of Theory Y

- The expenditure of physical and mental effort in work is as natural as play or rest. The average human being does not inherently dislike work. . . .
- External control and the threat of punishment are not the only means for bringing about effort toward organizational objectives. A person will exercise self-direction and self-control in the service of objectives to which he or she is committed. . . .
- The average human being learns, under proper conditions, not only to accept but to seek responsibility. . . .
- The capacity to exercise a relatively high degree of imagination, ingenuity, and creativity in the solution of organizational problems is widely, not narrowly, distributed in the population.
- Under the conditions of modern industrial life, the intellectual potentialities of the average human being are only partially utilized.

SOURCE: Douglas McGregor, *The Human Side of Enterprise* (New York: McGraw-Hill, 1960), 33–48.

IN THE LEAD   Mark Schmink, Dana Corp.

Dana Corp.'s plant in Stockton, California, makes truck chassis for Toyota, a contract the company won by promising to decrease prices by 2 percent within two years, with further decreases to follow. Mark Schmink, the founding plant manager, knew that meant finding efficiencies in the production process as well as providing good wages and benefits for employees who would be asked to use their minds as well as their bodies. Schmink wanted to create a "culture of inventiveness" in which employees were constantly coming up with new and better ways of working.

He began by hiring welders with no experience and training each one to perform every job in the plant. No employee had a permanent assignment, so that everyone was constantly doing something new and bringing a fresh perspective to bear. By moving all over the plant, workers could see problems all up and down the line, not just in one particular area. Schmink also opened a library in the plant and began offering tuition reimbursement to production workers, signaling that mental work was valued. He required that each worker submit two ideas a month, and more than 80 percent of them were put into action. As workers saw their ideas implemented, they became even more excited about proposing new ways to do things, questioning every procedure and routine, right down to the sequencing of individual welds.

To keep workers motivated toward goals, Schmink provided continuous feedback both by personally responding to every suggestion and by displaying minute-by-minute productivity figures on electronic signs on the plant floor. Every significant accomplishment was celebrated with a special occasion, such as a rib-eye lunch, a day of free sodas, or a family barbecue. Schmink rarely felt the need to coerce or control his workers to do their jobs; they were so fired up by the challenge that they were always looking for improvements. In addition, employees felt that they were truly valued, so they were eager to contribute.[25]

McGregor believed Theory Y to be a more realistic and productive approach for viewing subordinates and shaping leaders' attitudes. Studies exploring the relationship between leader attitudes and leadership success in general support his idea, although this relationship has not been carefully explored.[26]

COGNITIVE DIFFERENCES

The final area of individual differences we will explore is cognitive style. **Cognitive style** refers to how a person perceives, processes, interprets, and uses information. Thus, when we talk about cognitive differences, we are referring to varying approaches to perceiving and assimilating data, making decisions, solving problems, and relating to others.[27] Cognitive approaches are *preferences* that are not necessarily rigid, but most people tend to have only a few preferred habits of thought. One of the most widely recognized cognitive differences is between what we call left-brained versus right-brained thinking patterns.

Patterns of Thinking and Brain Dominance

Neurologists and psychologists have long known that the brain has two distinct hemispheres. Furthermore, science has shown that the left hemisphere controls movement on the body's right side and the right hemisphere controls movement on the left. In the 1960s and 1970s, scientists also discovered that the distinct hemispheres influence thinking, which led to an interest in what has been called left-brained versus right-brained thinking patterns. The left hemisphere is associated with logical, analytical thinking and a linear approach to problem-solving, whereas the right hemisphere is associated with creative, intuitive, values-based thought processes.[28] A recent J. C. Penney television commercial provides a simple illustration. The commercial shows a woman whose right brain is telling her to go out and spend money to buy fun clothes, while the left brain is telling her to be logical and save money. As another simplified example, people who are very good at verbal and written language (which involves a linear thinking process) are using the left brain, while those who prefer to interpret information through visual images are more right-brained. Katherine Sherwood, an artist who suffered a severe stroke that left her right side paralyzed, discovered a whole new approach to painting that has brought her widespread acclaim. Before the stroke, Sherwood's art was very logical and studied; now she creates paintings that are described as "raw and intuitive." Doctors and brain researchers believe that, by damaging a part of the left hemisphere responsible for logical reasoning, Sherwood's stroke freed up the rest of her mind to think more creatively and intuitively.[29]

Although the concept of right-brained versus left-brained thinking is not entirely accurate physiologically (not all processes associated with left-brained thinking are located in the left hemisphere and vice versa), this concept provides a powerful metaphor for two very different ways of thinking and decision making. It is also important to remember that everyone uses both left-brained and right-brained thinking, but to varying degrees.

More recently, these ideas have been broadened to what is called the **whole brain concept.**[30] Ned Herrmann began developing his concept of whole brain thinking while he was a manager at General Electric in the late 1970s and has expanded it through many years of research with thousands of individuals and organizations. The whole brain approach considers not only a person's preference for right-brained versus left-brained thinking, but also for conceptual versus experiential thinking. Herrmann's whole brain model thus identifies four quadrants of the brain that are related to different thinking styles. Again, while not entirely accurate physiologically, the whole brain model is an excellent metaphor for understanding differences in thinking patterns. Some people strongly lean toward using one quadrant in most situations, while others rely on two, three, or even all four styles of thinking.

An individual's preference for each of the four styles is determined through a survey called the *Herrmann Brain Dominance Instrument (HBDI),* which has been administered to hundreds of thousands of individuals. A simplified exercise to help you think about your own preferences appears in Exhibit 4.5. Before reading further, follow the instructions and complete the exercise to get an idea about your dominant thinking style according to

EXHIBIT 4.5

What's Your Thinking Style?

The following characteristics are associated with the four quadrants identified by Herrmann's whole brain model. Think for a moment about how you approach problems and make decisions. In addition, consider how you typically approach your work or class assignments and how you interact with others. Circle ten of the terms below that you believe best describe your own cognitive style. Try to be honest and select terms that apply to you as you are, not how you might like to be. There are no right or wrong answers.

A	B	C	D
Analytical	Organized	Friendly	Holistic
Factual	Planned	Receptive	Imaginative
Directive	Controlled	Enthusiastic	Intuitive
Rigorous	Detailed	Understanding	Synthesizing
Realistic	Conservative	Expressive	Curious
Intellectual	Disciplined	Empathetic	Spontaneous
Objective	Practical	Trusting	Flexible
Knowledgeable	Industrious	Sensitive	Open-Minded
Bright	Persistent	Passionate	Conceptual
Clear	Implementer	Humanistic	Adventurous

The terms in Column A are associated with logical, analytical thinking (Quadrant A); those in Column B with organized, detail-oriented thinking (Quadrant B); those in Column C with empathetic and emotionally based thinking (Quadrant C); and those in Column D with integrative and imaginative thinking (Quadrant D). Do your preferences fall primarily in one of the four columns, or do you have a more balanced set of preferences across all four? If you have a strong preference in one particular quadrant, were you surprised by which one?

Herrmann's whole brain model. Then, read the descriptions of each quadrant below. The whole brain model provides a useful overview of an individual's mental preferences, which in turn affect patterns of communication, behavior, and leadership.

Quadrant A is associated with logical thinking, analysis of facts, and processing numbers. A person who has a quadrant A dominance is rational and realistic, thinks critically, and likes to deal with numbers and technical matters. These people like to know how things work and to follow logical procedures. A leader with a predominantly A-quadrant thinking style tends to be directive and authoritative. This leader focuses on tasks and activities and likes to deal with concrete information and facts. Opinions and feelings are generally not considered as important as facts.

Quadrant B deals with planning, organizing facts, and careful detailed review. A person who relies heavily on quadrant B thinking is well-organized, reliable, and neat. These people like to establish plans and procedures and get things done on time. Quadrant-B leaders are typically conservative and highly traditional. They tend to avoid risks and strive for stability. Thus, they may insist on following rules and procedures, no matter what the circumstances are.

Quadrant C is associated with interpersonal relationships and affects intuitive and emotional thought processes. C-quadrant individuals are sensitive to others and enjoy interacting with and teaching others. They are typically emotional and expressive, outgoing, and supportive of others. Leaders with a predominantly quadrant-C style are friendly, trusting, and empathetic. They are concerned with people's feelings more than with tasks and procedures and may put emphasis on employee development and training.

Quadrant D is associated with conceptualizing, synthesizing, and integrating facts and patterns, with seeing the big picture rather than the details. A person with a quadrant-D preference is visionary and imaginative, likes to speculate, break the rules, and take risks, and may be impetuous. These people are curious and enjoy experimentation and playfulness. The D-quadrant leader is holistic, imaginative, and adventurous. This leader enjoys change, experimentation, and risk-taking, and generally allows followers a great deal of freedom and flexibility.

The model with its four quadrants and some of the mental processes associated with each is illustrated in Exhibit 4.6. Each style has positive and negative results for leaders and followers. There is no style that is necessarily better or worse, though any of the styles carried to an extreme can be detrimental. It is important to remember that every individual, even those with a strong preference in one quadrant, actually has a coalition of preferences from each of the four quadrants.[31] Therefore, leaders with a predominantly quadrant-A style may also have elements from one or more of the other styles, which affects their leadership effectiveness. For example, a leader with a strong A-quadrant preference might also have preferences from quadrant C, the interpersonal area, which would cause her to have concern for people's feelings even though she is primarily concerned with tasks, facts, and figures.

In addition, Herrmann believes people can learn to use their "whole brain," rather than relying only on one or two quadrants. His research indicates that very few, if any, individuals can be wholly balanced among the four quadrants, but people can be aware of their preferences and engage in activities and experiences that help develop the other quadrants. Leaders who reach the top of organizations often have well-balanced brains, according to Herrmann's research. In fact, the typical CEO has at least two, usually three, and

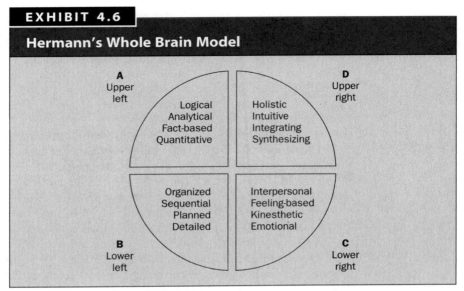

EXHIBIT 4.6

Hermann's Whole Brain Model

A Upper left	D Upper right
Logical Analytical Fact-based Quantitative	Holistic Intuitive Integrating Synthesizing
Organized Sequential Planned Detailed	Interpersonal Feeling-based Kinesthetic Emotional
B Lower left	C Lower right

SOURCE: Ned Hermann, *The Whole Brain Business Book*, (New York: McGraw-Hill, 1996), 15.

often four strong preferences and thus has a wide range of thinking options available to choose from. A broad range of thinking styles is particularly important at higher levels of organizations because leaders deal with a greater variety and complexity of people and issues.[32]

Understanding that individuals have different thinking styles can also help leaders be more effective in interacting with followers. Some leaders act as if everyone responds to the same material and behavior in the same way, but this isn't true. Some people prefer facts and figures whereas others want to know about relationships and patterns. Some followers prefer freedom and flexibility while others crave structure and order. At Nissan Design International, Jerry Hirshberg used an understanding of cognitive differences to change how he leads.

IN THE LEAD   **Jerry Hirshberg, Nissan Design International**

Jerry Hirshberg is a predominantly D-quadrant leader. He likes thinking broadly and dreaming big, deriving ideas intuitively—and he abhors tight structure and control. He once assumed that his employees would as well. Hirschberg wanted his designers to have the freedom to be creative, to take risks, and to innovate. Therefore, he was surprised when he learned that a few of his followers actually wanted and needed more structure in order to perform at their best.

Hirschberg had always assumed his employees would react to information and ideas the same way he did. He would throw huge amounts of information at them and expect them to respond intuitively and creatively. Some people, however, always reacted with hesitation, which Hirschberg originally interpreted as a resistance to innovation and change. However, over time, he came to realize that some of his designers simply wanted and needed time to "process" the information, and to develop more logical, analytical approaches to Hirschberg's intuitively derived ideas. When they were given this time, the employees returned with significant contributions and excellent plans that moved the project forward.

It didn't take Hirshberg long to recognize that the contributions of the more logical, analytical, and detail-oriented thinkers were just as critical to the success of a project as those of the intuitive, creative thinkers. Hirshberg turned his realization into a new approach to creativity at Nissan. He now hires designers in what he calls *divergent pairs*. He believes that by putting together two spectacularly gifted people who have different cognitive styles and see the world in different ways, he builds a creative tension that keeps the organization energized and provides unlimited potential for innovation. Essentially, Hirschberg mixes styles to create a "whole brain" company at Nissan Design International.[33]

As this example illustrates, leaders can shift their style and behavior to more effectively communicate with followers and to help them perform up to their full potential. Leaders can also recruit people with varied cognitive styles to help achieve goals.

Problem Solving Styles: The Myers-Briggs Type Indicator

Another approach to cognitive differences grew out of the work of psychologist Carl Jung. Jung believed that differences in individual behavior resulted from preferences in how we go about gathering and evaluating information for solving problems and making decisions.[34] One of the most widely used personality tests in the United States, the **Myers-Briggs Type Indicator (MBTI)**, is one way of measuring how individuals differ in these areas.[35] The MBTI has been taken by millions of people around the world and can help individuals better understand themselves and others.

The MBTI uses four different pairs of attributes to classify people in one of sixteen different personality types:

- **Introversion versus Extroversion:** This dimension focuses on where people gain interpersonal strength and mental energy. Extroverts (E) gain energy from being around others and interacting with others, whereas introverts (I) gain energy by focusing on personal thoughts and feelings.

- **Sensing versus Intuition:** This identifies how a person absorbs information. Those with a sensing preference (S) gather and absorb information through the five senses, whereas intuitive people (N) rely on less direct perceptions. Intuitives, for example, focus more on patterns, relationships, and hunches than on direct perception of facts and details.

- **Thinking versus Feeling:** This dimension relates to how much consideration a person gives to emotions in making a decision. Feeling types (F) tend to rely more on their values and sense of what is right and wrong, and they consider how a decision will affect other people's feelings. Thinking types (T) tend to rely more on logic and be very objective in decision making.

- **Judging versus Perceiving:** The judging versus perceiving dimension concerns an individual's attitudes toward ambiguity and how quickly a person makes a decision. People with a judging preference like certainty and closure. They enjoy having goals and deadlines and tend to make decisions quickly based on available data. Perceiving people, on the other hand, enjoy ambiguity, dislike deadlines, and may change their minds several times before making a final decision. Perceiving types like to gather a large amount of data and information before making a decision.

The various combinations of these preferences result in sixteen unique personality types. At the end of this chapter, you will have a chance to complete an exercise that will identify your MBTI personality type. In addition, there are a number of exercises available on the Internet that can help people determine their preferences according to the MBTI. Each person has developed unique strengths and weaknesses as a result of their preferences for introversion versus extroversion, sensing versus intuition, thinking versus feeling, and judging versus perceiving. As with the whole brain approach, MBTI types should not be considered ingrained or unalterable. People's awareness of their preferences, training, and life experiences can cause them to change their preferences over time.

In recent years, application of the MBTI in leadership studies has increased rapidly.[36] There is no "leader type," and all sixteen of the MBTI types can function effectively as leaders. As with the four quadrants of the whole brain model, leaders can learn to use their preferences and balance their approaches to best suit followers and the situation. However, research reveals some interesting, although tentative, findings. For example, although extroversion is often considered an important trait for a leader, leaders in the real world are about equally divided between extroverts and introverts. In regard to the sensing versus intuition dimension, data reveal that sensing types are in the majority in fields where the focus is on the immediate and tangible (for example, construction, banking, manufacturing). However, in areas that involve breaking new ground or long-range planning, intuitive leaders are in the majority. Thinking (as opposed to feeling) types are more common among leaders in business and industry as well as in the realm of science. In addition, thinking types appear to be chosen more often as managers even in organizations that value "feeling," such as counseling centers. Finally, one of the most consistent findings is that judging types are in the majority among the leaders studied.

Thus, based on the limited research, the two preferences that seem to be most strongly associated with successful leadership are thinking and judging. However, this doesn't mean that people with other preferences cannot be effective leaders. Much more research needs to be done before accurate conclusions can be reached about the relationship between MBTI types and leadership. One area in which research may eventually offer insight is the relationship between cognitive styles and two types of leadership that rely heavily on the individual leader's personal characteristics: charismatic leadership and transformational leadership. Although characteristics of followers and the situation also play a significant role, these two leadership styles rely strongly on the individual leader's personal qualities and cognitive style.

PERSONALITY AND LEADERSHIP STYLE: THE ROLE OF CHARISMA

Charismatic leadership has long been of great interest to researchers studying political leadership, social movements, and religious cults. In recent years, attention has also been given to the impact of charismatic leadership in organizations. Charisma is difficult to define. It has been called "a fire that ignites followers' energy and commitment, producing results above and beyond the call of duty."[37] **Charismatic leaders** have the ability to inspire and motivate people to do more than they would normally do, despite obstacles and personal sacrifice. In describing the charismatic leader, one business writer says, "He persuades people—subordinates, peers, customers, even the S.O.B. you both work for—to do things they'd rather not. People charge over the hill for him. Run through fire. Walk barefoot on broken glass. He doesn't demand attention, he commands it."[38]

EXHIBIT 4.7

Have You Got Charisma?

This short quiz will help you determine whether you have characteristics that are associated with charismatic leaders. Circle the answer that best describes you.

1. I am most comfortable thinking in
   a. Generalities
   b. Specifics

2. I worry most about
   a. Current competition
   b. Future competition

3. I tend to focus on
   a. The opportunities I've missed
   b. The opportunities I've seized

4. I prefer to
   a. Promote traditions and procedures that have led to success in the past
   b. Suggest new and unique ways of doing things

5. I tend to ask
   a. How can we do this better?
   b. Why are we doing this?

6. I believe
   a. There's always a way to minimize risk.
   b. Some risks are too high.

Charismatic leaders have an emotional impact on people because they appeal to both the heart and the mind. They may speak emotionally about putting themselves on the line for the sake of a mission. When Arthur Martinez took over as CEO of Sears in 1992, he knew he was facing big problems to rescue its sinking retail unit. To lure top talent, Martinez put himself in the role of evangelist, enrolling people in a mission. He met personally with almost every applicant for senior-level positions and told them, "This is one of the greatest adventures in business history. . . . You have to be courageous, filled with self-confidence. If we do it, we'll be wealthier, yes. But more than that, we'll have incredible psychic gratification. How can you not do it?" Martinez assembled one of the best executive teams in retailing, persuading some people who previously had no interest in changing jobs.[39] Used wisely and ethically, charisma can lift the entire organization's level of performance. Charismatic leaders can raise people's conscious-

---

EXHIBIT 4.7

Have You Got Charisma? *(continued)*

7. I tend to persuade people by using
   a. Emotion
   b. Logic

8. I prefer to
   a. Honor traditional values and ways of thinking
   b. Promote unconventional beliefs and values

9. I would prefer to communicate via
   a. A written report
   b. A one-page chart

10. I think this quiz is
    a. Ridiculous
    b. Fascinating

The following answers are associated with charismatic leadership:

1. a;   2. b;   3. a;   4. b;   5. b;   6. a;   7. a;   8. b;   9. b;   10. b

If you responded in this way to seven or more questions, you have a high charisma quotient and may have the potential to be a charismatic leader. If you answered this way to four or fewer questions, your charisma level is considered low. Do you believe a person can develop charisma?

SOURCE: Based on "Have You Got It?" a quiz that appeared in Patricia Sellers, "What Exactly Is Charisma?" *Fortune* January 15, 1996, 68–75. The original quiz was devised with the assistance of leadership expert Jay Conger.

ness about new possibilities and motivate them to transcend their own interests for the sake of the team, department, or organization. Exhibit 4.7 provides a short quiz to help you determine whether you have the potential to be a charismatic leader. One of the best known charismatic leaders in the business world is Herb Kelleher, chairman and former CEO of Southwest Airlines.

IN THE LEAD   **Herb Kelleher, Southwest Airlines**

To say that Herbert Kelleher is an oddball among top executives of major corporations is an understatement. He's known for drinking Wild Turkey and chain-smoking cigarettes, riding a Harley, and dressing up as Elvis or the Easter

Bunny to entertain employees. He once settled an argument with a fellow CEO for the use of a disputed slogan, by convincing the other guy to arm-wrestle for it rather than go to court. When it comes right down to it, it seems as if Kelleher can influence almost anyone to do almost anything.

As CEO, Kelleher inspired thousands of employees to be as passionate about Southwest Airlines as he is. Talking about his work, Kelleher says, "I love it, I love it—I sure as heck do." Even while going through extensive radiation treatment for prostate cancer, Kelleher never missed a day of work. That kind of passion rubbed off on people throughout the company, creating an environment where people go above and beyond the call of duty for the sake of the company and its customers. When Kelleher sent a letter to the home of every Southwest employee asking them to help cut costs, they responded immediately. Kelleher wrote to each employee after the cost of jet fuel rose dramatically, pointing out that Southwest's profitability was in jeopardy and asking that each worker help out by saving $5 a day. Within six weeks, employees had implemented ideas that saved the company more than $2 million. Kelleher also recognized the importance of individual differences and the varied gifts that people can bring to an organization. He encouraged employees to let their own unique personalities come out in serving customers. "I give people license to be themselves and motivate others in that way . . ." Kelleher says. "You don't have to fit into a constraining mode at work. . . ."

Southwest hasn't lost a dime since 1973, and its profit margins are the best in the industry. While other airlines have suffered bankruptcies, crippling strikes, and even failure, Southwest has thrived. Kelleher gives the credit to Southwest's employees. "There's no magic formula," he says. "It's just a bunch of people taking pride in what they're doing." Part of the success, no doubt, is due to Kelleher's charismatic leadership.[40]

Herb Kelleher galvanizes people to action by infusing his leadership with his own passion for the work, thus tapping into followers' emotions as well as their minds. In addition, his charisma extends beyond Southwest. At meetings of business executives, he is sometimes treated like a celebrity. When he enters the room, almost every head turns to watch him. Not everyone can develop the personal appeal of Herb Kelleher. However, charismatic leadership is not all about charm, personality, or unconventional behavior. Although charisma itself cannot be learned, there are aspects of charismatic leadership that anyone can use. For one thing, charisma comes from pursuing activities that you genuinely love, as with Herb Kelleher. Charismatic leaders are engaging their emotion in everyday work life, which makes them energetic, enthusiastic, and attractive to others. Understanding charismatic leadership qualities and behavior can help anyone become a stronger leader.

What Makes a Charismatic Leader

In today's turbulent business environment, there is growing interest in how charismatic leaders build emotional attachment and commitment among followers. A number of studies have identified the unique qualities of charismatic leaders, documented the impact they have on followers, and described the behaviors that help them achieve remarkable results.[41] Exhibit 4.8 compares distinguishing characteristics of charismatic and noncharismatic leaders.[42]

Charismatic leaders create an atmosphere of change and articulate an idealized vision of a future that is significantly better than what now exists. They have an ability to communicate complex ideas and goals in clear, compelling ways, so that everyone from the vice president to the janitor can understand and identify with their message. Charismatic leaders inspire followers with an abiding faith, even if the faith can't be stated in specific goals that are easily attained. The faith itself becomes a "reward" to followers. Martin Luther King's "I Have a Dream" speech is an example of how leaders can motivate followers by inspiring hope and faith in a better future.[43] Charismatic leaders also act in unconventional ways and use unconventional means to transcend the status quo and create change. Charismatic leaders may sometimes seem like oddballs, but this image only enhances their appeal.

Charismatic leaders earn followers' trust by being willing to incur great personal risk. Putting themselves on the line affirms charismatic leaders as passionate advocates for the vision. According to a personal friend of the King family, Martin Luther King received death threats against himself and his family almost every day during the civil rights movement.[44] By taking risks, leaders can also enhance their emotional appeal to followers. Michael Jordan is a good example of how the nerve to take great personal risks can enhance charisma and likability. Jordan temporarily left a career as a highly successful basketball player to flounder in the game of baseball. Quaker Oats, which pays Jordan to promote Gatorade, surveyed consumers daily during Jordan's baseball career, and his emotional appeal never wavered. In fact, most people identified more personally with Jordan because he seemed more "human."[45]

The final characteristic of charismatic leaders is that their source of influence comes from personal power as opposed to position power. People like and identify with the leader and want to be like him or her. Followers respect and admire the leader because of the leader's knowledge, experience, or personal character, not because of a title or position in the organization. Although charismatic leaders may be in formal positions of authority, charismatic leadership

EXHIBIT 4.8

Distinguishing Characteristics of Charismatic and Noncharismatic Leaders

	Noncharismatic Leaders	Charismatic Leaders
Likableness:	Shared perspective makes leader likable	Shared perspective and idealized vision make leader likable and an honorable hero worthy of identification and imitation
Trustworthiness:	Disinterested advocacy in persuasion attempts	Passionate advocacy by incurring great personal risk and cost
Relation to status quo:	Tries to maintain status quo	Creates atmosphere of change
Future goals:	Limited goals not too discrepant from status quo	Idealized vision that is highly discrepant from status quo
Articulation:	Weak articulation of goals and motivation to lead	Strong and inspirational articulation of vision and motivation to lead
Competence:	Uses available means to achieve goals within framework of the existing order	Uses unconventional means to transcend the existing order
Behavior:	Conventional, conforms to norms	Unconventional, counter-normative
Influence:	Primarily authority of position and rewards	Transcends position; personal power based on expertise and respect and admiration for the leader

SOURCE: Jay A. Conger and Rabindra N. Kanungo and Associates, *Charismatic Leadership: The Elusive Factor in Organizational Effectiveness* (San Francisco: Jossey-Bass, 1988), 91.

transcends formal organizational position because the leader's influence is based on personal qualities rather than the power and authority granted by the organization.

The Black Hat of Charisma

One characteristic of charisma noted by most researchers is that it can be a curse as well as a blessing. Leaders such as Winston Churchill, John F. Kennedy, and Mohandes Gandhi exhibited tremendous charisma. So did leaders such as Adolf Hitler, Charles Manson, and Idi Amin. Charisma isn't always used to benefit the group, organization, or society. It can also be used for self-serving purposes, which leads to deception, manipulation, and exploitation of others. Because the basis of charisma is emotional rather than logical or rational, it is risky and potentially dangerous.[46]

One explanation for the distinction between charisma that results in positive outcomes and that which results in negative outcomes relates to the difference between *personalized* leaders and *socialized* leaders.[47] Leaders who react to organizational problems in terms of their own needs rather than the needs of the whole often act in ways that can have disastrous consequences for others. Personalized charismatic leaders are characterized as self-aggrandizing, nonegalitarian, and exploitative, whereas socialized charismatic leaders are empowering, egalitarian, and supportive. Personalized behavior is based on caring about self; socialized behavior is based on valuing others. Studies have shown that personalized charismatic leaders can have a significant detrimental impact on long-term organizational performance. Leaders who have been consistently successful in improving organizational performance exhibit a pattern of socialized behavior.[48]

TRANSACTIONAL VERSUS TRANSFORMATIONAL LEADERSHIP

Another type of leadership based largely on the leader's personal qualities is transformational leadership, which has a substantial impact on followers and can potentially renew an entire organization. One way to understand transformational leadership is to compare it to transactional leadership.[49]

Transactional Leadership

The basis of **transactional leadership** is a transaction or exchange process between leaders and followers. The transactional leader recognizes followers' needs and desires and then clarifies how those needs and desires will be satisfied in exchange for meeting specified objectives or performing certain duties. Thus, followers receive rewards for job performance, while leaders benefit from the completion of tasks.

Transactional leaders focus on the present and excel at keeping the organization running smoothly and efficiently. They are good at traditional management functions such as planning and budgeting and generally focus on the impersonal aspects of job performance. Transactional leadership can be quite effective. By clarifying expectations, leaders help build followers' confidence. In addition, satisfying the needs of subordinates may improve productivity and morale. However, because transactional leadership involves a commitment to "follow the rules," transactional leaders maintain stability within the organization rather than promoting change. Transactional skills are important for all leaders. However, in today's world, where organizational success often depends on continuous change, effective leaders also use a different approach.

Transformational Leadership

Transformational leadership is characterized by the ability to bring about significant change. Transformational leaders have the ability to lead changes in the organization's vision, strategy, and culture as well as promote innovation in products and technologies. Rather than analyzing and controlling specific transactions with followers using rules, directions, and incentives, transformational leadership focuses on intangible qualities such as vision, shared values, and ideas in order to build relationships, give larger meaning to separate activities, and provide common ground to enlist followers in the change process. Transformational leadership is based on the personal values, beliefs, and qualities of the leader rather than on an exchange process between leaders and followers. Transformational leadership differs from transactional leadership in four significant areas.[50]

1. *Transformational leadership develops followers into leaders.* Followers are given greater freedom to control their own behavior. Transformational leadership rallies people around a mission and defines the boundaries within which followers can operate in relative freedom to accomplish organizational goals. The transformational leader arouses in followers an awareness of problems and issues and helps people look at things in new ways so that productive change can happen.

2. *Transformational leadership elevates the concerns of followers from lower-level physical needs (such as for safety and security) to higher-level psychological needs (such as for self-esteem and self-actualization).* It is important that lower-level needs are met through adequate wages, safe working conditions, and other considerations. However, the transformational leader also pays attention to each individual's need for growth and development. Therefore, the leader sets examples and assigns tasks not only to meet immediate needs but also to elevate followers' needs and abilities to a higher level and link them to the organization's mission. Transformational leaders change followers so that they are empowered to change the organization.

3. *Transformational leadership inspires followers to go beyond their own self-interests for the good of the group.* Transformational leaders motivate people to do more than originally expected. They make followers aware of the importance of change goals and outcomes and, in turn, enable them to transcend their own immediate interests for the sake of the organizational mission. Followers admire these leaders, want to identify with them, and have a high degree of trust in them. However, transformational leadership motivates people not just to follow the leader personally but to believe in the need for change and be willing to make personal sacrifices for the greater purpose.

4. *Transformational leadership paints a vision of a desired future state and communicates it in a way that makes the pain of change worth the effort.*[51] The most significant role of the transformational leader may be to find a vision for the organization that is significantly better than the old one and to enlist others in sharing the dream. It is the vision that launches people into action and provides the basis for the other aspects of transformational leadership we have just discussed. Change can occur only when people have a sense of purpose as well as a desirable picture of where the organization is going. Without vision, there can be no transformation.

Whereas transactional leaders promote stability, transformational leaders create significant change in followers as well as in organizations. Leaders can learn to be transformational as well as transactional. Effective leaders exhibit both transactional and transformational leadership patterns. They accentuate not only their abilities to build a vision and empower and energize others, but also the transactional skills of designing structures, control systems, and reward systems that can help people achieve the vision.[52] One leader who reflects a balance of transactional and transformational leadership is Richard Kovacevich, CEO of Norwest Corp. Kovacevich has been called one of the best bankers in America because of his careful attention to the structures and systems that keep banks stable and profitable. However, he's also known for spouting radical notions such as "Banking is necessary, banks are not." Kovacevich has inspired his followers with a vision of transformation—of becoming the Wal-Mart of financial services—and it looks as if the company is well on its way. At Norwest, for example, the average customer buys nearly four financial products, as opposed to the industry average of two, which translates into approximately triple the amount of profit for Norwest. Kovacevich leads with slogans such as "Mind share plus heart share equals market share." Although some people may think it sounds hokey, Kovacevich and Norwest employees don't care. It's the substance behind the slogans that matters. Employees are rewarded for putting both their hearts and minds into their work. Kovacevich constantly tells employees that they are the heart and soul of Norwest and that only through their efforts can the company succeed.[53] By combining elements of both transactional and transformational leadership, Kovacevich has turned Norwest into a banking powerhouse.

SUMMARY AND INTERPRETATION

This chapter explores some of the individual differences that affect leaders and the leadership process. Individuals differ in many ways, including personality, values and attitudes, and styles of thinking and decision making. One model of personality, the Big Five personality dimensions, examines whether individuals score high or low on the dimensions of extroversion, agreeableness, conscientiousness, emotional stability, and openness to experience. Although there is some indication that a high degree of each of the personality dimensions is associated with successful leadership, individuals who score low on various dimensions may also be effective leaders. Two specific personality traits that have a significant impact on leader behavior are locus of control and authoritarianism.

Values are fundamental beliefs that cause a person to prefer that things be done one way rather than another. One way to think about values is in terms of instrumental and end values. End values are beliefs about the kinds of goals that are worth pursuing, while instrumental values are beliefs about the types of behavior that are appropriate for reaching goals. Values also affect an individual's attitudes. A leader's attitudes about self and others influence how the leader behaves toward and interacts with followers. Two sets of assumptions called Theory X and Theory Y represent two very different sets of attitudes leaders may hold about people in general.

Another area of individual differences is cognitive style. The whole brain concept explores a person's preferences for right-brained versus left-brained thinking and for conceptual versus experiential thinking. The model provides a powerful metaphor for understanding differences in thinking styles. Individuals can learn to use their "whole brain" rather than relying on one thinking style. Another way of looking at cognitive differences is the Myers-Briggs Type Indicator, which measures an individual's preferences for introversion versus extroversion, sensing versus intuition, thinking versus feeling, and judging versus perceiving.

Two leadership styles that rely strongly on the individual leader's personal characteristics are charismatic leadership and transformational leadership. Charismatic leaders have an emotional impact on people by appealing to both the heart and mind. They create an atmosphere of change, articulate an idealized vision of the future, communicate clearly, inspire faith and hope, and incur personal risks to influence followers. Charisma can be used to benefit organizations and society, but it can also be dangerous. Transformational leaders also create an atmosphere of change, and they inspire followers not just to follow them personally but to believe in the vision of organizational transformation. Transformational leaders inspire followers to go beyond their own self-interest for the good of the whole.

KEY TERMS

personality	agreeableness
Big Five personality dimensions	conscientiousness
extroversion	emotional stability

openness to experience   Theory X
locus of control   Theory Y
authoritarianism   cognitive style
values   whole brain concept
end values   Myers-Briggs Type Indicator
instrumental values   charismatic leader
perception   transactional leadership
attitude   transformational leadership
self-concept

DISCUSSION QUESTIONS

1. Extroversion is often considered a "good" quality for a leader to have. Why might introversion be considered an equally positive quality?

2. What might be some reasons the dimension of "openness to experience" correlates so strongly with historians' ratings of the greatest U.S. presidents but has been less strongly associated with business leader success? Do you think this personality dimension might be more important for business leaders of today than it was in the past? Discuss.

3. In which of the Big Five personality dimensions would you place the traits of locus of control and authoritarianism?

4. From Exhibit 4.3, identify four or five values (either instrumental or end values) that could be a source of conflict between leaders and followers. Explain.

5. How do a person's attitudes and assumptions about human nature in general affect his or her leadership approach? How might a leader's attitudes about him or herself alter or reinforce this approach?

6. Do you believe understanding your preferences according to the whole brain model can help you be a better leader? Discuss.

7. How can a leader use an understanding of brain dominance to improve the functioning of the organization?

8. Why do you think *thinking* and *judging* are the two characteristics from the Myers-Briggs Type Indicator that seem to be most strongly associated with effective leadership?

9. What do you consider the essential traits of a charismatic leader? Why is charismatic leadership considered potentially dangerous?

10. What are the primary differences between transactional and transformational leadership?

11. What personality dimensions, values, and attitudes might be particularly useful to an individual who wants to act as a transformational leader? Do you believe anyone can develop them? Discuss.

LEADERSHIP DEVELOPMENT: Personal Feedback

Personality Assessment: Jung's Typology and the Myers-Briggs Type Indicator

For each item below, circle either "a" or "b." In some cases, both "a" and "b" may apply to you. You should decide which is *more* like you, even if it is only slightly more true.

1. I would rather
   a. Solve a new and complicated problem
   b. Work on something that I have done before

2. I like to
   a. Work alone in a quiet place
   b. Be where "the action" is

3. I want a boss who
   a. Establishes and applies criteria in decisions
   b. Considers individual needs and makes exceptions

4. When I work on a project, I
   a. Like to finish it and get some closure
   b. Often leave it open for possible change

5. When making a decision, the most important considerations are
   a. Rational thoughts, ideas, and data
   b. People's feelings and values

6. On a project, I tend to
   a. Think it over and over before deciding how to proceed
   b. Start working on it right away, thinking about it as I go along

7. When working on a project, I prefer to
   a. Maintain as much control as possible
   b. Explore various options

8. In my work, I prefer to
   a. Work on several projects at a time, and learn as much as possible about each one
   b. Have one project that is challenging and keeps me busy

9. I often
   a. Make lists and plans whenever I start something and may hate to seriously alter my plans
   b. Avoid plans and just let things progress as I work on them

10. When discussing a problem with colleagues, it is easy for me
    a. To see "the big picture"
    b. To grasp the specifics of the situation

11. When the phone rings in my office or at home, I usually
    a. Consider it an interruption
    b. Don't mind answering it

12. The word that describes me better is
    a. Analytical
    b. Empathetic

13. When I am working on an assignment, I tend to
    a. Work steadily and consistently
    b. Work in bursts of energy with "down time" in between

14. When I listen to someone talk on a subject, I usually try to
    a. Relate it to my own experience and see if it fits
    b. Assess and analyze the message

15. When I come up with new ideas, I generally
    a. "Go for it"
    b. Like to contemplate the ideas some more

16. When working on a project, I prefer to
    a. Narrow the scope so it is clearly defined
    b. Broaden the scope to include related aspects

17. When I read something, I usually
    a. Confine my thoughts to what is written there
    b. Read between the lines and relate the words to other ideas

18. When I have to make a decision in a hurry, I often
    a. Feel uncomfortable and wish I had more information
    b. Am able to do so with available data

19. In a meeting, I tend to
    a. Continue formulating my ideas as I talk about them
    b. Only speak out after I have carefully thought the issue through

20. In work, I prefer spending a great deal of time on issues of
    a. Ideas
    b. People

21. In meetings, I am most often annoyed with people who
    a. Come up with many sketchy ideas
    b. Lengthen the meeting with many practical details

22. I tend to be
    a. A morning person
    b. A night owl

23. My style in preparing for a meeting is
    a. To be willing to go in and be responsive
    b. To be fully prepared and sketch out an outline of the meeting

24. In meetings, I would prefer for people to
    a. Display a fuller range of emotions
    b. Be more task-oriented

25. I would rather work for an organization where
    a. My job was intellectually stimulating
    b. I was committed to its goals and mission

26. On weekends, I tend to
    a. Plan what I will do
    b. Just see what happens and decide as I go along

27. I am more
    a. Outgoing
    b. Contemplative

28. I would rather work for a boss who is
    a. Full of new ideas
    b. Practical

In the following, choose the word in each pair that appeals to you more:

29. a. Social   b. Theoretical
30. a. Ingenuity   b. Practicality
31. a. Organized   b. Adaptable
32. a. Active   b. Concentration

Scoring

Count one point for each item listed below that you circled in the inventory.

Score For I	Score For E	Score For S	Score For N
2a	2b	1b	1a
6a	6b	10b	10a
11a	11b	13a	13b
15b	15a	16a	16b
19b	19a	17a	17b
22a	22b	21a	21b

| | 27b | 27a | 28b | 28a |
| | 32b | 32a | 30b | 30a |

Totals ____ ____ ____ ____

Circle the one with more points: **Circle the one with more points:**

I or E   S or N

(If tied on I/E, don't count #11)   *(If tied on S/N, don't count #16)*

Score for T	Score for F	Score for J	Score for P
3a	3b	4a	4b
5a	5b	7a	7b
12a	12b	8b	8a
14b	14a	9a	9b
20a	20b	18b	18a
24b	24a	23b	23a
25a	25b	26a	26b
29b	29a	31a	31b

Totals ____ ____ ____ ____

Circle the one with more points: **Circle the one with more points:**

T or F   J or P

(If tied on T/F, don't count #24)   *(If tied on J/P, don't count #23)*

Your Score Is: I or E _____ S or N _____ T or F _____ J or P _____

Your MBTI type is: _____ (example: INTJ; ESFP; etc.)

SOURCE: "Personality Assessment: Jung's Typology" in Dorothy Marcic, *Organizational Behavior: Experience and Cases,* 4th ed. (St. Paul, MN: West Publishing Co., 1995), 16–19. Copyright 1988 by Dorothy Marcic and Paul Nutt. All rights reserved. Used with permission.

Interpretation

The Myers-Briggs Type Indicator (MBTI), based on the work of psychologist Carl Jung, is the most widely used personality assessment instrument in the world. The MBTI, which was described in the chapter text, identifies sixteen different "types," shown with their dominant characteristics in the chart below.

Characteristics Frequently Associated with Each Type

Sensing Types

ISTJ

Quiet, serious, earn success by thoroughness and dependability. Practical, matter-of-fact, realistic, and responsible. Decide logically what should be done and work toward it steadily, regardless of distractions. Take pleasure in making everything orderly and organized—their work, their home, their life. Value traditions and loyalty.

ISTP

Tolerant and flexible, quiet observers until a problem appears, then act quickly to find workable solutions. Analyze what makes things work and readily get through large amounts of data to isolate the core of practical problems. Interested in cause and effect, organize facts using logical principles, value efficiency.

ESTP

Flexible and tolerant, they take a pragmatic approach focused on immediate results. Theories and conceptual explanations bore them—they want to act energetically to solve the problem. Focus on the here-and-now, spontaneous, enjoy each moment that they can be active with others. Enjoy material comforts and style. Learn best through doing.

ESTJ

Practical, realistic, matter-of-fact. Decisive, quickly move to implement decisions. Organize projects and people to get things done, focus on getting results in the most efficient way possible. Take care of routine details. Have a clear set of logical standards, systematically follow them and want others to also. Forceful in implementing their plans.

ISFJ

Quiet, friendly, responsible, and conscientious. Committed and steady in meeting their obligations. Thorough, painstaking, and accurate. Loyal, considerate, notice and remember specifics about people who are important to them, concerned with how others feel. Strive to create an orderly and harmonious environment at work and at home.

ISFP

Quiet, friendly, sensitive, and kind. Enjoy the present moment, what's going on around them. Like to have their own space and to work within their own time frame. Loyal and committed to their values and to people who are important to them. Dislike disagreements and conflicts, do not force their opinions or values on others.

ESFP

Outgoing, friendly, and accepting. Exuberant lovers of life, people, and material comforts. Enjoy working with others to make things happen. Bring common sense and a realistic approach to their work, and make work fun. Flexible and spontaneous, adapt readily to new people and environments. Learn best by trying a new skill with other people.

ESFJ

Warmhearted, conscientious, and cooperative. Want harmony in their environment, work with determination to establish it. Like to work with others to complete tasks accurately and on time. Loyal, follow through even in small matters. Notice what others need in their day-by-day lives and try to provide it. Want to be appreciated for who they are and for what

Intuitive Types

INFJ

Seek meaning and connection in ideas, relationships, and material possessions. Want to understand what motivates people and are insightful about others. Conscientious and committed to their firm values. Develop a clear vision about how best to serve the common good. Organized and decisive in implementing their vision.

INFP

Idealistic, loyal to their values and to people who are important to them. Want an external life that is congruent with their values. Curious, quick to see possibilities, can be catalysts for implementing ideas. Seek to understand people and to help them fulfill their potential. Adaptable, flexible, and accepting unless a value is threatened.

ENFP

Warmly enthusiastic and imaginative. See life as full of possibilities. Make connections between events and information very quickly, and confidently proceed based on the patterns they see. Want a lot of affirmation from others, and readily give appreciation and support. Spontaneous and flexible, often rely on their ability to improvise and their verbal fluency.

ENFJ

Warm, empathetic, responsive, and responsible. Highly attuned to the emotions, needs, and motivations of others. Find potential in everyone, want to help others fulfill their potential. May act as catalysts for individual and group growth. Loyal, responsive to praise and criticism. Sociable, facilitate others in a group, and provide inspiring leadership.

INTJ

Have original minds and great drive for implementing their ideas and achieving their goals. Quickly see patterns in external events and develop long-range explanatory perspectives. When committed, organize a job and carry it through. Skeptical and independent, have high standards of competence and performance—for themselves and others.

INTP

Seek to develop logical explanations for everything that interests them. Theoretical and abstract, interested more in ideas than in social interaction. Quiet, contained, flexible, and adaptable. Have unusual ability to focus in depth to solve problems in their area of interest. Skeptical, sometimes critical, always analytical.

ENTP

Quick, ingenious, stimulating, alert, and outspoken. Resourceful in solving new and challenging problems. Adept at generating conceptual possibilities and then analyzing them strategically. Good at reading other people. Bored by routine, will seldom do the same thing the same way, apt to turn to one new interest after another.

ENTJ

Frank, decisive, assume leadership readily. Quickly see illogical and inefficient procedures and policies, develop and implement comprehensive systems to solve organizational problems. Enjoy long-term planning and goal setting. Usually well informed, well read, enjoy expanding their knowledge and passing it on to others. Forceful in presenting their ideas.

Introverts

Extraverts

Remember that no one is a pure type; however, each individual has preferences for introversion versus extroversion, sensing versus intuition, thinking versus feeling, and judging versus perceiving. Based on your scores on the survey, read the description of your type in the chart. Do you believe the description fits your personality?

LEADERSHIP DEVELOPMENT: Cases for Analysis

International Bank

Top executives and board members of a large international bank in New York are meeting to consider three finalists for a new position. The winning candidate will be in a high-profile job, taking charge of a group of top loan officers who have recently gotten the bank into some risky financial arrangements in Latin America. The bank had taken a financial bath when the Mexican peso collapsed, and the board voted to hire someone to directly oversee this group of loan officers and make sure the necessary due diligence is done on major loans before further commitments are made. Although the bank likes for decisions to be made as close to the action level as possible, they believe the loan officers have gotten out of hand and need to be reined in. The effectiveness of the person in this new position is considered to be of utmost importance for the bank's future. After carefully reviewing resumés, the board selected six candidates for the first round of interviews, after which the list of finalists was narrowed to three. All three candidates seem to have the intellect and experience to handle the job. Before the second-round interview, the board has asked their regular consulting firm to review the candidates, conduct more extensive background checks, and administer personality tests. A summary of their reports on the three candidates follows:

A.M. This candidate has a relatively poor self-concept and exhibits a fear of the unknown. She is somewhat of an introvert and is uncomfortable using power openly and conspicuously. A.M.'s beliefs about others are that all people are inherently noble, kind, and disposed to do the right thing, and that it is possible to influence and modify the behavior of anyone through logic and reason. Once a person's shortcomings are pointed out to her, A.M. will try to help the person overcome them. She believes that all employees can be happy, content, and dedicated to the goals of the organization.

J. T. J.T. is an extrovert with a strong drive for achievement and power. He likes new experiences and tends to be impulsive and adventurous. He is very self-assured and confident in his own abilities, but highly suspicious of the motives and abilities of others. J. T. believes the average person has an inherent dislike for work and will avoid responsibility when possible. He is very slow to trust others, but does have the ability over time to develop close, trusting relationships. In general, though, J. T. believes most people must be coerced, controlled, and threatened to get them to do their jobs well and to the benefit of the organization.

F. C. This candidate is also an extrovert, but, while she is competitive, F. C. does not seem to have the strong desire for dominance that many extroverts exhibit. F. C. is also highly conscientious and goal-oriented, and will do whatever she believes is necessary to achieve a goal. F. C. has a generally positive attitude toward others, believing that most people want to do their best for the organization. F. C. does, though, seem to have a problem forming close, personal attachments. Her lively, outgoing personality enables her to make many superficial acquaintances, but she seems to distrust and avoid emotions in herself and others, preventing the development of close relationships.

SOURCE: This case is based on information in "Consultant's Report" in John M. Champion and Francis J. Bridges, *Critical Incidents in Management: Decision and Policy Issues,* 6th ed. (Homewood, IL: Irwin, 1989), 55–60, and James Waldroop and Timothy Butler, "Guess What? You're Not Perfect," *Fortune,* October 16, 2000, 415–420.

Questions

1. Based only on the consultant's summary, which of the three candidates would you select as a leader for the group of loan officers? Discuss and defend your decision.

2. The selection committee is more divided than before on who would be best for the job. What additional information do you think you would need to help you select the best candidate?

3. How much weight do you think should be given to the personality assessment? Do you believe personality tests can be useful in predicting the best person for a job? Discuss.

The Deadlocked Committee

Ned Norman tried to reconstruct, in his own mind, the series of events that had culminated in this morning's deadlocked committee meeting. Each of the members had suddenly seemed to resist any suggestions that did not exactly coincide with their own ideas for implementing the program under consideration. This sort of "stubbornness," as Norman considered it, was not like the normal behavior patterns of most committee participants. Of course, the comment during last week's meeting about "old fashioned seat-of-the-pants decision making" had ruffled a few feathers, but Ned didn't think that was why things had bogged down today.

Ned recalled starting this morning's session by stating that the committee had discussed several of the factors connected with the proposed expanded services program, and now it seemed about time to make a decision about which way to go. Robert Romany had immediately protested that they had barely scratched the surface of the possibilities for implementing the program. Then, both Hillary Thomas and David Huntington, who worked in the statistics department of Division B, had sided with Romany and insisted that more time was needed for in-depth research. Walter Weston had entered the fray by stating that this seemed a little uncalled for, since previous experience has clearly indicated that expansion programs such as this one should be implemented through selected area district offices. This had sparked a statement from Susan Pilcher that experience was more often than not a lousy teacher, which was followed by Todd Tooley repeating his unfortunate statement about old-fashioned decision making! Robert Romany had further heated things up by saying that it was obviously far better to go a little slower in such matters by trying any new program in one area first, rather than having the committee look "unprogressive" by just "trudging along the same old cow paths"!

At this point, Ned had intuitively exercised his prerogative as chairman to stop the trend that was developing. However, things were obviously so touchy among the members that they simply refused to either offer suggestions or support any that Ned offered for breaking the deadlock. Ned decided to approach each of the division directors for whom the various committee members worked. In each area he visited, he learned that the directors were already aware of the problems, and each one had his or her own ideas as to what should be done:

Division A: The director stated that he was not much in sympathy with people who wanted to make a big deal out of every program that came along. He recalled a similar problem years ago when the company first introduced decision support software, which was hailed as the manager's replacement in decision making. He noted that the software was still in use but that he had probably made better decisions as a result of his broad background and knowledge than any computer ever could. "When I've served as chair of a deadlocked committee," he said, "I simply made the decision and solved the problem. If you're smart, you'll do the same. You can't worry about everybody's feelings on this thing."

Division B: "I know you'll want to use the best available information in estimating any program's potential performance," the director of Division B told Ned. She sided with Hillary Thomas and David Huntington that an investigative approach was the only way to go. After all, the director said, it logically followed that a decision could be no better than the research effort behind it. She also told Ned that she had told Thomas and Huntington to go ahead and collect the data they needed. "My division will be footing the bill for this, so nobody can gripe about the cost aspects." she said. "Any price would be cheap if it awakens some of the people around here to the tremendous value of a scientific approach."

Division C: The director of Division C bluntly told Ned that he didn't really care how the decision was made. However, he thought the best course of action would be to carefully develop a plan and implement it a piece at a time. "That way," he said, "you can evaluate how it looks without committing the company to a full-scale expansion. It doesn't take a lot of figuring to figure that one out!"

Division D: "We've got a time problem here," the director of Division D said. "The committee simply can't look at all possible angles. They need to synthesize the information and understandings they have and make a decision based on two or three possible solutions."

SOURCE: This is a revised version of a case by W. D. Heier, "Ned Norman, Committee Chairman," in John E. Dittrich and Robert A. Zawacki, *People and Organizations: Cases in Management and Organizational Behavior* (Plano, TX: Business Publications, Inc., 1981), 9–11.

Questions

1. Based on the whole brain concept, what different thinking styles are represented by the committee members and division directors? Do you believe they can ever be brought together? Discuss.

2. Do you see ways in which Norman might use the ideas of transformational leadership to help resolve this dilemma and break the impasse?

3. If you were the chairman of this committee, what would you do? Discuss.

REFERENCES

1. Quentin Hardy, "All Carly, All the Time," *Forbes,* December 13, 1999, 138–144; and Peter Burrows and Peter Elstrom, "The Boss," *Business Week,* August 2, 1999, 76–84. (All quotes are from Hardy.)
2. J. M. Digman, "Personality Structure: Emergence of the Five-Factor Model," *Annual Review of Psychology* 41 (1990), 417–440; M. R. Barrick and M. K. Mount, "Autonomy as a Moderator of the Relationships Between the Big Five Personality Dimensions and Job Performance," *Journal of Applied Psychology,* February, 1993, 111–118; and J. S. Wiggins and A. L. Pincus, "Personality: Structure and Assessment," *Annual Review of Psychology* 43 (1992), 473–504.
3. Betsy Morris and Patricia Sellers, "What Really Happened at Coke?" *Fortune,* January 10, 2000, 114–116; and Betsy McKay, Nikhil Deogun, and Joanne Lublin, "Ivester Had All Skills of a CEO But One: Ear for Political Nuance," *The Wall Street Journal,* December 17, 1999, A1, A6.

4. Esther Wachs Book, "Leadership for the Millennium," *Working Woman,* March 1998, 29–34.

5. Jeremy Kahn, Iobox profile, in "Euro Entrepreneurs: Why is This Man Smiling?" *Fortune,* July 24, 2000, 183–196.

6. James B. Hunt, "Travel Experience in the Formation of Leadership: John Quincy Adams, Frederick Douglass, and Jane Addams," *The Journal of Leadership Studies* 7, no. 1 (2000): 92–106.

7. R. T. Hogan, G. J. Curphy, and J. Hogan, "What We Know About Leadership: Effectiveness and Personality", *American Psychologist* 49, no. 6 (1994): 493–504.

8. Randolph E. Schmid, "Psychologists Rate What Helps Make a President Great," *Johnson City Press,* August 6, 2000, 10; and "Personality and the Presidency" segment on NBC News with John Siegenthaler, Jr., August 5, 2000.

9. P. E. Spector, "Behavior in Organizations as a Function of Employee's Locus of Control," *Psychological Bulletin,* May 1982, 482–497; and H. M. Lefcourt, "Durability and Impact of the Locus of Control Construct," *Psychological Bulletin,* 1992, 112, 411–414

10. Ibid.; and J. B. Miner, *Industrial-Organizational Psychology* (New York: McGraw-Hill, 1992), 151.

11. Andy Serwer, "There's Something about Cisco," *Fortune,* May 15, 2000, 114–138; and John A. Byrne, "The Corporation of the Future," *Business Week,* August 31, 1998, 102–106.

12. T. W. Adorno, E. Frenkel-Brunswick, D. J. Levinson, and R. N. Sanford, *The Authoritarian Personality* (New York: Harper & Row, 1950).

13. Susan Caminiti, "What Team Leaders Need to Know," *Fortune,* February 20, 1995, 93–100.

14. E. C. Ravlin and B. M. Meglino, "Effects of Values on Perception and Decision Making: A Study of Alternative Work Value Measures," *Journal of Applied Psychology* 72 (1987): 666–673.

15. Robert C. Benfari, *Understanding and Changing Your Management Style* (San Francisco: Jossey-Bass, 1999), 172.

16. Milton Rokeach, *The Nature of Human Values* (New York: The Free Press, 1973); and M. Rokeach, *Understanding Human Values* (New York: The Free Press, 1979).

17. Carol Hymowitz, "For Many Executives, Leadership Lessons Started with Mom" (In the Lead column), *The Wall Street Journal,* May 16, 2000, B1.

18. Ibid.

19. Based on G. W. England and R. Lee, "The Relationship between Managerial Values and Managerial Success in the United States, Japan, India, and Australia," *Journal of Applied Psychology* 59 (1974): 411–419.

20. L. K. Gundry, J. R. Kickul, and C. W. Prather, "Building the Creative Organization," *Organizational Dynamics* (Spring 1994): 25–28; and J. S. Chatzky, "Changing the World," *Forbes,* March 2, 1992, 83–84. Thanks to Karen Hill for this example.

21. S. J. Breckler, "Empirical Validation of Affect, Behavior, and Cognition as Distinct Components of Attitudes," *Journal of Personality and Social Psychology,* May 1984, 1191–1205; and J. M. Olson and M. P. Zanna, "Attitudes and Attitude Change," *Annual Review of Psychology* 44 (1993): 117–154.

22. Parker J. Palmer, *Leading from Within: Reflections on Spirituality and Leadership* (Indianapolis: Indiana Office for Campus Ministries, 1990), and Diane Chapman Walsh, "Cultivating Inner Sources for Leadership," in *The Organization of the Future,* Frances Hesselbein, Marshall Goldsmith, and Richard Beckhard, eds. (San Francisco: Jossey-Bass, 1997), 295–302.

23. Based on Richard L. Hughes, Robert C. Ginnett, and Gordon J. Curphy, *Leadership: Enhancing the Lessons of Experience* (Boston: Irwin McGraw-Hill, 1999), 182–184.

24. Douglas McGregor, *The Human Side of Enterprise* (New York: McGraw-Hill, 1960).

25. Thomas J. Petzinger, Jr., "A Plant Manager Keeps Reinventing His Production Line" (The Front Lines column), *The Wall Street Journal,* September 19, 1997, B1.

26. J. Hall and S. M. Donnell, "Managerial Achievement: The Personal Side of Behavioral Theory," *Human Relations* 32 (1979): 77–101.

27. Dorothy Leonard and Susaan Straus, "Putting Your Company's Whole Brain to Work," *Harvard Business Review,* July-August 1997, 111–121.

28. Henry Mintzberg, "Planning on the Left Side and Managing on the Right," *Harvard Business Review,* July-August, 1976, 49–57; Richard Restak, "The Hemispheres of the Brain Have Minds of Their Own," *The New York Times,* January 25, 1976; and Robert Ornstein, *The Psychology of Consciousness* (San Francisco: W. H. Freeman, 1975).

29. Peter Waldman, "Master Stroke: A Tragedy Transforms a Right-Handed Artist Into a Lefty—and a Star," *The Wall Street Journal,* May 12, 2000, A1.

30. This discussion is based on Ned Herrmann, *The Whole Brain Business Book* (New York: McGraw Hill, 1996).

31. Herrmann, *The Whole Brain Business Book,* 103.

32. Herrmann, *The Whole Brain Business Book,* 179.

33. Leonard and Straus, "Putting Your Company's Whole Brain to Work"; and Katherine Mieszkowski, "Opposites Attract," *Fast Company,* December-January, 1998, 42, 44.

34. Carl Jung, *Psychological Types* (London: Routledge and Kegan Paul, 1923).

35. Otto Kroeger and Janet M. Thuesen, *Type Talk* (New York: Delacorte Press, 1988); Kroeger and Thuesen, *Type Talk at Work* (New York: Dell, 1992; "Conference Proceedings," The Myers-Briggs Type Indicator and Leadership: An International Research Conference, January 12–14, 1994; and S. K. Hirsch, *MBTI Team Member's Guide* (Palo Alto, Calif.: Consulting Psychologists Press, 1992).

36. Based on Mary H. McCaulley, "Research on the MBTI and Leadership: Taking the Critical First Step," Keynote Address, The Myers-Briggs Type Indicator and Leadership: An International Research Conference, January 12–14, 1994.

37. Katherine J. Klein and Robert J. House, "On Fire: Charismatic Leadership and Levels of Analysis," *Leadership Quarterly* 6, no. 2 (1995): 183–198.

38. Patricia Sellers, "What Exactly is Charisma?" *Fortune* 15 January 1996, 68–75.

39. Ibid.

40. Hal Lancaster, "Herb Kelleher Has One Main Strategy: Treat Employees Well," *The Wall Street Journal,* August 31, 1999, B1; and Katrina Brooker, "Can Anyone

Replace Herb?" *Fortune,* April 17, 2000, 186–192; Thomas A. Stewart, "Why Leadership Matters," *Fortune,* March 2, 1998, 71–82.

41. Jay A. Conger, Rabindra N. Kanungo and Associates, *Charismatic Leadership: The Elusive Factor in Organizational Effectiveness* (San Francisco: Jossey-Bass, 1988); Robert J. House and Jane M. Howell, "Personality and Charismatic Leadership," *Leadership Quarterly* 3, no. 2 (1992): 81–108; Klein and House, "On Fire: Charismatic Leadership and Levels of Analysis."

42. The following discussion is based primarily on Conger, et. al., *Charismatic Leadership.*

43. Boas Shamir, Michael B. Arthur, and Robert J. House, "The Rhetoric of Charismatic Leadership: A Theoretical Extension, A Case Study, and Implications for Future Research," *Leadership Quarterly* 5, no. 1 (1994): 25–42.

44. Richard L. Daft and Robert H. Lengel, *Fusion Leadership: Unlocking the Subtle Forces that Change People and Organizations* (San Francisco: Berrett-Koehler, 1998), 169.

45. Sellers, "What Exactly Is Charisma?"

46. Janice M. Beyer, "Taming and Promoting Charisma to Change Organizations," *The Leadership Quarterly* 10, No. 2 (1999): 307–330.

47. Robert J. House and Jane M. Howell, "Personality and Charismatic Leadership," *Leadership Quarterly* 3, no. 2 (1992): 81–108; and Jennifer O'Connor, Michael D. Mumford, Timothy C. Clifton, Theodore L. Gessner, and Mary Shane Connelly, "Charismatic Leaders and Destructiveness: An Historiometric Study," *Leadership Quarterly* 6, no. 4 (1995): 529–555.

48. O'Connor et. al. "Charismatic Leaders and Destructiveness."

49. The terms transactional and transformational leadership are from James MacGregor Burns, *Leadership* (New York: Harper & Row, 1978), and Bernard M. Bass, "Leadership: Good, Better, Best," *Organizational Dynamics* 13 (Winter 1985): 26–40.

50. Based on Bernard M. Bass, "Theory of Transformational Leadership Redux," *Leadership Quarterly* 6, no. 4 (Winter 1995): 463–478, and "From Transactional to Transformational Leadership: Learning to Share the Vision," *Organizational Dynamics* 18, no. 3 (Winter 1990): 19–31; Francis J. Yammarino, William D. Spangler, and Bernard M. Bass, "Transformational Leadership and Performance: A Longitudinal Investigation," *Leadership Quarterly* 4, no. 1 (Spring 1993): 81–102; and B. M. Bass, "Current Developments in Transformational Leadership," *The Psychologist-Manager Journal* 3, no. 1 (1999), 5–21.

51. Noel M. Tichy and Mary Anne Devanna, *The Transformational Leader* (New York: John Wiley & Sons, 1986), 265–266.

52. Manfred F. R. Kets De Vries, "Charisma in Action: The Transformational Abilities of Virgin's Richard Branson and ABB's Percy Barnevik," *Organizational Dynamics,* Winter 1998, 7–21.

53. Bethany McLean, "Is This Guy the Best Banker in America?" *Fortune,* July 6, 1998, 126–128.

CHAPTER OUTLINE

YOUR LEADERSHIP CHALLENGE

After reading this chapter, you should be able to:

- Be aware of the mental models that guide your behavior and relationships.

- Engage in independent thinking by staying mentally alert, thinking critically, and being mindful rather than mindless.

- Start to break out of categorized thinking patterns and open your mind to new ideas and multiple perspectives.

- Begin to apply systems thinking and personal mastery to your activities at school or work.

- Exercise emotional intelligence in your relationships, including being self-aware, managing your emotions, motivating yourself, displaying empathy, and applying social skills.

- Apply the difference between motivating others based on fear and motivating others based on love.

Leadership Mind and Heart

Norman Mayne, CEO of Dorothy Lane Markets (DLM), got a lot of strange looks back in 1995 when he started talking about firing customers. Mayne came up with the radical idea of weeding out people who weren't regular DLM shoppers and focusing relentless energy on the market's best customers, rewarding them for their loyalty with great grocery deals as well as perks such as free turkeys at Thanksgiving and Christmas, bouquets of flowers, and tickets to concerts. Today, Club DLM is the most innovative customer loyalty program in the supermarket industry.

Mayne no longer runs print advertising, which once cost the company $5,000 to $10,000 a week. "Whenever we ran those ads, offering a special on pork-and-beans, all we did was attract 'cherry pickers,'" he says. "It was a headache for [our employees] and for our regular customers." Mayne also no longer keeps close track of prices at Kroger or other chain stores, choosing to focus on customers rather than on the competition. DLM now sends out a monthly newsletter to the company's top 9,000 customers. Different versions of the newsletter are targeted to different spending levels and offer different savings coupons. In addition, targeted postcard mailings go out four to six times a year. Naturally, Dorothy Lane still has to worry about competition, but it has found more intelligent ways to respond.

A consumer advisory board (members have their pictures posted at the front of DLM's main store) makes sure the company stays in touch with what customers want and need. In addition to the customer loyalty program, DLM sponsors events such as Hawaiian luaus and contests for members of the Kid's Club. The company delivers groceries—at a loss—to around 175 elderly customers who have shopped at the market all their lives. "We run this business with our hearts," explains Mayne, whose father started Dorothy Lane Markets as a roadside stand in 1948.

Mayne puts as much energy toward motivating employees and making them feel important as he does toward pleasing customers. Some staff members, even those with back-room jobs, have become almost like local celebrities because they have a chance to interact with customers at wine tastings, jazz nights, or other events. Employees are committed to showing care and respect for Club DLM customers because the company shows care and respect for them. According to Mayne, "It's not in our culture to be complacent in dealing with a customer—or with an employee."[1]

Norman Mayne came up with a new model for doing business at Dorothy Lane Markets, one that makes relationships with employees and regular customers a priority. Throughout the business world, leaders are beginning to talk about building work relationships based on caring, trust, and respect. Recall that one of the transformations we discussed in Chapter 1 is a shift from focusing on things to focusing on relationships. Peter Drucker, a writer who is widely read by practicing managers, has been stressing the importance of people and relationships for years. Wayne Calloway, former CEO of PepsiCo, when asked the secret to his company's competitiveness, once said, "The three Ps: people, people, people." Even Jack Welch of General Electric, who was once called the toughest boss in America, has mandated that he and his senior executives must get softer, more human, and more collegial.[2] Many organizations have a growing appreciation for the fact that the strength of relationships with employees, customers, suppliers, and competitors is just as important as formal rules, contracts, plans, and even profits. In a time of rapid change, leaders focus on personal relationships as a way to bind people together.

Making relationships rather than rules and schedules a priority is not easy for traditional managers who have been accustomed to thinking emotions should be left outside the company gate. However, smart leaders are increasingly aware that human emotion is the most basic force in organizations and that acknowledging and respecting employees as whole people can enhance organizational performance. People cannot be separated from their emotions, and it is through emotion that leaders generate employee commitment to shared vision and mission, values and culture, and caring for the work and each other.

This chapter and the next explore current thinking about the importance of leaders becoming whole people by exploring the full capacities of their mind and spirit. By doing so, they help others reach their full potential and contribute fully to the organization. We will first examine what we mean by leader capacity. Then we will expand on some of the ideas introduced in the previous chapter to consider how the capacity to shift our thinking and feeling can help leaders alter their behavior, influence others, and be more effective. We will discuss perception and the concept of mental models, and look at how qualities such as independent thinking, an open mind, and systems thinking are important for leaders. Then we take a closer look at human emotion as illustrated in the concept of emotional intelligence and the emotions of love versus fear in leader-follower relationships. The next chapter will turn to spirit as reflected in moral leadership and courage.

LEADER CAPACITY VERSUS COMPETENCE

Traditionally, effective leadership, like good management, has been thought of as competence in a set of skills; once these specific skills are acquired, all one has to do to succeed is put them into action. However, as we all know from personal experience, working effectively with other people requires much more than practicing specific, rational skills; it often means drawing on subtle aspects of ourselves—our thoughts, beliefs, or feelings—and appealing to those aspects in others. Particularly in today's environment, skills competence is no longer enough. While organizational issues such as production schedules, structure, finances, costs, profits, and so forth are important, in a time of uncertainty and change organizations need more. Key issues include how to give people a sense of meaning and purpose when major shifts occur almost daily; how to make employees feel valued and respected in an age of downsizing and job uncertainty; and how to keep morale and motivation high in the face of rapid change and the stress it creates.

In this chapter, rather than discussing competence, we will explore a person's *capacity* for mind and heart. Whereas competence is limited and quantifiable, capacity is unlimited and defined by the potential for expansion and growth.[3] **Capacity** means the potential each of us has to do more and be more than we are now. Leadership capacity goes beyond learning the skills for organizing, planning, or controlling others. It also involves something deeper and more subtle than the leadership traits and styles we discussed in Chapters 2 and 3. Living, working, and leading based on our capacity means using our whole selves, including intellectual, emotional, and spiritual abilities and understandings. A broad literature has emphasized that being a whole person means operating from mind, heart, spirit, and body.[4] Although we can't "learn" capacity the way we learn a set of skills, we can expand and develop leadership capacity. For example, just as the physical capacity of our lungs is increased through regular aerobic exercise, the capacities of the mind, heart, and spirit can be expanded through conscious development and regular use. In the previous chapter, we introduced some ideas about how individuals think, make decisions, and solve problems based on values, attitudes, and patterns of thinking. This chapter builds on some of those ideas to provide a broader view of the leadership capacities of mind and heart.

MENTAL MODELS

A mental model can be thought of as an internal picture of the world that affects a leader's actions and relationships with others. Many of our values, attitudes, and beliefs have become so deeply ingrained and so basic to our picture of the world that we aren't even aware that they cause us to take the same approaches to people and situations time and again. **Mental models** are deep-seated assumptions, values, attitudes, beliefs, biases, and prejudices that determine how leaders make sense of the world.[5] Leaders should be aware of how these elements affect their thinking and may cause "blind spots" that limit their understanding. Mental models govern how leaders interpret their experiences and the actions they take in response to people and situations. Two important components of mental models are assumptions and perception.[6]

Assumptions

In the previous chapter, we discussed two very different sets of attitudes and assumptions that leaders may have about subordinates, called Theory X and Theory Y, and how these assumptions affect leader behavior. A leader's assumptions naturally are part of his or her mental model. Someone who assumes that people can't be trusted will act very differently in a situation than someone who has the assumption that people are basically trustworthy. Leaders also have assumptions about events, situations, and circumstances as well as about people. For example, consider the different assumptions of Dick Michaux and his son Rick. The 56-year-old father is CEO of AvalonBay Communities, which has $3 billion of assets such as land, construction machinery, and so forth. His 30-year-old son Rick left a good job at Motorola to become CEO of a start-up trying to develop Internet-based wireless systems for maintenance workers. Rick's intention to run up big losses in pursuit of rapid growth makes sense to his e-commerce-savvy colleagues, but it goes against every assumption his traditional bricks-and-mortar-based father has about how to run a successful business: plan carefully, don't make mistakes, earn a profit.[7] Many organizations whose leaders operated on those traditional assumptions were hurt when Internet-based competitors began stealing market share. Some observers suggest that in today's world of rapid and discontinuous change, the greatest factor determining the success of leaders and their organizations is the ability to shift one's mind-set, or mental model, about how to do business.[8]

Leaders can learn to regard their assumptions as temporary ideas rather than fixed truths. The more aware a leader is of his or her assumptions, the more the leader understands how assumptions guide behavior. In addition, the leader can begin to question whether long-held assumptions fit the reality of the situation. Questioning assumptions can lead to successful new approaches to people and business, as it did for Norman Mayne at Dorothy Lane Markets, described in the opening example. Most business owners assume, as Mayne did, that all customers should be valued. By questioning that basic assumption and "firing" his lousy customers to focus on the best ones, Mayne put DLM on course to increased profitability and improved the work lives of his employees.

Perception: How Leaders Interpret Experience

As described in the previous chapter, perception is the process people use to make sense out of the environment by selecting, organizing, and interpreting information from the environment. There are many different ways of processing and interpreting information, which means that perception can vary widely from individual to individual. In terms of the Myers-Briggs psychological types described in the previous chapter, for example, people with a sensing preference base their perceptions largely on what they consider the facts and details of a situation, while intuitive types may rely more on impressions. Perceptions become part of a person's mental model, determining how a leader views people, situations, and events.

Perception occurs so naturally and spontaneously that we rarely think about it. However, perception can be broken down into a step-by-step process, as illustrated in Exhibit 5.1. First, we observe information (sensory data) from the environment through our senses. Next, our mind screens the data and selects only certain items to process further. Third, we organize the selected data into meaningful patterns for interpretation and response. We are all aware of the environment, but not everything in it is equally important to our perception. We tune in to some data (such as a familiar voice off in the distance) and tune out other data (such as paper shuffling next to us). What a person selects to pay attention to depends on a number of factors, including characteristics of the individual as well as characteristics of the stimuli. For example, a leader's values, attitudes, personality, and past experiences all affect the selection of stimuli or sensory data. In addition, characteristics of the data itself affect selection. People tend to notice something that stands out from surrounding stimuli, such as a loud noise in a quiet room. Something that is different from what we're accustomed to also gets noticed more. Thus, a leader might notice an employee who dresses in brightly colored ethnic clothing when everyone

EXHIBIT 5.1

The Perception Process

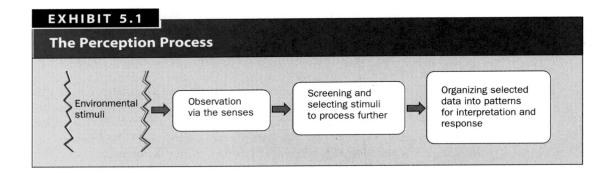

Environmental stimuli → Observation via the senses → Screening and selecting stimuli to process further → Organizing selected data into patterns for interpretation and response

else in the office wears suits. Furthermore, depending on the leader's values, beliefs, and assumptions, this perception can lead to either a positive or negative impression of the employee.

A leader needs to be aware of various factors that affect perception and influence his or her thinking. By being aware, leaders can avoid some perceptual distortions that can be detrimental to the leadership process. One such distortion is **stereotyping,** which is the tendency to assign a person to a group or broad category and then to attribute widely held generalizations about the group to the individual. Stereotypes prevent leaders from getting to know people as individuals and often prevent the individual from contributing fully to the organization. Joe Booker learned all about the power of stereotypes, but his own values and mental model enabled him to build a highly successful leadership career. As the only African American at an Air Force school in Mississippi, Booker was routinely ignored by instructors who held negative stereotypes about minorities. Rather than giving up, Booker only worked harder and ended up scoring tops in his class. He faced similar prejudices at his first assignment at Keeler Air Force Base. Booker overcame stereotypes by taking on the most difficult assignments and becoming an expert, which brought him positive attention. He always focused on where he wanted to go in his career and what jobs could take him there. Since those early days, he has served as CEO of two successful Silicon Valley companies and recently joined another start-up as vice president of operations for Alteon Systems.[9]

Becoming aware of assumptions and perceptions and understanding how they influence emotions and actions is the first step toward being able to shift mental models and see the world in new ways.[10] Leaders can learn to break free from outdated mental models. They can recognize that what worked yesterday may not work today. Following conventional wisdom about "how things have always been done" may be the surest route to failure in a fast-changing environment. As Larry Bossidy, who recently retired as CEO of AlliedSignal, said, "One of the wonderful things about business: You have to forget what you know. If I like the business model I have now, I'm not going to like it in five years."[11] Rear Admiral Albert H. Konetzni is bringing a new mental model to his work with the U.S. Navy's Pacific submarine fleet.

IN THE LEAD   ## Rear Admiral Albert H. Konetzni, U.S. Navy

The U.S. Navy is facing a personnel crisis. Despite the largest pay raise in history, recruitment is dismal, junior sailors are streaming out of the service, and the Navy is struggling to field full crews on many of its ships and subs. Officials often blame the strong economy, while some critics fault the military's recruiting strategies. Rear Admiral Albert H. Konetzni, however, thinks it's something more basic: the assumptions, perceptions, and mind-sets of top officers. Adm. Konetzni has brought a new mental model to the military that has sailors in his fleet signing up for a second tour of duty at twice the rate of the rest of the Navy.

When Adm. Konetzni took command of the Pacific submarine fleet two years ago, his first conclusion was that to keep his sailors, he needed to make sure they had time for a life outside the Navy between their grueling six-month-long deployments. The old mental model was that submarine commanders expected hard work, long hours, and near-perfection. A long-standing joke is that SSN, the acronym the Navy uses to designate its attack submarines, stands for "Saturdays, Sundays, and Nights," a reference to the long hours sailors spend working in port. Within weeks of taking command, Konetzni ordered that crews should work from 8 A.M. to 4 P.M. in port. He used $500,000 from his spare-parts budget to hire civilians to paint subs and fix the galleys, and spent an additional $12,000 from the travel budget on a conveyor belt to load boxes onto ships (rather than using a line of sailors to do the work). He declared that some subs, even though they had high certification scores or got a lot of praise from top officials, were "unsuccessful" because sailors were miserable and just waiting for their tour to be over so they could leave the Navy. Says Commander Dick Pusateri, the Pacific fleet's lead chaplain: "The admiral was telling us that taking care of people means something, even if we've been pretending it does not."

Adm. Konetzni has made a number of other changes, some of them quite controversial. For example, he has struggled to find ways to save sailors who would previously have been kicked out of the Navy because of psychological or disciplinary problems. Some question the wisdom of bending so far to make sailors' lives easier. Adm. Konetzni believes, however, that the Navy can "find the square hole for the square peg," and thus keep more sailors. Despite criticisms, there's no doubt that the new approach is having some positive results. The percentage of Pacific fleet sailors who sign up for a second tour of duty has doubled in the two years since Adm. Konetzni took over, morale is high, and there's no indication that the fleet's ability to execute its mission is diminished. "People enjoy coming to work now," said Chief Petty Officer Anthony B. Kostner. "I don't think they did before."[12]

Leaders like Admiral Konetzni are constantly questioning the status quo, looking for new ideas, and encouraging novel solutions to problems. They question their own mental models and encourage others to do the same. Issues of the mind are more critical to effective leadership than ever.

DEVELOPING A LEADER'S MIND

How do leaders make the shift to a new mental model? The leader's mind can be developed beyond the nonleader's in four critical areas: independent thinking, open-mindedness, systems thinking, and personal mastery. Taken together, these four disciplines provide a foundation that can help leaders examine their mental models and overcome blind spots that may limit their leadership effectiveness and the success of their organizations.

Independent Thinking

Independent thinking means questioning assumptions and interpreting data and events according to one's own beliefs, ideas, and thinking, not according to pre-established rules, routines, or categories defined by others. People who think independently are willing to stand apart, to have opinions, to say what they think, and to determine a course of action based on what they personally believe rather than on what other people think. To think independently means staying mentally alert, thinking critically, being mindful rather than mindless. **Mindfulness** can be defined as the process of continuously re-evaluating previously learned ways of doing things in the context of evolving information and shifting circumstances.[13] It is the opposite of mindlessness, which means blindly accepting rules and labels created by others. Mindless people let others do the thinking for them.

In the chaotic world of organizations, everything is constantly changing. What worked in one situation may not work the next time. In these conditions, mental laziness and accepting others' answers can hurt the organization and all its members. Leaders apply critical thinking to explore a situation, problem, or question from multiple perspectives and integrate all the available information into a possible solution. When leaders think critically, they question all assumptions, vigorously seek divergent opinions, and try to give balanced consideration to all alternatives.[14] Thinking independently and critically is hard work, and most of us can easily relax into temporary mindlessness, accepting black-and-white answers and relying on standard ways of doing things.

Leaders need to stay mentally alert, keep thinking, and keep asking questions.

Leslie Wexner, who opened the first Limited clothing store in 1963 and now presides over a company that includes thousands of specialty stores and brands such as Express, Victoria's Secret, and Abercrombie & Fitch, advises leaders to "keep your mental muscle loose."[15] Wexner embarked on a personal odyssey to change his own thinking and his organization's approach to the marketplace after the company lost touch with customers in the early 1990s.

Open-Mindedness

One approach to independent thinking is to try to break out of the mental boxes, the categorized thinking patterns we have been conditioned to accept as correct. Mind potential is released when we open up to new ideas and multiple perspectives, when we can get outside our mental box. John Keating, the private school teacher portrayed in a 1989 movie, *Dead Poets Society,* urged his students to stand on their desks to get a new perspective on the world: "I stand on my desk to remind myself we must constantly look at things a different way. The world looks different from here."

The power of the conditioning that guides our thinking and behavior is illustrated by what has been called the Pike Syndrome. In an experiment, a northern pike is placed in one half of a large glass-divided aquarium, with numerous minnows placed in the other half. The hungry pike makes repeated attempts to get the minnows, but succeeds only in battering itself against the glass, finally learning that trying to reach the minnows is futile. The glass divider is then removed, but the pike makes no attempt to attack the minnows because it has been conditioned to believe that reaching them is impossible. When people assume they have complete knowledge of a situation because of past experiences, they exhibit the Pike Syndrome, a rigid commitment to what was true in the past and a refusal to consider alternatives and different perspectives.[16]

Leaders have to forget many of their conditioned ideas to be open to new ones. This openness—putting aside preconceptions and suspending beliefs and opinions—can be referred to as "beginner's mind." Whereas the expert's mind rejects new ideas based on past experience and knowledge, the beginner's mind reflects the openness and innocence of a young child just learning about the world. The value of a beginner's mind is captured in the story told in this chapter's Living Leadership box.

Nobel prize-winning physicist Richard Feynman, one of the most original scientific minds of the twentieth century, illustrates the power of the beginner's mind. Feynman's IQ was an unremarkable 125. The heart of his genius was a childlike curiosity and a belief that doubt was the essence of learning and knowing. Feynman was always questioning, always uncertain, always starting over, always resisting any authority that prevented him from doing his own thinking and exploring.[17]

LIVING LEADERSHIP

An Empty Sort of Mind

Reflecting on how Winnie the Pooh found Eeyore's missing tail:

"An Empty sort of mind is valuable for finding pearls and tails and things because it can see what's in front of it. An Overstuffed mind is unable to. While the clear mind listens to a bird singing, the Stuffed-Full-of-Knowledge-and-Cleverness mind wonders what *kind* of bird is singing. The more Stuffed Up it is, the less it can hear through its own ears and see through its own eyes. Knowledge and Cleverness tend to concern themselves with the wrong sorts of things, and a mind confused by Knowledge, Cleverness, and Abstract Ideas tends to go chasing off after things that don't matter, or that don't even exist, instead of seeing, appreciating, and making use of what is right in front of it."

Benjamin Hoff, *The Tao of Pooh* (New York: E. P. Dutton, 1982), 146–147.

Effective leaders strive to keep open minds and cultivate an organizational environment that encourages curiosity. They understand the limitations of past experience and reach out for diverse perspectives. These leaders move away from a mind-set that sees any questioning of their ideas as a threat to a mind-set that encourages everyone throughout the organization to openly debate assumptions, confront paradoxes, question perceptions, and express feelings.[18]

To encourage open-mindedness at Xerox Corporation's Palo Alto Research Center, chief scientist John Seely Brown has a two-hour lunch with his senior team every Friday where they reflect on what went right during the week, what went wrong, and how they can learn from it. Brown began videotaping important meetings so he could try to avoid sending out nonverbal cues, such as squinting his eyes or stiffening his body, that could block open conversation. The weekly meetings help Brown broaden his mind to encompass ideas and issues far beyond his own thinking.[19] At McKinsey & Co., all 700 partners spend a week together every six months. Rajat Gupta, worldwide managing director, reads poetry during his closing talk because, as he puts it, poetry and literature "help us think in more well-rounded ways. . . . Poetry helps us reflect on the important questions: What is the purpose of our business? What are our values? Poetry helps us recognize that we face tough questions and that we seldom have perfect answers."[20]

Some companies, such as Microsoft, Southwest Airlines, and Manco, make curiosity and interest in learning a more important hiring criterion than experience or expertise. Leaders can also support and reward people who are willing to ask questions, stretch boundaries, experiment, and keep learning. At Manco, an adhesives company, employees can enroll in any outside course they choose, whether it's business management or basketweaving, and be reimbursed as long as they pass the course. CEO Jack Krahl's rationale is that "It lets people know . . . that one of the highest values at Manco is to be curious and to allow curiosity to take place."[21]

Bernard Bass, who has studied charismatic and transformational leadership, talks about the value of intellectual stimulation—which means arousing followers' thoughts and imagination as well as stimulating their ability to identify and solve problems creatively.[22] People admire leaders who challenge them to think and learn, to break out of the box of conditioned thinking and be open to new, inspiring ideas and alternatives.

Systems Thinking

Systems thinking means seeing patterns in the organizational whole instead of just the parts, and learning to reinforce or change system patterns.[23] Traditional managers have been trained to solve problems by breaking things down into discrete pieces, and the success of each piece is believed to add up to the success of the whole. But it is the *relationship* among the parts that form the whole that counts. Systems thinking enables leaders to look for patterns of movement over time and focus on the qualities of rhythm, flow, direction, shape, and networks of relationships that accomplish the work of an organization. Systems thinking is a mental discipline and framework for seeing patterns and interrelationships.

It is important to see organizational systems as a whole because of their complexity. Complexity can overwhelm leaders, undermining confidence. When leaders can see the structures that underlie complex situations, they can facilitate improvement. But it requires a focus on the big picture. Leaders can develop what David McCamus, former Chairman and CEO of Xerox Canada, calls "peripheral vision"—the ability to view the organization through a wide-angle lens, rather than a telephoto lens—so that they perceive how their decisions and actions affect the whole.[24]

An important element of systems thinking is to discern circles of causality. Peter Senge, author of *The Fifth Discipline,* argues that reality is made up of circles rather than straight lines. For example, Exhibit 5.2 shows circles of influence for producing new products. In the circle on the left, a high-tech firm grows rapidly by pumping out new products quickly. New products increase revenues, which enable the further increase of the R&D budget to add more new products.

But another circle of causality is being influenced as well. As the R&D budget grows, the engineering and research staff increases. The burgeoning technical staff becomes increasingly hard to manage. The management burden falls on senior engineers, who provide less of their time for developing new products, which slows product development time. The slowing of product development time has a negative impact on new products, the very thing that

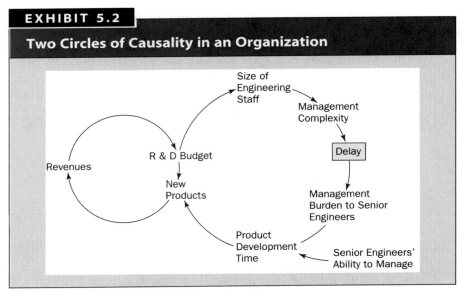

EXHIBIT 5.2

Two Circles of Causality in an Organization

SOURCE: From *The Fifth Discipline: The Art and Practice of the Learning Organization* by Peter M. Senge, 97. Copyright © 1990 by Peter M. Senge. Used by permission of Doubleday, a division of Bantam Doubleday Dell Publishing Group, Inc.

created organizational success. Maintaining product development time in the face of increasing management complexity depends upon senior engineers' management ability. Thus, understanding the circle of causality enables leaders to allocate resources to the training and development of engineering leadership as well as directly to new products. Without an understanding of the system, top leaders would fail to understand why increasing R&D budgets can actually increase product development time and reduce the number of new products coming to market.

The other element of systems thinking is learning to influence the system with reinforcing feedback as an engine for growth or decline. In the example of new products, after managers see how the system works, they can allocate revenues to speed new products to market, either by hiring more engineers, or by training senior engineers in management and leadership skills. They can guide the system when they understand it conceptually. Without this kind of understanding, managers will hit blockages in the form of seeming limits to growth and resistance to change because the large complex system will appear impossible to manage. Systems thinking is a significant solution.

Personal Mastery

Another concept introduced by Senge is *personal mastery,* a term he uses to describe the discipline of personal growth and learning, of mastering yourself in a way that facilitates your leadership and achieves desired results.[25] Organizations can grow and learn only when the people who make up the organization are growing and learning.

Personal mastery embodies three qualities—personal vision, facing reality, and holding creative tension. First, leaders engaged in personal mastery know and clarify what is important to them. They focus on the end result, the vision or dream that motivates them and their organization. They have a clear vision of a desired future, and their purpose is to achieve that future. One element of personal mastery, then, is the discipline of continually focusing and defining what one wants as their desired future and vision.

Second, facing reality means a commitment to the truth. Leaders are relentless in uncovering the mental models that limit and deceive them and are willing to challenge assumptions and ways of doing things. These leaders are committed to the truth, and will break through denial of reality in themselves and others. Their quest for truth leads to a deeper awareness of themselves and of the larger systems and events within which they operate. Commitment to the truth enables them to deal with reality, which increases the opportunity to achieve the results they seek.

Third, often there is a large gap between one's vision and the current situation. The gap between the desired future and today's reality, say between the dream of starting a business and the reality of having no capital, can be discouraging. But the gap is the source of creative energy. Acknowledging and living with the disparity between the truth and the vision, and facing it squarely, is the source of resolve and creativity to move forward. The effective leader resolves the tension by letting the vision pull reality toward it, in other words, by reorganizing current activities to work toward the vision. The leader works in a way that moves things toward the vision. The less effective way is to let reality pull the vision downward toward it. This means lowering the vision, such as walking away from a problem or settling for less than desired. Settling for less releases the tension, but also engenders mediocrity. Leaders with personal mastery learn to accept both the dream and the reality simultaneously, and to close the gap by moving the organization toward the dream.

All five elements of mind are interrelated. Independent thinking and open-mindedness improve systems thinking and enable personal mastery, helping leaders shift and expand their mental models. Since they are all interdependent, leaders working to improve even one element of their mental approach can move forward in a significant way toward mastering their mind and becoming more effective.

EMOTIONAL INTELLIGENCE—LEADING WITH HEART AND MIND

Psychologists and other researchers, as well as leaders in all walks of life, are increasingly recognizing the critical importance of emotional intelligence—the ability to connect effectively with people. Some have suggested that emotion, more than intellectual ability, drives our thinking and decision making, as well as our interpersonal relationships.[26] Emotional understanding and skills impact our success and happiness in our work as well as in our personal lives. Leaders can harness and direct the power of emotions to improve employee satisfaction, morale, and motivation, as well as to enhance organizational effectiveness. Some leaders act as if people leave their emotions at home when they come to work, but we all know this isn't true. "There are companies that don't want people to talk about their personal lives," says Paula Lawlor of Medi-Health Outsourcing. "But I say, 'Bring it on.' If people can get something off their chests for an hour, then I've got them for the next 10."[27]

Silicon Valley companies, including Intel, Sun Microsystems, and Netscape, regularly send managers to the Growth and Leadership Center (GLC), where they learn to use emotional intelligence to build better relationships. Nick Kepler, director of technology development at Advanced Micro Devices Inc., was surprised to learn how his emotionless approach to work was intimidating people and destroying rapport. Raymond Wice, now Lucent Technologies Inc.'s director of engineering in San Jose, used GLC's coaching to help him overcome a crippling introversion that was stifling his career. Wice, who used to eat his lunches alone and make a beeline to his office hoping no one would talk to him, was given regular assignments that helped him overcome his mistrust of people and relationships. Says GLC coach Ron Steck, "He was on the verge of being overlooked, and now he's running the biggest department in his organization."[28] In fact, according to GLC, 85 percent of its clients are promoted within a year of the training or receive increased responsibility of their own choosing.[29] In an environment where relationships with employees and customers are becoming more important than technology and material resources, interest in developing leaders' emotional intelligence will likely continue to grow. This chapter's Leader's Bookshelf describes how leaders can use emotional intelligence to develop healthier and more productive work relationships.

What Are Emotions?

There are hundreds of emotions and more subtleties of emotion than there are words to explain them. One important ability for leaders is to understand the range of emotions people have and how these emotions may manifest themselves. Many researchers accept eight categories or "families" of emotions, as

LEADER'S BOOKSHELF

PeopleSmart: Developing Your Interpersonal Intelligence

Mel Silberman with Freda Hansburg

"Working people smart means that all members of an organization focus on what's important between people and avoid what is of little value," says workplace psychologist Mel Silberman. Silberman believes developing interpersonal intelligence is a lifelong process. He wrote *PeopleSmart: Developing Your Interpersonal Intelligence* as a guide to the process of building healthier and more productive relationships. Silberman, with the assistance of psychologist Freda Hansburg, offers a clear plan focused on acquiring eight critical interpersonal skills.

People-Smart Skills

The first chapter of the book gives the reader a chance to assess his or her own people-smart skills, or "PQ" rating. Then, each chapter focuses on developing skills in eight areas, including:

- **Understanding People.** "How well you understand others has considerable impact on how successful you will be in every arena," writes Silberman. He suggests some ways to better understand what makes people tick: listen actively, empathize, and acknowledge other viewpoints; clarify meaning by asking open-ended questions that can get at underlying emotions; learn to interpret behavior by recognizing people's differences in style and motivation.

- **Asserting Your Needs.** Being people smart also means you have to "be your own person." People-smart individuals understand themselves, set limits, and are straightforward with their needs, interests, and motivations. Failure to be assertive leads to frustration,

which can cause you to become angry at others and lose the calm and confidence you need to be your best.

- **Resolving Conflict.** Interpersonally intelligent people get conflict right out in the open, but they do it in a calm and reasonable manner. When emotions are running high, the people-smart person can step back and examine what is bothering him as well as the other person. By understanding his or her own feelings and empathizing with the other person, the people-smart individual can begin to offer creative solutions to the conflict.

- **Shifting Gears.** People-smart people are flexible and resilient. They understand "that there are different strokes for different folks." They change relationships not by trying to change the other person but by changing their own behavior in the relationship. It takes courage and self-awareness to be able to step out of old ruts and habits and do things in a new and different way.

A Guide to Action

PeopleSmart is sharply focused on action. Each chapter provides a skill-building process for developing interpersonal intelligence in each of the eight areas. The process is summed up as "Want It, Learn It, Try It, and Live It." The authors provide reasons for developing the skill, practical ways to develop it, exercises to put it into practice, and ideas for living the new skill every day so that it continues to grow. Everyone is in the people business—at home, work, school, and with friends. This book provides a powerful guide for becoming more effective in every relationship.

PeopleSmart: Developing Your Interpersonal Intelligence, by Mel Silberman with Freda Hansburg, is published by Berrett-Koehler Publishers.

illustrated in Exhibit 5.3.[30] These categories do not resolve every question about how to categorize emotions, and scientific debate continues. The argument for there being a set of core emotions is based partly on the discovery that specific facial expressions for four of them (fear, anger, sadness, and enjoyment) are universally recognized. People in cultures around the world have been found to recognize these same basic emotions when shown photographs of facial expressions. The primary emotions and some of their variations follow.

- *Anger:* fury, outrage, resentment, exasperation, indignation, animosity, annoyance, irritability, hostility, violence.

- *Sadness:* grief, sorrow, gloom, melancholy, self-pity, loneliness, dejection, despair, depression.

- *Fear:* anxiety, apprehension, nervousness, concern, consternation, wariness, edginess, dread, fright, terror, panic.

- *Enjoyment:* happiness, joy, relief, contentment, delight, amusement, pride, sensual pleasure, thrill, rapture, gratification, satisfaction, euphoria.

- *Love:* acceptance, respect, friendliness, trust, kindness, affinity, devotion, adoration, infatuation.

EXHIBIT 5.3

Eight Families of Emotions

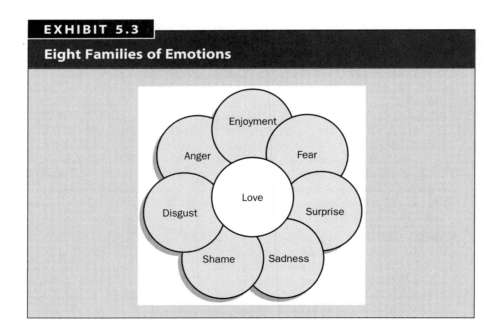

- *Surprise:* shock, astonishment, amazement, wonder.

- *Disgust:* contempt, disdain, scorn, abhorrence, aversion, distaste, revulsion.

- *Shame:* guilt, embarrassment, chagrin, remorse, humiliation, regret, mortification, contrition.

Leaders who are attuned to their own feelings and the feelings of others can use their understanding to enhance the organization.

The Components of Emotional Intelligence

Five basic components of emotional intelligence are important to organizational leaders.[31]

Self-awareness, which is the basis for all the other components, means being aware of what you are feeling, being conscious of the emotions within yourself. People who are in touch with their emotions are better able to guide their own lives. Leaders can be in touch with their emotions in order to interact effectively and appreciate emotions in others. Leaders with a high level of self-awareness learn to trust their "gut feelings" and realize that these feelings can provide useful information about difficult decisions. Answers are not always clear as to whether to propose a major deal, let an employee go, reorganize a business, or revise job responsibilities. When the answers are not available from external sources, leaders have to rely on their own feelings.

Managing emotions is the second key component, which means the leader is able to balance his or her own moods so that worry, anxiety, fear, or anger do not get in the way of what needs to be done. Leaders who can manage their emotions perform better because they are able to think clearly. Managing emotions does not mean suppressing or denying them but understanding them and using that understanding to deal with situations productively.[32] Leaders first recognize a mood or feeling, think about what it means and how it affects them, and then choose how to act.

Motivating oneself is the ability to be hopeful and optimistic despite obstacles, setbacks, or even outright failure. This ability is crucial for pursuing long-term goals in life or in business. Martin Seligman, a professor of psychology at the University of Pennsylvania, once advised the MetLife insurance company to hire a special group of job applicants who tested high on optimism but failed the normal sales aptitude test. Compared to salespeople who passed the regular aptitude test but scored high on pessimism, the "optimistic" group made 21 percent more sales in their first year and 57 percent more in the second.[33]

Empathy, the fourth component, means being able to put yourself in someone else's shoes, to recognize what others are feeling without them needing to tell you. Most people never tell us what they feel in words but rather in tone of voice, body language, and facial expression. Empathy is built from self-awareness; being attuned to one's own emotions makes it easier to read and understand the feelings of others.

Social skill, the ability to connect to others, build positive relationships, respond to the emotions of others, and influence others, is the final component of emotional intelligence. Leaders use social skills to understand interpersonal relationships, handle disagreements, resolve conflicts, and bind people together for a common purpose. The ability to build relationships is essential in modern team-based organizations, but it is important for effective leadership in all organizations. Jerrold L. Miller, president of Earl Industries, Inc., a $35 million ship-repair business, explained that project managers who cannot handle relationships "really cost us a lot of money." When managers habitually say things to upset shipyard workers, Miller says, "the guys on the job are not as motivated to make this fellow look good. . . . They don't really care if his job is falling a little bit behind."[34]

Paul Wieand revamped his entire approach to leadership and founded the Center for Advanced Emotional Intelligence after he lost his job at Independence Bancorp.

IN THE LEAD   ### Paul Wieand, Center for Advanced Emotional Intelligence

Paul Wieand became president of Bucks County Bank at the age of 33, then masterminded mergers that tripled its size and turned it into a major regional institution. A year after the merger, the renamed Independence Bancorp ranked third in the nation on performance on assets. Wieand's future, as well as that of his organization, looked bright. Yet, only a few years later, he was forced to resign, and his world fell apart.

Today, Wieand sees how his arrogance and insensitivity contributed to his downfall. Instead of cultivating the older, established bankers of the institutions that Wieand had acquired, for example, he tried to force them out by freezing their salaries, taking away their responsibilities, and installing younger managers above them in the hierarchy. He refused to defer to the board of directors, instead pushing his own ideas and plans with little consideration for their feelings. "I started thinking that I knew better than everyone else," he now says. Wieand believes a lot of executives begin defining themselves by their "positions" and lose touch with their emotions. They begin to think they always know best, become intolerant of others' weaknesses, and grow insensitive to how their actions affect other people.

After he was fired, Weiand began reading extensively—some books by management thinkers like Peter Drucker, but mostly books by psychologists—to help him understand why running a bank was so easy intellectually but so hard emotionally. He enrolled in graduate school, pursuing a PhD in psychology. While working with patients in a psychiatric ward who had extremely high IQs but almost nonexistent social skills, he began developing his idea of "the learning leader." "I saw that everyone—whether they're patients in a psych ward or executives in a corporation—wants the same things in life: to be recognized, to be cared for, and to be given an opportunity to grow. And if you're authentic and trustful, people will realize that and they'll respond. . . ."

Wieand opened the Center for Advanced Emotional Intelligence to help leaders change how they think, process their emotions, and communicate with others. At the Center, leaders learn how to shift from leading by fear and intimidation to leading with heart. Still haunted by the pain he caused years ago at Independence Bancorp, Wieand sees his work as a sort of penance. "Being a leader is a hard job—maybe the hardest job there is," he says. "But once you've chosen it, you have a moral obligation to be your best self."[35]

Implications for Leadership

How is emotional intelligence related to effective leadership? For one thing, a leader's emotional abilities and understandings play a key role in charismatic leadership behavior, as described in the previous chapter.[36] Charismatic leaders generally hold strong emotional convictions about their personal values and beliefs and are emotionally expressive in dealing with followers. In addition, these leaders exhibit self-confidence, determination, and persistence in the face of adversity.

A high level of self-awareness, combined with the ability to manage one's own emotions, enables a leader to display self-confidence and earn the respect and trust of followers. In addition, the ability to manage or temporarily restrain one's emotions can enable a leader to objectively consider the needs of others over his or her own immediate feelings. Giving in to strong feelings of anger or depression, for example, may intensify a self-centered focus on one's own needs and limit the ability of the leader to understand the needs of others or see things from other perspectives.

The emotional state of the leader impacts the entire group, department, or organization. Leaders who are able to maintain balance and keep themselves motivated are positive role models to help motivate and inspire those around them. The energy level of the entire organization increases when leaders are optimistic and hopeful. The ability to empathize with others and to manage interpersonal relationships also contributes to motivation and inspiration because it helps leaders create feelings of unity and team spirit.

Perhaps most importantly, emotional intelligence enables leaders to recognize and respect followers as whole human beings with feelings, opinions, and ideas of their own. Empathy allows leaders to treat followers as individuals with unique needs, abilities, and dreams. Empathetic leaders can use their social skills to help followers grow and develop, see and enhance their self-image and feelings of self-worth, and help meet their needs and achieve their personal goals.

Emotionally intelligent leaders can have a positive impact on organizations by helping employees grow, learn, and develop; creating a sense of purpose and meaning; instilling unity and team spirit; and building relationships of trust and respect that allow each employee to take risks and fully contribute to the organization. Leaders who lead with the heart often can take the organization to a higher level of motivation and performance. In the final section of this chapter, we will focus on two key emotional categories and examine how leaders' emphasis on either *fear* or *love* impacts followers and the organization.

LEADING WITH LOVE VERSUS LEADING WITH FEAR

You wouldn't expect a high-ranking military officer to go around spouting talk about love, but that's exactly what Rear Admiral Al Konetzni (described earlier in this chapter) does. One of his favorite phrases is "I love you guys." He repeats variations of it dozens of times a day—to fellow admirals, sailors, and others he comes in contact with. Konetzni's leadership approach, of course, reflects his own personality and style—not all leaders would feel comfortable telling their employees they love them. However, many are finding that an environment that shows respect and trust for people is much more effective than one in which people are fearful.

Traditionally, leadership in many organizations has been based on fear. An unspoken notion among many senior-level executives is that fear is a good thing and benefits the organization.[37] Indeed, fear can be a powerful motivator. When organizational success depended primarily on people mindlessly following orders, leading with fear often met the organization's needs. Today, however, success depends on the knowledge, mind-power, commitment, and enthusiasm of everyone in the organization. In a tight labor market, a fear-based organization loses its best people, and the knowledge they take with them, to other firms. In addition, even if people stay with the organization, they typically don't perform up to their real capabilities.

One major drawback of leading with fear is that it creates avoidance behavior, because no one wants to make a mistake, and this inhibits growth and change. Leaders can learn to bind people together for a shared purpose through more positive forces such as caring and compassion, listening, and connecting to others on a personal level. The emotion that attracts people to take risks, learn, grow, and move the organization forward comes from love, not fear.

Showing respect and trust not only enables people to perform better; it also allows them to feel emotionally connected with their work so that their lives are richer and more balanced. Executives can rely on negative emotions such as fear to fuel productive work, but by doing so they may slowly destroy people's spirits, which ultimately is bad for employees and the organization.[38]

Fear in Organizations

The workplace can hold many kinds of fear, including fear of failure, fear of change, fear of personal loss, and fear of the boss. All of these fears can prevent employees from doing their best, from taking risks, from challenging and changing the status quo. Fear gets in the way of people feeling good about their work, themselves, and the organization. It can create an atmosphere in which people feel powerless, so that their confidence, commitment, enthusiasm, imagination, and motivation are diminished.[39]

ASPECTS OF FEAR   A particularly damaging aspect of fear in the workplace is that it can weaken trust and communication. Employees feel threatened by repercussions if they speak up about work-related concerns. A survey of employees in twenty-two organizations around the country found that 70 percent of them "bit their tongues" at work because they feared repercussions. Twenty-seven percent reported that they feared losing their credibility or reputation if they spoke up. Other fears reported were lack of career advancement, possible damage to the relationship with their supervisor, demotion or losing their job, and being embarrassed or humiliated in front of others.[40] When people are afraid to speak up, important issues are suppressed and problems hidden. Employees are afraid to talk about a wide range of issues. These "undiscussables" can range from the poor performance of a coworker to concerns over benefits to suggestions for organizational improvement. However, by far the largest category of undiscussables is the behavior of executives, particularly their interpersonal and relationship skills. When fear is high, managers destroy the opportunity for feedback, blinding them to reality and denying them the chance to correct damaging decisions and behaviors.

RELATIONSHIP WITH LEADERS   Leaders control the fear level in the organization. We all know from personal experience that it is easier to report bad news to some people than to others. A boss or teacher who is understanding and caring is much easier to approach than one who is likely to blow up and scream at us. The relationship between an employee and supervisor is the primary factor determining the level of fear experienced at work. The legacy of fear and mistrust associated with traditional hierarchies in which bosses gave orders and employees jumped to obey "or else" still colors organizational life. Leaders are responsible for creating a new environment that enables people to feel safe speaking their minds. Leaders can act from love rather than fear to free employees and the organization from the chains of the past.

Bringing Love to Work

When leaders act from their own fear, they create fear in others. Organizations have traditionally rewarded people for strong qualities such as rational thinking, ambition, and competitiveness. These qualities are important, but their overemphasis has left many organizational leaders out of touch with their softer, caring, creative capabilities, unable to make emotional connections with others and afraid to risk showing any sign of "weakness." A leader's fear can manifest itself in arrogance, selfishness, deception, unfairness, and disrespect for others.[41]

Leaders can learn to develop their capacity for the positive emotions of love and caring. Former president Ronald Reagan was a master at leading with love, and the country responded. He openly showed his deep love for his wife and publicly displayed tender feelings on the beach at Normandy and at the funeral services for the dead astronauts following the *Challenger* disaster.[42] C. William Pollard, chairman of ServiceMaster, credits the success of the organization he leads with his partner Carlos Cantu partly to an environment based on love rather than fear.

IN THE LEAD   ## C. William Pollard, ServiceMaster

ServiceMaster is a successful, dynamic company that cleans and maintains hospitals, schools, and other buildings. It's not a glamorous industry, and many of the jobs are menial and mundane—cleaning toilets, scrubbing floors, killing bugs. Entry-level employees are frequently uneducated, unskilled, and (as Pollard puts it), "more often than not, unnoticed."

But ServiceMaster has instilled their employees with a sense of dignity, responsibility, and meaningfulness by treating each worker with respect. Employees are well-trained, provided with quality tools and materials, and then empowered to make their own decisions—to do whatever is needed to provide top-notch service. Leaders at the company don't see their jobs as just getting people to perform at work. Instead, they see their role as helping employees become whole people—helping them grow as individuals who contribute not only at work but also at home and in the community. They care about how employees feel about themselves, about their work, and about the people they work with. ServiceMaster also insists that leaders make themselves available—they are out and about talking to followers, listening to their concerns, and their doors are always open.

Pollard describes the impact that leading with love has on workers by contrasting the attitudes of two service workers:

> "During a trip to Leningrad in 1989, I met a custodian named Olga. She had the job of mopping a lobby floor in a large hotel. I took an interest in her and her task and engaged her in conversation. . . . The reality of Olga's task was to perform the fewest motions in the greatest amount of time until the day was over. . . . No one had taken the time to teach or equip Olga or to care about her as a person. She was lost in a system that did not care. Work was just a job that had to be done.
>
> By contrast, I had an experience just a few days later while visiting a hospital that ServiceMaster serves in London, England. As I was introduced to one of the housekeepers as the chairman of ServiceMaster, she put her arms around me and gave me a big hug. . . . She then showed me all that she had accomplished in cleaning patient rooms, providing a detailed "before and after" ServiceMaster description. She was proud of her work . . . Someone had cared enough to show her the way and recognize her efforts when the task was done. She was looking forward to the next accomplishment."[43]

ServiceMaster believes in the worth and dignity of each person as an individual, and leaders put that value into action by creating and sustaining an environment that allows people to grow and develop. Leading with love rather than fear has also helped ServiceMaster grow rapidly.

We all know there are different kinds of love—for example, the love of a mother for her child, romantic love, brotherly love, or the love of country. Most of us have experienced at least one kind of love in our lives and therefore know the tremendous power it can have. Despite its power, the "L" word is often looked upon with suspicion in the business world.[44] However, there are a number of aspects of love that are directly relevant to work relationships and organizational performance.

Love as motivation is the force within that enables people to feel alive, connected, energized, and "in love" with life and work. Western cultures place great emphasis on the mind and the rational approach. However, it is the heart rather than the mind that powers people forward. Recall a time when you wanted to do something with all your heart, and how your energy and motivation flowed freely. Also recall a time when your head said you had to do a task, but your heart was not in it. Motivation is reduced, perhaps to the point of procrastination. Moreover, emotional attachments bind people together to jointly pursue a shared vision with creativity and enthusiasm. When leaders connect with their own emotions, they can connect with other people and create webs of relationships that release this emotional energy.

Love as feelings involves attraction, fascination, and caring for people, work, or other things. This is what people most often think of as love, particularly in relation to romantic love between two people. However, love as feelings is also relevant in work situations. Feelings of compassion and caring for others are a manifestation of love, as are forgiveness, sincerity, respect, and loyalty, all of which are important for healthy working relationships. One personal feeling is *bliss*, best articulated for the general public by Joseph Campbell in his PBS television series and companion book with Bill Moyers, *The Power of Myth*.[45] Finding your bliss means doing things that make you light up inside, things you do for the sheer joy of doing rather than for the material rewards. Most of us experience moments of this bliss when we become so absorbed in enjoyable work activities that we lose track of time. This type of feeling and caring about work is a major source of charisma. Everyone becomes more charismatic to others when they pursue an activity they truly care about.

Love as action means more than feelings; it is translated into behavior. Stephen Covey points out that in all the great literature, love is a verb rather than a noun.[46] Love is something you do, the sacrifices you make and the giving of yourself to others. The feelings of compassion, respect, and loyalty, for example, are translated into acts of friendliness, teamwork, cooperation, listening, and serving others. Feelings of unity and cooperation in organizations by leaders or followers translate into acts of helping, cooperation, sharing, and understanding. Sentiments emerge as action.

Why Followers Respond to Love

Leaders who lead with love have extraordinary influence because they meet five unspoken employee needs. Most people yearn for more than a paycheck from their jobs. The five unspoken requests are:

- Hear and understand me.

- Even if you disagree with me, please don't make me wrong.

- Acknowledge the greatness within me.

- Remember to look for my loving intentions.

- Tell me the truth with compassion.[47]

When leaders address these subtle emotional needs directly, people typically respond by loving their work and becoming emotionally engaged in solving problems and serving customers. Enthusiasm for work and the organization increases. People want to believe that their leaders genuinely care. From the followers' point of view, love versus fear has different motivational potential.

- **Fear-based motivation:** I need a job to pay for my basic needs (fulfilling lower needs of the body). You give me a job, and I will give you just enough to keep my job.

- **Love-based motivation:** If the job and the leader make me feel valued as a person and provide a sense of meaning and contribution to the community at large (fulfilling higher needs of heart, mind, and body), then I will give you all I have to offer.[48]

Many examples throughout this book will illustrate what happens when positive emotion is used. One management consultant went so far as to advise that finding creative ways to love could solve every imaginable leadership problem.[49] Rational thinking is important, but leading with love can build trust, stimulate creativity, inspire commitment, and create boundless energy in an organization.

SUMMARY AND INTERPRETATION

Leaders use intellectual as well as emotional capabilities and understandings to guide organizations through today's turbulent environment and help employees feel energized, motivated, and cared for in the face of rapid change, confusion, and job insecurity. Leaders can expand the capacities of their minds and hearts through conscious development and practice.

Leaders should be aware of how their mental models affect their thinking and may cause "blind spots" that limit understanding. Two components of mental models are assumptions and perceptions. Becoming aware of mental models is a first step toward being able to see the world in new and different ways. Four key issues important to expanding and developing a leader's mind are independent thinking, open-mindedness, systems thinking, and personal mastery. Leaders should also understand the importance of emotional intelligence. Five basic components of emotional intelligence are self-awareness, managing emotions, motivating oneself, empathy, and social skills. Emotionally intelligent leaders can have a positive impact on organizations by helping employees grow, learn, and develop; creating a sense of purpose and meaning; instilling unity and team spirit; and basing relationships on trust and respect, which allows employees to take risks and fully contribute to the organization.

Traditional organizations have relied on fear as a motivator. While fear does motivate people, it prevents people from feeling good about their work and often causes avoidance behavior. Fear can reduce trust and communication so that important problems and issues are hidden or suppressed. Leaders can choose to lead with love instead of fear. Love can be thought of as a motivational force that enables people to feel alive, connected, and energized; as feelings of liking, caring, and bliss; and as actions of helping, listening, and cooperating. Each of these aspects of love has relevance for organizational relationships. People respond to love because it meets unspoken needs for respect and affirmation. Rational thinking is important to leadership, but it takes love to build trust, creativity, and enthusiasm.

KEY TERMS

capacity	systems thinking	empathy
mental models	personal mastery	social skill
stereotyping	self-awareness	fear-based motivation
independent thinking	managing emotions	love-based motivation
mindfulness	motivating oneself	

DISCUSSION QUESTIONS

1. How do you feel about developing the emotional qualities of yourself and other people in the organization as a way to be an effective leader? Discuss.

2. Do you agree that people have a capacity for developing their minds and hearts beyond current competency? Can you give an example? Discuss.

3. What are some specific reasons leaders need to be aware of their mental models?

4. Discuss the similarity and differences between mental models and open-mindedness.

5. What is the concept of personal mastery? How important is it to a leader?

6. Which of the five elements of emotional intelligence do you consider most essential to an effective leader? Why?

7. Consider fear and love as potential motivators. Which is the best source of motivation for soldiers during a war? For members of a new product development team? For top executives at a media conglomerate? Why?

8. Have you ever experienced love and/or fear from leaders at work? How did you respond?

LEADERSHIP DEVELOPMENT: PERSONAL FEEDBACK

Emotional Intelligence

For each item below, rate how well you are able to display the ability described. Before responding, try to think of actual situations in which you have had the opportunity to use the ability.

Very Slight Ability   **Moderate Ability**   **Very Much Ability**

1   2   3   4   5

1. Associate different internal physiological cues with different emotions.
2. Relax when under pressure in situations.
3. "Gear up" at will for a task.
4. Know the impact that your behavior has on others.
5. Initiate successful resolution of conflict with others.
6. Calm yourself quickly when angry.
7. Know when you are becoming angry.
8. Regroup quickly after a setback.
9. Recognize when others are distressed.
10. Build consensus with others.
11. Know what senses you are currently using.
12. Use internal "talk" to change your emotional state.
13. Produce motivation when doing uninteresting work.
14. Help others manage their emotions.
15. Make others feel good.
16. Identify when you experience mood shifts.
17. Stay calm when you are the target of anger from others.
18. Stop or change an ineffective habit.
19. Show empathy to others.
20. Provide advice and emotional support to others as needed.
21. Know when you become defensive.
22. Know when you are thinking negatively and head it off.
23. Follow your words with actions.
24. Engage in intimate conversations with others.
25. Accurately reflect people's feelings back to them.

Scoring

Sum your responses to the twenty-five questions to obtain your overall emotional intelligence score. Your score for self-awareness is the total of questions 1, 6, 11, 16, and 21. Your score for managing emotions is the total of questions 2, 7, 12, 17, and 22. Your score for motivating yourself is the sum of questions 3, 8, 13, 18, and 23. Your score for empathy is the sum of questions 4, 9, 14, 19, and 24. Your score for social skill is the sum of questions 5, 10, 15, 20, and 25.

Interpretation

This questionnaire provides some indication of your emotional intelligence. If you received a total score of 100 or more, you are certainly considered a person with high emotional intelligence. A score from 50 to 100 means you have a good platform of emotional intelligence from which to develop your leadership capability. A score below 50 indicates that you realize that you are probably below average in emotional intelligence. For each of the five components of emotional intelligence—self-awareness, managing emotions, motivating one's self, empathy, and social skill—a score above 20 is considered high, while a score below 10 would be considered low. Review the discussion earlier in this chapter of the five components of emotional intelligence and think about what you might do to develop those areas where you scored low. Compare your scores to those of other students. What will you do to improve your scores?

SOURCE: Adapted from Hendrie Weisinger, *Emotional Intelligence at Work* (San Francisco: Jossey-Bass, 1998), 214–215.

LEADERSHIP DEVELOPMENT: Cases for Analysis

The New Boss

Sam Nolan clicked the mouse for one more round of solitaire on the computer in his den. He'd been at it for more than an hour, and his wife had long ago given up trying to persuade him to join her for a movie or a rare Saturday night on the town. The mind-numbing game seemed to be all that calmed Sam down enough to stop agonizing about work and how his job seemed to get worse every day.

Nolan was Chief Information Officer at Century Medical, a large medical products company based in Connecticut. He had joined the company four years ago and since that time Century had made great progress integrating technology into its systems and processes. Nolan had already led projects to design and build two highly successful systems for Century. One was a benefits-administration system for the company's human resources department. The other was a complex Web-based purchasing system that streamlined the process of purchasing supplies and capital goods. Although the system had been up and running for only a few months, modest projections were that it would save Century nearly $2 million annually. The new Web-based system dramatically cut the time needed for processing requests and placing orders. Purchasing managers now had more time to work collaboratively with key stakeholders to identify and select the best suppliers and negotiate better deals.

Nolan thought wearily of all the hours he had put in developing trust with people throughout the company and showing them how technology could not only save time and money but also support team-based work, encourage open information sharing, and give people more control over their own jobs. He smiled briefly as he recalled one long-term HR employee, 61-year-old Ethel Moore. She had been terrified when Nolan first began showing her the company's intranet, but she was now one of his biggest supporters. In fact, it had been Ethel who had first approached him with an idea about a Web-based job posting system. The two had pulled together a team and developed an idea for linking Century managers, internal recruiters, and job applicants using artificial intelligence software on top of an integrated Web-based system. When Nolan had presented the idea to his boss, executive vice-president Sandra Ivey, she had enthusiastically endorsed it. Within a few weeks the team had authorization to proceed with the project.

But everything began to change when Ivey resigned her position six months later to take a plum job in New York. Ivey's successor, Tom Carr, seemed to have little interest in the project. During their first meeting, Carr had openly referred to the project as a waste of time and money. He immediately disapproved several new features suggested by the company's internal recruiters, even though the project team argued that the features could double internal hiring and save millions in training costs. "Just stick to the original plan and get it done. All this stuff needs to be handled on a personal basis anyway," Carr countered. "You can't learn more from a computer than you can talking to real people—and as for internal recruiting, it shouldn't be so hard to talk to people if they're already working right here in the company." Carr seemed to have no understanding of how and why technology was being used. He became irritated when Ethel Moore referred to the system as "Web-based." He boasted that he had never visited Century's intranet site and suggested that "this Internet fad" would blow over in a year or so anyway. Even Ethel's enthusiasm couldn't get through to him. "Technology is for those people in the IS department. My job is people and yours should be too." Near the end of the meeting, Carr even jokingly suggested that the project team should just buy a couple of good filing cabinets and save everyone some time and money.

Nolan sighed and leaned back in his chair. The whole project had begun to feel like a joke. The vibrant and innovative human resources department his team had imagined now seemed like nothing more than a pipe dream. But despite his frustration, a new thought entered Nolan's mind: "Is Carr just stubborn and narrow-minded or does he have a point that HR is a people business that doesn't need a high-tech job posting system?"

SOURCE: Based on Carol Hildebrand, "New Boss Blues," *CIO Enterprise,* Section 2, November 15, 1998, 53–58; and Megan Santosus, "Advanced Micro Devices' Web-Based Purchasing System," *CIO,* Section 1, May 15, 1998, 84. A version of this case originally appeared in Richard L. Daft, *Organization Theory and Design,* 7th ed. (Cincinnati, OH: South-Western College Publishing, 2001), 270–271.

Questions

1. Describe the two different mental models represented in this story.

2. What are some of the assumptions and perceptions that shape the mindset of Sam Nolan? Of Tom Carr?

3. Do you think it is possible for Carr to shift to a new mental model? If you were Sam Nolan, what would you do?

The USS Florida

The atmosphere in a Trident nuclear submarine is generally calm and quiet. Even pipe joints are cushioned to prevent noise that might tip off a pursuer. The Trident ranks among the world's most dangerous weapons—swift, silent, armed with 24 long-range missiles carrying 192 nuclear warheads. Trident crews are the cream of the Navy crop, and even the sailors who fix the plumbing exhibit a white-collar decorum. The culture aboard ship is a low-key, collegial one in which sailors learn to speak softly and share close quarters with an ever-changing roster of shipmates. Being subject to strict security restrictions enhances a sense of elitism and pride. To move up and take charge of a Trident submarine is an extraordinary feat in the Navy—fewer than half the officers qualified for such commands ever get them. When Michael Alfonso took charge of the USS *Florida,* the crew welcomed his arrival. They knew he was one of them—a career Navy man who joined up as a teenager and moved up through the ranks. Past shipmates remembered him as basically a loner, who could be brusque but generally pleasant enough. Neighbors on shore found Alfonso to be an unfailingly polite man who kept mostly to himself.

The crew's delight in their new captain was short-lived. Commander Alfonso moved swiftly to assume command, admonishing his sailors that he would push them hard. He wasn't joking—soon after the *Florida* slipped into deep waters to begin a postoverhaul shakedown cruise, the new captain loudly and publicly reprimanded those whose performance he considered lacking. Chief Petty Officer Donald MacArthur, chief of the navigation division, was only one of those who suffered Alfonso's anger personally. During training exercises, MacArthur was having trouble keeping the boat at periscope depth because of rough seas. Alfonso announced loudly, "You're disqualified." He then precipitously relieved him of his diving duty until he could be recertified by extra practice. Word of the incident spread quickly. The crew, accustomed to the Navy's adage of "praise in public, penalize in private," were shocked. It didn't take long for this type of behavior to have an impact on the crew, according to Petty Officer Aaron Carmody: "People didn't tell him when something was wrong. You're not supposed to be afraid of your captain, to tell him stuff. But nobody wanted to."

The captain's outbursts weren't always connected with job performance. He bawled out the supply officer, the executive officer, and the chief of the boat because the soda dispenser he used to pour himself a glass of Coke one day contained Mr. Pibb instead. He exploded when he arrived unexpected at a late-night meal and found the fork at his place setting missing. Soon, a newsletter titled *The Underground* was being circulated by the boat's plumbers, who used sophomoric humor to spread the word about the captain's outbursts over such petty matters. By the time the sub reached Hawaii for its "Tactical Readiness Evaluation," an intense week-long series of inspections by staff officers, the crew was almost completely alienated. Although the ship tested well, inspectors sent word to Rear Admiral Paul Sullivan that something seemed to be wrong on board, with severely strained relations between captain and crew. On the Trident's last evening of patrol, much of the crew celebrated with a film night—they chose *The Caine Mutiny* and *Crimson Tide*, both movies about Navy skippers who face mutinies and are relieved of command at sea. When Humphrey Bogart, playing the captain of the fictional USS *Caine*, exploded over a missing quart of strawberries, someone shouted, "Hey, sound familiar?"

When they reached home port, the sailors slumped ashore. "Physically and mentally, we were just beat into the ground," recalls one. Concerned about reports that the crew seemed "despondent," Admiral Sullivan launched an informal inquiry that eventually led him to relieve Alfonso of his command. It was the first-ever firing of a Trident submarine commander. "He had the chance of a lifetime to experience the magic of command, and he squandered it," Sullivan said. "Fear and intimidation lead to certain ruin." Alfonso himself seemed dumbfounded by Admiral Sullivan's actions, pointing out that the USS *Florida* under his command posted "the best-ever grades assigned for certifications and inspections for a postoverhaul Trident submarine."

SOURCE: Thomas E. Ricks, "A Skipper's Chance to Run a Trident Sub Hits Stormy Waters," *The Wall Street Journal,* November 20, 1997, A1, A6.

Questions

1. Analyze Alfonso's impact on the crew in terms of love versus fear. What might account for the fact that he behaved so strongly as captain of the USS *Florida?*

2. Which do you think a leader should be more concerned about aboard a nuclear submarine—high certification grades or high-quality interpersonal relationships? Do you agree with Admiral Sullivan's decision to fire Alfonso? Discuss.

3. Discuss Commander Alfonso's level of emotional intelligence in terms of the five components listed in the chapter. What advice would you give him?

REFERENCES

1. Scott Kirsner, "Dorothy Lane Loves Its Customers," *Fast Company,* June 1999, 76–78.

2. Lester C. Thurow, "Peter's Principles," *Boston Magazine,* January 1998, 89–90; Michele Morris, "The New Breed of Leaders: Taking Charge in a Different Way," *Working Woman,* March 1990, 73–75; and Stanley Bing, "Executive Shelf Life," *Esquire,* June 1992, 69–70.

3. Robert B. French, "The Teacher as Container of Anxiety: Psychoanalysis and the Role of Teacher," *Journal of Management Education* 21, No. 4 (November 1997), 483–495.

4. This basic idea is found in a number of sources, among them: Jack Hawley, *Reawakening the Spirit in Work* (San Francisco: Berrett-Koehler, 1993); Aristotle, *The Nicomachean Ethics,* trans. by the Brothers of the English Dominican Province, rev. by Daniel J. Sullivan (Chicago: Encyclopedia Britannica, 1952); Alasdair MacIntyre, *After Virtue: A Study in Moral Theory* (Notre Dame, IN: University of Notre Dame Press, 1984); and Stephen Covey, *The Seven Habits of Highly Effective People: Powerful Lessons in Personal Change* (New York: Fireside Books/Simon & Schuster, 1990).

5. Peter M. Senge, *The Fifth Discipline: The Art and Practice of the Learning Organization* (New York: Doubleday, 1990); and Peter Senge with Art Kleiner, Charlotte Roberts, Richard Ross, George Roth, and Bryan Smith, *The Dance of Change: The Challenges of Sustaining Momentum in Learning Organizations* (New York: Currency/Doubleday, 1999), 32, 184–185.

6. This discussion is based partly on Robert C. Benfari, *Understanding and Changing Your Management Style* (San Francisco: Jossey-Bass, 1999), 66–93.

7. George Anders, "Can Old-School CEO and Wired Progeny Bridge Internet Gap?" *The Wall Street Journal,* June 15, 1999, A1, A6.

8. Geoffrey Colvin, "The Most Valuable Quality in a Manager," *Fortune,* December 29, 1997, 279–280; and Marlene Piturro, "Mindshift," *Management Review,* May 1999, 46–51.

9. Hal Lancaster, "Take on Tough Jobs, Assess Your Own Work, and Other Life Lessons" (Managing Your Career column), *The Wall Street Journal,* December 7, 1999, B1.

10. Benfari, *Understanding and Changing Your Management Style,* 76.

11. Thomas A. Stewart, "How to Leave It All Behind," *Fortune,* December 6, 1999, 345–348.

12. Greg Jaffe, "How Admiral Konetzni Intends to Mend Navy's Staff Woes," *The Wall Street Journal,* July 6, 2000, A1, A6.

13. Ellen Langer and John Sviokla, "An Evaluation of Charisma from the Mindfulness Perspective," unpublished manuscript, Harvard University. Part of this discussion is also drawn from Richard L. Daft and Robert H. Lengel, *Fusion Leadership: Unlocking the Subtle Forces that Change People and Organizations* (San Francisco: Berrett-Koehler, 1998).

14. T. K. Das, "Educating Tomorrow's Managers: The Role of Critical Thinking," *The International Journal of Organizational Analysis* 2, No. 4 (October 1994), 333–360.

15. Rebecca Quick, "A Makeover That Began at the Top," *The Wall Street Journal,* May 25, 2000, B1, B4.

16. The Pike Syndrome has been discussed in multiple sources.

17. James Gleick, *Genius: The Life and Science of Richard Feynman* (New York: Pantheon Books, 1992).

18. Chris Argyris, *Flawed Advice and the Management Trap* (New York: Oxford University Press, 2000); and Eileen C. Shapiro, "Managing in the Cappuccino Economy" (review of *Flawed Advice*), *Harvard Business Review,* March-April 2000, 177–183.

19. Anna Muoio, ed. "The Art of Smart" (Unit of One column), *Fast Company,* July-August 1999, 85–102.

20. Quoted in *Fast Company,* September 1999, 120.

21. Oren Harari, "Mind Matters," *Management Review,* January 1996, 47–49.

22. Bernard M. Bass, *Leadership and Performance Beyond Expectations* (New York: The Free Press, 1985); and *New Paradigm Leadership: An Inquiry into Transformational Leadership* (Alexandria, VA: U.S. Army Research Institute for the Behavioral and Social Sciences, 1996).

23. This section is based on Peter M. Senge, *The Fifth Discipline: The Art and Practice of the Learning Organization* (New York: Doubleday, 1990).

24. Peter M. Senge, Charlotte Roberts, Richard B. Ross, Bryan J. Smith, and Art Kleiner, *The Fifth Discipline Fieldbook* (New York: Currency/Doubleday, 1994), 87.

25. Senge, *The Fifth Discipline.*
26. Daniel Goleman, *Emotional Intelligence: Why It Can Matter More Than IQ* (New York: Bantam Books, 1995); Pamela Kruger, "A Leader's Journey," *Fast Company,* June 1999, 116–129; Hendrie Weisinger, *Emotional Intelligence at Work* (San Francisco: Jossey-Bass, 1998).
27. Donna Fenn, "Personnel Best," *Inc.,* February 2000, 75–83.
28. Michelle Conlin, "Tough Love for Techie Souls," *Business Week,* November 29, 1999, 164–170.
29. Ibid.
30. This section is based largely on Daniel Goleman, *Emotional Intelligence: Why It Can Matter More Than IQ* (New York: Bantam Books, 1995), 289–290.
31. Based on Goleman, *Emotional Intelligence;* Sharon Nelton, "Emotions in the Workplace" *Nation's Business,* February 1996, 25–30; and Lara E. Megerian and John J. Sosik, "An Affair of the Heart: Emotional Intelligence and Transformational Leadership," *The Journal of Leadership Studies* 3, No. 3 (1996), 31–48.
32. Hendrie Weisinger, *Emotional Intelligence at Work* (San Francisco: Jossey-Bass, 1998).
33. Alan Farnham, "Are You Smart Enough to Keep Your Job?" *Fortune,* January 15, 1996, 34–47.
34. Nelton, "Emotions in the Workplace."
35. Pamela Kruger, "A Leader's Journey," *Fast Company,* June 1999, 116–129.
36. Based on Megerian and Sosik, "An Affair of the Heart."
37. Kathleen D. Ryan and Daniel K. Oestreich, *Driving Fear Out of the Workplace: How to Overcome the Invisible Barriers to Quality, Productivity, and Innovation* (San Francisco: Jossey-Bass, 1991).
38. David E. Dorsey, "Escape from the Red Zone," *Fast Company,* April/May 1997, 116–127.
39. This section is based on Ryan and Oestreich, *Driving Fear Out of the Workplace;* and Therese R. Welter, "Reducing Employee Fear: Get Workers and Managers to Speak Their Minds," *Small Business Reports,* April 1991, 15–18.
40. Ryan and Oestreich, *Driving Fear Out of the Workplace,* 43.
41. Donald G. Zauderer, "Integrity: An Essential Executive Quality," *Business Forum,* Fall 1992, 12–16.
42. Marshall Manley, "Going Beyond 'the Issues'," *Newsweek,* January 18, 1988, 8.
43. C. William Pollard, "The Leader Who Serves," in *The Leader of the Future,* Frances Hesselbein, Marshall Goldsmith, and Richard Beckhard, eds. (San Francisco: Jossey-Bass 1996), 241–248.
44. Jack Hawley, *Reawakening the Spirit at Work* (San Francisco: Berrett-Koehler, 1993), 55; and Rodney Ferris, "How Organizational Love Can Improve Leadership," *Organizational Dynamics,* 16, No. 4 (Spring 1988), 40–52.
45. Joseph Campbell with Bill Moyers, *The Power of Myth* (New York: Doubleday, 1988).

46. Stephen R. Covey, *The Seven Habits of Highly Effective People: Powerful Lessons in Personal Change* (New York: Fireside/Simon & Schuster, 1990), 80.
47. Hyler Bracey, Jack Rosenblum, Aubrey Sanford, and Roy Trueblood, *Managing from the Heart* (New York: Dell Publishing, 1993), 192.
48. Madan Birla with Cecilia Miller Marshall, *Balanced Life and Leadership Excellence* (Memphis, TN: The Balance Group, 1997), 76–77.
49. Ferris, "How Organizational Love Can Improve Leadership."

CHAPTER OUTLINE

YOUR LEADERSHIP CHALLENGE

After reading this chapter, you should be able to:

- Combine a rational approach to leadership with a concern for people and ethics.

- Recognize your own stage of moral development and ways to accelerate your moral maturation.

- Apply the principles of stewardship and servant leadership.

- Know and use mechanisms that enhance an ethical organizational culture.

- Recognize courage in others and unlock your own potential to live and act courageously.

Courage and Moral Leadership

During the waning months of World War II, a young man climbed atop the roof of a train ready to start for Auschwitz. Ignoring shouts—and later bullets—from Nazis and soldiers of the Hungarian Arrow Cross, he began handing fake Swedish passports to the astonished Jews inside and ordering them to walk to a caravan of cars marked in Swedish colors. By the time the cars were loaded, the soldiers were so dumbfounded by the young man's actions that they simply stood by and let the cars pass, carrying to safety dozens of Jews who had been headed for the death camps.

Virtually alone in Hungary, one of the most perilous places in Europe in 1944, Raoul Wallenberg worked such miracles on a daily basis, using as his weapons courage, self-confidence, and his deep, unwavering belief in the rightness of his mission. His deeds inspired hope, courage, and action in many people who otherwise felt powerless. Wallenberg became a symbol of good in a world dominated by evil, and a reminder of the hidden strength of the human spirit. No one knows how many people he directly or indirectly saved from certain death, though it is estimated at more than 100,000.

Wallenberg was thirty-two years old in 1944, a wealthy, politically connected, upper-class Swede from a prominent, well-respected family. When asked by the U.S. War Refugee Board to enter Hungary and help stop Hitler's slaughter of innocent civilians, Wallenberg had everything to lose and nothing to gain. Yet he left his life of safety and comfort to enter Hungary under cover as a diplomat, with the mission of saving as many of Hungary's Jews as possible. Wallenberg boldly demanded—and was granted—a great deal of latitude in the methods he would use. He personally conceived the plan to use false Swedish passports and designed them himself as masterpieces of the formal, official-looking pomp that so impressed the Nazis. Later, as Wallenberg plunged into the midst of the struggle to free Jews from the trains and death marches, he convinced his enemies to accept such things as library cards and laundry tickets as Swedish passports. The Nazi and Hungarian Arrow Cross soldiers, accustomed to yielding unquestioningly to authority, yielded to Wallenberg on the strength of his character, personal authority, and courage.

Wallenberg never returned from Hungary, but apparently was captured as a suspected anti-Soviet spy, and died in a Soviet prison. He gave up his life fighting for a cause he believed in, and his actions made a real difference in the world. In the Avenue of the Righteous, a grove of trees planted in Israel to memorialize those who risked their lives to help Jews during the Holocaust, Wallenberg's medal summarizes his mission with the words, "Whoever saves a single soul, it is as if he had saved the whole world."[1]

Raoul Wallenberg emerged from a dismal period in human history as a courageous leader who made the ultimate sacrifice for what he believed. Most leaders never have the opportunity to save lives, and few leaders help as many people as Wallenberg did. In recognition of this fact, Congress made Wallenberg only the second person ever to be awarded honorary U.S. citizenship (the other was Winston Churchill). On that occasion, one television commentator spoke for millions when he said, "It is human beings such as Raoul Wallenberg that make life worth living." The principles of leadership he demonstrated are valuable to anyone who aspires to make a real and positive difference in the world.

One of the primary lessons from Wallenberg's life is that being a real leader means learning who you are and what you stand for, and then having the courage to act. Leaders demonstrate confidence and commitment in what they believe and what they do. A deep devotion to a cause or a purpose larger than one's self sparks the courage to act. In addition, Wallenberg's story demonstrates that leadership has less to do with using other people than with *serving* other people. Placing others ahead of oneself is a key to successful leadership, whether in politics, war, education, sports, social services, or business.

This chapter explores ideas related to courage and moral leadership. In the previous chapter, we discussed mind and heart, two of the three elements that come together for successful leadership. This chapter focuses on the third element, spirit—on the ability to look within, to contemplate the human condition, to think about what is right and wrong, to see what really "matters" in the world, and to have the courage to stand up for what is worthy and right. We will begin by examining the situation in which most organizations currently operate and the dilemma leaders face in the modern world. The next sections will discuss how leaders develop the capacity for moral reasoning and examine the importance of stewardship and servant leadership. We will then examine the ways in which leaders can create an ethical climate in their organizations. The final sections of the chapter will explore what courage means and how leaders develop the courage needed for moral leadership to flourish.

MORAL LEADERSHIP TODAY

In recent years, numerous companies, including Prudential Insurance, Archer-Daniels-Midland, and Centennial Technology, have been charged with breaches of ethical or legal standards, including price fixing and insider trading. Sears, which has already endured one scandal concerning its auto centers, was recently hit with another lawsuit alleging that the company charged customers for tire balancing that wasn't done. W. R. Grace & Co. and its former subsidiary Baker & Taylor, a national book distributor, admitted no wrongdoing but recently paid millions of dollars to settle allegations that they overcharged schools, libraries, and government agencies for books that were discounted by publishers.[2] The world of cyberspace is opening new avenues for potential ethical lapses. Alibris, an online bookseller specializing in rare books, pled guilty to a charge of intercepting e-mail messages sent by Amazon.com to customers. Former iVillage executives have accused the company of cheating employees out of promised stock options and engaging in inappropriate accounting practices that inflate revenues.[3] In a Gallup poll asking about the trustworthiness of six American institutions, only the U.S. government scored lower than U.S. corporations.[4]

The Ethical Climate in U.S. Business

Ethical and legal lapses occur at all levels of the U.S. workforce. More than 54 percent of human resource professionals polled by the Society for Human Resource Management and the Ethics Resource Center reported observing employees lying to supervisors or coworkers, falsifying reports or records, or abusing drugs or alcohol while on the job.[5] Moreover, 48 percent of workers admit to ethical violations ranging from abuse of sick leave to theft of cash or merchandise. The Association of Certified Fraud Examiners, a trade group, estimates that unethical or criminal acts by employees cost U.S. businesses more than $400 billion a year.[6]

When organizational leaders operate from principles of selfishness and greed, many employees come to see unethical behavior as okay. Several years ago, managers at Bausch & Lomb's Hong Kong division say they resorted to corrupt practices such as faking sales and shipping products that customers never ordered because of intense pressure from top managers to maintain sales and earnings growth.[7] Companies that encourage their employees to do the right thing—and whose leaders model that behavior—have fewer ethical problems. Clark Construction Company of Lansing, Michigan, which operates in an industry known for litigation, has never sued or been sued in its fifty-year history because leaders set and maintain high ethical standards.[8] In general, employees will be as ethical in doing their jobs as their leaders are in performing their own duties.

Virtually every survey about the qualities most desired in a leader reports honesty and integrity as the most important attributes.[9] Unfortunately, the public perception of business and political leaders is dismal. Fifty-five percent of the American public believe the vast majority of corporate executives are dishonest, and 59 percent believe white-collar crime occurs on a regular basis.[10] However, the news is not all bad. In an encouraging shift of public opinion, only 15 percent of U.S. workers believe dishonesty and selfishness are a necessary byproduct of business.[11] The public is tired of unethical and socially irresponsible business practices. Leaders are responsible for improving the cultures and systems that lead to ethical lapses. One example is how Peter Holt has made ethical values a core part of his organization's culture.

IN THE LEAD   Peter Holt, Holt Companies

Peter Holt believes everyone at the Holt Companies, from the CEO on down, is responsible for upholding the organization's ethics. Ethical values are woven into the organizational culture, and Holt continually works to renew the values and signal his total commitment to them.

Holt began developing his approach to ethics in the mid-1980s after joining the company founded by his great-grandfather a century ago. He first involved the entire workforce in determining a set of core values that would guide everything the company did. The final list puts ethical values—being honest, showing integrity, being consistent, and providing fair treatment—at the top, followed in order by values of attaining success through meeting goals, achieving continuous improvement, commitment to the long-term health of the company, and pursuing new strategic opportunities through creativity and change.

All new employees attend a two-day training program, where they learn about the values and discuss values-related cases and dilemmas. In addition, the Holt Companies presents a two-day ethics awareness course for all managers and supervisors. Most importantly, Peter Holt visits each of the firm's locations twice a year to meet with employees, disclose financial information, answer questions, and talk about the importance of each employee upholding Holt's core values every day in every action. The close involvement of the CEO and other top leaders has contributed to an environment of candor and respect between management and workers. Importantly, Holt's evaluation and reward systems are also tied to how well managers and employees live the values in their everyday actions.[12]

By integrating ethics throughout the organization, leaders make personal and organizational integrity a part of day-to-day business. Holt's ethical leadership approach was not an overnight success; it took several years to develop the trust that is central to an ethical culture. However, when employees are convinced that ethical values play a key role in all leadership decisions and actions, they can also commit to making ethics a part of their everyday behavior.

The Leadership Dilemma

Leaders shape the ethical choices and decisions of followers in the workplace. However, leaders may face a dilemma because of a perceived conflict between the realm of business and the realm of ethics. As philosopher Peter Koestenbaum, who has consulted with leaders at some of the world's largest companies, puts it: "How do we cope with a brutal business reality and still preserve human values? How do we handle competition without becoming either the kind of fool who allows it to crush us or the kind of fool who forgets people?"[13]

The domain of business is one of hard, measurable facts—market studies, production costs, managed inventory, stock value, profit and loss statements, and rational analysis. Ethics, on the other hand, is in the "soft" almost impossible to measure realm of human meaning, purpose, quality, significance, and values. Whereas the realm of business can be dissected, diagnosed, and compared, the realm of ethics doesn't lend itself to precise interpretation, comparison, and evaluation.[14] Modern society has created a forced separation between the two, but there is a growing recognition of the need to bring them back together. Business cannot be separated from the basic human issue of how people treat one another. The same moral and ethical questions that confront individuals also face businesses and other organizations. As Henry Ford, Sr., once said, "For a long time people believed that the only purpose of industry was to make a profit. They are wrong. Its purpose is to serve the general welfare."[15] The challenge for today's leadership is to merge the hard and the soft, the rational and the ethical, to create organizations that profit while truly "serving the general welfare." This chapter's Leader's Bookshelf argues for a spiritual foundation to business that can strengthen organizations and enrich the lives of employees.

EXHIBIT 6.1

Comparing Personal Qualities of Purely Rational versus Ethical Leaders

Rational Leader	Ethical Leader
Concerned primarily with self and own goals and career advancement	Considers others equal to self, shows concern for development of others
Uses power for personal gain or impact	Uses power to serve others
Promotes own personal vision	Aligns vision with followers' needs and aspirations
Denounces critical or opposing views	Considers and learns from criticism
Demands decisions be accepted without question	Stimulates followers to think independently and to question the leader's view
Insensitive to followers' needs	Coaches, develops, and supports followers, shares recognition with others
Relies on convenient external moral standards to satisfy self-interests	Relies on internal moral standards to satisfy organizational and societal interests

SOURCE: Jane M. Howell and Bruce J. Avolio, "The Ethics of Charismatic Leadership: Submission or Liberation?" *Academy of Management Executive* 6, No. 2 (1992), 43–54.

Ethical leadership does not mean ignoring profit and loss, production costs, and so forth. Ethical leadership combines a concern for the rational measures of performance with a recognition of the importance of treating people right every day. Exhibit 6.1 compares the characteristics of leaders who follow a strictly rational self-interest approach with those who take an ethical approach. Rational leadership focuses primarily on self, whereas ethical leadership is about others. Ethical leadership is the primary route through which organizations become ethical. A first step toward developing into an ethical leader is recognizing the stages of moral development.

BECOMING A MORAL LEADER

Is leadership moral or amoral? If leadership is merely a set of practices, with no association with right or wrong, it would be amoral. But all leadership practices can be used for good or evil and thus have a moral dimension. Leaders choose whether to act in ways that diminish others or in ways that inspire and

LEADER'S BOOKSHELF

Managing with the Wisdom of Love: Uncovering Virtue in People and Organizations

Dorothy Marcic

The changes and challenges faced by today's organizations have spurred a new leadership paradigm based on concepts such as vision, commitment, empowerment, and accountability. All of these concepts, argues Dorothy Marcic, can become more than just words when leaders recognize that work—like life and personal relationships—is enriched by a spiritual foundation. Quoting extensively from major religious texts, Marcic illustrates the similar messages in a variety of religions and demonstrates the application of this spiritual wisdom to organizations. By citing figures of faith such as Buddha, Jesus Christ, and Bahá'u'lláh, the founder of the Baha'i tradition, Marcic distills five "new management virtues" that can provide a necessary balance among the physical, intellectual, emotional, volitional (willingness to change for the better), and spiritual dimensions of work.

New Management Virtues

These five virtues form a philosophical and spiritual foundation for the issues leaders struggle with every day and for the relationships between a leader and others.

- **Trustworthiness** This virtue corresponds to the organizational issue of accountability or stewardship. It means being honest, behaving ethically, and building relationships with customers and employees based on integrity.

- **Unity** Unity is the foundation for shared vision, commitment, and reciprocity. Unity in action means seeking unanimity in important decisions, satisfying customers, going from controlling to coaching.

- **Respect and Dignity** An attitude of respect and dignity is the basis for true empowerment. Leaders listen, act as coaches and mentors, create self-determining teams, and reward and appreciate workers for their contributions.

- **Justice** The virtue of justice corresponds to equal opportunity and profit sharing in organizations. Leading with justice means treating everyone fairly, eliminating barriers to equal opportunity, and providing equitable compensation and profit sharing.

- **Service and Humility** In organizations, service corresponds to the emphasis on quality and customer satisfaction. Truly serving others means being a servant to employees and customers. Leaders who embrace the virtue of service and humility share power, admit mistakes, and trust others.

Virtues at Work

When leaders go about their work and relate to others according to a spiritual foundation, they cultivate virtue in others by creating a balance in the work lives of organizational members. Marcic emphasizes that spirituality is not a quick fix but a process that takes time, commitment, and effort. Leaders can make a commitment to long-term organizational health and base their behavior on these five virtues to develop happier, more committed employees and stronger organizations.

Managing with the Wisdom of Love, by Dorothy Marcic, is published by Jossey-Bass.

motivate others to develop to their full potential as employees and as human beings.[16] **Moral leadership** is about distinguishing right from wrong and doing right, seeking the just, the honest, the good, and the right conduct in its practice. Leaders have great influence over others, and moral leadership gives life to others and enhances the lives of others. Immoral leadership takes away from others in order to enhance oneself.[17] Leaders who would do evil toward others, such as Hitler, Stalin, or Cambodia's Pol Pot, are immoral, while Raoul Wallenberg typifies the height of moral leadership. Moral leadership uplifts people, enabling them to be better than they were without the leader.

Specific personality characteristics such as ego strength, self-confidence, and a sense of independence may enable leaders to behave morally in the face of opposition. Moreover, leaders can develop these characteristics through their own hard work. For example, Raoul Wallenberg made a concentrated effort to understand his enemies. His understanding of the Nazis' fear of those who displayed power gave him the self-confidence to act with authority even when he felt vulnerable.[18]

Viktor Frankl was in one of the death camps in Nazi Germany, and he learned that people have choices about whether or not to behave morally.

> We who lived in concentration camps can remember the men who walked through the huts comforting the others, giving away their last piece of bread. They may have been few in number, but they offer sufficient proof that everything can be taken from a man but one thing: the last of the human freedoms—to choose one's attitude in any given set of circumstances. To choose one's own way.
>
> And there were always choices to make. Every day, every hour, offered the opportunity to make a decision, a decision which determined whether you would or would not submit to those powers which threatened to rob you of your very self, your inner freedom. . . .[19]

A leader's capacity to make moral choices is related to the individual's level of moral development.[20] Exhibit 6.2 shows a simplified illustration of one model of personal moral development. At the **preconventional level,** individuals are concerned with receiving external rewards and avoiding punishments. They obey authority to avoid detrimental personal consequences. A person at this level is motivated solely by self-interest. Modern psychology believes that children who don't receive sufficient love and nurturing spend the rest of their lives filling that need through money, material goods, and over-achievement to gain the recognition of others. The basic orientation toward the world is one of taking what one can get. Someone with this orientation in a leadership position would tend to be autocratic toward others and use the position for personal advancement.

At level two, the **conventional level,** people learn to conform to the expectations of good behavior as defined by colleagues, family, friends, and

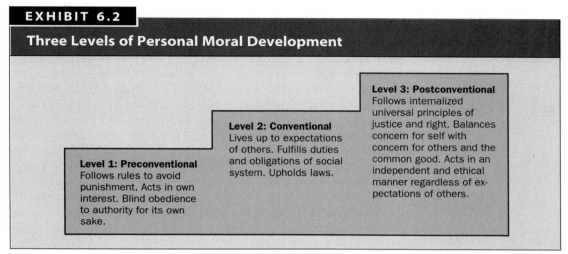

EXHIBIT 6.2

Three Levels of Personal Moral Development

Level 3: Postconventional
Follows internalized universal principles of justice and right. Balances concern for self with concern for others and the common good. Acts in an independent and ethical manner regardless of expectations of others.

Level 2: Conventional
Lives up to expectations of others. Fulfills duties and obligations of social system. Upholds laws.

Level 1: Preconventional
Follows rules to avoid punishment. Acts in own interest. Blind obedience to authority for its own sake.

SOURCE: Based on Lawrence Kohlberg, "Moral Stages and Moralization: The Cognitive-Developmental Approach," in *Moral Development and Behavior: Theory, Research, and Social Issues,* ed. Thomas Likona (Austin, TX: Holt, Rinehart and Winston, 1976), 31–53; and Jill W. Graham, "Leadership, Moral Development, and Citizenship Behavior," *Business Ethics Quarterly* 5, No. 1 (January 1995), 43–54.

society. People at this level follow the rules, norms, and values in the corporate culture. If the rules are to not steal, cheat, make false promises, or violate regulatory laws, a person at the conventional level will attempt to obey. They adhere to the norms of the larger social system. However, if the social system says it is okay to inflate bills to the government, or make achieving the bottom line more important than integrity, people at the conventional level will often go along with that norm also. Often, when organizations do something illegal, many managers and employees are simply going along with the system.[21]

At the postconventional or **principled level,** leaders are guided by an internalized set of principles universally recognized as right or wrong. People at this level may even disobey rules or laws that violate these principles. These internalized values become more important than the expectations of other people in the organization or community. Recall from Chapter 2's discussion of integrity how Roy Vagelos "broke the rules" by giving away a drug to cure river blindness, putting the lives of poor children in developing nations above the short-term interests of Merck's shareholders. Or consider Martin Luther King, Jr., who broke what he considered unjust laws and spent time in jail to serve a higher cause of universal dignity and justice. A leader at this level is visionary, empowering, and committed to serving others and a higher cause.

Most adults operate at level two, and some have not advanced beyond level one. Only about 20 percent of American adults reach the third, postconventional level of moral development, although most of us have the capacity to do so. People at level three are able to act in an independent, ethical manner regardless of expectations from others inside or outside the organization. Impartially applying universal standards to resolve moral conflicts balances self-interest with a concern for others and for the common good. Research has consistently found a direct relationship between higher levels of moral development and more ethical behavior on the job, including less cheating, a tendency toward helpfulness to others, and the reporting of unethical or illegal acts, known as whistleblowing.[22] Leaders can use an understanding of these stages to enhance their own and followers' moral development and to initiate ethics training programs to move people to higher levels of moral reasoning. When leaders operate at level three of moral development, they focus on higher principles and encourage others to think for themselves and expand their understanding of moral issues.

LEADERSHIP CONTROL VERSUS SERVICE

Assumptions about the relationship between leaders and followers are changing dramatically, and the concept of leadership is expanding. What is a leader's moral responsibility toward followers? Is it to limit and control them to meet the needs of the organization? Is it to pay them a fair wage? Or is it to enable them to grow and create and expand themselves as human beings? William Pollard, chairman of ServiceMaster (described in the previous chapter) believes it is immoral to take away an employee's right to make decisions and take action. He sees leaders as having a moral responsibility to help employees grow and develop their full potential, which means giving them the skills, information, tools, and authority they need to act independently.[23]

Much of the thinking about leadership today implies that moral leadership encourages change toward developing followers into leaders, thereby developing their potential rather than using a leadership position to control or limit followers. Exhibit 6.3 illustrates a continuum of leadership thinking and practice. Traditional organizations were based on the idea that the leader is in charge of subordinates and the success of the organization depends on leader control over followers. In the first stage, subordinates are passive—not expected to think for themselves but simply to do as they are told. Stage two in the continuum involves subordinates more actively in their own work. Stage three is stewardship, which represents a significant shift in mind-set by moving responsibility and authority from leaders to followers. Servant leadership represents a stage beyond stewardship, where leaders give up control and make a

EXHIBIT 6.3

Continuum of Leader-Follower Relationships

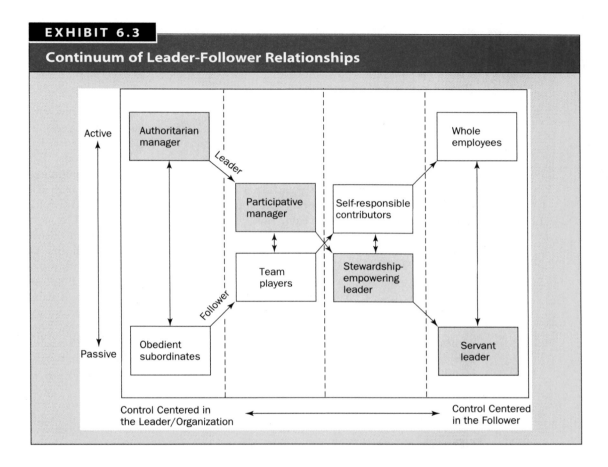

choice to serve employees. In the following sections, we will discuss each stage of this leadership continuum.

Authoritarian Management

The traditional understanding of leadership is that leaders are good managers who direct and control their people. Followers are obedient subordinates who follow orders. In Chapter 2, we discussed the autocratic leader, who makes the decisions and announces them to subordinates. Power, purpose, and privilege reside with those at the top of the organization. At this stage, leaders set the strategy and goals, as well as the methods and rewards for attaining them. Organizational stability and efficiency are paramount, and followers are routinized and controlled along with machines and raw materials. Subordinates are given no voice in creating meaning and purpose for their work and no discretion as to how they perform their jobs. This leadership mind-set emphasizes tight top-down control, employee standardization and specialization, and management by impersonal measurement and analysis.

Participative Management

Since the 1980s, many organizations have made efforts to actively involve employees. Leaders have increased employee participation through employee suggestion programs, participation groups, and quality circles. Teamwork has become an important part of how work is done in many organizations. The success of Japanese firms that emphasize employee involvement encouraged many U.S. organizations to try participatory management practices in response to increased global competition. One study, sponsored by the Association for Quality and Participation, revealed that over 70 percent of the largest U.S. corporations have adopted some kind of employee participation program. However, most of these programs do not redistribute power and authority to lower-level workers.[24] The mind-set is still paternalistic in that top leaders determine purpose and goals, make final decisions, and decide rewards. Employees are expected to make suggestions for quality improvements, act as team players, and take greater responsibility for their own jobs, but they are not allowed to be true partners in the enterprise. Leaders are responsible for outcomes, but they may act as mentors and coaches. They have given up some of their control, but they are still responsible for the morale, emotional well-being, and performance of subordinates, which can lead to treating followers as if they are not able to think for themselves.[25]

Stewardship

Stewardship is a pivotal shift in leadership thinking. Employees are empowered to make decisions and they have control over how they do their own jobs. Leaders give workers the power to influence goals, systems, and structures and become leaders themselves. **Stewardship** supports the belief that leaders are deeply accountable to others as well as to the organization, without trying to control others, define meaning and purpose for others, or take care of others.[26] In fact, stewardship has been called an alternative to leadership because the spotlight is on the people actually doing the work, making the product, providing the service, or working directly with the customer. Four principles provide the framework for stewardship.

1. *Reorient toward a partnership assumption.* Partnership can happen only when power and control shift away from formal leaders to core workers. Partners have a right to say "no" to one another. They are totally honest with one another, neither hiding information nor protecting the other from bad news. In addition, partners (leaders and followers) are jointly responsible for defining vision and purpose and jointly accountable for outcomes.

2. *Localize decisions and power to those closest to the work and the customer.* Decision-making power and the authority to act should reside right at the point where the work gets done. This means reintegrating the "managing" and the "doing" of work, so that everyone is doing some of the core work of the organization part of the time. Nobody gets paid simply to plan and manage the work of others.

3. *Recognize and reward the value of labor.* The reward systems tie everyone's fortunes to the success of the enterprise. Stewardship involves redistributing wealth by designing compensation so that core workers can make significant gains when they make exceptional contributions. Everyone earns their pay by delivering real value, and the organization pays everyone as much as possible.

4. *Expect core work teams to build the organization.* Teams of workers who make up the core of the organization or division define goals, maintain controls, create a nurturing environment, and organize and reorganize themselves to respond to a changing environment and the marketplace they serve.

Stewardship leaders guide the organization without dominating it and facilitate followers without controlling them. Stewardship allows for a relationship between leaders and followers in which each makes significant, self-responsible contributions to organizational success. In addition, it gives followers a chance to use their minds, bodies, and spirits on the job, thereby allowing them to be more "complete" human beings.

Stewardship leaders can help organizations thrive in today's rapidly changing environment because they tap into the energy and commitment of followers. Although the ideas we have discussed may sound new, an early management thinker, Mary Parker Follett, captured the spirit of stewardship eighty years ago when she described the type of leader who motivated her.

> The skillful leader, then, does not rely on personal force; he controls his group not by dominating but by expressing it. He stimulates what is best in us; he unifies and concentrates what we feel only gropingly and scatteringly, but he never gets away from the current of which we and he are both an integral part. He is a leader who gives form to the inchoate energy in every man. The person who influences me most is not he who does great deeds but he who makes me feel I can do great deeds.[27]

Servant Leadership

Servant leadership takes stewardship assumptions about leaders and followers one step further. Robert Wood Johnson, who built Johnson & Johnson from a small private company into one of the world's greatest corporations, summarized his ideas about management in the expression "to serve." In a statement called "Our Management Philosophy," Wood went on to say, "It is the duty of the leader to be a servant to those responsible to him."[28] Wood died more than thirty years ago, but his beliefs about the moral responsibility of a leader are as fresh and compelling (and perhaps as controversial) today as they were when he wrote them. **Servant leadership** is leadership upside-down. Servant leaders transcend self-interest to serve the needs of others, help others grow and develop, and provide opportunity for others to gain materially and emotionally. The fulfillment of others is the servant leader's principal aim.

Servant leadership was first described by Robert Greenleaf in his book, *Servant Leadership*. Greenleaf began developing his ideas after reading Hermann Hesse's novel, *Journey to the East*. The central character of the story is Leo, who appears as a servant to a group of men on a journey. Leo performs the lowliest, most menial tasks to serve the group, and he also cheers them with his good spirits and his singing. All goes well until Leo disappears, and then the journey falls into disarray. Years later, when the narrator is taken to the headquarters of the Order that had sponsored the original journey, he encounters Leo again. There, he discovers that Leo is in fact the titular head of the Order—a great leader, not the lowly "servant" the travelers had thought him to be.[29] Hesse's fictional character is the epitome of the servant leader, and some doubt whether real human beings functioning in the real world of organizations can ever achieve Leo's level of selflessness in service to others. However, many leaders, such as Robert Wood Johnson of Johnson & Johnson and William Pollard of ServiceMaster, have shown that leaders can operate from Greenleaf's basic precepts of servant leadership:[30]

1. *Put service before self-interest.* Servant leaders make a conscious choice to use their gifts in the cause of change and growth for other individuals and for the organization. The desire to help others takes precedence over the desire to achieve a formal leadership position or to attain power and control over others. The servant leader calls for doing what is good and right for others even if it does not "pay off" financially. In this view, the organization exists as much to provide meaningful work to the person as the person exists to perform work for the organization.

2. *Listen first to affirm others.* The servant leader doesn't have answers; he asks questions. One of the servant leader's greatest gifts to others is listening, fully understanding the problems others face, and affirming his confidence in others. The servant leader tries to figure out the will of the group and then further it however he can. The leader doesn't impose his or her will on others. By understanding others, the leader can contribute to the best course of action.

3. *Inspire trust by being trustworthy.* Servant leaders build trust by doing what they say they will do, being totally honest with others, giving up control, and focusing on the well-being of others. They share all information, good and bad, and they make decisions to further the good of the group rather than their own interests. In addition, trust grows from trusting others to make their own decisions. Servant leaders gain trust because they give everything away—power, control, rewards, information, and recognition. Trust allows others to flourish.

4. *Nourish others and help them become whole.* Vaclev Havel, former playwright, dissident, and prisoner of the Soviet regime, who served as president of Czechoslovakia after the Soviet withdrawal, once said, "The salvation of this human world lies nowhere else than in the human heart, in the human power to reflect, in human meekness, and in human responsibility."[31] Servant leaders help others find the power of the human spirit and accept their responsibilities. This requires an openness and willingness to share in the pain and difficulties of others. Being close to people also means leaders make themselves vulnerable to others and are willing to show their own pain and humanity.

Servant leadership can mean something as simple as encouraging others in their personal development and helping them understand the larger purpose in their work. When Linda Burzynski became president of Molly Maid International, she learned about servant leadership from one of her cleaners. Posing as a new member of the cleaning crew, Burzynski entered a home with her partner, Dawn, to find dishes piled high, food spilled on countertops, clothes and magazines strewn about, and pet hair everywhere. Surveying the mess, Burzynski was ready to walk out, but Dawn explained that the woman who owned the house was going through a divorce and dealing with three rebellious teenage sons. "She's barely hanging on," said Dawn, and having a clean house gave her a sense of order and control. Burzynski noticed that Dawn seemed to take extra care because she knew she was helping the woman with more than just her household chores. Burzynski says she learned that day about the power of being a servant to her employees and helping them find larger meaning in their difficult jobs.[32] Another example of a leader who puts service to workers first is Bob Thompson of Thompson-McCully Company.

IN THE LEAD   ## Bob Thompson, Thompson-McCully Co.

Bob Thompson started an asphalt company in his basement with $3,500 and developed it into a road-building powerhouse. When he sold the company forty years later, he did something that flabbergasted people—he distributed $128 million of the proceeds to his 550 employees—the salesmen and secretaries, gravel pit workers and road crews, even some retirees and widows. He also paid the taxes, so that the eighty or so workers who were given a million dollars would actually reach that magical milestone.

Thompson knows road-building is a tough business; people often put in 14-hour days, six days a week, working with 300-degree asphalt under 99-degree sun. His workers describe Thompson as a no-nonsense boss who is very driven and demanding—but they emphasize that he is always fair and always willing to listen. His ability to empathize with employees and treat them like human beings instead of like pieces of road-building equipment has helped Thompson maintain experienced, quality workers in a difficult and competitive industry. When he decided to sell the business, Thompson carefully chose a buyer who would not break up the company and fire workers. His first bit of good news for employees was that they wouldn't lose their jobs and that he'd be staying on to run the business even after the sale. He could have taken the money from the sale and never looked back, but that wasn't even an option for a man who had always genuinely believed that without the dedication of his employees he wouldn't have had a business to run.

Thompson knew people would be happy when they got their checks, but he really can't understand what the fuss is all about. "It's sharing good times, that's really all it is," he says. "We're dependent on people, so it would just not be fair not to do it."[33]

For leaders like Bob Thompson, leadership contains a strong moral component. Servant leaders truly value and respect others as human beings, not as objects of labor. To fully trust others relies on an assumption that we all have a moral duty to one another.[34] To make the choice for service requires a belief in a purpose higher than acquiring more material goods for oneself. Raoul Wallenberg, described at the beginning of the chapter, made the choice for service when he exchanged a comfortable life of privilege for war-torn Hungary. Organizational leaders can act from moral values rather than from greed, selfishness, and fear. Indeed, Greenleaf believed that many people have the capacity for servant leadership. He said the greatest enemy to organizations and to society is fuzzy thinking on the part of good, intelligent, vital people who "have the potential to lead but do not lead, or who choose to follow a nonservant."[35]

BUILDING AN ETHICAL CULTURE

Leaders who operate from the principles of stewardship and servant leadership are uniquely qualified to create ethical cultures within organizations. Because they demonstrate and act from high moral standards, they engender high standards in others. Despite the corporate realities of fear, greed, apathy, and divisiveness, these leaders act from their moral values and encourage others to bring their own ethical and spiritual values to work with them. Having the conviction and courage to stand up for one's beliefs is especially important in today's complex world where issues are seldom clear-cut.

All leaders face situations where right and wrong are hard to define. These ethical dilemmas often involve a conflict between the needs of the part and the whole—for example, the individual versus the organization, or the organization versus society as a whole. The way in which leaders approach ethical issues sets the tone for the rest of the organization. In Chapter 14 we will discuss in detail how leaders shape organizational culture, including ethical values. Culture exerts a powerful influence on employee behavior. In ethical organizations, employees believe that if they violate the ethical values they will not fit in or their jobs may be in jeopardy. Organizations such as Johnson & Johnson, General Mills, and Levi Strauss are known for setting high ethical standards as part of the organizational culture, and those high standards are based on the belief that organizations have an obligation to benefit society as well as themselves.

The leader's behavior is an important tool for shaping ethical values. The single most important factor in ethical decision making in organizations is whether top leaders show a commitment to ethics in their talk and their behavior. Employees learn about the values that are important in the organization by watching leaders. Ryder Systems' Tony Burns puts ethical values into action to demonstrate the importance of giving something back to the community.

| IN THE LEAD | Tony Burns, Ryder Systems |

Two days after Hurricane Andrew swept through South Florida, leaving thousands homeless, Ryder Systems' corporate offices in Miami resembled command central on the edge of a war zone. Because United Way's power had been knocked out, they set up in Ryder's cafeteria. In the lobby, Ryder employees could sign up for on-the-spot interest-free company loans of up to $10,000. An army of volunteers sorted food and clothing, much of it to be delivered by the 500 yellow trucks Ryder loaned for free to various relief agencies.

At the heart of this humanitarian activity was M. Anthony Burns, Ryder's Chairman, President, and CEO. Burns himself delivered supplies to employees whose homes were destroyed and joined work crews going house to house repairing roofs. Employees volunteered to work half a day at Ryder and half a day in the community—seven days a week from sunup to sundown for three

EXHIBIT 6.4

Ten Ways to Enhance Ethical Leadership

1. Establish a code of ethics or code of responsible business conduct.
2. Require all employees to verify that they've read and understand the code.
3. Integrate ethics into all performance evaluations.
4. Recognize and reward ethical behavior.
5. Establish a confidential ethics hotline or advisory service.
6. Incorporate ethics questions into employee opinion surveys.
7. Show and discuss videos that deal with ethical dilemmas.
8. Launch an ethics column in the employee newsletter.
9. Use on-line menu-driven answers to queries about ethical problems.
10. Hold open forums on ethics with top leaders.

SOURCE: The Canadian Clearinghouse for Consumer and Corporate Ethics, *www.interactive.yorku.ca/ ethicscan/eem.html,* as published in Nancy Croft Baker, "Heightened Interest in Ethics Education Reflects Employer, Employee Concerns," *Corporate University Review* (May/June 1997), 6-9.

months. No one in the South Florida area was surprised by Ryder's contribution during the crisis. Burns has had a long-standing commitment to public service, which earned him the Humanitarian of the Year award from the Greater Miami chapter of the American Red Cross. He has also created an atmosphere for service within the company. Harvey Mogul, president of the United Way of Dade County, characterizes Burns as "very intense, very focused, and absolutely ethical. There's not a local cultural or social institution that has not been impacted by his leadership."

Burns modestly deflects the praise heaped upon him, and credits "a very good organization here at Ryder." However, he doesn't mind talking about his values and where they came from—Burns says he learned the values of hard work, integrity, service, and commitment as a boy growing up in a devout Mormon family in Nevada. His parents lived by the code of absolute honesty and integrity. Burns' commitment to helping others may have come from his grandfather, who "always thought the best thing you could do was giving service to other people." Burns deeply believes that a corporation has a responsibility to give something back to the community, and he also recognizes that doing so pays dividends. "I really think being a good citizen and offering opportunity to all people is not only the absolute right thing to do, it's also great business. Customers want to do business with you, and employees want to work here."[36]

Leaders like Tony Burns demonstrate the importance of serving people and society as well as the bottom line. Leaders are responsible for creating and sustaining a culture that emphasizes the importance of ethical behavior and service within the organization for all employees every day. They do this most clearly by behaving ethically themselves. There are a number of mechanisms leaders can also use to create an ethical organizational culture. Exhibit 6.4 lists ten ways to enhance ethical leadership.

LEADERSHIP COURAGE

Leadership demands courage. In particular, the moral leadership we have been discussing in this chapter requires that leaders reach deep within themselves and find the fortitude and courage to stand up for their beliefs. However, for many leaders, particularly those working in large organizations, the importance of courage is easily obscured—the main thing is to get along, fit in, and do whatever brings promotions and pay raises. In a world of stability and abundance, it was easy to forget even the *meaning* of courage, so how can leaders know where to find it when they need it? In the following sections, we will examine the nature of leadership courage and discuss some ways courage is expressed in organizations. The final section of the chapter will explore the sources of leadership courage.

What Is Courage?

Many people know intuitively that courage can carry you through deprivation, ridicule, and rejection and enable you to achieve something about which you care deeply. Courage is both a moral and a practical matter for leaders. Years of stability and abundance misled American businesses into thinking that courage isn't needed in the business world. The lesson executives learned to advance in their careers was: "Keep your nose clean. Don't fail. Let someone else take the risk. Be careful. Don't make mistakes." Such a philosophy is no longer beneficial. Indeed, the courage to take risks has always been important for living a full, rewarding life, as discussed in the Living Leadership box. For today's organizations, things are constantly changing, and leaders thrive by solving problems through trial and error. They create the future by moving forward in the face of uncertainty, by taking chances, by acting with courage.[37] The defining characteristic of **courage** is the ability to step forward through fear. Courage doesn't mean the absence of doubt or fear, but the ability to act in spite of them.

In fact, if there were no fear or doubt, courage would not be needed. People experience all kinds of fears, including fear of death, mistakes, failure, embarrassment, change, loss of control, loneliness, pain, uncertainty, abuse,

LIVING LEADERSHIP

Is It Worth the Risk?

To *laugh* . . . is to risk appearing the fool.

To *weep* . . . is to risk appearing sentimental.

To *reach out* . . . is to risk involvement.

To *expose feelings* . . . is to risk exposing your true self.

To *place your ideas and dreams before a crowd* . . . is to risk rejection.

To *love* . . . is to risk not being loved in return.

To *live* . . . is to risk dying.

To *hope* . . . is to risk despair.

To *try* . . . is to risk failure.

But risks must be taken, because the greatest hazard in life is to risk nothing.

Those who risk nothing do nothing and have nothing.

They may avoid suffering and sorrow,

But they cannot learn, feel, change, grow, or love.

Chained by their certitude, they are slaves; they have forfeited their freedom.

Only one who risks in free.

—————————

© Janet Rand

---

rejection, success, and public speaking. It is natural and right for people to feel fear when real risk is involved, whether the risk be losing your life, losing your job, losing the acceptance of peers, or losing your reputation. But many fears are learned and prevent people from doing what they want. True leaders step through these learned fears to accept responsibility, take risks, make changes, speak their minds, and fight for what they believe.

Courage means accepting responsibility. Leaders make a real difference in the world when they are willing to step up and take personal responsibility. Some people just let life happen to them; leaders make things happen. They do not expect others to tell them what to do or give them permission to act. Courageous leaders create opportunities to make a difference in their organizations and communities. Consider the courage Carol Roberts showed at Memphis, Tennessee-based International Paper.

IN THE LEAD   ## Carol Roberts, International Paper

Carol Roberts faced a test of her courage almost immediately after being hired as vice president of people development at International Paper. Although the company had all sorts of processes in place for employee development, managers weren't following through. Roberts realized that managers at the company weren't really helping people develop and grow, and were thus limiting the progress and growth of the organization.

As a new female manager in a male-dominated industry, Roberts knew she'd be taking a huge risk to speak up, but she stepped through her fear and called thirty-three of the company's top leaders together for a two-day off-site meeting to discuss the problem. She soon learned her fear was justified. The company's CEO, John Dillon, questioned her entire agenda, emphasizing that the company already had feedback mechanisms in place. Although he allowed the meeting to proceed, Dillon made it clear he had serious reservations about her plans. Roberts didn't sleep a wink the night before the retreat began. "There I was," she says, "new to the job, calling in vice presidents and general managers of a $20 billion global company and telling them they weren't doing enough to develop their employees. If I didn't engage them properly—if my effort flopped—I was dead."

Roberts decided to trust that other managers in the company also recognized that employee development was weak, so she opened the meeting by asking for help rather than criticizing the job that had been done in the past. Although it also took courage to admit that she didn't have solutions, the approach proved to be right on target. The managers quickly focused on steps toward positive change, which Carol was now responsible for selling to Dillon and other top executives. Ultimately, her efforts proved successful. At the company's Human Issues and Management Conference, the CEO proudly highlighted the improvements in employee development that resulted from the off-site meeting.[38]

By having the courage to speak up and accept responsibility, Carol Roberts made a real difference in her organization. However, she realizes that her efforts could have failed miserably. Leaders also openly take responsibility for their failures and mistakes, rather than avoiding blame or shifting it to others. The acceptance of responsibility in many of today's large, bureaucratic organizations seems nonexistent. In one large agency of the federal government, for example, the slightest mistake created a whirlwind of blaming, finger pointing, and extra effort to avoid responsibility. The absence of courage froze the agency to the point that many employees were afraid to even do their routine tasks.[39]

Courage means nonconformity. Leadership courage means going against the grain, breaking traditions, reducing boundaries, and initiating change. Leaders do not play it safe by following rules designed for an earlier time. They're willing to take risks and they encourage others to do so. At Trilogy Software, for example, new employees go through a three-month "boot camp" where they learn to take risks, accept failure, admit mistakes, and move forward to take more risks. Trilogy's founder and CEO, Joe Liemandt, who dropped out of Stanford to start the company, rewards employees for their hard work with activities such as a trip to Las Vegas. There, Liemandt challenges them to take a $2,000 bet at the roulette table—Trilogy will put up the cash and losers will have their paychecks reduced for several months to cover it. Liemandt wants all Trilogy's employees to understand that taking risks and suffering the consequences are a crucial part of business in a fast-paced industry.[40] Leaders at FedEx also encourage risk-taking among all employees. For example, the company is downright proud of ZapMail, a program that, around 15 years ago, put expensive fax machines in key FedEx offices and had those offices act as middlemen for same-day fax delivery. The program was a complete failure and reportedly cost the company as much as $300 million. ZapMail is celebrated because it shows that leaders at FedEx are willing to go against the status quo, take risks, and change.[41]

Going against the status quo is difficult. It's often easier to stay with what is familiar, even if it will lead to certain failure, than to initiate bold change. A naval aviator once said that many pilots die because they choose to stay with disabled aircraft, preferring the familiarity of the cockpit to the unfamiliarity of the parachute.[42] Similarly, many leaders hurt their organizations and their own careers by sticking with the status quo rather than facing the difficulty of change. Most leaders initiating change find some cooperation and support, but they also encounter resistance, rejection, loneliness, and even ridicule. Taking chances means making mistakes, enduring mockery or scorn, being outvoted by others, and sometimes failing miserably. Courageous leaders are willing to disagree with the boss, persist with a new idea, and sacrifice the approval of others in the pursuit of a dream.

Courage means pushing beyond the comfort zone. To take a chance and improve things means leaders have to push beyond their comfort zone. According to Barry Diller, the former chairman of Paramount Pictures, Fox, Inc., and QVC, Inc., his secret to success is to "plunge into the uncomfortable; push, or be lucky enough to have someone push you, beyond your fears and your sense of limitations. That's what I've been doing . . . overcoming my discomfort as I go along."[43] At Trilogy Software, employees learn early to push beyond their comfort zone. During their training period, recruits are assigned to teams and work on projects about which they know little or nothing. Two women with no marketing experience were assigned to develop a marketing plan, which was deemed a complete failure by Liemandt. But the project built their courage because it required them to push beyond their comfort zone. When people go beyond the comfort zone, they encounter an invisible "wall of fear." They may encounter it when about to ask someone for a date, confront the boss, break off a relationship, launch an expensive project, or change careers. Facing the invisible wall of fear is when courage is needed most.

Courage means asking for what you want and saying what you think. Leaders have to speak out to influence others. However, the desire to please others—especially the boss—can sometimes block the truth. Everyone wants approval, so it is difficult to say things when you think others will disagree or disapprove. Author and scholar Jerry Harvey tells a story of how members of his extended family in Texas decided to drive forty miles to Abilene for dinner on a hot day when the car air conditioning did not work. They were all miserable. Talking about it afterward, each person admitted they had not wanted to go but went along to please the others. The *Abilene Paradox* is the name Harvey uses to describe the tendency of people to not voice their true thoughts because they want to please others.[44] A top executive at Pepsi-Cola once said: "One of the things we look for when we are assessing people on their way up is 'Do they have a point of view? Do they have the guts to recommend what might be unpopular solutions to things?' "[45] Courage means speaking your mind even when you know others may disagree with you and may even deride you. Courage also means asking for what you want and setting boundaries. It is the ability to say no to unreasonable demands from others, as well as the ability to ask for what you want to help achieve the vision. When Ronald Shaw was hired as president of Pilot Pen, he insisted on autonomy in order to make the struggling company profitable. By asking for what he wanted, Shaw guided Pilot from sales of $1.2 million to sales of $81 million and a healthy profit.[46]

Courage means fighting for what you believe. Courage means fighting for valued outcomes that benefit the whole. Leaders take risks, but they do so for a higher purpose. Wallenberg did not risk his life just for the thrill of it; he risked it for a cause he deeply believed in: the dignity of human life. Taking risks that do not offer the possibility of valued outcomes is at best foolish and at worst evil. Courage doesn't mean doing battle to destroy the weak, trample the powerless, or crush things that are valued by others. It does mean doing what you believe is right, even when this opens you up to failure and personal sacrifice. One good example of a courageous leader in the business world is Lawrence Fish, who has experienced both failure and success by doing what he believes is right.

IN THE LEAD   ## Lawrence Fish, Citizens Financial Group

Lawrence Fish, CEO of Citizens Financial Group, Inc., is a man who has known both success and failure as a result of his unconventional approaches and ethical beliefs. His effort to rescue the Bank of New England ended in defeat with the bank's sale to Fleet Financial Group. However, Fish's unconventional ideas have led to success at Citizens. Under his leadership, Citizens has grown more than seven-fold to become the second largest commercial banking company in New England and one of the thirty-five largest in the United States. According to Cornelius Hurley, a banking consultant in Boston, Fish has "put together a powerhouse." Yet when he talks about the company, Fish says, "If we just make money, we'll fail."

Fish is widely known for his volunteer efforts and commitment to the community. He once donated half of his salary to Drake University in Iowa, his alma mater. When he was offered the job at Citizens, he postponed taking it for three months so he could work in a shelter for abused kids—washing walls, feeding children, reading stories. He also serves as founding chairman of the Rhode Island Commission for National and Community Service, which is recognized as one of the most creative and successful Americorps programs in the country.

Fish's approach at Citizens is to turn the conventional wisdom of banking on its head. Unlike most big banks, Citizens courts working-class customers and specializes in the human touch rather than promoting fancy electronic devices and new technology. Although the bank has all the modern conveniences, including online banking, Fish believes banking the old-fashioned way—with a human touch—is the best way to long-term profitability. He gives local bank executives the freedom to decide how to make loans rather than insisting on approval from the home office. He makes a point of writing a thank-you note to at least one employee a day, and he encourages his staff to spend part of their time caring for babies with AIDS. He is sometimes derided for "having too much heart" or "being too soft." However, Anat Bird, a banking consultant in New York, says Citizens' success shows there is still room for banks that operate efficiently but with a heart.

In the world of business, Fish believes there's more to life than material success. It's a belief that goes back to 1968, when he graduated from Harvard Business School. Rather than heading for Wall Street, the nonconformist Fish ended up at a remote ashram in northern India, where he lived as an ascetic for a year. "There are forces that brought me to India that are still with me," he says. "Ultimately, what matters is the good that we do."[47]

Moral Courage

Lawrence Fish is an example of the many people working in organizations who have the courage to be unconventional, to do what they think is right, to dare to treat employees and customers as whole human beings who deserve respect. Balancing profit with people, selfishness with service, and control with stewardship requires individual moral courage.

Moral leadership requires courage. To practice moral leadership, leaders have to know themselves, understand their strengths and weaknesses, know what they stand for, and often be nonconformists. Honest self-analysis can be painful, and acknowledging one's limitations in order to recognize the superior abilities of others takes personal strength of character. In addition, moral leadership means building relationships, which requires sharing yourself, listening, having significant personal experiences with others, and making yourself vulnerable—qualities that frighten many people. The quest for emotional strength requires people to overcome their deepest fears and to accept emotions as a source of strength rather than weakness. True power lies in the emotions that connect people. By getting close and doing what is best for others—sharing the good and the bad, the pain and anger as well as the success and the joy—leaders bring out the best qualities in others.[48]

One example of this in practice is when William Peace had to initiate a layoff as general manager of the Synthetic Fuels Division of Westinghouse. To make the division attractive to buyers, executives made a painful decision to cut any jobs not considered essential. Peace had the courage to deliver the news about layoffs personally. He took some painful blows in the face-to-face meetings he held with the workers to be laid off, but he believed that allowing them to vent their grief and anger at him and the situation was the moral thing to do. His action sent a message to the remaining workers that, even though layoffs were necessary, leaders valued each of them as individuals. Because the workers recognized that layoffs were a last resort and the executive team was doing everything they could to save as many jobs as possible, they rededicated themselves to helping save the division. A buyer was found and the company had the opportunity to rehire half of those who had been laid off. Everyone contacted agreed to come back because the humane way they had been treated overcame negative feelings about the layoff.[49] For Peace, the courage to practice moral leadership gained respect, renewed commitment, and higher performance, even though he suffered personal rejection in the short run. Standing up for one's beliefs often entails great risk and tremendous courage. Nowhere is this more evident than in the case of ethical whistleblowing.

Opposing unethical conduct requires courage. **Whistleblowing** means employee disclosure of illegal, immoral, or unethical practices in the organization.[50] Although whistleblowing is more widespread in recent years, it is still risky for employees, who can lose their jobs, be ostracized by coworkers, or be transferred to lower-level positions. For example, when Curtis Overall reported nearly 200 broken screws at the bottom of a massive ice condenser system at TVA's Watts Bar nuclear plant, he lost his job and security clearance and endured an escalating series of threats, which eventually caused him to seek treatment for stress and depression. Although he eventually won his job back, he left again after a fake bomb was planted in his pickup truck. The Nuclear Regulatory Commission is still investigating the situation at Watts Bar.[51]

Although some whistleblowers believe nothing bad will happen to them because they are "doing the right thing," most realize they may suffer financially and emotionally from their willingness to report unethical conduct on the part of bosses or coworkers.[52] They step forward to tell the truth despite a jumble of contradictory emotions and fears. As one professor put it, "Depending upon the circumstances, including our own courage, we can choose to act and be ethical both as individuals and as leaders."[53] Choosing to act courageously means conflicting emotions—whistleblowers may feel an ethical obligation to report the wrongdoing but may also feel disloyal to their boss and coworkers. Some may do battle within themselves about where their responsibility lies. Robert A. Bugai, who challenged college marketers on unethical business practices in the early 1980s, warns that there are considerable costs involved—"mentally, financially, physically, emotionally, and spiritually." However, when asked if he'd do it again, he says, "You bet."[54]

SOURCES OF PERSONAL COURAGE

How does a leader find the courage to step through fear and confusion, to act despite the risks involved? All of us have the potential to live and act courageously, if we can push through our own fears. Most of us have learned fears that limit our comfort zone and stand in the way of being our best and accomplishing our goals. We have been conditioned to follow the rules, not rock the boat, to "go along" with things we feel are wrong so others will like and accept us. There are a number of ways people can unlock the courage within themselves, including committing to a cause they believe in, connecting with others, welcoming failure as a natural and beneficial part of life, and harnessing anger.

BELIEF IN A HIGHER PURPOSE   Courage comes easily when we fight for something we really believe in. Service to a larger vision or purpose gives people the courage to step through fear. For someone to risk his life as Raoul Wallenberg did requires a profound conviction that there is a greater good than the self. In organizations, too, courage depends on belief in a higher vision. A leader who is concerned only with his own career advancement would not be willing to report wrongdoing for fear of losing his position. On the other hand, after the 1986 *Challenger* explosion that killed seven crew members, concern about the safety of astronauts was the higher purpose that led John W. Young, the chief of NASA's astronaut office, to publicly blow the whistle about safety-related problems in the NASA system.[55] Sometimes courage can increase simply by getting clear on what higher purpose you are seeking. V. Cheryl Womack, founder of VCW, Inc. in Kansas City, Missouri, tries to help employees find their own courage by asking each of them to write a personal mission statement which is reviewed annually and linked to company mission and goals.[56]

CONNECTION WITH OTHERS   Caring about others and having support from others is a potent source of courage in a topsy-turvy world. Caring about the people who work with and for her was a source of courage for Cindy Olson, vice president of contract settlement in Enron's Capital and Trade Commercial Support Group. When Olson was asked to put the bulk of her job on the back burner and sign on as a leader with a major back-office re-engineering project, she knew there were career risks involved. She was new in her position and hadn't yet mastered her duties. Everyone expected the re-engineering effort would be difficult and thankless, and would result in lost jobs. She had the choice to say no; however, partly because she was concerned about the impact of re-engineering on the people on the front line, Olson stepped forward and assumed the difficulties and additional responsibilities.[57] The support of others is also a source of courage. People who feel alone in the world take fewer risks because they have more to lose.[58] Being part of an organizational team that is supportive and caring, or having a loving and supportive family at home, can reduce the fear of failure and help people take risks they otherwise wouldn't take.

WELCOMING FAILURE   Thomas Moore, author of *Care of the Soul,* talks about the importance of "befriending a problem rather than making an enemy of it."[59] Failure can play a creative role in work and in life. Success and failure are two sides of the same coin; one cannot exist without the other. A child learns to ride a bicycle by failing and trying again and again. Today, many people want success to arrive without difficulties, problems, and struggles. However, accepting failure enables courage. When people accept failure and are at peace with the worst possible outcome, they find they have the fortitude to move forward. Leaders know that failure can lead to success and that the pain of learning strengthens individuals and the organization. Both Walt Disney and Henry Ford had early business ventures go bankrupt, but both went on to achieve major success. Sharon McCollick was hired for a top sales and planning position at a hot software startup partly because she had started a business and failed. Company leaders liked the fact that she had been willing to take the risks associated with starting a designer apparel business and then move forward after the failure. Even people who invested in her business and lost money say they'd do it again. "She tried and failed and so what?" said one backer. "The next time, my bet's on her."[60] McCollick believes that having hit rock bottom and survived has given her greater courage. In addition, she radiates self-confidence because she is no longer terrified of failure. There is evidence that with repeated practice, people can overcome fears such as a fear of flying or fear of heights. Practice also enables people to overcome fear of risk-taking in their work. Every time you push beyond your comfort zone, every time you fail and try again, you build psychological strength and courage.

HARNESSING FRUSTRATION AND ANGER   If you have ever been really angry about something, you know that it can cause you to forget about fear of embarrassment or fear that others won't like you. In organizations, we can also see the power of frustration and anger. Glenn McIntyre used his anger and frustration to start a new life and a new business. After he was paralyzed in a motorcycle accident, McIntyre first used his anger to overcome thoughts of suicide and begin intensive physical therapy. Later, frustration over how poorly hotels served handicapped guests led him to start a consulting firm, Access Designs. The firm helps hotels such as Quality Suites and Renaissance Ramada redesign their space to be more usable for disabled travelers.[61] People in organizations can harness their anger to deal with difficult situations. When someone has to be fired for just cause, a supervisor may put if off until some incident makes her angry enough to step through the fear and act. Sometimes, outrage over a perceived injustice can give a mild-mannered person the courage to confront the boss head on.[62] Getting mad at yourself may be the motivation to change. Anger, in moderate amounts, is a healthy emotion that provides energy to move forward. The challenge is to harness anger and use it appropriately.

SUMMARY AND INTERPRETATION

This chapter has explored a number of ideas concerning moral leadership and leadership courage. People want honest and trustworthy leaders. However, leaders face a dilemma because modern society has created a separation between business and ethics. The world of business is one of rationality and hard measurable facts, whereas the realm of ethics concerns human meaning, purpose, significance, and values. But more and more, ethics is being recognized as an essential part of business. For leaders to create ethical organizations requires that they themselves be honest, ethical, and principled.

One personal consideration for leaders is the level of moral development. Leaders use an understanding of the stages of moral development to enhance their own as well as followers' personal moral growth. Leaders who operate at higher stages of moral development focus on the needs of followers and universal ethical principles.

Ideas about control versus service between leaders and followers are changing and expanding, reflected in a continuum of leader-follower relationships. The continuum varies from authoritarian managers to participative managers to stewardship to servant leadership.

Leaders who operate from the principles of stewardship and servant leadership can help build ethical organizations. All leaders face ethical dilemmas. Leaders shape the ethical culture of the organization most clearly by their behavior. They can also use a number of formal mechanisms to create ethical organizations.

The final sections of the chapter discussed leadership courage and how leaders can find their own courage. Courage means the ability to step forward through fear, to accept responsibility, to take risks and make changes, to speak your mind, and to fight for what you believe. Two expressions of courage in organizations are moral leadership and ethical whistleblowing. Sources of courage include belief in a higher purpose, connection with others, experience with failure, and harnessing anger.

KEY TERMS

moral leadership	principled level	courage
preconventional level	stewardship	whistleblowing
conventional level	servant leadership	

DISCUSSION QUESTIONS

1. If you were in a position similar to Raoul Wallenberg, what do you think you would do? Why?
2. Explain the dilemma between business and ethics. Do you feel a similar dilemma in your life as a student? As an employee?
3. If most adults are at a conventional level of moral development, what does this mean for their potential for moral leadership?
4. Do you feel that the difference between authoritarian leadership and stewardship should be interpreted as a moral difference? Discuss.
5. Should serving others be placed at a higher moral level than serving oneself? Discuss.
6. If you find yourself avoiding a situation or activity, what can you do to find the courage to move forward? Explain.
7. If it is immoral to prevent those around you from growing to their fullest potential, are you being moral?
8. Do you have the courage to take a moral stand that your peers and even authority figures will disagree with? Why?

LEADERSHIP DEVELOPMENT: Personal Feedback

Moral Leadership

Think about situations in which you either assumed or were given a leadership role in a group or organization. Imagine your own courage and moral standards as a leader. To what extent does each of the following statements characterize your leadership?

1 = very little
2 = somewhat
3 = a moderate amount
4 = a great deal
5 = very much

_____ 1. My actions meet the needs of others before my own.

_____ 2. I create a sense of community.

_____ 3. I am a symbol of integrity and honesty.

_____ 4. I give people a lot of discretion.

_____ 5. I let others know my values and beliefs.

_____ 6. I give away credit and recognition to others.

_____ 7. I enable others to feel ownership for their work.

_____ 8. I encourage the growth of others, expecting nothing in return.

_____ 9. My choices reflect a larger moral purpose.

_____10. I display high moral standards and values for others.

_____11. I give up control to show that I trust others.

_____12. I risk substantial personal loss to achieve the vision.

_____13. I take personal risks to defend my beliefs.

_____14. I say no even if I have a lot to lose.

_____15. I am assertive about what I believe.

_____16. My actions are linked to higher values.

_____17. I often act against the opinions and approval of others.

_____18. I quickly tell people the truth, even when it is negative.

_____19. I speak out against organizational injustice, bureaucracy, complacency, or corruption.

_____20. I stand up to offensive people.

Scoring

Each of these questions pertains to courage and moral leadership. Calculate your total score by summing the scores for all twenty answers.

Interpretation

This questionnaire pertains to both courage and moral leadership. It provides some indication of the extent to which you infuse your leadership with moral values and risk-taking to uphold those values. If you received a score of 80 or higher, you would be considered a courageous moral leader. A score of below 40 indicates that either you have been avoiding moral issues or you have not been in situations that challenged your moral courage. A score of 40 to 80 means that you are using courage to assert moral leadership. Keep up the good work, but continue trying to improve. Is your score consistent with your understanding of your own strengths and weaknesses? Compare your score to that of other students. What might you do to improve your scores?

LEADERSHIP DEVELOPMENT: Cases for Analysis

Young Leaders Council

Gehan Rasinghe was thrilled to be appointed to the Young Leaders Council at Werner & Burns, a large consulting and financial management firm located in Boston. When Rasinghe had first joined the firm he'd had a hard time fitting in, with his accented English and quiet manner. However, through hard work and persistence, he had overcome many obstacles, made many friends, and worked his way up in the organization. He had been in a leadership position as an account manager for two years, and he particularly loved working with new employees and helping them find their niche in the company and develop greater skills and confidence. His employee evaluations by both superiors and subordinates had been exceptional, and Rasinghe himself was pleased with his success as a leader.

Now, this! The purpose of the Young Leaders Council was to provide a training ground for young executives at Werner-Burns and help them continue to improve their leadership skills. In addition, top executives and the Board used the Council as a way to evaluate the potential of young managers for higher-level positions. Everyone knew that a good showing on the Council often resulted in a promotion. Typically, an appointment to the Council was for a one-year period, with new members added every six months on a rotating basis. Occasionally, some members would stay an additional six months, based on the results of an appraisal process personally introduced by the CEO. The process involved each member of the Council being rated by each of the other members on four criteria: 1) general intelligence and knowledge of the business; 2) creativity and innovativeness; 3) co-operation and team spirit; and 4) adherence to company values.

Rasinghe was attending his fifth monthly meeting when several members of the Council raised a concern about the rating system. They felt that it was being forced on the group, was controlled by top management, and was not used as a fair and accurate rating of each member's abilities but just as a way "to pat your buddies on the back," as his colleague Cathy Patton put it. Most of the other members seemed to agree with their arguments, at least to some degree. Rasinghe agreed that the system was flawed, but he was surprised by their suggestion for a solution. One member made an informal motion that in the next appraisal every member of the Council should simply give every other member the highest rating in each category.

Rasinghe quickly considered what to do as the chairman called for a show of hands from those in favor of the motion. His gut feeling is that such a "solution" to the problem of the rating system would be dishonest and unethical, but he remembers what it felt like to be an "outsider," and he doesn't want to be there again.

SOURCE: Based on "Junior Board," in John M. Champion and Francis J. Bridges, *Critical Incidents in Management,* rev. ed., (Homewood, IL: Irwin, 1969), 106–107.

Questions

1. What personal and organizational factors might influence Rasinghe's decision?

2. Do you believe it would take courage for Rasinghe to vote against the motion? What sources of courage might he call upon to help him vote his conscience?

3. What do you think about the current rating system? If you were in Rasinghe's position, what would you do? Discuss.

The Boy, the Girl, the Ferryboat Captain, and the Hermits

There was an island, and on this island there lived a girl. A short distance away there was another island, and on this island there lived a boy. The boy and the girl were very much in love with each other.

The boy had to leave his island and go on a long journey, and he would be gone for a very long time. The girl felt that she must see the boy one more time before he went away. There was only one way to get from the island where the girl lived to the boy's island, and that was on a ferryboat that was run by a ferryboat captain. And so the girl went down to the dock and asked the ferryboat captain to take her to the island where the boy lived. The ferryboat captain agreed and asked her for the fare. The girl told the ferryboat captain that she did not have any money. The ferryboat captain told her that money was not necessary: "I will take you to the other island if you will stay with me tonight."

The girl did not know what to do, so she went up into the hills on her island until she came to a hut where a hermit lived. We will call him the first hermit.

She related the whole story to the hermit and asked for his advice. The hermit listened carefully to her story, and then told her, "I cannot tell you what to do. You must weigh the alternatives and the sacrifices that are involved and come to a decision within your own heart."

And so the girl went back down to the dock and accepted the ferryboat captain's offer.

The next day, when the girl arrived on the other island, the boy was waiting at the dock to greet her. They embraced, and then the boy asked her how she got over to his island, for he knew she did not have any money. The girl explained the ferryboat captain's offer and what she did. The boy pushed her away from him and said, "We're through. That's the end. Go away from me. I never want to see you again," and he left her.

The girl was desolate and confused. She went up into the hills of the boy's island to a hut where a second hermit lived. She told the whole story to the second hermit and asked him what she should do. The hermit told her that there was nothing she could do, that she was welcome to stay in his hut, to partake of his food, and to rest on his bed while he went down into the town and begged for enough money to pay the girl's fare back to her own island.

When the second hermit returned with the money for her, the girl asked him how she could repay him. The hermit answered, "You owe me nothing. We owe this to each other. I am only too happy to be of help." And so the girl went back down to the dock and returned to her own island.

Questions

1. List in order the characters in this story that you like, from most to least. What values governed your choices?
2. Rate the characters on their level of moral development. Explain.
3. Evaluate each character's level of courage. Discuss.

REFERENCES

1. John C. Kunich and Richard I. Lester, "Profile of a Leader: The Wallenberg Effect," *The Journal of Leadership Studies* 4, No. 3 (Summer 1997), 5–19.
2. Michael J. McCarthy, "An Ex-Divinity Student Works on Searching the Corporate Soul," *The Wall Street Journal,* June 18, 1999, B1; Michael J. Sniffen, "Millions Recovered in Settlement Over Books," *Johnson City Press,* August 3, 2000, 10.
3. Jeffrey L. Seglin, "Dot.con," *Forbes ASAP,* February 21, 2000, 135; Jerry Useem, "New Ethics . . . or No Ethics?" *Fortune,* March 20, 2000, 82–86; and Jeremy Kahn, "Presto Chango! Sales Are Huge!" *Fortune,* March 20, 2000, 90–96.
4. William J. Morin, "Silent Sabotage: Mending the Crisis in Corporate Values," *Management Review,* July 1995, 10–14.
5. Geanne Rosenberg, "Truth and Consequences," *Working Woman,* July-August 1998, 79–80.
6. Del Jones, "Doing the Wrong Thing: 48% of Workers Admit to Unethical or Illegal Acts," *USA Today,* April 4, 1997, 1A, 2A; McCarthy, "An Ex-Divinity Student Works on Searching the Corporate Soul."
7. Mark Maremont with Joyce Barnathan, "Blind Ambition: How the Pursuit of Results Got Out of Hand at Bausch & Lomb," *Business Week,* October 23, 1995, 78–92.
8. Jones, "Doing the Wrong Thing."
9. James M. Kouzes and Barry Z. Posner, *Credibility: How Leaders Gain and Lose It, Why People Demand It* (San Francisco: Jossey-Bass, 1993), 255.
10. Al Gini, "Moral Leadership and Business Ethics," *The Journal of Leadership Studies* 4, No. 4 (Fall 1997), 64–81.
11. Jones, "Doing the Wrong Thing."
12. Linda Klebe Treviño and Katherine A. Nelson, *Managing Business Ethics: Straight Talk About How to Do It Right,* 2nd ed. (New York: John Wiley & Sons, 1999), 274–283.
13. Polly LaBarre, "Do You Have the Will to Lead?" (an interview with Peter Koestenbaum), *Fast Company,* March 2000, 222–230.
14. Gini, "Moral Leadership and Business Ethics."
15. Henry Ford, Sr., quoted by Thomas Donaldson, *Corporations and Morality* (Prentice-Hall, Inc., 1982), 57 in Al Gini, "Moral Leadership and Business Ethics," 64–81.
16. Donald G. Zauderer, "Integrity: An Essential Executive Quality," *Business Forum,* Fall 1992, 12–16; and LaBarre, "Do You Have the Will to Lead?"
17. Kouzes and Posner, *Credibility: How Leaders Gain and Lose It, Why People Demand It.*
18. Kunich and Lester, "Profile of a Leader: The Wallenberg Effect," 15.
19. Viktor E. Frankl, *Man's Search for Meaning* (New York: Pocket Books, 1959), 104.

20. Lawrence Kolhberg, "Moral Stages and Moralization: The Cognitive Developmental Approach," in Thomas Likona, ed. *Moral Development and Behavior: Theory, Research, and Social Issues* (Austin, TX: Holt, Rinehart and Winston, 1976), 31–53; Jill W. Graham, "Leadership, Moral Development, and Citizenship Behavior," *Business Ethics Quarterly* 5, No. 1 (January 1995), 43–54; James Weber, "Exploring the Relationship between Personal Values and Moral Reasoning," *Human Relations* 46, No. 4 (April 1993), 435–463; and Duane M. Covrig, "The Organizational Context of Moral Dilemmas: The Role of Moral Leadership in Administration in Making and Breaking Dilemmas," *The Journal of Leadership Studies* 7, No. 1 (2000): 40–59.

21. Tom Morris, *If Aristotle Ran General Motors* (New York: Henry Holt, 1997).

22. James Weber, "Exploring the Relationship Between Personal Values and Moral Reasoning," *Human Relations* 46, No. 4 (April 1993), 435–463.

23. C. William Pollard, "The Leader Who Serves," in *The Leader of the Future,* Frances Hesselbein, Marshall Goldsmith, and Richard Beckhard, eds. (San Francisco: Jossey-Bass 1996), 241–248.

24. Peter Block, "Reassigning Responsibility," *Sky,* February 1994, 26–31; and David P. McCaffrey, Sue R. Faerman, and David W. Hart, "The Appeal and Difficulty of Participative Systems," *Organization Science* 6, No. 6 (November-December 1995), 603–627.

25. Block, "Reassigning Responsibility."

26. This discussion of stewardship is based on Peter Block, *Stewardship: Choosing Service Over Self-Interest* (San Francisco: Berrett-Koehler Publishers, 1993), 29–31; and Block, "Reassigning Responsibility."

27. Mary Parker Follett, from *The New State* (1918), as quoted in David K. Hurst, "Thoroughly Modern—Mary Parker Follett," *Business Quarterly* 56, No. 4 (Spring 1992), 55–58.

28. Lawrence G. Foster, *Robert Wood Johnson—The Gentleman Rebel* (Lemont, PA: Lillian Press, 1999); and John Cunniff, "Businessman's Honesty, Integrity Lesson for Today," *Johnson City Press,* May 28, 2000.

29. Robert K. Greenleaf, *Servant Leadership: A Journey into the Nature of Legitimate Power and Greatness* (Mahwah, N.J.: Paulist Press, 1977), 7.

30. The following is based on Greenleaf, *Servant Leadership,* and Walter Kiechel III, "The Leader as Servant," *Fortune,* May 4, 1992, 121–122.

31. Quoted in Parker J. Palmer, *Leading from Within: Reflections on Spirituality and Leadership* (Indianapolis: Indiana Office for Campus Ministries, 1990), 2.

32. Marcia Heroux Pounds, "Execs Should Head For Trenches to Find Out How Business Works," *The Tennessean,* May 9, 1999, 2H.

33. Sharon Cohen, "Boss Treats His Workers Like a Million Bucks—By Giving It To Them," *Johnson City Press,* September 12, 1999, 28; and Michelle Singletary, "Saluting a Generous Spirit, *The Washington Post,* August 1, 1999, H1.

34. LaRue Tone Hosmer, "Trust: The Connecting Link between Organizational Theory and Philosophical Ethics," *Academy of Management Review* 20, No. 2 (April 1995), 379–403.

35. Greenleaf, *Servant Leadership*, 45.
36. John Grossmann, "A Whirlwind of Humanity," *Sky*, January 1997, 96–101.
37. Richard L. Daft and Robert H. Lengel, *Fusion Leadership: Unlocking the Subtle Forces that Change People and Organizations* (San Francisco: Berrett-Koehler, 1998).
38. Michael Warshaw, "Open Mouth, Close Career?" *Fast Company*, December 1998, 240.
39. Daft and Lengel, *Fusion Leadership*, 155.
40. Evan Ramstad, "How Trilogy Software Trains Its Raw Recruits to Be Risk Takers," *The Wall Street Journal*, September 21, 1998, A1, A10.
41. Seth Godin, "Guillotine or Rack?" *Fast Company*, October 1999, 341–344.
42. Reported in Nido R. Qubein, *Stairway to Success: The Complete Blueprint for Personal and Professional Achievement* (New York: John Wiley & Sons, 1997).
43. Barry Diller, "The Discomfort Zone," *Inc.*, November 1995, 19–20.
44. Jerry B. Harvey, *The Abilene Paradox and Other Meditations on Management* (Lexington, MA: Lexington Books, 1988), 13-15.
45. Lester Korn, *The Success Profile: A Leading Headhunter Tells You How to Get to the Top* (New York: Simon & Schuster, 1988).
46. Laurie Kretchmar, "Fortune People," *Fortune*, April 20, 1992, 185–186.
47. Joseph Rebello, "Radical Ways of Its CEO Are a Boon to Bank," *The Wall Street Journal*, March 20,1995, B1, B2; and Profile of Lawrence W. Fish, *www.citizensbank.com*, accessed on August 11, 2000.
48. A. J. Vogl, "Risky Work," an interview with Max DePree, *Across the Board*, July/August 1993, 27–31.
49. William H. Peace, "The Hard Work of Being a Soft Manager," *Harvard Business Review*, November-December 1991, 40–47.
50. Janet P. Near and Marcia P. Miceli, "Effective Whistle-Blowing," *Academy of Management Review* 20, No. 3 (1995), 679–708.
51. "Tiny Screws Cause Woes for TVA Whistle-Blower," *The Tennessean*, December 21, 1998, 3B.
52. Hal Lancaster, "Workers Who Blow the Whistle on Bosses Often Pay a High Price," *The Wall Street Journal*, July 18, 1995, B1.
53. Richard P. Nielsen, "Changing Unethical Organizational Behavior," *The Executive*, May 1989, 123–130.
54. Barbara Ettorre, "Whistleblowers: Who's the Real Bad Guy?" *Management Review*, May 1994, 18–23.
55. Nielsen, "Changing Unethical Organizational Behavior."
56. Charles Burck, "Succeeding with Tough Love," *Fortune*, November 29, 1993, 188.
57. Jon R. Katzenbach and the RCL Team, *Real Change Leaders: How You Can Create Growth and High Performance at Your Company* (New York: Times Business/Random House 1995), 107–108.
58. James M. Kouzes and Barry Z. Posner, *The Leadership Challenge: How to Get Extraordinary Things Done in Organizations* (San Francisco: Jossey-Bass, 1988).

59. Thomas Moore, "The Soul of Work," *Business Ethics,* March/April 1993, 6–7.

60. Thomas Petzinger Jr. "She Failed. So What? An Entrepreneur Finds Her Prestige Rising" (The Front Lines column), *The Wall Street Journal,* October 31, 1997, B1.

61. Michael Warshaw, ed., "Great Comebacks," *Success,* July/August 1995, 33–46.

62. Ira Cheleff, *The Courageous Follower: Standing Up To and For Our Leaders* (San Francisco: Berrett-Koehler, 1995).

CHAPTER OUTLINE

YOUR LEADERSHIP CHALLENGE

After reading this chapter, you should be able to:

- Recognize your followership style and take steps to become a more effective follower.

- Understand the leader's role in developing effective followers.

- Apply the principles of courageous followership, including responsibility, service, challenging authority, participating in change, and knowing when to leave.

- Implement the strategies for effective followership at school or work.

- Know what followers want and contribute to building a community among followers.

Followership

In the closing months of the Vietnam War, Army lieutenant John Richards was charged with dangerous daily assignments to search out and destroy the enemy. At a time when most American troops had been withdrawn, and soldiers could see that the war had already been lost, Richards and his platoon were ordered to continue fighting.

The lieutenant knew that following orders meant almost certain death for some of his men—and for no apparent reason. Unlike some platoons that patrolled American bases and continued fighting to protect American soldiers, Richards could find no justification for risking the lives of those under his command. Yet, although he felt a duty to protect his men from unnecessary risk, to disobey direct orders from his commanding officers wasn't an option for Richards. He knew the military depends on discipline and respect for the chain of command, and he wasn't willing to break the commitment he had pledged when he joined the army. Some of his followers, however—particularly young draftees—didn't share Richards' willingness to risk their lives simply for the sake of the military institution and its code of discipline and honor.

Faced with this seemingly unsolvable dilemma—to follow orders he disagreed with and place his men at unnecessary risk, or to disobey direct orders from his superiors, thus breaking a commitment he strongly felt—Richards began to seek a middle ground. Eventually, after long, hard discussions with the soldiers, Richards allowed the platoon to break into two groups. One group, made up of soldiers who felt compelled to honor the military's norms and standards of discipline, would continue to fight and risk their lives. The other group, aided by Richards and the others in the fighting unit, would stay out of combat as best they could. Each group respected the decision of the other, and by working together most of Richards' men made it home.

Richards' solution to the problem required him to go beyond his formal authority—and it involved risk to his own career as well as to the lives of his men. For example, although Richards technically followed his superiors' orders, he found a way to "get around" those orders and honor the duty he felt to the soldiers who didn't want to fight. Richards also knew, though, that the decision could backfire and result in the loss of more rather than fewer men. He had to make a difficult decision based on his own beliefs and understanding of the situation, without the support and authorization of his superiors.[1]

John Richards was both a leader and a follower in Vietnam, and his story illustrates how leadership and followership are closely intertwined. As a leader, Richards listened to his soldiers' concerns and honored his duty to protect them from unnecessary harm. As a follower, he found the courage to think critically, act independently, and risk failure by developing a creative solution without formal authorization and support. Richards' courage and initiative are hallmarks of both effective followership and leadership.

Followership is an important consideration for both leaders and followers. In this chapter we will examine the nature of the follower's role, the different styles of followership that individuals express, and the definition of a courageous follower. This chapter also explores the sources of courage and power that are available to followers, the strategies for effective followership, and how leaders can help develop effective followers. Finally, we will look at the consequential role of followers in building community within their organizations.

THE ROLE OF FOLLOWERS

Followership is important in the discussion of leadership for several reasons. First, leadership and followership are fundamental roles that individuals shift into and out of under various conditions. Everyone—leaders included—is a follower at one time or another in their lives. Indeed, most individuals, even those in a position of authority, have some kind of boss or supervisor. Individuals are more often followers than leaders.[2]

Second, recall that the definition of a leader from Chapter 1 referred to an influence relationship among leaders and followers. This means that in a position of leadership, an individual is influenced by the actions and the attitudes of followers. In fact, the contingency theories introduced in Chapter 3 are based on how leaders adjust their behavior to fit situations, especially their followers. Thus, the nature of leader-follower relationships involves reciprocity, the mutual exchange of influence.[3] The followers' influence upon a leader can enhance the leader or underscore the leader's shortcomings.[4]

Third, many of the qualities that are desirable in a leader are the same qualities possessed by an effective follower. In addition to demonstrating initiative, independence, commitment to common goals, and courage, a follower can provide enthusiastic support of a leader, but not to the extent that the follower fails to challenge the leader who threatens the values or objectives of the organization.[5] This is not very different from the role of leader. Both leader and follower roles are proactive; together they can achieve a shared vision. As in the opening example, the military often provides insight into the interaction of leadership and followership. A performance study of U.S. Navy personnel found that the outstanding ships were those staffed by followers who supported their leaders but also took initiative and did not avoid raising issues or concerns with their superiors.[6] D. Michael Abrashoff, former commander of the USS *Benfold*, recognized as one of the best ships in the Navy, always encouraged his followers to speak up. To Abrashoff, the highest boss should be the sailor who does the work—the follower—not the person with the most stripes on his or her uniform. Even though Abrashoff has moved on to a top post at the Space and Naval Warfare Systems Command, he believes the effective followership demonstrated by the crew of the *Benfold* will continue. "The people on this ship know that they are part owners of this organization. . . . And they now have the courage to raise their hands and to get heard. That's almost irreversible."[7] In any organization, leaders can help develop effective followers, just as effective followers develop better leaders. The performance of followers, leaders, and the organization are variables that depend on one another.

The trend toward empowerment discussed in Chapter 1, and the growing importance of knowledge workers in determining the success of organizations, make the process of followership particularly relevant today. The reciprocal partnership that makes up the leader-follower relationship warrants increasing attention as power and decision-making authority is increasingly pushed to lower levels in organizations.

Styles of Followership

After extensive interviews with leaders and followers, Robert E. Kelley described five styles of followership.[8] These followership styles are categorized according to two dimensions, as illustrated in Exhibit 7.1. The first dimension is

EXHIBIT 7.1

Followership Styles

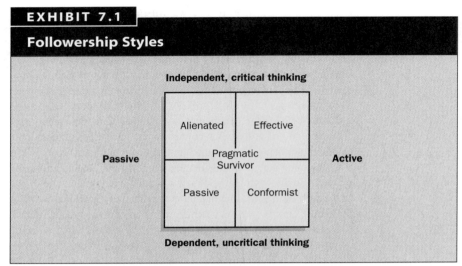

Independent, critical thinking

Alienated	Effective

Pragmatic Survivor

Passive	Conformist

Passive   **Active**

Dependent, uncritical thinking

SOURCE: Adapted from *The Power of Followership* by Robert E. Kelley, 97. Copyright © 1992 by Consultants to Executives and Organizations, Ltd. Used by Permission of Doubleday, a division of Random House, Inc.

the quality of independent, **critical thinking** versus dependent, **uncritical thinking.** Independent thinking recalls our discussion of mindfulness in Chapter 5; independent critical thinkers are mindful of the effects of people's behavior on achieving organizational goals. They are aware of the significance of their own actions and the actions of others. They can weigh the impact of decisions on the vision set forth by a leader and offer constructive criticism, creativity, and innovation. Conversely, a dependent, uncritical thinker does not consider possibilities beyond what he or she is told, does not contribute to the cultivation of the organization, and accepts the leader's ideas without thinking.

According to Kelley, the second dimension of followership style is active versus passive behavior. An active individual participates fully in an organization, engages in behavior that is beyond the limits of the job, demonstrates a sense of ownership, and initiates problem solving and decision making. A passive individual is characterized by a need for constant supervision and prodding by superiors. Passivity is often regarded as laziness; a passive person does nothing that is not required and avoids added responsibility.

The extent to which one is active or passive and is a critical, independent thinker or a dependent, uncritical thinker determines whether he or she is an alienated follower, a passive follower, a conformist, a pragmatic survivor, or an effective follower, as shown in Exhibit 7.1.

The **alienated follower** is a passive, yet independent, critical thinker. Alienated followers are often effective followers who have experienced setbacks and obstacles, perhaps promises broken by superiors. Thus, they are capable, but they focus exclusively on the shortcomings of the organization and other people. Often cynical, alienated followers are able to think independently, but they do not participate in developing solutions to the problems or deficiencies they see. For example, Barry Paris spent over ten years writing on and off for the *Pittsburgh Post-Gazette,* where he was known for his bad attitude and lack of enthusiasm and teamwork. Eventually Paris realized that he wasted that time ruminating over what he perceived as the hypocrisy of journalistic objectivity. "I could never resign myself to it," says Paris. Thus, rather than doing his best and trying to help others maintain standards of integrity, he allowed hostility and cynicism to permeate his work.[9]

The **conformist** participates actively in the organization but does not utilize critical thinking skills in his or her task behavior. In other words, a conformist typically carries out any and all orders regardless of the nature of those tasks. The conformist participates willingly, but without considering the consequences of what he or she is being asked to do—even at the risk of contributing to a harmful endeavor. A conformist is only concerned with avoiding conflict. Indeed, this style often results from rigid rules and authoritarian environments in which leaders perceive subordinate recommendations as a challenge or threat. When Kelley, the author who developed the two dimensions of followership, was consulted about how to improve employee creativity and innovation for an oil company, he discovered that each office was virtually identical, owing to strict company policies that prohibited individual expression. This is specifically the kind of environment that suppresses effective followership and creates conformists.[10]

The **pragmatic survivor** has qualities of all four extremes—depending on which style fits with the prevalent situation. This type of follower uses whatever style best benefits his or her own position and minimizes risk. Pragmatic survivors often emerge when an organization is going through desperate times, and followers find themselves doing whatever is needed to get themselves through the difficulty. Within any given company, some 25 to 35 percent of followers tend to be pragmatic survivors, avoiding risks and fostering the status quo, often for political reasons. Government appointees often demonstrate this followership style because they have their own agenda and a short period of time in which to implement it. They may appeal to the necessary individuals, who themselves have a limited time to accomplish goals, and are therefore willing to do whatever is necessary to survive in the short run.[11]

The **passive follower** exhibits neither critical, independent thinking nor active participation. Being passive and uncritical, this type of follower displays neither initiative nor a sense of responsibility. Their activity is limited to what they are told to do, and they accomplish things only with a great deal of supervision. Passive followers leave the thinking to their leaders. Often, however, this style is the result of a leader who expects and encourages passive behavior.

Followers learn that to show initiative, accept responsibility, or think creatively is not rewarded, and may even be punished by the leader, so they grow increasingly passive. Passive followers are often the result of leaders who are overcontrolling of others and who punish mistakes.[12]

The **effective follower** is both a critical, independent thinker and active in the organization. Effective followers behave the same toward everyone, regardless of their position in the organization. They do not try to avoid risk or conflict. Rather, effective followers have the courage to initiate change and put themselves at risk or in conflict with others, even their leaders, to serve the best interest of the organization.

Characterized by both mindfulness and a willingness to act, effective followers are essential for an organization to be effective. They are capable of self-management, they discern strengths and weaknesses in themselves and in the organization, they are committed to something bigger than themselves, and they work toward competency, solutions, and positive impact. Effective followers are far from powerless—and they know it. Therefore, they do not despair in their positions, nor do they resent or manipulate others. The Living Leadership box provides highlights from a speech given by Nelson Mandela that underscores his meaning of effective followership.

LIVING LEADERSHIP

Our Deepest Fear

Our deepest fear is not that we are
Inadequate, Our deepest fear is that we are
Powerful beyond measure.

It is our light, not our darkness, that most
Frightens us.

We ask ourselves, who am I to be brilliant,
Gorgeous, talented and fabulous?

Actually, who are you NOT to be?
You are a child of God.
Your playing small doesn't serve the world.

There's nothing enlightened about shrinking

So that other people won't feel insecure
Around you.

We were born to make manifest the glory . . .
that is within us.

It's not just in some of us; it's in everyone.
And as we let our own light shine, we
Unconsciously give other people permission
To do the same.

As we are liberated from our own fear, our
Presence automatically liberates others.

SOURCE: From the 1994 Inaugural Speech of Nelson Mandela.

The Leader's Role in Developing Effective Followers

Researchers Charles Manz and Henry Sims proposed that leaders can develop effective followers through a process called **self-management leadership,** which means leading others to lead themselves.[13] Empowerment of employees and the use of self-directed teams have increased the importance of followers who can think critically and independently and are capable of taking action to improve the organization. Self-management leadership calls for leaders to share power and responsibility with their subordinates in such a way that everyone becomes a leader. Leaders act as coaches and mentors, show trust in others, remove barriers to learning, and offer encouragement and support. Developing leaders throughout the organization enables the company to react quickly to threats and opportunities.

Leaders who practice self-management leadership do not try to control employee behavior, but coach employees to think critically about their own performance and judge how well they are accomplishing tasks and achieving goals. Leaders also make sure employees have the information they need to perform effectively and an understanding of how their jobs are relevant to attaining the organization's vision. By linking individual jobs with larger organizational goals, employees have a framework within which to act. Self-management leadership hinges on providing employees with this directed autonomy.[14] Consider how leaders at Royal Dutch/Shell have empowered effective followers through self-management leadership.

IN THE LEAD   ### Steve Miller, Royal Dutch/Shell

After joining Shell's Committee of Managing Directors, the group of top leaders who guide the day-to-day activities of the Royal Dutch/Shell Group of Companies, Steve Miller watched as the company struggled to transform itself one layer of management at a time. After two years of reorganizing, downsizing, and attending management seminars and workshops, profits had edged up slightly, but employee morale was in the pits and workers out in the field were conducting business as usual. Miller thought the best way to truly transform was to reach around the resistant bureaucracy and directly involve employees on the front lines, or as he phrases it, "at the coal face." To truly bring about lasting change, Miller believed leaders should "find the way to empower these frontline people, to challenge them, to provide them with the resources they need, and then to hold them accountable. Once the folks at the grass roots find that they own the problem, they find that they also own the answer."

Starting in 1997, Miller devoted more than 50 percent of his time to working directly with grassroots employees. He and his colleagues worked with a cross-section of Shell people from more than twenty-five countries, representing more than 85 percent of Shell's retail sales volume. Six- to eight-person cross-functional teams from various operating companies attended intense "retailing boot camp," where they learned to think like business people and act like leaders. Teams were given assignments that helped them learn to think critically and apply their knowledge to solving business problems. Although many of the teams were initially resistant, they gradually developed an enthusiasm and belief in their own abilities that sparked amazing creativity and led to solid results in the business. Employees saw that they truly had the ability—and the power—to change things for the better.

"The truth is," says Miller, "it's scary at first. It's scary for me. It's scary for the team. But the track record has been incredible." Productivity and profitability have improved, but most important is the increased morale and energy level of people throughout the company. Top-level leaders have had to give up traditional control, but they now get almost immediate feedback from the front lines, helping the whole company keep in touch with the marketplace and customer needs. In addition, the energy of followers has spread upward, re-energizing the entire organization. According to Miller, the people at the coal face "taught us to believe in ourselves again."[15]

Empowerment of frontline employees is a strong trend in organizations, and there are more and more situations that call for self-management leadership, but there has been little research to test the effectiveness of this new approach. As with other styles of leadership, it is likely that self-management leadership is effective for some, but not for all, situations. However, all leaders can act in ways that encourage followers to think independently and be willing to take risks, challenge their leaders, and initiate change for the benefit of the organization. This chapter's Leader's Bookshelf describes principles from the U.S. Marine Corps for cultivating leadership abilities in people at all levels.

THE COURAGEOUS FOLLOWER

Recall the discussion of the importance of courage to leadership from Chapter 6. Courage is found in both effective leaders and followers. Indeed, a willingness to take risks, to challenge authority, and to believe one's own ideas are equal to or better than one's superior typically marks a follower as a future leader.[16] The role of followership includes responsibility, service, challenging authority, participating in change, and knowing when it is time to leave an organization.[17] All of these components of followership require courage.

Corps Business: The 30 Management Principles of the U.S. Marines

David H. Freedman

Many people still think of the U.S. Marine Corps as an autocratic, hidebound organization with mindlessly aggressive Marines ready to hurl themselves into battle under the orders of abusive officers. Nothing could be further from the truth, according to David Freedman, author of *Corps Business*. Through observations and interviews with more than 100 Marines of all ranks, Freedman discovered a highly innovative, nimble, almost freewheeling organization—and one of the best leadership training programs for business in the twenty-first century.

Principles for Leadership in Dynamic Environments

The ability to react quickly and effectively under conditions brewing with complex, unpredictable, and fast-changing threats is the Marines' specialty. How do they do it? By cultivating leaders at all levels. Here are a few lessons from the Marines:

- **Lead by end-state and intent.** Tell followers what needs to be accomplished and why; then leave the details to them. People need to fully understand the mission and the reasons behind it, but they are the ones who need to make the day-to-day, minute-to-minute decisions about how to reach the goal.

- **Allow for authority on demand.** The Marines still use a classic military-style organizational pyramid, but they've made a crucial modification. Under critical circumstances, people at even the lowest level have the authority to make any and all decisions necessary to accomplish the mission. One example comes from the Gulf War, when a corporal's squad was pinned down by an Iraqi machine-gunner. With no "higher-ups" immediately available, the corporal decided to take action on his own. He took half his squad around the gunner's side and took him by surprise. Taking the time to check with superiors could have meant death for most squad members.

- **Make every decision-making experience a learning experience.** The Marines are extraordinarily tolerant of most types of mistakes, because they recognize that taking risks and making mistakes is not only "part of the job," but also the best possible learning experience. In training, the Marines purposefully push people outside their comfort zones, but guard against pushing them over the line into failure. This approach encourages a self-assurance that is necessary for people to be willing to step forward in the face of danger and uncertainty.

- **Preserve your core purpose and values.** Followers need a solid context within which to make decisions and take action. The Marines stress core values such as perseverance, integrity, loyalty, and personal accountability. In addition, there are long-standing and clearly defined standards that Marines follow in decision making. Although many decisions have to be made quickly and based largely on "gut instinct," they are made within the context of standards and values ingrained in the minds and hearts of all Marines.

Training with the Marines

With vivid stories and a colorful cast of characters, this book sometimes reads like a military thriller. However, the real value for leaders is in the clearly defined principles and how they can be applied to any organization. Freedman also offers examples of how companies such as FedEx and Coca-Cola have used some of these principles, providing a "real world" view for business leaders.

Corps Business: The 30 Management Principles of the U.S. Marines, by David H Freedman, is published by HarperBusiness.

Courage to Assume Responsibility

A courageous follower derives a sense of personal responsibility from the acknowledgment of ownership in the organization and the mission that the organization serves. By assuming responsibility for their own behavior and its impact on the organization, courageous followers do not presume that a leader or an organization will provide them with security, permission to act, or personal growth. Instead, courageous followers initiate the opportunities through which they can achieve personal fulfillment, exercise their potential, and provide the organization with the fullest extent of their capabilities. At Spartan Motors, for example, Larry Karkau and Tim Williams spent a year and a half tinkering over the production of a low-cost chassis for a high-end motor home. The project presented a number of difficulties with no quick solutions in sight, which had already led competing companies to give up on the idea, so company leaders discussed abandoning the project with Karkau and Williams. But Karkau insisted that their efforts be continued. "I was real candid about it. I knew this would work," says Karkau. Williams and Karkau had the courage to assume responsibility for the time and expense of their project, and it paid off. Eventually, they had a product that cost $500,000 but reaped $30 million in sales in one year.[18]

Courage to Serve

A courageous follower discerns the needs of the organization and actively seeks to serve those needs. Just as leaders can serve others, as discussed in the previous chapter, so can followers. A courageous follower provides strength to the leader by supporting the leader's decisions and by contributing to the organization in areas that complement the leader's position. By displaying the courage to serve others over themselves, followers act for the common mission of the organization with a passion that equals that of a leader. Wade R. Fenn, a rising star at Best Buy Co., used to wage a campaign of rebellion and discontent behind the scenes whenever his boss didn't take his advice and suggestions. However, with the help of an industrial psychologist, Fenn is developing the courage to serve both his superiors and subordinates. Now, he looks for ways to support his boss and make contributions in areas where his input is most needed. At one workshop, which was designed for potential CEOs and COOs from organizations around the country, Fenn says he "learned to admire Tonto, because he always pulled the Lone Ranger out of danger."[19]

Courage to Challenge

Courageous followers do not sacrifice the purpose of the organization or their personal ethics in order to maintain harmony and minimize conflict. On the contrary, courageous followers take a stand against the leader's actions and decisions when that behavior contradicts the best interest of the organization, or their own integrity. They are not afraid of the consequences of their challenge, believing that emotional reactions and conflict are worth risking to meet the needs of those served by the organization. For example, David C. Fannin, a vice president at Sunbeam, had the courage to challenge CEO Al Dunlap when he believed Dunlap's methods were hurting the company. Fannin was a member of Dunlap's inner circle and had been handsomely rewarded for his loyalty and commitment to his boss. However, Fannin became disillusioned with Dunlap's arrogant approach and his promotion of aggressive sales and accounting practices that artificially inflated revenues and profits. After investigating the situation, Fannin discovered that Sunbeam was headed for a crisis, and he had the courage to speak up. "Had he not come forward," said one board member, "it would have been extraordinarily difficult for us to act. He was the quiet hero. He really put his neck out."[20] Good leaders want followers who are willing to challenge them. Lou Gertsner hired Larry Ricciardi as senior vice president and corporate counsel at IBM even though he knew Ricciardi would constantly challenge his thinking and decisions (the two have worked together at various companies for more than twenty years). According to another former colleague, Ricciardi is "sort of a fearless fighter about what he believes in. . . . He's both extremely bright and extremely willing to express his opinion."[21]

Courage to Participate in Transformation

Courageous followers view the struggle of corporate change and transformation as a mutual experience shared by all members of the organization. When an organization undergoes a difficult transformation, courageous followers support the leader and the organization. They are not afraid to confront the changes and work toward reshaping the organization. David Chislett, of Imperial Oil's Dartmouth, Nova Scotia refinery, was faced with this test of courage. The refinery was the least efficient in the industry and the Board of Directors gave management nine months to turn things around. Chislett was asked to give up his management position and return to the duties of a wage earner as part of an overall transformation strategy. He and many others agreed to the request, thereby contributing to the success of the refinery's transformation.[22]

Courage to Leave

Often organizational or personal changes create a situation in which a follower must withdraw from a particular leader-follower relationship. Courageous followers are not afraid to depart because they do not rely on their leaders or their organizations to provide them with self-worth. When courageous followers are faced with a leader or an organization unwilling to make necessary changes, it is time to take their support elsewhere. For example, Dianne Martz had the courage to leave a job as sales manager for a pharmaceutical company when she learned about the company's practice of withholding information, which helped sales but not the customer. She discovered that HIV was present in a clotting factor for hemophilia patients, and that doctors and the pharmaceuticals industry had known about it for two years before they told anyone. As the mother of a hemophiliac son, Martz could not justify her participation in the company. She left to start her own company that would seek out and provide complete information on every hemophilia treatment option available, as well as provide meaningful jobs for people living with hemophilia or HIV.[23]

Another reason for leaving is a person's desire to move on to another phase of his or her life. Sometimes people know they need new challenges, but they have a hard time finding the courage to leave a comfortable job where they may be quite happy and have many friends and valued colleagues. Paul Birch found the courage to begin a new career by helping others be courageous at British Airways.

IN THE LEAD   Paul Birch, British Airways

During a long career with British Airways, Paul Birch worked on everything from mergers to marketing. But perhaps his favorite job was that of the "corporate jester." Birch had for some years been trying to leave the company, feeling that it was time for something new. Yet, every time he would try to leave, his boss would come up with an interesting job that kept him there. The last time he announced it was time for him to leave, the boss just asked, "What would it take to keep you?" With nothing to lose, Birch wrote out a job description for someone who would constantly question authority, challenge convention, and promote honesty and courage.

Birch had been inspired by the character of the Fool in *King Lear.* "One of the roles of the jester is to declare, 'Just because you're the boss doesn't mean that you know better,'" Birch says. "The jester's role is to draw attention to things that are going wrong, to stir things up." Having a job designed specifically to do that made it easier for Birch to act as a voice of truth, to "say the unsayable and think the unthinkable." In addition, his job involved helping others speak up, take risks, and look for creative new approaches. At first, Birch had only limited success in provoking creativity and change, but gradually people became more willing to disagree with their bosses or propose off-the-wall ideas. However, a funny thing happened as Birch matured in his role: People started responding to him with comments such as, "You *would* say that, wouldn't you? That's your role." People began to ignore what Birch said because he was the "official jester."

The realization helped Birch finally take the step and resign from British Airways. He now had a vision of working as a consultant to help other organizations cut through fear and complacency and encourage people throughout the organization to be courageous. "When things go wrong," he says, "employees usually have a good idea of how to fix them. You need to create a state in which they've got the commitment and the courage to do something."[24]

Sources of Follower Courage

The ability to consciously put oneself at risk requires a great deal of personal courage. Risk is often a necessary condition for effective follower efforts toward change. For example, research comparing urban schools revealed that the most effective schools had principals and teachers who assumed control without receiving authority from the district level, or who initiated change in their schools through direct insubordination.[25] Thus, the achievement of change is a process that entails risky behavior, such as challenging a leader, making a transformation, or leaving an unfulfilling situation. Chapter 6 discussed several sources of personal courage that are available to both leaders and followers.

Effective followers find courage from numerous sources.[26] Individuals gain strength from their personal philosophical or religious beliefs. A vision of the future—who and where they hope to be—can provide individuals with the courage to follow a difficult course of action. Often an event from the past that tested the courage of an individual makes future courageous behavior easier. The personal values of an individual can serve as a foundation for the courage to act. A commitment to peers and a deep concern for others can enable individuals to brave the risks demanding a change toward fairness. In the same vein, an outrage about injustice toward self or others can fuel the fire of a courageous act.

DEVELOPING PERSONAL POTENTIAL

Followers can grow in courage when they develop and apply personal leadership qualities in both their private and work lives. One well-known and widely acclaimed approach to helping people deal courageously with life's changes and challenges is Stephen Covey's *The 7 Habits of Highly Effective People*.[27] Covey defines a habit as the intersection of knowledge, skill, and desire. His approach to personal and interpersonal effectiveness includes seven habits arranged along a maturity continuum from dependence to independence to interdependence, as illustrated in Exhibit 7.2. Each habit builds on the previous one so that individuals grow further along the maturity continuum as they develop these personal effectiveness habits.

In organizations, many people fall into a mind-set of dependency, expecting someone else to take care of everything and make all the decisions. The *dependent* person is comparable to the passive follower we described earlier, displaying neither initiative nor a sense of personal responsibility. Dependent people expect someone else to take care of them and blame others when things go wrong. An *independent* person, on the other hand, has developed a sense of self-worth and an attitude of self-reliance. Independent people accept personal responsibility and get what they want through their own actions. To be a truly effective follower—or leader—requires a further step to *interdependence*, the realization that the best things happen by working cooperatively with others, that life and work are better when one experiences the richness of close interpersonal relationships.

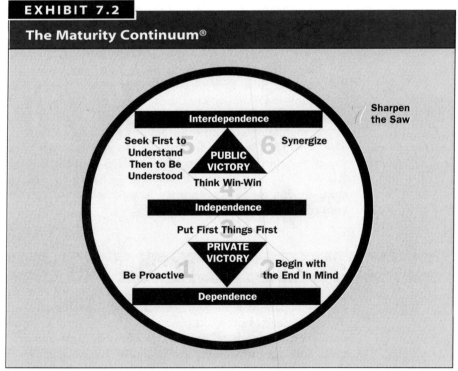

EXHIBIT 7.2

The Maturity Continuum®

From Dependence to Independence

Covey's first three habits deal with self-reliance and self-mastery. Covey calls these *private victories* because they involve only the individual follower growing from dependence to independence, not the follower in relationship with others.[28]

Habit 1: Be Proactive® Being proactive means more than merely taking initiative; it means being responsible for your own life. Proactive people recognize that they have the ability to choose and to act with integrity. They don't blame others or life's circumstances for their outcomes. Eleanor Roosevelt was talking about being proactive when she observed that, "No one can make you feel inferior without your consent."[29] Proactive people know that it is not what happens to them but how they respond to it that ultimately matters.

Habit 2: Begin with the End in Mind® This means to start with a clear mental image of your destination. For each individual, beginning with the end in mind means knowing what you want, what is deeply important to you, so that you can live each day in a way that contributes to your personal vision. In addition to clarifying goals and plans, this habit entails establishing guiding principles and values for achieving them.

Habit 3: Put First Things First® This habit encourages people to gain control of time and events by relating them to their goals and by managing themselves. It means that, rather than getting tangled up dealing with things, time, and activities, we should focus on preserving and enhancing *relationships* and on accomplishing *results*.

Effective Interdependence

The first three habits build a foundation of independence, from which one can move to interdependence—caring, productive relationships with others—which Covey calls *public victories*. Moving to effective interdependence involves open communication, effective teamwork, and building positive relationships based on trust, caring, and respect, topics that are discussed throughout this book. No matter what position you hold in the organization, when you move to interdependence, you step into a leadership role.

Habit 4: Think Win-Win® To think win-win means understanding that without cooperation, the organization cannot succeed. When followers understand this, they co-operate in ways that ensure their mutual success and allow everyone to come out a winner. Win-win is a frame of mind and heart that constantly seeks agreements or solutions that are mutually beneficial and satisfying.

Habit 5: Seek First to Understand, Then to Be Understood® This principle is the key to effective communication. Many people don't listen with the intent to understand; they are too busy thinking about what they want to say. Seeking first to understand requires being nonjudgmental and able to empathize with the other person's situation. *Empathetic listening* gets inside another person's frame of reference so that you can better understand how that person feels. Communication will be discussed in detail in Chapter 8.

Habit 6: Synergize® Synergy is the combined action that occurs when people work together to create new alternatives and solutions. In addition, the greatest opportunity for synergy occurs when people have different viewpoints, because the differences present new opportunities. The essence of synergy is to value and respect differences and take advantage of them to build on strengths and compensate for weaknesses.

Habit 7: Sharpen the Saw® This habit encompasses the previous six—it is the habit that makes all the others possible. "Sharpening the saw" is a process of using and continuously renewing the physical, mental, spiritual, and social aspects of your life. To be an effective follower or an effective leader requires living a balanced life. For example, Larry Ricciardi of IBM, introduced earlier, is an avid traveler and voracious reader who likes to study art, literature, and history. He once spent eighteen months learning everything he could about the Ottoman Empire just because he "realized he knew nothing about the Ottoman Empire." He also likes to read tabloids in addition to his daily fare of *The Wall Street Journal.* On business trips, he scouts out side trips to exotic or interesting sites, and he likes to take adventurous vacations with his family and friends. Ricciardi loves his job, but he also loves exploring other aspects of life.[30]

SOURCES OF POWER

Another issue of concern is how followers gain and use power in organizations. Formal leaders typically have more power than followers do. Nevertheless, effective followers participate fully in organizations by culling power from the available sources. Even the lowest-level follower has personal and position-based sources of power that can be used to generate upward influence, thereby impacting the organization and establishing a mutually beneficial relationship with leaders.[31] Personal sources of power include knowledge, expertise, effort, and persuasion. Position sources of power include location, information, and access.

Personal Sources

A knowledgeable follower possesses skills and talents that are a valuable resource to the leader and to the organization. Such a follower is of real value, and his or her departure would be a loss. *Knowledge* is a source of upward influence. In addition, a follower who has a demonstrated record of performance often develops *expertise* and in this way can influence decisions. A record of successes and a history of contributions can garner expert status for followers, from which followers can derive the power to influence operations and establish themselves as a resource to the leader. The power to influence is also associated with the *effort* put forth by a follower. By demonstrating a willingness to learn, to accept undesirable projects, and to initiate activities beyond the scope of expected effort, a follower can gain power in an organization.[32] Tim Chapman was hired by Spartan Motors during his senior year of high school. By age 20, he was the head electrical engineer, troubleshooting and consorting with key vendors. "I guess I'm willing to learn," says Chapman.[33]

Followers can also use persuasion as a source of personal power. *Persuasion* refers to the direct appeal to leaders in an organization for desired outcomes.[34] In addition to being direct, speaking truthfully to a leader can be a source of power for effective followers.[35] Rob Hummel, head of international post-production at Dreamworks SKG, once promoted an employee who was known for being "difficult" because he always challenged his superiors. The fact that this follower was willing to speak truthfully to higher-ups based on his own knowledge and creative brilliance gave him increased power.[36] Power doesn't always come from titles or seniority in the organization; sometimes it comes from one's knowledge and contributions.

Position Sources

Often the formal position of a follower in an organization can provide sources of power. For example, the location of a follower can render him or her *visible* to numerous individuals. A *central location* provides influence to a follower, because the follower is known to many and contributes to the work of many. Similarly, a position that is key to the *flow of information* can establish that position and the follower in it as critical—thus, influential—to those who seek the information. Access to people and information in an organization provides the follower in the position a means to establish relationships with others. With a *network of relationships,* a follower has greater opportunity to persuade others and to make powerful contributions to numerous organizational processes.

STRATEGIES FOR EFFECTIVE FOLLOWERSHIP

Most followers at some point complain about the leader's deficiencies, such as the leader's failure to listen, to encourage, or to recognize followers' efforts.[37] Perfection is impossible for leaders. However, followers can be effective in spite of their leaders by employing strategies that transform the greatest barrier to effective followership: the leader-follower relationship. Most relationships between leaders and followers are characterized by some emotion and behavior based on authority and submission. Leaders are authority figures and may play a disproportionately large role in the mind of a follower. Followers may find themselves being overcritical of their leaders, or rebellious, or passive. Irvin D. Yalom, a professor of psychiatry and author of the novels *Lying on the Couch* and *When Nietzsche Wept*, once had a patient in group therapy who ranted at great length about her boss who never listened and refused to pay her any respect. Interestingly, this woman's complaints persisted through three different jobs and three different bosses.[38] The relationships between leaders and followers are not unlike those between parents and children, and individuals may engage old family patterns when entering into leader-follower relationships.[39] Effective followers, conversely, may perceive themselves as the equals of their leaders, not inherently subordinate.[40] Exhibit 7.3 illustrates the strategies that enable followers to overcome the authority-based relationship and develop an effective, respectful relationship with their leaders.

Be a Resource for the Leader

Effective followers align themselves to the purpose and the vision of the organization. They ask the leader about vision and goals and help achieve them. They understand their impact on the organization's achievement. In this way, followers are a resource of strength and support for the leader. This alignment

EXHIBIT 7.3

Ways to Influence Your Leader

Be a Resource for the Leader
What are leader's needs?
Zig where leader zags
Tell leader about you
Align self to team purpose/vision

Help the Leader be a Good Leader
Ask for advice
Tell leader what you think
Find things to thank leader for

Build a Relationship
Ask about leader at your level/position
Welcome feedback and criticism, such as "What experience led you to that opinion?"
Ask leader to tell you company stories

View the Leader Realistically
Give up idealized leader images
Don't hide anything
Don't criticize leader to others
Disagree occasionally

involves understanding the leader's position, that is, his or her goals, needs, and constraints. Thus, an effective follower can complement the leader's weaknesses with the follower's own strengths.[41] Similarly, effective followers indicate their personal goals and the resources they bring to the organization. Effective followers inform their leaders about their own ideas, beliefs, needs, and constraints. The more leaders and followers can know the day-to-day activities and problems of one another, the better resources they can be for each other. For example, one group of handicapped workers took advantage of a board meeting to issue rented wheelchairs to the members, who then tried to move around the factory in them. Realizing what the workers faced, the board got the factory's ramps improved, and the handicapped workers became a better resource for the organization.[42]

Help the Leader Be a Good Leader

Advice from a leader can be helpful in cultivating followers' abilities. Furthermore, asking a leader for advice enables the leader to give advice. If a leader senses that his or her advice is well regarded, the leader is likely to give effective advice rather than unsympathetic criticism. Effective followers help their leaders be good leaders by simply telling their leaders what they need in order to be good followers.

A leader can become a better leader when followers compliment and thank their leader for things well done.[43] If a leader knows what followers appreciate, the leader is more likely to continue the appreciated behavior. Similarly, if ineffective or destructive actions are not congratulated, they may taper off. Thus, thanking leaders for helpful behaviors and being honest when leaders are counterproductive is an effective way to communicate the need for a leader to change. For example, an emergency room nurse who constantly dealt with a temperamental doctor did not resist the tantrums he aimed at the nurses. After she began to thank him when he did not become angry, his temper flared less regularly.[44]

Build a Relationship with the Leader

Effective followers work toward a genuine relationship with their leaders, which includes developing trust and speaking honestly on the basis of that trust.[45] By building a relationship with a leader, a follower makes every interaction more meaningful to the organization. Furthermore, the relationship is imbued with mutual respect rather than authority and submission. Wes Walsh used mindful initiatives to create a relationship with his boss that maximized his own upward influence.

IN THE LEAD Wes Walsh

When Wes Walsh came under an autocratic manager, his position predecessor warned him to either stay away from the infamously autocratic boss, or else be prepared to give up any influence over the unit operations. Walsh decided to ignore this advice. Instead, he started dropping by his boss's office on a regular basis to discuss production progress. Walsh also sought approval on very small matters because they were virtually impossible for his boss to oppose. Walsh continued these frequent, informal interactions over a lengthy period of time before moving on to more consequential matters.

Eventually, major projects had to be addressed. For example, an increase in the volume of materials processed had rendered Walsh's unit too slow and too limited to adequately serve the increased production. In response, Walsh first requested his boss to devote a couple of hours to him at some designated point in the near future. When the appointed time arrived, Walsh took his boss on a lengthy tour of the plant, pointing out the volume of material scattered about waiting to be processed. He supplemented this visual evidence with facts and figures.

The boss was compelled to acknowledge the problem. Thus, he asked for Walsh's proposal, which Walsh had carefully prepared beforehand. Although the boss had rejected identical proposals from Walsh's predecessor, this time the boss almost immediately approved the sum of $150,000 for updating the unit equipment.[46]

Walsh's conscious effort to interact and get his boss comfortable saying yes on small matters set a precedent for a pattern of respect that was not lost even on his autocratic superior.

Followers can generate respect by asking their leaders questions, such as about the leader's experiences in the follower's position and what the source was for specific feedback and criticism. Followers can also ply the leader for company stories.[47] By doing so, followers are getting beyond submissive behavior by asking leaders to be accountable for their criticism, to have empathy for the followers' position, and to share history about something both parties have in common—the organization. When Mary Kay Ash relates stories to her sales associates about her struggles prior to the founding of her cosmetics company, the associates repeat them to women all over the country. Women who have been underrated in the corporate world feel an immediate kinship because Ash is giving them the respect—and the opportunity—they are otherwise missing.[48]

View the Leader Realistically

To view leaders realistically means to give up idealized images of them. Understanding that leaders are fallible and will make many mistakes leads to acceptance. The way in which a follower perceives his or her boss is the foundation of their relationship. It helps to view leaders as they really are, not as followers think they should be.[49] For example, a follower must determine whether he or she is reading the leader accurately. One employee believed for a long time that his boss disliked him because she was ignoring him. In reality, she believed him to be the most competent member of the department, who did not require supervision like the rest of the crew.[50]

Similarly, effective followers present realistic images of themselves. Followers do not try to hide their weaknesses or cover their mistakes, nor do they criticize their leaders to others.[51] Hiding things is symptomatic of conforming and passive followers. Criticizing leaders to others merely bolsters alienation, and reinforces the mind-set of an alienated follower. Only positive things about a leader should be shared with others. It is an alienated follower who complains without engaging in constructive action. Instead of criticizing a leader to others, it is far more constructive to directly disagree with a leader on occasions relevant to the operation of the organization.

WHAT FOLLOWERS WANT

Research indicates that followers have expectations about what constitutes a desirable leader.[52] Exhibit 7.4 shows the top four choices in rank order based on surveys of followers about what they desire in leaders and colleagues.

Followers want their leaders to be honest, forward-thinking, inspiring, and competent. A leader must be worthy of trust, envision the future of the organization, inspire others to contribute, and be capable and effective in matters that will affect the organization. In terms of competence, leadership roles may shift from the formal leader to the person with particular expertise in a given area.

Followers want their fellow followers to be honest and competent, but also dependable and cooperative. Thus, desired qualities of colleagues share two qualities with leaders—honesty and competence. However, followers themselves want followers to be dependable and cooperative, rather than forward-thinking and inspiring. The hallmark that distinguishes the role of leadership from the role of followership, then, is not authority, knowledge, power, or other conventional notions of what a follower is not. Rather, the distinction lies in the clearly defined leadership activities of fostering a vision and inspiring others to achieve that vision. Vision will be discussed in detail in Chapter 13.

EXHIBIT 7.4

Rank Order of Desirable Characteristics

Desirable Leaders Are	Desirable Colleagues (Followers) Are
Honest	Honest
Forward-thinking	Cooperative
Inspiring	Dependable
Competent	Competent

SOURCE: Adapted from James M. Kouzes and Barry Z. Posner, *Credibility: How Leaders Gain and Lose It, Why People Demand It* (San Francisco, CA: Jossey-Bass Publishers, 1993), 255.

Organizations that can boast of effective followers tend to have leaders who deal primarily with change and progress.[53] Followers do not want to find themselves subjected to authority that would make them alienated, passive, pragmatic, or conforming. They perceive their role to differ from their leader's primarily in terms of the leadership responsibilities of foresight and inspiration. The survey results in Exhibit 7.4 underscore the basis of this chapter—leaders and followers are acting in two different roles at any given moment, but effective behaviors often overlap.

BUILDING A COMMUNITY OF FOLLOWERS

Significantly, dependability and cooperation are necessary for the followers' role in building a sense of community. Leaders are often encouraged to achieve community in their organizations, especially if it is becoming a learning organization. Yet community building is firmly within the purview of followers too. The learning organization, which will be described in Chapter 15, depends on community, wherein all people feel encouraged, respected, and committed to a common purpose. In a community, people are able to communicate openly with one another, maintain their uniqueness, and be firmly committed to something larger than selfish interests. In short, a group of effective followers provides the basis for community. It is not by coincidence that effective followers and effective community members share certain characteristics. Historically, communities of all sorts were based on service, informed participation, and individual contributions.[54] Thus, the follower who has the courage to serve, who is an active, critical thinker, and who maximizes his or her contributions encourages a sense of community to develop in an organization.

Characteristics of a community include inclusivity, realism, and shared leadership.[55] Effective followers encourage these traits as they enact their followership roles.

INCLUSIVITY   In a community, everyone belongs. Individuality and different points of view are encouraged. However, community focuses on the whole rather than the parts, and people emphasize what binds them together rather than what separates them. Effective followers speak honestly when their convictions differ from others. This courage often stems from the belief in the inherent equality between themselves, other followers, and their leaders—that is wholeness. Effective followership facilitates an environment built on individual differences, which results in realism, and the equal worth of those differences, which leads to shared leadership.

CONVERSATION   Conversation is how people make and share the meanings that are the basis of community. In a thriving community, conversation across traditional boundaries strengthens bonds of trust and commitment. One special type of communication, **dialogue,** means that each person suspends his attachment to a particular viewpoint so that a deeper level of listening, synthesis, and meaning evolves from the whole community. Individual differences are acknowledged and respected, but the group searches for an expanded collective perspective.[56] Dialogue will be explained more thoroughly in Chapter 9. Only through conversation can people build collaboration and collective action so they move together on a common path.

REALISM   By including everyone's point of view, a community is realistic. A community includes people with very different perspectives and encourages people to speak up. Thus, community members appreciate the whole of any issue or problem, and the resulting conclusions are typically more sensible, creative, and well-rounded.

SHARED LEADERSHIP   In a community, a leader is one among many equals. Decentralization is an essential aspect of true community, and decisions are reached by consensus. A community creates a "safe" place, so that anyone feels free to step forward as a leader. Like plugs of zoysia grass planted far apart that eventually meld together into a beautiful carpet of lawn, effective followers who share leadership throughout an organization meld together to make good things happen.[57]

SUMMARY AND INTERPRETATION

As organizations continue the trend toward empowering employees, the important role of followers can be recognized. People are followers more often than leaders, and effective leaders and followers share similar characteristics. An effective follower is both active and an independent thinker. Being an effective follower depends on not becoming alienated, conforming, passive, nor a pragmatic survivor. Leaders can develop effective followers through self-management leadership.

Courage is vital to effective followership. Effective followers display the courage to assume responsibility, to serve, to challenge, to participate in transformation, and to leave when necessary. Followers also are aware of their own power and its sources, which include personal and position sources. Strategies for being an effective follower include being a resource, helping the leader be a good leader, building a relationship with the leader, and viewing the leader realistically.

Followers want both their leaders and their colleagues to be honest and competent. However, they want their leaders also to be forward-thinking and inspirational. The two latter traits distinguish the role of leader from follower. Followers want to be led, not controlled. Conversely, followers want their peers to be dependable and cooperative. These features help develop community, which enables followers to prosper and to share leadership in organizations.

KEY TERMS

critical thinking	pragmatic survivor	synergy
uncritical thinking	passive follower	dialogue
alienated follower	self-management leadership	
conformist	effective follower	

DISCUSSION QUESTIONS

1. Discuss the role of a follower. Why do you think so little emphasis is given to followership compared to leadership in organizations?

2. Compare the alienated follower with the passive follower. Can you give an example of each? How would you respond to each if you were a leader?

3. Do you think self-management leadership should be considered a leadership style? Why or why not?

4. Which of the five courageous actions of a follower do you feel is most important to an effective follower? Least important? How does a follower derive the courage and power to be effective? Discuss.

5. As a follower, from what sources do you derive courage? Discuss.

6. Describe the strategy for effective followership that you most prefer. Explain.

7. What do the traits followers want in leaders and in other followers tell us about the roles of each? Discuss.

8. How might the characteristics of effective followership contribute to building community? Discuss.

9. Is the courage to leave the ultimate courage of a follower compared to the courage to participate in transformation? Which would be hardest for you?

LEADERSHIP DEVELOPMENT: Personal Feedback

The Power of Followership

For each statement below, please use the six-point scale to indicate the extent to which the statement describes you. Think of a specific but typical followership situation and how you acted.

0	1	2	3	4	5	6
Rarely			Occasionally			Almost Always

_____ 1. Does your work help you fulfill some societal goal or personal dream that is important to you?

_____ 2. Are your personal work goals aligned with the organization's priority goals?

_____ 3. Are you highly committed to and energized by your work and organization, giving them your best ideas and performance?

_____ 4. Does your enthusiasm also spread to and energize your coworkers?

_____ 5. Instead of waiting for or merely accepting what the leader tells you, do you personally identify which organizational activities are most critical for achieving the organization's priority goals?

_____ 6. Do you actively develop a distinctive competence in those critical activities so that you become more valuable to the leader and the organization?

_____ 7. When starting a new job or assignment, do you promptly build a record of successes in tasks that are important to the leader?

_____ 8. Can the leader give you a difficult assignment without the benefit of much supervision, knowing that you will meet your deadline with highest-quality work and that you will "fill in the cracks" if need be?

_____ 9. Do you take the initiative to seek out and successfully complete assignments that go above and beyond your job?

_____ 10. When you are not the leader of a group project, do you still contribute at a high level, often doing more than your share?

_____ 11. Do you independently think up and champion new ideas that will contribute significantly to the leader's or the organization's goals?

_____ 12. Do you try to solve the tough problems (technical or organizational), rather than look to the leader to do it for you?

_____ 13. Do you help out other coworkers, making them look good, even when you do not get any credit?

_____ 14. Do you help the leader or group see both the upside potential and downside risks of ideas or plans, playing the devil's advocate if need be?

_____ 15. Do you understand the leader's needs, goals, and constraints, and work hard to meet them?

_____ 16. Do you actively and honestly own up to your strengths and weaknesses rather than put off evaluation?

_____ 17. Do you make a habit of internally questioning the wisdom of the leader's decision rather than just doing what you are told?

_____ 18. When the leader asks you to do something that runs contrary to your professional or personal preferences, do you say "no" rather than "yes"?

_____ 19. Do you act on your own ethical standards rather than the leader's or the group's standards?

_____ 20. Do you assert your views on important issues, even though it might mean conflict with your group or reprisals from the leader?

Scoring

Questions 1, 5, 11, 12, 14, 16, 17, 18, 19, and 20 measure "independent thinking." Sum your answers and write your score below.

Questions 2, 3, 4, 6, 7, 8, 9, 10, 13, and 15 measure "active engagement." Sum your answers and write your score below.

Independent Thinking Total Score = _____

Active Engagement Total Score = _____

Interpretation

These two scores indicate how you carry out your followership role. A score of 20 or below is considered low. A score of 40 or higher is considered high. A score between 20 and 40 is in the middle. Based on whether your score is high, middle, or low, assess your followership style below.

Followership Style	Independent Thinking Score	Active Engagement Score
Effective	High	High
Alienated	High	Low
Conformist	Low	High
Pragmatist	Middling	Middling
Passive	Low	Low

How do you feel about your follower style? Compare your style to others. What might you do to be more effective as a follower?

SOURCE: From Robert E. Kelley, *The Power of Followership: How to Create Leaders People Want to Follow and Followers Who Lead Themselves,* 89–97. Copyright © 1992 by Consultants to Executives and Organizations, Ltd. Used by permission of Doubleday, a division of Random House, Inc.

LEADERSHIP DEVELOPMENT: Cases for Analysis

General Products Britain

Carl Mitchell was delighted to accept a job in the British branch office of General Products, Inc., a consumer products multinational. Two months later, Mitchell was miserable. The problem was George Garrow, the general manager in charge of the British branch, to whom Mitchell reported.

Garrow had worked his way to the general manager position by "keeping his nose clean" and not making mistakes, which he accomplished by avoiding controversial and risky decisions.

As Mitchell complained to his wife, "Any time I ask him to make a decision, he just wants us to dig deeper and provide thirty more pages of data, most of which are irrelevant. I can't get any improvements started."

For example, Mitchell believed that the line of frozen breakfasts and dinners he was in charge of would be more successful if prices were lowered. He and his four product managers spent weeks preparing graphs and charts to justify a lower price. Garrow reviewed the data but kept waffling, asking for more information. His latest request for weather patterns that might affect shopping habits seemed absurd.

Garrow seemed terrified of departing from the status quo. The frozen breakfast and dinner lines still had 1970s-style packaging, even though they had been reformulated for microwave ovens. Garrow would not approve a coupon program in March because in previous years coupons had been run in April. Garrow measured progress not by new ideas or sales results but by hours spent in the office. He arrived early and shuffled memos and charts until late in the evening and expected the same from everyone else.

After four months on the job, Mitchell made a final effort to reason with Garrow. He argued that the branch was taking a big risk by avoiding decisions to improve things. Market share was slipping. New pricing and promotion strategies were essential. But Garrow just urged more patience and told Mitchell that he and his product managers would have to build a more solid case. Soon after, Mitchell's two best product managers quit, burned out by the marathon sessions analyzing pointless data without results.

Questions

1. How would you evaluate Mitchell as a follower? Evaluate his courage and style.
2. If you were Mitchell, what would you do now?
3. If you were Garrow's boss and Mitchell came to see you, what would you say?

Trams Discount Store

"Things are different around here" were the first words Jill heard from her new manager. Mr. Tyler was welcoming Jill back to another summer of working at Trams, a nationwide discount store. Jill was not at all thrilled with the prospect of another summer at Trams, but jobs were hard to find.

Reluctantly, Jill had returned to work the 6:00 P.M. to 10:00 P.M. shift at Trams, where she worked in the ladies' and children's apparel department. Her job consisted of folding clothes, straightening up the racks, and going to the registers for "price checks." Jill's stomach tied in knots as she remembered her previous work experience at Trams. She was originally hired because management had found that college students work hard, and work hard Jill did. Her first boss at Trams was Ms. Williams, who had strict rules that were to be adhered to or else you were fired. There was to be no talking between employees, or to friends and family who entered the store. Each of the four girls who worked the night shift was assigned a section of the department and was held responsible for it. With the clientele and the number of price checks, it was almost impossible to finish the work, but each night Jill would race against the clock to finish her section. Ms. Williams was always watching through a one-way mirror, so everyone was alert at all times. It seemed there wasn't a minute to breathe—her twenty-minute break (and not a minute more!) was hardly enough to recover from the stress of trying to beat the clock.

As Jill talked to Mr. Tyler, she sensed that things really were different. She was introduced to the other girls she'd be working with and, to her surprise, they all seemed to know one another well and enjoy working at Trams. Mr. Tyler then left a little after 6 P.M., leaving the night shift with no supervision! One of the girls explained that they all worked as a team to get the work done. There was constant chatter, and her coworkers seemed eager to get to know her and hear about her experiences at college. It was hard for Jill at first, but she gradually became used to talking and working. The girls teased her a bit for working so hard and fast and rushing back to the department at the end of her allotted twenty minutes of break time.

At first, Jill was appalled by the amount of goofing off the girls did, but as time passed she began to enjoy it and participate. After all, the work got done with time to spare. Maybe things weren't quite as neat as before—and the store manager had alerted the department that sales were down—but no one had asked the girls to change their behavior. Everyone, including Jill, began taking longer and longer breaks. Some of the girls even snacked on the sales floor, and they were becoming sloppier and sloppier in their work. Jill liked the relaxed atmosphere, but her work ethic and previous training made it hard for her to accept this. She felt responsible for the decline in sales, and she hated seeing the department so untidy. She began to make a few suggestions, but the other girls ignored her and began excluding her from their bantering. She even talked to Mr. Tyler, who agreed that her suggestions were excellent, but he never said anything to the others. Their behavior grew more and more lax. None of the girls did her job completely, and breaks often stretched to an hour long. Jill knew the quality of her own work went down as well, but she tried hard to keep up with her own job and the jobs of the others. Again, Trams became a nightmare.

The final straw came when her coworker Tara approached Jill and asked her to change the price tag on a fashionable tank top to $2 and then "back her up" at the register. Jill replied that the tag said $20, not $2. Tara explained that she worked hard, did her job, and never received any reward. The store owed her this "discount." Jill adamantly refused. Tara changed the price tag herself, went to the register to ring it up, and called Jill a college snob. Jill knew it was time for her to act.

SOURCE: Adapted from "Things are Different Around Here," prepared by Ann Marie Calacci, with the assistance of Frank Yeandel, in John E. Dittrich and Robert A. Zawacki, *People and Organizations: Cases in Management and Organizational Behavior* (Plano, TX: Business Publications, Inc., 1981), 72–75.

Questions

1. What types of follower courage does Jill need in this situation?

2. If you were Jill, what actions would you take first? If that didn't produce results, what would you do second? Third?

3. How might Jill use this experience to develop her personal potential?

REFERENCES

1. Ronald A. Heifetz, *Leadership Without Easy Answers* (Cambridge, MA: The Belknap Press of Harvard University Press, 1994), 203–204.
2. Robert E. Kelley, "In Praise of Followers," *Harvard Business Review,* November/December 1988, 142–148.
3. Bernard M. Bass, *Bass & Stodgill's Handbook of Leadership,* 3rd ed. (New York: Free Press, 1990).
4. Ira Chaleff, *The Courageous Follower: Standing Up To and For Our Leaders* (San Francisco, CA: Berrett-Koehler, 1995).
5. Ira Chaleff, "Learn the Art of Followership," *Government Executive,* February 1997, 51.
6. D. E. Whiteside, *Command Excellence: What It Takes to Be the Best!,* Department of the Navy, Washington, DC: Naval Military Personnel Command, 1985.
7. Polly LaBarre, "'The Most Important Thing a Captain Can Do Is to See the Ship From the Eyes of the Crew,'" *Fast Company,* April 1999, 115–126.
8. Robert E. Kelley, *The Power of Followership* (New York: Doubleday, 1992).
9. Ibid., 101.
10. Ibid., 111–112.
11. Ibid., 117–118.
12. Ibid., 123.
13. Charles C. Manz and Henry P. Sims, Jr., "Leading Workers to Lead Themselves: The External Leadership of Self-Managing Work Teams," *Administrative Science Quarterly,* March 1987, 106–129; and Charles C. Manz, *Mastering Self-Leadership: Empowering Yourself for Personal Excellence* (Englewood Cliffs, NJ: Prentice-Hall, 1992).

14. Robert C. Ford and Myron D. Fottler, "Empowerment: A Matter of Degree," *Academy of Management Executive* 9 (1995), 21–31.
15. Richard Pascale, "Change How You Define Leadership, and You Change How You Run a Company," *Fast Company,* April-May 1998, 110–120.
16. Howard Gardner, *Leading Minds* (New York: Basic Books, 1995), 286.
17. Chaleff, *The Courageous Follower: Standing Up To and For Our Leaders.*
18. Edward O. Welles, "The Shape of Things to Come," *Inc.,* February 1992, 66–74.
19. Joann S. Lublin, "Building a Better CEO," *The Wall Street Journal,* April 14, 2000, B1, B4.
20. John A. Byrne, "How Al Dunlap Self-Destructed," *Business Week,* July 6, 1998, 58–65.
21. Ira Sager with Diane Brady, "Big Blue's Blunt Bohemian," *Business Week,* June 14, 1999, 107–112.
22. Merle MacIsaac, "Born Again Basket Case," *Canadian Business,* May 1993, 38–44.
23. Dianne Martz, "Hard Lessons, Well Learned," *Inc.,* December 1993, 29–30.
24. Curtis Sittenfeld, "He's No Fool (But He Plays One Inside Companies)," *Fast Company,* November 1998, 66, 68.
25. Kofi Lomotey and Austin D. Swanson, "Restructuring School Governance: Learning from the Experiences of Rural and Urban Schools," in *Educational Leadership in an Age of Reform,* Stephen L. Jacobson and James A. Conway, eds. (White Plains, NY: Longman 1990), 65–82.
26. Chaleff, *The Courageous Follower: Standing Up To and For Our Leaders.*
27. Stephen R. Covey, *The 7 Habits of Highly Effective People: Powerful Lessons in Personal Change* (New York: Simon & Schuster 1989).
28. This discussion of the seven habits is based on Covey, *The 7 Habits of Highly Effective People;* and Don Hellriegel, John W. Slocum, Jr., and Richard Woodman, *Organizational Behavior,* 8th ed. (Cincinnati, OH: South-Western College Publishing, 1998), 350–352.
29. Stephen R. Covey, *The 7 Habits of Highly Effective People* (New York: Fireside edition/Simon & Schuster, 1990), 72.
30. Sager with Brady, "Big Blue's Blunt Bohemian."
31. David C. Wilson and Graham K. Kenny, "Managerially Perceived Influence Over Interdepartmental Decisions," *Journal of Management Studies* 22 (1985), 155–173; Warren Keith Schilit, "An Examination of Individual Differences as Moderators of Upward Influence Activity in Strategic Decisions," *Human Relations* 39 (1986), 933-953; David Mechanic, "Sources of Power of Lower Participants in Complex Organizations," *Administrative Science Quarterly* 7 (1962), 349–364.
32. Peter Moroz and Brian H. Kleiner, "Playing Hardball in Business Organizations," *IM,* January/February 1994, 9–11.
33. Welles, "The Shape of Things to Come."
34. Warren Keith Schilit and Edwin A. Locke, "A Study of Upward Influence in Organizations," *Administrative Science Quarterly* 27 (1982), 304–316.
35. Chaleff, *The Courageous Follower: Standing Up To and For Our Leaders.*
36. "Open Mouth, Open Career," sidebar in Michael Warshaw, "Open Mouth, Close Career?" *Fast Company,* December 1998, 240ff.

37. Len Schlesinger, "It Doesn't Take a Wizard to Build a Better Boss," *Fast Company*, June/July 1996, 102–107.
38. Irvin D. Yalom, M.D., with Ben Yalom, "Mad About Me," *Inc.*, December 1998, 37–38.
39. Frank Pittman, "How to Manage Mom and Dad," *Psychology Today*, November/December 1994, 44–74.
40. Kelley, "In Praise of Followers."
41. Chaleff, *The Courageous Follower: Standing Up To and For Our Leaders*.
42. Christopher Hegarty, *How to Manage Your Boss* (New York: Ballantine 1985), 147.
43. Ibid.
44. Ibid., 107–108.
45. Chaleff, *The Courageous Follower: Standing Up To and For Our Leaders*.
46. Peter B. Smith and Mark F. Peterson, *Leadership, Organizations and Culture* (London: Sage Publications, 1988), 144–145.
47. Pittman, "How to Manage Mom and Dad."
48. Alan Farnham, "Mary Kay's Lessons in Leadership," *Fortune*, September 20, 1993, 68–77.
49. Hegarty, *How to Manage Your Boss*.
50. Ibid., 49.
51. Pittman, "How to Manage Mom and Dad."
52. James M. Kouzes and Barry Z. Posner, *Credibility: How Leaders Gain and Lose It, Why People Demand It* (San Francisco: Jossey-Bass, 1993).
53. Kelley, "In Praise of Followers."
54. Juanita Brown and David Isaacs, "Building Corporations as Communities: The Best of Both Worlds," in *Community Building: Renewing Spirit & Learning in Business*, Kazimierz Gozdz, ed. (San Francisco: Sterling & Stone, Inc., 1995), 69–83.
55. M. Scott Peck, *The Different Drum: Community Making and Peace* (New York: Touchstone, 1987).
56. Brown and Isaacs, "Building Corporations as Communities"; Glenna Gerard and Linda Teurfs, "Dialogue and Organizational Transformation," in Kazimierz Gozdz, ed., *Community Building* (San Francisco: Sterling & Stone, Inc., 1995), 142–153; and Edgar G. Schein, "On Dialogue, Culture, and Organizational Learning," *Organizational Dynamics*, Autumn 1993, 40–51.
57. Brown and Isaacs, "Building Corporations as Communities."

The Leader as Relationship Builder

CHAPTER OUTLINE

YOUR LEADERSHIP CHALLENGE

After reading this chapter, you should be able to:

- Recognize and apply the difference between intrinsic and extrinsic rewards.

- Motivate others by meeting their higher-level needs.

- Apply needs-based theories of motivation.

- Implement individual and systemwide rewards.

- Avoid the disadvantages of "carrot-and-stick" motivation.

- Implement empowerment by providing the five elements of information, knowledge, discretion, meaning, and rewards.

Motivation and Empowerment

With the hectic Christmas season approaching, leaders at Growing Green were especially concerned about keeping their staff energized and motivated. But morale was in the pits at the corporate plantscaping firm located in St. Louis, and the company continued to lose employees. Growing Green was facing its first major crisis.

Joel and Teri Pesapane started the company from scratch and had always made all the decisions. Employees had to check with Joel about every detail, from what to spray on a particular plant to whether it was time to fertilize a ficus tree. The company was bumping against a growth ceiling, turning away business because the two owners wanted to handle every new account. The Pesapanes had read about the results of empowerment at larger companies and wondered if it could help their small firm through its growing pains. As an experiment, they asked employees to decide whether the company's gift shop should continue to sell Christmas decorations and if so, to propose better ways to do it. Sales were weak and the Pesapanes had considered discontinuing the items. Employees, however, researched how other companies succeeded with seasonal items and came up with a plan that revived sales—and employee motivation. "We did a comprehensive analysis and succeeded in turning around the business," says Donald Thieman. "Even more important, we could all take credit for the outcome. Suddenly, everybody was excited about Christmas instead of dreading it."

Since that first experiment, the Pesapanes have empowered teams of workers to handle almost all of the firm's decisions. Small action teams have authority in specific areas, such as bidding for new business, handling plant installations, maintaining customer sites, or handling administrative functions. One member from each of the action teams serves on Growing Green's management team. Teri and Joel are no longer involved in the teams' day-to-day work, acting instead to provide leadership and guidance as needed.

The shift to empowered work teams wasn't easy, but the Pesapanes believe the results were worth the effort. Employees who wanted more control over their own work thrived in the new environment. The reputation of the firm soared as a result of energized, motivated teams who were committed to completing jobs on time and on budget, helping Growing Green win contracts with major clients such as the St. Louis Galleria, the Monsanto Company, the Hyatt Regency St. Louis, and St. Charles Riverfront Station. The Pesapanes are no longer afraid of stepping aside and letting their employees run the show. As Joel explains it, "We want our people to grow, just like our plants."[1]

Joel and Teri Pesapane improved motivation at Growing Green by putting emphasis on cultivating people as well as plants. By giving employees more control over their work, the leaders revived morale and improved job satisfaction, helping their small firm continue to grow and thrive. Empowerment of lower-level employees is a powerful trend in today's organizations, and one reason for this is the favorable impact that true empowerment can have on employee motivation.

This chapter will explore motivation in organizations and examine how leaders can bring out the best in organizational followers. We will examine the difference between intrinsic and extrinsic rewards and how they meet the needs of followers. Individuals have both lower and higher needs, and there are different methods of motivation to meet those needs. The chapter presents several theories of motivation, with particular attention to the differences between leadership and conventional management methods for creating a motivated workforce. The final sections of the chapter explore empowerment and other recent motivational tools that do not rely on traditional reward and punishment methods.

LEADERSHIP AND MOTIVATION

Most of us get up in the morning, go to school or work, and behave in ways that are predictably our own. We usually respond to our environment and the people in it with little thought as to why we work hard, enjoy certain classes, or find some recreational activities so much fun. Yet all these behaviors are motivated by something. **Motivation** refers to the forces either internal or external to a person that arouse enthusiasm and persistence to pursue a certain course of action. Employee motivation affects productivity, and so part of a leader's job is to channel followers' motivation toward the accomplishment of the organization's vision and goals.[2] The study of motivation helps leaders understand what prompts people to initiate action, what influences their choice of action, and why they persist in that action over time.

Exhibit 8.1 illustrates a simple model of human motivation. People have basic needs, such as for food, recognition, or monetary gain, that translate into an internal tension that motivates specific behaviors with which to fulfill the need. To the extent that the behavior is successful, the person is rewarded when the need is satisfied. The reward also informs the person that the behavior was appropriate and can be used again in the future.

The importance of motivation, as illustrated in Exhibit 8.1, is that it can lead to behaviors that reflect high performance within organizations. Recent studies have found that high employee motivation and high organizational performance and profits go hand in hand.[3] Leaders may use motivation theory to help satisfy followers' needs and simultaneously encourage high work performance. When workers are not motivated to achieve organizational goals, the fault is often the leader's.

EXHIBIT 8.1

A Simple Model of Motivation

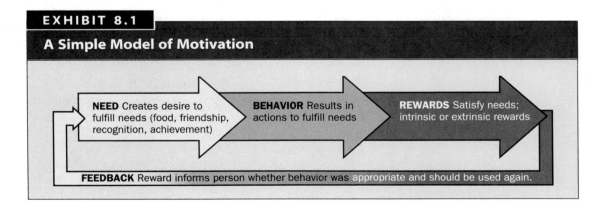

NEED Creates desire to fulfill needs (food, friendship, recognition, achievement)

BEHAVIOR Results in actions to fulfill needs

REWARDS Satisfy needs; intrinsic or extrinsic rewards

FEEDBACK Reward informs person whether behavior was appropriate and should be used again.

Intrinsic and Extrinsic Rewards

Rewards can be either intrinsic or extrinsic, systemwide or individual. Exhibit 8.2 illustrates the categories of rewards, combining intrinsic and extrinsic rewards with those that are applied systemwide or individually.[4] **Intrinsic rewards** are the internal satisfactions a person receives in the process of performing a particular action. Solving a problem to benefit others may fulfill a personal mission, or the completion of a complex task may bestow a pleasant feeling of accomplishment. An intrinsic reward is internal and under the control of the individual, such as to engage in task behavior to satisfy a need for competency and self-determination.

Conversely, **extrinsic rewards** are given by another person, typically a supervisor, and include promotions and pay increases. Because they originate externally as a result of pleasing others, extrinsic rewards compel individuals to engage in a task behavior for an outside source that provides what they need, such as money to survive in modern society. Consider, for example, the difference in motivation for polishing a car if it belongs to you versus if you work at a car wash. Your good feelings from making your own car shine would be intrinsic. However, buffing a car that is but one of many in a day's work requires the extrinsic reward of a paycheck.[5]

Rewards can be given systemwide or on an individual basis. **Systemwide rewards** apply the same to all people within an organization or within a specific category or department. **Individual rewards** may differ among people within the same organization or department. An extrinsic, systemwide reward could be insurance benefits or vacation time available to an entire organization

---

EXHIBIT 8.2

Examples of Intrinsic and Extrinsic Rewards

	Extrinsic	Intrinsic
Individual	Large merit increase	Feeling of self-fulfillment
System-wide	Insurance benefits	Pride in being part of a "winning" organization

SOURCE Adapted from Richard M. Steers, Lyman W. Porter, and Gregory A. Bigley, *Motivation and Leadership at Work,* 6th ed. (New York: McGraw-Hill, 1996), 498. Reprinted with permission of the McGraw-Hill Companies.

or category of people, such as those who have been with the organization for two years or more. An intrinsic, systemwide reward would be the sense of pride that comes from within by virtue of contributing to a "winning" organization. An extrinsic, individual reward is a promotion or a bonus check. An intrinsic, individual reward would be a sense of self-fulfillment that an individual derives from his or her work.

Although extrinsic rewards are important, leaders work especially hard to enable followers to achieve intrinsic rewards—both individually and systemwide. Employees who get intrinsic satisfaction from their jobs often put forth increased effort. In addition, as we described in Chapter 1, leaders genuinely care about others and want them to feel good about their work. Leaders create an environment that brings out the best in people. We all know that people voluntarily invest time and energy in activities they enjoy, such as hobbies, charitable causes, or community projects. On the job, employees may always have to perform some activities they don't particularly like, but leaders try to match followers with jobs and tasks that provide individual intrinsic rewards. They also strive to create an environment where people feel valued and feel that they are contributing to something worthwhile, helping followers achieve systemwide intrinsic rewards. For example, Bennett and Patricia Kopp, owners of a Charley's Steakery franchise in Knoxville, Tennessee, have always put employees first. They created an environment where their young workers feel they are part of a family that cares about them as individuals. In an industry where workers are hard to find and even harder to keep, the Kopps still have all the employees they started the deli with six years ago. Workers rarely are late or fail to show up for work because they are motivated by intrinsic as well as extrinsic rewards.[6] In an extensive survey conducted by the Gallup Organization, researchers found that the way leaders create engaged employees and high performance has very little to do with extrinsic rewards such as pay and benefits, and much more to do with creating an environment in which people flourish. This chapter's Leader's Bookshelf tells more.

Higher versus Lower Needs

Intrinsic rewards appeal to the "higher" needs of individuals, such as accomplishment, competence, fulfillment, and self-determination. Extrinsic rewards appeal to the "lower" needs of individuals, such as material comfort and basic safety and security. Exhibit 8.3 outlines the distinction between conventional management and leadership approaches to motivation based on people's needs. Conventional management approaches often appeal to an individual's lower, basic needs and rely on extrinsic rewards and punishments—carrot-and-stick methods—to motivate subordinates to behave in desired ways. These approaches are effective, but they are based on controlling the behavior of people by manipulating their decisions about how to act. The higher needs of

LEADER'S BOOKSHELF

First, Break All the Rules: What the World's Greatest Managers Do Differently

Marcus Buckingham and Curt Coffman

Money can't buy employee commitment and motivation, increased performance, or greater profits. That's the conclusion Gallup researchers reached following two mammoth studies carried out over the last twenty-five years. During the studies, researchers talked to more than 80,000 managers and a million employees in 400 companies. The results are reported by Marcus Buckingham and Curt Coffman in their book, *First, Break All the Rules.* The strength of a workplace, they say, depends on factors such as whether employees know what is expected of them, have the right tools and information to do their jobs, get to do what they do best, have their opinions heard and considered, and feel that someone at work truly cares about them. That is, it depends largely on leadership.

Great Leaders Create Great Companies

Based on results of the second phase of the Gallup studies, Buckingham and Coffman offer some guidelines for how leaders build strong workplaces by creating environments that allow people to flourish.

■ **Recognize that you have no control.** The first step is for leaders to understand that they actually have less control than their subordinates. It is only through other people that leaders can accomplish anything in the organization. "Each individual employee can decide what to do and what not to do. He can decide the hows, the whens, and the with whoms. For good or for ill, he can make things happen." The leader's job is to channel each employee's motivation toward the accomplishment of organizational goals.

■ **Build on the talents of employees.** Each employee arrives at an organization with a unique set of needs, motivations, and talents. Great leaders "try to draw out what was left in, not put in what was left out." Rather than trying to get people to do things they aren't suited for and don't enjoy, leaders spend loads of time trying to recognize the unique qualities and talents each person brings to the workplace and how those qualities can benefit the organization. By treating each employee as an individual, leaders can put people in the right positions, which provides intrinsic rewards to every employee every day.

■ **Focus people on performance.** Organizations achieve their purpose and goals only when employees perform well. Great leaders clearly define performance outcomes and then let each person find his or her own route toward those outcomes. The authors argue that the most efficient way to turn each individual's talents into high performance is to help employees find their own "path of least resistance" by doing things in a way that works for them.

The Bottom Line

By putting people in the right jobs, clearly defining outcomes, and then getting out of the way, the leader "creates a hero in every role." But does all this have a real impact on performance and profitability? The authors offer compelling statistical evidence that it does. Companies where employees gave high marks to the company on the survey qualities consistently showed higher profits and better financial performance. When employees are more engaged and motivated, they—and their organizations—thrive.

First, Break All the Rules, by Marcus Buckingham and Curt Coffman, is published by Simon & Schuster.

EXHIBIT 8.3

Needs of People and Motivation Methods

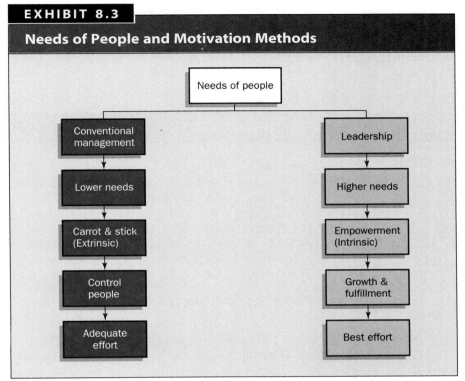

SOURCE: Adapted from William D. Hitt, *The Leader-Manager: Guidelines for Action* (Columbus, OH: Battelle Press, 1988), 153.

people may be unmet in favor of utilizing their labor in exchange for external rewards. Under conventional management, people perform adequately to receive the "carrot," or avoid the "stick," since they will not necessarily derive intrinsic satisfaction from their work.

Leaders often try to motivate others by providing them with the opportunity to satisfy higher needs and become intrinsically rewarded. Remember that the source of an intrinsic reward is internal to the follower. Thus, what is intrinsically rewarding to one individual may not be so to another. One way in which leaders try to enable all followers to achieve intrinsic rewards is by giving them more control over their own work and the power to affect outcomes. When leaders empower others, allowing them the freedom to determine their own actions, subordinates reward themselves intrinsically for good performance. They may become creative, innovative, and develop a greater commitment to their objectives. So motivated, they often achieve their best possible performance.

Ideally, work behaviors should satisfy both lower and higher needs as well as serve the mission of the organization. Unfortunately, this is often not the case. The leader's motivational role, then, is to create a situation that integrates the needs of people—especially higher needs—and the fundamental objectives of the organization.

NEEDS-BASED THEORIES OF MOTIVATION

Needs-based theories emphasize the needs that motivate people. At any point in time, people have basic needs such as those for food, achievement, or monetary reward. These needs are the source of an internal drive that motivates behavior to fulfill the needs. An individual's needs are like a hidden catalog of the things he or she wants and will work to get. To the extent that leaders understand worker needs, they can design the reward system to reinforce employees for directing energies and priorities toward attainment of shared goals.

Hierarchy of Needs Theory

Probably the most famous needs-based theory is the one developed by Abraham Maslow.[7] Maslow's **hierarchy of needs theory** proposes that humans are motivated by multiple needs and those needs exist in a hierarchical order, as illustrated in Exhibit 8.4, wherein the higher needs cannot be satisfied until the lower needs are met. Maslow identified five general levels of motivating needs.

- **Physiological** The most basic human physiological needs include food, water, and sex. In the organizational setting, these are reflected in the needs for adequate heat, air, and base salary to ensure survival.

- **Safety** Next is the need for a safe and secure physical and emotional environment and freedom from threats—that is, for freedom from violence and for an orderly society. In an organizational workplace, safety needs reflect the needs for safe jobs, fringe benefits, and job security.

- **Belongingness** People have a desire to be accepted by their peers, have friendships, be part of a group, and be loved. In the organization, these needs influence the desire for good relationships with coworkers, participation in a work team, and a positive relationship with supervisors.

- **Esteem** The need for esteem relates to the desires for a positive self-image and for attention, recognition, and appreciation from others.

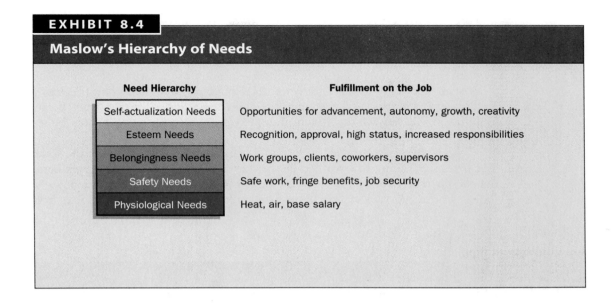

EXHIBIT 8.4

Maslow's Hierarchy of Needs

Need Hierarchy	Fulfillment on the Job
Self-actualization Needs	Opportunities for advancement, autonomy, growth, creativity
Esteem Needs	Recognition, approval, high status, increased responsibilities
Belongingness Needs	Work groups, clients, coworkers, supervisors
Safety Needs	Safe work, fringe benefits, job security
Physiological Needs	Heat, air, base salary

Within organizations, esteem needs reflect a motivation for recognition, an increase in responsibility, high status, and credit for contributions to the organization.

■ **Self-Actualization** The highest need category, self-actualization, represents the need for self-fulfillment: developing one's full potential, increasing one's competence, and becoming a better person. Self-actualization needs can be met in the organization by providing people with opportunities to grow, be empowered and creative, and acquire training for challenging assignments and advancement.

According to Maslow's theory, physiology, safety, and belonging are deficiency needs. These low-order needs take priority—they must be satisfied before higher-order, or growth needs, are activated. The needs are satisfied in sequence: Physiological needs are satisfied before safety needs, safety needs are satisfied before social needs, and so on. A person desiring physical safety will devote his or her efforts to securing a safer environment and will not be concerned with esteem or self-actualization. Once a need is satisfied, it declines in importance and the next higher need is activated. When a union wins good pay and working conditions for its members, basic needs will be met; union members may then want to have social and esteem needs met in the workplace.

Two-Factor Theory

Frederick Herzberg developed another popular theory of motivation called the *two-factor theory*.[8] Herzberg interviewed hundreds of workers about times when they were highly motivated to work and other times when they were dissatisfied and unmotivated to work. His findings suggested that the work characteristics associated with dissatisfaction were quite different from those pertaining to satisfaction, which prompted the notion that two factors influence work motivation.

The two-factor theory is illustrated in Exhibit 8.5. The center of the scale is neutral, meaning that workers are neither satisfied nor dissatisfied. Herzberg believed that two entirely separate dimensions contribute to an employee's behavior at work. The first dimension, called **hygiene factors,** involves the

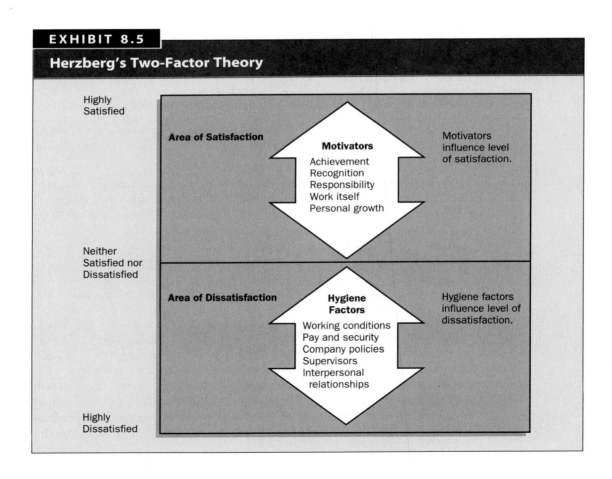

EXHIBIT 8.5

Herzberg's Two-Factor Theory

Highly Satisfied

Area of Satisfaction

Motivators
Achievement
Recognition
Responsibility
Work itself
Personal growth

Motivators influence level of satisfaction.

Neither Satisfied nor Dissatisfied

Area of Dissatisfaction

Hygiene Factors
Working conditions
Pay and security
Company policies
Supervisors
Interpersonal relationships

Hygiene factors influence level of dissatisfaction.

Highly Dissatisfied

presence or absence of job dissatisfiers, such as working conditions, pay, company policies, and interpersonal relationships. When hygiene factors are poor, work is dissatisfying. This is similar to the concept of deficiency needs described by Maslow. Good hygiene factors remove the dissatisfaction, but they do not in themselves cause people to become highly satisfied and motivated in their work.

The second set of factors does influence job satisfaction. **Motivators** fulfill high-level needs and include achievement, recognition, responsibility, and opportunity for growth. Herzberg believed that when motivators are present, workers are highly motivated and satisfied. Thus, hygiene factors and motivators represent two distinct factors that influence motivation. Hygiene factors work in the area of lower-level needs, and their absence causes dissatisfaction. Unsafe working conditions or a noisy working environment will cause people to be dissatisfied; but their correction will not cause a high level of work enthusiasm and satisfaction. Higher-level motivators such as challenge, responsibility, and recognition must be in place before employees will be highly motivated to excel at their work.

The implication of the two-factor theory for leaders is clear. The leader's role is to go beyond the removal of dissatisfiers to the use of motivators to meet higher-level needs and propel employees toward greater achievement and satisfaction. Consider how Rick Born strives to meet employees' higher-level needs at Born Information Services.

IN THE LEAD   Rick Born, Born Information Services

Rick Born built his company around a critical issue facing organizations in the technology-consulting industry: keeping good employees. To differentiate his company as "the very best company to work for," Born offers good salaries and benefits such as tuition reimbursement, revenue sharing, stock options, generous health and dental plans, bonuses, and even a clothing allowance for new employees. However, he knew that wasn't enough. To truly motivate employees and keep them energized and committed to the company, Born needed to provide higher-level motivators as well.

One way Born meets employees' higher-level needs is through the work itself. From the beginning, he chose to focus on cutting-edge technologies, passing up a huge chunk of business with potential clients using older technologies. "We didn't want to do mundane, boring work that wouldn't take our employees anywhere," Born says. He recognized that the really good people in the industry wanted to work on new stuff, not "yesterday's snooze." Another step Born took was to build a $20 million corporate technology center, to give consultants who are between projects a chance to stay on top of their skills. In the company's most recent employee satisfaction survey, career advancement, including the opportunity to work with emerging technologies, ranked first in the employees' list of the key drivers of motivation and satisfaction.

Consultants at Born are also motivated by their high level of responsibility. Rick Born and other top leaders don't micromanage. Consultants are treated like the professionals they are, and many of them feel as if they are running their own business. However, to keep consultants from burning out when they're working for extended periods at clients' sites—and to make sure they know that the company cares about them—Born created the position of "staff manager." The only job of staff managers is to take care of consultants. They have done everything from "dealing with a client who was verbally abusing a consultant" to arranging an extended leave of absence for a consultant who hadn't visited his native country for twenty years.

Rick Born continues his quest to understand and respond to employees' higher-level needs. At Born Information Services, employees get a sense of achievement and accomplishment from working on cutting-edge technologies, and they thrive on the opportunity to expand their knowledge through extensive career and training opportunities.[9]

Acquired Needs Theory

Another needs-based theory was developed by David McClelland. The **acquired needs theory** proposes that certain types of needs are acquired during an individual's lifetime. In other words, people are not born with these needs but may learn them through their life experiences.[10] Three needs are most frequently studied.

- *Need for achievement*—the desire to accomplish something difficult, attain a high standard of success, master complex tasks, and surpass others.

- *Need for affiliation*—the desire to form close personal relationships, avoid conflict, and establish warm friendships.

- *Need for power*—the desire to influence or control others, be responsible for others, and have authority over others.

For more than twenty years, McClelland studied human needs and their implications for management. People with a high need for achievement tend to enjoy work that is entrepreneurial and innovative. People who have a high need for affiliation are successful "integrators," whose job is to coordinate the work of people and departments.[11] Integrators include brand managers and project managers, positions that require excellent people skills. A high need for power is often associated with successful attainment of top levels in the organizational hierarchy. For example, McClelland studied managers at AT&T for sixteen years and found that those with a high need for power were more likely to pursue a path of continued promotion over time.

Needs-based theories focus on underlying needs that motivate how people behave. The hierarchy of needs theory, the two-factor theory, and the acquired needs theory all identify the specific needs that motivate people. Leaders can work to meet followers' needs and hence elicit appropriate and successful work behaviors.

OTHER MOTIVATIONAL THEORIES

Three additional motivation theories, the reinforcement perspective, expectancy theory, and equity theory, focus primarily on extrinsic rewards and punishments. Relying on extrinsic rewards and punishments is sometimes referred to as the "carrot-and-stick" approach.[12] The behavior that produces a desired outcome is rewarded with "carrots," such as a pay raise or a promotion. Conversely, undesirable or unproductive behavior brings the "stick," such as a demotion or withholding a pay raise. Carrot-and-stick approaches tend to focus on lower needs, although higher needs can sometimes also be met.

Reinforcement Perspective on Motivation

The reinforcement approach to employee motivation sidesteps the deeper issue of employee needs described in the needs-based theories. **Reinforcement theory** simply looks at the relationship between behavior and its consequences by changing or modifying followers' on-the-job behavior through the appropriate use of immediate rewards or punishments.

Behavior modification is the name given to the set of techniques by which reinforcement theory is used to modify behavior.[13] The basic assumption underlying behavior modification is the **law of effect,** which states that positively reinforced behavior tends to be repeated, and behavior that is not reinforced tends not to be repeated. **Reinforcement** is defined as anything that causes a certain behavior to be repeated or inhibited. Four ways in which leaders use reinforcement to modify or shape employee behavior are: positive reinforcement, negative reinforcement, punishment, and extinction.

Positive reinforcement is the administration of a pleasant and rewarding consequence following a behavior. A good example of positive reinforcement is immediate praise for an employee who arrives on time or does a little extra in his or her work. The pleasant consequence will increase the likelihood of the excellent work behavior occurring again.

Negative reinforcement is the withdrawal of an unpleasant consequence once a behavior is improved. Sometimes referred to as *avoidance learning,* negative reinforcement means people learn to perform the desired behavior by avoiding unpleasant situations. A simple example would be when a supervisor stops reprimanding an employee for tardiness once the employee starts getting to work on time.

Punishment is the imposition of unpleasant outcomes on an employee. Punishment typically occurs following undesirable behavior. For example, a supervisor may berate an employee for performing a task incorrectly. The supervisor expects that the negative outcome will serve as a punishment and reduce the likelihood of the behavior recurring. The use of punishment in organizations is controversial and often criticized because it fails to indicate the correct behavior.

Extinction is the withdrawal of a positive reward, meaning that behavior is no longer reinforced and hence is less likely to occur in the future. If a perpetually tardy employee fails to receive praise and pay raises, he or she will begin to realize that the behavior is not producing desired outcomes. The behavior will gradually disappear if it is continually not reinforced.

Leaders can reinforce behavior after each and every occurrence, which is referred to as *continuous reinforcement,* or they can choose to reinforce behavior intermittently, which is referred to as *partial reinforcement.* With partial reinforcement, the desired behavior is reinforced often enough to make the employee believe the behavior is worth repeating, but not every time it is demonstrated. Continuous reinforcement can be very effective for establishing new behaviors, but research has found that partial reinforcement is more effective for maintaining behavior over extended time periods.[14]

Some leaders have applied reinforcement theory very effectively to shape followers' behavior. For example, Frank Bohac, CEO of Computer Systems Development in Albuquerque, New Mexico, has used positive reinforcement by rewarding his employees with computers, vacations, and even horses.[15] Another company where leaders have successfully applied reinforcement theory is Emerald Packaging in Union City, California.

IN THE LEAD   Kevin Kelly, Emerald Packaging Inc.

Emerald Packaging is a family-owned business that prints plastic bags for prepackaged salads and other vegetables. The company employs about 100 people and is the tenth largest manufacturer in Union City, California, located about thirty miles southeast of San Francisco.

Kevin Kelly, vice president of operations for Emerald, and other leaders wanted to fire up employees by developing a positive reinforcement scheme that would motivate and reward workers. The plan at Emerald includes the following:

1. *Monthly Quality Award.* Each month, managers pick the best print job in the plant from samples submitted by printing press employees. The winning press operator gets $100 and the operator's helper wins $50.

2. *Safety Program.* When the company has three or fewer minor accidents and no lost-time accidents in one quarter, leaders raffle off $1,000, provide workers with company shirts and jackets, and buy lunch for everyone. If employees make it through the entire year with only twelve minor accidents and no lost-time injuries, the company raffles a total of $10,000 to three winners and throws a party for all employees.

3. *Profit-Sharing Plan.* A certain percentage of operating profit is set aside into a bonus pool, which is shared among employees.

Has Emerald's plan for reinforcing correct behaviors worked? Kelly reports that customer returns for poor quality are down 75 percent over last year. The quality rewards of $50–100 are substantial enough to get employees' attention and make it worth their while to put increased effort into producing a high-quality print job. So far, safety results are also impressive. During the first five months of the program, the company had only one minor accident. Employees are much more careful about how they conduct themselves on the job because no one wants to derail the raffle.

Interestingly, the profit-sharing plan has been less effective. In fact, Kelly believes it has simply put more money in employees' pockets without motivating more desirable behaviors. He thinks tying the reward to operating profit made it too remote for most employees to pay much attention to. Although the company still uses profit sharing, Kelly now prefers to use positive reinforcement that is tied more directly to specific employee behaviors.[16]

Expectancy Theory

Expectancy theory suggests that motivation depends on individuals' mental expectations about their ability to perform tasks and receive desired rewards. Expectancy theory is associated with the work of Victor Vroom, although a number of scholars have made contributions in this area.[17] Expectancy theory is concerned not with understanding types of needs but with the thinking process that individuals use to achieve rewards. Consider Betty Bradley, a university student with a strong desire for an A on her accounting exam. Betty's motivation to study for the exam will be influenced by her expectation that hard study will truly lead to an A on the exam. If Betty believes she cannot get an A on the exam, she will not be motivated to study exceptionally hard.

Expectancy theory is based on the relationship among the individual's effort, the possibility of high performance, and the desirability of outcomes following high performance. These elements and the relationships among them are illustrated in Exhibit 8.6. The E > P expectancy is the probability that putting effort into a task will lead to high performance. For this expectancy to be high, the individual must have the ability, previous experience, and necessary tools, information, and opportunity to perform. The P > O expectancy involves whether successful performance will lead to the desired outcome. If this expectancy is high, the individual will be more highly motivated. Valence refers to the value of outcomes to the individual. If the outcomes that are available from high effort and good performance are not valued by an employee, motivation will be low. Likewise, if outcomes have a high value, motivation will be higher. A simple example to illustrate the relationships in Exhibit 8.6 is Alfredo Torres, a salesperson at Diamond Gift Shop. If Alfredo believes that increased

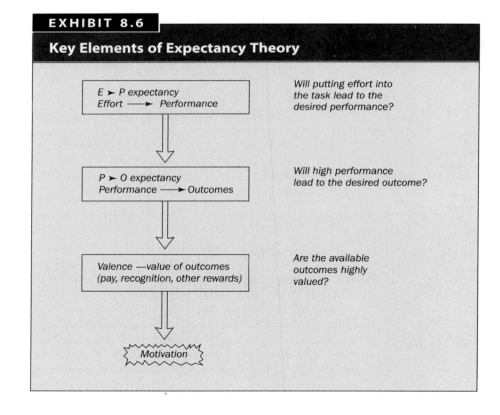

EXHIBIT 8.6

Key Elements of Expectancy Theory

E ➤ P expectancy
Effort ⟶ Performance

Will putting effort into the task lead to the desired performance?

P ➤ O expectancy
Performance ⟶ Outcomes

Will high performance lead to the desired outcome?

Valence —value of outcomes (pay, recognition, other rewards)

Are the available outcomes highly valued?

Motivation

selling effort will lead to higher personal sales, his E > P expectancy would be considered high. Moreover, if he also believes that higher personal sales will lead to a promotion or pay raise, the P > O expectancy is also high. Finally, if Alfredo places a high value on the promotion or pay raise, valence is high and he will be highly motivated. For an employee to be highly motivated, all three factors in the expectancy model must be high.[18]

Like the path-goal theory of leadership described in Chapter 3, expectancy theory is personalized to subordinates' needs and goals. A leader's responsibility is to help followers meet their needs while attaining organizational goals. One employee may want to be promoted to a position of increased responsibility, and another may want a good relationship with peers. To increase motivation, leaders can increase followers' expectancy by clarifying individual needs, providing the desired outcomes, and ensuring that individuals have the ability and support needed to perform well and attain their desired outcomes.

An example of expectancy theory at work occurs at Lincoln Electric Co., where leaders cite the expectation of rewards for hard work as the reason their four plants have remained competitive for more than a century. The 2,000 workers are paid by the piece and receive no vacation or sick pay. Wages are based on ratings of skill, effort, and responsibility for each job. Employees know they must produce quality goods in order to make any money. In addition to keeping the company's absenteeism at half the national average, the reinforcement system enables employees at Lincoln to earn up to three times that of their counterparts at other companies.[19]

Equity Theory

Sometimes employees' motivation is affected not only by their expectancies and the rewards they receive, but also by their perceptions of how fairly they are treated in relation to others. **Equity theory** proposes that people are motivated to seek social equity in the rewards they expect for performance.[20] According to the theory, if people perceive their rewards as equal to what others receive for similar contributions, they will believe they are treated fairly and will be more highly motivated. When they believe they are not being treated fairly and equitably, motivation will decline.

People evaluate equity by a ratio of inputs to outcomes. That is, employees make comparisons of what they put into a job and the rewards they receive relative to those of other people in the organization. Inputs include such things as education, experience, effort, and ability. Outcomes include pay, recognition, promotions, and other rewards. A state of equity exists whenever the ratio of one person's outcomes to inputs equals the ratio of others' in the work group. Inequity occurs when the input/outcome ratios are out of balance, such as when an employee with a high level of experience and ability receives the same salary as a new, less educated employee. One example is from the J. Peterman Company before it slid into bankruptcy. John Peterman had created a comfortable, creative culture where employees were highly motivated to work together toward common goals. However, when the company began to grow rapidly, Peterman found himself having to hire people very quickly—and he often had to offer them higher salaries than those of his current employees to match what they were making elsewhere. In addition, when making important decisions, leaders tended to pay more attention to the ideas and thoughts of the new staff than they did the "old timers." Long-time employees felt slighted, and motivation declined significantly. Employees were no longer willing to put in the extra effort they once had because of a perceived state of inequity.[21]

This discussion provides only a brief overview of equity theory. The theory's practical use has been criticized because a number of key issues are unclear. However, the important point of equity theory is that, for many people, motivation is influenced significantly by relative as well as absolute rewards. The concept reminds leaders that they should be cognizant of the possible effects of perceived inequity on follower motivation and performance.

THE CARROT-AND-STICK CONTROVERSY

Reward and punishment motivation practices dominate organizations; as many as 94 percent of companies in the United States engage in practices that reward performance or merit with pay.[22] In addition, many companies regard their incentive programs as successful. For example, U.S. Healthcare, a health maintenance organization (HMO), pays physicians who meet performance goals up to an additional 28 percent of their regular monthly premium. This HMO earned the highest quality care rating of any in the United States.[23]

Financial incentives can be quite effective. For one thing, giving employees pay raises or bonuses can signal that leaders value their contributions to the organization. Some researchers argue that using money as a motivator almost always leads to higher performance.[24] However, despite the testimonies of numerous organizations that enjoy successful incentive programs, the arguments against the efficacy of carrot-and-stick methods are growing. Critics argue that extrinsic rewards are neither adequate nor productive motivators and may even work against the best interest of organizations. Reasons for this criticism include the following.

1. *Extrinsic rewards diminish intrinsic rewards.* The motivation to seek an extrinsic reward, whether a bonus or approval, leads people to focus on the reward, rather than on the work they do to achieve it.[25] Reward seeking of this type necessarily diminishes the intrinsic satisfaction people receive

from the process of working. Numerous studies have found that giving people extrinsic rewards undermines their interest in the work itself.[26] When people lack intrinsic rewards in their work, their performance levels out; it stays just adequate to reach the reward. In the worst case, people perform hazardously, such as covering up an on-the-job accident to get a bonus based on a safety target. In addition, with extrinsic rewards, individuals tend to attribute their behavior to extrinsic rather than intrinsic factors, diminishing their own contributions.[27]

2. *Extrinsic rewards are temporary.* Bestowing outside incentives on people might ensure short-term success, but not long-term quality.[28] The success of reaching immediate goals is quickly followed by the development of unintended consequences. Because people are focusing on the reward, the work they do holds no interest for them, and without interest in their work, the potential for exploration, innovation, and creativity disappears.[29] The current deadline may be met, but better ways of working will not be discovered.

3. *Extrinsic rewards assume people are driven by lower needs.* The perfunctory rewards of praise and pay increases tied only to performance presumes that the primary reason people initiate and persist in actions is to satisfy lower needs. However, behavior is also based on yearning for self-expression, and on self-esteem, self-worth, feelings, and attitudes. A survey of employees at *Fortune* magazine's "100 Best Companies to Work For in America" found that the majority mentioned intrinsic rather than extrinsic rewards as their motivation. Although many of these workers had been offered higher salaries elsewhere, they stayed where they were because of such motivators as a fun, challenging work environment; flexibility that provided a balance between work and personal life; and the potential to learn, grow, and be creative.[30] Offers of an extrinsic reward do not encourage the myriad behaviors that are motivated by people's need to express elements of their identities. Extrinsic rewards focus on the specific goals and deadlines delineated by incentive plans rather than enabling people to facilitate their vision for a desired future, that is, to realize their possible higher need for growth and fulfillment.[31]

4. *Organizations are too complex for carrot-and-stick approaches.* The current organizational climate is marked by uncertainty and high interdependence among departments and with other organizations. In short, the relationships and the accompanying actions that are part of organizations are overwhelmingly complex.[32] By contrast, the carrot-and-stick plans are quite simple, and the application of an overly simplified incentive plan to a highly complex operation usually creates a misdirected system.[33] It is difficult for leaders to interpret and reward all the behaviors that employees need to demonstrate to keep complex organizations successful over the

LIVING LEADERSHIP

On the Folly of Rewarding A While Hoping for B

Managers who complain about the lack of motivation in workers might do well to examine whether the reward system encourages behavior different from what they are seeking. People usually determine which activities are rewarded and then seek to do those things, to the virtual exclusion of activities not rewarded. Nevertheless, there are numerous examples of fouled-up systems that reward unwanted behaviors, while the desired actions are not being rewarded at all.

In sports, for example, most coaches stress teamwork, proper attitude, and one-for-all spirit. However, rewards are usually distributed according to individual performance. The college basketball player who passes the ball to teammates instead of shooting will not compile impressive scoring statistics and will be less likely to be drafted by the pros. The big-league baseball player who hits to advance the runner rather than to score a home run is less likely to win the titles that guarantee big salaries. In universities, a primary goal is the transfer of knowledge from professors to students; yet professors are rewarded primarily for research and publication, not for their commitment to good teaching. Students are rewarded for making good grades, not necessarily for acquiring knowledge, and may resort to cheating rather than risk a low grade on their college transcript.

In business, there are often similar discrepancies between the desired behaviors and those rewarded. For example, see the table below.

What do a majority of managers see as the major obstacles to dealing with fouled-up reward systems?

1. The inability to break out of old ways of thinking about reward and recognition. This includes entitlement mentality in workers and resistance by management to revamp performance review and reward systems.

2. Lack of an overall systems view of performance and results. This is particularly true of systems that promote subunit results at the expense of the total organization.

3. Continuing focus on short-term results by management and shareholders.

Motivation theories must be sound because people do what they are rewarded for. But when will organizations learn to reward what they say they want?

SOURCE: Steven Kerr, "An Academy Classic! On the Folly of Rewarding A, While Hoping for B," and "More on the Folly," *Academy of Management Executive* 9, no. 1 (1995), 7–16.

Managers Hope For	But They Reward
Teamwork and collaboration	The best individual performers
Innovative thinking and risk taking	Proven methods and not making mistakes
Development of people skills	Technical achievements and accomplishment
Employee involvement and empowerment	Tight control over operations and resources
High achievement	Another year's routine effort
Commitment to quality	Shipping on time, even with defects
Long-term growth	Quarterly earnings

long term. Thus, extrinsic motivators often wind up rewarding behaviors that are the opposite of what the organization wants and needs. While managers may espouse long-term growth, they wind up rewarding quarterly earnings; thus, workers are motivated to act for quick returns for themselves. Consider this chapter's Living Leadership box.

5. *Carrot-and-stick approaches destroy people's motivation to work as a group.* Extrinsic rewards and punishments create a culture of competition versus a culture of co-operation.[34] In a competitive environment, people see their goal as individual victory, as making others appear inferior. Thus, one person's success is a threat to another's goals. Furthermore, sharing problems and solutions is out of the question when co-workers may use your weakness to undermine you, or when a supervisor might view the need for assistance as a disqualifier for rewards. The organization is less likely to achieve excellent performance from employees who are mistrustful and threatened by one another. In contrast, replacing the carrot-and-stick with methods based on meeting higher *as well as* lower needs enables a culture of collaboration marked by compatible goals; all the members of the organization are trying to achieve a shared vision. Without the effort to control behavior individually through rigid rewards, people can see co-workers as part of their success. Each person's success is mutually enjoyed because every success benefits the organization. When leaders focus on higher needs, they can make everyone feel valued, which facilitates excellent performance.

The conflicts that arose among workers at Lantech illustrate how the competition for rewards led to the demise of collaboration. Luckily, leaders understood how to fix the problem.

| IN THE LEAD | **Patrick Lancaster III, Lantech Corporation** |

Patrick Lancaster III is convinced that the negative consequences on Lantech of incentive pay programs are greater than any motivational benefit. For nearly three decades, Lancaster has adopted, modified, and abandoned various incentive programs at his packaging machine manufacturing company. His first plan involved a bonus pool from which employees were rewarded based on evaluations of one another's performance. The first six months saw a rapid rise in productivity. However, stress, insecurity, and the competition for the bonus pool took its toll; productivity fell steadily. Too much focus by employees on the reward and the threat of a bad evaluation from a fellow worker compromised their ability to co-operate and perform together. Then Lancaster rewarded several division managers with profit percentages based on their division sales growth. One of the unforeseen consequences of this plan was a sudden overconcern with tasks believed to directly increase sales growth. The quality of customer service diminished because it wasn't rewarded directly. Moreover, managers started fighting to attribute expenses to other divisions in order to maximize their own profit. One argument was about where to bill the toilet paper used in the common areas. Lancaster was spending 95 percent of his time resolving conflicts rather than serving clients.

Lancaster also tried linking rewards to the number of sales calls per day. He discovered, however, that even when the call records had not been "inflated," the employees believed everyone else was doing so anyway. Eventually, Lancaster realized that most workers simply resented the manipulation implicit in the attempt to control their behavior with rewards.[35]

Now Lantech operates with a very simple profit-sharing plan. Everyone shares in the overall success of Lantech. According to Lancaster, the difference now is that he does not consider the plan a motivation incentive. He attributes Lantech's success to the feelings of accomplishment, job satisfaction, and empowerment that his associates receive from the positive culture he has sought to engender at Lantech.[36]

Some incentive programs are successful, especially when the people involved are actually motivated by money and lower needs. One way for leaders to address the carrot-and-stick controversy is to understand a program's strengths and weaknesses and acknowledge the positive but limited effects of extrinsic motivators. A leader also appeals to people's higher needs, and no subordinate should have work that does not offer some self-satisfaction as well as a yearly pay raise. Furthermore, rewards can be directly linked to behavior promoting the higher needs of both individuals and the organization, such as rewarding quality, long-term growth, or a collaborative culture.[37]

EMPOWERMENT

A significant way in which leaders can meet the higher motivational needs of subordinates is to shift power down from the top of the organizational hierarchy and share it with subordinates. They can decrease the emphasis on incentives designed to affect and control subordinate behavior and instead attempt to share power with organizational members to achieve shared goals. **Empowerment** is power sharing, the delegation of power or authority to subordinates in the organization.[38] Recall from Chapter 1 that the shift from control to empowerment is one of the new realities today's effective leaders respond to.

Leaders are shifting from efforts to control behavior through carrot-and-stick approaches to providing employees with the power, information, and authority that enables them to find greater intrinsic satisfaction with their work. Leaders provide their followers with an understanding of how their jobs are important to the organization's mission and performance, thereby giving them a direction within which to act freely.[39] Consider the effect empowerment has on motivation at General Electric's aircraft engine factory in Durham, North Carolina.

IN THE LEAD   ## GE/Durham

At General Electric's aircraft engine factory in Durham, North Carolina, nine teams of workers build some of the world's most powerful jet engines, including the ones that keep Air Force One running. The plant manager is the only supervisor in the factory, and teams are given only one directive—the deadline for when their next engine is due to be shipped. The teams themselves make all other decisions. For example, they decide who does what job each day, how to make the manufacturing process more efficient, and what to do about slackers. It is the teams on the shop floor, not bosses in the front office, who write the assembly process, figure out the schedule, order tools and parts, and perform any other jobs necessary, including keeping the plant clean and the machinery and tools in good order. Each team "owns" an engine from beginning to end. The team is responsible for every step of the process from the time when parts are unpacked to the moment a completed engine is loaded on a truck for shipment.

Obviously, to work in such an environment means employees have to be highly skilled. GE/Durham is the only one of the company's engine plants that requires job candidates to be FAA-certified mechanics, for example. Then, everyone learns to assemble different parts of the engine. Employees have a high level of responsibility and strive every day to produce perfect jet engines. The philosophy of continuous improvement permeates the plant—employees don't think their job is to make jet engines but to make jet engines *better*.

Some of the factory's workers remember what it was like to work in a place where they were expected to check their minds at the door and follow strict rules and procedures. The difference at GE/Durham is reflected in the words of mechanic Duane Williams, talking about his first six months on the job: "I was never valued that much as an employee in my life. I had never been at the point where I couldn't wait to get to work. But here, I couldn't wait to get to work every day."[40]

As at GE/Durham, the autonomy of empowered employees can create flexibility that is an enormous advantage for a company.[41]

Reasons for Empowerment

What are the organizational advantages of having empowered workers? One study suggests that empowering workers enables leaders to create a unique organization with superior performance capabilities.[42] The strategic advantages are intimately linked to the motivation that empowerment unleashes among employees, and by extension, the overall effort of an organization.

First, empowerment provides strong motivation because it meets the higher needs of individuals. Research indicates that individuals have a need for *self-efficacy*, which is the capacity to produce results or outcomes, to feel they are effective.[43] Most people come into an organization with the desire to do a good job, and empowerment enables leaders to release the motivation already there. The employee reward is intrinsic—a sense of personal mastery and competence. Increased responsibility motivates most people to strive to do their best. One employee described the sense of accomplishment that even a simple task can provide: "One boss told me, 'These all need to go in boxes and be labeled, crated, and taken to the garage by this afternoon—and when you're done, I have something else you can help us with.' Then he went away. That made me feel like an important part of the process and told me he trusted me to do it right. I had an incentive to not let him down, to prove I could come through on my own."[44]

Second, empowerment actually increases the total amount of power in an organization. To say that leaders give power away to subordinates is somewhat inaccurate; leaders actually share power, creating a bigger overall power base. Simply put, if everyone in the organization has power, then the organization is more powerful.[45] The freedom from overcontrol allows subordinates to utilize their talents and abilities in ways that were otherwise constrained. Empowered employees use more of themselves to do their jobs.

Recall how Joel and Teri Pesapane, described at the beginning of this chapter, gave their employees at Growing Green opportunities to use their skills and abilities in new ways. The Pesapanes' overly controlling leadership had led to a "juggling crisis." Joel and Teri were no longer able to be involved in every detail and handle every potential new account. The shift to shared power and companywide participation freed them to concentrate on the big picture and freed their employees to apply previously untapped talents and abilities.

Third, leaders benefit from the additional capabilities employee participation brings to the organization. For one thing, leaders can devote more time to vision and the big picture. For another, empowerment takes the pressure off because subordinates are able to respond better and more quickly to the markets they serve.[46] Frontline workers often have a better understanding than do leaders of how to improve a work process, satisfy a customer, or solve a production problem.

Elements of Empowerment

In general, increased power and responsibility leads to greater motivation, increased employee satisfaction, and decreased turnover and absenteeism. In a recent survey, for example, empowerment of workers, including increased job responsibility, authority to define their work, and power to make decisions, was found to be the most dramatic indicator of workplace satisfaction.[47]

The first step toward effective empowerment is effective hiring and training. Leaders look for people who have the ability as well as the desire to make a genuine contribution to the organization and then provide them with the training they need to excel. For example, at GE/Durham, described earlier, there is a significant emphasis on selection and training because the organization needs people who can perform complex tasks. However, having a team of competent employees isn't enough. Five elements must be in place before employees can be truly empowered to perform their jobs successfully: information, knowledge, discretion, meaning, and rewards.[48]

1. *Employees receive information about company performance.* In companies where employees are fully empowered, no information is secret. Meritor, a components manufacturer, goes to great lengths to help employees understand companywide business measures and gives them regular information about the performance of individual businesses and plants.[49]

2. *Employees receive knowledge and skills to contribute to company goals.* Companies train employees to have the knowledge and skills they need to personally contribute to company performance. Knowledge and skills lead to competency—the belief that one is capable of accomplishing one's job successfully.[50] For example, regular quality awareness workshops are held at Chrysler Canada's assembly plant in Bramalea, Ontario, so that employees can initiate quality improvements on their own.

3. *Employees have the power to make substantive decisions.* Many of today's most competitive companies are giving workers the power to influence work procedures and organizational direction through quality circles and self-directed work teams. Teams of tank house workers at BHP Copper Metals in San Manuel, Arizona, identify and solve production problems and determine how best to organize themselves to get the job done. In addition, they can even determine the specific hours they need to handle their own workloads. For example, an employee could opt to work for four hours, leave, and come back to do the next four.[51]

4. *Employees understand the meaning and impact of their jobs.* Empowered employees consider their jobs important and personally meaningful and see themselves as influential in their work roles.[52] Understanding the connection between one's day-to-day activities and the overall vision for the organization gives a subordinate a sense of direction, an idea of what his or her job means. It enables employees to fit their actions to the vision and have an active influence on the outcome of their work.[53] For example, Xerox gives its workers what the company calls "line of sight" training, in which employees familiarize themselves with how their job fits into upstream and downstream activities, all the way to the customer. The training helps empowered employees make better decisions that contribute to the company's overall goals.[54]

5. *Employees are rewarded based on company performance.* Studies have revealed the important role of fair reward and recognition systems in supporting empowerment. By affirming that employees are progressing toward goals, rewards help to keep motivation high.[55] Leaders are careful to examine and redesign reward systems to support empowerment and teamwork. Two ways in which organizations can financially reward employees based on company performance are through profit sharing and employee stock ownership plans (ESOPs). At W. L. Gore and Associates, makers of Gore-Tex, compensation takes three forms—salary, profit sharing, and an associates stock ownership program.[56] Unlike traditional carrot-and-stick approaches, these rewards focus on the performance of the group rather than individuals. Joe Cabral, CEO of Chatsworth Products Inc., a small company that makes support gear for computer networks, uses an ESOP because it "gets everyone pulling in the same direction. Everybody wants the company to do the best it possibly can."[57] Furthermore, rewards are just one component of empowerment rather than the sole basis of motivation.

Empowerment Applications

Many of today's organizations are implementing empowerment programs, but they are empowering workers to varying degrees. At some companies, empowerment means encouraging employee ideas while managers retain final authority for decisions; at others it means giving frontline workers almost complete power to make decisions and exercise initiative and imagination.[58]

Current methods of empowering workers fall along a continuum as shown in Exhibit 8.7. The continuum runs from a situation where frontline workers have no discretion (such as on a traditional assembly line) to full empowerment where workers even participate in formulating organizational strategy. An example of full empowerment is when self-directed teams are given the power to hire, discipline, and dismiss team members and to set compensation

EXHIBIT 8.7

The Empowerment Continuum

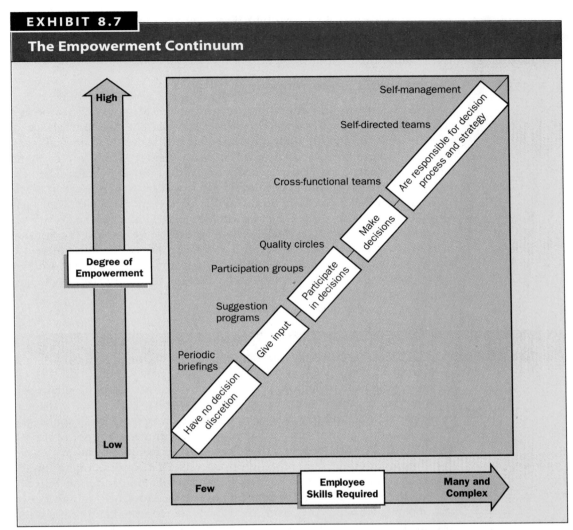

High

Degree of
Empowerment

Low

Self-management

Self-directed teams

Cross-functional teams

Quality circles

Participation groups

Suggestion
programs

Periodic
briefings

Are responsible for decision
process and strategy

Make
decisions

Participate
in decisions

Give input

Have no decision
discretion

Few | Employee
Skills Required | Many and
Complex

SOURCE: Based on Robert C. Ford and Myron D. Fottler, "Empowerment: A Matter of Degree," *Academy of Management Executive* 9, No. 3 (1995), 21–31; Lawrence Holpp, "Applied Empowerment," *Training* (February 1994), 39–44; and David P. McCaffrey, Sue R. Faerman, and David W. Hart, "The Appeal and Difficulties of Participative Systems," *Organization Science* 6, No. 6 (November-December 1995), 603–627.

rates. Few organizations have moved to this level of empowerment. One that has is Semco, a $160 million South American company involved in manufacturing, services, and e-business. Majority owner Ricardo Semler believes that people will act in their own, and by extension, the organization's best interests if they're given complete freedom. Semco allows its 1300 employees to choose what they do, where and when they do it, and even how they get paid for it. Semco has remained highly successful and profitable under a system of complete empowerment for more than twenty years.[59]

Implementing Empowerment

Empowerment programs can be difficult to implement in established organizations because they destroy hierarchies and upset the familiar balance of power. A study of *Fortune* 1000 companies found that the empowerment practices that have diffused most widely are those that redistribute power and authority the least, for example, quality circles or job enrichment, because managers can keep decision authority.[60] Also, workers sometimes balk at the added responsibility freedom brings. Most organizations begin with small steps. For example, at Recyclights, a small Minneapolis-based company that recycles fluorescent lights, CEO Keith Thorndyke first gave employees control of their own tasks. As employees' skills grew, they developed a greater interest in how their jobs fit into the total picture. Thorndyke recognized that workers wanted to shape corporate strategy, so he engaged their participation in company goal setting.[61]

ORGANIZATIONWIDE MOTIVATIONAL PROGRAMS

Leaders can motivate organizational members using other recent programs that are more than the carrot-and-stick approaches described earlier in this chapter, but may be less than full empowerment: employee ownership, paying for knowledge, gainsharing, pay for performance, and job enrichment. Forms of "at risk" pay are becoming more common than fixed salary in many companies.

Employee ownership occurs on two levels. First, empowerment can result in a psychological commitment to the mission of an organization whereby members act as "owners" rather than employees. Secondly, by owning stock in the companies for which they work, individuals are motivated to give their best performances. After SAIC, the largest private information technology firm in the United States, acquired Telcordia Technologies, it extended its stock programs to the new employees. Employee ownership is changing the culture at Telcordia, according to one leader: "People are taking a more proprietary interest in the performance of the company."[62] Stock options have become common among major corporations as well as small, Internet-based companies. The workers' vested interest in seeing the stock rise motivates them to perform well. Additionally, stock options give workers a sign that their employer acknowledges each person's role in the organization.[63]

Pay for knowledge programs base an employee's salary on the number of task skills he or she possesses. Employees are motivated to acquire more skills to increase their salaries. A workforce in which individuals skillfully perform numerous tasks is more flexible and efficient. At BHP Copper Metals, for example, leaders devised a pay-for-skills program that supported the move to teamwork. Employees can rotate through various jobs to build their skills and earn a higher pay rate. Rates range from entry-level workers to lead operators. Lead operators are those who have demonstrated a mastery of skills, the ability to teach and lead others, and effective self-directed behavior.[64]

Gainsharing is a method of encouraging teamwork among employees by rewarding groups for reaching productivity improvement goals. A gainsharing program at Meritor rewards employees based on the performance of their own unit as well as on overall company performance. Gainsharing proved to be a powerful incentive for teamwork.[65]

Pay for performance, which links at least a portion of employees' monetary rewards to results or accomplishments, is a significant trend in today's organizations. Gainsharing is one type of pay for performance, but many companies are devising other ways to give employees a chance to earn more money based on higher performance. Other examples of pay for performance include profit sharing, bonuses, and merit pay. In addition to the potential for greater income, pay for performance can give employees a greater sense of control over the outcome of their efforts. At Semco, described earlier, employees choose how they are paid based on eleven compensation options, which can be combined in various ways. Exhibit 8.8 lists Semco's eleven ways to pay. Semco leaders indicate that the flexible pay plan encourages innovation and risk-taking and motivates employees to perform in the best interest of the company as well as themselves.

Job enrichment incorporates high-level motivators into the work, including job responsibility, recognition, and opportunities for growth, learning, and achievement. In an enriched job, the employee controls resources needed to perform well and makes decisions on how to do the work. One way to enrich an oversimplified job is to enlarge it, that is, to extend the responsibility to cover several tasks instead of only one.

Leaders at Ralcorp's cereal manufacturing plant in Sparks, Nevada, enriched jobs by combining several packing positions into a single job and cross-training employees to operate all of the packing line's equipment. Employees were given both the ability and the responsibility to perform all the various functions in their department, not just a single task. In addition, line employees are responsible for all screening and interviewing of new hires as well as training and advising one another. They also manage the production flow to and from their upstream and downstream partners—they understand the entire production process so they can see how their work affects the quality and productivity of employees in other departments. Ralcorp invests heavily in training to be sure employees have the needed operational skills as well as the ability to make decisions, solve problems, manage quality, and contribute to continuous improvement. Enriched jobs have improved employee motivation and

EXHIBIT 8.8

Semco's Eleven Ways to Pay

Semco, a South American company involved in manufacturing, services, and e-business, lets employees choose how they are paid based on eleven compensation options:

1. Fixed salary

2. Bonuses

3. Profit sharing

4. Commission

5. Royalties on sales

6. Royalties on profits

7. Commission on gross margin

8. Stock or stock options

9. IPO/sale warrants that an executive cashes in when a business unit goes public or is sold

10. Self-determined annual review compensation in which an executive is paid for meeting self-set goals

11. Commission on difference between actual and three-year value of the company

SOURCE: Ricardo Semler, "How We Went Digital Without a Strategy," *Harvard Business Review*, September-October 2000, 51–58.

satisfaction, and the company has benefited from higher long-term productivity, reduced costs, and happier employees.[66]

SUMMARY AND INTERPRETATION

This chapter introduced a number of important ideas about motivating people in organizations. Individuals are motivated to act to satisfy a range of needs. The leadership approach to motivation tends to focus on the higher needs of employees. The role of the leader is to create a situation in which followers' higher needs and the needs of the organization can be met simultaneously.

Needs-based theories focus on the underlying needs that motivate how people behave. Maslow's hierarchy of needs proposes that individuals satisfy lower needs before they move on to higher needs. Herzberg's two-factor theory holds that dissatisfiers must be removed and motivators then added to satisfy employees. McClelland asserted that people are motivated differently depending on which needs they have acquired. Other motivation theories, including the reinforcement perspective, expectancy theory, and equity theory, focus primarily on extrinsic rewards and punishments, sometimes called "carrot-and-stick" methods of motivation. The reinforcement perspective proposes that behavior can be modified by the use of rewards and punishments. Expectancy theory is based on the idea that a person's motivation is contingent upon his or her expectations that a given behavior will result in desired rewards. Equity theory proposes that individuals' motivation is affected not only by the rewards they receive but also by their perceptions of how fairly they are treated in relation to others. People are motivated to seek social equity in the rewards they expect for performance.

Although carrot-and-stick methods of motivation are pervasive in North American organizations, many critics argue that extrinsic rewards undermine intrinsic rewards, bring about unintended consequences, are too simple to capture organizational realities, and replace workplace co-operation with unhealthy competition.

An alternative approach to carrot-and-stick motivation is that of empowerment, by which subordinates know the direction of the organization and have the autonomy to act as they see fit to go in that direction. Leaders provide employees with the knowledge to contribute to the organization, the power to make consequential decisions, and the necessary resources to do their jobs. Empowerment typically meets the higher needs of individuals. Other organizationwide motivational programs include employee ownership, pay-for-knowledge, gainsharing, pay for performance, and job enrichment.

KEY TERMS

motivation	motivators	punishment
intrinsic rewards	acquired needs theory	extinction
extrinsic rewards	reinforcement theory	expectancy theory
systemwide rewards	behavior modification	equity theory
individual rewards	law of effect	empowerment
hierarchy of needs theory	reinforcement	employee ownership
hygiene factors	positive reinforcement	pay for knowledge
job enrichment	negative reinforcement	gainsharing
		pay for performance

DISCUSSION QUESTIONS

1. Describe the kinds of needs that people bring to an organization. How might a person's values and attitudes, as described in Chapter 4, influence the needs he or she brings to work?

2. What is the relationship among needs, rewards, and motivation?

3. What do you see as the leader's role in motivating others in an organization?

4. Do you believe it is possible to increase the total amount of power in an organization? Discuss.

5. What is the carrot-and-stick approach? Do you think that it should be minimized in organizations? Why?

6. What are the features of the reinforcement and expectancy theories that make them seem like carrot-and-stick methods for motivation? Why do they often work in organizations?

7. Why is it important for leaders to have a basic understanding of equity theory? Can you see ways in which some of today's popular compensation trends, such as gainsharing or pay for performance, might contribute to perceived inequity among employees? Discuss.

8. What are the advantages of an organization with empowered employees? Why might some individuals *not* want to be empowered?

9. Do you agree that hygiene factors, as defined in Herzberg's two-factor theory, cannot provide increased satisfaction and motivation? Discuss.

10. Would you rather work for a leader who has a high need for achievement, high need for affiliation, or high need for power? Why?

LEADERSHIP DEVELOPMENT: Personal Feedback

Your Approach to Motivating Others

Think about times when you have tried to motivate others or how you might behave in a leadership role. Describe how often you act or think in the way indicated by each of the following statements, according to the following scale: VI = very infrequently; I = infrequently; S = sometimes; F = frequently; VF = very frequently

		VI	I	S	F	VF
1.	I ask the other person what he or she is hoping to achieve in the situation.	1	2	3	4	5

	VI	I	S	F	VF
2. I attempt to figure out if the person has the ability to do what I need done.	1	2	3	4	5
3. When another person is heel-dragging, it usually means he or she is lazy.	5	4	3	2	1
4. I explain exactly what I want to the person I'm trying to motivate.	1	2	3	4	5
5. I like to give the person a reward up front so . he or she will be motivated	5	4	3	2	1
6. I give lots of feedback when another person is performing a task for me.	1	2	3	4	5
7. I try to belittle the person enough so that he or she will be intimidated into doing what I need done.	5	4	3	2	1
8. I make sure that the other person feels fairly treated.	1	2	3	4	5
9. I figure that if I smile nicely, I can get the other person to work as hard as I need.	5	4	3	2	1
10. I attempt to get what I need done by instilling fear in the other person.	5	4	3	2	1
11. I specify exactly what needs to be accomplished.	1	2	3	4	5
12. I generously praise people who help me get my work accomplished.	1	2	3	4	5
13. A job well done is its own reward. I therefore keep praise to a minimum.	5	4	3	2	1
14. I make sure to let people know how well they have done in meeting my expectations on a task.	1	2	3	4	5
15. To be fair, I attempt to reward people similarly no matter how well they have performed.	5	4	3	2	1
16. When somebody doing work for me performs well, I recognize his or her accomplishments promptly.	1	2	3	4	5
17. Before giving somebody a reward, I attempt to find out what would appeal to that person.	1	2	3	4	5
18. I make it a policy not to thank somebody for doing a job they are paid to do.	5	4	3	2	1
19. If people do not know how to perform a task, motivation will suffer.	1	2	3	4	5
20. If properly laid out, many jobs can be self-rewarding.	1	2	3	4	5

Scoring

Add the circled numbers to obtain your total score and record it here: _____

Interpretation

Your score represents how much knowledge and understanding you have about how to motivate people in today's workplace.

90–100: Exceptional knowledge and understanding of how to motivate others. Continue to build on your solid motivational skills.

50–89: Average knowledge and understanding. A good base to build on; with study and experience, you can develop advanced motivational skills.

20–49: Very low knowledge and understanding. Without greatly expanding your knowledge of motivation theory and techniques, you will not function well as a motivator in today's workplace.

Are you surprised by your score, or does it reflect how you feel about yourself as a motivator? Compare and discuss your score, and the questionnaire, with other students.

SOURCE: From D. Whetten and K. Cameron, *Developing Management Skills,* 2nd ed. (Addison-Wesley Educational Publishers Inc., 1984), 336–337. Copyright 1984, Addison-Wesley Educational Publishers.

LEADERSHIP DEVELOPMENT: Cases for Analysis

The Parlor

The Parlor, a local franchise operation located in San Francisco, serves sandwiches and small dinners in an atmosphere reminiscent of the "roaring twenties." Period fixtures accent the atmosphere and tunes from a mechanically driven, old-time player piano greet one's ears upon entering. Its major attraction, however, is a high-quality, old-fashioned soda fountain that specializes in superior ice cream sundaes and sodas. Fresh, quality sandwiches are also a popular item. Business has grown steadily during the seven years of operation.

The business has been so successful that Richard Purvis, owner and manager, decided to hire a parlor manager so that he could devote more time to other business interests. After a month of quiet recruitment and interviewing, he selected Paul McCarthy, whose prior experience included the supervision of the refreshment stand at one of the town's leading burlesque houses.

The present employees were unaware of McCarthy's employment until his first day on the job, when he walked in unescorted (Purvis was out of town) and introduced himself.

During the first few weeks, he evidenced sincere attempts at supervision and seemed to perform his work efficiently. According to his agreement with Purvis, he is paid a straight salary plus a percentage of the amount he saves the business monthly, based on the previous month's operating expenses. All other employees are on a straight hourly rate.

After a month on the job, McCarthy single-mindedly decided to initiate an economy program designed to increase his earnings. He changed the wholesale meat supplier and lowered both his cost and product quality in the process. Arbitrarily, he reduced the size and portion of everything on the menu, including those fabulous sundaes and sodas. He increased the working hours of those on the minimum wage and reduced the time of those employed at a higher rate. Moreover, he eliminated the fringe benefit of a one-dollar meal credit for employees who work longer than a five-hour stretch, and he cut out the usual 20 percent discount on anything purchased by the employees.

When questioned by the owner about the impact of his new practices, McCarthy swore up and down that there would be no negative effect upon the business. Customers, though, have begun to complain about the indifferent service of the female waitresses and the sloppy appearance of the male soda fountain clerks—"Their hair keeps getting in the ice cream." And there has been almost a complete turnover among the four short-order cooks who work two to a shift.

Ron Sharp, an accounting major at the nearby university, had been a short-order cook on the night shift for five months prior to McCarthy's arrival. Conscientious and ambitious, Ron enjoys a fine work record, and even his new boss recognizes Ron's superiority over the other cooks—"The best we got."

Heavy customer traffic at the Parlor has always required two short-order cooks working in tandem on each shift. The work requires a high degree of interpersonal co-operation in completing the food orders. An unwritten and informal policy is that each cook would clean up his specific work area at closing time.

One especially busy night, Ron's fellow cook became involved in a shouting match with McCarthy after the cook returned five minutes late from his shift break. McCarthy fired him right on the spot and commanded him to turn in his apron. This meant that Ron was required to stay over an extra half-hour to wash the other fellow's utensils. He did not get to bed until 3 A.M. But McCarthy wanted him back at the store at 9 A.M. to substitute for a daytime cook whose wife reported him ill. Ron was normally scheduled to begin at 4 P.M. However, when Ron arrived somewhat sleepily at 10 A.M. (and after an 8 A.M. accounting class), McCarthy was furious. He thereupon warned Ron, "Once more and you can look for another job. If you work for me, you do things my way or you don't work here at all." "Fine with me," fired back Ron as he slammed his apron into the sink. "You know what you can do with this job!"

The next day, McCarthy discussed his problems with the owner. Purvis was actually very upset. "I can't understand what went wrong. All of a sudden, things have gone to hell."

SOURCE: Bernard A. Deitzer and Karl A. Schillif, *Contemporary Incidents in Management* (Columbus, OH: Grid, Inc., 1977), 167–168. Reprinted by permission of John Wiley & Sons, Inc.

Questions

1. Contrast the beliefs about motivation held by Purvis and McCarthy.
2. Do you consider either Purvis or McCarthy a leader? Discuss.
3. What would you do now if you were in Purvis' position? Why?

Cub Scout Pack 81

Things certainly have changed over the past six years for Cub Scout Pack 81. Six years ago, the pack was on the verge of disbanding. There were barely enough boys for an effective den, and they had been losing membership for as long as anyone could remember. The cub master was trying to pass his job onto any parent foolish enough to take the helm of a sinking ship, and the volunteer fire department that sponsored the pack was openly considering dropping it.

But that was six years ago. Today the pack has one of the largest memberships of any in the Lancaster/Lebanon Council. It has started its own Boy Scout troop, into which the Webelos can graduate, and it has received a presidential citation for its antidrug program. The pack consistently wins competitions with other packs in the Council, and the fire department is very happy about its sponsorship. Membership in the pack is now around sixty cubs at all levels, and they have a new cub master.

"Parents want their boys to be in a successful program," says Cub Master Mike Murphy. "Look, I can't do everything. We depend on the parents and the boys to get things done. Everybody understands that we want to have a successful program, and that means we all have to participate to achieve that success. I can't do it all, but if we can unleash the energy these boys have, there isn't anything in the Cub Scout Program we can't do!"

It was not always like that. "About five years ago we placed fourth for our booth in the Scout Expo at the mall," says Mike. "Everybody was surprised! Who was Pack 81? We were all elated! It was one of the best things to happen to this pack in years. Now, if we don't win at least something, we're disappointed. Our kids expect to win, and so do their parents."

Fourth place at the Scout Expo eventually led to several first places. Success leads to success, and the community around Pack 81 knows it.

"Last year, we made our annual presentation to the boys and their parents at the elementary school. We were with several other packs, each one trying to drum up interest in their program. When everyone was finished, the boys and their parents went over to the table of the pack that most interested them. We must have had well over half of the people at our table. I was embarrassed! They were standing six or seven deep in front of our table, and there was virtually nobody in front of the others."

SOURCE: "Case IV: Cub Scout Pack 81," in *2001–02 Annual Editions: Management,* Fred H. Maidment, ed. (Guilford, CT: McGraw-Hill/Dushkin, 2001), 130.

Questions

1. What are some of Mike Murphy's basic assumptions about motivation?
2. Why do you think he has been so successful in turning the organization around?
3. How would you motivate people in a volunteer organization such as the Cub Scouts?

REFERENCES

1. Barbara B. Buchholz and Margaret Crane, "Nurturing the Team Spirit at Growing Green," *Your Company,* Spring, 1995, 11–16.

2. Michael West and Malcolm Patterson, "Profitable Personnel," *People Management,* January 8, 1998, 28–31; Richard M. Steers and Lyman W. Porter, eds. *Motivation and Work Behavior,* 3rd ed. (New York: McGraw-Hill, 1983); Don Hellriegel, John W. Slocum, Jr., and Richard W. Woodman, *Organizational Behavior,* 7th ed. (St. Paul, MN: West Publishing Co., 1995), 170; and Jerry L. Gray and Frederick A. Starke, *Organizational Behavior: Concepts and Applications,* 4th ed. (New York: Macmillan, 1988), 104–105.

3. Linda Grant, "Happy Workers, High Returns," *Fortune,* January 12, 1998, 81; Elizabeth J. Hawk and Garrett J. Sheridan, "The Right Staff," *Management Review,* June 1999, 43–48; and West and Patterson, "Profitable Personnel."

4. Richard M. Steers, Lyman W. Porter, and Gregory A. Bigley, *Motivation and Leadership at Work,* 6th ed. (New York: McGraw-Hill, 1996), 496–498.

5. Steven Bergals, "When Money Talks, People Walk," *Inc.,* May 1996, 25–26.

6. Thomas Love, "Yes, Virginia, There Are Good Workers," *Nation's Business,* December 1998, 12.

7. Abraham F. Maslow, "A Theory of Human Motivation," *Psychological Review* 50 (1943): 370–396.

8. Frederick Herzberg, "One More Time: How Do You Motivate Employees?" *Harvard Business Review* (January-February 1968), 53–62.

9. Donna Fenn, "Redesign Work," *Inc.,* June 1999, 75–84.

10. David C. McClelland, *Human Motivation* (Glenview, IL: Scott Foresman, 1985).

11. David C. McClelland, "The Two Faces of Power," in *Organizational Psychology,* D. A. Colb, I. M. Rubin, and J. M. McIntyre, eds. (Englewood Cliffs, NJ: Prentice-Hall, 1971), 73–86.

12. Alfie Kohn, "Why Incentive Plans Cannot Work," *Harvard Business Review,* September-October 1993, 54–63; A. J. Vogl, "Carrots, Sticks, and Self-Deception," (an interview with Alfie Kohn), *Across the Board,* January 1994, 39–44; and Alfie Kohn, "Challenging Behaviorist Dogma: Myths about Money and Motivation," *Compensation and Benefits Review,* March-April 1998, 27, 33–37.

13. H. Richlin, *Modern Behaviorism* (San Francisco: Freeman, 1970); B. F. Skinner, *Science and Human Behavior* (New York: Macmillan, 1953); Alexander D. Stajkovic and Fred Luthans, "A Meta-Analysis of the Effects of Organizational Behavior Modification on Task Performance 1975–1995," *Academy of Management Journal,* October 1997, 1122–1149; F. Luthans and R. Kreitner, *Organizational Behavior Modification and Beyond,* 2nd ed., (Glenview, IL: Scott Foresman, 1985).

14. Luthans and Kreitner, *Organizational Behavior Modification and Beyond;* L. M. Saari and G. P. Latham, "Employee Reaction to Continuous and Variable Ratio Reinforcement Schedules Involving a Monetary Incentive," *Journal of Applied Psychology* 67 (1982): 506–508; and R. D. Pritchard, J. Hollenback, and

P. J. DeLeo, "The Effects of Continuous and Partial Schedules of Reinforcement on Effort, Performance, and Satisfaction," *Organizational Behavior and Human Performance* 25 (1980): 336–353.

15. Fred Goodman, "Suite Smarts," *Success,* January 1998, 11.

16. Kevin Kelly, "Firing Up the Team," *Business Week Frontier,* May 24, 1999, 32.

17. Victor H. Vroom, *Work and Motivation* (New York: Wiley, 1969); B. S. Gorgopoulos, G. M. Mahoney, and N. Jones, "A Path-Goal Approach to Productivity," *Journal of Applied Psychology* 41 (1957), 345–353; and E. E. Lawler III, *Pay and Organizational Effectiveness: A Psychological View* (New York: McGraw-Hill, 1981).

18. Richard M. Daft and Richard M. Steers, *Organizations: A Micro/Macro Approach* (Glenview, IL: Scott, Foresman, 1986).

19. Anita Lienert, "A Dinosaur of A Different Color," *Management Review,* February 1995, 24–29.

20. J. Stacy Adams, "Injustice in Social Exchange," in *Advances in Experimental Social Psychology,* 2nd ed., L. Berkowitz, ed. (New York: Academic Press, 1965); and J. Stacy Adams, "Toward an Understanding of Inequity," *Journal of Abnormal and Social Psychology,* November 1963, 422–436.

21. John Peterman, "The Rise and Fall of the J. Peterman Company," *Harvard Business Review,* September-October 1999, 59–66.

22. Vogl, "Carrots, Sticks, and Self-Deception."

23. James M. Kouzes and Barry Z. Posner, *The Leadership Challenge* (San Francisco, CA: Jossey-Bass, 1995).

24. Nina Gupta and Jason D. Shaw, "Let the Evidence Speak: Financial Incentives *Are* Effective!!" *Compensation and Benefits Review,* March/April 1998, 26, 28–32.

25. Vogl, "Carrots, Sticks, and Self-Deception," 40; and Alfie Kohn, "Incentives Can Be Bad for Business," *Inc.,* January 1998, 93–94.

26. Kohn, "Challenging Behaviorist Dogma."

27. Jerry L. Gray and Frederick A. Starke, *Organizational Behavior: Concepts and Applications,* 4th ed. (New York, NY: Merrill, 1988).

28. Richard M. Steers, Lyman W. Porter, and Gregory A. Bigley, *Motivation and Leadership at Work,* 6th ed. (New York: McGraw-Hill, 1996), 512.

29. Steers, Porter, and Bigley, *Motivation and Leadership at Work,* 517; Vogl, "Carrots, Sticks, and Self-Deception," 40.

30. Steers, Porter, and Bigley, *Motivation and Leadership at Work,* 154-157; Anne Fisher, "The 100 Best Companies to Work for in America," *Fortune,* January 12, 1998, 69–70.

31. William D. Hitt, *The Leader-Manager: Guidelines for Action* (Columbus, OH: Battelle Press, 1988), 153.

32. Steers, Porter, and Bigley, *Motivation and Leadership at Work,* 520–525.

33. Vogl, "Carrots, Sticks, and Self-Deception," 43.

34. Kouzes and Posner, *The Leadership Challenge,* 153.

35. Patrick R. Lancaster III, "Incentive Pay Isn't Good for Your Company," *Inc.,* September 1994, 23–24; Peter Nulty, "Incentive Pay Can Be Crippling," *Fortune,* November 13, 1995, 235.

36. Nulty, "Incentive Pay Can Be Crippling."

37. Kouzes and Posner, *The Leadership Challenge*, 282.
38. Edwin P. Hollander and Lynn R. Offerman, "Power and Leadership in Organizations," *American Psychology* 45 (February 1990), 179–189.
39. Robert C. Ford and Myron D. Fottler, "Empowerment: A Matter of Degree," *Academy of Management Executive* 9 (1995), 21–31.
40. Charles Fishman, "Engines of Democracy," *Fast Company*, October 1999, 174–202.
41. David P. McCaffrey, Sue R. Faerman, and David W. Hart, "The Appeal and Difficulties of Participative Systems," *Organization Science* 6, No. 6 (November-December 1995), 603–627.
42. David E. Bowen and Edward E. Lawler III, "Empowering Service Employees," *Sloan Management Review* (Summer 1995), 73–84.
43. Jay A. Conger and Rabindra N. Kanungo, "The Empowerment Process: Integrating Theory and Practice," *Academy of Management Review* 13 (1988): 471–482.
44. Richard Lalibert, "For Love, Not Money: Ten Ways to Make Your Minimum-Wage Employees Passionate About Their Work," *Success*, August 1998, 63–65.
45. Arnold S. Tannenbaum and Robert S. Cooke, "Organizational Control: A Review of Studies Employing the Control Graph Method," in *Organizations Alike and Unalike*, Cornelius J. Lamners and David J. Hickson, eds., (Boston: Rutledge and Keegan Paul, 1980), 183–210.
46. McCaffrey, Faerman and Hart, "The Appeal and Difficulties of Participative Systems."
47. "Great Expectations?" *Fast Company*, November 1999, 212–224.
48. Bowen and Lawler, "Empowering Service Employees."
49. Hawk and Sheridan, "The Right Staff."
50. Gretchen Spreitzer, "Social Structural Characteristics of Psychological Empowerment," *Academy of Management Journal* 39, No. 2 (April 1996), 483–504.
51. Glenn L. Dalton, "The Collective Stretch," *Management Review*, December 1998, 54–59.
52. Gretchen M. Spreitzer, "Psychological Empowerment in the Workplace: Dimensions, Measurement, and Validation," *Academy of Management Journal* 38, No. 5 (October 1995), 1442.
53. Spreitzer, "Social Structural Characteristics of Psychological Empowerment."
54. Bowen and Lawler, "Empowering Service Employees."
55. Roy C. Herrenkohl, G. Thomas Judson, and Judith A. Heffner, "Defining and Measuring Employee Empowerment," *The Journal of Applied Behavioral Science* 35, No. 3 (September 1999): 373–389.
56. Frank Shipper and Charles C. Manz, "Employee Self-Management Without Formally Designated Teams: An Alternative Road to Empowerment," *Organizational Dynamics* (Winter 1992), 48–61.
57. Steve Kaufman, "ESOPs' Appeal on the Increase," *Nation's Business*, June 1997, 43–44.
58. Ford and Fottler, "Empowerment: A Matter of Degree."
59. Ricardo Semler, "How We Went Digital Without a Strategy," *Harvard Business Review*, September-October 2000, 51–58.

60. McCaffrey, Faerman, and Hart, "The Appeal and Difficulties of Participative Systems."
61. Michael Barrier, "The Changing Face of Leadership," *Nation's Business,* January 1995, 41–42.
62. Kerry Capell, "Options for Everyone," *Business Week,* July 22, 1996, 80–88.
63. Larry Armstrong, "Where Owners and Workers See Eye to Eye," *Business Week,* June 21, 1999, 160–162.
64. Dalton, "The Collective Stretch."
65. Hawk and Sheridan, "The Right Staff."
66. Dalton, "The Collective Stretch."

CHAPTER OUTLINE

YOUR LEADERSHIP CHALLENGE

After reading this chapter, you should be able to:

- Act as a communication champion rather than just as an information processor.

- Use key elements of effective listening and understand why listening is important to leader communication.

- Recognize and apply the difference between dialogue and discussion.

- Select an appropriate communication channel for your leadership message.

- Use communication feedback and realize its importance for leadership.

Leadership Communication

In December of 1955, Martin Luther King, Jr., was installed as president of the new Montgomery Improvement Association. That same evening, he was called upon to address a crowd of thousands about the bus boycott that had begun only days earlier. In his impromptu speech, King referred to his audience as people "tired of being pushed out of the glittering sunlight of life's July and left standing amidst the chill of an alpine November." He reminded the audience of Rosa Parks' arrest and conviction for refusing to give up her bus seat to a white person. He commended her integrity; her action was a move toward justice and reflected a belief that all Americans are entitled to basic rights and privileges. King pointed out that the bus boycott was a means of protest with similar integrity. The boycott was nonviolent, it required patience, and it rested on the expectation of equal treatment of all people—values King had preached in his sermons as a minister.

The audience rallied in agreement, and under King's guidance 50,000 citizens of Montgomery, Alabama participated in the boycott for the duration of the protest, despite the fact that most of those same citizens needed to ride the buses to get to and from work.

King's actions over the next several months were a witness of his sincerity to the protestors. He was the first to be arrested for participating in the boycott. His home was bombed the same day as his arrest. Despite these tribulations, he declared his determination inviolate. The boycott continued.

After nearly a year of protest, the U.S. Supreme Court ruled that Alabama's segregation laws were indeed unconstitutional. The boycott ended in victory, and King declared the verdict a leap of progress for the entire American population.[1]

What made King's first public role in a political drama so powerful that it ignited the support of thousands? How did King manage to maintain the support of so many people over a long period of hardship? Much of King's impact occurred the moment he gave his first speech. With his initial words, King created the parameters of a social movement. He discerned that the audience was tired of injustice. His metaphor contrasting summer sunshine with winter winds made the experience of racism tangible, felt upon the skin of each person in the crowd. King stood before the crowd and directed their collective attention to the immediate situation—Parks' action and the decision to boycott. Then he defined the significance of the boycott by comparing it to the incident on the bus—in effect, every boycotter was Rosa Parks.

King was thrust into a position of leadership where others looked to him for direction and inspiration. As he endured arrest and violence against his family without changing course, he symbolized his message of determination in the face of hardship. He communicated with both words and actions a vision and possibility of equality. King's followers wanted a future based on basic religious values and American ideals, a future King motivated them to work for and helped them see. For thousands, Martin Luther King, Jr., created a purpose and an identity that had not existed before.

In the previous chapter, we discussed motivation and reviewed some of the ways in which leaders motivate followers toward the accomplishment of the organization's goals. As this story of Martin Luther King, Jr., clearly illustrates, motivation depends greatly on a leader's ability to communicate effectively. In fact, leadership cannot happen without effective communication. The styles of leadership we have discussed in earlier chapters of this book, particularly charismatic and transformational leadership, depend on powerful communication. Recall that leadership means influencing people to bring about change toward a vision, or desirable future for the organization. Leaders communicate to share the vision with others, inspire and motivate them to strive toward the vision, and build the values and trust that enable effective working relationships and goal accomplishment.

Successful leader communication also includes deceptively simple components, such as actively listening to others. Today's fast-paced environment does not always provide time for the listening and reflection that good communication requires.[2] A recent study showed that although leaders at a majority of companies agree that communication is a priority, less than half bother to tailor their messages to employees, customers, or suppliers, and even fewer seek feedback from those constituencies. Furthermore, investors appear to have a better idea of the vision and mission of companies than do employees.[3]

This chapter will describe the tools and skills that overcome the communication deficit pervading today's organizations and the broader social world. We will also examine how leaders can use communication skills to make a difference in their organizations and the lives of followers.

HOW LEADERS COMMUNICATE

Leadership means communicating with others in such a way that they are influenced and motivated to perform actions that further common goals and lead toward desired outcomes. **Communication** is a process by which information and understanding are transferred between a sender and a receiver, such as between a leader and an employee. The key elements of the communication process are shown in Exhibit 9.1. The leader initiates a communication by *encoding* a thought or idea, that is, by selecting symbols (such as words) with which to compose and transmit a message. The message is the tangible formulation of the thought or idea sent to the receiver, and the *channel* is the medium by which the message is sent. The channel could be a formal report, a telephone call, an e-mail message, or a face-to-face conversation. The receiver *decodes* the symbols to interpret the meaning of the message. Encoding and decoding are potential sources for communication errors because individual differences, knowledge, values, attitudes, and background act as filters and may create "noise" when translating from symbols to meaning. Finally, *feedback* occurs when a receiver responds to the leader's communication with a return message. Feedback is a powerful aid to communication because it enables the leader to determine whether the receiver correctly interpreted the message. Effective communication involves both the transference and the mutual understanding of information.[4] The process of sending, receiving, and feedback to test understanding underlies both management and leadership communication.

Management Communication

A manager's primary role is that of "information processor." Managers spend some 80 percent of each working day in communication with others.[5] In other words, forty-eight minutes of every hour are spent in meetings, on the telephone, or talking informally with others. Managers scan their environments for important written and personal information, gathering facts, data, and ideas, which in turn are sent to subordinates and others who can use them. A manager then receives subordinate messages and feedback to see if "noise" interfered with translation, and determines whether to modify messages for accuracy.

EXHIBIT 9.1

A Basic Model of the Communication Process

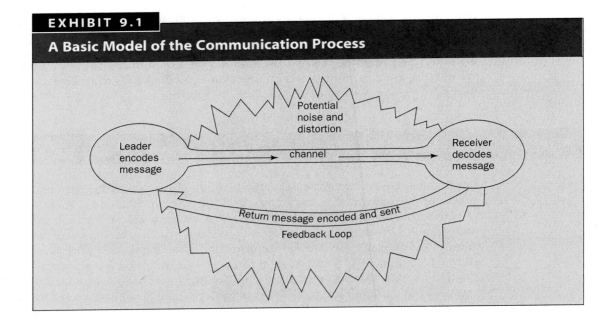

Managers have a huge communication responsibility directing and controlling an organization. Communication effectiveness lies in accuracy of formulation, with less "noise" as one determinant of success. Managers communicate facts, statistics, and decisions. Effective managers establish themselves at the center of information networks to facilitate the completion of tasks. Leadership communication, however, serves a different purpose.

Leader Communication

While leader communication also includes the components of sending, receiving, and feedback, it is different from management communication. Leaders often communicate the big picture—the vision, as defined in Chapter 1—rather than facts and pieces of information. Whereas a manager acts as an information processor to disseminate data accurately, a leader can be seen as a communication champion.[6] A **communication champion** is philosophically grounded in the belief that communication is essential to building trust and gaining commitment to the organizational vision. Learning, problem solving, decision making, and strategizing are all oriented around and stem from the vision. Furthermore, communication champions visibly and symbolically engage in communication-based activities. Whether they walk around asking and answering questions or thoughtfully listen to a subordinate's problem, the actions of champions convey a commitment to communication. For example, top leaders at Weirton Steel act as communication champions by participating in every team training session—a significant commitment in an 8000-employee organization.[7] At the end of each session, CEO Robert Loughead and other top leaders, along with the president of the union, listen to team members' reactions to the training, their feelings about management and the union, and their ideas for how they would improve the company. Besides being a good opportunity for the exchange of information, the participation of top leaders is a powerful symbol that teamwork is valued at Weirton. However, communication isn't just about occasional meetings, formal speeches, or presentations. Leaders actively communicate through both words and actions every day. Regular communication is essential for building personal relationships with followers.

Exhibit 9.2 shows the leader-as-communication-champion model. Through the efforts of listening with pure concentration on the needs of others, and the discernment of underlying messages, leaders gather what they need to communicate. Active listening requires that leaders temporarily drop their personal agendas and give their full attention to speakers. Discernment involves recognizing the needs that followers, for whatever reason, are unable to articulate.

Leader communication actions include directing others' attention toward the vision and values of an organization. Leaders can use many communication methods including rich channels of communication, stories, metaphors, informality, openness, and dialogue. For example, in communicating his message about the federal budget, President Ronald Reagan spoke of a trillion dollars in terms of stacking it next to the Empire State Building. Framed this way, the message redefined the meaning of a trillion dollars, and took on a new reality for the audience. Historical and contemporary leaders as diverse as Reagan, Martin Luther King, Jr., Golda Meir, Bill Gates, and Carly Fiorina all share the ability to powerfully communicate their messages to followers and others.

EXHIBIT 9.2

The Leader as Communication Champion

CREATING AN OPEN COMMUNICATION CLIMATE

Open communication means sharing all types of information throughout the company, especially across functional and hierarchical levels. Open communication runs counter to the traditional flow of selective information downward from supervisors to subordinates. But leaders want communication to flow in all directions. People throughout the organization need a clear direction and an understanding of how they can contribute.[8] Leaders break down conventional hierarchical and departmental boundaries that may be barriers to communication, enabling them to convey a stronger awareness of and commitment to organizational vision, goals, and values. In an open climate, a leader's communication of the vision "cascades" through an organization, as explained in Exhibit 9.3. Consistent and frequent communication brings follower acceptance and understanding. Open communication also builds trust, which is an essential element in effective leader-follower relationships because it inspires collaboration and commitment to common goals.[9] A. W. Chesterton Co., a manufacturer of valves and seals in Stoneham, Massachusetts, holds quarterly meetings where employees can ask CEO Jim Chesterton about anything and everything. Departments, divisions, and subsidiaries meet and exchange information on a regular basis. Chesterton believes open communication is vital to the creation of a trusting work environment. Other leaders agree. In a recent

EXHIBIT 9.3

Why Open the Communication Climate?

An open climate is essential for cascading vision, and cascading is essential because:

Natural Law 1: You Get What You Talk About
A vision must have ample 'air time' in an organization. A vision must be shared and practiced by leaders at every opportunity.

Natural Law 2: The Climate of an Organization Is a Reflection of the Leader
A leader who doesn't embody the vision and values doesn't have an organization that does.

Natural Law 3: You Can't Walk Faster Than One Step at a Time
A vision is neither understood nor accepted overnight. Communicating must be built into continuous, daily interaction so that over time followers will internalize it.

SOURCE: Based on Bob Wall, Robert S. Slocum, and Mark R. Sobol, *Visionary Leader* (Rocklin, CA: Prima Publishing, 1992), 87–89.

survey, more than 50 percent of executives reported that open communication is essential for building trust.[10]

Leaders also want an open communication climate because it helps employees understand how their actions interact with and affect others in the organization, which makes them more effective followers. Open communication encompasses the recent trend toward "open-book management," which means sharing financial information with all employees to engender an attitude of employee ownership. Recall from the previous chapter that when employees feel a sense of ownership in the company, they are more highly motivated to achieve goals. In addition, when employees have access to complete information, they make decisions that are good for the company. For example, leaders at Tampa-based AmeriSteel say opening the books and training all employees to understand the numbers helped cut the cost of converting a ton of scrap steel into a ton of finished steel from $145 to $127.[11] The open-book management program helped workers understand how every decision and action affects organizational success.

Communication across traditional boundaries enables leaders to hear what followers have to say, which means the organization gains the benefit of all employees' minds. The same perspectives batted back and forth between top executives don't lead to effective change, the creation of a powerful shared vision, or the network of personal relationships that keep organizations thriving. New voices and continuous conversation involving a broad spectrum of people revitalize and enhance communication.[12] One company that believes in open communication, with information flowing in all directions and including everyone in the organization, is IDEO Product Development.

IN THE LEAD   ## David Kelley, IDEO Product Development

David Kelley, president of IDEO, the firm that has designed cutting-edge products for such clients as Apple Computer, PepsiCo, and Eli Lilly, is devoted to "unfettered conversation." He and other leaders have searched for ways to blast open the hierarchical and departmental boundaries that block the flow of communication.

IDEO has designed its physical work space to provide maximum opportunity for open communication. There are few special executive areas or status symbols. Meeting spaces are arranged to make everyone feel comfortable enough to speak up, contribute ideas, and ask questions. In addition, walls are transparent, so anyone can see what's going on and drop in to participate or pull out a colleague for a quick chat. Studio work areas are also open, so colleagues can visually eavesdrop on other projects, as well as plug into neighboring conversations.

IDEO's leaders were so committed to the concept of an open environment that they hired a behavioral scientist, Peter Coughlan, who first carefully analyzed what employees were already doing—how they interacted with one another and what design elements could support the informal interaction that already existed. Employees were also asked for their opinions about what areas of the office best supported interaction and creative collaboration. Video cameras were positioned to allow office designers to analyze traffic flow and usage patterns. This careful approach helped IDEO design a casual, informal atmosphere that truly encourages continuous conversations that cross traditional boundaries. Too often, Kelley says, leaders and companies "are just faking an informal conversation. It's staged. It's not spontaneous, so you never really know what's on anyone's mind."[13]

Leaders such as David Kelley continually look for ways to promote open communication. Open communication improves the operations of a company, builds trust, spreads knowledge, and provides a foundation for communicating vision, values, and other vital big-picture information.

LISTENING AND DISCERNMENT

One of the most important tools in a leader's communication tool kit is listening, both to followers and customers. Many leaders now believe that important information flows from the bottom up, not top down, and that a crucial component of leadership is to listen effectively.[14] A listener is responsible for message reception, which is a vital link in the communication process. **Listening** involves the skill of grasping and interpreting a message's genuine meaning. Only then can a leader's response be on target. Listening is an activity; it requires attention, energy, and skill.

Many people do not listen effectively. They concentrate on formulating what they are going to say next rather than on what is being said to them. Our listening efficiency, as measured by the amount of material understood and remembered by subjects forty-eight hours after listening to a ten-minute message, is, on average, no better than 25 percent.[15]

What constitutes good listening? Exhibit 9.4 gives ten keys to effective listening and illustrates a number of ways to distinguish a bad listener from a good one. A key to effective listening is focus. A good listener's total attention is focused on the message; he isn't thinking about an unrelated problem in the purchasing department, how much work is piled up on his desk, or what to have for lunch. A good listener also listens actively, finds areas of interest, is flexible, works hard at listening, and uses thought speed to mentally summarize, weigh, and anticipate what the speaker says.

EXHIBIT 9.4

Ten Keys to Effective Listening

Keys	Poor Listener	Good Listener
1. Listen actively	Is passive, laid back	Asks questions; paraphrases what is said
2. Find areas of interest	Tunes out dry subjects	Looks for opportunities, new learning
3. Resist distractions	Is easily distracted	Fights distractions; tolerates bad habits; knows how to concentrate
4. Capitalize on the fact that thought is faster than speech	Tends to daydream with slow speakers	Challenges, anticipates, summarizes; listens between lines to tone of voice
5. Be responsive	Is minimally involved	Nods; shows interest, positive feedback
6. Judge content, not delivery	Tunes out if delivery is poor	Judges content; skips over delivery errors
7. Hold one's fire	Has preconceptions; argues	Does not judge until comprehension is complete
8. Listen for ideas	Listens for facts	Listens to central themes
9. Work at listening	No energy output; faked attention	Works hard; exhibits active body state, eye contact
10. Exercise one's mind	Resists difficult material in favor of light, recreational material	Uses heavier material as exercise for the mind

SOURCE: Adapted from Sherman K. Okum, "How to Be a Better Listener," *Nation's Business* (August 1975), 62; and Philip Morgan and Kent Baker, "Building a Professional Image: Improving Listening Behavior," *Supervisory Management* (November 1985), 34–38.

The act of good listening affirms others, builds trust, and suppresses personal judgments that shape perceptions. Merrill Lynch superbroker Richard F. Green explained the importance of listening to his success: "If you talk, you'll like me. If I talk, I'll like you—but if I do the talking, my business will not be served."[16] By not interrupting people when they talk, and by not plying them with his business agenda, Green builds long-term relationships with his clients.

Being a good listener expands a leader's role in the eyes of others and enhances the leader's influence. A new CEO at Griffin Hospital in Derby, Connecticut, started actively listening to employees and patients when it became clear that the community hospital would have to change to survive against larger, more aggressive competitors. CEO Patrick Charmel implemented virtually every requested change, including installing wooden rather than steel handrails in hallways, banning fluorescent bulbs in favor of soft, indirect lighting, and adding cozy, home-style kitchens within easy access of all patient rooms. In addition, every patient now takes part in a detailed "case conference" with doctors, nurses, and other caregivers. They're encouraged to look at their medical charts and given detailed literature about their condition. Employees throughout the hospital are authorized to make decisions and take actions within their area of expertise based on the best interest of the patient.[17] By listening to the needs of patients and employees, and subsequently responding to those needs, Charmel transformed Griffin Hospital—as well as the relationships between leaders and employees and between employees and patients. This kind of transformation is what leader listening—indeed, communication—is all about.

Active listening is not only necessary during times of crisis or change, but is a daily, ongoing part of a leader's communication. At Home Depot, leaders believe listening is the only possible way to meet customer needs. Greg McMillan, head of the Seattle store's garden department, spends his days listening to customers' fears and helping them overcome their biggest do-it-yourself worries. "People come in with a lot of fear," McMillan says. "All I'm doing is empowering them [by listening]." Home Depot leaders encourage this type of listening from the top to the bottom of the organization, stressing that listening and communication take precedence over just "making a sale."[18]

The characteristics of good listening hold true within organizations as well. For example, Jack Stack, CEO of Springfield Remanufacturing Corp. (SRC) learned from an outside poll that employees in the Heavy Duty Division did not feel that leaders were listening to them. Although SRC had been a pioneer in the use of open-book management, communications were poor because employees were not being heard. Stack immediately took steps to solve the problem. In addition, he set up an employee satisfaction committee, made up of eighteen shop-floor volunteers. Leaders began regularly auditing the division with a goal of improving leader listening skills and reducing to zero the percentage of demoralized employees.[19]

The connection between personal satisfaction and being listened to, whether one is a customer or an employee, is not a mystery. When people sense that they have been heard, they simply feel better. Dr. Robert Buckman, a cancer specialist who teaches other doctors, as well as businesspeople, how to break bad news, says you have to start by listening. "The trust that you build just by letting people say what they feel is incredible," Buckman says.[20] Few things are as maddening to people as not being listened to by doctors or other professionals. In the business world, customers are often infuriated when their requests are ignored or they are told they can't be accommodated, signals that nobody is listening to their needs. Furthermore, when leaders fail to listen to employees, it sends the signal, "you don't matter," which decreases employee commitment and motivation.

Listening is a requirement for leader communication, for doing better work, and for enabling others to do better work. Tom Peters, the famous management author and consultant, says that executives can become good listeners by observing the following: Effective listening is engaged listening; ask dumb questions; break down barriers by participating with employees in casual get-togethers; force yourself to get out and about; provide listening forums; take notes; promise feedback—and deliver.[21]

Dialogue

Dialogue is what you get when active listening spreads throughout an organization. A dialogue occurs when a group of good listeners convene. The "roots of dialogue" are *dia* and *logos*, which can be thought of as *stream of meaning*. In **dialogue,** people together create a stream of shared meaning that enables them to understand each other and share a view of the world.[22] People may start out as polar opposites, but by actively listening and talking authentically to one another, they discover their common ground, common issues, and common dreams on which they can build a better future.

Most of us have a tendency to infuse everything we hear with our own opinions rather than being genuinely open to what others are saying. In addition, traditional business values in the United States and most other Western countries reward people for forcefully asserting their own ideas and opinions and trying to discredit or contradict others.[23] But people can engage in dialogue only when they come to a conversation free of prejudgments, personal agendas, and "right" answers. Participants in a dialogue do not presume to know the outcome, nor do they sell their convictions.

One way to understand the distinctive quality of dialogue is to contrast it with discussion.[24] Exhibit 9.5 illustrates the differences between a dialogue and a discussion. Typically, the intent of a discussion is to present one's own point of view and persuade others in the group to adopt it. A discussion is often resolved by logic or by "beating down" opposing viewpoints. Dialogue, on the other hand, requires that participants suspend their attachments to a particular point of view so that a deeper level of listening, synthesis, and meaning can emerge from the group. A dialogue's focus is to reveal feelings and build common ground, with the emphasis on inquiry rather than advocacy. Consider how Henry Bertolon, cofounder and CEO of NECX, introduced dialogue into the company to improve communication.

EXHIBIT 9.5

Dialogue and Discussion: The Differences

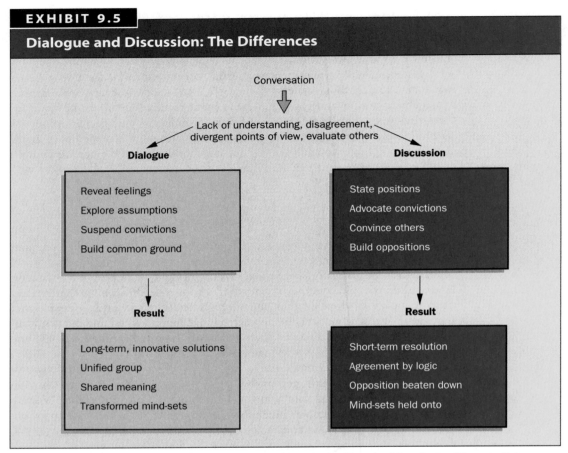

SOURCE: Adapted from Edgar Schein, "On Dialogue, Culture, and Organizational Learning," *Organizational Dynamics* (Autumn 1993), 46.

IN THE LEAD   Henry Bertolon, NECX

From the outside, everything looked rosy at NECX, a leading independent distributor of semiconductors and other computer products. However, CEO Henry Bertolon could see that the company was suffering from the strain of rapid growth and beginning to come apart at the seams. "We'd have meetings that just melted down," he says. "Everyone would scream at each other and then leave."

Bertolon hired Wil Calmas, a psychologist with an MBA, to help solve NECX's communication problems. Calmas set up a one-day-a-week program to get people talking—and listening—to one another on a deeper, authentic level. The day begins with a 90-minute meeting of top leaders. There's never a formal agenda—people are encouraged to express fear, hostility, frustration, secret wishes, whatever feelings are affecting their lives and work. The early morning meeting is just the beginning of a day-long series of dialogues among NECX employees from all ranks and departments. The sales department became so adept at dialogue that they quickly began meeting on their own, without Calmas's guidance.

Bertolon is convinced that the sessions have had a positive impact on communication, interpersonal relationships, and the bottom line. In a fast-growing business, he believes that getting people communicating in a way that builds shared understanding and meaning is critical to success. The dialogue sessions created a safe environment for people to reveal their feelings, explore ideas, and build common ground. It also keeps them loose, flexible, and open to new ideas—ready to respond to the rapid changes taking place all around them.[25]

Both forms of communication, dialogue and discussion, can result in organizational change. However, the result of a discussion is limited to a specific topic being deliberated, whereas the result of dialogue is characterized by group unity, shared meaning, and transformed mind-sets. This kind of result is far-reaching. A new, common mind-set is not the same thing as agreement, because it creates a reference point from which subsequent communication can start. As new and deeper solutions are developed, a trusting relationship is built among communicators, as occurred at NECX, and this is important to all communication episodes that follow. Dialogue thus transforms communication and, by extension, the organization. The Leader's Bookshelf offers some tips for bringing about successful dialogue.

Discernment

One of the most rewarding kinds of listening involves **discernment.** By this kind of listening, a leader detects the unarticulated messages hidden below the surface of spoken interaction, complaints, behavior, and actions. A discerning leader pays attention to patterns and relationships underlying the organization and those it serves.

Richard Teerlink, CEO of Harley-Davidson, used discernment to help turn around the company. Through the innovative Harley Owners Group (HOG) rallies, Teerlink has the opportunity to mingle with many of the 360,000 members nationwide. He attends the rallies, talks with owners, listens

The Magic of Dialogue: Transforming Conflict Into Cooperation

Daniel Yankelovich

Most leaders are highly skilled at talking. Many are even excellent at listening. But very few, argues Daniel Yankelovich, know how to engage in dialogue. Yankelovich believes this skill is becoming not only useful but essential for today's leaders—as they strive to create webs of relationships that replace the traditional command-and-control hierarchy, as they try to repair the damaged morale and weakened trust that may have resulted from years of downsizing, and as they strive to align everyone in implementing a shared vision for the organization's future.

In his book, *The Magic of Dialogue*, Yankelovich offers some basic guidelines and strategies for creating successful dialogue.

Strategies for Dialogue

The heart of Yankelovich's book outlines fifteen strategies that can help leaders create dialogue and bridge the "understanding gap" that threatens to tear apart many of today's organizations. These strategies include:

- **Introduce the three core requirements of dialogue.** Dialogue cannot exist without three conditions: (1) participants must be treated as equals; (2) everyone must listen with empathy; and (3) assumptions must be brought into the open. The other strategies are designed to help leaders meet these three core requirements.

- **Bring forth your own assumptions before speculating on those of others.** When leaders are willing to open up first, it becomes easier for other participants to express their assumptions. Leaders can also evaluate and be critical of their assumptions, which shows the leader in a vulnerable light and helps others develop greater self-awareness of their own potential prejudices.

- **Err on the side of including people who disagree.** It's much easier to engage in conversation or discussion with people who agree with you. However, true dialogue requires seeking out a variety of viewpoints.

- **Focus on conflicts between value systems, not people.** Leaders take care not to stereotype people because of individual or subcultural differences in value systems. They help bring conflicting values into the open and focus participants on looking at the "good" or "bad" of values in light of specific issues the organization faces.

- **When appropriate, express the emotions that accompany strongly held values.** A key to the "magic of dialogue" is that it reaches deep into people's personal convictions. The expression of strong emotions can sometimes make dialogue uncomfortable, but it also brings people to a higher level of understanding.

Conclusion

Taken together, the fifteen strategies presented in *The Magic of Dialogue* serve as a blueprint for using dialogue to work out disagreements and enhance mutual understanding. The real magic of dialogue is that it can create a sense of community that lasts far beyond a specific meeting, thereby transforming everyday working relationships.

The Magic of Dialogue: Transforming Conflict Into Cooperation, by Daniel Yankelovich, is published by Simon & Schuster.

LIVING LEADERSHIP

Discerning Feelings

Caotang said:

There is essentially nothing to leadership but to carefully observe people's conditions and know them all, in both upper and lower echelons.

When people's inner conditions are thoroughly enough understood, then inside and outside are in harmony. When above and below communicate, all affairs are set in order. This is how leadership is made secure.

If the leader cannot minutely discern people's psychological conditions, and the feeling of those below is not communicated above, the above and below oppose each other and matters are disordered. This is how leadership goes to ruin.

It may happen that a leader will presume upon intellectual brilliance and often hold to biased views, failing to comprehend people's feelings, rejecting community counsel and giving importance to his own authority, neglecting public consideration and practicing private favoritism—all of this causes the road of advance in goodness to become narrower and narrower, and causes the path of responsibility for the community to become fainter and fainter.

Such leaders repudiate whatever they have never before seen or heard, and become set in their ways, to which they are habituated and by which they are veiled. To hope that the leadership of people like this would be great and far-reaching is like walking backward trying to go forward.

SOURCE: Thomas Cleary, translator, *Zen Lessons: The Art of Leadership* (Boston, Mass.: Shambhala Publications 1989), 83–84.

to what they have to say, and takes note of the ideas they toss his way. Teerlink thus determined how to give more people a reason to use Harley products. He discerned that people really seek relief from the stresses of daily life when they buy a Harley. The company is selling a sense of freedom and independence more than providing motorcycles and related products. This feeling of escaping the daily grind was not something stated to him by customers, but something Teerlink was able to discern from what he encountered while strolling among and listening to rally members.[26]

A leader hears the undercurrents that have yet to emerge.[27] Remember how Martin Luther King, Jr., discerned a readiness to fight injustice in his audience, a frustration just beginning to surface to which he subsequently gave definition and organization? Discernment is a critical skill for leaders because it enables them to tap into the unarticulated, often deep-seated needs, desires, and hopes of followers and customers. This chapter's Living Leadership box considers discernment as the essence of leadership.

RICH COMMUNICATION CHANNELS

A **channel** is a medium by which a communication message is carried from sender to receiver. Leaders have a choice of many channels through which to communicate to subordinates. A leader may discuss a problem face-to-face, use the telephone, write a memo or letter, use e-mail, or put an item in a newsletter, depending on the nature of the message. In addition, new communication media such as Web pages, intranets, and extranets have expanded leaders' options for communicating to followers as well as the organization's customers, clients, or shareholders. Recent research has attempted to explain how leaders select communication channels to enhance communication effectiveness.[28] The research has found that channels differ in their capacity to convey information. Just as a pipeline's physical characteristics limit the kind and amount of liquid that can be pumped through it, a communication channel's physical characteristics limit the kind and amount of information that can be conveyed among people. The channels available to leaders can be classified into a hierarchy based on information richness. **Channel richness** is the amount of information that can be transmitted during a communication episode. The hierarchy of channel richness is illustrated in Exhibit 9.6.

The richness of an information channel is influenced by three characteristics: (1) the ability to handle multiple cues simultaneously; (2) the ability to facilitate rapid, two-way feedback; and (3) the ability to establish a personal focus for the communication. Face-to-face discussion is the richest medium, because it permits direct experience, multiple information cues, immediate feedback, and personal focus. Face-to-face discussions facilitate the assimilation of broad cues and deep, emotional understanding of the situation. For example, Tony Burns, CEO of Ryder Systems, Inc., likes to handle things face-to-face: "You can look someone in the eyes. You can tell by the look in his eyes or the inflection of his voice what the real problem or question or answer is."[29]

Telephone conversations are next in the richness hierarchy. Eye contact, gaze, posture, and other body language cues are missing, but the human voice still carries a tremendous amount of emotional information. Electronic messaging, or e-mail, which lacks both visual and verbal cues, is increasingly being used for communications that were once handled over the telephone. E-mail has improved the speed and reduced the cost of long-distance communication in particular. Rather than playing "phone tag," a leader or employee can send an e-mail message to communicate necessary information. A recent survey by Ohio State University researchers found that about half of the respondents reported making fewer telephone calls since they began using e-mail. However, respondents also said they preferred the telephone or face-to-face conversations for expressing affection, giving advice, or communicating difficult news.[30] De-

EXHIBIT 9.6

A Continuum of Channel Richness

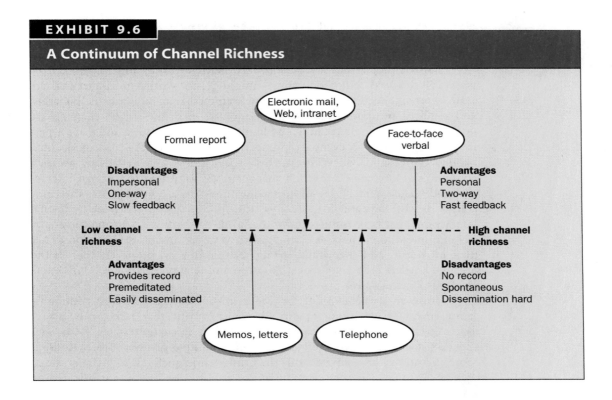

spite many of the advantages of e-mail, its proliferation has contributed to *poorer* communication in many organizations. Employees who work in offices down the hall from one another will often send e-mail rather than communicating face to face. One employee reported that he was fired via e-mail—by a manager who sat five feet away in the same office.[31]

Other forms of electronic communication, such as video conferencing, recognize the need for channel richness, allowing for voice as well as body language cues. A lower level of richness is offered by the World Wide Web and company intranets, but these have opened new avenues for keeping in touch with employees and customers. An intranet enables leaders to disseminate certain types of information to a huge number of employees simultaneously, such as a traditional company newsletter might. Company Web pages are increasingly being used to keep in closer touch with customers, suppliers, or partners, and unlike print media, the Web allows for rapid feedback. The companies that are most successful in using the Web are those that supplement electronic media with the human touch. At some Web sites, customers are immediately greeted by a person offering help. Land's End Inc. has operators on hand who can instantly interact with customers to answer questions and help them make selections.[32]

Written media that are personalized, such as notes and letters, can be personally focused, but they convey only the cues written on paper and are slow to provide feedback. Impersonal written media, including fliers, bulletins, and standard computer reports, are the lowest in richness. The channels are not focused on a single receiver, use limited information cues, and do not permit feedback. Paul Stevenson, president and CEO of ATI Medical, Inc., banned the practice of writing memos to encourage employees to use rich communication channels. He felt that memos substituted for human interaction and wasted valuable decision-making time. Stevenson attributes the company's yearly increase in sales to the productive and timely personal interactions that have resulted from the no-memo policy.[33] Lacking memos as a communication channel, ATI employees must communicate in person to get their ideas out, and they build strong relationships with one another in the process. Leaders recognize that innovation and teamwork are the by-products of using rich channels.

However, it is important for leaders to understand that each communication channel has advantages and disadvantages, and that each can be an effective means of communication in the appropriate circumstances.[34] Channel selection depends on whether the message is routine or nonroutine. Routine communications are simple and straightforward, such as a product price change. Routine messages convey data or statistics or simply put into words what people already understand and agree on. Routine messages can be efficiently communicated through a channel lower in richness. Written or electronic communications also are effective when the audience is widely dispersed or when the communication is "official" and a permanent record is required.[35] On the other hand, nonroutine messages typically concern issues of change, conflict, or complexity that have great potential for misunderstanding. Nonroutine messages often are characterized by time pressure and surprise. Leaders can communicate nonroutine messages effectively only by selecting a rich channel.

Consider a CEO trying to work out a press release with public relations people about a plant explosion that injured fifteen employees. If the press release must be ready in three hours, the communication is truly nonroutine and forces a rich information exchange. The group will meet face-to-face, brainstorm ideas, and provide rapid feedback to resolve disagreement and convey the correct information. If the CEO has three days to prepare the release, less information capacity is needed. The CEO and public relations people might begin developing the press release with an exchange of memos and telephone calls.

The leadership key is to select a channel to fit the message. During a major acquisition, one firm elected to send senior executives to all major work sites, where 75 percent of the acquired workforce met the officials in person. The results were well worth the time and expense of the personal appearances. Participating leaders claimed that the workers saw them as understanding and willing to listen—people they would not mind working for.[36] On the other hand, consider the executive who addressed a letter "Dear Team" to inform employees in his department that they would be required to make significant changes to achieve a new corporate quality goal of zero defects. Although the letter indicated that the supervisor realized this would "not be welcome news," it directs employees to renew their commitment to quality and pull together as a team. The letter concludes with a P.S.: "As of tomorrow, I will be on vacation in Hawaii for the next four weeks and out of reach." If you were a member of this supervisor's team, how would you feel about such a communication? Most leader communication by its very nature is comprised of nonroutine messages. Although leaders maximize the use of all channels, they don't let anything substitute for the rich face-to-face channel when important issues are at stake.

Sometimes a channel conveys more than the simple message content, a symbolic meaning to the receiver of which the leader must be aware. In other words, members of an organization attach meaning to the channel itself. Reports and memos—low richness channels—typically convey formality and legitimize a message. Personal visits from a leader or other rich channels are seen as a sign of teamwork.[37] The supervisor who sent a form letter about new quality standards is not likely to inspire teamwork among members of his department. In addition, his communication could be interpreted as a signal that he is less than committed to both the new standards and the welfare of his employees. The very modes of communication, then, are symbolic, as when students gauge the importance of a topic based on the amount of time a professor spends talking about it, or when an individual experiences indignation at receiving a "Dear John" letter instead of having a relationship terminated in person.

STORIES AND METAPHORS

The Ute Indians of Utah, as well as other native tribes, made the best storytellers their tribal leaders.[38] Why? Because storytelling is a powerful means of persuasion and influence. Stories enable leaders to connect with people on an emotional as well as an intellectual level. In addition, telling stories helps people make sense of complex situations, inspires action, and brings about change in ways that other forms of communication cannot.

Leaders have to be conscious of the language they use in all situations. Just being aware of the terminology they choose and the definitions and context they create is one way leaders enhance communications with others. For example, when Federal Express acquired airfreight rival Flying Tiger Lines Inc., the careers and trust of employees in both companies were at stake. Leaders deliberately chose the word "merger" rather than acquisition to define the situation, easing concerns over job security from the beginning.[39] Thus, even simple language choices make a tremendous difference for leadership. However, it is by using language rich in metaphor and storytelling that leaders can create a deep and lasting effect on others.

It is in the leader's purview to direct followers' attention to the values that underlie the organization, to define the meaning of situations and objectives, and to give visionary messages in ways that make them palpable and meaningful to organizational members. People seek meaning in their daily work and want to understand their role in the larger context of the organization. It is up to leaders to provide that context for followers, to frame activity with discrete meaning.[40] By using language rich in metaphor and storytelling, leaders can make sense of situations in ways that will be understood similarly throughout the organization.

For example, Jack Welch, CEO of General Electric, refers to the huge global company as "the grocery store," conveying an image of the grandfatherly Welch slipping on an apron, leaning on a gleaming countertop, and chatting with employees and customers. This vivid image imparts a basic principle Welch believes is crucial to GE's success: When it comes to personalized service, you should run a large business the same way you'd run a small neighborhood market.[41]

Telling stories is a powerful way to relay a message because a story evokes both visual imagery and emotion, which helps employees connect with the message and the key values. People are almost always able to apply some aspect of the story to themselves, and a story is often much more convincing and more likely to be remembered than a simple directive or a batch of facts and figures.[42]

Stories can bind people together and create a shared sense of purpose and meaning.[43] In addition, stories enhance the connection between leader and followers. Great leaders such as Martin Luther King, Jr., described at the beginning of this chapter, almost instinctively rely on stories to connect with followers. However, almost everyone can learn to be an effective storyteller. Companies such as IBM, Coca-Cola, and Royal Dutch/Shell have sent managers to workshops to learn about the advantages of stories as a way to transmit cultural values and promote change.[44] Rolf Jensen, director of the Copenhagen Institute for Futures Studies, asserts that in the twenty-first century, people will place increasing importance on the "language of emotion," and that companies will thrive on the basis of their stories and myths. One leader who agrees is Anita Ward, vice president of Cambridge Technology

Partners. An anthropologist by training, Ward uses stories to help employees cope with dramatic change. "Campfire stories," she says, "turn experience into narratives, people into heroes, and new ideas into enduring traditions."[45]

Len Riggio, CEO of Barnes & Noble, also leads effectively with stories. As an outsider to the bookstore business, Riggio came to Barnes & Noble with a vision of shedding the elitist image of the past and becoming a populist institution. He used stories of his experiences growing up in a predominantly Italian neighborhood in Brooklyn, including his father's stint as a prize fighter, to help convey his vision to employees. Riggio's innovations and the commitment of followers to his vision transformed the company.[46]

Some people believe that the true impact of a leader depends primarily on the stories he or she tells and how followers receive them.[47] Evidence for the compatibility of stories with human thinking was demonstrated by a study at the Stanford Business School.[48] The point was to convince MBA students that a company practiced a policy of avoiding layoffs. For some students, only a story was used. For others, statistical data were provided that showed little turnover compared to competitors. For other students, statistics and stories were combined, and yet other students were shown the company's policy statement. Of all these approaches, students presented with the story alone were most convinced about the avoiding layoffs policy.

SYMBOLS AND INFORMAL COMMUNICATION

Leaders don't just communicate stories in words. They also *embody* the stories in the way that they live their lives and what they seek to inspire in others.[49] Leaders are watched, and their appearance, behavior, actions, and attitudes are symbolic to others. Martin Luther King, Jr., was a symbol to the Montgomery, Alabama boycotters. King himself stood for something abstract, a commitment. That King seemed impervious to bombs and arrests communicated something to his followers—perseverance and possibility. His actions held important meanings to supporters and adversaries alike.

Symbols are a powerful tool for communicating what is important. Therefore, leaders are aware of what they signal to others in addition to verbal messages. Indeed, **nonverbal communication,** that is, messages transmitted through action and behavior, accounts for over one half of the entire message received in a personal encounter.[50] People interpret leader actions as symbols, just as they attach meaning to words.

In interpreting a leader's nonverbal cues, followers determine the extent to which a leader's actions correspond with his or her verbal messages. Jack Welch's stories about customer service carry significant weight because followers can see that he lives the values conveyed in the stories every day. If a leader talked about customer service but spent no time with customers, followers would likely place little value on service. Research suggests that if there is a discrepancy between a person's verbal and nonverbal communication, the nonverbal is granted more weight by the interpreter.[51] For example, a whole week after delivering an impassioned software development pitch to a group of investors, entrepreneur Michael Damphousse still had no takers. It wasn't until he took the advice of a friend and quit his job that $150,000 rolled in for his start-up project.[52] Verbally, Damphousse communicated effectively, but investors considered his recent promotion within his firm to mean that he wasn't committed to the project. His resignation corresponded to his verbal message, prompting the investors to reconsider. Leaders use actions to symbolize their vision and draw attention to specific values and ideas.

Informal communication is built into an open communication climate and includes interactions that go beyond formal, authorized channels. Informal communication is important not only because it can be symbolic of leader vision, but also because it has great impact on participants. For example, consider how much more memorable the quarterly results were for Mattel employees when former CEO John Amerman used a rap song to deliver them instead of a memo.[53] Another example of informal communication is "management by wandering around (MBWA)" presented in the books *In Search of Excellence* and *A Passion for Excellence*.[54] MBWA means that leaders leave their offices and speak directly to employees as they work. These impromptu encounters send positive messages to followers. In addition, the communication is richer, therefore likely to make a lasting impression in both directions. When E. Grady Bogue became interim chancellor at Louisiana State University, one of the first things he did was walk through the departments on campus. He wound up in the biology building, where he enjoyed an extended tour of the facility by a faculty member he ran across. Bogue remarked that he learned an enormous amount about the university operations and the strengths and weaknesses of the biology program that was "more direct, personal and meaningful than any written communication might have conveyed."[55] Thus, both leaders and followers benefit from informal channels.

FEEDBACK AND LEARNING

When a leader listens, chooses a communication channel, directs attention, or creates a story, he or she does so with a desired outcome in mind. A leader must decide to what extent the desired outcome is reflected in his or her message. Whether it is an expression of company values, a quarterly financial report, or work performance, an outcome can be evaluated for the reflection of leader intent and objective. **Feedback** occurs when a leader uses evaluation and communication to help individuals and the organization learn and improve.

Feedback is an essential tool for leadership communication.[56] As an evaluation, feedback enables leaders to determine whether they have been successful or unsuccessful in communicating with others. Feedback is crucial for the closure of a communication loop. This is not to say that communication ends with feedback, but that only by evaluating the success of a communication can leaders reformulate and increase the effectiveness of subsequent messages, signals, and organizational practices. By understanding feedback as a process of communication with a systematic improvement component, leaders can increase their communication effectiveness, and use this awareness to develop followers and improve the organization. The result of feedback is change—change in the follower and change in the organization.

The feedback process involves four elements, as illustrated in Exhibit 9.7. **Observations** are visible occurrences, either subordinate behavior or

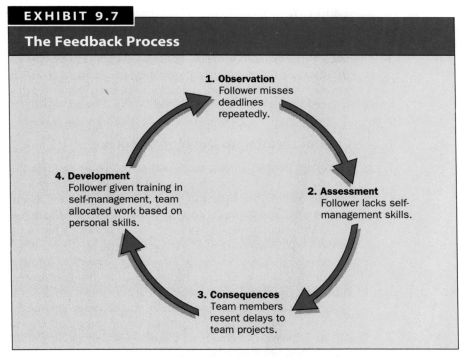

EXHIBIT 9.7

The Feedback Process

1. Observation
Follower misses deadlines repeatedly.

2. Assessment
Follower lacks self-management skills.

3. Consequences
Team members resent delays to team projects.

4. Development
Follower given training in self-management, team allocated work based on personal skills.

SOURCE: Adapted from Mary Mavis, "Painless Performance Evaluations," *Training and Development,* October 1994, 40–44.

results of organizational activity. An **assessment** is the interpretation of observed behaviors, an evaluation of the results in terms of vision and goals. A **consequence** refers to the outcome of what was observed, and can include both actual consequences and the consequences possible if no change takes place. **Development** refers to the sustainment or improvement of behaviors. Leaders communicate what they observe, how they assess it, what consequences it has, and how to effectively address the observed behavior and consequence. Each element is communicated from the leader to the individual or organization.[57]

Furthermore, the development becomes an observation in the next communication loop. For example, a leader who observes development and assesses it positively may consequently promote the responsible subordinate. Thus, feedback enables communication to form a continuous loop. Leaders use these elements to provide feedback that facilitates growth for followers and organizations.

Despite the importance of feedback to leadership communication, often it is neglected. Remember the research presented at the beginning of this chapter that found even though most companies feel that communication is a priority, few of them utilize feedback to employees in their communication process. Indeed, operationalizing feedback can seem daunting because it potentially involves many sources. A single individual might receive feedback from supervisors, coworkers, and customers. Leaders focus feedback on both the individual and organization; they use it to develop the capacities of followers, and to teach the organization how to better reach its objectives.

Communicating to Develop Followers

Generally people do not enjoy either receiving or giving evaluative feedback. To receive criticism makes people defensive, and to give criticism makes people responsible for their judgments and leaves them open to fire. There are several ways for leaders to optimize the use of feedback and yet minimize the "conflict" that it typically connotes, such as using a previously accepted goal to support leader assessment.[58] Using elements of storytelling in these situations can also help. For example, a subordinate as well as a leader learns more from examining the *story* of what happened and why than from conventional evaluation procedures that may seem like a "chewing out from the boss."[59]

Primarily, a leader must clarify for everyone involved the purpose of the feedback—to congratulate efforts and outcomes that support the shared vision and to improve the efforts and outcomes that do not. Thus, leaders can recognize the opportunity for both positive and negative evaluations. Communication that is limited to moments of shortcoming runs the risk of demoralizing followers. Furthermore, the more communication takes place, the better equipped followers become to do their work, which is a significant source of development.

Organizational Learning

Just as feedback is a communication tool for developing followers, it is also an important means by which organizations can learn from their mistakes and improve the work they do. Leaders who enlist the whole organization to review the outcomes of activities can quickly discover what does and does not work. This provides an additional source of information for leaders. The U.S. Army uses organizational feedback in significant ways to promote whole-system learning.

IN THE LEAD   **U.S. Army**

At the National Training Center near Death Valley, California, U.S. Army troops engage in a simulated battle: the "enemy" has sent unmanned aerial vehicles (UAVs) to gather targeting data. When the troops fire upon the UAVs, they reveal themselves to the "opposition forces" hidden nearby, and are defeated. Now that the exercise is over, the real learning begins. Unit members and their superiors hold "after action reviews." After reviewing the ingredients of this battle, General William Hartzog suggested that decoy UAVs might be just the thing to get an enemy to reveal his location. His observation amounts to a lesson for the entire Army.

This process of weeding out mistakes, of innovating, and of learning from experience is known in the Army as a lessons-learned system. A systematic review of action after it has taken place yields a lesson, whether it is the application of a high-tech UAV or simply how to mask a vehicle using terrain. The Army stockpiles lessons such as these and disseminates them throughout the combat forces.

The lessons do not come just from the training ground. The Center for Army Lessons Learned (CALL) sends experts to soldiers in the field to conduct after-action reviews. The resulting lessons are collected. In 1994, CALL compiled twenty-six lessons in Haiti for the incoming replacement troops, who confronted twenty-three of the scenarios within the first few months. Fortunately, they had learned what to do. In Bosnia the following year, lessons were sent to all units every seventy-two hours—and shared with the multinational peace-keepers.

The Army has come to depend on the results of the lessons-learned system for organizational learning. A case study by the Harvard Business School concluded that the process is what enables the Army to minimize mistakes and create success in an efficient way.[60]

In this example the organization is learning by communicating feedback about the consequences of field operations. Compiling what is learned and using communication feedback creates an improved organization. The success of the Army's system for organizational learning has inspired corporations to adopt after action reviews. Bill Goodspeed, of J. M. Huber Corporation's wood-products division, claims to see concrete results after only two months of after-action reviews with customers.[61]

Communication feedback is dynamic and continuous. It serves to develop followers and organizations, giving closure to each innovation within an organization and enhancing performance with each subsequent loop. Leaders cannot guide their organizations effectively, nor can they fully communicate, without feedback. As asserted by long-time university leader E. Grady Bogue, "Leaders are teachers. Teachers are learners."[62]

SUMMARY AND INTERPRETATION

Effective communication is an essential element of leadership. Leaders make choices about how to communicate with others. In an organization, the shift to open communication is far-reaching in its effect. An open climate paves the way for more opportunities to communicate with followers; more practice at listening actively and discerning the messages waiting to emerge; more opportunities to use rich channels; and more chances to build trust and commitment to the vision through informal communication and symbolic actions. In addition, a conscious choice to communicate through stories, metaphors, and meaningful language enables a leader to direct attention to specific ideas, define the parameters of organizational values, and have longer lasting impact on followers. Finally, using feedback as an essential tool for communication provides the leader a means by which to develop followers and transform organizations.

KEY TERMS

communication	discernment	observations
communication champion	channel	assessment
open communication	channel richness	consequence
listening	nonverbal communication	development
dialogue	feedback	

DISCUSSION QUESTIONS

1. How do you think leadership communication differs from conventional management communication?

2. If you were to evaluate an organization based on the degree of open communication climate, what things would you look for? Discuss.

3. A manager in a communication class remarked, "Listening seems like minimal intrusion of oneself into the conversation, yet it also seems like more work." Do you agree or disagree? Discuss.

4. How does dialogue differ from discussion? Give an example of each from your experience.

5. Some senior executives believe they should rely on written information and computer reports because these yield more accurate data than face-to-face communications do. Do you agree? Discuss.

6. Why is "management by wandering around" considered effective communication?

7. If you were to communicate symbolically with your team to create a sense of trust and team work, what would you do?

8. Is speaking accurately or listening actively the more important communication skill for leaders? Discuss.

9. Why is storytelling such a powerful means of communication for a leader? Can you give examples from your own experience of leaders who have used metaphor and story? What was the effect on followers?

LEADERSHIP DEVELOPMENT: Personal Feedback

Listening Self-Inventory

Go through the following questions, filling in yes or no next to each question. Mark each as truthfully as you can in light of your behavior in the last few meetings or gatherings you attended.

1. _____ I frequently attempt to listen to several conversations at the same time.

2. _____ I like people to give me only the facts and then let me make my own interpretation.

3. _____ I sometimes pretend to pay attention to people.

4. _____ I consider myself a good judge of nonverbal communications.

5. _____ I usually know what another person is going to say before he or she says it.

6. _____ I usually end conversations that don't interest me by diverting my attention from the speaker.

7. _____ I frequently nod, frown, or whatever to let the speaker know how I feel about what he or she is saying.

8. _____ I usually respond immediately when someone has finished talking.

9. _____ I evaluate what is being said while it is being said.

10. _____ I usually formulate a response while the other person is still talking.

11. _____ The speaker's "delivery" style frequently distracts me from the content.

12. _____ I usually ask people to clarify what they have said rather than guess at the meaning.

13. _____ I make a concerted effort to understand other people's points of view.

14. _____ I frequently hear what I expect to hear rather than what is actually said.

15. _____ Most people feel that I have understood their point of view even when we disagree.

Scoring

The correct answers according to communication theory are as follows: No for questions 1, 2, 3, 5, 6, 7, 8, 9, 10, 11, 14. Yes for questions 4, 12, 13, 15.

Interpretation

If you missed only one or two questions, you strongly approve of your own listening habits and you are on the right track to becoming an effective listener in your role as leader. If you missed three or four questions, you have uncovered some doubts about your listening effectiveness, and your knowledge of how to listen has some gaps. If you missed five or more questions, you probably are not satisfied with the way you listen, and your followers and coworkers may not feel you are a good listener either. Work on improving your active listening skills.

LEADERSHIP DEVELOPMENT: Cases for Analysis

The Superintendent's Directive

Educational administrators are bombarded by possible innovations at all educational levels. Programs to upgrade math, science, and social science education, state accountability plans, new approaches to administration, and other ideas are initiated by teachers, administrators, interest groups, reformers, and state regulators. In a school district, the superintendent is the key leader; in an individual school, the principal is the key leader.

In the Carville City School District, Superintendent Porter has responsibility for eleven schools—eight elementary, two junior high, and one high school. After attending a management summer course, Porter sent an e-mail directive to each principal stating that every teacher in their building was required to develop a set of performance objectives for each class they taught. These objectives were to be submitted one month after the school opened, and copies were to be forwarded to the superintendent's office. Porter also wrote that he had hired the consultant who taught the summer management course to help teachers write objectives during their annual opening in-service day of orientation work.

Mr. Weigand, Principal of Earsworth Elementary School, sent his teachers the following memo: "Friends, Superintendent Porter has asked me to inform you that written performance objectives for your courses must be handed in one month from today. This afternoon at the in-service meeting, you will receive instruction in composing these objectives."

In response, one teacher sent a note asking, "Is anything wrong with our teaching? Is this the reason we have to spend hours writing objectives?"

Another teacher saw Weigand in the hall and said, "I don't see how all this objectives business will improve my classroom. It sounds like an empty exercise. In fact, because of the time it will take me to write objectives, it may hurt my teaching. I should be reading on new developments and working on lesson plans."

In response to these and other inquiries, Principal Weigand announced to the teachers with a follow-up memo, "I was told to inform all of you to write performance objectives. If you want to talk about it, contact Dr. Porter."

SOURCE: Based on Robert C. Mills, Alan F. Quick, and Michael P. Wolfe, *Critical Incidents in School Administration* (Midland, MI: Pendell Publishing Co., 1976).

Questions

1. Evaluate the communications of Porter and Weigand. To what extent do they communicate as leaders? Explain.
2. How would you have handled this if you were Superintendent Porter?
3. How would you have handled the communication if you were the principal of Earsworth Elementary School? Why?

Imperial Metal Products

Imperial Metal Products, a mid-sized manufacturing company located in the Southeast, makes wheel rims for automobiles. With forty-two furnaces on the production floor, the temperature often reaches well over 100 degrees Fahrenheit. Even employees who work in the lab complain of the heat because they have to venture onto the production floor numerous times a day to take metal samples from the furnaces.

A year ago, the top executive team recommended to the Board that the employee lounge, located at the far end of the production floor near the plant manager's office, be air-conditioned. Company profits had been good, and the managers wanted to do something to show appreciation for employees' good work. The Board enthusiastically approved the proposal and the work was completed within a month.

At the end of the fiscal year, the top management team met to review the company's operations for the past year. Profits were higher than ever, and productivity for the past year had been excellent. The team unanimously agreed that the employees deserved additional recognition for their work, and they considered ways to show management's appreciation. Robb Vaughn suggested that it might be interesting to see what workers thought about the action managers took last year to have the lounge air-conditioned. Everyone agreed, and the human resources director, Amy Simpkins, was instructed to send a questionnaire to a sample of employees to get their reaction to the air-conditioned lounge. The team agreed to meet in six weeks and review the results.

Simpkins mailed a simple form to 100 randomly selected employees with the following request: "Please state your feelings about the recently air-conditioned employee lounge." The response rate was excellent, with 96 forms being returned. Simpkins classified the responses into the following categories and presented her report to the top management team:

1. I thought only managers could use the lounge.   25
2. I didn't know it was air-conditioned.   21
3. If management can spend that kind of money, they should pay us more.   21
4. The whole plant should be air-conditioned.   10
5. I never use the lounge anyway.   8
6. OK   8
7. Miscellaneous comments   3

Top managers were shocked by the responses. They had expected a majority of the employees to be grateful for the air conditioning. One of the managers suggested that it was useless to do anything else for employees, since it wouldn't be appreciated anyway. Another argued, however, that top managers just needed to communicate better with plant workers. She suggested posting flyers on the bulletin boards announcing that the lounge was now air-conditioned, and perhaps putting a memo in with employees' next paycheck. "They slave away eight or nine hours a day in that heat; at least we need to let them know they have a cool place to take a break or eat lunch!" she pointed out. "And if we plan to do another 'employee appreciation' project this year, maybe we should send out another questionnaire and ask people what they want."

SOURCE: Based on "The Air Conditioned Cafeteria," in John M. Champion and John H. James, *Critical Incidents in Management: Decision and Policy Issues,* 6th ed. (Homewood, IL: Irwin, 1989), 280–281.

Questions

1. How would you rate the communication climate at Imperial Metal Products?

2. What channels do you think top managers should use to improve communications and both keep employees informed as well as learn about what they are thinking?

3. If you were a top manager at Imperial, what is the first step you would take? Why?

REFERENCES

1. Howard Gardner, *Leading Minds: An Anatomy of Leadership* (New York: Basic Books, 1995), 204–208.
2. Cynthia Crossen, "Blah, Blah, Blah," *The Wall Street Journal,* July 10, 1997; Paul Roberts, "Live! From Your Office! It's . . ." *Fast Company,* October 1999, 151–170; and Cathy Olofson, "Can We Talk? Put Another Log on the Fire," *Fast Company,* October 1999, 86.
3. Peter Lowry and Byron Reimus, "Ready, Aim, Communicate," *Management Review,* July 1996.
4. Bernard M. Bass, *Bass & Stogdill's Handbook of Leadership,* 3rd ed. (New York: The Free Press, 1990).
5. Henry Mintzberg, *The Nature of Managerial Work* (New York: Harper & Row, 1973).
6. Mary Young and James E. Post, "Managing to Communicate, Communicating to Manage: How Leading Companies Communicate with Employees," *Organizational Dynamics* (Summer 1993), 31-43; and Warren Bennis and Burt Nanus, *Leaders: The Strategies for Taking Charge* (New York: Harper & Row, 1985).
7. Excerpt from Peter B. Grazier, "Before It's Too Late: Employee Involvement . . . An Idea Whose Time Has Come," *Pete's Corner* by Peter B. Grazier, *http://www.teambuilding.com.*
8. John Luthy, "New Keys to Employee Performance and Productivity," *Public Management,* March 1998, 4–8.
9. Mirta M. Martin, "Trust Leadership," *The Journal of Leadership Studies* 5, No. 3 (1998), 41–49.
10. "What Is Trust," results of a survey by Manchester Consulting, reported in Jenny C. McCune, "That Elusive Thing Called Trust," *Management Review,* July-August 1998, 10–16.
11. Julie Carrick Dalton, "Between the Lines: The Hard Truth About Open-Book Management," *CFO,* March 1999, 58–64.
12. Gary Hamel, "Killer Strategies That Make Shareholders Rich," *Fortune,* June 23, 1997, 70–84.
13. Roberts, "Live! From Your Office!"; and David M. Kelley, "Performing Rapid Innovation Magic: Ten Secrets of a Modern Merlin," in *Straight from the CEO: The World's Top Business Leaders Reveal Ideas That Every Manager Can Use,* G. William Dauphinais and Colin Price, Price Waterhouse, eds. (New York: Simon & Schuster, 1998), 271–281.
14. C. Glenn Pearce, "Doing Something About Your Listening Ability," *Supervisory Management,* March 1989, 29–34; and Tom Peters, "Learning to Listen," *Hyatt Magazine,* Spring 1988, 16–21.
15. Gerald M. Goldhaber, *Organizational Communication,* 4th ed. (Dubuque, IA: Wm. C. Brown, 1980), 189.
16. Monci Jo Williams, "America's Best Salesman," *Fortune,* October 26, 1987, 122–134.

17. David H. Freedman, "Intensive Care," *Inc.*, February 1999, 72–80.

18. Roberts, "Live! From Your Office!"

19. Jack Stack, "Measuring Morale," *Inc.*, January 1997, 29–30.

20. Curtis Sittenfeld, "Good Ways to Deliver Bad News," *Fast Company*, April 1999, 58, 60.

21. Tom Peters, "Learning to Listen."

22. David Bohm, *On Dialogue* (Ojai, CA: David Bohm Seminars, 1989).

23. Bill Isaacs, *Dialogue and the Art of Thinking Together* (New York: Doubleday, 1999); and "The Art of Dialogue," column in Roberts, "Live! From Your Office!"

24. Based on Glenna Gerard and Linda Teurfs, "Dialogue and Organizational Transformation," in *Community Building: Renewing Spirit and Learning in Business*, Kazimierz Gozdz, ed. (New Leaders Press, 1995).

25. Scott Kirsner, "Want to Grow? Hire a Shrink!" *Fast Company*, December-January 1998, 68, 70.

26. R. B. L., "Selling the Sizzle," *Fortune*, June 23, 1997, 80.

27. Joseph Jaworski, *Synchronicity: the Inner Path of Leadership* (San Francisco, CA.: Berrett-Koehler, 1996).

28. Robert H. Lengel and Richard L. Daft, "The Selection of Communication Media as an Executive Skill," *Academy of Management Executive* 2 (August 1988), 225–232; and Richard L. Daft and Robert Lengel, "Organizational Information Requirements, Media Richness and Structural Design," *Managerial Science* 32 (May 1986), 554–572.

29. Ford S. Worthy, "How CEOs Manage Their Time," *Fortune*, January 18, 1988, 88–97.

30. "E-mail Can't Mimic Phone Calls," *Johnson City Press*, September 17, 2000, 31.

31. Anne Fisher, "Readers Weigh in on Rudeness and Speechmaking" (Ask Annie column), *Fortune*, January 10, 2000, 194.

32. Tom Davenport, "Tuning In to Channel Four," *CIO*, Section 1, August 1, 1999, 30-32; Timothy J. Mullaney, "Needed: The Human Touch," *Business Week E.biz*, December 13, 1999, EB 53-EB 54.

33. "Enforcing a No-Memo Policy," *Small Business Report*, July 1988, 26–27.

34. Ronald E. Rice, "Task Analyzability, Use of New Media, and Effectiveness: A Multi-Site Exploration of Media Richness," *Organizational Science* 3, No. 4 (November 1994), 502–527.

35. Richard L. Daft, Robert H. Lengel, and Linda Klebe Treviño, "Message Equivocality, Media Selection and Manager Performance: Implications for Information Systems," *MIS Quarterly* 11 (1987), 355–368.

36. Young and Post, "Managing to Communicate, Communicating to Manage."

37. Jane Webster and Linda Klebe Treviño, "Rational and Social Theories as Complementary Explanations of Communication Media Choices: Two Policy Capturing Studies," *Academy of Management Journal*, December 1995, 1544–1572.

38. David M. Boje, "Learning Storytelling: Storytelling to Learn Management Skills," *Journal of Management Education* 15, No. 3 (August 1991): 279–294.
39. Young and Post, "Managing to Communicate, Communicating to Manage."
40. Linda Smircich and Gareth Morgan, "Leadership: The Management of Meaning," *Journal of Applied Behavioral Science* 18 (November 3, 1982): 257–273.
41. Robert F. Dennehy, "The Executive as Storyteller," *Management Review,* March 1999, 40–43.
42. Ibid.
43. Beverly Kaye and Betsy Jacobson, "True Tales and Tall Tales: The Power of Organizational Storytelling," *Training and Development,* March 1999, 45–50.
44. Dennehy, "The Executive as Storyteller;" and Elizabeth Weil, "Every Leader Tells a Story," *Fast Company,* June-July 1998, 38–39.
45. Cathy Olofson, "To Transform Culture, Tap Emotion," *Fast Company,* April 1999, 54.
46. Dennehy, "The Executive as Storyteller."
47. Gardner, *Leading Minds.*
48. J. Martin and M. Powers, "Organizational Stories: More Vivid and Persuasive than Quantitative Data," in B. M. Staw, ed., *Psychological Foundations of Organizational Behavior* (Glenview, IL: Scott Foresman, 1982), 161–168.
49. Gardner, *Leading Minds.*
50. Albert Mehrabian, *Silent Messages* (Belmont, CA: Wadsworth, 1971); and Albert Mehrabian, "Communicating Without Words," *Psychology Today,* September 1968, 53–55.
51. I. Thomas Sheppard, "Silent Signals," *Supervisory Management,* March 1986, 31–33.
52. Edward O. Welles, "Why Every Company Needs a Story," *Inc.,* May 1996, 69.
53. Peter Richardson and D. Keith Denton, "Communicating Change," *Human Resource Management* (Summer 1996), 203–216.
54. Thomas H. Peters and Robert J. Waterman, Jr., *In Search of Excellence* (New York: Harper & Row, 1982); and Tom Peters and Nancy Austin, *A Passion for Excellence: The Leadership Difference* (New York: Random House, 1985).
55. Grady Bogue, *Leadership by Design: Strengthening Integrity in Higher Education* (San Francisco, CA: Jossey-Bass, Inc., 1994), 81.
56. John C. Kunich and Richard I. Lester, "Leadership and the Art of Feedback: Feeding the Hands that Back Us," *The Journal of Leadership Studies* 3, No. 4 (1996), 3–22.
57. Mary Mavis, "Painless Performance Evaluations," *Training & Development,* October 1994, 40–44.
58. R. Hughes, R. Ginnett, and R. Curphy, *Leadership: Enhancing the Lessons of Experience* (Homewood, IL: Irwin, 1993), 209-215.

59. Thomas A. Stewart, "The Cunning Plots of Leadership" (The Leading Edge column), *Fortune,* September 7, 1998, 165–166.
60. Thomas E. Ricks, "Army Devises System to Decide What Does, and Does Not, Work," *The Wall Street Journal,* May 23, 1997, A1; and Stephanie Watts Sussman, "CALL: A Model for Effective Organizational Learning," *Strategy,* Summer 1999, 14–15.
61. Ricks, "Army Devises System to Decide What Does, and Does Not, Work."
62. Bogue, *Leadership by Design,* 143.

CHAPTER OUTLINE

YOUR LEADERSHIP CHALLENGE

After reading this chapter, you should be able to:

- Turn a group of individuals into a collaborative team that achieves high performance through shared mission and collective responsibility.

- Develop and apply the personal qualities of effective team leadership.

- Understand and handle the stages of team development and forms of interdependence.

- Guide cultural norms and values to influence team cohesiveness.

- Handle conflicts that inevitably arise among members of a team.

Leading Teams

The battle lines were drawn: On one side, the Los Angeles Lakers, looking for their first National Basketball Association championship since 1988; on the other, the Indiana Pacers, playing in the finals for the first time in the team's history. In the end, the Lakers prevailed, clinching the title in Game 6. But almost everyone recognized that both teams played with a spirit and heart that made them winners. Both teams struggled for years to reach this point, and they made it largely because, as one half-time commentator put it, "These players believe in their coaches."

The coach of the winning Lakers, Phil Jackson, had previously led the Chicago Bulls to six NBA championships, but many critics dismissed his coaching ability. Anyone could win, they said, with basketball's greatest player, Michael Jordan, on the team. Now people are taking a second look as Jackson smoothly guided the Lakers to their first NBA championship in twelve years. Jackson bases his leadership approach on Native American and Eastern spiritual principles, stressing awareness, compassion, and the importance of selfless team play to achieve victory. His greatest strength is an ability to get wealthy, pampered, and sometimes conceited young players to pull together mentally and spiritually to achieve a common goal. "It's been cool with Phil," Laker Kobe Bryant says. "He's opened our minds up, expanded the game of basketball beyond Xs and Os, to the point where it's really mental. It's about bonding, and about communication—a lot of it nonverbal—with one another."

The coach on the other side of the court, Larry Bird with the Indiana Pacers, showed the same passionate team leadership in his final coaching season as he showed in his first, when he took a struggling group of players and turned them into one of the NBA's finest teams. The Pacers may have lost the championship, but they never lost their team spirit. Bird instilled players with a vision of being the best, established clear goals and standards of performance, worked players hard on the practice court, and then let them do their jobs rather than micromanaging from the sidelines. "My whole thing is preparedness," Bird says. "But I feel that once the game starts, let the players play the game."

Both Jackson and Bird expected each player to bring his own sense of commitment and personal responsibility to the game. In addition, both insisted on open and honest communication as the only way everyone could come together around a shared purpose. By focusing on the spirit of teamwork, the coaches cultivated the leadership abilities of everyone on the team. Phil Jackson and Larry Bird offer lessons in leadership not only in the world of pro basketball but also in today's high-pressure, team-based workplace.[1]

Coaching a pro basketball team may seem very different from leading a group of people in an organization, but both require similar leadership skills and qualities. Particularly in today's changing organizations, the ability to inspire and support teamwork is critical to effective leadership. From the assembly line to the executive suite, from large businesses such as BP Amoco and Microsoft to small companies like Growing Green, discussed in Chapter 8, teams are becoming the basic building block of organizations.

The use of teams has increased dramatically in response to new competitive pressures, the need for greater flexibility and speed, and a desire to give employees more opportunities for involvement and decision making. Recent data show that nearly half of *Fortune* 1000 companies use teams, and 60 percent plan to increase the use of teams in the near future. Teamwork has become the most frequent topic taught in company training programs. In a study of 109 Canadian organizations, 42 percent reported widespread team-based activity and only 13 percent reported little or no team activity.[2]

Teams present greater leadership challenges and opportunities than does the traditional hierarchical organization. Every team member has to develop some leadership capability. This chapter explores team leadership in today's organizations. We will define various types of teams, examine the personal changes people make to become good team leaders, and discuss how leaders can help teams be more effective. We will also discuss the role of information technology in expanding teamwork options. Then we examine such characteristics as team size, interdependence, cohesiveness, and culture. The final sections of the chapter look at the role of leadership in guiding team development and handling conflict.

TEAMS IN ORGANIZATIONS

The concept of teamwork is a fundamental change in the way work is organized. More and more companies are recognizing that the best way to meet the challenges of higher quality, faster service, and total customer satisfaction is through an aligned, coordinated, and committed effort by all employees.[3] At the Frito-Lay plant in Lubbock, Texas, team members handle everything from potato processing to equipment maintenance. Each team has authority to select new hires, determine crew scheduling, and discipline team members who are not pulling their load. The four owners of Crescent Manufacturing in Fremont, Ohio, run their company as a team, switching jobs among themselves as the company's needs change. At Massachusetts General Hospital, the emergency trauma team performs so smoothly that the team switches leaders seamlessly, depending on the crisis at hand. With each new emergency, direction may come from a doctor, intern, nurse, or technician—whoever is particularly experienced with the problem.[4]

Teams such as the one at Massachusetts General are self-directed and anyone may assume a leadership role. Others operate without a traditional hierarchy but have designated team leaders who play a central role in guiding the team's work. For example, when the United States Information Agency's Bureau of Information reorganized into teams, managers were assigned as team leaders of each of the twenty-one work teams. Now, rather than "issuing orders and breathing down people's necks," as one manager put it, team leaders are responsible for guiding teams in ironing out problems and making decisions together.[5] Still other teams function within the traditional vertical hierarchy. In this section, we will first define teams and examine the types of teams that exist in organizations.

What Is a Team?

A **team** is a unit of two or more people who interact and coordinate their work to accomplish a specific team goal.[6] This definition has three components. First, teams are made up of two or more people. Teams can be large, but most have fewer than fifteen people. Second, people in a team work together regularly. People who do not interact regularly, such as those waiting in line at the company cafeteria or riding together in the elevator, do not comprise a team. Third, people in a team share a goal, whether it be to build a car, design a new laptop computer, or write a textbook. Today's students are frequently assigned to complete assignments in teams. In this case, the shared goal is to complete the task and receive an acceptable grade. However, in many cases, student teams are provided with a great deal of structure in terms of team roles and responsibilities, time frame, activities, and so forth. In a work setting, these elements are often much more ambiguous and have to be worked out within the team.

A team is a group of people, but the two are not equal. A professor, coach, or employer can put together a *group* of people and never build a *team*. The sports world is full of stories of underdog teams that have won championships against a group of players who were better individually but did not

---

LIVING LEADERSHIP

Lessons from Geese

Fact 1: As each goose flaps its wings, it creates an "uplift" for the birds that follow. By flying in a "V" formation, the whole flock adds 71 percent greater flying range than if each bird flew alone.

Lesson: People who share a common direction and sense of community can get where they are going quicker and easier because they are traveling on the thrust of one another.

Fact 2: When a goose falls out of formation, it suddenly feels the drag and resistance of flying alone. It quickly moves back into formation to take advantage of the lifting power of the bird immediately in front of it.

Lesson: If we have as much sense as a goose, we stay in formation with those headed where we want to go. We are willing to accept their help and give our help to others.

Fact 3: When the lead goose tires, it rotates back into the formation and another goose flies to the point position.

Lesson: It pays to take turns doing the hard tasks and sharing leadership. Like geese, people are interdependent on each other's skills, capa-

bilities, and unique arrangements of gifts, talents, or resources.

Fact 4: The geese flying in formation honk to encourage those up front to keep up their speed.

Lesson: We need to make sure our honking is encouraging. In groups where there is encouragement, the production is much greater. The power of encouragement (to stand by one's heart or core values and encourage the heart and core of others) is the quality of honking we seek.

Fact 5: When a goose gets sick, wounded, or shot down, two geese drop out of the formation and follow it down to help and protect it. They stay until it dies or is able to fly again. Then, they launch out with another formation or catch up with the flock.

Lesson: If we have as much sense as geese, we will stand by each other in difficult times as well as when we are strong.

SOURCE: 1991 · Organizational Development Network. Original author unknown

EXHIBIT 10.1

Differences Between Groups and Teams

Group	Team
Has a designated, strong leader	Shares or rotates leadership roles
Individual accountability	Mutual and individual accountability (accountable to each other)
Identical purpose for group and organization	Specific team vision or purpose
Performance goals set by others	Performance goals set by team
Works within organizational boundaries	Not inhibited by organizational boundaries
Individual work products	Collective work products
Organized meetings, delegation	Mutual feedback, open-ended discussion, active problem-solving

SOURCES: Based on Jon R. Katzenbach and Douglas K. Smith, "The Discipline of Teams," *Harvard Business Review* (March-April 1995), 111–120; and Milan Moravec, Odd Jan Johannessen, and Thor A. Hjelmas, "Thumbs Up for Self-Managed Teams," *Management Review* (July-August 1997), 42–47 (chart on 46).

make up a better team.[7] Only when people sublimate their individual needs and desires and synthesize their knowledge, skills, and efforts toward accomplishment of a communal goal do they become a team. This chapter's Living Leadership illustrates the spirit and power of teamwork.

The team concept implies a sense of shared mission and collective responsibility. Exhibit 10.1 lists the primary differences between groups and teams. A team achieves high levels of performance through shared leadership, purpose, and responsibility by all members working toward a common goal. Teams are characterized by equality; in the best teams, there are no individual "stars" and everyone sublimates individual ego to the good of the whole.

TYPES OF TEAMS

All organizations are made up of groups of people who work together to accomplish specific goals. You may have learned about the fundamentals of group development and behavior in a previous management or organizational behavior course. Keep in mind that not all organizations use teams as they are defined in Exhibit 10.1, but many of the leadership ideas presented here can also be effectively applied in leading other types of groups.

In this section, we will look at three fundamental types of teams used in today's organizations: functional teams, cross-functional teams, and self-directed teams. In addition, we will consider the growing use of *virtual teams* and *global teams*. The types of teams are illustrated in Exhibit 10.2.

Functional Teams

A **functional team** is part of the traditional vertical hierarchy. This type of team is made up of a supervisor and his or her subordinates in the formal chain

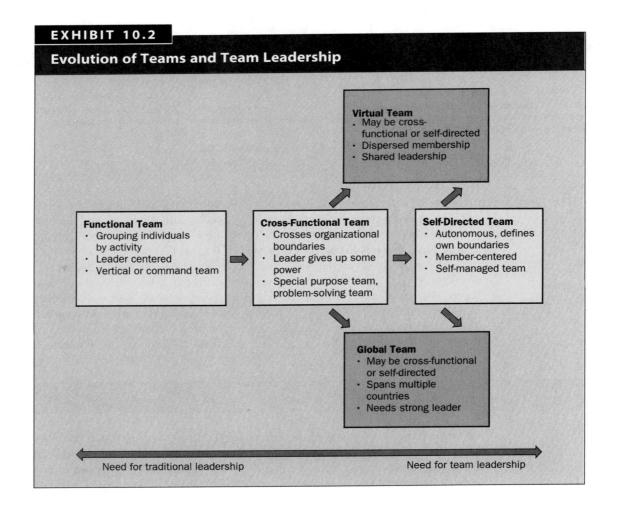

EXHIBIT 10.2

Evolution of Teams and Team Leadership

Virtual Team
- May be cross-functional or self-directed
- Dispersed membership
- Shared leadership

Functional Team
- Grouping individuals by activity
- Leader centered
- Vertical or command team

Cross-Functional Team
- Crosses organizational boundaries
- Leader gives up some power
- Special purpose team, problem-solving team

Self-Directed Team
- Autonomous, defines own boundaries
- Member-centered
- Self-managed team

Global Team
- May be cross-functional or self-directed
- Spans multiple countries
- Needs strong leader

Need for traditional leadership ←————————————→ Need for team leadership of command. Sometimes called a *vertical team* or a *command team,* the functional team may in some cases include three or four levels of hierarchy within a department. Typically, a functional team makes up a single department in the organization. For example, the quality control department at Blue Bell Creameries in Brenham, Texas, is a functional team that tests all incoming ingredients to make sure only the best products go into the company's ice cream. A financial analysis department, a human resources department, and a sales department are all functional or vertical teams. Each is created by the organization within the vertical hierarchy to attain specific goals through members' joint activities. Functional teams exist in most organizations, but they are on the decline as companies look for ways to better serve customers and increase speed, flexibility, and quality.

Cross-Functional Teams

As the name implies, **cross-functional teams** are made up of members from different functional departments within the organization. Employees are generally from about the same hierarchical level in the organization, although cross-functional teams sometimes cross vertical as well as horizontal boundaries. Cross-functional teams typically have a specific team leader and lead change projects, such as creating a new product in a manufacturing organization or developing an interdisciplinary curriculum in a middle school. Cross-functional teams are generally involved in projects that affect several departments and therefore require that many views be considered. For example, at GE Lighting Co. in Cleveland, Ohio, a cross-functional team with members from information technology, finance, and several other departments oversaw an ambitious systems-integration project that spanned operations in the United States and Canada.[8] Commercial Casework, a $10 million woodworking and cabinetry shop in Fremont, California, used a cross-functional team to research and design the company's bonus plan.

Cross-functional teams facilitate information sharing across functional boundaries, generate suggestions for coordinating the departments represented, develop new ideas and solutions for existing organizational problems, and assist in developing new practices or policies. The members of one type of cross-functional team, the *problem-solving* or *process-improvement* team, meet voluntarily to discuss ways to improve quality, efficiency, and the work environment. Their recommendations are proposed to top executives for approval. Another type of cross-functional team is the *special purpose* team, which is created outside the formal organization structure to undertake a project of special importance or creativity. For example, US Airways set up a special purpose team made up of mechanics, flight attendants, reservations agents, ramp workers, luggage attendants, aircraft cleaners, and others to plan and design a low-fare airline to compete with the expansion of Southwest Airlines into the east.[9]

The team was separated from the formal organization to give it time and autonomy to innovate successfully. Cross-functional teams are often an organization's first step toward greater employee participation and empowerment. These teams may gradually evolve into self-directed teams, which represent a fundamental change in how work is organized.

Evolution to Self-Directed Teams

Exhibit 10.2 illustrates the evolution of teams and team leadership. The functional team represents grouping individuals by common skill and activity within the traditional structure. Leadership is based on the vertical hierarchy. In cross-functional teams, members have more freedom from the hierarchy, but the team typically is still leader-centered and leader-directed. The leader is most often assigned by the organization and is usually a supervisor or manager from one of the departments represented on the team. Leaders do, however, have to give up some of their control and power at this stage in order for the team to function effectively.

In the highest stage of evolution, team members work together without the direction of managers, supervisors, or assigned team leaders.[10] Self-directed teams are member- rather than leader-centered and directed. Hundreds of companies, including Consolidated Diesel, Industrial Light and Magic, the Mayo Clinic, and Edy's Grand Ice Cream, are using self-directed teams as a way to increase the participation and enthusiasm of lower-level workers. Self-directed teams enable workers to feel challenged, find their work meaningful, and develop a strong sense of identity with the organization.[11]

Self-directed teams typically consist of five to twenty members who rotate jobs to produce an entire product or service or at least one complete aspect or portion of a product or service (for example, engine assembly or insurance claim processing).[12] Self-directed teams often are long-term or permanent in nature, although many of today's fast-moving companies also use temporary self-directed teams that come together to work on a specific project and then disband when their work is done. For example, at SEI Investments, all work is distributed among 140 self-directed teams. Some are permanent, such as those that serve major customers or focus on specific markets. Others, however, are designed to work on short-term projects or problems. Most employees belong to one "base team" and to three or four ad hoc teams.[13] Self-directed teams typically include three elements:

1. The team includes workers with varied skills and functions and the combined skills are sufficient to perform a major organizational task, thereby eliminating barriers among departments and enabling excellent coordination.

2. The team is given access to resources such as information, financial resources, equipment, machinery, and supplies needed to perform the complete task.

3. The team is empowered with decision-making authority, which means that members have the freedom to select new members, solve problems, spend money, monitor results, and plan for the future.

In self-directed teams, members take over duties such as scheduling work or vacations, ordering materials, and evaluating performance. Teams work with minimum supervision, and members are jointly responsible for conflict resolution and decision making. Many self-directed teams elect one of their own to serve as team leader, and the leader may change each year. Some teams function without a designated leader, so anyone may play a leadership role depending on the situation. In either case, equality and empowerment are key values in organizations based on self-directed teams. At SEI, the only power is the "power of persuasion." There are no titles or hierarchy to symbolize power and authority. Anyone can set up a team, but is then responsible for marshaling the resources and persuading others to participate. In discussing his style of leadership, CEO Al West says, "I lead where I figure it really matters and I let other people lead where it matters to them."[14]

Organizations are integrating a variety of team approaches into their operations. Industrial Light & Magic (ILM) uses teams of artists and animators to create visual effects for such movies as *Star Wars: The Phantom Menace* and *The Perfect Storm*.[15] At Radius, a hot new restaurant in Boston's financial district, the kitchen is made up of team work stations, such as a meat station, fish station, pastry station, and so forth. Team members at each station are responsible for the entire procedure to prepare their part of the meal. The teams work at a station for six months and then rotate to another.[16]

Virtual Teams

An exciting new approach to teamwork that has resulted from advances in information technology, shifting employee expectations, and the globalization of business is the virtual team. A **virtual team** is made up of geographically or organizationally dispersed members who are linked primarily through advanced information and telecommunications technologies.[17] Team members use e-mail, voice mail, videoconferencing, Internet and intranet technologies, and various types of collaboration software to perform their work rather than meeting face-to-face. With what economist William Knoke, author of *Bold New World*, calls "the technology of placelessness," it no longer matters whether team members are located down the hall or across the hemisphere. For example, at Schneider Automation Inc., program manager Allan Tate works with a virtual team whose members are located in France, Germany, and the United States.[18]

The increasing use of virtual teams is related to the transformations going on in organizations that were introduced in Chapter 1, including an emphasis on change and the strategic use of new technologies, a shift to collaborative forms of working, the growing importance of relationships in a knowledge-based economy, and the trend toward empowerment and greater participation of diverse employees. New technology enables the communication of richer, more complex information and removes the barriers of time and distance that have traditionally defined organization structures. In addition, information that was once available only to top leaders can quickly and easily be shared throughout the organization, helping to push decision making to lower levels. Increasingly, today's best employees, who may be located anywhere in the world, are demanding greater technological sophistication as well as more flexibility in how they perform their work. Thus, many organizations are feeling a pressure to increase opportunities for virtual teams.

Virtual teams, sometimes called *distributed teams,* may be temporary cross-functional teams pulled together to work on specific problems, or they may be long-term or permanent self-directed teams. Virtual teams may also include suppliers, customers, and even competitors to pull together the best minds to complete a specific project. Team leadership is typically shared or altered, depending on the area of expertise needed at each stage of the project. In addition, team membership in virtual teams may change fairly quickly, depending on the tasks to be performed. For example, two young entrepreneurs started a new advertising agency made up entirely of ever-shifting virtual teams.

IN THE LEAD   Robin Smith and Steven Hess, Host Universal

Robin Smith always loved the advertising business, but hated the ad-agency business. He felt that most agencies were overstaffed and inefficient, and he knew from experience that many good ideas got lost in bureaucratic paper shuffling. He began dreaming of a new kind of organization—a virtual ad agency—that would focus all its energies on developing innovative solutions for clients. Rather than running an agency full of employees, the company would contract work out to small ad hoc teams that offered the best combination of talent for each particular project.

Two years later, Smith and his partner Steven Hess had built a network of thirty-five creative professionals—art directors, writers, producers, and so forth—and formed them into idea teams for some eighty different advertising projects for clients such as Kellogg, the Body Shop, Volkswagen, and British Telecom. The organization itself consists only of Smith and Hess; everyone else is a freelance professional, hired on a project-by-project basis. Smith and Hess work to put the right combination of people together for each project. Then, the team works directly for and is paid directly by the client. Host Universal takes a percentage off the top for finding clients and putting together the right team.

The virtual team approach enables Host to take on numerous projects at once and get them done quickly because each team is staffed with the people who can produce the best ideas for each situation. "We create links between people," Hess says. "We give people the chance to create great ideas very quickly with other great people."[19]

Global Teams

Virtual teams are sometimes also global teams. **Global teams** are work teams made up of members whose activities span multiple countries.[20] Generally, global teams fall into two categories: intercultural teams, whose members come from different countries or cultures and meet face to face, and virtual global teams, whose members remain in separate locations around the world and conduct their work electronically.[21] For example, lengthy phone calls, frequent e-mail, and weekly videoconferences provided the lifeline between global team members creating the Texas Instruments C82 digital signal processor.[22] The research department at BT Labs has 660 researchers spread across the United Kingdom and several other countries. The researchers work in global virtual teams that investigate virtual reality, artificial intelligence, and other advanced information technologies.[23]

Global teams can present enormous challenges. Leaders have to bridge gaps of time, distance, and culture. In some cases, members speak different languages, use different technologies, and have different beliefs about authority, time orientation, decision making, and so forth. Cultural differences can significantly affect team working relationships. The next chapter will discuss global diversity and cultural differences in more detail.

Effective team leadership becomes even more critical when dealing with global teams. For example, when team members are bound by a common, shared purpose, it can serve to bridge culture and distance gaps. Organizations and leaders also have to invest the time and resources to adequately educate employees. They have to make sure all team members appreciate and understand cultural differences, are focused on goals, and understand their responsibilities to the team. For a global team to be effective, all team members have to be willing to deviate somewhat from their own values and norms and establish new norms for the team.[24] One model for global team effectiveness, called the GRIP model, suggests that leaders focus on developing clarity and

Mastering Virtual Teams: Strategies, Tools, and Techniques That Succeed

Deborah L. Duarte and Nancy Tennant Snyder

Technology and globalization have created an environment in which many of today's teams communicate virtually, across boundaries of time, geography, culture, language, and organizations. Deborah L. Duarte, a consultant and assistant professor at The George Washington University, and Nancy Tennant Snyder, Chief Learning Officer for Whirlpool Corporation, wrote their book, *Mastering Virtual Teams,* to provide specific guidelines and strategies for leaders and members of virtual and global teams, emphasizing the skills needed to work effectively across technical, functional, and cultural boundaries.

Myths and Realities of Virtual Team Leadership

Many people have been thrust into the role of virtual team leader with little preparation, and they often distort ideas of what it takes to be effective. By identifying some of the myths regarding virtual teams, leaders can begin to develop the competencies they need to be successful.

Myth 1: Virtual Team Members Can Be Left Alone. Even though team members may be spread out across the world, it is a mistake to believe people can perform effectively without coordinating their efforts with other members and the leader. Good virtual team leaders are very explicit concerning how the team will communicate and how decisions will be made. They also develop effective monitoring and coaching skills to help people work well in a virtual environment.

Myth 2: The Complexity of Using Technology to Communicate Across Boundaries is Exaggerated. Not so. The problems of communicating and collaborating across time, distance, and organizations are immense and can't be solved by technology alone. Leaders must align and balance the use of technology and face-to-face interaction with the team's tasks and life cycle as well as team members' backgrounds.

Myth 3: Building Trust and Networking Are Relatively Unimportant in Virtual Teamwork. "One of the biggest mistakes a virtual team leader can make is to underestimate the power of trust." Good virtual team leaders build trust by setting and maintaining values, boundaries, and consistency. They never forget that work is accomplished through *people*, not technology. Networking. Keeping people informed, and soliciting input from all team members, partners, and customers is an essential part of a virtual team leader's job.

Myth 4: Every Aspect of Virtual Teams Should Be Planned Organized, and Controlled. Some leaders believe that everything should be carefully managed to avoid surprises, but too much control can destroy a virtual team's progress. Virtual teams operate in rapidly changing environments. Leaders face a constant tension between balancing structure and accountability with adaptability.

A Practical Focus

The authors indicate that as many as 80 percent of today's companies use virtual teams. *Mastering Virtual Teams* is divided into three sections that focus on their unique inherent complexities, their creation, and their operation. Each section provides clear, practical tools and advice for how to be a successful leader or member of a virtual team. Helpful checklists and practical exercises are combined with real-life examples and vignettes based on the authors' own experiences and research with real-life virtual teams.

Mastering Virtual Teams, by Deborah L. Duarte and Nancy Tennant Snyder, is published by Jossey-Bass.

common understanding in four areas: goals, relationships, information sharing, and work processes, thus helping the team "get a grip" on its collaborative work at a high level.[25]

The use of virtual and global teams is likely to grow as companies look for ways to harness knowledge and respond faster to increased global competition. Some scholars have suggested that twenty-first-century organizations may come to resemble amoebas—collections of workers, often connected electronically, who are divided into ever-changing teams that can best exploit the organization's unique resources, capabilities, and core competencies.[26] This chapter's Leader's Bookshelf discusses some of the myths and realities of leading virtual and global teams. In the following sections, we look at the challenges facing all team leaders. Clearly, developing a smoothly functioning team-based organization requires a different approach to leadership than that used in traditional hierarchical companies.

TEAM LEADERSHIP

There are two key aspects of team leadership. First are the personal qualities team leaders need. Second is how leaders use team characteristics and processes to guide team effectiveness.

The Team Leader's Personal Role

Successful teams begin with confident and effective team leaders. However, leading a team requires a shift in mind-set and behavior for those who are accustomed to working in traditional organizations where managers make the decisions. Most people can learn the new skills and qualities needed for team leadership, but it is not always easy. To be effective team leaders, people have to be willing to change themselves, to step outside their comfort zone and let go of many of the assumptions that have guided their behavior in the past. Here we will discuss five changes leaders can make to develop a foundation for effective team leadership.

LEARN TO RELAX AND ADMIT YOUR IGNORANCE   Team leaders don't have to know everything, and they can't always be in control. To be effective, team leaders let go of two counterproductive beliefs that are a legacy of the command-and-control system:

- If you don't know, don't ask.
- Don't look vulnerable.

Effective team leaders *do* ask—they aren't afraid to show that they don't know everything and they openly admit their mistakes. Although it is hard for many traditional managers to believe, admitting and learning from mistakes earns the respect of team members faster than almost any other behavior.[27]

In many cases, team leaders don't fully understand their teammates' jobs. For example, Bruce Moravec had mastered his technical discipline during seven years as a manufacturing engineer at Boeing. But when he was asked to lead the 757 Stretch Project—a team that would design a new fuselage for the Boeing 757—he knew he had to gain the respect and confidence of people who worked in areas he knew little about. "You don't want to pretend you're more knowledgeable about subjects other people know more about," Moravec says. "That dooms you to failure. I tell my people we all have different roles. My job is to pull things together. They're the experts."[28] For traditional managers who have spent years pretending they have all the answers, hiding their mistakes, and feeling in control, the move to team leader can be frightening. The first step to becoming effective in the new role is to let go and relax. Then, leaders can determine their own strengths and how those strengths can benefit the team.

TAKE CARE OF TEAM MEMBERS The leader sets the tone for how team members treat one another and their customers. Rather than always thinking about oneself and how to get the next promotion or salary increase, effective team leaders spend their time taking care of team members. Most team members share the critically important needs for recognition and support.[29] Leaders frequently overlook how important it is for people to feel that their contribution is valued, and they may especially forget to acknowledge the contributions of lower-level support staff. One woman who has held the same secretarial position for many years attributes her high enthusiasm to her team leader: "For the last several years, our team of four has reported to him. At the end of each day—no matter how hectic or trying things have been—he comes by each of our desks and says, 'Thank you for another good day.' "[30]

Team members also need to feel that their leader will go to the wall for them and back them up. Top executives expect the team leader to represent the organization's needs to the team. However, the leader is also responsible for representing the team's needs to the organization, getting the team what it needs to effectively do the job, and being a champion for the team. Leaders take the heat so team members don't have to.

COMMUNICATE Good communication skills are essential for team leadership—but this doesn't mean just learning how to express oneself clearly. It means, first and foremost, learning to listen as described in Chapter 9. Effective team leaders ask more questions than they answer. By asking the right questions, leaders help team members solve problems and make decisions. In addition, leaders help team members focus on the issues, encourage balanced participation in team meetings, summarize differences and agreements, and brainstorm alternative ideas, all of which require careful listening.[31]

For global teams and virtual teams, communication presents even greater challenges. The potential for communication errors is increased because of cultural and language differences as well as the use of electronic communication channels. People can't communicate face-to-face and may have trouble developing the trust that is essential for effective communication. Mobil Corp. leaders have virtual global team members gather in one location at the beginning of any new project so they can begin to build personal relationships, gain an understanding of goals and their responsibilities, and determine the ground rules by which the team will communicate.[32]

LEARN TO TRULY SHARE POWER   Team leaders embrace the concept of teamwork in deeds as well as words. This means sharing power, information, and responsibility. It requires leaders to have faith that team members will make the best decisions, even though those decisions might not be the ones the leader would have made. It is not always easy for a leader to let go and trust the team, as the leader of a sales team discovered. Having received a limited number of much-coveted tickets to a golf outing, he turned them over to the team, with the suggestion that they give one of the tickets to a manager from another department. When the team decided to give the tickets to exceptionally hardworking team members instead, the leader exploded. After he saw and admitted his mistake, and openly discussed it with the team, the sales team pulled together again.[33]

Effective team leaders recognize that it is example, not command, that holds a team together. They learn that helping team members be happier and more productive means thinking less about what they can do and more about what they can stop doing.[34]

RECOGNIZE THE IMPORTANCE OF SHARED PURPOSE AND VALUES   Building a team means creating a community united by shared values and commitment. It is at heart a spiritual undertaking.[35] To promote teamwork, leaders use ritual, stories, ceremonies, and other symbolism to create meaning for team members and give them a sense of belonging to something important. Phil Jackson, described at the beginning of this chapter, understands this aspect of team leadership. When he was coach of the Chicago Bulls, Jackson referred to the Bulls' team room as "the room where the spirit of the team takes form." Jackson uses symbols and stories to help team members feel intimately connected to one another and to feel that they're engaged in something almost sacred.[36]

Team leaders are responsible for facilitating a team vision and culture that works within and becomes a part of the larger organizational culture. Teams are successful only if they serve the organization's needs. In addition to developing personal qualities, team leaders work to ensure that the team's efforts benefit the organization.

Guiding Team Effectiveness

A number of factors are associated with workteam effectiveness, as illustrated in Exhibit 10.3. **Team effectiveness** can be defined as achieving four performance outcomes—innovation/adaptation, efficiency, quality, and employee satisfaction.[37] Innovation/adaptation means the degree to which teams impact the organization's ability to rapidly respond to environmental needs and changes. Efficiency pertains to whether the team helps the organization attain goals using fewer resources. Quality refers to achieving fewer defects and exceeding customer expectations. Satisfaction pertains to the team's ability to maintain employee commitment and enthusiasm by meeting the personal needs of its members.

Performance is influenced by team characteristics, including the type of team, the size of the team, team diversity, and the degree of team interdependence. These characteristics influence team dynamics, which in turn affect performance outcomes. Team leaders should understand and handle task and socio-emotional needs, the stages of team development, team norms, and team cohesiveness and conflict. Performance outcomes are influenced by the ability of leaders to guide teams through these processes in a positive manner.

Team leaders influence the factors described in Exhibit 10.3. We have already discussed the types of teams and personal qualities needed for team leadership. In the following sections, we will examine characteristics of teams and internal team dynamics.

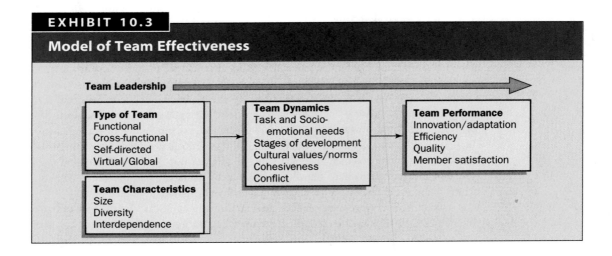

EXHIBIT 10.3

Model of Team Effectiveness

Team Leadership

Type of Team
Functional
Cross-functional
Self-directed
Virtual/Global

Team Characteristics
Size
Diversity
Interdependence

Team Dynamics
Task and Socio-
    emotional needs
Stages of development
Cultural values/norms
Cohesiveness
Conflict

Team Performance
Innovation/adaptation
Efficiency
Quality
Member satisfaction

UNDERSTANDING TEAM CHARACTERISTICS

Teams in organizations have certain characteristics that are important to team dynamics and performance. Three characteristics of particular concern to leaders are team size, diversity, and interdependence.

Size

The ideal size of workteams is thought to be seven, although variations from five to twelve are associated with high performance. These teams are large enough to take advantage of diverse skills, yet small enough to permit members to feel an intimate part of a community. Even teams of much greater size can be effective, and information technology has contributed to the ability of larger teams to maintain close contact, interact regularly, and share information. In general, however, as a team increases in size it becomes harder for each member to interact with and influence the others.

A summary of research on size suggests that small teams show more agreement, ask more questions, and exchange more opinions. Members want to get along with one another. Small teams report more satisfaction and enter into more personal discussions, and members feel a greater sense of cohesiveness and belonging. Large teams (generally defined as twelve or more members) tend to have more disagreements and differences of opinion. Subgroups often form and conflicts among them may occur. Demands on leaders are greater in large teams because there is less member participation. Large teams also tend to be less friendly and members do not feel that they are part of a cohesive community.[38] As a general rule, it is more difficult to satisfy members' needs in large teams, forcing leaders to work harder to keep members focused and committed to team goals.

Diversity

Since teams require a variety of skills, knowledge, and experience, it seems likely that heterogeneous teams would be more effective because members bring diverse abilities and information to bear on a project or problem. In general, research supports this idea, showing that heterogeneous teams produce more innovative solutions to problems than do homogeneous teams.[39] Diversity within a team can be a source of creativity. In addition, diversity can contribute to a healthy level of conflict that leads to better decision making. Some conflict helps to prevent "groupthink," in which people are so committed to a cohesive team that they are reluctant to express contrary opinions. Among top management teams, for example, low levels of conflict are associated with poor decision making. Furthermore, many of these low-conflict teams reflect little diversity among members.[40]

However, despite the value of some conflict, conflict that is too strong or is not handled appropriately can limit team members' satisfaction and performance. Diversity provides fertile ground for disagreements and disputes that may be based on personal rather than team issues.[41] Racial and national differences in particular can interfere with team interaction and performance, particularly in the short term.[42] Teams made up of racially and culturally diverse members tend to have more difficulty learning to work well together, but, with effective leadership and conflict resolution, the problems seem to dissipate over a period of time. The benefits and challenges of diversity will be discussed in detail in the next chapter.

Interdependence

Interdependence means the extent to which team members depend on each other for information, resources, or ideas to accomplish their tasks. Tasks such as performing surgery or directing military operations, for example, require a high degree of interaction and exchange, whereas tasks such as assembly-line manufacturing require very little.[43]

Three types of interdependence can affect teams: pooled, sequential, and reciprocal.[44]

In **pooled interdependence,** the lowest form of interdependence, members are fairly independent of one another in completing their work, participating *on* a team, but not *as* a team.[45] They may share a machine or a common secretary, but most of their work is done independently. An example might be a sales team, with each salesperson responsible for his or her own sales area and customers, but sharing the same appointment secretary. Salespersons need not interact to accomplish their work and little day-to-day coordination is needed.[46]

Sequential interdependence is a serial form wherein the output of one team member becomes the input to another team member. One member must perform well in order for the next member to perform well, and so on. Because team members have to exchange information and resources and rely upon one another, this is a higher level of interdependence. An example might be an engine assembly team in an automobile plant. Each team member performs a separate task, but his work depends on the satisfactory completion of work by other team members. Regular communication and coordination is required to keep work running smoothly.

The highest level of interdependence, **reciprocal interdependence,** exists when team members influence and affect one another in reciprocal fashion. The output of team member A is the input to team member B, and the output of team member B is the input back again to team member A. Reciprocal interdependence characterizes most teams performing knowledge-based work. Writing a technical manual, for example, rarely moves forward in a logical, step-by-step fashion. It is more like "an open-ended series of to-and-fro collaborations, iterations, and reiterations" among team members.[47] The emergency trauma team at Massachusetts General Hospital is another good example of reciprocal interdependence. Team members provide a variety of coordinated services in combination to a patient. Intense coordination is needed and team members are expected to "cover" their teammates, adjusting to each individual's strengths and weaknesses and to the changing demands of the specific problem at hand. On reciprocal teams, each individual member makes a contribution, but only the team as a whole "performs."[48]

According to a study of athletic teams, baseball, football, and basketball have differences that clearly illustrate these three levels of interdependence.

| IN THE LEAD | Athletic Team Interdependence |

Baseball, football, and basketball differ significantly in the degree of interdependence among team players. Baseball is low in interdependence, football is medium, and basketball is high.

An old baseball saying is, "Up at bat, you're totally alone." In baseball, interdependence among team players is low and can be defined as pooled. Each member acts independently, taking a turn at bat and playing his or her own position. When interaction does occur, it is only between two or three players, as in a double play. Players often practice and develop their skills individually and each strives to be successful as an individual. As Pete Rose put it, "Baseball is a team game, but nine men who reach their individual goals make a nice team."

In football, interdependence tends to be sequential. The line first blocks the opponents to enable the backs to run or pass. Plays are performed sequentially from first down to fourth down. Each player has an assignment that fits together with the assignments of other team members, and the various assignments are coordinated to achieve victory.

Basketball represents the highest level of interdependence and tends to be reciprocal. The game is free-flowing, and the division of labor is less precise than in other sports. Each player is involved in both offense and defense. The ball flows back and forth among players, and teammates must learn to adapt to the flow of the game and to one another as events unfold. Each game of basketball is like a riddle and the players in the thick of the action are the ones who have to solve it.

Interdependence among players is a primary difference among these three sports. Baseball is organized around an autonomous individual, football around groups that are sequentially interdependent, and basketball around the free flow of reciprocal players.[49]

Leaders are responsible for facilitating the degree of coordination and communication needed among team members, depending on the level of team interdependence. True team leadership, which involves empowering the team to make decisions and take action, is especially important to high performance when team interdependence is high. However, for teams with low interdependence, traditional leadership, individual rewards, and granting authority and power to individuals rather than the team may be appropriate.[50]

One of a team leader's most important jobs is to get the team designed right, by considering such factors as size, diversity, and interdependence. The quality of team design has a significant impact on the success of self-directed teams.[51] Team dynamics also affect performance and member satisfaction.

LEADING TEAM DYNAMICS

In this section, we will discuss team dynamics and interactions that change over time and can be influenced by team leaders. These include task and socio-emotional roles, the stages of team development, norms, and cohesiveness. Team conflict will be discussed in the next section.

Meeting Task and Socio-Emotional Needs

An important part of leading team dynamics is ensuring that the needs for both task accomplishment and team members' socio-emotional well-being are met. Recall from Chapter 2 the discussion of task-oriented and people-oriented leadership behaviors. Task-oriented behavior places primary concern on tasks and production and is generally associated with higher productivity, while people-oriented behavior emphasizes concern for followers and relationships and is associated with higher employee satisfaction.

For a team to be successful over the long term, it must both maintain its members' satisfaction and accomplish its task. These requirements are met through two types of team leadership roles, as illustrated in Exhibit 10.4. A *role* may be thought of as a set of behaviors expected of a person occupying a certain position, such as that of team leader. The **task-specialist role** is associated with behaviors such as initiating new ideas or different ways of considering problems; evaluating the team's effectiveness by questioning the logic, facts, or practicality of proposed solutions; seeking information to clarify tasks,

EXHIBIT 10.4

Two Types of Team Leadership Roles

Task-Specialist Behavior	Socio-Emotional Behavior
Propose solutions and initiate new ideas	Encourage contributions by others; draw out others' ideas by showing warmth and acceptance
Evaluate effectiveness of task solutions; offer feedback on others' suggestions	Smooth over conflicts between members; reduce tension and help resolve differences
Seek information to clarify tasks, responsibilities, and suggestions	Be friendly and supportive of others; show concern for members' needs and feelings
Summarize ideas and facts related to the problem at hand	Maintain standards of behavior and remind others of agreed-upon norms and standards for interaction
Energize others and stimulate the team to action	Seek to identify problems with team interactions or dysfunctional member behavior; ask for others' perceptions

SOURCE: Based on Robert A. Baron, *Behavior in Organizations,* 2nd ed. (Boston: Allyn & Bacon, 1986); and Don Hellriegel, John W. Slocum, Jr., and Richard W. Woodman, *Organizational Behavior,* 8th ed. (Cincinnati, OH: South-Western College Publishing, 1998), 244; and Gary A. Yukl, *Leadership in Organizations,* 4th ed. (Upper Saddle River, NJ: Prentice Hall, 1998): 384-387.

responsibilities, and suggestions; summarizing facts and ideas for others; and stimulating others to action when energy and interest wanes. The **socio-emotional role** includes behaviors such as facilitating the participation of others and being receptive to others' ideas; smoothing over conflicts between team members and striving to reduce tensions; showing concern for team members' needs and feelings; serving as a role model and reminding others of agreed-upon standards for interaction and cooperation; and seeking to identify problems with team interactions or dysfunctional member behaviors.[52]

Ideally, a team leader plays both task-specialist and socio-emotional roles. By satisfying both types of needs, the leader gains the respect and admiration of others. However, a leader may find it necessary to put more emphasis on one role over another. For example, if many members of the team are highly task-oriented, the leader may put more emphasis on meeting socio-emotional needs. On the other hand, when most members seem to emphasize relationships, the leader will need to be more task-oriented to ensure that the team performs its tasks and meets its goals. It is the leader's responsibility to make sure both types of needs are met, whether through the leader's own behaviors or through the actions and behaviors of other team members. A well-balanced team does best over the long term because it is personally satisfying for members and also promotes the successful accomplishment of team tasks and goals.

Team Development

After a team has been created, it goes through distinct stages of development.[53] Effective team leaders realize that new teams are different from mature teams. If you have participated in teams to do class assignments, you probably noticed that the team changed over time. In the beginning, members have to get to know one another, establish some order, divide responsibilities, and clarify tasks. These activities help members become part of a smoothly functioning team. The challenge for leaders is to recognize the stages of development and help teams move through them successfully.

Research suggests that teams develop over several stages. One model describing these stages is shown in Exhibit 10.5. These four stages typically occur in sequence, although there can be overlap. Each stage presents team members and leaders with unique problems and challenges.

FORMING   The **forming** stage of development is a period of orientation and getting acquainted. Team members find out what behavior is acceptable to others, explore friendship possibilities, and determine task orientation. Uncertainty is high because no one knows what the ground rules are or what is expected of them. Members will usually accept whatever power or authority is offered by either formal or informal leaders. The leader's challenge at this stage of development is to facilitate communication and interaction among team members to help them get acquainted and establish guidelines for how the team will work together. It is important at this stage that the leader try to make everyone feel comfortable and like a part of the team. Leaders can draw out shy or quiet team members to help them establish relationships with others.

STORMING   During the **storming** stage, individual personalities emerge more clearly. People become more assertive in clarifying their roles. This stage is marked by conflict and disagreement. Team members may disagree over their perceptions of the team's mission or goals. They may jockey for position or form subgroups based on common interests. The team is characterized by a general lack of unity and cohesiveness. It is essential that teams move beyond this stage or they will never achieve high performance. The leader's role is to encourage participation by each team member and help them find their common vision and values. Members need to debate ideas, surface conflicts,

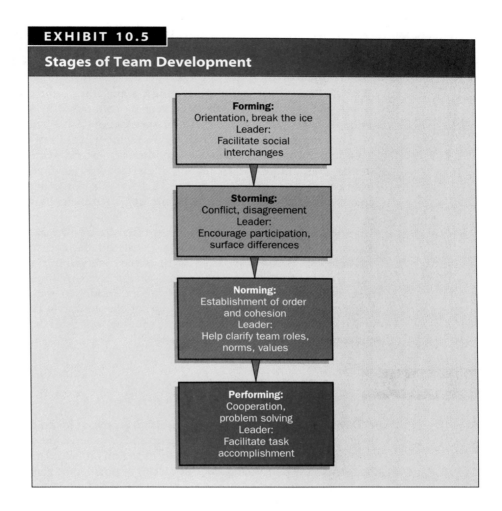

EXHIBIT 10.5

Stages of Team Development

Forming:
Orientation, break the ice
Leader:
Facilitate social
interchanges

Storming:
Conflict, disagreement
Leader:
Encourage participation,
surface differences

Norming:
Establishment of order
and cohesion
Leader:
Help clarify team roles,
norms, values

Performing:
Cooperation,
problem solving
Leader:
Facilitate task
accomplishment

disagree with one another, and work through the uncertainties and conflicting perceptions about team tasks and goals. Team leaders often play a stronger socio-emotional role during the forming and storming stages.

NORMING   At the **norming** stage, conflict has been resolved and team unity and harmony emerge. Consensus develops as to who the natural team leaders are and members' roles are clear. Team members come to understand and accept one another. Differences are resolved and members develop a sense of cohesiveness. This stage typically is of short duration and moves quickly into the next stage. The team leader should emphasize openness within the team and continue to facilitate communication and clarify team roles, values, and expectations.

PERFORMING   During the **performing stage,** the major emphasis is on accomplishing the team's goals. Members are committed to the team's mission. They interact frequently, coordinate their actions, and handle disagreements in a mature, productive manner. Team members confront and resolve problems in the interest of task accomplishment. At this stage, the team leader should concentrate on facilitating high task performance and helping the team self-manage to reach its goals. Leader behavior may shift to a stronger task-specialist role, although it is essential that socio-emotional needs continue to be met.

The stages of team development often have to be accelerated in virtual teams. Studies of virtual teams suggest that the first two stages, forming and storming, are best accomplished at the same time and in the same place, or at least via videoconferencing.[54] Bringing people together for a couple of days of team building can help teams move more rapidly to the performing stage. Leaders at McDevitt Street Bovis, one of the country's largest construction management firms, strive to accelerate the stages of team development to help put teams on a solid foundation.

IN THE LEAD   McDevitt Street Bovis

McDevitt Street Bovis credits its team-building process for quickly and effectively unifying teams, circumventing damaging and time-consuming conflicts, and preventing lawsuits related to major construction projects. The goal is to take the team to the performing stage as quickly as possible by giving everyone an opportunity to get to know one another, explore the ground rules, and clarify roles, responsibilities and expectations.

Rather than the typical construction project characterized by conflicts, frantic scheduling, and poor communications, Bovis wants its collection of contractors, designers, suppliers, and other partners to function like a true team—putting the success of the project ahead of their own individual interests. The team is first divided into separate groups that may have competing objectives—such as the clients in one group, suppliers in another, engineers and architects in a third, and so forth—and asked to come up with a list of their goals for the project. Although interests sometimes vary widely in purely accounting terms, there are almost always common themes. By talking about conflicting goals and interests, as well as what all the groups share, facilitators help the team gradually come together around a common purpose and begin to develop shared values that will guide the project. After jointly writing a mission statement for the team, each party says what it expects from the others, so that roles and responsibilities can be clarified. The intensive team-building session helps take members quickly through the forming and storming stages of development, but meetings continue all the way through the project to keep relationships strong and to keep people on target toward achieving the team mission. "We prevent conflicts from happening," says facilitator Monica Bennett. Leaders at McDevitt Street Bovis believe building better teams builds better buildings.[55]

Team Norms

Another important aspect of team dynamics is the development of team norms. **Norms** are acceptable standards of behavior that are shared by team members.[56] Norms tell team members what they ought and ought not to do in certain situations. Over time, all teams develop norms that guide member behavior. When agreed to and accepted by everyone, norms shape the behavior of the team and may further or inhibit the achievement of the team's goal.

Team norms begin to develop in the first interactions among members of a new team.[57] In addition, norms that apply to both day-to-day behavior and team performance gradually evolve as the team does its work. By understanding the three primary ways in which norms develop—critical events, primacy, and explicit statements and symbols—leaders can help shape norms that will help the team successfully meet its goals and keep team members committed and satisfied with being part of the team.

CRITICAL EVENTS   Norms often arise around critical incidents in the team's history and the way in which team members respond.[58] One example occurred when an employee at a forest products plant was injured while standing too close to a machine being operated by a teammate. This led to a norm that team members regularly monitor one another to make sure all safety rules are observed and that no one other than the operator gets within five feet of any machine. Any critical event can lead to the creation of norms that guide team behavior. At Xerox, Tom Ruddy developed a special deck of playing cards to help teams develop norms. Team members agree how they should respond to a critical incident and then write this norm on a card. Team members can "play" the card if someone on the team goes against the norm; eventually, people internalize the appropriate and accepted behavior.[59]

PRIMACY   Primacy means that the first behaviors that occur in a team often set a precedent for later team expectations. The first team meeting at a paper manufacturing plant set an unproductive norm regarding employee participation. The team leader raised an issue and turned it over to the team for discussion. As members offered solutions and alternatives, the leader responded to each with a friendly, "Yes, but what if . . ." response. As team members began trying to guess what solution the leader wanted, the leader began asking more and more leading questions to help them arrive at that solution. The pattern became so ingrained that team members dubbed staff meetings the "Guess What I Think" game.[60]

SYMBOLS AND EXPLICIT STATEMENTS Leaders or team members can use symbols as well as explicit statements to instill norms. At Sony Computer Entertainment America, PlayStation game design teams use language as well as symbolism to reinforce the norm that designers should be left alone to do their work without interference. One sign announces: "We don't mean to sound rude, but for development security reasons, visitors are not allowed past this point." For emphasis, storm troopers from *Star Wars* stand guard outside the cubicle.[61]

Explicit statements can be a highly effective way for leaders to influence norms. Roger Greene of the software company Ipswitch Inc., who doesn't want employees "burning the midnight oil," is constantly lecturing people on the need to take more personal days and vacation time. At Ipswitch, people don't get rewarded for being workaholics, and Greene's explicit statements support the norm that employees should live a balanced life. Explicit statements are especially effective for changing norms. When Richard Boyle at Honeywell wanted to develop a more relaxed, casual atmosphere, he wrote a memo called "Loosening Up the Tie." The explicit statement officially relaxed the excessive formality, gradually creating a new norm. Leaders' use of symbols and language to shape cultural norms and values will be discussed in greater detail in Chapter 14.

Team Cohesiveness

Team **cohesiveness** is defined as the extent to which members stick together and remain united in the pursuit of a common goal.[62] Members of highly cohesive teams are committed to team goals and activities, feel that they are involved in something significant, and are happy when the team succeeds. Members of less cohesive teams are less concerned about the team's welfare. Cohesiveness is generally considered an attractive feature of teams.

DETERMINANTS OF COHESIVENESS Leaders can use several factors to influence team cohesiveness. One is team *interaction*. The greater the amount of contact between team members and the more time they spend together, the more cohesive the team. Through frequent interaction, members get to know one another and become more devoted to the team. Another factor is *shared* *mission and goals.* When team members agree on purpose and direction, they will be more cohesive. The most cohesive teams are those that feel they are involved in something immensely relevant and important—that they are embarking on a journey together that will make the world better in some way. An aerospace executive, recalling his participation in an advanced design team, put it this way: "We even walked differently than anybody else. We felt we were way out there, ahead of the whole world."[63] A third factor is *personal attraction* to the team, meaning members find their common ground and have similar attitudes and values and enjoy being together. Members like and respect one another.

The organizational context can also affect team cohesiveness. When a team is in moderate *competition* with other teams, its cohesiveness increases as it strives to win. Finally, *team success* and the favorable evaluation of the team's work by outsiders add to cohesiveness. When a team succeeds and others in the organization recognize this success, members feel good and their commitment to the team will be higher.

CONSEQUENCES OF TEAM COHESIVENESS   The consequences of team cohesiveness can be examined according to two categories: morale and performance. As a general rule, employee *morale* is much higher in cohesive teams because of increased communication, a friendly atmosphere, loyalty, and member participation in decisions and activities. High team cohesiveness has almost uniformly positive effects on the satisfaction and morale of team members.[64]

With respect to team *performance,* it seems that cohesiveness and performance are generally positively related, although research results are mixed. Cohesive teams can sometimes unleash enormous amounts of employee energy and creativity. One explanation for this is the research finding that working in a team increases individual motivation and performance. *Social facilitation* refers to the tendency for the presence of other people to enhance an individual's motivation and performance. Simply interacting with others has an energizing effect.[65] In relation to this, one study found that cohesiveness is more closely related to high performance when team interdependence is high, requiring frequent interaction, coordination, and communication, as discussed earlier in this chapter.[66]

Another factor influencing performance is the relationship between teams and top leadership. One study surveyed more than 200 workteams and correlated job performance with cohesiveness.[67] Highly cohesive teams were more productive when team members felt supported by organizational leaders and less productive when they sensed hostility and negativism from leaders. The support of leaders contributes to the development of high performance norms, whereas hostility leads to team norms and goals of low performance. At Southwest Airlines, highly cohesive teams are supported by top leaders.

IN THE LEAD   Southwest Airlines

At Southwest Airlines, teamwork is built through the Crew Resource Management (CRM) program, implemented by the aviation industry to reduce air carrier accidents. The program is derided by employees at many airlines as *Cockpit* Resource Management, since the attitude of most airlines is that flight safety is in the hands of the pilot.

Not so at Southwest. The successful airline focuses on teams, not individuals, as the driving force behind the company. The entire team is responsible for flight safety, from flight attendants and pilots to ground crews and baggage handlers. Training emphasizes communication and mutual understanding of each team member's role in ensuring a safe flight. Each member understands the time constraints, expectations, and particular problems of other workers. For example, dispatchers observe pilots in flight simulation training and pilots learn about the time constraints of baggage handlers.

Southwest's top leadership has demonstrated total commitment to team training and responsibility since the CRM program began in 1985. The combination of team cohesiveness and leadership support has made Southwest's workers the most productive in the industry and the company a benchmark for flight safety.[68]

As we discussed earlier in this chapter, one aspect of a team leader's job is to represent the organization's needs to the team and the team's needs to the organization. Leaders can sometimes revive a team and shift them toward higher performance norms by recruiting even one senior leader as a sponsor who shows interest in and concern about the team's work. "Get one of them excited," says Joe Bonito, a consultant and team leader at Pfizer Pharmaceuticals. "If you can show the boss that your team is doing something unique, something that will create a competitive advantage, the boss will want to become the de facto sponsor."[69]

HANDLING TEAM CONFLICT

The final characteristic of team dynamics is team conflict. Of all the skills needed for effective team leadership, none is more important than handling the conflicts that inevitably arise among members. Conflict can arise between members of a team or between one team and another.

Conflict refers to hostile or antagonistic interaction in which one party attempts to thwart the intentions or goals of another. Conflict is natural and occurs in all teams and organizations. However, too much conflict can be destructive, tear relationships apart, and interfere with the healthy exchange of ideas and information needed for team development and cohesiveness.[70]

Causes of Conflict

Leaders can be aware of several factors that cause conflict among individuals or teams. Whenever teams compete for scarce resources, such as money, information, or supplies, conflict is almost inevitable. Conflicts also emerge when task responsibilities are unclear. People may disagree about who has responsibility for specific tasks or who has a claim on resources, and leaders help members reach agreement. Another reason for conflict is simply because individuals or teams are pursuing conflicting goals. For example, individual salespeople's targets may put them in conflict with one another and with the sales manager. Finally, it sometimes happens that two people simply do not get along with one another and will never see eye to eye on any issue. Personality clashes are caused by basic differences in personality, values, and attitudes, as described in Chapter 4, and can be particularly difficult to deal with. Sometimes, the only solution is to separate the parties and reassign them to other teams where they can be more productive.

Styles to Handle Conflict

Teams as well as individuals develop specific styles for dealing with conflict, based on the desire to satisfy their own concerns versus the other party's concerns. Exhibit 10.6 describes five styles of handling conflict. How an individual approaches conflict is measured along two dimensions: *assertiveness* and *cooperation*. Effective leaders and team members vary their style to fit a specific situation, as each style is appropriate in certain cases.[71]

1. The *competing style,* which reflects assertiveness to get one's own way, should be used when quick, decisive action is vital on important issues or unpopular actions, such as during emergencies or urgent cost cutting.

2. The *avoiding style,* which reflects neither assertiveness nor cooperativeness, is appropriate when an issue is trivial, when there is no chance of winning, when a delay to gather more information is needed, or when a disruption would be costly.

3. The *compromising style* reflects a moderate amount of both assertiveness and cooperativeness. It is appropriate when the goals on both sides are

EXHIBIT 10.6

A Model of Styles to Handle Conflict

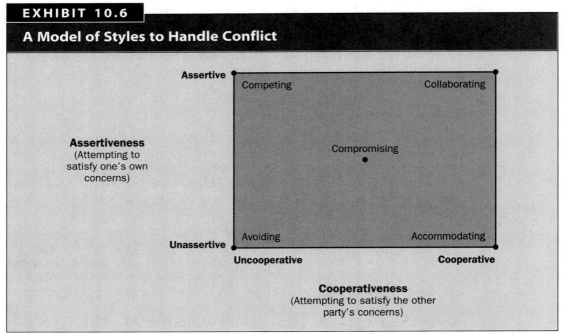

SOURCE: Adapted from Kenneth Thomas, "Conflict and Conflict Management," in *Handbook of Industrial and Organizational Behavior,* ed. M. D. Dunnette (New York: John Wiley, 1976), 900. Used by permission of Marvin D. Dunnette.

equally important, when opponents have equal power and both sides want to split the difference, or when people need to arrive at temporary or expedient solutions under time pressure.

4. The *accommodating style* reflects a high degree of cooperativeness, which works best when people realize that they are wrong, when an issue is more important to others than to oneself, when building social credits for use in later discussions, or when maintaining cohesiveness is especially important.

5. The *collaborating style* reflects both a high degree of assertiveness and of cooperativeness. This style enables both parties to win, although it may require substantial dialogue and negotiation. The collaborating style is important when both sets of concerns are too important to be compromised, when insights from different people need to be merged into an overall solution, or when the commitment of both sides is needed for a consensus.

Other Approaches

The various styles of handling conflict illustrated in Exhibit 10.6 are especially effective for an individual to use when he or she disagrees with another. But what can a team leader do when conflict erupts among others? Research suggests several techniques that help resolve conflicts among people or teams.

VISION A compelling vision can pull people together. A vision is for the whole team and cannot be attained by one person. Its achievement requires the cooperation of conflicting parties. To the extent that leaders can focus on a larger team or organizational vision, conflict will decrease because the people involved see the big picture and realize they must work together to achieve it.

BARGAINING/NEGOTIATING Bargaining and negotiating mean that the parties engage one another in an attempt to systematically reach a solution. They attempt logical problem solving to identify and correct the conflict. This approach works well if the individuals can set aside personal animosities and deal with conflict in a businesslike way.

MEDIATION Using a third party to settle a dispute involves mediation. A mediator could be a supervisor, another team leader, or someone from the human resources department. The mediator can discuss the conflict with each party and work toward a solution. If a solution satisfactory to all parties cannot be reached, the parties may be willing to turn the conflict over to the mediator and abide by his or her solution.

FACILITATING COMMUNICATION One of the most effective ways to reduce conflict is to help conflicting parties communicate openly and honestly. As conflicting parties exchange information and learn more about one another, suspicions diminish and teamwork becomes possible. A particularly promising avenue for reducing conflict is through dialogue, as discussed in Chapter 9. Dialogue asks that participants suspend their attachments to their own viewpoint so that a deeper level of listening, synthesis, and meaning can evolve from the interaction. Individual differences are acknowledged and respected, but rather than trying to figure out who is right or wrong, the parties search for a joint perspective.

Each of these approaches can be helpful in resolving conflicts between individuals or teams. Effective leaders use a combination of these on a regular basis—such as articulating a larger vision and continuously facilitating communication—to keep conflict at a minimum while the team moves forward.

SUMMARY AND INTERPRETATION

Teams are a reality in most organizations, and leaders are called upon to facilitate teams rather than manage direct report subordinates. Functional teams typically are part of the traditional organization structure. Cross-functional teams, including problem-solving teams, process-improvement teams, and special purpose teams, often represent an organization's first move toward greater team participation. Cross-functional teams may evolve into self-directed teams, which are member- rather than leader-centered and directed. Two recent types of teams, virtual teams and global teams, have resulted from advances in technology, changing employee expectations, and the globalization of business. New technology both supports teamwork and increases the pressures on organizations to expand opportunities for employee participation and the widespread sharing of information.

Successful teams begin with effective team leaders. People typically have to change themselves to become effective team leaders. Five principles that provide a foundation for team leadership are: relax and admit mistakes; take care of team members; communicate; truly share power; and recognize the shared-values nature of teamwork. Several other factors are associated with team effectiveness, such as the type of team, size, diversity, and interdependence, as well as team cohesiveness, roles, norms, conflict, and stages of development.

All teams experience some conflict because of scarce resources, ambiguous responsibilities, faulty communication, goal conflicts, power and status differences, or personality clashes. Handling team conflict is one of the most important skills of team leadership.

KEY TERMS

team	pooled interdependence	performing
functional team	sequential interdependence	norm
cross-functional team	reciprocal interdependence	cohesiveness
self-directed team	task-specialist role	conflict
virtual team	socio-emotional role	
global team	forming	
team effectiveness	storming	
interdependence	norming	

DISCUSSION QUESTIONS

1. What is the difference between a "team" and a "group"? Describe your personal experience with each.

2. Discuss the differences between a cross-functional team and a self-directed team.

3. Why do you think organizations are increasingly using virtual and global teams? Would you like to be a member or leader of a virtual global team? Why or why not?

4. Why might a person need to go through significant personal changes to be an effective team leader? What are some of the changes required?

5. Describe the three levels of interdependence and explain how they affect team leadership.

6. Which is more important to team effectiveness—the task-specialist role or the socio-emotional role? Discuss.

7. What are the stages of team development? How can a team leader best facilitate the team at each stage?

8. Think about a team or group of which you have been a member, either at work or at your university. Can you identify some of the team's cultural norms and values?

9. Discuss the relationship between team cohesiveness and performance.

10. What style of handling conflict do you typically use? Can you think of instances where a different style might have been more productive?

LEADERSHIP DEVELOPMENT: Personal Feedback

Assess Your Team Leadership Skills

Answer the following questions based on what you have done, or think you would do, related to the situations and attitudes described.

	Mostly True	Mostly False
1. I am more likely to handle a high-priority task than assign it to the team.	_____	_____
2. A team leader should always be open to new ideas and information from team members.	_____	_____

	Mostly True	Mostly False
3. It makes sense to stay somewhat aloof from the team, so you can make a tough decision when necessary.	_____	_____
4. I would prefer to share leadership, encouraging people to take initiative at appropriate times for the benefit of the team.	_____	_____
5. An important part of leading a team is to keep members informed almost daily of information that could affect their work.	_____	_____
6. Building trust is an important part of leading a team.	_____	_____
7. I like to do things my own way and in my own time.	_____	_____
8. If my team were adding a new member, I would want the person to be interviewed by the entire team.	_____	_____
9. Some of the best ideas are likely to come from team members rather than the leader.	_____	_____
10. I dislike it intensely when a team member challenges my position on an issue.	_____	_____
11. I try to help each team member find a way to make a significant contribution to the project.	_____	_____
12. I typically explain to team members what methods they should use to accomplish an assigned task.	_____	_____
13. If I were out of the office for a week, most of the important work of the team would get accomplished anyway.	_____	_____
14. Delegation of tasks is something that is (or would be) very difficult for me.	_____	_____
15. When a team member comes to me with a problem, I tend to jump right in with a proposed solution.	_____	_____

Scoring

The answers for effective team leadership are as follows:

1. Mostly false	6. Mostly true	11. Mostly true
2. Mostly true	7. Mostly false	12. Mostly false
3. Mostly false	8. Mostly true	13. Mostly true
4. Mostly true	9. Mostly true	14. Mostly false
5. Mostly true	10. Mostly false	15. Mostly false

Interpretation

If your score is 12 or higher, you most likely are (or would be) a highly effective team leader. If your score is 6 or lower, you have an authoritarian approach to leadership that could cause difficulty in a team leadership role. Team leadership requires that the leader learn to share power, information, and responsibility. An authoritarian approach blocks rather than supports teamwork and the accomplishment of team goals. If you scored low on this exercise, you can use the implied suggestions in these questions, along with the information in this chapter, to help shift your leadership approach. Team leadership is becoming a critical skill for leaders in all organizations.

SOURCE: Adapted from "What Style of Leader Are You or Would You Be?" in Andrew J. DuBrin, *Leadership: Research Findings, Practice, and Skills,* 3rd ed. (Boston, MA: Houghton Mifflin Company, 2001), 126–127.

LEADERSHIP DEVELOPMENT: Cases for Analysis

Valena Scientific Corporation

Valena Scientific Corporation (VSC) is a large manufacturer of health care products. The health care market includes hospitals, clinical laboratories, universities, and industries. Clinical laboratories represent 52 percent of VSC's sales. Laboratories are located in hospitals and diagnostic centers where blood tests and urine analyses are performed for physicians. Equipment sold to laboratories can range from a five-cent test tube to a $195,000 blood analyzer.

By 1980, the industry experienced a move into genetic engineering. Companies such as Genentech Corporation and Cetus Scientific Laboratories were created and staffed with university microbiologists. These companies were designed to exploit the commercial potential for gene splicing.

Senior executives at VSC saw the trend developing and decided to create a Biotech Research Program. Skilled microbiologists were scarce, so the program was staffed with only nine scientists. Three scientists were skilled in gene splicing, three in recombination, and three in fermentation. The specialties reflected the larger departments to which they were assigned. However, they were expected to work as a team on this program. Twenty technicians were also assigned to the program to help the scientists.

Senior management believed that the biotech research program could be self-managed. For the first eighteen months of operation, everything went well. Informal leaders emerged among the scientists in gene splicing, recombination, and fermentation. These three informal leaders coordinated the work of the three groups, which tended to stay separate. For example, the work typically started in the gene-splicing group, followed by work in recombination, and then in fermentation. Fermentation was used to breed the bacteria created by the other two groups in sufficient numbers to enable mass production.

During the summer of 1983, the biotech research program was given a special project. Hoffman-LaRoche was developing leukocyte interferon to use as a treatment against cancer. VSC contracted with Hoffman-LaRoche to develop a technique for large-scale interferon production. VSC had only six months to come up with a production technology. Scientists in each of the subgroups remained in their own geographical confines and began immediately to test ideas relevant to their specialty. In September, the informal group leaders met and discovered that each group had taken a different research direction. Each of the subgroups believed their direction was best and the informal leaders argued vehemently for their positions, rather than change to another direction. Future meetings were conflict-laden and did not resolve the issues. When management became aware of the crisis, they decided to appoint a formal leader to the program.

On November 15, a Stanford professor with extensive research experience in recombinant DNA technology was hired. His title was Chief Biologist for the Biotech Research Program, and all project members reported to him for the duration of the interferon project.

The chief biologist immediately took the nine scientists on a two-day retreat. He assigned them to three tables for discussions, with a member from each subgroup at each table, so they had to talk across their traditional boundaries. He led the discussion of their common ground as scientists, and of their hopes and vision for this project. After they developed a shared vision, the group turned to scientific issues and in mixed groups discussed the ideas that the VSC subgroups had developed. Gradually, one approach seemed to have more likelihood of success than the others. A consensus emerged, and the chief biologist adopted the basic approach that would be taken in the interferon project. Upon their return to VSC, the technicians were brought in and the scientists explained the approach to them. At this point, each subgroup was assigned a set of instructions within the overall research plan. Firm deadlines were established based upon group interdependence. Weekly progress reports to the chief biologist were required from each group leader.

Dramatic changes in the behavior of the scientists were observed after the two-day retreat. Communication among groups became more common. Problems discovered by one group were communicated to other groups so that effort was not expended needlessly. Subgroup leaders coordinated many solutions among themselves. Lunch and coffee gatherings that included several members of the subgroups began to appear. Group leaders and members often had daily discussions and cooperated on research requirements. Enthusiasm for the department and the interferon project was high, and cohesion seemed especially strong.

SOURCE: Adapted from Richard L. Daft, *Organization Theory and Design*, 5th ed., 474–477. Copyright 1995 West Publishing. Used by permission of South-Western College Publishing, a division of International Thomson Publishing Inc., Cincinnati, Ohio 45227.

Questions

1. Was the research program a group or a team? What type of team were they (functional, cross-functional, self-directed)? Explain.
2. Did the interdependence among the subgroups change with the interferon project? What were the group norms before and after the retreat?
3. What factors account for the change in cohesiveness after the chief biologist took over?

Burgess Industries

Managers at Burgess Industries, one of the few remaining garment manufacturing companies in eastern North Carolina, are struggling to improve productivity and profits. If things don't get better, they and their 650 employees will be out of work. Top executives have been evaluating whether to close the plant, which makes pants for several different clothing companies, and move production to Mexico. However, everyone hopes to keep the North Carolina factory going. The latest effort to turn things around is a shift to teamwork.

Top executives directed managers to abandon the traditional assembly system, where workers performed a single task, such as sewing zippers or attaching belt loops. In the new team system, teams of thirty to thirty-five workers coordinate their activities to assemble complete garments. People were given training to help master new machinery and also attended a brief team-building and problem-solving seminar prior to the shift to teamwork. Approximately fifty workers at a time were taken off the production floor for an afternoon to attend the seminars, which were spread over a month's time. As an introduction to the seminar, employees were told that the new team system would improve their work lives by giving them more autonomy, eliminating the monotony of the old assembly system, and reducing the number of injuries people received from repeating the same task over and over.

The pay system was also revised. Previously, workers were paid based on their total output. A skilled worker could frequently exceed his or her quota of belt loops or fly stitching by 20 percent or more, which amounted to a hefty increase in pay. In the new system, people are paid based on the total output of the team. In many cases, this meant that the pay of top performers went down dramatically because the productivity of the team was adversely affected by slower, inexperienced, or inefficient team members. Skilled workers were frustrated having to wait for slower colleagues to complete their part of the garment, but they resented having to pitch in and help out the less skilled workers to speed things up. Supervisors, unaccustomed to the team system, provided little direction beyond telling people they needed to resolve work flow and personality issues among themselves. The idea was to empower employees to have more control over their own work.

So far, the experiment in teamwork has been a dismal failure. The quantity of garments produced per hour has actually declined 25 percent from pre-team levels. Labor costs have gone down, but morale is terrible. Threats and insults are commonly heard on the factory floor. One seamstress even had to restrain a coworker who was about to throw a chair at a team member who constantly griped about "having to do everyone else's work."

SOURCE: Based on information reported in N. Munk, "How Levi's Trashed a Great American Brand," *Fortune,* April 12, 1999, 83–90; and R. King, "Levi's Factory Workers Are Assigned to Teams, and Morale Takes a Hit," *The Wall Street Journal,* May 20, 1998, A1, A6.

Questions

1. Why do you think the experiment in teamwork at Burgess Industries has been unsuccessful? Consider the definition of teams, team characteristics and team dynamics, and issues of leadership.

2. If you were a consultant to Burgess, what would you recommend managers do to promote more effective teamwork?

3. How would you alleviate the conflicts that have developed among employees?

REFERENCES

1. Dennis McCafferty, "Managing to Win," *USA Weekend,* April 24-26, 1998, 4–6; "Bird Leaves Pacers with Head Held High," Associated Press report, *Johnson City Press,* June 20, 2000, 20; "Coach Bio: Phil Jackson," *http://www.nba.com/lakers/bios/coach.html* accessed on May 19, 2000; Paul Buker, "The Man with the Jewelry," *OregonLive,* Monday, May 22, 2000, *http://www.oregonlive.com* accessed on May 22, 2000; Brian S. Moskal, "Running with the Bulls," *IW,* January 8, 1996, 26–34; Charley Rosen, "No More Bull," *Cigar Aficionado,* September-October 1998, *http://www.cigaraficionado.com/Cigar/Aficionado/people/fe1098.html;* "The NBA at 50: Phil Jackson," *http://nba.com/history/jackson_50.html.*

2. James Wallace Bishop and K. Dow Scott, "How Commitment Affects Team Performance," *HR Magazine,* February 1997, 107–111; "Training in the 1990s," *The Wall Street Journal,* March 1, 1990, B1; Patricia Booth, "Embracing the Team Concept," *Canadian Business Review* (Autumn 1994), 10–13.

3. Jeffrey Pfeffer, "Producing Sustainable Competitive Advantage through the Effective Management of People," *Academy of Management Executive* 9, No. 1 (1995), 55–72.

4. Wendy Zellner, "No More Same Ol'-Same Ol'," *Business Week,* October 17, 1994, 95–96; Michael Barrier, "However You Slice It," *Nation's Business,* June 1996, 16; Kenneth Labich, "Elite Teams Get the Job Done," *Fortune,* February 19, 1996, 90–99.

5. Mark A. Abramson, "First Teams," *Government Executive,* May 1996, 53–58.

6. Carl E. Larson and Frank M. J. LaFasto, *Team Work* (Newbury Park, CA: Sage, 1989).

7. Lee G. Bolman and Terrence E. Deal, "What Makes a Team Work?" *Organizational Dynamics,* August 1992, 34–44.

8. Laton McCartney, "A Team Effort," *IW,* December 18, 1995, 65–72.

9. Susan Carey, "US Air 'Peon' Team Pilots Start-Up of Low-Fare Airline," *The Wall Street Journal,* March 24, 1998, B1.

10. Pierre van Amelsvoort and Jos Benders, "Team Time: A Model for Developing Self-Directed Work Teams," *International Journal of Operations and Production Management* 16, No. 2 (1996), 159–170.

11. Jeanne M. Wilson, Jill George, and Richard S. Wellins, with William C. Byham, *Leadership Trapeze: Strategies for Leadership in Team-Based Organizations* (San Francisco: Jossey-Bass, 1994).

12. Booth, "Embracing the Team Concept."

13. Scott Kirsner, "Every Day, It's a New Place," *Fast Company,* April-May 1998, 130–134.

14. Ibid.

15. Cheryl Dahle, "Xtreme Teams," *Fast Company,* November 1999, 310–326.

16. Gina Imperato, "Their Specialty? Teamwork," *Fast Company,* January-February 2000, 54, 56.

17. The discussion of virtual teams is based on Anthony M. Townsend, Samuel M. DeMarie, and Anthony R. Hendrickson, "Virtual Teams: Technology and the Workplace of the Future," *Academy of Management Executive* 12, No. 3 (August 1998), 17–29; and Deborah L. Duarte and Nancy Tennant Snyder, *Mastering Virtual Teams* (San Francisco: Jossey-Bass, 1999).

18. Amy Helen Johnson, "Teamwork Made Simple," *CIO*, Section 1, November 1, 1999, 86–92.

19. Keith H. Hammonds, "This Virtual Agency Has Big Ideas," *Fast Company*, November 1999, 70, 72.

20. Mary O'Hara-Devereaux and Robert Johansen, *Globalwork: Bridging Distance, Culture, and Time* (San Francisco: Jossey-Bass, 1994); Charles C. Snow, Scott A. Snell, Sue Canney Davison, and Donald C. Hambrick, "Use Transnational Teams to Globalize Your Company," *Organizational Dynamics* 24, No. 4 (Spring 1996), 50–67.

21. Charlene Marmer Solomon, "Building Teams Across Borders," *Global Workforce*, November 1998, 12–17.

22. James Daly, "Digital Cowboys," *Forbes ASAP*, February 26, 1996, 62.

23. Jane Pickard, "Control Freaks Need Not Apply," *People Management*, February 5, 1998, 49.

24. Sylvia Odenwald, "Global Work Teams," *Training and Development*, February 1996, 54–57; and Debby Young, "Team Heat," *CIO*, Section 1, September 1, 1998, 43–51.

25. O'Hara-Devereaux and Johansen, *Globalwork: Bridging Distance, Culture, and Time*, 227–228.

26. R. Duane Ireland and Michael A. Hitt, "Achieving and Maintaining Strategic Competitiveness in the 21st Century: The Role of Strategic Leadership," *Academy of Management Executive* 13, No. 1 (1999), 43–57.

27. Wilson, et. al., *Leadership Trapeze*, 14.

28. Eric Matson, "Congratulations, You're Promoted. (Now What?)," *Fast Company*, June-July 1997, 116–130.

29. Mark Sanborn, *TeamBuilt: Making Teamwork Pay* (New York: MasterMedia Limited, 1992), 99–101.

30. Sanborn, *TeamBuilt: Making Teamwork Pay*, 100.

31. Lawrence Holpp, "New Roles for Leaders: An HRD Reporter's Inquiry," *Training & Development*, March 1995, 46–50.

32. Solomon, "Building Teams Across Borders."

33. J. Thomas Buck, "The Rocky Road to Team-Based Management," *Training & Development*, April 1995, 35-38; Wilson, et. al., *Leadership Trapeze*, 15–16.

34. Bolman and Deal, "What Makes a Team Work?"; Stratford Sherman, "Secrets of HP's 'Muddled' Team," *Fortune*, March 18, 1996, 116–120.

35. Based on Bolman and Deal, "What Makes a Team Work?"

36. Brian S. Moskal, "Running with the Bulls," *IW*, January 8, 1996, 26–34.

37. Dexter Dunphy and Ben Bryant, "Teams: Panaceas or Prescriptions for Improved Performance," *Human Relations* 49, No. 5 (1996), 677–699; and Susan G. Cohen, Gerald E. Ledford, and Gretchen M. Spreitzer, "A Predictive Model of

Self-Managing Work Team Effectiveness," *Human Relations* 49, No. 5 (1996), 643–676.

38. For research findings on group size, see M. E. Shaw, *Group Dynamics,* 3rd ed. (New York: McGraw-Hill, 1981); G. Manners, "Another Look at Group Size, Group Problem-Solving and Member Consensus," *Academy of Management Journal* 18 (1975), 715–724; and Albert V. Carron and Kevin S. Spink, "The Group Size-Cohesion Relationship in Minimal Groups," *Small Group Research* 26, No. 1 (February 1995), 86–105.

39. Warren E. Watson, Kamalesh Kumar, and Larry K. Michaelsen, "Cultural Diversity's Impact on Interaction Process and Performance: Comparing Homogeneous and Diverse Task Groups," *Academy of Management Journal* 36 (1993), 590–602; Gail Robinson and Kathleen Dechant, "Building a Business Case for Diversity," *Academy of Management Executive* 11, No. 3 (1997), 21–31; R. A. Guzzo and G. P. Shea, "Group Performance and Intergroup Relations in Organizations," in M. D. Dunnette and L. M. Hough, eds., *Handbook of Industrial & Organizational Psychology,* 2nd ed., Vol. 3 (Palo Alto, CA: Consulting Psychologists Press, 1992), 288–290; and David A. Thomas and Robin J. Ely, "Making Differences Matter: A New Paradigm for Managing Diversity," *Harvard Business Review,* September-October 1996, 79–90.

40. Kathleen M. Eisenhardt, Jean L. Kahwajy, and L. J. Bourgeois III, "Conflict and Strategic Choice: How Top Management Teams Disagree," *California Management Review* 39, No. 2 (Winter 1997), 42–62

41. Dora C. Lau and J. Keith Murnighan, "Demographic Diversity and Faultlines: The Compositional Dynamics of Organizational Groups," *Academy of Management Review* 23, No. 2 (1998), 325–340; and K. A. Jehn, "A Multimethod Examination of the Benefits and Detriments of Intragroup Conflict," *Administrative Science Quarterly* 40 (1995), 256–282.

42. Watson, Kumar, and Michaelsen, "Cultural Diversity's Impact on Interaction Process and Performance."

43. Stanley M. Gully, Dennis J. Devine, and David J. Whitney, "A Meta-Analysis of Cohesion and Performance: Effects of Level of Analysis and Task Interdependence," *Small Group Research* 26, No. 4 (November 1995), 497–520.

44. James Thompson, *Organizations in Action* (New York: McGraw-Hill, 1967).

45. Peter F. Drucker, *Managing in a Time of Great Change* (New York: Truman Talley Books/Dutton, 1995), 98.

46. Ibid.

47. Thomas A. Stewart, "The Great Conundrum—You vs. the Team," *Fortune,* November 25, 1996, 165–166.

48. Labich, "Elite Teams"; and Drucker, *Managing in a Time of Great Change,* 101.

49. Robert W. Keidel, "Team Sports Models as a Generic Organizational Framework," *Human Relations* 40 (1987), 591–612; Robert W. Keidel, "Baseball, Football, and Basketball: Models for Business, *Organizational Dynamics* (Winter 1984), 5–18; Richard L. Daft and Richard M. Steers, *Organizations: A Micro-Macro Approach* (Glenview, IL: Scott, Foresman, 1986); and Peter M. Drucker, *Managing in a Time of Great Change,* 97–102.

50. Robert C. Liden, Sandy J. Wayne, and Lisa Bradway, "Connections Make the Difference," *HR Magazine,* February 1996, 73.

51. Ruth Wageman, "Critical Success Factors for Creating Superb Self-Managing Teams," *Organizational Dynamics,* Summer 1997, 49–61.

52. Based on Robert A. Baron, *Behavior in Organizations,* 2nd ed. (Boston: Allyn & Bacon, 1986); Don Hellriegel, John W. Slocum, Jr., and Richard W. Woodman, *Organizational Behavior,* 8th ed. (Cincinnati, OH: South-Western College Publishing, 1998), 244; and Gary A. Yukl, *Leadership in Organizations,* 4th edition (Upper Saddle River, NJ: Prentice Hall, 1998), 384–387.

53. Kenneth G. Koehler, "Effective Team Management," *Small Business Report,* July 19, 1989, 14–16; Connie J. G. Gersick, "Time and Transition in Work Teams: Toward a New Model of Group Development," *Academy of Management Journal* 31 (1988), 9–41; and John Beck and Neil Yeager, "Moving Beyond Myths," *Training & Development,* March 1996, 51–55.

54. Ron Young, "The Wide-Awake Club," *People Management,* February 5, 1998, 46–49.

55. Thomas Petzinger Jr., "Bovis Team Helps Builders Construct a Solid Foundation" (The Front Lines column), *The Wall Street Journal,* March 21, 1997, B1.

56. Cohen, Ledford, and Spreitzer, "A Predictive Model of Self-Managing Work Team Effectiveness."

57. Kenneth Bettenhausen and J. Keith Murnighan, "The Emergence of Norms in Competitive Decision-Making Groups," *Administrative Science Quarterly* 30 (1985), 350–372.

58. Edgar H. Schein, "Organizational Culture," *American Psychologist* 45, No. 2 (February 1990), 109–119.

59. Mark Fischetti, "Team Doctors, Report to ER!" *Fast Company,* February-March 1998, 170–177.

60. Wilson, et. al., *Leadership Trapeze,* 12.

61. Paul Roberts, "Sony Changes the Game," *Fast Company,* August-September 1997, 116–128.

62. Carron and Spink, "The Group Size-Cohesion Relationship in Minimal Groups."

63. Harold J. Leavitt and Jean Lipman-Blumen, "Hot Groups," *Harvard Business Review,* (July-August 1995), 109–116.

64. Dorwin Cartwright and Alvin Zander, *Group Dynamics: Research and Theory,* 3rd ed. (New York: Harper & Row, 1968); Eliot Aronson, *The Social Animal* (San Francisco: W. H. Freeman, 1976); and Thomas Li-Ping Tang and Amy Beth Crofford, "Self-Managing Work Teams," *Employment Relations Today* (Winter 1995/96), 29–39.

65. Tang and Crofford, "Self-Managing Work Teams."

66. Gully, Devine, and Whitney, "A Meta-Analysis of Cohesion and Performance: Effects of Level of Analysis and Task Interdependence."

67. Stanley E. Seashore, *Group Cohesiveness in the Industrial Work Group* (Ann Arbor, MI: Institute for Social Research, 1954).

68. Connie Bovier, "Teamwork: The Heart of the Airline," *Training,* June 1993, 53–58; and Tang and Crofford, "Self-Managing Work Teams," 34–35.

69. Fischetti, "Team Doctors, Report to ER!"
70. Koehler, "Effective Team Management"; and Dean Tjosvold, "Making Conflict Productive," *Personnel Administrator* 29 (June 1984), 121.
71. This discussion is based on K. W. Thomas, "Towards Multidimensional Values in Teaching: The Example of Conflict Behaviors," *Academy of Management Review* 2 (1977), 487.

CHAPTER OUTLINE

YOUR LEADERSHIP CHALLENGE

After reading this chapter, you should be able to:

- Apply an awareness of the dimensions of diversity and multicultural issues in your everyday life.

- Encourage and support diversity to meet organizational needs.

- Consider the role of cultural values and attitudes in determining how to deal with employees from different cultures or ethnic backgrounds.

- Reduce the difficulties faced by minorities in organizations.

- Break down your personal barriers that may stand in the way of enhancing your level of diversity awareness and appreciation.

Developing Leadership Diversity

Lloyd David Ward is known as a master motivator who listens as carefully as he speaks. His ability to challenge people's thinking without putting them on the defensive, to find areas of common ground, and to unite people toward a shared vision mark him as a gifted and inspiring leader. As PepsiCo Inc. CEO Roger Enrico explained: "He is a good thinker, but he is an exceptional leader." Yet, despite Ward's leadership abilities, it's been a long, hard road from a three-room house with no running water to the executive office at Maytag Corporation. When Ward took over as CEO of Maytag in 1999, he became only the second African American ever to lead a major U.S. corporation.

Ward's story is one of success against all odds, and it reflects the deep-seated racism and discrimination that still pervades much of U.S. society and organizations. Ward refused to let it stand in his way. "There are many who are systematically excluded," he says. "[But] the oppressed have to overcome the prejudices of society. Knock on the door, pull on the handle, and, if you have to, dismantle the hinge." Ward's entire life has been spent overcoming challenges—from his impoverished upbringing and a college roommate who told Ward not to touch any of his things to later facing the hostility of white factory workers and being passed over for promotions he felt he deserved. Yet Ward decided at the start of his career that he wanted to someday be the CEO of a major corporation—an ambition that seemed as likely in the early 1970s as a black president of the United States—and he has achieved his goal through hard work, determination, and drive.

As a successful African American leader, one of Ward's driving passions is to motivate and inspire others, particularly minorities, to excellence. At work, he refers to himself as the coach because he likes teaching others and helping them succeed. His passion also extends to the community. While working for Frito-Lay in Dallas, he persuaded the company to adopt a struggling high school. Ward led a group of employees in tutoring and mentoring the students, brought in local pro athletes to give pep talks, and rewarded students with a trip to an amusement park in the corporate jet. Today, he's playing a major role in an initiative to boost high-school graduation rates among African American high school students to 100 percent. It's an ambitious target, but Ward's never been afraid to set his sights high. "Just because you can't see how to get someplace doesn't mean you don't set the goal."[1]

The face of organizations in America is beginning to change, with women and minorities slowly moving into upper-level leadership positions. However, there are still many challenges for creating diverse organizations. One of the most important roles for leaders in the coming years will be developing a solid base of diverse leadership talent. "In any organization in America, you will see diversity at the bottom of the house," says Roberta (Bobbi) Gutman, vice president and director of global diversity at Motorola. "But to get it higher up takes the clout and the wingspan of company leadership."[2]

Diversity in terms of race, gender, religion, ethnicity, age, nationality, sexual orientation, physical and mental ability, and so forth, is a fact of life for today's organizations. In the United States, the population, the workforce, and the customer base are changing dramatically. According to U.S. Department of Labor statistics, the workforce will soon be dominated by female and minority workers. In addition, there has been a slow but emphatic shift in our attitudes toward racial, ethnic, cultural, or other "differences." In the past, the United States was seen as a "melting pot" where people of different national origins, races, ethnicity, and religions came together and blended to resemble one another. Opportunities for advancement in society and in organizations favored people who fit easily into the mainstream culture. Many times immigrants chose desperate measures, such as changing their last names, abandoning their native languages, and sacrificing their own unique cultures. People were willing to assimilate in order to get ahead.

Today, however, the burden of adaptation rests more on the organization than on the individual. People of different races, nationalities, genders, sexual orientations, religions, and so forth, are no longer willing to give up or hide their own values, beliefs, and ways of doing things in order to fit in. The social landscape of the United States has changed dramatically over the past several decades. This chapter's Leader's Bookshelf examines the role of women in this transformation.

In addition, the tightest labor market in thirty years has left many U.S. companies scrambling to fill even low-level jobs. Human resource departments are increasingly recruiting from a wider, more diverse field, including older workers, the disabled, and welfare recipients, as well as racial and ethnic minorities. Companies are looking for ways to attract and retain these diverse workers, which often means changing the organizational culture. Carlton Yearwood, director of diversity management at Allstate, points out that whereas diversity programs in the past were usually aimed at assimilating cultural differences, the focus today is on accepting differences and finding a way to bring workforce differences together to benefit the organization.[3]

In addition to the increasing heterogeneity of the U.S. population, organizations—and employees—are increasingly operating on a global playing field, which means that people of different races and nationalities are working and living together at an unprecedented level.[4] Talented, educated knowledge workers seek opportunities all over the world, just as organizations search the world for the best minds to help them compete in a global economy. In the previous chapter, we discussed global teams, made up of people from around the world. Radha Basu, for example, leads teams of Hewlett-Packard software writers who work in the U.S., Australia, England, Germany, India, Japan, and Switzerland. Schering AG, the German pharmaceuticals company, employs 56 percent of its 22,000 workers outside its home country. Even the smallest organizations today are often enmeshed with suppliers, competitors, and customers from all over the world.

Successful leaders in an increasingly diverse world have a responsibility to acknowledge and value cultural differences and understand how diversity affects organizational operations and outcomes.[5] This chapter explores the topic of diversity and multiculturalism. We will first define diversity and explore the need for diversity in today's organizations. Then we will look at new styles of leadership and the multicultural challenges brought about by globalization. We will also examine some of the specific challenges facing minority employees and leadership initiatives for supporting and valuing diversity in the workplace.

Everyday Revolutionaries: Working Women and the Transformation of American Life

Sally Helgesen

Sally Helgesen boldly claims that women are the driving force in the transformation of American society. In this study of the lives of women in Naperville, Illinois, Helgesen argues that the life choices women have made over the past few decades have radically changed the workplace, the community, and the nation. Thus, any woman who has ever entered the workforce is an "everyday revolutionary."

Helgesen contrasts domesticity, work, social and religious life, and family composition in 1990s Naperville with William Whyte's classic 1957 study of nearby Park Forest, Illinois. Whyte's "Organization Man" was a wing-tipped, suited junior executive living in a community characterized by sameness, from family configuration to worship, commuting patterns, cars, houses, and leisure activities. The new typical American, Helgesen asserts, is the working woman, whose choices have contributed to the significant diversity that permeates suburban America.

From Well-Defined to Ill-Defined

The society of the Organization Man was characterized by predictable adult life stages and similar choices and experiences of everyone, particularly those of the same age. Today, the well-defined lives of the Organization Man and his neighbors have lost their predictability and given way to lives that individuals find difficult to categorize.

The end of uniformity. Domestic life is more heterogeneous than ever, with a combination of single parents, childless couples, blended families, and a greater range of ages at which marriage and childbearing occur. Careers are also no longer character-ized by stable, linear progress. Women are often in and out of the workforce, and they garner skills and contacts in their communities during their years at home that contribute to the opportunities that arise and the path their careers may follow.

The end of time. When women entered the workforce in significant numbers, the amount of time for other endeavors necessarily dwindled. The pace of business and the demands of multiple life spheres mean that every minute must count. Increasingly particularized needs have given rise to niche products and services, which expand women's options but also increase the time needed to make purchasing decisions.

The beginning of opportunity. The erosion of exclusive male privilege and the increasing need for expert talent and knowledge-based work have given women more opportunities than ever before. Women's concerns have contributed to the work-from-home options made available by an increasing number of employers. The disintegration of the distinction between work and home provides women with an opportunity to manage their tasks in a way that is most coherent for them.

Transformations

The participation of women in the economy has brought about a number of transformations in the basic social organizations of homes, families, and workplaces. Women's approach to work has traditionally been very different, says Helgesen, because they have not been socialized as the Organization Man was. Indeed, the practical approach of women to organizing tasks and the necessity to accommodate women's needs has resulted in a social landscape that is radically different from the predictable, patterned life stages of 1950s society.

Everyday Revolutionaries: Working Women and the Transformation of American Life, by Sally Helgesen, is published by Doubleday.

DIVERSITY TODAY

At 3Com Corporation's modem factory in Morton Grove, Illinois, sixty-five different national flags are displayed, each representing the origin of at least one person who has worked at the plant. The factory's 1200 workers speak more than twenty languages, including Tagalog, Chinese, and Gujarati. On the plant floor, employees must learn to mingle and cooperate, but in the company lunchroom, they often cluster into ethnic and linguistic groups. Semifreddi's, a $7.1 million artisan-bread bakery in Emeryville, California, has only 100 employees, but most of them come from Mexico, Laos, China, Peru, Cambodia, Yemen, and Vietnam. CEO Tom Frainier had to hire translators to help him communicate with workers.[6] In Silicon Valley, where at least one-third of scientists and engineers are immigrants from Europe, Latin America, the Middle East, and Asia, Jesse Jackson has criticized organizations for the low participation of blacks and Hispanics.[7] These examples illustrate both the challenge of diversity and its value for today's organizations.

Definition of Diversity

Workforce diversity means a workforce made up of people with different human qualities or who belong to various cultural groups. From the perspective of individuals, **diversity** refers to differences among people in terms of dimensions such as age, ethnicity, gender, or race. It is important to remember that diversity includes everyone, not just racial or ethnic minorities.

Several important dimensions of diversity are illustrated in Exhibit 11.1. This "diversity wheel" shows the myriad combinations of traits that make up diversity. The inside wheel represents primary dimensions of diversity, which include inborn differences or differences that have an impact throughout one's life.[8] Primary dimensions are core elements through which people shape their self-image and world view. These dimensions are age, race, ethnicity, gender, mental or physical abilities, and sexual orientation. Turn the wheel and these primary characteristics match up with various secondary dimensions of diversity.

Secondary dimensions can be acquired or changed throughout one's lifetime. These dimensions tend to have less impact than those of the core but nevertheless affect a person's self-definition and worldview and have an impact on how the person is viewed by others. For example, Gulf War veterans may have been profoundly affected by their military experience and may be perceived differently from other people. An employee living in a public housing project will be perceived differently from one who lives in an affluent part of town. Secondary dimensions such as work style, communication style, and educational or skill level are particularly relevant in the organizational setting.[9]

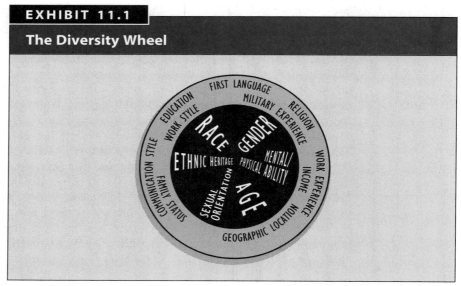

EXHIBIT 11.1

The Diversity Wheel

SOURCE: Marilyn Loden, *Implementing Diversity* (Homewood, IL: Irwin, 1996). Used with permission.

The challenge for organizational leaders is to recognize that each person can bring value and strengths to the workplace based on his or her own unique combination of diversity characteristics. Organizations establish workforce diversity programs to promote the hiring, inclusion, and promotion of diverse employees and to ensure that differences are accepted and respected in the workplace.

The Reality of Diversity

Attitudes toward diversity are changing partly because they have to—organizations are recognizing and welcoming cultural differences as a result of significant changes in our society, including globalization and the changing workforce.[10] The average worker is older now, and many more women, people of color, and immigrants are entering the workforce. Immigration accounted for nearly half of the increase in the labor force in the 1990s and immigrants likely will constitute an increasing share of workers in the coming decades.[11] Figures from the Bureau of Labor Statistics indicate that the number of immigrant workers jumped to 15.7 million in 1999, up 17 percent from three years earlier, and immigrants now make up 12 percent of the total U.S. workforce.[12] In addition, during the first decade of the twenty-first century, minorities will make up about 40 percent of people entering the U.S. workforce, with many of those first-generation immigrants and almost two-thirds female. By 2020, it is estimated that women will comprise fully half of the total full-time U.S. workforce. White males, the majority of workers in the past, already make up less than half the U.S. workforce.[13]

The other factor contributing to increased acceptance of diversity is globalization. In today's world, ideas, capital investments, products, services, and people flow freely and rapidly around the world. Some large multinational corporations, including Canada's Northern Telecom, U.S.-based Coca-Cola, Switzerland's Nestlé, and France's Carrefour, all get a large percentage of their sales from outside their home countries. In this global environment, foreign-born people with global experience have been appointed to lead such U.S. companies as Ford, Gerber, NCR, and Heinz.[14] An unprecedented number of foreign-born CEOs now run major companies in the United States, Britain, and several other countries.[15] Employees with global experience and cultural sensitivity are in high demand in many industries, and almost every employee is dealing with a wider range of cultures than ever before. For example, in the 1970s, most McKinsey & Co. consultants were American. By 1999, McKinsey's chief partner was a foreign national (Rajat Gupta from India), only 40 percent of consultants were American, and the firm's foreign-born consultants came from forty different countries.[16] Companies that ignore diversity will struggle to stay competitive in the global marketplace of the twenty-first century.

The Need for Organizational Diversity

Top leaders of organizations are responding to diversity and new attitudes for a number of reasons beyond the simple fact that shifting demographics make it necessary to do so. There is no question that the workforce is changing and organizations have to change to reflect the new workforce composition. However, there are a number of other reasons leaders need to incorporate and support diversity.

Organizations use internal diversity to meet the needs of diverse customers. Culture plays an important part in determining the goods, entertainment, social services, and household products that people use and buy. A Glass Ceiling Commission study noted that two out of every three people in the United States are minority-group members or females or both, so organizations are recruiting minority employees who can understand how diverse people live and what they want and need.[17] Many companies are developing targeted marketing initiatives aimed at fast-growing minority groups. For example, both Avon and Maybelline have successfully marketed cosmetics to African Americans and Hispanic Americans by hiring members of these minority groups as marketing managers.[18] Diverse employees can also help an organization build better relationships with customers. Consider the benefits Allstate Insurance Company has gained from its diversity initiatives.

IN THE LEAD   Allstate Insurance Company

"Being in a relationship business, how can you not look like and sound like your clients?" asks Phil Lawson, vice president of sales for Allstate Insurance. "It's an obvious competitive advantage when you can mirror the clients that you serve."

Allstate actively recruits, develops, and promotes diverse employees. Its percentages of minority employees, female executives, and minority executives are all well above the national average. However, the company's concept of diversity is a broad one that goes beyond race and gender to include diversity in terms of age, religion, sexual orientation, disability, and other dimensions as well.

Allstate's diversity initiatives have earned the company a string of awards, such as the "1999 Best Companies for Hispanics to Work," the "1998 Top 10 Companies for Minority Managers," and the "1997 Best Companies for Working Mothers." They've also led to some solid business results. A study by Simmons Research Group found that Allstate is the No. 1 life and auto insurer among African Americans and the No. 1 homeowner's and life insurance firm among Hispanic Americans. Allstate's internal measurement systems show a steady increase in the customer base and growing levels of customer satisfaction.

The company's diverse workforce has enabled Allstate to establish solid relationships with culturally and ethnically diverse communities. At the Sunnyside neighborhood office in Queens, New York, one of the most ethnically diverse communities in the country, customers often relate to sales reps like members of their family, consulting them on problems that may have no relation to insurance. Mike Kalkin, the agent who heads up the office (and who is himself from an immigrant family), often recruits employees from within the community because they understand the local people's unique needs. A different situation exists at a northwestern Arkansas office, where a growing retired population means placing more emphasis on serving the needs of older customers.

"We want to outperform the competition," says Joan Crockett, senior vice president for human resources. "[For us] the best talents are diverse because the customers are."[19]

Another need for diversity, also reflected at Allstate, is to develop employee and organizational potential. When organizations support diversity, people feel valued for what they can bring to the organization, which leads to higher morale. It can also produce better relationships at work when employees develop the skills to understand and accept cultural differences. Allstate's diversity training emphasizes that employees can expect to be treated with respect and dignity, but they are also expected to treat others the same way and to develop their business as well as relationship skills to help Allstate succeed.

By seriously recruiting and valuing individuals without regard to race, nationality, gender, age, sexual preference, or physical ability, organizations can attract and retain the best human talent. As mentioned earlier, the U.S. has been experiencing an extremely tight labor market. A strong economy combined with a shrinking labor force meant employees could pick and choose their employers. Companies scrambled to find workers, particularly for entry-level jobs and jobs in fast-growing high-tech industries. In a labor-short environment, "a company that has a reputation for valuing all people does have an advantage," says Solomon Trujillor, CEO of US West, which ranked number 14 on *Fortune* magazine's list of "America's 50 Best Companies for Asians, Blacks, and Hispanics."[20] Organizations looking for the best people have fewer options than in previous years, and the available labor pool is much more diverse. For example, disabled workers can find new opportunities in a tight labor market. Organizations such as Crestar Bank, Honeywell, IBM, and Charles Schwab have developed policies and programs to encourage greater recruitment of disabled workers.[21]

Finally, diversity develops greater organizational flexibility. For one thing, diversity within an organization provides a broader and deeper base of experience for problem solving, creativity, and innovation. Bell Atlantic CEO Ivan Seidenberg promotes diversity at his company primarily because he believes diverse groups make better decisions and bring the creativity and innovation needed to keep pace with massive changes in technology and competition. "If everybody in the room is the same," Seidenberg says, "you'll get a lot fewer arguments and a lot worse answers."[22]

Diversity of thought is essential to today's learning organization, which will be described in Chapter 15. Competitive pressures are challenging all leaders to create organizational environments that foster and support creative thinking and sharing of diverse viewpoints. Diverse groups tend to be more creative than homogeneous groups in part because of the different perspectives people can bring to the problem or issue. One study reported that companies that are high on creativity and innovation have a higher percentage of women and nonwhite male employees than less innovative companies.[23]

One aspect of diversity that is of particular interest in organizations is the way in which women's style of leadership may differ from men's. As women move into higher positions in organizations, it has been observed that they often use a style of leadership that is highly effective in today's turbulent, culturally diverse environment.[24]

WAYS WOMEN LEAD

Leadership traits traditionally associated with white, American-born males include aggressiveness or assertiveness, rational analysis, and a "take charge" attitude. Male leaders tend to be competitive and individualistic and prefer working in vertical hierarchies. They rely on formal authority and position in their dealings with subordinates.

Although women may also demonstrate these traits, research has found that in general, women tend to be more concerned with consensus building, inclusiveness, participation, and caring. Female leaders such as Linda Johnson Rice, president and CEO of Johnson Publishing Company, which owns *Ebony, Jet,* and Fashion Fair Cosmetics, are often more willing to share power and information, to empower employees, and to strive to enhance workers' feelings of self-worth. As Rice puts it, "It is the creative process that I find stimulating, sitting down and letting ideas flow among the different groups. I love the interaction with people."[25]

Professor and author Judy B. Rosener has called this style **interactive leadership**.[26] The leader favors a consensual and collaborative process, and influence derives from relationships rather than position power and authority. Some psychologists have suggested that women may be more relationship-oriented than men because of different psychological needs stemming from early experiences. This difference between the relationship orientations of men and women has sometimes been used to suggest that women cannot lead effectively because they fail to exercise power. However, whereas male leaders may associate effective leadership with a top-down command-and-control process, women's interactive leadership seems appropriate for the future of diversity and learning organizations. Deborah Kent provides an excellent example of the interactive leadership style.

IN THE LEAD   Deborah S. Kent, Ford Motor Company

As plant manager at Ford's assembly plant in Avon Lake, Ohio, Deborah S. Kent's goal is to treat people the way she wants to be treated. Kent is the first woman to head a vehicle assembly plant for Ford. One way top leaders in the U.S. auto industry are trying to regain the industry's competitive edge and reputation for quality is by using a more diverse workforce. As aging factory workers retire, companies are recruiting a wider range of employees whose brainpower and diverse ideas give the company an edge in the fierce global market.

Kent's leadership style is appropriate for just such an organization. Because she is open to all opinions and accessible to all workers, Kent quickly became an energizing force among both peers and subordinates at the Avon Lake factory. When she talks to people, she says, "Give me some feedback and some eye contact. Don't look away from me and say, 'Okay, we have to do this because she says so.' Let's talk about it."

Kent spends a lot of time walking the assembly line, learning from the workers who do the job every day. As plant manager, she is often called upon to make spur-of-the-moment decisions with millions of dollars weighing in the balance. She relies on her gut instincts, on her twenty years of experience in the auto industry, and on what she learns from workers. As she puts it, "It does no good to have a diverse workforce if you don't listen to their opinions and thoughts. I treat people the way I want to be treated."[27]

Kent believes an interactive, nurturing style of leadership is essential for today's organizations, but she doesn't think this type of leadership is gender-specific.

The values associated with interactive leadership, such as inclusion, relationship building, and caring, are generally considered "feminine" values, but they are emerging as valuable qualities for both male and female leaders in the twenty-first century.[28] Many of the "new ideas" being touted by management consultants and business authors have been practiced as a normal way of working by women leaders and business owners for years. For example, a review of research indicates that women leaders in general are more participative and less autocratic, behaviors that are considered well-suited for today's organizations and the new reality for leadership outlined in Chapter 1 of this book.[29]

As illustrated in Exhibit 11.2, one survey of followers rated women leaders significantly higher than men on several characteristics that are crucial for developing fast, flexible, learning organizations. Female leaders were rated as having more idealized influence, providing more inspirational motivation, being more individually considerate, and offering more intellectual stimulation.[30] *Idealized influence* means that followers identify with and want to emulate the leader; the leader is trusted and respected, maintains high standards, and is considered to have power because of who she is rather than what position she holds. *Inspirational motivation* is derived from the leader who appeals emotionally and symbolically to employees' desire to do a good job and help achieve organizational goals. *Individual consideration* means each follower is treated as an individual but all are treated equitably; individual needs are recognized and assignments are delegated to followers to provide learning opportunities. *Intellectual stimulation* means questioning current methods and challenging employees to think in new ways. In addition, women leaders were

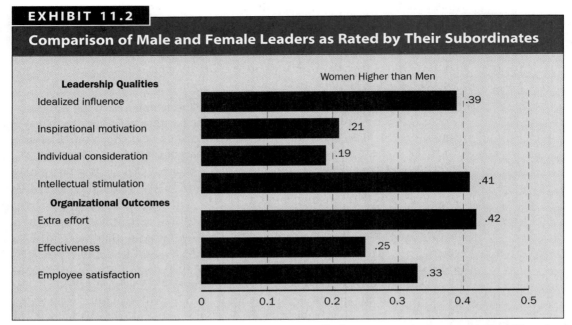

EXHIBIT 11.2

Comparison of Male and Female Leaders as Rated by Their Subordinates

Women Higher than Men

Leadership Qualities

Idealized influence .39

Inspirational motivation .21

Individual consideration .19

Intellectual stimulation .41

Organizational Outcomes

Extra effort .42

Effectiveness .25

Employee satisfaction .33

0   0.1   0.2   0.3   0.4   0.5

NOTE: Ratings of leaders were on a scale of 1–5. Women leaders were rated higher, on average, by the amount indicated for each item.
SOURCE: Based on Bernard M. Bass and Bruce J. Avolio, "Shatter the Glass Ceiling: Women May Make Better Managers," *Human Resource Management* 33, No. 4 (Winter 1994), 549–560.

judged by subordinates as more effective and satisfying to work for and were considered able to generate extra levels of effort from employees.

Again, the interactive leadership style is not exclusive to women. Any leader can learn to adopt a more inclusive style by paying attention to nonverbal behavior and developing skills such as listening, empathy, cooperation, and collaboration.[31]

GLOBAL DIVERSITY

One of the most rapidly increasing sources of diversity in North American organizations is globalization, which means hiring employees in many countries. Globalization means that organizations are confronting diversity issues across a broader stage than ever before. To handle the challenges of global diversity, leaders can develop cross-cultural understanding, the ability to build networks, and the understanding of geopolitical forces. Two significant aspects of global diversity are the sociocultural environment and communication differences.

The Sociocultural Environment

Social and cultural factors are even more perplexing than political and economic factors in foreign countries. For organizations operating globally, cultural differences may provide more potential for difficulties and conflicts than any other source. For example, although an alliance between U.S.-based Upjohn and Pharmacia, based in Stockholm, Sweden, with operations in Italy, seemed like a marriage made in heaven, the merger has floundered because of a clash of cultures. Upjohn leaders scheduled a series of meetings for July and August, unaware that Swedes typically take vacation the entire month of July and Italians the entire month of August. The Swedish partners were annoyed that the Americans had scheduled the meetings, and the Americans were annoyed that they had to cancel them because of their colleagues' vacation plans.[32] Only time will tell if leaders can sort out these cultural differences.

National cultures are intangible, pervasive, and difficult to comprehend. However, it is imperative that leaders in international organizations understand local cultures and deal with them effectively.

SOCIAL VALUE SYSTEMS   Research done by Geert Hofstede on IBM employees in forty countries discovered that mind-set and cultural values on issues such as individualism versus collectivism strongly influence organizational and employee relationships and vary widely among cultures.[33] Exhibit 11.3 shows examples of how countries rate on four significant dimensions.

- *Power distance* High **power distance** means people accept inequality in power among institutions, organizations, and individuals. Low power distance means people expect equality in power. Countries that value high power distance are Malaysia, the Philippines, and Panama. Countries that value low power distance include Denmark, Austria, and Israel.

- *Uncertainty avoidance* High **uncertainty avoidance** means that members of a society feel uncomfortable with uncertainty and ambiguity and thus support beliefs and behavior that promise certainty and conformity. Low uncertainty avoidance means that people have a high tolerance for the unstructured, the unclear, and the unpredictable. High uncertainty avoidance cultures include Greece, Portugal, and Uruguay. Singapore and Jamaica are two countries with low uncertainty avoidance values.

EXHIBIT 11.3				
Rank Orderings of 10 Countries Along Four Dimensions of National Value System				
Country	**Power**[a]	**Uncertainty**[b]	**Individualism**[c]	**Masculinity**[d]
Australia	7	7	2	5
Costa Rica	8 (tie)	2 (tie)	10	9
France	3	2 (tie)	4	7
West Germany	8 (tie)	5	5	3
India	2	9	6	6
Japan	5	1	7	1
Mexico	1	4	8	2
Sweden	10	10	3	10
Thailand	4	6	9	8
United States	6	8	1	4

[a]1 = highest power distance
10 = lowest power distance
[b]1 = highest uncertainty avoidance
10 = lowest uncertainty avoidance
[c]1 = highest individualism
10 = highest collectivism
[d]1 = highest masculinity
10 = highest femininity

SOURCE: From Dorothy Marcic, *Organizational Behavior and Cases*, 4th ed. (St. Paul, MN: West, 1995). Based on Geert Hofstede, *Culture's Consequences* (London: Sage Publications, 1984); and *Cultures and Organizations: Software of the Mind* (New York:McGraw-Hill, 1991).

- *Individualism and collectivism* **Individualism** reflects a value for a loosely knit social framework in which individuals are expected to take care of themselves. **Collectivism** is a preference for a tightly knit social framework in which people look out for one another and organizations protect their members' interests. Countries with individualist values include the United States, Great Britain, and Canada. Countries with collectivist values are Guatemala, Ecuador, and Panama.

- *Masculinity and femininity* **Masculinity** reflects a preference for achievement, heroism, assertiveness, work centrality, and material success. **Femininity** reflects the values of relationships, cooperation, group decision making, and quality of life. Japan, Austria, Mexico, and Germany are countries with strong masculine values. Countries with strong feminine values include Sweden, Norway, Denmark, and the former Yugoslavia. Both men and women subscribe to the dominant value in masculine or feminine cultures.

Social value differences can significantly affect leadership, working relationships, and organizational functioning. Terry Neill, a managing partner at Andersen Consulting's London-based change management practice, uses Hofstede's findings in his work with companies. Based on his experiences with global companies such as Unilever PLC, Shell Oil, and British Petroleum, Neill points out that the Dutch, Irish, Americans, and British are generally quite comfortable with open argument. However, Japanese and other Asian employees often feel uneasy or even threatened by such directness.[34] In many Asian countries, leaders perceive the organization as a large family and emphasize cooperation through networks of personal relationships. In contrast, leaders in Germany and other central European countries typically strive to run their organizations as impersonal well-oiled machines.[35] How leaders handle these and other cultural differences has tremendous impact on the satisfaction and effectiveness of diverse employees.

OTHER CULTURAL CHARACTERISTICS   Other cultural characteristics that can affect international leadership are language, religion, attitudes, social organization, and education. Some countries, such as India, are characterized by *linguistic pluralism,* meaning several languages are spoken there. Other countries may rely heavily on spoken rather than written language. Religion includes sacred objects, philosophical attitudes toward life, taboos, and rituals. Attitudes toward time, space, authority, and achievement can all affect organizations. People from urban cultures tend to follow rigid time schedules, for example, while those from rural cultures are less concerned with clock time, which can lead to disputes regarding tardiness. In some cultures, the amount of space an employee is given to work in is a status symbol, while other cultures treat space as inconsequential. Elements of social organization include kinship and families, status systems, and opportunities for social mobility. For example, leadership in Japan is a way to move up in the social "pecking order." Age commands more status and respect in Europe and the Middle East than in the United States.[36]

Leaders working in a global context have found that these cultural differences cannot be ignored. Leaders at Chrysler and Daimler-Benz AG, which merged to form Daimler-Chrysler, are learning the impact social and cultural factors can have on an organization.

IN THE LEAD   DaimlerChrysler

Two years after the former Daimler-Benz AG and Chrysler Corporation joined to form DaimlerChrysler, the new organization remains essentially two separate companies, one German and one American. The traditional top-down authoritarian culture of Daimler-Benz almost immediately conflicted with Chrysler's more open culture. The desirable goal of combining the precision of German engineering and control with an American-style environment of open communications between leaders and employees has so far not been achieved.

Many American workers perceive their German colleagues as rigid, formal, and humorless. As one German expatriate said, Americans seem to characterize the Germans as "running around in steel helmets and always saying 'Yes, General.'" On the other hand, German employees are accused of stereotyping Americans as "cowboys who shoot from the hip." The Germans think Americans make decisions much too quickly; they prefer a more analytical, systematic approach. The Americans think the Germans are too slow-moving and inflexible. Another problem in merging the two companies has been the difficulty in persuading American workers to accept expatriate assignments. Chrysler was a much less globalized company than Daimler-Benz, and leaders are having a hard time convincing American workers of the value of global experience. Many don't want to leave their nice homes in the Midwest for smaller apartments or houses in Germany, where real estate is much more expensive. Despite a generous pay package, the company struggled to fill just sixty expatriate assignments.

Daimler-Benz leaders point out that they successfully blended two cultures at the Mercedes-Benz plant in Vance, Alabama, which CEO Andreas Renschler refers to as "a melting pot of styles." The organization faced the same cultural difficulties there, only on a smaller scale. Leaders are hoping to use what they learned about working with another culture there to help smooth the merger with Chrysler.[37]

Many organizations have discovered that cultural differences create more barriers than any other factor to successful communication and collaboration in organizations. However, the potential rewards to overcoming these barriers are significant. The most successful organizations in a global world are those that can operate in a truly global fashion, blending different races, nationalities, and ethnic groups into a powerful whole. Dieter Schmeier of Schering AG, the German pharmaceuticals company, struggled mightily with cultural differences during a diverse team program at Harvard, where he worked and lived in a dorm with executives from the United States, Australia,

Canada, China, India, the Philippines, and South Africa. However, the experience convinced him that there was tremendous learning power in cultural diversity. He returned to Germany with a plan to mix Schering employees from numerous cultures so they could grow and become multicultural "through a critical mass of associations with strangers." Schmeier believes his company's future depends on embracing cultural diversity.[38]

Leadership Implications

Leaders can be aware of cultural and subcultural differences in order to lead effectively in a diverse environment. Chapter 3 examined contingency theories of leadership that explain the relationship between leader style and a given situation. It is important for leaders to recognize that culture impacts both style and the leadership situation. For example, in cultures with high uncertainty avoidance, a leadership situation with high task structure as described in Chapter 3 is favorable, but those in low uncertainty avoidance cultures prefer less structured work situations.

In addition, how behavior is perceived differs from culture to culture. To criticize a subordinate in private directly is considered appropriate behavior in individualistic societies such as the United States. However, in Japan, which values collectivism over individualism, the same leader behavior would be seen as inconsiderate. Japanese employees lose face if they are criticized directly by a supervisor. The expectation is that people will receive criticism information from peers rather than directly from the leader.[39] Research into how the contingency models apply to cross-cultural situations is sparse. However, all leaders need to be aware of the impact culture may have and consider cultural values in their dealings with employees. As we move into the twenty-first century, global leadership skills, cultural sensitivity, and the flexibility to adapt to different ways of thinking and behaving will become increasingly important.

CHALLENGES MINORITIES FACE

Valuing diversity and enabling all individuals to develop their unique talents is difficult to achieve. **Ethnocentrism,** the belief that one's own culture and subculture are inherently superior to other cultures, is a natural tendency of most people.[40] Moreover, the organizational climate in the United States still tends to reflect values, behaviors, assumptions, and expectations based on the experience of a rather homogeneous, white, middle-class male workforce. Many leaders relate to people in the organization as if everyone shares similar values, beliefs, motivations, and attitudes about work and life. This assumption is typically false even when dealing with people who share the same cultural background. Ethnocentric viewpoints combined with a standard set of cultural assumptions and practices create a number of challenges for minority employees and leaders.

UNEQUAL EXPECTATIONS/DIFFERENCE AS DEFICIENCY The one-best-way approach leads to a mind-set that views difference as deficiency or dysfunction.[41] The perception by most career women and minorities is that no matter how many college degrees they earn, how many hours they work, how they dress, or how much effort and enthusiasm they invest, they are never considered to "have the right stuff." For example, a Hispanic executive, in discussing the animosity he felt at one job, said, "The fact that I graduated first in my class didn't make as much difference as the fact that I looked different."[42] If the standard of quality were based, for instance, on being white and male, anything else would be seen as deficient. This dilemma is often difficult for white men to understand because most of them are not intentionally racist and sexist. IBM set up eight task forces—one each for white males, African Americans, Asians, disabled people, gays and lesbians, Hispanics, Native Americans, and women. When asked to define their primary objective, the leader of the white male group announced that his team's objective was to make sure the other seven groups didn't see them as the problem. "He made the comment humorously, so everybody laughed," said Ted Childs, an African American who serves as IBM's vice president of global workforce diversity. "But we also saw the value of his comment. . . . That provided a foundation for enormous thought—and enormous cooperation."[43] Many men feel extremely uncomfortable with the prevailing attitudes and stereotypes, but don't know how to change them. These attitudes are deeply rooted in our society as well as in our organizations. Only through conscious leadership such as that at IBM can the status quo be changed.

Women and minorities also generally feel that they are not evaluated by the same standards as their male counterparts. For example, where having a family is often considered a plus for a male executive, it is perceived as a hindrance for a woman who wants to reach the top. One term heard frequently is the *mommy track,* which implies that a woman's commitment to her children limits her commitment to the company or her ability to handle the rigors of corporate leadership.[44]

LIVING BICULTURALLY Research on differences between whites and blacks has focused on issues of biculturalism and how it affects employees' access to information, level of respect and appreciation, and relation to superiors and subordinates. **Biculturalism** can be defined as the sociocultural skills and attitudes used by racial minorities as they move back and forth between the dominant culture and their own ethnic or racial culture.[45] More than ninety years ago, W. E. B. DuBois referred to this as a "double-consciousness. . . . One always feels his twoness—an American, a Negro; two souls, two thoughts, two unreconciled strivings. . . ."[46] In general, African Americans feel less accepted in their organizations, perceive themselves to have less discretion on their jobs, receive lower ratings on job performance, experience lower levels of job satisfaction, and reach career plateaus earlier than whites.

Racism in the workplace often shows up in subtle ways—the disregard by a subordinate for an assigned chore; a lack of urgency in completing an important assignment; the ignoring of comments or suggestions made at a meeting. Black leaders often struggle daily with the problem of delegating authority and responsibility to employees who show them little respect. Other minority groups struggle with biculturalism as well. They find themselves striving to adopt behaviors and attitudes that will help them be successful in the white-dominated corporate world while at the same time maintaining their ties to their racial or ethnic community and culture. J. D. Hokoyama started a nonprofit organization to teach Asian Americans how to be bicultural.

IN THE LEAD   ## J. D. Hokoyama, Leadership Education For Asian Pacifics, Inc.

Asian Americans who aspire to leadership positions are often frustrated by the stereotype that they are hard workers but not executive material. Many times Asian Americans are perceived as too quiet or not assertive enough. One Chinese American woman says her boss claimed she wasn't strong enough for an executive-level job because she didn't raise her voice in discussions as he did.

J. D. Hokoyama, a 47-year-old Japanese American, started a nonprofit organization to try to change these perceptions. Hokoyama runs workshops to alert Asian Americans to the ways in which their communication style may hold them back in the American workplace. Participants are taught to use more eye contact, start more sentences with "I," and use more assertive body language. Many Asian Americans are offended by the implication that they should abandon their cultural values to succeed. Hokoyama, however, looks at this as a way to help more Asian Americans adjust their style so they can move into leadership positions. Pauline Ho, a senior technical staff member at Sandia National Laboratories, agrees. She has seen the obstacles her parents and other immigrants faced and knows how difficult it is to succeed in the mainstream culture: "They want to get ahead, but they don't understand what they should be doing."

Hokoyama says Asian Americans and other minorities should not have to give up their own culture; however, he believes that only by understanding the differences between Asian values and mainstream American values can more Asians and Asian Americans move into leadership positions.[47]

The workshops offered by Leadership Education for Asian Pacifics, Inc. are a sad commentary on the opportunities for minorities in America's organizations. Many minorities feel they have a chance for career advancement only by becoming bicultural or abandoning their native cultures altogether. Culturally sensitive leadership can work to remove these barriers.

THE GLASS CEILING   Another issue is the **glass ceiling,** an invisible barrier that separates women and minorities from top leadership positions. They can look up through the ceiling, but prevailing attitudes are invisible obstacles to their own advancement. Although a few women and minorities have recently moved into highly visible top leadership positions, evidence that the glass ceiling still exists is that most women and minorities are clustered at the bottom of the organizational hierarchy. Even in the technology sector, where opportunities for diverse employees are considered more abundant, only 7 percent of top officers in *Fortune* 500 technology firms are female. Overall, women make up 12.5 percent of corporate officers in *Fortune* 500 companies, and 7.3 percent of managers in line positions. Statistics for women of color are even more dismal. Although women of color make up 23 percent of the U.S. women's workforce, they account for only 14 percent of the women in all management positions.[48] Moreover, about 65 percent of women of color surveyed said they plan to leave their management positions because of their organizations' failure to address subtle bias in the workplace.[49]

Women and minorities also earn considerably less than their male peers, with women of color earning the least. As women move up the career ladder, the wage gap widens; at the level of vice president, a woman's average salary is 42 percent less than that of her male counterpart.[50]

The glass ceiling persists because top-level corporate culture in most organizations still revolves around traditional management thinking, a vertical hierarchy populated by white, American-born males, who often hire and promote people who look, act, and think like them. Although hiring and promotion patterns may be well intended, women and minority employees are often relegated to less visible positions and projects; hence, their work fails to come to the attention of top executives. Recent research has suggested the existence of "glass walls" that serve as invisible barriers to important lateral movement within the organization. Glass walls bar experience in areas such as line supervision or general management that would enable women and minorities to advance to senior-level positions.[51] In general, women and minorities feel that they must work harder and perform at higher levels than their white male counterparts in order to be noticed, recognized, fully accepted, and promoted.

THE OPPORTUNITY GAP   In some cases, people fail to advance to higher levels in organizations because they don't have the necessary education and skills. A final challenge is the lack of opportunities for many minorities to obtain the same level of education as white, American-born individuals. Only 62 percent of Hispanics, the fastest growing segment of the U.S. population, complete high school. Both African Americans and Hispanics lag behind whites in college attendance, and only 10 percent of adults with disabilities have graduated from college.[52] Eric Adolphe, president and CEO of Optimus Corporation, who managed to stay in college because of a scholarship from the National Association Council for Minorities in Engineering, recalls many of the kids he grew up with in New York City: "There are a lot of people more gifted than myself who never made it—not because of their lack of ability, but because of their lack of opportunity."[53] Many African Americans and other minorities also have fewer skills because of inadequate inner city schools and lack of exposure to the ideas, technologies, and disciplines that are needed to succeed in today's knowledge-based organizations. There is not yet a level playing field in our schools and in society, which is in turn reflected in unequal opportunities for diverse employees in organizations. Some companies and leaders, such as Lloyd Ward, described at the beginning of this chapter, are taking the lead to ensure that minorities get the education, skills, and opportunities they need to participate fully in today's economy.

LEADERSHIP INITIATIVES TOWARD ORGANIZATIONAL DIVERSITY

One goal for today's global organizations is to ensure that *all* employees—women, ethnic and racial minorities, gay people, the disabled, the elderly, as well as white males—are given equal opportunities in the workplace.[54] Strong, culturally sensitive leadership can move organizations toward diversity, where all people are valued and respected for the unique abilities they can bring to the workplace.

Organizational Stages of Diversity Awareness

Organizations as well as individuals vary in their sensitivity and openness to other cultures, attitudes, values, and ways of doing things. Exhibit 11.4 shows a model of five organizational stages of diversity awareness and action.[55] The continuum ranges from meeting the minimum legal requirements regarding affirmative action and sexual harassment to valuing diversity as an inherent part of the organizational culture.

Stage 1 organizations and leaders consider themselves successful if their legal record is good. Women and minorities are viewed primarily as a "problem"

EXHIBIT 11.4

Evolution of Organizational Diversity Awareness and Action

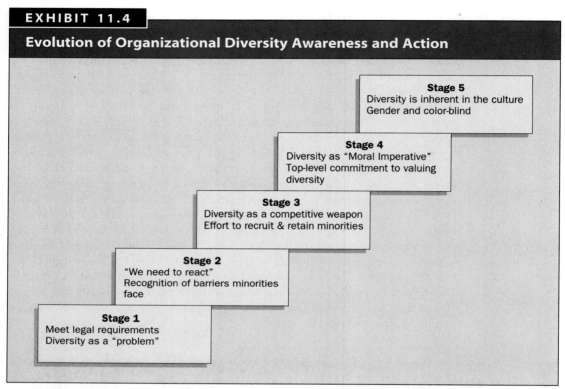

Stage 5
Diversity is inherent in the culture
Gender and color-blind

Stage 4
Diversity as "Moral Imperative"
Top-level commitment to valuing
diversity

Stage 3
Diversity as a competitive weapon
Effort to recruit & retain minorities

Stage 2
"We need to react"
Recognition of barriers minorities
face

Stage 1
Meet legal requirements
Diversity as a "problem"

SOURCE: Adapted from *America's Competitive Secret: Utilizing Women as a Management Strategy*, p. 142 by Judy B. Rosener. Copyright 1995 by J. B. Rosener. Used by permission of Oxford University Press, Inc.

that must be dealt with, and typically there are only a few minorities in executive-level jobs to meet legal requirements. At Stage 2, leaders become aware that women and minorities face challenges not faced by white males, and that higher absenteeism and turnover rates among minorities are detrimental to the organization. However, awareness is seldom translated into action until the organization moves into Stage 3. Leaders become proactive and acknowledge that addressing issues of gender, race, disability, and so forth, is important not just for the minority employees but for the health of the organization. They recognize that women and minorities can bring needed insight into developing and marketing products for new customers, so they look for ways to attract and retain high-quality minority employees. In Stage 3 organizations, more women and minorities make it to high-level positions, and the organization begins providing some diversity awareness training to all employees. The motivation for diversity at Stage 3 is to remain competitive.

When the organization reaches Stage 4, there is a top-level leadership commitment to broad equality and community. Leaders rectify the undervaluation and underutilization of women and minorities. Top leaders allocate significant resources for diversity training and other programs to bring about organizational change. A genuine attempt is made to develop policies and practices that are inclusive rather than exclusive, and executives at all levels are generally required to provide evidence that they are recruiting, retaining, and promoting quality female and minority employees. For example, at Allstate Insurance, described earlier, leaders are held responsible for proactive hiring and promotion. In addition, a "diversity index" that probes how well leaders are "walking the talk" about a bias-free workplace, cultural sensitivity, respect for all individuals, and so forth, determines 25 percent of a manager's merit pay.

Stage 5 organizations are gender- and color-blind. All employees are judged on their competence, and stereotypes and prejudices are completely erased. No group of employees feels different or disadvantaged. This stage represents the ideal organization. Although it may seem unreachable, many of today's best organizations are striving to reach this stage. Ernst & Young LLP, one of the Big Five professional services firms, illustrates the evolution of a company through the stages of diversity awareness.

IN THE LEAD   Ernst & Young LLP

Ernst & Young has long had a sterling reputation in the field of accounting and consulting services, but the firm is striving to become a leader in diversity as well. Like most organizations, Ernst & Young once viewed diversity primarily as a matter of complying with EEO and affirmative action laws (Stage 1 of diversity awareness). However, even though leaders worked hard to bring women and minorities into the organization, they began to realize that E&Y was losing female and minority professionals at a much higher rate than white males. Top leaders authorized a two-year study to help them understand the pressures that minority groups were feeling and how to address them (Stage 2).

In Stage 3 of diversity awareness, E&Y's chairman and CEO Phil Laskawy launched two diversity initiatives: the Office of Minority Recruitment and Retention, under the leadership of Allen A. Boston, a partner and African American, and the Office for Retention, directed by Deborah K. Holmes, a lawyer who had been involved in the diversity study. The first objective was to increase recruitment and retention of women and minorities as a way to remain competitive. The diversity initiatives have made significant progress. By 1999, 7 percent of Ernst & Young's partners and senior managers were members of minority groups, and the percentage of minorities recruited each year had risen from around 10 percent to around 24 percent. The number of women in senior positions is also edging up.

Now, Ernst & Young is moving into Stage 4 of diversity awareness and action. Top leaders have allocated significant resources to training and mentoring programs, work-life balance initiatives, and other programs. Even more significantly, through Boston's efforts the company is providing for minority scholarships and programs at both undergraduate and graduate institutions. The company also sponsors two organizations that give minority high school students a chance to get an inside look at the accounting and engineering professions. By encouraging closer ties between E&Y and universities and minority organizations, Boston hopes to give young minority members opportunities they otherwise might not have. Ernst & Young is still early in Stage 4, but leaders are committed to keep the firm moving in the right direction— toward full equality and opportunity for everyone.[56]

Barriers to Evolution

Leaders face a number of personal and organizational barriers to achieving a high level of diversity awareness, acceptance, and appreciation. Four of these barriers are discussed below.[57]

ETHNOCENTRISM Recall that ethnocentrism is the belief that one's own group and subculture are inherently superior to other groups and cultures. Viewing one's own culture as the best culture is a natural tendency among most people and contributes to cultural cohesiveness. However, ethnocentrism makes it difficult to value diversity because it tends to produce a monoculture, a culture that accepts only one way of doing things and one set of values and beliefs. The goal for organizations seeking cultural diversity is to develop *ethnorelativism*, or the belief that all groups, cultures, and subcultures are inherently equal.

STEREOTYPES AND PREJUDICE Carried to an extreme, ethnocentrism becomes outright prejudice, which is perhaps the single biggest obstacle to providing equal opportunities for women and minorities. *Prejudice* can be defined as the tendency to view people who are different from the mainstream in terms of sex, race, ethnic background, or physical ability as being deficient. Prejudice is the assumption, without evidence, that minorities are inherently inferior, less competent at their jobs, and less suitable for leadership positions. Recent surveys have found that stereotypes are still prevalent in our society, and prejudice is a contributing factor in most other barriers to accepting and valuing diversity in the workplace.[58]

THE "WHITE MALE" CLUB The work environment for many minorities is lonely, unfriendly, and stressful, which is partly attributed to the so-called white male club. Particularly in executive-level positions, women and minorities are heavily outnumbered by white men, many of whom treat them differently from the way they treat their white male colleagues. Women and minorities may be excluded, often unintentionally, from social functions, lunches, and even regular office banter. In addition, there are few role models or mentors for women and minorities trying to reach senior-level positions. Minorities feel they have no one to talk to about their fears, their mistakes, and even their ideas for the organization. They have difficulty fitting into the white male club, yet if they remain isolated, they are perceived as aloof and arrogant.

THE PARADOX OF DIVERSITY Leaders also face a significant challenge in simultaneously promoting diversity and maintaining a strong, unified corporate culture.[59] Homogeneous organizations provide a firmer basis for building a strong culture, which is considered critical to organizational success. One reason is that, in general, people feel more comfortable and satisfied dealing with others who are like themselves. Also, in many communities, ethnic groups still do not interact socially, and this carries over into unfamiliarity and discomfort in the workplace. Diverse racial and ethnic groups within a work environment can be competitive with and even antagonistic toward one another, and the time and energy leaders spend dealing with interpersonal issues dramatically increases in a diverse environment. Leaders have to work harder than ever to unite employees around a common purpose while also allowing individual differences to flourish.

ACTUAL CULTURAL DIFFERENCES Finally, real cultural differences can cause problems in the workplace. As we discussed earlier in the chapter, culture influences attitudes toward such things as time, physical space, and authority. Leaders may face enormous challenges in relating to employees from different cultures. For example, most organizations will not accept routine tardiness or absenteeism from employees simply because their time orientation is culturally different from the mainstream values.

As another example of how cultural differences complicate leadership, one supervisor declined a gift from a new employee, an immigrant who wanted to show gratitude for her job. He was concerned about ethics and explained the company's policy about not accepting gifts. The employee was so insulted that she quit, even though she desperately needed the work.[60] The potential for communication difficulties is much greater in heterogeneous groups, leading to misunderstandings, conflict, and anxiety for leaders as well as employees.

LEADERSHIP SOLUTIONS

In the past, the pressure to change has been on the new employee coming into the workplace. Today, however, the idea that diverse individuals have to assimilate into the mainstream culture is dead. The pressure is now on organizations to change, and strong leadership is needed. Many of today's leaders have had little experience with people different from themselves and are unprepared to deal with emerging diversity in the workplace. The benefits of diversity are not automatic, and working with people different from oneself can be difficult and frustrating. Without strong leadership, increased cultural diversity can lead to decreased work effort and lower organizational performance. The Living Leadership box urges leaders to first clear their own minds of prejudice.

Leading Diverse Organizations

To successfully lead in diverse organizations, leaders must develop personal characteristics that support diversity. Four characteristics have been identified as important for leadership of diverse organizations.[61]

- A personal, long-range vision that recognizes and supports a diverse organizational community. Leaders should have long-term plans to include employees of various ethnic and cultural groups, races, ages, and so on at all levels of the organization. In addition, they express the vision through symbols and rituals that reinforce the value of a diverse workforce.

- A broad knowledge of the dimensions of diversity and awareness of multicultural issues. Leaders need a basic knowledge of the primary dimensions of diversity as discussed earlier in this chapter: age, race, ethnicity, gender, mental or physical abilities, and sexual orientation, as well as some understanding of secondary dimensions. Knowledge is also put into action through the use of inclusive language and showing respect for differences.

- An openness to change themselves. Leaders in diverse organizations encourage feedback from their employees, can accept criticism, and are willing to change their behavior.

- Mentoring and empowerment of diverse employees. Leaders take an active role in creating opportunities for all employees to use their unique abilities. They also offer honest feedback and coaching as needed, and they reward those in the organization who show respect to culturally different employees.

LIVING LEADERSHIP

Good Leadership

Lingyuan said:

"Good leaders make the mind of the community their mind, and never let their minds indulge in private prejudices. They make the eyes and ears of the community their eyes and ears, and never let their eyes and ears be partial.

"Thus are they ultimately able to realize the will of the community and comprehend the feelings of the community.

"When they make the mind of the community their own mind, good and bad are to the leaders what good and bad are to the community. Therefore the good is not wrongly so, and the bad is unmistakably so.

"Then why resort to airing what is in your own mind, and accepting the flattery of others?

"Once you use the community's ears and eyes for your ears and eyes, then the people's perceptivity is your own—thus it is so clear nothing is not seen, nothing is not heard.

"So then why add personal views and stubbornly invite hypocrisy and deception from others?

"When they expressed their own hearts and added their own views, the accomplished sages were striving to find their own faults, to have the same wishes as the people of the community, and to be without bias."

SOURCE: Thomas Cleary, trans., *Zen Lessons: The Art of Leadership* (Boston: Shambhala Press, 1989), 45–46. Used with permission.

Once leaders examine and change themselves, they can lead change in the organization. In the following sections, we will briefly discuss two major actions that can help organizations stretch to accommodate and support increasing cultural diversity: changing corporate culture and providing diversity training.

CHANGING CORPORATE CULTURE   A leader's ability to create and communicate a shared vision and values for the organization becomes even more critical in an organization made up of diverse individuals. Leaders are also challenged to ensure that the organizational culture is continually open to new and different ideas and ways of doing things, while maintaining a focus on the common purpose and vision.[62] Shaping culture and values will be discussed in detail in Chapter 14.

Today's organizational cultures for the most part reflect the white male model of doing business. As a result of this mismatch between the dominant culture and the growing employee population of minorities and women, many employees' talents and abilities are not being fully used. To help an organization thrive in today's increasingly diverse environment, leaders should develop a culture that supports the inclusion and full participation of all individuals, regardless of race, gender, age, cultural or ethnic group, physical ability, or other characteristics. One way leaders begin to shift cultural values is by using symbols, such as encouraging and celebrating the promotion of minorities. They also examine the unwritten rules and assumptions in the organization. What are the values that exemplify the existing culture? What are the myths and stereotypes about minorities? Are unwritten rules communicated from one person to another in ways that exclude women and minority workers?

The most important element in changing the corporate culture to one that values diversity is leadership. The commitment of top leaders has been essential to changing the culture at Texaco.

IN THE LEAD   Peter Bijur, Texaco

Peter Bijur, CEO of Texaco, knew that nothing less than a total overhaul of the culture could begin to erase Texaco's image as the embodiment of corporate racism. Texaco paid a whopping $175 million to settle a racial discrimination suit, but the details that came out during and after the settlement hurt even more. Besides exposing blatant acts of racism by Texaco managers and employees, the incident also revealed examples of institutional racism, such as hundreds of minority employees being paid less than the minimum salary for their job category. Bijur moved quickly and decisively. "I drew a line in the sand and said that we will not tolerate disrespect," Bijur says. "Some people acted inappropriately; they are no longer here."

Texaco is in the midst of a remarkable transformation, which some experts believe could make the company a model for diversity. A detailed, well-scripted plan for changing the corporate culture was hammered out by Texaco executives in collaboration with members of an independent task force required by the lawsuit to monitor the company's diversity efforts. Bijur set specific goals with specific timetables, and he made it clear to top executives as well as managers and supervisors throughout the company that their future career advancement would be determined by how well they implemented the new diversity initiatives. Compensation is also tied to how effectively managers "create openness and inclusion in the work place."

To further spur culture change, Bijur recruited several eminent African Americans to join Texaco's top ranks. Recruiting African American executives wasn't easy in the wake of the racial discrimination scandal, but Bijur's ardent personal commitment to changing Texaco's culture convinced them to join in the quest. "It's obvious that top-of-the-house commitment is there and will remain there," said Angela E. Vallot, a top Washington, D.C. attorney who came on board to head up Texaco's diversity programs.

Texaco still has a long way to go, but Bijur—and many others both inside and outside the company—see concrete signs of a major cultural shift.[63]

EXHIBIT 11.5

Stages of Personal Diversity Awareness

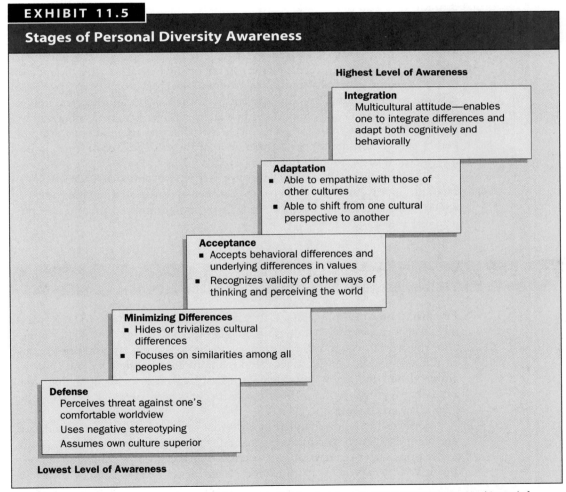

Highest Level of Awareness

Integration
Multicultural attitude—enables one to integrate differences and adapt both cognitively and behaviorally

Adaptation
- Able to empathize with those of other cultures
- Able to shift from one cultural perspective to another

Acceptance
- Accepts behavioral differences and underlying differences in values
- Recognizes validity of other ways of thinking and perceiving the world

Minimizing Differences
- Hides or trivializes cultural differences
- Focuses on similarities among all peoples

Defense
Perceives threat against one's comfortable worldview
Uses negative stereotyping
Assumes own culture superior

Lowest Level of Awareness

SOURCE: Based on M. Bennett, "A Developmental Approach to Training for Intercultural Sensitivity," *International Journal of Intercultural Relations* 10 (1986), 179–196.

DIVERSITY AWARENESS TRAINING Many organizations provide **diversity awareness training** to help employees become aware of their own cultural boundaries, their prejudices and stereotypes, so they can learn to work together successfully. Leaders in these companies understand that their future competitiveness may depend on how well they handle diversity issues.[64]

People vary in their sensitivity and openness to other cultures and ways of doing things. Exhibit 11.5 shows a model of five stages of individual diversity awareness, which are roughly comparable to the organizational stages shown in Exhibit 11.4. The continuum ranges from a defensive, ethnocentric attitude to a complete understanding and acceptance of people's differences. The model can help leaders assess their own and employees' openness to change. People at different levels may require different kinds of training. A primary aim of diversity awareness training is to help people recognize that their own hidden and overt biases direct their thinking about specific individuals and groups. Diversity awareness programs also focus on helping people of varying backgrounds communicate effectively with one another and understand the language and context used in dealing with people from other cultural groups. One of the most important aspects of diversity training is to bring together people of differing perspectives so that they can engage in learning new interpersonal communication skills.

Diversity presents many challenges, yet it also provides leaders with an exciting opportunity to build organizations as integrated communities in which all people feel encouraged, respected, and committed to common purposes and goals.

SUMMARY AND INTERPRETATION

The main point of this chapter is that diversity is a fact of life in today's world, and leaders can create change in organizations to keep up. The U.S. population, the workforce, and the customer base are changing. In addition, people of different national origins, races, and religions are no longer willing to be assimilated into the mainstream culture. Organizations are also operating in an increasingly global world, which means dealing with diversity on a broader stage than ever before.

Dimensions of diversity are both primary, such as age, gender, and race, and secondary, such as education, marital status, and religion. There are several reasons why organizations are recognizing the need to value and support diversity. Diversity helps organizations build better relationships with diverse customers and helps develop employee potential. Diversity provides a broader and deeper base of experience for creativity and problem solving, which is essential to building learning organizations. One aspect of diversity of particular interest is women's style of leadership, referred to as interactive leadership. The values associated with interactive leadership, such as inclusion, relationship building, and caring, are emerging as valuable qualities for both male and female leaders in the twenty-first century.

Another important idea in this chapter is global diversity. Leaders can be aware of the impact culture may have and consider cultural differences in their dealings with followers. Within organizations, people who do not fit the mainstream white, U.S.-born, male culture face a number of challenges, including unequal expectations, the need to live biculturally, the glass ceiling, and the opportunity gap.

Organizations generally evolve through stages of diversity awareness and action, ranging from minimum efforts to meet affirmative action guidelines to valuing diversity as an integral part of organizational culture. The barriers to successful evolution include ethnocentrism, prejudice, the so-called "White Male" club, the paradox of diversity, and actual cultural differences. Strong, culturally sensitive leadership is the only way organizations can move through the stages of diversity awareness. Leaders first change themselves by developing personal characteristics that support diversity. They use these personal characteristics to change the organization. The ultimate goal for leaders in the twenty-first century is to build organizations as integrated communities in which all people feel encouraged, respected, and committed to common purposes and goals.

KEY TERMS

workforce diversity
diversity
interactive leadership
power distance
uncertainty avoidance

individualism
collectivism
masculinity
femininity

ethnocentrism
biculturalism
glass ceiling
diversity awareness training

DISCUSSION QUESTIONS

1. How might a leader's role and responsibility change as a company becomes more diverse? Explain.

2. How might diversity within the organization ultimately lead to better problem solving and greater creativity?

3. What is interactive leadership and why may this approach be increasingly important in the twenty-first century?

4. Discuss ways in which low power distance as a social value among followers could affect their interaction with leaders who display high power distance.

5. Why do you think the glass ceiling persists in organizations?

6. What is the paradox of diversity and how could it be a barrier to valuing and supporting diversity within organizations?

7. In preparing organizations to accept and value diversity, do you think leaders should focus primarily on changing the underlying culture or on diversity awareness training? Discuss.

8. Recall a company you worked for. At what stage of diversity awareness (refer to Exhibit 11.4) was it? Explain.

9. Do you think people and organizations can ever become gender and color-blind? Discuss.

LEADERSHIP DEVELOPMENT: Personal Feedback

A Passive Bias Quiz

	Yes	No
1. What you notice first about people around you are the characteristics that make them different from you.	___	___
2. You make it a general rule never to discuss the subjects of race, ethnicity, politics, age, religion, gender, and sexuality when you are at work.	___	___
3. When others make bigoted remarks or jokes, you either laugh or say nothing because you don't want to seem sensitive or self-righteous.	___	___
4. When you see media that are targeted at an ethnic, gender, or religious group that you do not represent, you usually ignore them.	___	___
5. When you look for a mentor or protégé, you pick someone like yourself.	___	___
6. If someone tells you about a cultural difference that you have never heard of, you rarely ask questions.	___	___
7. You are affiliated with organizations that practice subtle discrimination, but you say nothing because you didn't create the rules.	___	___
8. Before you hire someone for a position, you have a vague picture in mind of what the ideal candidate would look like.	___	___

9. Your conversations make use of phrases like "you people" or "our kind."   ___ ___

10. You avoid talking about cultural differences when dealing with people different from you because you're afraid of saying the wrong thing.   ___ ___

11. When complimenting someone from a different background, you might tell them, "You are nothing like the others" or "I really don't think of you as a _____."   ___ ___

12. There are people in your organization whom you like and respect but whom you would feel uncomfortable introducing to your family or close friends.   ___ ___

Scoring:

Give yourself five points for each "yes" answer.

Interpretation:

The appropriate score for today's world is "0." However, if you scored less than 20, you're probably making a good attempt to eliminate personal passive bias. A score of 20 to 40 means you need to watch it—you reveal passive bias that is inappropriate in organizations and society. If you scored more than 40, your level of bias could get you into trouble. You should definitely consider ways to become more diversity-aware and culturally sensitive.

SOURCE: Adapted from Lawrence Otis Graham, *Proversity: Getting Past Face Values and Finding the Soul of People* (John Wiley & Sons, 1997). Used with permission of Lawrence Otis Graham.

LEADERSHIP DEVELOPMENT: Cases for Analysis

Northern Industries

Northern Industries asked you, a consultant in organizational change and diversity management, to help them resolve some racial issues that, according to president Jim Fisher, are "festering" in their manufacturing plant in Springfield, Massachusetts. Northern Industries is a family-owned enterprise that manufactures greeting cards and paper and plastic holiday decorations. It employs 125 people full time, including African Americans and Asians. About 80 percent of the full-time workforce is female. During the peak production months of September and January (to produce orders primarily for Christmas/Hanukah and Mother's Day), the company runs a second shift and adds about fifty part-time workers, most of whom are women and minorities.

All orders are batch runs made to customer specifications. In a period of a week, it is not unusual for seventy different orders to be filled requiring different paper stocks, inks, plastics, and setups. Since these orders vary greatly in size, the company has a long-term policy of giving priority to high-volume customers and processing other orders on a first-come first-served basis. Half a dozen of the company's major customers have been doing business with Northern for more than twenty years, having been signed on by Jim Fisher's father (now retired).

To begin your orientation to the company, Fisher asks his Production Manager, Walter Beacon, to take you around the plant. Beacon points out the production areas responsible for each of the various steps in the manufacture of a greeting card, from purchasing to printing to quality control and shipping. The plant is clean, but the two large printing rooms, each the workplace for about twenty-five workers, are quite noisy. You catch snatches of the employees' conversations there, but you cannot figure out what language they are speaking. In the shipping and receiving department you notice that most workers are black, perhaps African American. Beacon confirms that eight out of ten of the workers in that department are black males, and that their boss, Adam Wright, is also African American.

It has been previously arranged that you would attend a meeting of top management in order to get a flavor of the organizational culture. The president introduces you as a diversity consultant and notes that several of his managers have expressed concerns about potential racial problems in the company. He says, "Each of the minority groups sticks together. The African Americans and Orientals rarely mix. Recently there has been a problem with theft of finished product, especially on the second shift, and we had to fire a Thai worker." Fisher has read a lot lately about "managing diversity" and hopes you will be able to help the company. Several managers nod their heads in agreement.

Fisher then turns his executive team to its daily business. The others present are the general manager, personnel manager (the only woman), sales manager, quality control manager, production manager (Beacon), and the shipping and receiving manager (the only nonwhite manager). Soon an angry debate ensues between the sales and shipping/receiving managers. It seems that orders are not being shipped quickly enough, according to the sales manager, and several complaints have been received from smaller customers about the quality of the product. The shipping/receiving manager argues that he needs more hands to do the job, and that the quality of incoming supplies is lousy. While this debate continues, the other managers are silent and seemingly uncomfortable. Finally one of them attempts to break up the argument with a joke about his wife. Fisher and the other men laugh loudly, and the conversation shifts to other topics.

SOURCE: Copyright 1991 by Rae Andre of Northeastern University. Used with permission.

Questions

1. What recommendations would you make to Northern's leaders to help them move toward successfully managing diversity issues?

2. If you were the shipping and receiving or personnel manager, how do you think you would feel about your job? Discuss some of the challenges you might face at Northern.

3. Refer to Exhibit 11.5. Based on the information in the case, at what stage of personal diversity awareness do leaders at Northern seem to be? Discuss.

The Trouble with Bangles

Leela Patel was standing by her machine as she had for eight hours of each working day for the past six years. Leela was happy; she had many friends among the 400 or so women at the food processing plant. Most of them were of Indian origin like herself, although Asian women formed less than a fifth of the female workforce. Leela was a member of a five-woman team that reported to supervisor Bill Evans.

Leela saw Evans approaching now, accompanied by Jamie Watkins, the shop steward. "Hello, Leela; we've come to explain something to you," Evans began. "You must have heard about the accident last month when one of the girls caught a bangle in the machine and cut her wrist. Well, the Safety Committee has decided that no one will be allowed to wear any bangles, engagement rings, earrings, or necklaces at work—only wedding rings, sleepers for pierced ears, and wristwatches will be allowed. So I'm afraid you'll have to remove your bangles." Leela, as was her custom, was wearing three bangles, one steel, one plastic, and one gold. All the married Asian women wore bangles, and many of the English girls had also begun wearing them. Leela explained that she was a Hindu wife and the bangles were important to her religion.

"Don't make a fuss, Leela," Evans said between clenched teeth. "I've already had to shout at Hansa Patel and Mira Desai. Why can't you all be like Meena Shah? She didn't mind taking her bangles off; neither did the English girls." Leela could see that Evans was very angry so, almost in tears, she removed the bangles. When the two had moved off, however, she replaced the gold bangle and carried on with her work.

Within two or three days, the plant manager, Sam Jones, noticed that all the Asian women were wearing their bangles again—some, in fact, were wearing more than ever before. "I'm staggered by the response which this simple, common-sense restriction on the wearing of jewelry has brought," Jones remarked to the regional race relations employment advisor. "I have had several deputations from the Asian women protesting the ban, not to mention visits by individuals on the instruction of their husbands. In addition, I've just had a letter from something called the Asian Advisory Committee, asking that the ban be lifted until we meet with their representatives. The strength of this discontent has prompted me to talk to you. Jewelry constitutes both a safety and a hygiene hazard on this site, so it must be removed. And I'm afraid if I talk to this Asian Committee, they'll turn out to be a bunch of militants who'll cause all sorts of trouble. At the same time, we can't afford any work stoppages. What do you suggest?"

Several days later, the advisor had arranged for Mr. Singh from the local Council for Community Relations to talk to Jones and other managers. Singh explained that in his opinion there were no obstacles arising from *religious* observance that prevented implementation of the ban on bangles. However, he pointed out, the bangles do have a custom base which is stronger than the English tradition base for wedding rings. "The bangles are a mark not only of marriage but of the esteem in which a wife is held by her husband. The more bangles and the greater their value, the higher her esteem and the greater her social standing. The tradition also has religious overtones, since the wearing of bangles by the wife demonstrates that each recognizes the other as "worthy" in terms of the fulfillment of their religious obligations. This position is further complicated in that women remove their bangles if they are widowed, and some fear that the removal of the bangles may lead to their husbands' deaths."

SOURCE: Adapted from "Bangles," in Allan R. Cohen, Stephen L. Fink, Herman Gadon, and Robin D. Willits, *Effective Behavior in Organizations: Cases, Concepts, and Student Experiences,* 7th ed. (Burr Ridge, IL: McGraw-Hill Irwin, 2001), 413–414.

Questions

1. What is your initial reaction to this story? Why do you think you had this reaction?

2. Based on this limited information, how would you rate this organization in terms of developing leadership diversity? Discuss.

3. If you were a top manager at this company, how would you handle this problem?

REFERENCES

1. David Leonhardt, "The Saga of Lloyd Ward," *Business Week,* August 9, 1999, 58–70.
2. "Diversity in the New Millennium," *Working Woman,* September 2000, Special Advertising Section.
3. Louisa Wah, "Diversity at Allstate: A Competitive Weapon," *Management Review,* July-August 1999, 24–30.

4. Based on G. Pascal Zachary, "Mighty is the Mongrel," *Fast Company,* July 2000, 270–284.

5. Frances J. Milliken and Luis I. Martins, "Searching for Common Threads: Understanding the Multiple Effects of Diversity in Organizational Groups," *Academy of Management Review* 21, No. 2 (1996), 402–433.

6. Timothy Aeppel, "A 3Com Factory Hires a Lot of Immigrants, Gets Mix of Languages," *The Wall Street Journal,* March 30, 1998, A1; Mike Hofman, "Lost in the Translation," *Inc.,* May 2000, 161–162.

7. Roger O. Crockett, with Andy Reinhardt, Peter Burrows, and Leah Nathans Spiro, "Jesse's New Target: Silicon Valley," *Business Week,* July 12, 1999, 111–112.

8. Marilyn Loden and Judy B. Rosener, *Workforce America!* (Homewood, IL: Business One Irwin, 1991); and Marilyn Loden, *Implementing Diversity* (Homewood, IL: Irwin, 1996).

9. Milliken and Martins, "Searching for Common Threads."

10. C. Keen, "Human Resource Management Issues in the '90s," *Vital Speeches* 56, No. 24 (1990), 752–754.

11. Richard W. Judy and Carol D'Amico, *Workforce 2020: Work and Workers in the 21st Century* (Indianapolis, IN: Hudson Institute, 1997).

12. Steven Greenhouse, N.Y. Times News Service, "Influx of Immigrants Having Profound Impact on Economy," *Johnson City Press,* September 4, 2000, 9.

13. Judy and D'Amico, *Workforce 2020.*

14. Alan Farnham, "Global—or Just Globaloney?" *Fortune,* June 27, 1994, 97–100; William C. Symonds, Brian Bremner, Stewart Toy, and Karen Lowry Miller, "The Globetrotters Take Over," *Business Week,* July 8, 1996, 46–48; Carla Rapoport, "Nestlé's Brand Building Machine," *Fortune,* September 19, 1994, 147–156; and "Execs with Global Vision," *USA Today,* International Edition, February 9, 1996, 12B.

15. Zachary, "Mighty is the Mongrel."

16. Ibid.

17. Sharon Nelton, "Nurturing Diversity," *Nation's Business,* June 1995, 25–27.

18. Gail Robinson and Kathleen Dechant, "Building a Business Case for Diversity," *Academy of Management Executive* 11, No. 3 (1997), 21–31.

19. Wah, "Diversity at Allstate: A Competitive Weapon."

20. Geoffrey Colvin, "The 50 Best Companies for Asians, Blacks, and Hispanics," *Fortune,* July 19, 1999, 53–58.

21. John Williams, "The New Workforce," *Business Week,* March 20, 2000, 64–70.

22. Colvin, "The 50 Best Companies."

23. Taylor H. Cox, *Cultural Diversity in Organizations* (San Francisco: Berrett-Koehler, 1994).

24. Judy B. Rosener, *America's Competitive Secret: Women Managers* (New York: Oxford University Press, 1995), and "Ways Women Lead," *Harvard Business Review,* November-December 1990, 119–125; Sally Helgesen, *The Female Advantage: Women's Ways of Leadership* (New York: Currency/Doubleday, 1990); Joline Godfrey, "Been There, Doing That," *Inc.,* March 1996, 21–22; Chris Lee, "The Feminization of Management," *Training,* November 1994, 25–31; and Bernard M. Bass and Bruce J. Avolio, "Shatter the Glass Ceiling: Women May Make Better Managers," *Human Resource Management* 33, No. 4 (Winter 1994), 549–560.

25. Dawn Hill, "Women Leaders Doing It Their Way," *New Woman,* January 1994, 78.
26. Based on Judy B. Rosener, *America's Competitive Secret: Women Managers* (New York: Oxford University Press, 1997), 129–135.
27. Lena Williams, "A Silk Blouse on the Assembly Line? (Yes, the Boss's)," *The New York Times,* February 5, 1995, Business Section, 7.
28. Helgesen, *The Female Advantage.*
29. Julie Indvik, "Women and Leadership," in Peter G. Northouse, *Leadership: Theory and Practice,* 2nd ed. (Thousand Oaks, CA: Sage, 2001), 215–247.
30. Bass and Avolio, "Shatter the Glass Ceiling."
31. M. Fine, F. Johnson, and M. S. Ryan, "Cultural Diversity in the Workforce," *Public Personnel Management* 19 (1990), 305–319; and Hill, "Women Leaders Doing It Their Way."
32. R. Frank and T. Burton, "Culture Clash Causes Anxiety for Pharmacia and Upjohn Inc.," *The Wall Street Journal,* February 4, 1997, A1, A12.
33. Geert Hofstede, "The Interaction between National and Organizational Value Systems," *Journal of Management Studies* 22 (1985), 347–357; and "The Cultural Relativity of the Quality of Life Concept," *Academy of Management Review* 9 (1984), 389–398.
34. Debby Young, "Team Heat," *CIO,* Section 1, September 1, 1998, 43–51.
35. Geert Hofstede, "Cultural Constraints in Management Theories," excerpted in Dorothy Marcic and Sheila M. Puffer, *Management International: Cases, Exercises, and Readings* (St. Paul, MN: West Publishing, 1994), 24.
36. Gilbert W. Fairholm, *Leadership and the Culture of Trust* (Westport, CT: Praeger, 1994), 187–188.
37. J. Ball, "DaimlerChrysler's Transfer Woes," *The Wall Street Journal,* August 24, 1999, B1, B2; "DaimlerChrysler Moves Shift Power to Germans," *Columbus Dispatch,* September 25, 1999, E1, E2; Douglas A. Blackmon, "A Factory in Alabama is the Merger in Microcosm," *The Wall Street Journal,* May 8, 1998, B1; and Justin Martin, "Mercedes: Made in Alabama," *Fortune,* July 7, 1997, 150–158.
38. Zachary, "Mighty is the Mongrel."
39. Harry C. Triandis, "The Contingency Model in Cross-Cultural Perspective," in Martin M. Chemers and Roya Ayman, eds., *Leadership Theory and Research: Perspectives and Directions* (San Diego, CA: Academic Press, Inc., 1993), 167–188; and Peter B. Smith and Mark F. Peterson, *Leadership, Organizations, and Culture: An Event Management Model* (London: Sage, 1988).
40. G. Haight, "Managing Diversity," *Across the Board* 27, No. 3 (1990), 22–29.
41. This section is based on Rosener, *America's Competitive Secret,* 33–34.
42. Ann Morrison, *The New Leaders: Guidelines on Leadership Diversity in America* (San Francisco: Jossey-Bass, 1992), 37.
43. Keith H. Hammonds, "Difference is Power," *Fast Company,* July 2000, 258–266.
44. Deborah L. Jacobs, "Back from the Mommy Track," *The New York Times,* October 9, 1994, F1, F6.
45. Robert Hooijberg and Nancy DiTomaso, "Leadership in and of Demographically Diverse Organizations," *Leadership Quarterly* 7, No. 1 (1996), 1–19.
46. W. E. B. DuBois, *The Souls of Black Folks* (Chicago: Chicago University Press, 1903), quoted in Hooijberg and DiTomaso, "Leadership in and of Demographically Diverse Organizations."

47. Vivian Louie, "For Asian-Americans, A Way to Fight a Maddening Stereotype," *The New York Times,* August 8, 1993, 9.

48. Debra E. Meyerson and Joyce K. Fletcher, "A Modest Manifesto for Shattering the Glass Ceiling," *Harvard Business Review,* January-February 2000, 127-136; and Eileen Alt Powell, "Survey: Women Make Up 12.5 Percent of Fortune 500 Executives," AP report, *Johnson City Press,* November 14, 2000.

49. "Diversity in the New Millennium," *Working Woman,* September 2000, Special Advertising Section.

50. C. Solomon, "Careers under Glass," *Personnel Journal* 69, No. 4 (1990), 96-105; and *Population Profile of the United States 1995,* U.S. Department of Commerce, Bureau of the Census, July 1995.

51. Meyerson and Fletcher, "A Modest Manifesto for Shattering the Glass Ceiling"; Julie Amparano Lopez, "Study Says Women Face Glass Walls as Well as Glass Ceiling," *The Wall Street Journal,* March 3, 1992, B1, B2; and Joann S. Lublin, "Women at Top Still Are Distant from CEO Jobs," *The Wall Street Journal,* February 28, 1996, B1, B8.

52. U.S. Department of Labor, *Futurework: Trends and Challenges for Work in the 21st Century.*

53. "Diversity: Developing Tomorrow's Leadership Today," *Business Week,* December 20, 1999, Special Advertising Section.

54. Renee Blank and Sandra Slipp, "The White Male: An Endangered Species?" *Management Review,* September 1994, 27-32; and Nelton, "Nurturing Diversity."

55. Based on Rosener, *America's Competitive Secret,* 142-148.

56. "Ernst & Young LLP: An Aggressive Approach," in "Diversity Today: Developing and Retaining the Best Corporate Talent," *Fortune,* June 21, 1999, Special Advertising Section.

57. Based on Fairholm, *Leadership and the Culture of Trust,* 189-192; Cox, *Cultural Diversity in Organizations;* and Morrison, *The New Leaders,* 29-56.

58. Morrison, *The New Leaders,* 35.

59. Based on Nicholas Imparato and Oren Harari, *Jumping the Curve: Innovation and Strategic Choice in an Age of Transition* (San Francisco: Jossey-Bass, 1994), 186-203.

60. Lennie Copeland, "Learning to Manage a Multicultural Workforce," *Training,* May 25, 1988, 48-56.

61. Martin M. Chemers and Roya Ayman, *Leadership Theory and Research: Perspectives and Directions* (San Diego, CA: Academic Press, 1993), 209.

62. Fairholm, *Leadership and the Culture of Trust,* 194.

63. Kenneth Labich, "No More Crude at Texaco," *Fortune,* September 6, 1999, 205-212.

64. Jenny C. McCune, "Diversity Training: A Competitive Weapon," *Management Review,* June 1996, 25-28.

CHAPTER OUTLINE

YOUR LEADERSHIP CHALLENGE

After reading this chapter, you should be able to:

- Recognize your natural leadership frame of reference and how you can expand your perspective.

- Use power and politics to help accomplish important organizational goals.

- Identify types and sources of power in organizations and know how to increase power through political activity.

- Use the influence tactics of rational persuasion, emotional appeal, symbolic action, building coalitions, expanding networks, and being assertive.

Leadership Power and Influence

When Cindy Casselman first began working at Xerox headquarters, she noticed that company communications weren't so good. Most of the company's employees would read about a big acquisition or a drop in earnings in the newspaper before they ever heard about it from the company. Even though Casselman wanted to change that by developing an intranet site that would be a haven of free speech and open information, she had little formal power and authority. Still, she formed a makeshift budget to explore ideas, got the approval of her direct supervisor, and put together a volunteer team that she called the Sanctioned Covert Operation (SCO).

Casselman knew that many people inside Xerox would feel threatened by her idea, so she began selling the project by emphasizing the benefits that would accrue to whomever she was talking to at the time. For example, to a manager at Xerox Business Services, Casselman presented the intranet as a place to test virtual reality delivery of documents; to a worker in the information management division, she sold it as a place to showcase a new technology architecture he had developed. By positioning her idea in different ways to different people, blending her goals with the goals of others, Casselman gradually built a network of allies all around the huge corporation.

On Xerox Teamwork Day, Chairman Paul Allaire proudly described the company's newest internal communications tool—the WebBoard. Today, thanks to Casselman and the SCO team, 85,000 Xerox employees can visit this lively intranet site to read up-to-the minute news about internal developments, talk with other workers, and generally stay connected with what's going on in the company. Casselman herself has been promoted to executive assistant to the head of corporate research and technology. "The WebBoard raised my profile and proved that I could follow through on an ambitious project and form the relationships needed to support the project," Casselman says. "It definitely helped me win my new job."[1]

Even though Cindy Casselman had little formal power at Xerox, she influenced others to do what was needed to accomplish a goal beneficial to the organization. By surrounding herself with a network of people who supported her idea for a company intranet, Casselman gained power and influence beyond her formal position.

Recall that one of the key elements in the definition of leadership is *influence*. A central concern for leaders is getting other people to do what is necessary to reach specific goals. Some do so by exercising their formal position of authority in the organization. Others, such as Martin Luther King, described in Chapter 9, and Raoul Wallenberg, described in Chapter 6, do so by demonstrating the courage to take personal risks. Another way in which leaders gain power and influence is through political activity, such as building a coalition, as Cindy Casselman did at Xerox. This chapter explores the topic of leadership power and influence in detail. The chapter opens with a consideration of leadership frames of reference and how a political approach to leadership combines with other leadership philosophies. We will also examine the concepts of power and influence, look at some sources and types of power, and outline ways leaders exercise power and influence through political activity. Finally, we will briefly consider some ethical aspects of using power and influence.

LEADERSHIP FRAMES OF REFERENCE

A **frame** is a perspective from which a leader views the world. The concept of frames of reference calls attention to the way people gather information, make decisions, and exercise power. The four frames of reference, illustrated in Exhibit 12.1 as a set of stairsteps, are structural, human, political, and symbolic. These frames of reference determine how situations are defined and what actions are taken.[2] Leaders often begin with a limited structural perspective of the organization and develop the other frames based on their own personal development and experience with the organization. One study found the struc-

EXHIBIT 12.1

Four Organizational Frames of Reference

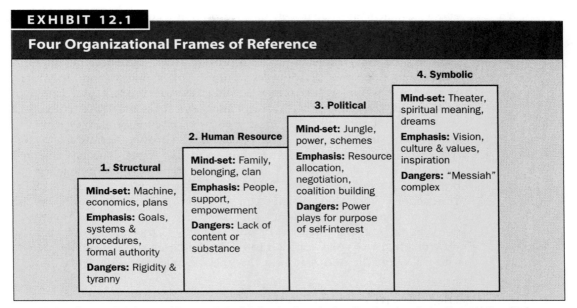

SOURCE: Based on Lee G. Bolman and Terrence E. Deal, *Reframing Organizations* (San Francisco: Jossey-Bass, 1991); and Bolman and Deal, "Leadership and Management Effectiveness: A Multi-Frame, Multi-Sector Analysis," *Human Resource Management* 30, No. 4 (Winter 1991), 509–534. Thanks to Roy Williams for suggesting the stair sequence.

tural frame of reference was used about 60 percent of the time, while the symbolic frame was used only about 20 percent of the time.[3]

Each frame of reference has strengths and weaknesses, and effective leaders strive for a balanced perspective so that all the needs of the organization are met. Previous chapters of this book have dealt primarily with leadership approaches relating to the first two frames (structural and human resource). This chapter examines leadership as a political process. The final chapters of the book will focus on the symbolic frame, considering how leaders influence others through vision, culture, and values. Effective leaders balance their view of the organization by becoming aware of all four frames of reference, the importance of each, and how using multiple frames can help leaders better understand organizational needs and problems.

The Structural Frame

The organization as machine is the dominant image in the structural frame of reference. Leaders strive for machine-like efficiency and make decisions based on economic efficiency. Plans and goals are the primary tools of management, and leaders generally rely heavily on the power and authority granted through their organizational position to influence others.

The **structural frame** of reference places emphasis on goal setting and clarifying job expectations as a way to provide order, efficiency, and continuity. Leaders emphasize clear job descriptions, specific policies and procedures, and the view of the organization as a rational system. Leaders value hard data and analysis, keep an eye on the bottom line, and stress adherence to accepted standards, conformity to rules, and the creation of administrative systems as a way to bring order and logic to the organization. Clarity of direction and control of results are important characteristics in this frame. The task-oriented leadership styles described in Chapter 2 and some of the contingency approaches discussed in Chapter 3 illustrate the structural frame of reference. Transactional leadership, described in Chapter 5, also relies heavily on the structural frame. Structure, plans, and rationality are needed in all organizations, but not to the exclusion of other frames. Carried to an extreme, the structural frame of reference leads to rigidity and even tyranny among leaders, who will quote the rules and insist that they be followed to the letter.[4]

The Human Resource Frame

According to the **human resource frame** of reference, people are the organization's most valuable resource. This frame defines problems and issues in interpersonal terms and looks for ways to adjust the organization to meet human needs. Leaders do not rely solely on the power of their position to exert influence. Instead, they focus on relationships and feelings (recall the discussion of emotional intelligence in Chapter 5) and lead through empowerment and support, as described in the empowerment section of Chapter 8 and in our discussion of moral leadership in Chapter 6. Leaders also encourage open communication (Chapter 9), teamwork (Chapter 10), and the development of diverse employees (Chapter 11).

Effective leaders use the human resource perspective to involve others and give them opportunities for personal and professional development. They value people, are visible and accessible, and serve others. The images in this view are a sense of family, belonging, and the organization as a clan. This frame of reference, however, can also lead to ineffectiveness if leaders are wishy-washy and always bending to the whims of others, in essence using caring and participation as an excuse to avoid leadership responsibility.[5]

The Political Frame

The **political frame** of reference views organizations as arenas of ongoing conflict or tension over the allocation of scarce resources. Leaders spend their time networking and building alliances and coalitions to influence decisions. These leaders consciously strive to build a power base, and they frequently exercise both personal and organizational power to achieve their desired results. Carried to an extreme, the political frame of reference can lead to deception, dishonesty, and power plays for purposes of individual self-interest. However, effective political leaders typically use their negotiating, bargaining, and coalition-building skills to serve organizational needs.[6]

Power and politics are an important, although often hidden, part of all organizations. The mind-set in the political frame is to be aware of the organization as a jungle. Power is a reality, and political schemes are a natural part of organizational life. Embracing this frame, although not to the exclusion of the other frames, is an important part of effective leadership in most organizations. The remaining sections of this chapter will examine the political approach to leadership in more detail.

The Symbolic Frame

To use full leadership potential requires that leaders also develop a fourth frame of reference—the **symbolic frame,** in which leaders perceive the organization as a system of shared meaning and values.[7] Rather than relying only on formal power and the use of politics, the symbolic leader focuses on shared vision, culture, and values to influence others and lead the organization. We have touched on topics related to the symbolic frame of reference throughout this book. For example, charismatic and transformational leadership, described in Chapter 4, rely heavily on this frame. The communication chapter (Chapter 9) discussed how leaders use stories and symbols to build shared values, and Chapter 11 touched on changing cultural values to support diversity. The symbolic frame of reference will be explored in more depth in the remaining chapters of this book. Chapter 13 will focus on how leaders create and communicate a vision for the organization, and Chapter 14 will look closely at building and changing organizational culture. In Chapter 15, we will examine how leaders design learning organizations, including shaping the values required to promote continuous learning and change. The final chapter of the book looks specifically at the topic of leading change.

Symbolic leaders frequently inspire people to higher levels of performance and commitment; however, this frame of reference can also lead to problems when used exclusively. One danger of relying too heavily on the symbolic frame is that leaders develop a "messiah" complex. The focus shifts to the leader rather than the organization and all its members (recall our discussion of the "black hat of charisma" in Chapter 4). Symbols can also be used for dishonest, unethical, and self-serving purposes. Symbolic leaders are effective when they articulate a vision that is widely shared and understood, and when they support the deepest values and concerns of followers. The leader thinks in terms of the organization as theater, is concerned with spirit and meaning, and focuses on harnessing people's dreams and desires for the benefit of everyone and the organization.

Each of the four frames illustrated in Exhibit 12.1 provides significant possibilities for enhancing leadership effectiveness, but each is incomplete. Leaders can understand their own natural frame of reference and recognize its limitations. In addition, they can learn to integrate multiple frames to fully use their leadership potential. Not every leader can develop abilities in all areas. However, effective leaders "understand their own strengths, work to expand them, and build teams that together can provide leadership in all four modes—structural, human resource, political, and symbolic."[8]

POWER, INFLUENCE, AND LEADERSHIP

One distinction in the four frames of reference is how leaders gain and use power and influence. Power may be one of the most important concepts in the study of leadership. However, getting a grasp on the meaning of the terms power and influence can be difficult.[9]

Power is an intangible force in organizations. It cannot be seen, but its effect can be felt. Power is often defined as the potential ability of one person (or department) to influence other persons (or departments) to carry out orders[10] or to do something they otherwise would not have done.[11] Other definitions stress that power is the ability to achieve goals or outcomes that power holders desire.[12] The achievement of desired outcomes is the basis of the definition used here. **Power** is the ability of one person or department in an organization to influence other people to bring about desired outcomes. It is the potential to influence others within the organization with the goal of attaining desired outcomes for power holders. Potential power is realized through the processes of politics and influence.[13] Sometimes, the terms power and influence are used synonymously, but there are distinctions between the two. Basically, **influence** is the effect a person's actions have on the attitudes, values, beliefs, or actions of others. Whereas power is the capacity to cause a change in a person, influence may be thought of as the degree of actual change. Although we usually think of power and influence as belonging to the leader, in reality they result from the interaction of leaders and followers in specific situations. As we learned in Chapter 7 on followership, followers may influence a leader's behavior in any number of ways, for better or worse. Later in this chapter, we will examine some specific *influence tactics* that may be used to change another's attitudes or behavior. Leaders can improve their effectiveness by understanding the various types and sources of power as well as the influence tactics they or their followers may use.

Five Types of Leader Power

Power is often described as a personal characteristic, but as described above, organizational position also influences a leader's power. Most discussions of power include five types that are available to leaders.[14]

The five types of leader power are illustrated in Exhibit 12.2. The first three—legitimate, reward, and coercive power—may all be considered types of *position power* that are defined largely by the organization's policies and procedures. A person's position in the organization determines what amount of power he or she has, particularly in regard to the ability to reward or punish subordinates to influence their behavior. However, it is important to remember that position power and leadership are not the same thing. As we discussed in Chapter 1, a person may hold a formal position of authority and yet not be a leader. Effective leaders don't rely solely on formal position to influence others to accomplish goals. Two sources of *personal power,* called expert power and referent power, are based on the leader's special knowledge or personal characteristics.

LEGITIMATE POWER   **Legitimate power** is the authority granted from a formal position in an organization. For example, once a person has been selected as a supervisor, most workers understand that they are obligated to follow his or her direction with respect to work activities. Subordinates accept this source

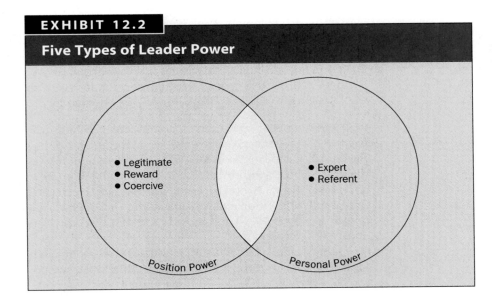

EXHIBIT 12.2

Five Types of Leader Power

- Legitimate
- Reward
- Coercive

- Expert
- Referent

Position Power

Personal Power

of power as legitimate, which is why they comply. Certain rights, responsibilities, and prerogatives accrue to anyone holding a formal leadership position. Followers accept the legitimate rights of formal leaders to set goals, make decisions, and direct activities. Most North Americans accept the legitimate right of appointed leaders to direct an organization.

REWARD POWER   This kind of power stems from the authority to bestow rewards on other people. For example, appointed leaders may have access to formal rewards, such as pay increases or promotions. Moreover, organizations allocate huge amounts of resources downward from top leaders. Leaders control resources and their distribution. Lower-level followers depend on leaders for the financial and physical resources to perform their tasks. Leaders with **reward power** can use rewards to influence subordinates' behavior.

COERCIVE POWER   The opposite of reward power is **coercive power.** It refers to the power to punish or recommend punishment. Supervisors have coercive power when they have the right to fire or demote subordinates, criticize, or withdraw pay increases. For example, if Paul, a salesman, does not perform as well as expected, his supervisor has the coercive power to criticize him, reprimand him, put a negative letter in his file, and hurt his chance for a raise. Coercive power is the negative side of legitimate and reward power.

EXPERT POWER   Power resulting from a leader's special knowledge or skill regarding tasks performed by followers is referred to as **expert power.** When a leader is a true expert, subordinates go along with recommendations because of his or her superior knowledge. Leaders at supervisory levels often have experience in the production process that gains them promotion. At top management levels, however, leaders may lack expert power because subordinates know more about technical details than they do. Experts may use their knowledge to influence or place limits on decisions made by people above them in the organization.[15] Furthermore, specialized information may be withheld or divulged in ways designed to achieve particular outcomes desired by the leaders.[16]

REFERENT POWER   This kind of power comes from leader personality characteristics that command followers' identification, respect, and admiration so they want to emulate the leader. When workers admire a supervisor because of the way she deals with them, the influence is based on referent power. **Referent power** depends on the leader's personal characteristics rather than on a formal title or position and is visible in the area of charismatic leadership as described in Chapter 4. The Living Leadership box talks about the far-reaching impact of referent power.

One leader who illustrates both expert and referent power is Rachel Hubka of Rachel's Bus Company. Although Hubka has strong position power, she does not rely on it as her primary means of influencing followers.

LIVING LEADERSHIP

The Ripple Effect

Do you want to be a positive influence in the world? First, get your own life in order. Ground yourself in the single principle so that your behavior is wholesome and effective. If you do that, you will earn respect and be a powerful influence.

Your behavior influences others through a ripple effect. A ripple effect works because everyone influences everyone else. Powerful people are powerful influences.

If your life works, you influence your family.

If your family works, your family influences the community.

If your community works, your community influences the nation.

If your nation works, your nation influences the world.

If your world works, the ripple effect spreads throughout the cosmos.

SOURCE: John Heider, *The Tao of Leadership: Leadership Strategies for a New Age* (New York: Bantam Books, 1985), 107. Copyright 1985 Humanic Ltd., Atlanta, GA. Used with permission.

IN THE LEAD   ## Rachel Hubka, Rachel's Bus Company

In 1978, Rachel Hubka joined Chicago-based Stewart's Bus Company as a dispatcher and immediately set herself the task of learning every job in the company. Her passion for the job not only stood her in good stead as she scrubbed floors and performed other mundane chores, but also helped her master the complex routing system for scheduling school buses, develop the skills for hiring and training drivers, develop and implement a safety program, and generally become an expert in school bus operations. When Stewart's owners put the company up for sale, Hubka bought it and changed the name to Rachel's Bus Company.

Hubka often has to hire people with marginal work histories as drivers, but she gives them comprehensive training and treats them like professionals. Employees respect Hubka's leadership because of her expert knowledge of the company's operations. She understands the details and difficulties of every job in the company, in addition to having a firm grasp on the big picture and where she wants to take the organization in the future. Hubka also illustrates referent power. People genuinely like her, and they like the "teaching environment" she has created at the company. There is no chain of command at Rachel's Bus Company, and Hubka's door is always open to any employee—to talk about anything. She is known as a great listener who is able to engage others in meaningful conversation. She encourages employees with entrepreneurial dreams to follow them, and she takes pride when employees leave her company to start their own businesses.

Employees admire and respect Hubka for her hard work, dedication, and knowledge of the business, as well as the way she treats everyone with respect and empathy. Although she also uses rewards to influence subordinates, her strong expert and referent power means Hubka has found little need to use coercive power.[17]

Responses to the Use of Power

Leaders use the various types of power to influence others to do what is necessary to accomplish organizational goals. The success of any attempt to influence is a matter of degree, but there are three distinct outcomes that may result from the use of power: compliance, resistance, and commitment, as illustrated in Exhibit 12.3.[18]

When people successfully use position power (legitimate, reward, coercive), the response is compliance. **Compliance** means that people follow the directions of the person with power, whether or not they agree with those directions. They will obey orders and carry out instructions even though they may not like it. The problem is that in many cases, followers do just enough work as is necessary to satisfy the leader and may not contribute their full potential. In addition, if the use of position power, especially the use of coercion, exceeds a level people consider legitimate, people may resist the attempt to influence. **Resistance** means that employees will deliberately try to avoid carrying out instructions or they will attempt to disobey orders. Thus, the effectiveness of leaders who rely solely on position power is limited.

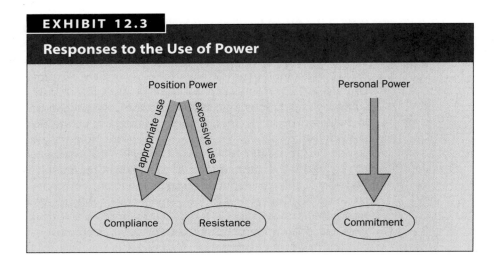

EXHIBIT 12.3

Responses to the Use of Power

Position Power

Personal Power

appropriate use

excessive use

Compliance   Resistance   Commitment

The follower response most often generated by personal power (expert, referent) is commitment. **Commitment** means that followers adopt the leader's viewpoint and enthusiastically carry out instructions. Needless to say, commitment is preferred to compliance or resistance. Although compliance alone may be enough for routine matters, commitment is particularly important when the leader is promoting change. Change carries risk or uncertainty, and follower commitment helps to overcome fear and resistance associated with change efforts. Successful leaders exercise both personal and position power to influence others.

The Role of Dependency

You probably know from personal experience that when a person has control over something that others want and need, he or she gains power. A simple example is a star high school quarterback graduating at a time when there are few excellent quarterbacks coming out of high schools. The star will be courted by numerous colleges who will vie for his interest and make increasingly attractive offers to entice him to sign on with their team.

One of the key aspects of power is that it is a function of dependence—that is, the greater Individual B's dependence on Individual A, the greater power A will have over B. People in organizations, as elsewhere, have power because other people depend on them—for information, resources, cooperation, and so forth. The more people depend on someone, the greater that person's power.[19] The nature of dependency relationships between leaders and subordinates in organizations changed in recent years because of low unemployment and a tight labor market. When good jobs are plentiful, people in organizations are less willing to put up with overbearing or incompetent bosses because they feel they can always find another job. That is, they feel less dependence on the supervisor. For example, several employees in a Bank of Montreal administrative unit, after suffering the harsh command-and-control style of their boss for years, took their complaints to a top executive. Even though executives had considered the manager a rising star in the organization, he was told to change his way of interacting with subordinates. When he refused, the bank "made it easy for him" to quit with a severance package.[20] In this case, the employees had greater power than their manager. Conversely, when jobs are hard to come by and unemployment is high, organizational leaders have greater power over employees because most people are dependent on the organization for their livelihood. They know that if they lose their job it might be very difficult to find another one. This type of dependency primarily affects a leader's position power, which is based on formal authority and the ability to bestow rewards and punishments. Today's leaders find that they must gain and exercise personal power to a greater extent. Often, people stay in a job where they admire and respect their leader

The 9 Natural Laws of Leadership

Warren Blank

Warren Blank applies principles of quantum physics to the contemporary business environment to arrive at nine "natural laws" that he believes hold true for all leaders. Using examples from real companies, this book explores what it means to be a leader, when and how leadership emerges, how leaders and followers influence one another, and how people can tap the unseen sources of leadership power. The book also includes practical action steps to help the reader develop leadership potential.

The Nine Natural Laws

To fully understand and master the process of leadership, according to Blank, requires understanding nine fundamental laws.

1. **Leaders operate outside the boundaries of organizationally defined procedures.** Leadership is about change, not about maintaining the status quo. Leaders need courage to stir things up and keep things moving.

2. **Leadership involves risk and uncertainty.** Leaders live without a safety net. They accept that ambiguity and chaos are a natural part of the leadership territory.

3. **Leadership is a field of interaction.** Leadership is a relationship between leaders and followers. Leadership is not a person, a position, or a program, but something that happens when a leader and followers connect.

4. **Leadership occurs as an event.** Leader-follower interactions happen as discrete occurrences, with each having a beginning, a middle, and an end. Thus, leadership occurs throughout organizations, with numerous leaders gaining followers in a variety of situations.

5. **Leaders use influence beyond formal authority.** Leadership influence does not extend from a person's position in the organizational hierarchy. Instead it is personal and arises from the interactions of a leader and followers.

6. **Not everyone will follow a leader's initiative.** All leaders face limits, and no leader will ever have everyone's support.

7. **Consciousness—the capacity to process information—creates leadership.** Leadership begins with an idea that might resolve a problem or exploit an opportunity. The ability to process information and create meaning from it is the underlying source of leadership power.

8. **Leadership is a self-referral process.** Leaders and followers process information from their own subjective, internal frame of reference. Leaders can expand their consciousness so that they operate from a more unified, enlightened state. If they are narrow-minded, their perception is limited and distorted.

9. **A leader has willing followers.** Voluntary followers are the underlying element that defines all leaders in all situations.

Developing Quantum Leadership

Blank calls his view of leadership based on natural laws "quantum leadership." To clarify his definition, he contrasts quantum leaders with classical managers. However, he emphasizes that managers can learn to be quantum leaders. Throughout the book, he offers action ideas to help the reader develop quantum leadership capacities, such as learning to deal with risk and uncertainty. The final chapter summarizes ideas and offers tips for expanding consciousness and leadership potential.

The 9 Natural Laws of Leadership, by Warren Blank, is published by AMACOM, a division of American Management Association.

even though they could make more money working somewhere else. This chapter's Leader's Bookshelf points out that leadership is much more than a job title and asserts that leaders can tap their personal power by understanding the "natural laws of leadership."

Dependency in organizations is related primarily to a person's control over resources. As illustrated in Exhibit 12.4, dependency is greatest for resources that are high on three characteristics—importance, scarcity, and nonsubstitutability.[21] People in the organization must perceive the resource to be *important*—that is, if nobody wants what you've got, it's not going to create dependency. Resources can be important for a variety of reasons. For example, they may be essential elements of a key product, they may directly generate sales, or they may be critical to reducing or avoiding uncertainty for the organization's top decision makers. Chief information officers have gained a tremendous amount of power in many organizations because of the critical role of information technology in today's business world.

Scarcity refers to whether the resource is easy or difficult to obtain. A resource that is difficult or expensive to acquire is more valuable and creates more dependency than one that is widely available. Leaders and employees with expert specialized knowledge illustrate this aspect of dependency. In companies moving to an e-commerce strategy, young computer-literate managers often have more power than senior leaders with no computer expertise.

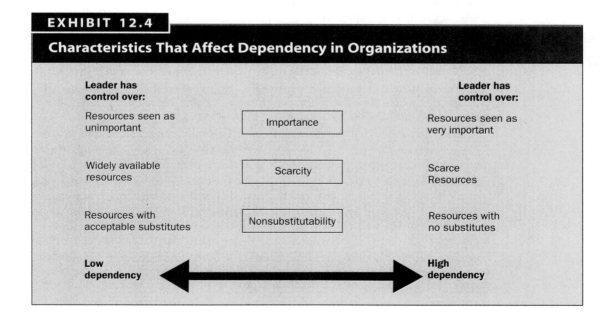

EXHIBIT 12.4

Characteristics That Affect Dependency in Organizations

Leader has control over:		Leader has control over:
Resources seen as unimportant	Importance	Resources seen as very important
Widely available resources	Scarcity	Scarce Resources
Resources with acceptable substitutes	Nonsubstitutability	Resources with no substitutes
Low dependency	⟵———————⟶	**High dependency**

Succeeding in e-commerce has become a critical issue for many companies, which has opened the doors for those with Internet skills to gain power over more senior executives who have failed to acquire the skills needed to help the organization compete in this new environment.

The third characteristic, *nonsubstitutability*, means that leaders or employees with control over resources with no viable substitute will have more power. These resources may include knowledge and expertise as well as access to people with high power. For example, an executive secretary who has daily access to the CEO may have more power than middle managers who must compete for a few minutes of the top leader's time.

SOURCES OF LEADER POWER IN ORGANIZATIONS

An understanding of dependency provides the foundation for examining several sources of leader power in organizations. The five types of power we discussed earlier are derived from either formal position or the leader's personal qualities. These sources provide a basis for much of a leader's influence. In organizations, however, additional sources of power and influence have been identified. The strategic contingencies theory identifies power sources not linked to the specific person or position, but to the role the leader plays in the overall functioning of the organization.[22] Sources of power in this regard are interdepartmental dependency, control over information, centrality, and coping with uncertainty, as illustrated in Exhibit 12.5.

INTERDEPARTMENTAL DEPENDENCY   One key source of leader power in many organizations is interdepartmental dependency. Materials, resources, and information may flow between departments in one direction. In such cases, leaders in the department receiving resources will have less power than those in the department that provides them. For example, consider the case of leaders at a cigarette factory.[23]   One might expect that the production department would be more powerful than the maintenance department, but this was not the case in a cigarette plant near Paris. The production of cigarettes was a routine process. The machinery was automated. On the other hand, maintenance department workers and their leaders were responsible for repair of the automated machinery, which was a complex task, and they had many years of experience. Because the maintenance department had the ability to fix unpredictable assembly-line breakdowns, production managers became dependent on maintenance, and maintenance leaders called the shots about machine repair and assembly line maintenance.

EXHIBIT 12.5

Strategic Contingencies That Affect Leader Power in Organizations

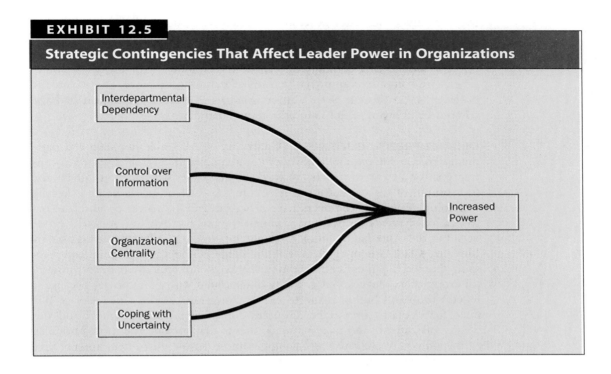

CONTROL OVER INFORMATION   Despite the trend toward empowerment and broader information-sharing, the fact remains that some people will almost always have access to more information than others. Control over information—which involves both access to information and control over how and to whom it is distributed—is an important source of power for leaders. Most leaders recognize that information is a primary business resource and that by controlling what information is collected, how it is interpreted, and how it is shared, they can influence how decisions are made.[24] To some extent, access to information is determined by a person's position in the organization. Top leaders typically have access to more information than do lower-level supervisors or other employees. They can release information selectively to influence others and shape actions and decisions. However, control over information can also be a source of power for lower-level leaders and employees. Employees who have exclusive access to information needed by leaders to make decisions gain power as a result. For example, top executives may be dependent on the operating manager for analyzing and interpreting complex operations data.

Some leaders actively seek to increase their power by gaining control over information. At a not-for-profit organization that sponsors a regional book fair, the fair's coordinator developed contacts with publishing houses that gave her early access to information about new books and authors who would be touring the country. She could selectively provide information to the executive director and steering committee to shape the content of the program. Sometimes, the committee approved authors that the coordinator wanted on the program, even though these authors might not have been chosen had the committee known the full slate of potential participants.

ORGANIZATIONAL CENTRALITY   Centrality reflects a leader's or a department's role in the primary activity of an organization.[25] One measure of centrality is the extent to which the work of the leader's department affects the final output of the organization. At a company such as Intel, which is heavily technology-oriented, engineers have a high degree of power because the organization depends on them to maintain the technical superiority of its products. On the other hand, engineers at a company such as Procter & Gamble or Kimberly-Clark, where marketing is the name of the game, have a lower degree of power. In these organizations, marketers are typically the most powerful group of employees.[26] Centrality is associated with more power because it reflects the contribution made to the organization. At the University of Illinois, for example, important resources come from research grants and the quality of students and faculty. Departments that provide the most resources to the university are rated as having the most power. Also, departments that generate large research grants are more powerful because the grants contain a sizable overhead payment to university administration.[27]

COPING WITH UNCERTAINTY   The environment can change swiftly and create uncertainty and complexity for leaders. In the face of uncertainty, little information is available to leaders on appropriate courses of action. Leaders in departments that cope well with this uncertainty will increase their power.[28] When market research personnel accurately predict changes in demand for new products, they gain power and prestige because they have reduced a critical uncertainty. Consider the following example of Crystal Manufacturing Corporation.

IN THE LEAD   Crystal Manufacturing

Although union influence has been declining in recent years, unions are still seeking to extend their membership to new organizations. A new union is a crucial source of uncertainty for many manufacturing firms. It can be a countervailing power to management in decisions concerning wages and working conditions.

The workers in Crystal Manufacturing Corporation voted to become part of the Glassmakers Craft Union. Management had been aware of union organizing activities, but it had not taken the threat seriously. No one had acted to forecast or prevent the formation of a union.

The presence of the union had potentially serious consequences for Crystal. Glassmaking is a delicate and expensive manufacturing process. The float-glass process cannot be shut down even temporarily except at great expense. A strike or walkout would mean financial disaster. Therefore, leaders decided that establishing a good working relationship with the union was critically important.

The industrial relations department learned to deal with the union. This department was responsible for coping with the uncertainties created by the new union. Its leader helped the industrial relations group quickly develop expertise in union relationships. It became the contact point on industrial relations matters for managers throughout the organization. The industrial relations leader developed a network throughout the organization and could bypass the normal chain of command on issues she considered important. Industrial relations had nearly absolute knowledge and control over union relations.[29]

At Crystal Manufacturing Corporation, the industrial relations leader coped with a critical uncertainty. She was also more central to the company's mission, and other managers depended on her. She took action to reduce uncertainty after it appeared. This action gave both her and the industrial relations department increased power.

INCREASING POWER THROUGH POLITICAL ACTIVITY

Another aspect of power is that it isn't enough to be performing central activities or coping with organizational uncertainties—one's efforts must also be recognized as important by others.[30] People who want to increase their power make sure their activities are visible and appreciated by others. Acquiring and using power is largely a political process. **Politics** involves activities to acquire, develop, and use power and other resources to obtain desired future outcomes when there is uncertainty or disagreement about choices.[31] Political behavior can be either a positive or negative force. Uncertainty and conflict are natural in organizations, and politics is the mechanism for accomplishing things that can't be handled purely through formal policies or position power.

Leaders use politics to increase their personal power in a number of ways. For one thing, power can come from doing things for other people that obligate them to reciprocate. Leaders find ways to be helpful to others, whether it be helping someone finish an unpleasant job or offering compassion and concern for a follower's personal problems. They may do favors for others whenever possible, which creates an obligation for others to return the favors in the future. Another way in which leaders increase their power is by seeking out greater responsibility, such as serving on committees or volunteering for difficult projects. This often enables them to make connections with powerful people in the organization and build their reputation among those people. When lower-level leaders are perceived as having "friends in higher places," their own power is increased.

Leaders may also increase their personal power by cultivating subordinates' feelings of friendship and loyalty. By being friendly and considerate, showing concern for others, demonstrating trust and respect, and treating people fairly, leaders gain referent power. Leaders may consciously hire subordinates who are likely to identify with the leader, which increases referent power.

Another political approach is called *impression management,* which means leaders seek to control how others perceive them. In other words, they strive to create an impression of greater power. A whole industry, known as "executive coaching," is aimed at helping leaders develop this ability. For example, coach Debra Benton helps executives at companies such as Mattel, Hewlett-Packard, and PepsiCo develop what she calls executive presence—"the impact you have when you walk into a room, a collection of subtle . . . visual cues, including everything from how your clothes fit to how you walk."[32] Impression management may include a wide variety of tactics. Subtle name-dropping can give the impression that a leader associates with high-status people. Likewise, flattery is a form of impression management that can help a person appear to be perceptive and pleasant. These political tactics can be helpful when they enable others to perceive a leader's value to the organization. However, they can also backfire if leaders are perceived as being insincere, dishonest, or arrogant. One example of the effective use of impression management is Steve Harrison, who at the age of 50 was afraid younger superiors as well as subordinates might perceive him as behind the times. Not only does Harrison make sure others know that he keeps up with current business issues, but he also peppers his informal conversations with references to his "youthful" hobbies of running and collecting electric guitars.[33]

POLITICAL TACTICS FOR ASSERTING INFLUENCE

The next issue is how leaders use their power to implement decisions, facilitate change, and pursue organizational goals. That is, leaders use power to influence others, which requires both skill and willingness. Much influence is interpersonal and one-on-one. This is social influence, which involves coalitions, rewards, and inspiration. Other influence has broader appeal, such as to influence the organization as a whole, or to influence those outside the organization. For example, Pat Means and Karen Hixson, who started the magazine *Turning Point* to focus on the positive aspects of African American life in Los Angeles, use their influence to "play a positive role in the development of African Americans." They have attracted prominent writers, artists, and activists that readers want to identify with. They refuse to accept advertising from alcohol or tobacco companies and make careful decisions about where the magazine will be sold.[34]

Within organizations, leaders call upon a variety of political tactics to get things done. Exhibit 12.6 lists six influence tactics that are important for leaders. All of these tactics involve the use of personal power, rather than relying solely on legitimate power or the use of rewards and punishments. Leaders frequently use a combination of influence strategies, and people who are perceived as having greater power typically use a wider variety of tactics.

1. *Use Rational Persuasion.* Perhaps the most frequently used influence tactic is rational persuasion, which means using facts, data, and logical arguments to persuade others that a proposed idea or request is the best way to complete a task or accomplish a desired goal. Rational persuasion can be effective regardless of whether the influence attempt is directed upward toward superiors, downward toward subordinates, or horizontally.[35] Most people have faith in facts and analysis.[36] Rational persuasion is most effective when a leader has technical knowledge and expertise related to the issue (expert power), although referent power is also used. Frequently, some parts of a rational argument cannot be backed up with facts and figures, so people have to believe in the leader's credibility to accept his or her argument.

EXHIBIT 12.6

Six Tactics for Asserting Influence

Use Rational Persuasion

Appeal to Ideals, Values, and Emotions

Use Symbolic Action

Build Coalitions

Expand Networks

Use Assertiveness

2. *Appeal to Ideals, Values, and Emotions.* In contrast to the logical approach of rational persuasion, this tactic involves using an emotional appeal to influence others.[37] The leader attempts to gain enthusiasm and commitment by arousing strong emotions or linking a proposal or request to followers' needs, hopes, ideals, and dreams. This tactic is frequently used by charismatic leaders, as described in Chapter 4. For example, Dolores Huerta, cofounder of the United Farm Workers Union, was described by a follower as having "a gift for making you believe in yourself. She has an ability to inspire you and urge you to do things you could not think were possible."[38]

Any leader can learn to appeal to people on an emotional level. Leaders may influence others by appealing to their desire to feel important, to feel useful, to fully use their skills and abilities, or to participate in something exciting or meaningful. This type of influence is critical for effective leadership, because it is primarily by appealing to ideals, values, and emotions that leaders rally people around an organizational vision. Clearly, this tactic depends greatly on a leader's active listening and discernment skills, because a leader has to understand the hopes, values, and longings of followers.

3. *Use Symbolic Action.* One way in which leaders appeal to people's emotions is through the use of rituals, stories, and other symbols. The use of metaphor and story enables leaders to tap into emotions and generate enthusiasm and commitment, as we discussed in the chapter on leadership communication. In addition, leaders use physical symbols, slogans, and ceremonies to persuade others of the higher purpose to be achieved through a desired course of action. The use of symbols to influence organizational culture and values will be discussed in detail in Chapter 14.

It is a leader's job to help people want to do what they need or have to do to help the organization prosper, and symbolic leadership is a subtle yet effective way to help people do the right thing.[39] Symbolic leadership touches the heart rather than the mind. By combining symbolic action with other, more rational appeals, leaders influence both the minds and emotions of followers.

4. *Build coalitions.* Coalition building means taking the time to talk with followers and other leaders to explain problems and describe the leader's point of view.[40] Most important decisions are made outside of formal meetings. Leaders consult with one another and reach a meeting of minds about a proposed change, decision, or strategy. Effective leaders are those who huddle with others, being willing to meet in groups of twos or threes to resolve key issues.[41] An important aspect of coalition building is to build positive social relationships. Social relationships are built on liking, trust, and respect. Reliability, trustworthiness, and the motivation to work

with others to achieve desired future outcomes are the desired use of politics.[42]

5. *Expand networks.* A leader's network of contacts can be expanded by reaching out to establish contact with additional people and by co-opting dissenters. The first approach is to build new alliances through the hiring, transfer, and promotion process. Identifying people, or placing people in key positions who are sympathetic to the desired outcomes of the leader can help achieve the leader's goals.[43] The second approach, *co-optation*, is the act of bringing a dissenter into one's network or coalition. Dissenters can be influenced if they are brought into the group. One example of co-optation occurred at a university. Several female professors were critical of the tenure and promotion process. They were appointed to a university committee to review promotion and tenure procedures. Once a part of the administrative process, they could see the administrative point of view and learned that administrators were not as evil as suspected. They were able to work with administration to create procedures that satisfied the interests of everyone.[44]

6. *Use Assertiveness.* Leaders can have influence simply by being clear about what they want and asking for it. If leaders do not ask, they seldom receive. Political activity is effective only when the leader's vision, goals, and desired changes are made explicit so the organization can respond. Leaders can use their courage to be assertive, saying what they believe to persuade others. An explicit proposal may be accepted simply because other people have no better alternatives. Also, an explicit proposal for change or for a specific decision alternative will often receive favorable treatment when other options are less well defined. Effective political behavior requires sufficient forcefulness and risk-taking to at least try to achieve desired outcomes.[45]

Being assertive is different from issuing orders and expecting them to be obeyed, as Larry Ellison learned at Oracle Corporation.

IN THE LEAD   **Larry Ellison, Oracle Corporation**

Even though he was the founder and chief executive of Oracle Corporation, Larry Ellison discovered that leading the company in a new direction required using more than his position power to influence employees. Oracle, a Silicon Valley powerhouse, made its reputation as a provider of database software, but leaders feared it would lose its edge as the Internet began to dominate information technology. Ellison had a vision that Oracle could apply Internet browsers to finding, analyzing, and reporting a company's data, rather than limiting these tasks to the traditional client-server tools. Before leaving for his summer vacation, Ellison issued orders that Oracle's employees should convert all products so that they could work as Internet applications, usable by any computer with Internet access and a browser. All client-server products would gradually be phased out.

When Ellison returned in the fall, he discovered that little had been done toward achieving his goal. Software developers weren't seriously working on the Internet applications, and salespeople were quietly telling customers that Oracle would continue to handle the old client-server products. Employees had not taken Ellison seriously about the new goals, perhaps interpreting his leaving on vacation as a symbol that he was not seriously committed to the goals himself. Ellison realized that he needed to exert more of his personal power to influence employees to work toward the new goal.

He began personally directing software development, using his physical presence and active, daily involvement as a symbol that the work was of the highest priority. He also found that as his involvement grew, his personal excitement about the vision grew. And, as Ellison's excitement about the work grew, so did his ability to inspire others by appealing to their values and ideals. Before long, software developers were turning out the new products Ellison had envisioned, and salespeople were enthusiastically explaining the new direction to customers. Ellison used his personal as well as position power to set Oracle on a new course, prompting a ZDNet online news story to proclaim, "Oracle is not your daddy's database company any more."[46]

ETHICAL CONSIDERATIONS IN USING POWER AND POLITICS

Harry Truman once said that leadership is the ability to get people to do what they don't want to do and like it.[47] His statement raises an important issue: Leadership can be an opportunity to use power and influence to accomplish important organizational goals, but power can also be abused. We all know that some people use power primarily to serve their own interests, at the expense of others and the organization. Recall from Chapter 4 our discussion of *personalized* versus *socialized* charismatic leaders. This distinction refers primarily to their approach to the use of power.[48] Personalized leaders are typically selfish, impulsive, and exercise power for their own self-centered needs and interests rather than for the good of the organization. Socialized leaders exercise power in the service of higher goals that will benefit others and the organization as a whole.

One specific area in which the unethical use of power has become of increasing concern for organizations is sexual harassment. People in organizations depend on one another—and especially on leaders—for many resources, including information, cooperation, and even their jobs. When access to resources seems to depend on granting sexual favors or putting up with sexually intimidating or threatening comments, the person in a dependent position is being personally violated, whether or not the leader actually withholds the resources. Partly in response to pressures from the courts, many organizations are developing policies and procedures that protect individuals from sexual harassment on the job and offer mechanisms for reporting complaints. Sexual harassment is not just unethical, it is illegal, and it is a clear abuse of power.

However, there are many other situations in organizations that are not so clear-cut, and leaders may sometimes have difficulty differentiating ethical from unethical uses of power and politics. Exhibit 12.7 summarizes some criteria that can guide ethical actions. First and foremost is the question of whether the action is motivated by self-interest or whether it is consistent with the organization's goals. At Phone.com, any employee can be terminated for a political act that is in the individual's own self-interest rather than in the interest of the company, or that harms another person in the company.[49] Once a leader answers this primary question, there are several other questions that can help determine whether a potential act is ethical, including whether it respects the rights of individuals and groups affected by it, whether it meets the standards of fairness, and whether the leader would want others to behave in the same way. If a leader answers these questions honestly, they can serve as a guide to

EXHIBIT 12.7

Guidelines for Ethical Action

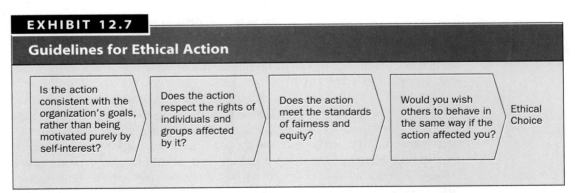

Is the action consistent with the organization's goals, rather than being motivated purely by self-interest?

Does the action respect the rights of individuals and groups affected by it?

Does the action meet the standards of fairness and equity?

Would you wish others to behave in the same way if the action affected you?

Ethical Choice

SOURCE: Based on G. F. Cavanaugh, D. J. Mobert, and M. Valasques, "The Ethics of Organizational Politics," *Academy of Management Journal,* June 1981, 363–374; and Stephen P. Robbins, *Organizational Behavior,* 8th ed. (Upper Saddle River, NJ: Prentice Hall, 1998), 422.

whether an intended political act is ethical. However, in the complex world of organizations, there will always be situations that are difficult to interpret. The most important point is for leaders to be aware of the ethical responsibilities of possessing power and take care to use their power to help rather than harm others.

SUMMARY AND INTERPRETATION

Leaders use various frames of reference to view the organization and its needs. Frames of reference determine how people gather information, make decisions, and exercise power. There are four frames of reference leaders may use: structural, human resource, political, and symbolic. Most leaders rely heavily on one or the other, but they can learn to use multiple frames of reference to expand their influence and better meet the needs of the organization.

This chapter focused largely on the political frame of reference. Power and politics are an important, though often hidden, part of all organizations. Power is the ability to influence others to reach desired outcomes. The best known types of power are legitimate, reward, expert, referent, and coercive, which are associated with a leader's position and personal qualities. Three distinct outcomes may result from the use of power to influence others: compliance, resistance, and commitment. The effective use of position power generally leads to follower compliance, whereas the excessive use of position power—particularly coercive power—may result in resistance. The follower response most often generated by personal power is commitment.

A key aspect of power is that it is a function of dependency, which is related to a person's control over resources. Dependency is greatest for resources that are highly important, scarce, and have no readily available substitutes. Leaders may gain power by contributing to the organization's purpose via interdepartmental dependencies, centrality, control over information, and coping with uncertainty.

Power is acquired, developed, and exercised through political activities. Political tactics for asserting influence include using rational persuasion, appealing to ideals, values and emotions, using symbolic action, building coalitions, expanding networks, and using assertiveness. Leadership action depends on forming effective social relationships and achieving the desired future through agreements and cooperation in today's complex world. One important consideration for leaders is how to use power and politics ethically and responsibly. Ethical leaders use power to serve the organization's goals, respect the rights of individuals and groups, and strive to be fair in their dealings with others.

KEY TERMS

frame	power	referent power
structural frame	influence	compliance
human resource frame	legitimate power	resistance
political frame	reward power	commitment
symbolic frame	coercive power	centrality
	expert power	politics

DISCUSSION QUESTIONS

1. Which organizational frame of reference do you most identify with? How do you think this frame of reference could be beneficial or detrimental to your leadership capability?

2. Discuss why symbolic leadership needs to be balanced by other leadership perspectives in order to meet organizational needs.

3. Do you agree that politics is a natural and healthy part of organizational life? Discuss.

4. What types and sources of power would be available to a leader of a student government organization? To a head nurse in a small hospital?

5. Do you think supervisors in discount stores such as Wal-Mart and Kmart have greater or less power over subordinates today than they had ten years ago? Discuss the reasons for your answer.

6. How does control over information give power to a person? Have you ever used control over information to influence a decision with friends or coworkers? Explain.

7. Describe ways in which you might increase your personal power.

8. Which of the six political tactics would you be most comfortable with as leader of a study group? Of a work team? Discuss.

LEADERSHIP DEVELOPMENT: Personal Feedback

Personal Power Profile

Below is a list of statements that describe behaviors that leaders in work organizations can direct toward their followers. Read each descriptive statement, thinking in terms of how you prefer to influence others. Mark the number that most closely represents how you feel. Use the following numbers for your answers.

1 = Strongly disagree   4 = Agree

2 = Disagree   5 = Strongly agree

3 = Neither agree nor disagree

To influence others, I would prefer to:

1. Increase their pay level	1 2 3 4 5
2. Make them feel valued	1 2 3 4 5
3. Give undesirable job assignments	1 2 3 4 5
4. Make them feel that I approve of them	1 2 3 4 5
5. Make them feel that they have commitments to meet	1 2 3 4 5
6. Make them feel personally accepted	1 2 3 4 5
7. Make them feel important	1 2 3 4 5
8. Give them good technical suggestions	1 2 3 4 5
9. Make the work difficult for them	1 2 3 4 5
10. Share my experience and/or training	1 2 3 4 5
11. Influence a pay increase	1 2 3 4 5
12. Make working here unpleasant	1 2 3 4 5
13. Make being at work distasteful	1 2 3 4 5
14. Make them feel that they should satisfy their job requirements	1 2 3 4 5
15. Provide them with sound job-related advice	1 2 3 4 5
16. Provide them with special benefits	1 2 3 4 5
17. Influence promotions	1 2 3 4 5
18. Give them the feeling that they have responsibilities to fulfill	1 2 3 4 5
19. Provide them with needed technical knowledge	1 2 3 4 5
20. Make them recognize that they have tasks to accomplish	1 2 3 4 5

Scoring

Compute your scores from the 20 questions according to the following procedure: Reward power—sum your responses to items 1, 13, 16, and 17. Coercive power—sum your responses to items 3, 9, 11, and 12. Legitimate power—sum your responses to questions 5, 14, 18, and 20. Referent power—sum your responses to questions 2, 4, 6, and 7. Expert power—sum your responses to questions 8, 10, 15, and 19.

Scores: Reward   =   _____   Coercive   =   _____   Legitimate   =   _____
Referent = _____ Expert = _____

Interpretation

A high score (16 and greater) on any of the five dimensions of power implies that you prefer to influence others by employing that particular form of power. A low score (8 and less) implies that you prefer not to employ this particular form of power to influence others. These scores represent your power profile.

SOURCE: Modified version of T. R. Hinkin and C. A. Schriesheim, "Development and Application of New Scales to Measure the French and Raven Bases of Social Power," *Journal of Applied Psychology* 74 (1989), 561–567, copyright (c) 1989 by the American Psychological Association, as appeared in Jon L. Pierce and John W. Newstrom, *Leaders and the Leadership Process: Readings, Self-Assessments, and Applications* (Chicago: Richard D. Irwin, 1995), 25–26.

LEADERSHIP DEVELOPMENT: Cases for Analysis

The Unhealthy Hospital

When Bruce Reid was hired as Blake Memorial Hospital's new CEO, the mandate had been clear: Improve the quality of care, and set the financial house in order.

As Reid struggled to finalize his budget for approval at next week's board meeting, his attention kept returning to one issue—the future of six off-site clinics. The clinics had been set up six years earlier to provide primary health care to the community's poorer neighborhoods. Although they provided a valuable service, they also diverted funds away from Blake's in-house services, many of which were underfunded. Cutting hospital personnel and freezing salaries could affect Blake's quality of care, which was already slipping. Eliminating the clinics, on the other hand, would save $256,000 without compromising Blake's internal operations.

However, there would be political consequences. Clara Bryant, the recently appointed commissioner of health services, repeatedly insisted that the clinics were an essential service for the poor. Closing the clinics could also jeopardize Blake's access to city funds. Dr. Winston Lee, chief of surgery, argued forcefully for closing the off-site clinics and having shuttle buses bring patients to the hospital weekly. Dr. Susan Russell, the hospital's director of clinics, was equally vocal about Blake's responsibility to the community, and suggested an entirely new way of delivering health care: "A hospital is not a building," she said, "it's a service. And wherever the service is needed, that is where the hospital should be." In Blake's case, that meant funding *more* clinics. Russell wanted to create a network of neighborhood-based centers for all the surrounding neighborhoods, poor and middle income. Besides improving health care, the network would act as an inpatient referral system for hospital services. Reid considered the proposal: If a clinic network could tap the paying public and generate more inpatient business, it might be worth looking into. Blake's rival hospital, located on the affluent side of town, certainly wasn't doing anything that creative. Reid was concerned, however, that whichever way he decided, he was going to make enemies.

SOURCE: Based on Anthony R. Kovner, "The Case of the Unhealthy Hospital," *Harvard Business Review*, September-October 1991, 12–25.

Questions

1. What sources of power does Reid have in this situation? Do you believe using legitimate power to implement a decision would have a positive effect at Blake Memorial? Discuss.

2. What political tactics might you use to resolve this dilemma?

3. How might Reid's predominant frame of reference influence his actions? Consider how he might act based on each of the four frames.

Waite Pharmaceuticals

Amelia Lassiter is chief information officer at Waite Pharmaceuticals, a large California-based company. In an industry where it generally takes $500 million and ten to twelve years to bring a new drug to market, companies such as Waite are always looking for ways to increase productivity and speed things up. After about eight months on the job, Lassiter suggested to company president James Hsu that Waite implement a new global knowledge-sharing application that promises to cut development time and costs in half. She has done extensive research on knowledge-sharing systems, and has talked closely with an IT director at global powerhouse Novartis, a company on the cutting edge in pharmaceuticals and animal health care, as well as other diverse products. The Novartis director believes the knowledge-sharing system plays an important role in that company's competitiveness.

Hsu presented the idea to the Board of Directors, and everyone agreed to pursue the project. He has asked Lassiter to investigate firms that could assist Waite's IT department in developing and implementing a global knowledge-sharing application that would be compatible with Waite's existing systems. Hsu explained that he wants to present the information to the Board of Directors for a decision next month.

Lassiter identified three major firms that she believed could handle the work and took a summary of her findings to Hsu's office, where she was greeted by

Lucy Lee, a young, petite, attractive woman who served as a sort of executive assistant to Hsu. Word was that the relationship between Lee and Hsu was totally proper, but besides the value of her good looks, no one in the company could understand why she was working there. Her lack of talent and experience made her a liability more than a help. She was very deferential to Hsu, but condescending to everyone else. Lee was a constant source of irritation and ill will among managers throughout the company, but there was no doubt that the only way to get to Hsu was through Lucy Lee. Lee took the information from Lassiter and promised the president would review it within two days.

The next afternoon, Hsu called Lassiter to his office and asked why Standard Systems, a small local consulting firm, was not being considered as a potential provider. Lassiter was surprised—Standard was known primarily for helping small companies computerize their accounting systems. She was not aware that they had done any work related to knowledge-sharing applications, particularly on a global basis. Upon further investigation into the company, she learned that Standard was owned by an uncle of Lucy Lee's, and things began to fall into place. Fortunately, she also learned that the firm did have some limited experience in more complex applications. She tried to talk privately with Hsu about his reasons for wanting to consider Standard, but Hsu insisted that Lee participate in all his internal meetings. At their most recent meeting, Hsu insisted that Standard be included for possible consideration by the Board.

During the next two weeks, representatives from each company met with Hsu, his two top executives, and the IT staff to explain their services and give demonstrations. Lassiter had suggested that the Board of Directors attend these presentations, but Hsu said they wouldn't have the time and he would need to evaluate everything and make a recommendation to the Board. At the end of these meetings, Lassiter prepared a final report evaluating the pros and cons of going with each firm and making her first and second-choice recommendations. Standard was dead last on her list. Although the firm had some excellent people and a good reputation, it was simply not capable of handling such a large and complex project.

Lassiter offered to present her findings to the Board, but again, Hsu declined her offer in the interest of time. "It's best if I present them with a final recommendation; that way, we can move on to other matters without getting bogged down with a lot of questions and discussion. These are busy people." The board meeting was held the following week. Lassiter was shocked when the president returned from the meeting and informed her that the board had decided to go with Standard Systems as the consulting firm for the knowledge-sharing application.

SOURCE: Based on "Restview Hospital," in Gary Yukl, *Leadership,* 4th ed. (Upper Saddle River, NJ: Prentice Hall, 1998), 203–204; "Did Somebody Say Infrastructure?" in Polly Schneider, "Another Trip to Hell," *CIO,* February 15, 2000, 71–78; and Joe Kay, "Digital Diary," Part I, *www.forbes.com/asap/2000/,* accessed on November 19, 2000.

Questions

1. How would you explain the Board's selection of Standard Systems?
2. Discuss the types, sources, and relative amount of power for the three main characters in this story.
3. How might Lassiter have increased her power and influence over this decision? If you were in her position, what would you do now?

REFERENCES

1. Michael Warshaw, "The Good Guy's (and Gal's) Guide to Office Politics," *Fast Company,* April-May 1998, 157–178.
2. Based on Lee G. Bolman and Terrence E. Deal, *Reframing Organizations: Artistry, Choice, and Leadership* (San Francisco: Jossey-Bass, 1991), and "Leadership and Management Effectiveness: A Multi-Frame, Multi-Sector Analysis," *Human Resource Management* 30, No. 4 (Winter 1991), 509–534.
3. Bolman and Deal, "Leadership and Management Effectiveness."
4. Richard D. Heimovics, Robert D. Herman, and Carole L. Jurkiewicz Coughlin, "Executive Leadership and Resource Dependence in Nonprofit Organizations: A Frame Analysis," *Public Administration Review* 53, No. 5 (September-October 1993), 419–427.
5. Bolman and Deal, *Reframing Organizations,* 431.
6. Jeffrey Pfeffer, *Managing with Power: Politics and Influence in Organizations* (Boston, MA: Harvard Business School Press, 1992); and Peter Moroz and Brian H. Kleiner, "Playing Hardball in Business Organizations," *IM* (January-February 1994), 9–11.
7. Bolman and Deal, "Leadership and Management Effectiveness."
8. Bolman and Deal, *Reframing Organizations,* 445.
9. James MacGregor Burns, *Leadership* (New York: Harper & Row, 1978); and Earle Hitchner, "The Power to Get Things Done," *National Productivity Review* 12 (Winter 1992/93), 117–122.
10. Robert A. Dahl, "The Concept of Power," *Behavioral Science* 2 (1957), 201–215.
11. W. Graham Astley and Paramijit S. Pachdeva, "Structural Sources of Intraorganizational Power: A Theoretical Synthesis," *Academy of Management Review* 9 (1984), 104–113; and Abraham Kaplan, "Power in Perspective," in Robert L. Kahn and Elise Boulding, eds., *Power and Conflict in Organizations* (London: Tavistock, 1964), 11–32.

12. Gerald R. Salancik and Jeffrey Pfeffer, "The Bases and Use of Power in Organizational Decision Making: The Case of the University," *Administrative Science Quarterly* 19 (1974), 453–473.

13. Earle Hitchner, "The Power to Get Things Done."

14. John R. P. French, Jr. and Bertram Raven, "The Bases of Social Power," in *Group Dynamics,* D. Cartwright and A. F. Zander, eds. (Evanston, IL: Row Peterson, 1960), 607–623.

15. Jeffrey Pfeffer, *Power in Organizations* (Marshfield, MA: Pitman Publishing, 1981).

16. Erik W. Larson and Jonathan B. King, "The Systemic Distortion of Information: An Ongoing Challenge to Management," *Organizational Dynamics,* 24, No. 3 (Winter 1996), 49-61; Thomas H. Davenport, Robert G. Eccles, and Lawrence Prusak, "Information Politics," *Sloan Management Review,* Fall 1992, 53–65.

17. Michael E. McGill and John W. Slocum, Jr., "A *Little* Leadership, Please?" *Organizational Dynamics,* Winter 1998, 39–49.

18. Gary A. Yukl and T. Taber, "The Effective Use of Managerial Power," *Personnel,* March-April 1983, 37–44.

19. R. E. Emerson, "Power-Dependence Relations," *American Sociological Review* 27 (1962), 31–41.

20. Sue Shellenbarger, "Workers, Emboldened by Tight Job Market, Take on Their Bosses," (Work & Family column), *The Wall Street Journal,* May 17, 2000, B1.

21. Henry Mintzberg, *Power In and Around Organizations* (Englewood Cliffs, NJ: Prentice-Hall, 1963).

22. Jeffrey Pfeffer, *Managing with Power: Politics and Influence in Organizations* (Boston: Harvard University Press, 1992); Gerald R. Salancik and Jeffrey Pfeffer, "Who Gets Power—and How They Hold onto It: A Strategic Contingency Model of Power," *Organizational Dynamics,* Winter 1977, 3–21; Pfeffer, *Power in Organizations;* Carol Stoak Saunders, "The Strategic Contingencies Theory of Power: Multiple Perspectives," *Journal of Management Studies* 27 (1990), 1–18.

23. Michel Crozier, *The Bureaucratic Phenomenon* (Chicago: University of Chicago Press, 1964).

24. Larson and King, "The Systemic Distortion of Information;" and Davenport, Eccles, and Prusak, "Information Politics."

25. D. J. Hickson, C. R. Hinings, C. A. Lee, R. C. Schneck, and J. M. Pennings, "A Strategic Contingencies Theory of Intraorganizational Power," *Administrative Science Quarterly* 16 (1971), 216–229.

26. Stephen P. Robbins, *Organizational Behavior,* 8th ed. (Upper Saddle River, NJ: Prentice Hall, 1998), 401.

27. Jeffrey Pfeffer and Gerald Salancik, "Organizational Decision Making as a Political Process: The Case of a University Budget," *Administrative Science Quarterly* (1974), 135–151.

28. Hickson, et al., "Strategic Contingencies Theory."

29. Based on Aaron Bernstein, "The Unions Are Learning to Hit Where It Hurts," *Business Week,* March 17, 1986, 112–114; and James Worsham, "Labor Comes Alive," *Nation's Business,* February 1996, 16–24.

30. Allan R. Cohen, Stephen L. Fink, Herman Gadon, and Robin D. Willits, *Effective Behavior in Organizations,* 7th ed. (New York: McGraw-Hill Irwin, 2001), 264; Rosabeth Moss Kanter, *Men and Women of the Corporation* (New York: Basic Books, 1977).

31. Pfeffer, *Power in Organizations,* 70.

32. Anne Fisher, "Ask Annie: Studying in Charm School, and Meeting Laggards," *Fortune,* June 7, 1999, 226.

33. Hal Lancaster, "For Some Managers, Hitting Middle Age Brings Uncertainties," *The Wall Street Journal,* April 20, 1999, B1.

34. Geoff Williams, "Making Headlines," *Entrepreneur,* September 1999, 114–117.

35. D. Kipnis, S. M. Schmidt, C. Swaffin-Smith, and I. Wilkinson, "Patterns of Managerial Influence: Shotgun Managers, Tacticians, and Bystanders," *Organizational Dynamics,* Winter 1984, 58–67.

36. Pfeffer, *Managing with Power,* Chapter 13.

37. Gary Yukl, *Leadership in Organizations,* 4th ed., (Upper Saddle River, NJ: Prentice-Hall, 1998), 209.

38. James Rainey, "The Eternal Soldadera," *Los Angeles Times Magazine,* August 15, 1999, 12–15, 35–37.

39. Pfeffer, *Managing with Power,* Chapter 15.

40. Pfeffer, *Power in Organizations,* 70.

41. V. Dallas Merrell, *Huddling: The Informal Way to Management Success* (New York: AMACON, 1979).

42. Donald J. Vredenburgh and John G. Maurer, "A Process Framework of Organizational Politics," *Human Relations* 37 (1984), 47–66.

43. Ibid.

44. Ibid.

45. Richard L. Daft, *Organization Theory and Design,* 6th ed. (Cincinnati, OH: South-Western College Publishing, 1998), Chapter 12.

46. Brent Schlender, "Larry Ellison: Oracle at Web Speed," *Fortune,* May 24, 1999, 128-133; and Mel Duvall, "Oracle Sings a New Tune," *Inter@ctive Week,* November 29, 1999 (downloaded from ZDNet, *www.zdnet.com,* December 15, 1999). With thanks to Karen Hill.

47. Quoted in Cohen, Fink, Gadon, and Willits, *Effective Behavior in Organizations,* 254.

48. For a discussion of personalized and socialized power, see David C. McClelland, *Power: The Inner Experience* (New York: Irvington, 1975).

49. "Stop the Politics," *Forbes ASAP,* April 3, 2000, 126.

The Leader as Social Architect

CHAPTER OUTLINE

YOUR LEADERSHIP CHALLENGE

After reading this chapter, you should be able to:

- Explain the relationship among vision, mission, strategy, and implementation mechanisms.

- Create your personal leadership vision.

- Use the common themes of powerful visions in your life and work.

- Understand how leaders formulate and implement strategy.

- Apply the elements of effective strategy.

Creating Vision and Strategic Direction

Nobody took Michael Dell seriously when he was building PCs in his dorm room instead of going to classes. But his fast, low-cost, build-to-order model eventually turned the world of computer manufacturing upside down and made Dell one of the richest people in America. His company, Dell Computer, grew 59 percent in fiscal year 1998, 48 percent in 1999, and 39 percent in 2000.

The Dell legend has awed and inspired young entrepreneurs and seasoned executives alike. Some say the legend is starting to fade. But Dell isn't worried, nor are his thousands of employees—they believe in Dell's vision that the company can once again come out of nowhere to destroy complacent competitors. Dell is still No. 1 in U.S. sales of desktops, notebooks, and workstations. In sales of Wintel servers, it ranks No. 2 behind Compaq, defying critics who said the company could never sell something so complicated over the telephone or through the Internet. Now, Dell wants to grab a bigger share of the future by developing low-cost storage systems and services to sell along with its hardware. To those who doubt that the company can compete in this new market, Dell says "Bring them on. We're coming right at them."

In his speeches to employees, Dell portrays his company as the good guy, a sort of corporate Robin Hood going into battle on behalf of customers against price gougers with huge offices, huge overhead, and clunky, outmoded ways of doing business. Employees rally to the battle cry. The company's primary weapons are Michael Dell's ability to align people with a vision and the skill of company leaders in executing the vision through sound strategy. Rather than focusing on radical new technology, Dell emphasizes speed, flexibility, and the discipline that enables the company to keep costs low, undercut competitors, and devour market share.

The annual employee meeting gives Michael Dell a chance to personally reinforce the vision in employees' minds. At the last meeting, he told a cheering crowd that Dell will be No. 1 in servers and storage, and "the premier Internet partner for customers around the world." Competitors beware—up to now, when Michael Dell says his company's employees will achieve something almost miraculous, they have.[1]

Regardless of Dell Computer's past success, Michael Dell knows he must constantly be looking forward. An important part of a leader's job is to set a course toward the future and get everyone in the organization moving in the same direction. Employee motivation and energy are crucial to the success of all organizations; the role of leadership is to focus everyone's energy on the same path. For Michael Dell, this means focusing employees on being the fastest, lowest-cost provider in order to "defeat the bad guys" and become No. 1 in servers, storage, and Internet services. At City Bank, the predecessor of Citigroup, it meant energizing employees to make the company "the most powerful, the most serviceable, the most far-reaching world financial institution that has ever been." That vision, articulated in 1915 by a small regional bank, motivated and inspired generations of workers until it was eventually achieved.[2]

One of leadership's primary functions is to create a compelling vision and develop a strategy to achieve it. Traditionally, in more stable times, top leaders defined the vision and organized human and material resources to reach it. In today's era of turbulent change, everyone in an organization must understand and support the vision so they can adapt their behaviors to achieving it.

In this chapter, we will first provide an overview of the leader's role in creating the organization's future. Then, we examine what vision is, the underlying themes that are common to effective visions, and how vision works on multiple levels. The distinction between vision and the organization's mission will also be explained. We will discuss how leaders formulate vision and strategy and the leader's contribution to actually achieving the vision. The last section discusses the impact this leadership has on organizations.

STRATEGIC LEADERSHIP

Superior organizational performance is not a matter of luck. It is determined largely by choices leaders make. Top leaders, like Michael Dell at Dell Computer, are responsible for knowing the organization's environment, considering what it might be like in five or ten years, and setting a direction for the future that everyone can believe in. In a fast-changing world, leaders are faced with a bewildering array of complex, ambiguous information, and no two leaders will see things the same way or make the same choices.

The complexity of the environment and the uncertainty of the future can overwhelm an executive. Thus, many are inclined to focus on internal organizational issues where they feel they have more control. It is easier and more comforting for leaders to focus on routine, operational issues where they can see instant results. In addition, years of downsizing and reengineering have reduced support staff in many organizations. Another problem is that many executives who have been accustomed to a command-and-control style of management get caught up in solving routine problems rather than allowing frontline workers to make decisions and take action on their own. One recent study looked at the time executives in various departments spend on long-term, strategic activities and found discouraging results. In the companies studied, 84 percent of finance executives' time, 70 percent of information technology executives' time, and 76 percent of operational managers' time is focused on routine, day-to-day activities.[3] Another study found that, on average, senior executives in today's organizations spend less than 3 percent of their energy on building a corporate perspective for the future, and in some companies, the average is less than 1 percent.[4]

The first, essential step to remaining competitive is to develop an understanding of the trends and discontinuities that can be used to gain an edge. Leaders such as Michael Dell, Jack Welch of General Electric, and Scott McNealy of Sun Microsystems are constantly looking toward the future. "All they do is chase opportunity," says Sander Flaum, chairman and CEO of Robert A. Becker Inc., a health-care strategic marketing firm. "They aren't afraid to go out of the box. . . . The great ones are always focused on discontinuity, not building the future based upon the past, but building a future on what [they] think it can be."[5] Leaders at Charles Schwab & Co. were among the first to spot the opportunities available for online securities trading. Charles Schwab and other top leaders recognized the Web's potential as early as 1995, the first year more personal computers were sold in the United States than television sets. Today, Charles Schwab has moved the core of its business online, gets 76 million hits a day, and has captured more than 40 percent of the assets invested in online trading accounts.[6]

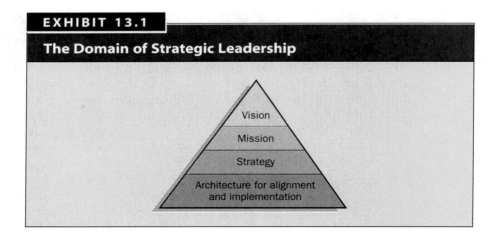

EXHIBIT 13.1

The Domain of Strategic Leadership

Thinking about how to meet future customer needs is more important now than ever. Globalization, deregulation, advancing technology, and changing demographics and lifestyles are profoundly altering the way businesses are perceived and operate. The world in 2010 will be different from the world of today, and leaders are responsible for determining how their organizations can fit into that world. No organization can thrive for long without a clear viewpoint and framework for the future.

Exhibit 13.1 illustrates the levels that make up the domain of strategic leadership. **Strategic leadership** is responsible for the relationship of the external environment to choices about vision, mission, strategy, and their implementation.[7] At the top of Exhibit 13.1 is a clear, compelling vision of where the organization wants to be in five to ten years. The vision reflects the environment and works in concert with the company's mission—its core values, purpose, and reason for existence. Strategy provides direction for translating the vision into action and is the basis for the development of specific mechanisms to help the organization achieve goals. Strategies are intentions, whereas implementation is through the basic organization architecture (structure, incentives) that makes things happen. Each level of the hierarchy in Exhibit 13.1 supports the level above it. Each part of this framework will be discussed in the remainder of this chapter.

LEADERSHIP VISION

A vision can be thought of as a dream for the future. Rebekka Weinstein, the daughter of an entrepreneur, has grown up with the dream of going into business for herself, of not being "harnessed and restricted by the corporate world." Her dream motivated her to study hard and achieve high academic honors at Richardson High School in Texas, which in turn enabled her to win a scholarship that will help finance her studies at Brown University. Moreover, Rebekka has already started her own jewelry-making business, creating custom pieces for individuals and selling original designs through the museum store at the Dallas Museum of Art and through a few independent retailers.[8] Rebekka's dream has played a powerful role in motivating her behavior and guiding her decisions and actions. Rebekka's dream is a personal one, but if her vision becomes a reality, she will someday have to create a vision that will inspire and motivate her employees as well as herself.

For organizations, a **vision** is an attractive, ideal future that is credible yet not readily attainable. A vision is not *just* a dream—it is an ambitious view of the future that everyone in the organization can believe in, one that can realistically be achieved, yet offers a future that is better in important ways than what now exists. In the 1950s, Sony Corporation wanted to "[b]ecome the company most known for changing the worldwide poor-quality image of Japanese products."[9] It may be hard to believe today, but in the 1950s this was a highly ambitious goal. Sometimes visions are brief, compelling, and slogan-like, easily communicated to and understood by everyone in the organization. For example, Coca-Cola's "A Coke within arm's reach of everyone on the planet" and Komatsu's "Encircle Caterpillar" serve to motivate all workers. Buy.com's "The lowest prices on earth" lets everyone inside and outside the organization know that the company is ruthlessly committed to being the price leader.[10] Exhibit 13.2 lists a few more brief vision statements that let people know where the organization wants to go in the future.

As these visions illustrate, a vision presents a challenge—it is an ambitious view of the future that requires employees to give their best. The City Bank vision mentioned earlier is another example: considering its size and strength at the time, City Bank's vision to become the most far-reaching bank in the world was highly ambitious, but it was eventually attained. Many successful organizations don't have short, easily communicated slogans, but their visions are powerful because leaders paint a compelling picture of where the organization wants to go. Microstrategy's Michael Saylor has created an ambitious, somewhat radical, vision that motivates employees and fires up customers.

IN THE LEAD   ## Michael Saylor, Microstrategy

Michael Saylor dreams of "a world where we have universal intelligence, and that will mean 10,000 intelligence dynamos. There ought to be dynamos everywhere, spinning data, always delivering the right information to the right person. I want to know when my wife's in the hospital or my boat is smacked or my equities are

EXHIBIT 13.2

Examples of Brief Vision Statements

Motorola: Become the premier company in the world.

Ritz-Carlton (Amelia Island) engineering department: To boldly go where no hotel has gone before—free of all defects.

Johnson Controls Inc.: Continually exceed our customers' increasing expectations.

New York City Transit: No graffiti.

Texas Commerce Bank: Eliminate what annoys our bankers and our customers.

AT&T Business and Commercial Services: Be our customers' best sales relationship.

Egon Zehnder: Be the worldwide leader in executive search.

SOURCE: These examples are from Jon R. Katzenbach and the RCL Team, *Real Change Leaders: How You Can Create Growth and High Performance in Your Company* (New York: Times Business, 1995), 68–70; Andrew Campbell and Sally Yeung, "Creating a Sense of Mission," *Long Range Planning,* August, 1991, 10–20; Alan Farnham, "State Your Values, Hold the Hot Air," *Fortune,* April 19, 1993, 117–124; and Christopher K. Bart, "Sex, Lies, and Mission Statements," *Business Horizons,* November-December 1997, 23–28.

in trouble or the government's unstable and something has happened to my hometown. I think that people will surrender their personal information to a centralized intelligence dynamo . . . because the cost of not doing so is an early death, an accidental death, a lack of opportunity, a lack of income, a lack of happiness."

Saylor gives some version of that little speech all the time. His company makes complex decision-support software that lets companies sift through massive amounts of data, ask complex questions, and get answers back in neat, easy-to-understand charts and graphs. But Saylor's vision is not to make software or even to beat competitors; it's to build a better world. His ability to sell the vision has earned him almost cult-like devotion from employees and customers alike. "He can make his products sound like they're the solution to world hunger," one analyst said.

To some people, Saylor sounds a little kooky, but his vision has kept Microstrategy a step ahead of rivals. Since the company started selling data-mining software in 1994, it has gone from losing money on $5 million in sales to netting $6 million on sales of $106 million in 1998. Microstrategy is now the fourth largest vendor of decision-support software. Employee turnover at the company is around 10 percent, surprisingly low for a software company. Saylor strongly believes in his long-term vision of the future, where his products will be used in limitless ways to improve the lives of the everyday working man and woman. He frequently talks about a future that spans generations and even considers a time when his company may no longer exist. What he's sure *will* exist, however, is the legacy of Microstrategy's dedication to mankind[11]

Michael Saylor started Microstrategy when he was twenty-four years old and fresh out of the Massachusetts Institute of Technology. Over the past decade, Saylor's ability to create and communicate a powerful vision has enabled him to build a solid organization that is one of today's leading software companies.

In Exhibit 13.3, vision is shown as a guiding star, drawing everyone in the organization along the same path toward the future. Taking the organization on this path requires leadership. Compare this to rational management (as described in Chapter 1), which leads to the status quo. When employees have a guiding vision, everyday decisions and actions throughout the organization respond to current problems and challenges in ways that move the organization toward the future rather than maintain the status quo.

EXHIBIT 13.3

The Nature of the Vision

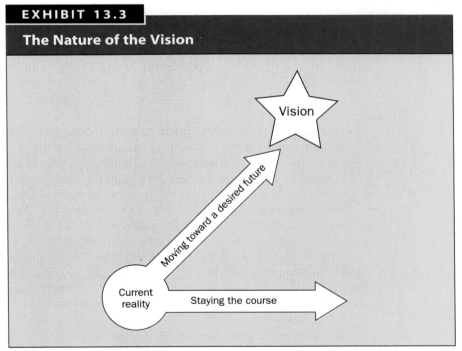

SOURCE: Based on William D. Hitt, *The Leader-Manager:Guidelines for Action* (Columbus, OH: Battelle Press, 1988).

What Vision Does

Vision works in a number of important ways. An effective vision provides a link between today and tomorrow, serves to energize and motivate employees toward the future, provides meaning for people's work, and sets a standard of excellence in the organization.[12]

VISION LINKS THE PRESENT TO THE FUTURE   Vision connects what is going on right now with what the organization aspires to. A vision is always about the future, but it begins with the here and now. Microstrategy employees, for example, create products that meet current organizational needs but they also strive to create products that may inspire other, broader applications for the future.

In organizations, the pressures to meet deadlines, make the big sale, solve immediate problems, and complete specific projects are very real. The problem for today's organizations is that managers spend most of their time dealing with current problems and little time contemplating and visualizing the future. Some have suggested that today's leaders need "bifocal vision," the ability to take care of the needs of today and meet current obligations while also aiming toward dreams for the future.[13] The ability to operate on both levels can be seen in a number of successful companies, such as DuPont. Top executives routinely review short-term operational goals with managers throughout the company, reflecting a focus on the present. However, DuPont has succeeded over the long haul because of its leaders' ability to look to the future and shift gears quickly to take advantage of new opportunities. Since its beginning, DuPont's business portfolio has shifted from gunpowder to specialty chemicals, and today, the company is moving into biotechnology and life sciences.[14]

VISION ENERGIZES PEOPLE AND GARNERS COMMITMENT   People want to feel enthusiastic about their work. A powerful vision frees people from the mundane by providing them with a challenge worthy of their best efforts. Many people commit their time and energy voluntarily to causes they believe in—a political campaign, the animal rights movement, environmental causes. These same people often leave their energy and enthusiasm at home when they go to work, because they don't have anything to inspire them. Employees are not generally willing to make emotional commitments just for the sake of increasing profits and enhancing shareholder wealth. Vision needs to transcend the bottom line because people are willing, and even eager, to commit to something truly worthwhile, something that makes life better for others or improves their communities.[15] Consider Henry Ford's original vision for Ford Motor Company:

> *I will build a motor car for the great multitude. . . . It will be so low in price that no man making a good salary will be unable to own one and*

enjoy with his family the blessings of hours of pleasure in God's open spaces. . . . When I'm through, everybody will be able to afford one, and everyone will have one. The horse will have disappeared from our highways, the automobile will be taken for granted [and we will give many people] employment at good wages.[16]

Employees were motivated and energized by Ford's vision because they saw an opportunity to make life better for themselves and others.

VISION GIVES MEANING TO WORK.   People need to find dignity and meaning in their work. Even people performing routine tasks can find pride in their work when they have a larger purpose for what they do. For example, a clerk who thinks of his job as "processing insurance claims" will feel very differently than one who thinks of her job as helping victims of fire or burglary put their lives back in order.[17] Michael Saylor's vision at Microstrategy is highly successful on this front. Many employees don't think of their job at Microstrategy as work, but as dedication to a cause. They know they're developing software that today helps a company such as McDonald's, for example, analyze which hamburger promotion is most successful with middle-class men, but they also believe they're developing products that will someday change the world.

One interesting finding is that younger employees often ask about a company's vision when interviewing for a job. According to Ann Weiser, vice president of human resources development at Kraft Foods, "Generation Xers demand a vision that conveys the big picture of what the organization stands for and how, or whether, they will fit in."[18]

VISION ESTABLISHES A STANDARD OF EXCELLENCE   Vision provides a measure by which employees can gauge their contributions to the organization. Most workers welcome the chance to see how their work fits into the whole. Think of how frustrating it is to watch a movie when the projector is out of focus. Today's complex, fast-changing business environment often seems just like that—out of focus.[19] A vision is the focus button. It clarifies an image of the future and lets people see how they can contribute. For example, salespeople at Nordstrom have a clear picture of superior customer service, so they can see how to serve customers better. A vision presents a challenge, asks people to go where they haven't gone before. Thus, it encourages workers to take risks and find new ways of doing things. The Living Leadership box discusses three qualities a powerful vision can inspire.

A good vision brings out the best by speaking to the hearts of employees, letting them be a part of something bigger than themselves. Consider how Walt Disney painted a picture of Disneyland that unified and energized employees.

IN THE LEAD   Walt Disney

Walt Disney created a clear picture of what he wanted Disneyland to be. His vision translated hopes and dreams into words and allowed employees to help create the future. Notice how the vision says nothing about making money—the emphasis is on a greater purpose that all employees could believe in.

"The idea of Disneyland is a simple one. It will be a place for people to find happiness and knowledge. It will be a place for parents and children to spend pleasant times in one another's company, a place for teachers and pupils to discover greater ways of understanding and education. Here the older generation can recapture the nostalgia of days gone by, and the younger generation can savor the challenge of the future. Here will be the wonders of Nature and Man for all to see and understand. Disneyland will be based upon and dedicated to the ideals, the dreams, and hard facts that have created America. And it will be uniquely equipped to dramatize these dreams and facts and send them forth as a source of courage and inspiration for all the world. Disneyland will be something of a fair, an exhibition, a playground, a community center, a museum of living facts, and a showplace of beauty and magic. It will be filled with the accomplishments, the joys and hopes of the world we live in. And it will remind us and show us how to make these wonders part of our lives."[20]

A clear, inspiring picture such as that painted by Walt Disney can have a powerful impact on people. His vision gave meaning and value to workers' activities. Painting a clear picture of the future is a significant responsibility of leaders, yet it cannot always be the leader's alone. To make a difference, a vision can be widely shared and is often created with the participation of others. Every good organizational vision is a shared vision. There are a number of other common themes that are found in powerful or transforming visions like the ones for Disneyland and Microstrategy.

Common Themes of Vision

Five themes are common to powerful, effective visions: they have broad, widely shared appeal; they help organizations deal with change; they encourage faith and hope for the future; they reflect high ideals; and they define both the organization's destination and the basic rules to get there.

VISION HAS BROAD APPEAL   One theme common to effective visions is a focus on people. Although it may be obvious that a vision can be achieved only through people, many visions fail to adequately involve employees. The vision cannot be the property of the leader alone.[21] The ideal vision is identified with the organization as a whole, not with a single leader or even a top leadership team. It "grabs

LIVING LEADERSHIP

Vision's Offspring

A compelling vision inspires and nurtures three qualities, here personified as individuals. Do you think followers would benefit from contact with the following "people" in an organization?

Clarity

My visits to Clarity are soothing now. He never tells me what to think or feel or do but shows me how to find out what I need to know . . . he presented me with a sketchbook and told me to draw the same thing every day until the drawing started to speak to me.

Commitment

Commitment has kind eyes. He wears sturdy shoes. . . . You can taste in [his] vegetables that the soil has been cared for. . . . He is a simple man, and yet he is mysterious. He is more generous than most people. His heart is open. He is not afraid of life.

Imagination

Some people accuse Imagination of being a liar. They don't understand that she has her own ways of uncovering the truth. . . . Imagination has been working as a fortuneteller in the circus. She has a way of telling your fortune so clearly that you believe her, and then your wishes start to come true. . . . Her vision is more complex, and very simple. Even with the old stories, she wants us to see what has never been seen before.

SOURCE: J. Ruth Gendler, *The Book of Qualities* (New York: Harper & Row, 1988). Used with permission.

---

people in the gut" and motivates them to work toward a common end.[22] It allows each individual to act independently but in the same direction.

VISION DEALS WITH CHANGE Visions that work help the organization achieve bold change. Vision is about action and challenges people to make important changes toward a better future. Change can be frightening, but a clear sense of direction helps people face the difficulties and uncertainties involved in the change process.

VISION ENCOURAGES FAITH AND HOPE Vision exists only in the imagination—it is a picture of a world that cannot be observed or verified in advance. The future is shaped by people who believe in it, and a powerful vision helps people believe that they can be effective, that there is a better future they can move to through their own commitment and actions. Vision is an emotional appeal to our fundamental human needs and desires—to feel important and useful, to believe we can make a real difference in the world.[23] John F. Kennedy's vision for NASA to send a man to the moon by the end of the 1960s was so powerful that hundreds of thousands of people throughout the world believed in a future they couldn't see.[24]

VISION REFLECTS HIGH IDEALS   Good visions are idealistic. Vision has power to inspire and energize people only when it paints an uplifting future. When Kennedy announced the "man on the moon" vision, NASA had only a small amount of the knowledge it would need to accomplish the feat. William F. Powers, who worked at NASA during the 1960s, later helped Ford Motor Company develop an idealistic vision for a new automobile. The vision to create the world's first high-volume, aerodynamically styled car that featured fuel economy (the 1980s Taurus) was a big risk for Ford at a time when the company was down and out. But leaders painted this as a chance not only to save the company but to establish a whole new path in automotive engineering, which helped to energize and motivate employees.[25]

VISION DEFINES THE DESTINATION AND THE JOURNEY   A good vision for the future includes specific outcomes that the organization wants to achieve. It also incorporates the underlying values that will help the organization get there. For example, at Dell Computer Corp., described at the beginning of the chapter, the values of speed and flexibility are built into the company's vision statement and into the corporate culture. "The culture is results," says Michael Dell. "It's 'Get it done.' It's 'Do whatever it takes.'" At Dell, goals that would be considered stretch targets anywhere else are just business as usual.[26] Giro Sport Design, a small company that manufactures bicycling products, wants to "become the Nike of the cycling industry," but it doesn't want to do so at any cost. Giro's complete vision statement is based on a set of guiding principles that emphasize making a positive impact on society.[27] As another example, a private business school might specify certain outcomes such as a top 20 ranking, placing 90 percent of students in summer internships, and getting 80 percent of students into jobs by June of their graduating year. Yet in the process of reaching those specific outcomes, the school wants to increase students' knowledge of business, values, and teamwork, as well as prepare them for lifelong learning. Additionally, the vision may espouse underlying values such as no separation between fields of study or between professors and students, a genuine concern for students' welfare, and adding to the body of business knowledge. A good vision includes both the desired future outcomes and the underlying values that set the rules for achieving them.[28]

A powerful vision can have a significant impact on an organization and its employees, but only if it is communicated clearly to everyone throughout the organization. Some companies, such as Merix Corp., a $140 million electronic interconnect supplier that was spun out of Tektronix in 1994, are experimenting with graphical vision statements that help people think in new, metaphorical ways about their work.

IN THE LEAD   Debi Coleman, Merix Corp.

Most of us have heard the saying that a picture is worth a thousand words. Leaders at Merix Corp., based in Forest Grove, Oregon, took the saying to heart and used graphics as a tool to articulate the company's strategic vision.

Chair and CEO Debi Coleman held a company retreat where employees talked about their feelings about Merix and where it should be headed. A consultant (David Sibbet, president and CEO of The Grove Consultants International) then mapped out the themes that emerged. The resulting graphical vision statement, shown in Exhibit 13.4, conveys the image of a futuristic company, going where no one has gone before, on the leading edge of technology. "Our single overriding goal is to be the best electronic interconnect company in the world," says Coleman. "This image conveys the power of that idea as well as the challenges. It also tells a story about Merix. It puts our core values and core competencies at the center of the company, tells the history of the company and our proud relationship to Tektronix, and identifies our suppliers and partners." The statement portrays Merix as a mother ship, moving fast in a fast-moving, complex industry, constantly sharing goods, information, and technology with suppliers and partners.

"Each of these images means something to us," Coleman continues. "If you could put this drawing on a computer and double-click on each image, underneath each one you'd find serious plans, strategies with time lines, and performance measures. If you look around Merix, this picture is on people's walls, on workbenches, even on T-shirts."[29]

Merix leaders believe the image in Exhibit 13.4 conveys the company's vision and worldview more powerfully than words ever could and that it becomes more personal and meaningful to employees. A visual statement can be more broadly shared—a written statement on posters and T-shirts wouldn't have the same aesthetic and emotional impact that the image has. Other companies are also using graphics as a tool to more vividly convey their visions. Particularly for younger employees, who are increasingly attuned to absorbing information via computer graphics rather than words on paper, graphical vision statements can be more compelling than a written or spoken statement.

A Vision Works at Multiple Levels

Most of the visions we have talked about so far are for the company as a whole. However, divisions, departments, and individuals also have visions, which are just as important and powerful. For example, the head of Corporate Audit for

EXHIBIT 13.4

Merix Vision Statement

Citicorp worked with his department to craft an elegant vision that stands on its own yet fits well within the broader Citicorp vision. One aspect of Corporate Audit's vision is to "shape the way the line thinks and acts about risk and control . . . and to take a leadership role outside of Citicorp in setting professional standards."[30] Benjamin Zander, world-renowned conductor of the Boston Philharmonic Orchestra, has a personal vision to "share the most powerful language ever devised by human beings" by putting a recording of Beethoven's Fifth Symphony in the hands of every person on earth.[31] Successful individuals usually have a clear mental picture of their vision and how to achieve it. People who do not have this clear vision of the future have less chance of success.

Top leaders of an effective organization develop a vision for the organization as a whole, and at the same time a project team leader five levels beneath the CEO can develop a vision with team members for a new product they are working on. Leaders of functional departments, divisions, and teams can use vision with the same positive results as do top leaders.

Consider the facility manager for a large corporation. His department received requests to fix toilets and air conditioners. The manager took this to mean that people cared about their physical space, which became the basis for his vision to "use physical space to make people feel good." People in his department started planting flowers outside office windows and created an environment that lifted people's spirits.[32] In innovative companies, every group or department creates its own vision, as long as the vision is in line with the overall company's direction. At the Ritz-Carlton hotel chain, each department in each hotel develops its own vision statement. People in the parking garage, engineering department, housekeeping, and the front desk all wrestle with their purpose, and develop a shared vision for their future.[33]

A clear mental picture of how to do something successfully is a tremendous advantage. When individuals have a clear vision, they become effective as leaders. Without the vision, a person's work in the moment may be disconnected from the higher goals. In talking about his work as conductor of the Boston Philharmonic, Benjamin Zander says that the leader's job is "to create a powerful vision that allows room for things to occur that are as yet undreamed of. The leader must hold the definition of the vision so clearly that all the players involved are able to align with it daily."[34]

When a vision for the organization as a whole is shared among individuals and departments, it has real impact. Therefore top leaders' real work is to share the vision with others, and to help them to develop their part of the vision so that everyone has the picture. As Peter Senge said in *The Fifth Discipline,* a shared vision changes people's relationship with the organization. It creates a common identity and allows each employee to look at a manager and think of "our company" rather than "their company." The vision becomes the common thread connecting people, involving them personally and emotionally in the organization.[35]

When every person understands and embraces a vision, the organization becomes self-adapting. Although each individual acts independently, everyone is working in the same direction. In the new sciences, this is called the principle of self-reference. **Self-reference** means that each element in a system will serve the goals of the whole system when the elements are imprinted with an understanding of the whole. Thus the vision serves to direct and control people for the good of themselves and the organization. Leaders at Dell Computer have imprinted the vision so clearly in employees' minds that one CEO who has studied the company says Dell is "like a living organism. It is constantly adapting and changing and finding ways to master its environment, as opposed to just respond to it. . . . Somehow Dell has been able to take speed and flexibility and build it into their DNA."[36]

To develop a shared vision, leaders share their personal visions with others and encourage others to express their dreams for the future. This requires openness, good listening skills, and the courage to connect with others on an emotional level. Good leaders give up the idea that vision emanates from only the top. A leader's ultimate responsibility is to be in touch with the hopes and dreams that drive employees and find the common ground that binds personal dreams into a shared vision for the organization. As one successful top leader put it, "My job, fundamentally, is listening to what the organization is trying to say, and then making sure it is forcefully articulated."[37] Another successful leader refers to leadership as "discovering the company's destiny and having the courage to follow it."[38]

MISSION

Mission is not the same thing as a company's vision, although the two work together. The **mission** is the organization's core broad purpose and reason for existence. It defines the company's core values and reason for being, and it provides a basis for creating the vision. Whereas vision is an ambitious desire for the future, mission is what the organization "stands for" in a larger sense. James Collins compares Zenith and Motorola to illustrate how knowing what the organization stands for helps companies adapt and grow. Both Zenith and Motorola were once successful makers of televisions. Yet while Zenith stayed there, Motorola continued to move forward—to making microprocessors, integrated circuits, and numerous other products—and became one of the most highly regarded companies in the country. The difference is that Motorola defined its mission as "applying technology to benefit the public," not as "making television sets."[39] Visions for the future should change and grow continuously, whereas the mission itself should persist in the face of change, as discussed in the Leader's Bookshelf. The mission defines the enduring character, values, and purpose of the organization.

LEADER'S BOOKSHELF

Built to Last: Successful Habits of Visionary Companies

James C. Collins and Jerry I. Porras

In a six-year study comparing eighteen companies that have experienced long-term success with eighteen similar companies that have not performed as well, James Collins and Jerry Porras found a key determining factor in the successful companies to be a culture in which employees share such a strong sense of purpose that they know in their hearts what is right for the company. *Built to Last* describes how companies such as 3M, Boeing, Wal-Mart, Merck, Nordstrom, Hewlett-Packard, and others have successfully adapted to a changing world without losing sight of the core values that guide the organization. Collins and Porras found that the successful companies were guided by a "core ideology"—values and a sense of purpose that go beyond just making money and that provide a guide for employee behavior.

Timeless Fundamentals
The book offers four key concepts that show how leaders can contribute to building successful companies.

- **Be a Clock Builder, Not a Time Teller.** Products and market opportunities are vehicles for building a great organization, not the other way around. Visionary leaders concentrate on building adaptive cultures and systems that remain strong despite changes in products, services, or markets.

- **Embrace the "Genius of the AND."** Successful organizations simultaneously embrace two extremes, such as continuity and change, stability and revolution, predictability and chaos.

- **Preserve the Core/Stimulate Progress.** The core ideology is balanced with a relentless drive for progress. Successful companies set ambitious goals and create an atmosphere that encourages experimentation and learning.

- **Seek Consistent Alignment.** Strive to make all aspects of the company work in unison with the core ideology. At Disneyland, employees are "cast members" and customers are "guests." Hewlett-Packard's policies reinforce its commitment to respect for each individual.

Conclusion
Built to Last offers important lessons on how leaders can build organizations that stand the test of time. By concentrating on the timeless fundamentals, organizations can adapt and thrive in a changing world.

Built to Last: Successful Habits of Visionary Companies, by James C. Collins and Jerry I. Porras, is published by Harper-Collins.

Typically the mission is made up of two critical parts: the core values and the core purpose. The *core values* guide the organization "no matter what." As Ralph Larsen, former CEO of Johnson & Johnson, explained it, "The core values embodied in our credo might be a competitive advantage, but that is not *why* we have them. We have them because they define for us what we stand for, and we would hold them even if they became a competitive *dis*advantage in certain situations."[40] Johnson & Johnson's core values led the company, for example, to voluntarily remove Tylenol from the market after the cyanide poisoning of some Tylenol capsule users, even though this act cost the company more than $100 million.

EXHIBIT 13.5

Merck's Mission Statement

Merck & Co., Inc. is a leading research-driven pharmaceutical products and services company. Merck discovers, develops, manufactures, and markets a broad range of innovative products to improve human and animal health. The Merck-Medco Managed Care Division manages pharmacy benefits for more than 40 million Americans, encouraging the appropriate use of medicines and providing disease management programs.

OUR MISSION

The mission of **Merck** is to provide society with superior products and services—innovations and solutions that improve the quality of life and satisfy customer needs—to provide employees with meaningful work and advancement opportunities and investors with a superior rate of return.

OUR VALUES

1. **Our business is preserving and improving human life.** All of our actions must be measured by our success in achieving this goal. We value above all our ability to serve everyone who can benefit from the appropriate use of our products and services, thereby providing lasting consumer satisfaction.

2. **We are committed to the highest standards of ethics and integrity.** We are responsible to our customers, to Merck employees and their families, to the environments we inhabit, and to the societies we serve worldwide. In discharging our responsibilities, we do not take professional or ethical shortcuts. Our interactions with all segments of society must reflect the high standards we profess.

3. **We are dedicated to the highest level of scientific excellence and commit our research to improving human and animal health and the quality of life.** We strive to identify the most critical needs of consumers and customers, we devote our resources to meeting those needs.

4. **We expect profits, but only from work that satisfies customer needs and benefits humanity.** Our ability to meet our responsibilities depends on maintaining a financial position that invites investment in leading-edge research and that makes possible effective delivery of research results.

5. **We recognize that the ability to excel—to most competitively meet society's and customers' needs—depends on the integrity, knowledge, imagination, skill, diversity, and teamwork of employees, and we value these qualities most highly.** To this end, we strive to create an environment of mutual respect, encouragement and teamwork—a working environment that rewards commitment and performance and is responsive to the needs of employees and their families.

SOURCE: http://www.merck.com/overview/philosophy.html

The mission also includes the company's *core purpose*. An effective purpose statement doesn't just describe products or services; it captures people's idealistic motivations for why the organization exists. The purpose of America Online is "to build a global medium as central to people's lives as the telephone or television . . . and even more valuable." Great Plains, a provider of integrated e-business solutions, which has recently earned Global Best Practices Awards in the categories of Exceeding Customer Expectations, Motivating and Retaining Employees, and Strategic Leadership, defines its core purpose as to "improve the lives and business success of partners and customers."

Many companies have mission statements that define what they stand for, including their core values and core purpose. For example, the mission statement of Medtronics includes the organization's purpose—to contribute to human welfare—as well as the values used to carry out the mission, including a commitment to unsurpassed quality and focused growth, recognizing the personal worth of each employee, being a good corporate citizen, and earning a fair profit.[41] Exhibit 13.5 shows the mission statement for Merck & Co., Inc. Read the mission statement and then consider how Merck's specific vision grows out of the company's mission and works with it:

> We will be the first drug maker with advanced research in every disease category. Our research will be as good as the science being done anywhere in the world. Our drugs won't be used by a single person who doesn't need them. Merck will continue to grow on a steady basis, bringing forth worthwhile products. . . .[42]

Some companies include the specific vision for the future as a part of their mission statements. However, it is important to remember that the vision continually grows and changes, while the mission endures. It serves as the glue that holds the organization together in times of change and guides strategic choices and decisions about the future.

STRATEGY FORMULATION

Strong missions and guiding visions are important, but they are not enough alone to make strong, powerful organizations. For organizations to succeed, they need ways to translate vision, values, and purpose into action, which is the role of strategy. Formulating strategy is the hard, serious work of taking a specific step toward the future. **Strategic management** is the set of decisions and actions used to formulate and implement specific strategies that will achieve a competitively superior fit between the organization and its environment so as to achieve organizational goals.[43] It is the leader's job to find this fit and translate it into action.

Strategy can be defined as the general plan of action that describes resource allocation and other activities for dealing with the environment and helping the organization attain its goals. In formulating strategy, leaders ask questions such as "Where is the organization now? Where does the organization want to be? What changes and trends are occurring in the competitive environment? What courses of action can help us achieve our vision?" Developing effective strategy requires actively listening to people both inside and outside the organization, as well as examining trends and discontinuities in the environment. In today's high tech and Web-based businesses, formulating innovative strategy often requires radical thinking because things change so quickly. Ted Waite of Gateway, for example, has pursued an innovative strategy to reinvent his company for the Internet generation. Gateway started as a maker of personal computers, but Waite casually remarks, "I'd be totally happy if I didn't sell a PC five years from now." Gateway has been moving away from reliance on PCs for years, including launching an Internet access service and venturing into the finance business with a package that lets a consumer pay monthly installments for a PC bundled with software, Internet access, in-home repair service, and the industry's first trade-in option. Waite's next step is to again break new ground by offering an array of Web appliances.[44]

Innovative thinking carries a lot of risk, but it can also help companies win big. Lloyd Hill, president and CEO of Applebee's Neighborhood Grill and Bar, decided an old-school company like his could also win big by thinking differently.

IN THE LEAD   Lloyd Hill, Applebee's Neighborhood Grill and Bar

Applebee's broke one of the cardinal rules of retailing, and it paid off in rapid growth and soaring sales. Rather than carefully spacing out restaurants so that the sales of one don't eat into the sales of another, Applebee's floods a territory with stores to gain brand recognition and market dominance. The strategy, which leaders call "conscious cannibalization," has helped Applebee's "come out of nowhere as a dominant player in the industry," says Lloyd Hill, president and CEO. Applebee's strategy also challenges conventional thinking in other ways. Instead of building bigger restaurants to handle larger crowds, Applebee's keeps its restaurants small, which means they're easier and cheaper to build, easier to fill on slow days, and provide a cozy atmosphere.

Applebee's wants to give customers a convenient, comfortable, high-value experience. "Our restaurants are about more than food," says Hill. "They're about inclusiveness, value, comfort, trust, and relationships." Information from customers helps Applebee's leaders keep track of big-picture trends as well as respond to specific problems quickly. Leaders also listen to employees. The "Hey, Lloyd" program provides a confidential way for any employee to send a message straight to the top. In addition, once a year, all 300 people in Applebee's corporate office work a shift at an Applebee's restaurant to learn what works and what doesn't from employees' perspectives. Last year, the CEO spent a day working as a busboy. Hill thinks the program keeps executives from losing track of what really matters to the success of the business: your products, your staff, and your customers.[45]

Applebee's leaders emphasize listening to people both inside and outside the organization because it keeps them in touch with a shifting environment. Listening is a key to breaking out of conventional thinking.

Strategy necessarily changes over time to fit environmental conditions. To remain competitive, leaders develop company strategies that focus on three qualities: core competencies, developing synergy, and creating value for customers.

Core Competence

An organization's **core competence** is something the organization does extremely well in comparison to competitors. Leaders try to identify the organization's unique strengths—what makes their organization different from others in the industry. At Amgen, a pharmaceutical company, strategy focuses on the company's core competence of high-quality scientific research. Rather than starting with a specific disease and working backwards, Amgen takes brilliant science and finds unique uses for it.[46] Dell Computer, described at the beginning of this chapter, has core competencies of speed and cost efficiency. Home Depot thrives because of a strategy focused on superior customer service. And Chase Brass Industries, a manufacturer of brass rods and steel tubing, has a core competence in the mastery of specific technologies and production processes.[47] In each case, leaders identified what their company does particularly well and built strategy around it.

Synergy

Synergy occurs when organizational parts interact to produce a joint effect that is greater than the sum of the parts acting alone. As a result the organization may attain a special advantage with respect to cost, market power, technology, or employee skills. PepsiCo's new "Power of One" strategy is aimed at leveraging the synergies of its soft drink and snack divisions to achieve greater market power. The business that drives PepsiCo these days is snack foods, with the Frito-Lay division enjoying near total dominance of the snack food market.

PepsiCo CEO Roger Enrico has used the company's clout with supermarkets to move Pepsi drinks next to Frito-Lay snacks on store shelves, increasing the chance that when shoppers pick up chips and soda, the soda of choice will be a Pepsi product. Enrico personally visited the heads of the twenty-five largest supermarket chains to sell the strategy. Leaders are betting that the strength of Frito-Lay can not only gain greater shelf space for Pepsi, but increased market share as well.[48]

Alliances between companies can be a source of synergy as well. For example, Erie Bolt, a small Erie, Pennsylvania company, teamed up with fourteen other area companies to give itself more muscle in tackling competitive global markets. Team members share equipment, customer lists, and other information that enables each small company to go after more business than it ever could without the team approach.[49]

Value Creation

Focusing on core competencies and attaining synergy helps companies create value for their customers. **Value** can be defined as the combination of benefits received and costs paid by the customer.[50] A product that is low cost but does not provide benefits is not a good value. For example, People Express Airlines initially made a splash with ultra-low prices, but travelers couldn't tolerate the airline's consistently late takeoffs at any price.[51] Delivering value to the customer is at the heart of strategy. Leaders at Gallo are involved in a strategic makeover to help the family firm use its core competencies to create better value for customers. Gallo, long famous for its inexpensive wines, produces one of every four bottles of wine sold in the U.S. Today, the company is pouring $100 million into Gallo of Sonoma, a line of upscale wines that the company hopes will fuel greater growth. However, value pricing is a key part of the Gallo of Sonoma strategy. As the low-cost producer, Gallo is able to consistently sell upscale wines for $1 to $30 less per bottle than comparable-quality competitors.[52]

STRATEGY IN ACTION

Strategy formulation integrates knowledge of the environment, vision, and mission with the company's core competence in such a way as to achieve synergy and create value for customers. When these elements are brought together, the company has an excellent chance to succeed in a competitive environment. But to do so, leaders have to ensure that strategies are implemented—that actual behavior within the organization reflects the desired direction.

Strategy is implemented through specific mechanisms, techniques, or tools for directing organizational resources to accomplish strategic goals. This is the basic architecture for how things get done in the organization. Some people argue that **strategy implementation** is the most important as well as the most difficult part of strategic management.[53] Strategy implementation involves using several tools or parts of the organization that can be adjusted to put strategy into action. Strong leadership is one of the most important tools for strategy implementation. Leaders motivate and influence others to adopt the behaviors needed for the new strategy. For example, the manager of a department store might implement a strategy of increased sales by using leadership to pump up morale, encouraging aggressive selling, being physically present on the sales floor, and speaking about the high sales goals to employees at every opportunity.

Strategy is also implemented through elements such as structural design, pay or reward systems, budget allocations, and organizational rules, policies, or procedures. For example, at ConAgra, maker of Healthy Choice and Banquet brands, CEO Philip B. Fletcher made changes to incentive pay systems and computerized the company's information systems to encourage commitment to a new strategy of cooperation and efficiency.[54] Another company reorganized its workforce into teams, each responsible for all details of a product for a single customer. Each group was a separate structural unit that could do whatever was necessary to adapt to changes in the product or customer. Dedicating these resources to customers provided extraordinary service.

Leaders are responsible for making decisions about changes in structure, systems, policies, and so forth, to support the company's strategic direction. Leaders make decisions every day—some large and some small—that support company strategy. Exhibit 13.6 provides a simplified model for how leaders make strategic decisions. The two dimensions considered are whether a particular choice will have a high or low strategic impact on the business and whether implementation of the decision will be easy or difficult. A change that both produces a high strategic impact and is easy to implement would be a leader's first choice for putting strategy into action. For example, when Emerson Electric Company wanted to pursue a high-growth strategy, one of the first things leaders did was change hiring practices and begin recruiting experienced marketers from companies such as Procter & Gamble, Johnson & Johnson, and Black & Decker to put more muscle into Emerson's industrial brands.[55] The decision had a tremendous impact because it gave Emerson the marketing talent it needed to pursue growth, but the change was relatively easy to implement. Pursuing growth through acquisitions, on the other hand, as Craig Barrett is now doing at Intel, recently purchasing Case Technology, Level One Communications, and NetBoost, is much more difficult to implement.[56] Mergers and acquisitions can present difficulties of blending production processes, accounting procedures, corporate cultures, and other aspects of

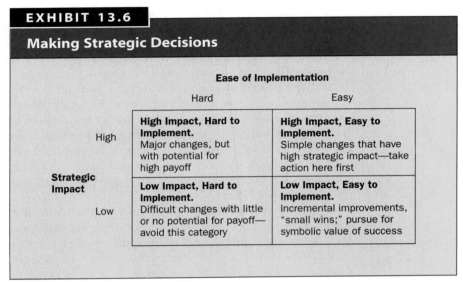

EXHIBIT 13.6

Making Strategic Decisions

	Ease of Implementation	
	Hard	Easy
Strategic Impact — High	**High Impact, Hard to Implement.** Major changes, but with potential for high payoff	**High Impact, Easy to Implement.** Simple changes that have high strategic impact—take action here first
Strategic Impact — Low	**Low Impact, Hard to Implement.** Difficult changes with little or no potential for payoff—avoid this category	**Low Impact, Easy to Implement.** Incremental improvements, "small wins;" pursue for symbolic value of success

SOURCE: Adapted from Amir Hartman and John Sifonis, with John Kador, *Net Ready: Strategies for the New E-conomy* (McGraw-Hill, 2000), 95.

the organizations into an effectively functioning whole. Leaders often initiate such major changes despite the difficulties because the potential strategic payoff is very high. A structural reorganization such as a shift to horizontal teams or breaking a corporation into separate divisions, as AT&T is now undergoing, also would fall into this category.

Leaders sometimes pursue activities that have a low strategic impact but which are relatively easy to implement. Incremental improvements in products, work processes, or techniques are examples. Over time, incremental improvements can have an important effect on the organization. In addition, small changes can sometimes be needed to symbolize improvement and success to people within the organization. It may be important for leaders to produce quick, highly visible improvements to boost morale, keep people committed to larger changes, or keep followers focused on the vision. For example, the manager of a purchasing department wanted to reengineer the purchasing process to increase efficiency and improve relationships with suppliers. He wanted requisitions and invoices to be processed within days rather than the several weeks it had been taking. Employees were skeptical that the department could ever meet the new standards and pointed out that some invoices currently awaiting processing were almost two months old. The manager decided to make some simple revisions in the flow of paperwork and employee duties which enabled the department to process all the old invoices so that no remaining invoice was more than a week old. This "small win" energized employees and helped keep them focused on the larger goal.[57] The positive attitude made implementation of the larger change much smoother.

The final category shown in Exhibit 13.6 relates to changes that are both difficult to implement and have low strategic impact. An illustration of a decision in this category was the attempt by new management at a highly successful mail-order clothing company to implement teams. In this case, the decision was not made to support a new strategic direction but simply to try out a new management trend—and it was a miserable failure that cost the organization much time, money, and employee good-will before the teams were finally disbanded.[58] Effective leaders strive to avoid making decisions that fall within this category.

THE LEADER'S CONTRIBUTION

Although good leadership for today's organizations calls for actively involving everyone in the organization, leaders are still ultimately responsible for establishing direction through vision and strategy. When leadership fails to provide direction, organizations flounder. For example, McDonald's is a well-managed company, but when franchisees saw per-store profits sink as much as 30 percent in the 1990s, they criticized leaders for their failure to provide vision and strategy. Among the responses to one survey was a request for "long-term focus on direction and identity of McDonald's, rather than expensive knee-jerk changes." Since Jack M. Greenberg took over as Chairman and CEO in 1998, he has been striving to provide the clear, focused direction McDonald's needs to stay strong in the future.[59] One of the most critical jobs of the leader is deciding the vision for the future and linking the future with strategic actions.

Stimulating Vision and Action

In the waiting lounge of a fine lakeside restaurant a sign reads, "Where there is no hope in the future, there is no power in the present." The owner explains its presence there by telling the story of how his small, picturesque village with its homes and businesses was sacrificed to make way for a flood-control project. After losing their fight to reverse the decision, most business leaders simply let their businesses decline and die. Soon, the only people who came to the village did so to eat at the cheery little diner, whose owner became the butt of jokes because he continued to work so hard. Everyone laughed when he chose to open a larger and fancier restaurant on the hill behind the village. Yet, when the flood-control project was finally completed, he had the only attractive restaurant on the edge of a beautiful, newly constructed lake that drew many tourists. Anyone could have found out, as he did, where the edge of the lake would be, yet most of the business owners had no vision for the future. The restaurant owner had a vision and he took action on it. Hopes and dreams for the future are what keep people moving forward. However, for leaders to make a real difference, they have to link those dreams with strategic actions. Vision has to be translated into specific goals, objectives, and plans so that employees know how to move toward the desired future. An old English churchyard saying applies to organizations as it does to life:

Life without vision is drudgery.
Vision without action is but an empty dream.
Action guided by vision is joy and the hope of the earth.[60]

Exhibit 13.7 illustrates four possibilities of leadership in providing direction. Four types of leader are described based on their attention to vision and attention to action. The person who is low both on providing vision and stimulating action is uninvolved, not really a leader at all. The leader who is all action and little vision is a Doer. He or she may be a hard worker and dedicated to the job and the organization, but the Doer is working blind. Without a sense of purpose and direction, activities have no real meaning and do not truly serve the organization, the employees, or the community. The Dreamer, on the other hand, is good at providing a big idea with meaning for self and others. This leader may effectively inspire others with a vision, yet he or she is weak on implementing strategic action. The vision in this case is only a dream, a fantasy, because it has little chance of ever becoming reality. To be an Effective Leader, one both dreams big *and* transforms those dreams into significant strategic action, either through his or her own activities or by hiring other

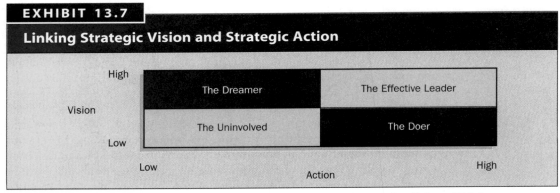

EXHIBIT 13.7

Linking Strategic Vision and Strategic Action

SOURCE: Based on William D. Hitt, *The Leader-Manager: Guidelines for Action* (Columbus, OH: Battelle Press, 1988), 7

leaders who can effectively implement the vision and strategy. For example, Michael Dell is well-known for his ability to hire the right leaders to take his vision and help make it a reality. Dell realizes that his talent lies primarily in painting the big picture, so he hires other leaders who are skilled at translating the vision and strategy into specific objectives and plans for employees to follow.

How Leaders Decide

To determine strategic direction for the future, leaders look inward, outward, and forward. Leaders scan both the internal and external organizational environment to identify trends, threats, and opportunities for the organization. Consider how Andrea Jung looked at changes and trends in the environment to develop a new strategic plan for Avon.

IN THE LEAD   ### Andrea Jung, Avon Products Inc.

Andrea Jung recently stood before thousands of Avon representatives and vowed that Avon Products Inc. can be as big in the beauty business as Walt Disney Co. is in entertainment. The audience rose to a standing ovation as Jung continued: "We will change the future of women around the world!"

Jung, who landed the top job at Avon in November of 1999, began formulating a new vision and strategy by looking at where Avon is now and where it needs to go in the future. One environmental trend of particular concern for Avon is that most women, particularly in the U.S., now work outside the home, making the company's traditional direct-sales approach seem destined to fade into history. Another trend is the explosion of the World Wide Web as a place for doing business. People no longer have the time or the desire to have a cup of coffee with the "Avon lady." Jung's vision for a new Avon is what she calls the "ultimate relationship marketer of products and services for women." She intends to rebuild the organization from the ground up, making it a source for anything and everything today's busy woman wants to buy. In addition, Avon will give women a choice of buying through a traditional representative, from a store, or over the Web.

Putting strategy into action involves a trial run of Avon kiosks in shopping malls, which are effectively luring younger customers who have never tried Avon products. Next up is a pending deal for a separate line of products to be sold at a "store-within-a-store" at a major retailer such as Wal-Mart or Kmart. The biggest bet, however, is on the Web. Jung has held focus groups with both Net-savvy and technologically illiterate sales reps to help plan the best way to merge an

Internet strategy with the company's Old Economy direct sales model. She has invested $60 million to build a Web site focused on sales reps and the full Avon catalog of products. Future plans call for adding nutritional supplements and vitamins to the product mix. Eventually, Avon may even offer expert financial services and legal advice targeted to women.

Jung believes Avon has an opportunity to provide a new kind of Web experience. "If we don't include [our sales reps] in everything we do, then we're just another retail brand, just another Internet site, and I don't see the world needing more of those," she says. Former CEO James E. Preston, who was Jung's mentor, praises her for having a "fresh take on what Avon could be." However, analysts warn that the key to moving Avon forward into an e-tailing future is careful, step-by-step execution. It remains to be seen whether Jung can successfully execute her strategy and reinvent Avon for a new generation, but so far most people are betting for rather than against her. As one investor put it, "at this point, it would be hard to give her anything less than A's."[61]

Leaders such as Andrea Jung recognize that organizations need both a broad and inspiring vision and an underlying plan for how to achieve it. To decide and map a strategic direction, leaders strive to develop industry foresight based on trends in technology, demographics, government regulation, and lifestyles that will help them identify new competitive advantages.[62]

One approach leaders take in setting a course for the future is through hard analysis. Situation analysis, for example, includes a search for SWOT—strengths, weaknesses, opportunities, and threats that affect organizational performance. Leaders using situation analysis obtain external information from a variety of sources, such as customers, government reports, suppliers, consultants, or association meetings. They gather information about internal strengths and weaknesses from sources such as budgets, financial ratios, profit and loss statements, and employee surveys. Another formula often used by companies is a five-force analysis developed by Michael Porter, who studied a number of businesses and proposed that strategy is often the result of five competitive forces: potential new entrants into an industry; the bargaining power of buyers; the bargaining power of suppliers; the threat of substitute products; and rivalry among competitors. By carefully examining these five forces, leaders can develop effective strategies to remain competitive.

Vision and strategy have to be based on a solid factual foundation, but too much rationality can get in the way of creating a compelling vision. When leaders rely solely on formal strategic planning, competitor analysis, or market research, they miss new opportunities. For example, when Ted Turner first talked about launching a 24-hour news and information channel in the 1970s, many dismissed him as delusional. Every source of conventional wisdom, from market research to broadcast professionals, said the vision was crazy and bound to fail. Yet Turner looked at emerging social and demographic trends, listened to his intuition, and launched a global network that generates 35 percent gross margins.[63] Sony has long been known for creating the future. As Sony's visionary leader Akio Morita puts it, "Our plan is to lead the public with new products rather than ask them what kinds of products they want. The public does not know what is possible, but we do."[64]

To formulate a vision, leaders also look inward to their hopes and dreams. Foresight and the ability to see future possibilities emerge not just from traditional strategic planning tools and formulas, but from curiosity, instinct and intuition, emotions, deep thinking, personal experience, and hope. To develop foresight, leaders view the world with a wide-angle lens, capturing bits and pieces of subtle information without shutting it off with "yeah, but" preconceptions.[65]

Another good reason for not relying too heavily on rational analysis is that rationality can kill a vision. Overly rational people have a hard time letting go and dreaming big. At Sewell Village Cadillac in Dallas, antique lamps are used instead of fluorescent lights. The expensive fixtures don't make sense in a rational, economic sense, but the setting captures people's imaginations, making the dealership seem special. To connect with people's deeper yearning for something great, vision can transcend the rational. Although it is based on reality, it comes from the heart rather than the head. One writer has suggested that leaders take a tip from Helen Keller, who was blind and deaf since early childhood and in order to see had to go out and touch the world, relying on instinct, emotion, and cues from others.[66]

THE LEADER'S IMPACT

When leaders link vision and strategy, they can make a real difference for their organization's future. A leader's greatest discretion is often over strategic vision and strategic action. Research has shown that strategic thinking and planning for the future can positively affect a company's performance and financial success.[67] Another study has shown that as much as 44 percent of the variance in profitability of major firms may be attributed to strategic leadership.[68] When Richard Teerlink took over as CEO of Harley Davidson, he saw the strategic opportunity to revive customers' emotional connections with the struggling company: "We symbolize the feeling of freedom and independence that people want in this stressful world." By capitalizing on the nostalgia of biking, creating the Harley Owners Group (HOG for short), and slapping the Harley logo on merchandise from deodorant to throw pillows, Teerlink revolutionized the company, translating an emotional bond into steadily increasing profits.[69]

One way leader impact has been evaluated is to examine whether top executive turnover makes a difference. Several studies of chief executive turnover have been conducted, including a sample of 167 corporations studied over a twenty-year period, 193 manufacturing companies, a large sample of Methodist churches, and retail firms in the United Kingdom.[70] These studies found that leader succession was associated with improved profits and stock prices and, in the case of churches, with improved attendance, membership, and donations. Although good economic conditions and industry circumstances play a part in improved performance for any organization, the top leader had impact beyond these factors. Overall, when research has been carefully done, top leader succession typically explains from 20 percent to 45 percent of the variance in organizational outcomes.[71]

More recent research has explored the notion of top leadership teams, as opposed to an individual executive. The makeup of the top leadership group is believed to affect whether an organization develops organizational capability and the ability to exploit strategic opportunities. A team provides diverse aptitudes and skills to deal with complex organizational situations. Many researchers believe the configuration of the top leadership team to be more important for organizational success than the characteristics of a single CEO. For example, the size, diversity, attitudes, and skills of the team affect patterns of communication and collaboration, which in turn affect company performance.[72]

The emerging focus on teams is more realistic in some ways than focusing on individual leadership. In a complex environment, a single leader cannot do all things. An effective team may have a better chance of identifying and implementing a successful strategy, of discerning an accurate interpretation of the environment, and of developing internal capability based on empowered employees and a shared vision. Without a capable and effectively interacting top leadership team, a company may not adapt readily in a shifting environment. Although research in the area of leader impact is still relatively limited, it does seem to affirm the belief that the choices leaders make have significant impact on an organization's performance.

SUMMARY AND INTERPRETATION

Leaders establish organizational direction through vision and strategy. They are responsible for studying the organization's environment, considering how it may be different in the future, and setting a direction everyone can believe in. The shared vision is an attractive, ideal future for the organization that is credible yet not readily attainable. A clear, powerful vision links the present and the future by showing how present actions and decisions can move the organization toward its long-range goals. Vision energizes employees and gives them an inspiring picture of the future to which they are eager to commit themselves. The vision can also give meaning to work and establish a standard of excellence by presenting a challenge that asks all workers to give their best.

The mission includes the company's core values and its core purpose or reason for existence. Visions for the future change, whereas the mission should persist, as does the enduring character of the organization.

Strategy is the serious work of figuring out how to translate vision and mission into action. Strategy is a general plan of action that describes resource allocation and other activities for dealing with the environment and helping the organization reach its goals. Like vision, strategy changes, but successful companies develop strategies that focus on core competence, develop synergy, and create value for customers. Strategy is implemented through the systems and structures that are the basic architecture for how things get done in the organization.

Leaders decide on direction through rational analysis as well as intuition, personal experience, and hopes and dreams. Leaders make a real difference for their organization only when they link vision to strategic action, so that vision is more than just a dream. Superior organizational performance is not a matter of luck. It is determined by the decisions leaders make.

KEY TERMS

strategic leadership	strategic management	value
vision	strategy	strategy formulation
self-reference	core competence	strategy implementation
mission	synergy	

DISCUSSION QUESTIONS

1. A management consultant said that strategic leaders are concerned with vision and mission, while strategic managers are concerned with strategy. Do you agree? Discuss.

2. A vision can apply to an individual, a family, a college course, a career, or decorating an apartment. Think of something you care about for which you want the future to be different from the present and write a vision statement for it.

3. If you worked for a company like Cisco Systems that has a strong vision for the future, how would that affect you compared to working for a company that did not have a vision?

4. Do you agree with the principle of self-reference? In other words, do you believe if people know where the organization is trying to go, they will make decisions that support the desired organizational outcome?

5. What does it mean to say that the vision can include a description of both the journey and the destination?

6. Many visions are written and hung on a wall. Do you think this type of vision has value? What would be required to imprint the vision within each person?

7. What is the difference between mission and vision? Can you give an example of each?

8. What is the difference between synergy and value creation with respect to strategy?

9. Strategic vision and strategic action are both needed for an effective leader. Which do you think you are better at doing? Why?

10. If a new top leader is hired for a corporation, and performance improves, to what extent do you think the new top leader was responsible compared to other factors? To what extent do you think a new coach is responsible if her basketball team did better after she took over?

LEADERSHIP DEVELOPMENT: PERSONAL FEEDBACK

Visionary Leadership

Think about a situation in which you either assumed or were given a leadership role in a group. Imagine your own behavior as leader. To what extent does each of the following statements characterize your leadership?

1 = very little

2

3 = a moderate amount

4

5 = very much

1. I have a clear understanding of where we are going.

2. I work to get others to be committed to our desired future.

3. I paint an interesting picture for my group.

4. I get the group to work together for the same outcome.

5. I initiate discussion with others about the kind of future I would like us to create together.

6. I clearly and repeatedly communicate a positive outlook for the group's future.

7. I look ahead and forecast what I expect in the future.

8. I show others how their interests can be realized by working toward a common vision.

9. I am excited and enthusiastic about future possibilities.

10. I make certain that the activities I manage are broken down into manageable chunks.

11. I seek future challenges for the group.

12. I spend time and effort making certain that people adhere to the values and outcomes that have been agreed on.

13. I inspire others with my ideas for the future.

14. I give special recognition when others' work is consistent with the vision.

Scoring

The odd-numbered questions pertain to creating a vision for the group. The even-numbered questions pertain to implementing the vision. Calculate your score for each set of questions. Which score is higher? Compare your scores with other students.

Interpretation

This questionnaire pertains to two dimensions of visionary leadership. Creating the vision has to do with whether you think about the future, whether you are excited about the future, and whether you engage others in the future. Implementing the vision is about the extent to which you communicate, allocate the work, and provide rewards for activities that achieve the vision. Which of the two dimensions is easiest for you? Are your scores consistent with your understanding of your own strengths and weaknesses? What might you do to improve your scores?

LEADERSHIP DEVELOPMENT: Cases for Analysis

Metropolis Police Department

You are in a hotel room watching the evening news as a local reporter interviews people who complain about abuse and mistreatment by police officers. These reports have been occurring in the news media with increasing frequency over the last three years. Some observers believe the problem is the police department's authoritarian style. Police managers encourage paramilitary values and a "them-against-us" attitude. The police orientation has been toward a spit-and-polish force that is efficient and tolerates no foolishness. The city believes that a highly professional, aloof police force is the best way to keep the city under control. Training emphasizes police techniques, the appropriate use of guns, and new technology, but there is no training on dealing with people. Several citizens have won large lawsuits against the police force, and many suits originated with minority groups. Critics believe the police chief is a major part of the problem. He has defended the rough actions of police officers, giving little public credence to complaints of abuse. He resists the community-oriented, people-friendly attitudes of other city departments. The chief has been considered insensitive toward minorities and has been heard to make disparaging public comments about African Americans, women, and Hispanics.

One vocal critic alleges that police brutality depends upon the vision and moral leadership set by the chief of police and lays responsibility for incidents of abuse on the current chief. Another critic believes there is a relationship between his intemperate remarks and the actions of police officers.

The reason you are in Metropolis, watching the news in a hotel room, is that you have been invited to interview for the job of police chief. The mayor and selected council members are preparing to fire the chief and name a replacement. You are thinking about what you would do if you took the job.

Questions

1. Identify themes that you would like to make a part of your vision for the police department.
2. If you get the job, how will you gain acceptance for your vision? How will you implement changes that will support the new vision and values?
3. Would you relish the challenge of becoming police chief of Metropolis? Why or why not?

The Visionary Leader

When Frank Coleman first began his job as president of Hi-Tech Aerostructures, most managers and employees felt a surge of hope and excitement. Hi-Tech Aerostructures is a fifty-year old family-owned manufacturing company that produces parts for the aircraft industry. The founder and owner had served as president until his health began to decline, and he felt the need to bring in someone from outside the company to get a fresh perspective. It was certainly needed. Over the past several years, Hi-Tech had just been stumbling along.

Coleman came to the company from a smaller business, but one with excellent credentials as a leader in advanced aircraft technology. He had a vision for transforming Hi-Tech into a world-class manufacturing facility. In addition to implementing cutting-edge technology, the vision included transforming the sleepy, paternalistic culture to a more dynamic, adaptive one and empowering employees to take a more active, responsible role in the organization. After years of just doing the same old thing day after day, vice president David Deacon was delighted with the new president and thrilled when Coleman asked him to head up the transformation project.

Deacon and his colleagues spent hours talking with Coleman, listening to him weave his ideas about the kind of company Hi-Tech could become. He assured the team that the transformation was his highest priority, and inspired them with stories about the significant impact they were going to have on the company as well as the entire aircraft industry. Together, the group crafted a vision statement that was distributed to all employees and posted all over the building. At lunchtime, the company cafeteria was abuzz with talk about the new vision. And when the young, nattily dressed president himself appeared in the cafeteria, as he did once every few weeks, it was almost as if a rock star had walked in.

At the team's first meeting with Coleman, Deacon presented several different ideas and concepts they had come up with, explaining the advantages of each for ripping Hi-Tech out of the past and slamming it jubilantly into the twenty-first century. Nothing, however, seemed to live up to Coleman's ambitions for the project—he thought all the suggestions were either too conventional or too confusing. After three hours the team left Coleman's office and went back to the drawing board. Everyone was even more fired up after Coleman's closing remarks about the potential to remake the industry and maybe even change the world.

Early the next day, Coleman called Deacon to his office and laid out his own broad ideas for how the project should proceed. "Not bad," thought Deacon, as he took the notes and drawings back to the team. "We can take this broad concept and really put some plans for action into place." The team's work over the next few months was for the most part lively and encouraging. Whenever Coleman would attend the meetings, he would suggest changes in many of their specific plans and goals, but miraculously, the transformation plan began to take shape. The team sent out a final draft to colleagues and outside consultants and the feedback was almost entirely positive.

The plan was delivered to Coleman on a Wednesday morning. When Deacon had still not heard anything by Friday afternoon, he began to worry. He knew Coleman had been busy with a major customer, but the president had indicated his intention to review the plan immediately. Finally, at 6 P.M., Coleman called

Deacon to his office. "I'm afraid we just can't run with this," he said, tossing the team's months of hard work on the desk. "It's just . . . well, just not right for this company."

Deacon was stunned. And so was the rest of the team when he reported Coleman's reaction. In addition, word was beginning to get out around the company that all was not smooth with the transformation project. The cafeteria conversations were now more likely to be gripes that nothing was being done to help the company improve. Coleman assured the team, however, that his commitment was still strong; they just needed to take a different approach. Deacon asked that Coleman attend as many meetings as he could to help keep the team on the right track. Nearly a year later, the team waited in anticipation for Coleman's response to the revised proposal.

Coleman called Deacon at home on Friday night. "Let's meet on this project first thing Monday morning," he began. "I think we need to make a few adjustments. Looks like we're more or less headed in the right direction, though." Deacon felt like crying as he hung up the phone. All that time and work. He knew what he could expect on Monday morning. Coleman would lay out his vision and ask the team to start over.

SOURCE: Based on "The Vision Failed," Case 8.1 in Peter G. Northouse, *Leadership—Theory and Practice,* 2nd ed. (Thousand Oaks, CA: Sage, 2001), 150–151; and Joe Kay, "My Year at a Big High Tech Company," *Forbes ASAP,* May 29, 2000, 195–198; "Digital Diary (My Year at a Big High Tech Company)," *www.forbes.com/asap/2000/* accessed on November 19, 2000; and "Digital Diary, Part Two: The Miracle," *Forbes ASAP,* August 21, 2000, 187–190.

Questions

1. How effective would you rate Coleman as a visionary leader? Discuss.
2. Where would you place Coleman on the chart of types of leaders in Exhibit 13.7? Where would you place Deacon?
3. If you were Deacon, what would you do?

REFERENCES

1. Betsy Morris, "Can Michael Dell Escape The Box?" *Fortune,* October 16, 2000, 92–110.
2. James C. Collins and Jerry I. Porras, "Building Your Company's Vision," *Harvard Business Review* September-October 1996, 65–77.
3. Louisa Wah, "The Dear Cost of 'Scut Work,'" *Management Review,* June 1999, 27–31.
4. Gary Hamel and C. K. Prahalad, "Seeing the Future First," *Fortune,* September 5, 1994, 64–70.

5. Quoted in Wah, "The Dear Cost of 'Scut Work.'"

6. Nanette Byrnes and Paul C. Judge, "Internet Anxiety," *Business Week,* June 28, 1999, 79–88.

7. Ray Maghroori and Eric Rolland, "Strategic Leadership: The Art of Balancing Organizational Mission with Policy, Procedures, and External Environment," *The Journal of Leadership Studies* No. 2 (1997), 62–81.

8. Suzanne Martin, "Family Inspires a Bright Future for Young Entrepreneur," *Self-Employed America* September-October 1997, 12–13.

9. Collins and Porras, "Building Your Company's Vision."

10. J. William Gurley, "Buy.com May Fail, But If It Succeeds, Retailing May Never Be the Same," *Fortune,* January 11, 1999, 150–152.

11. Daniel Roth, "The Value of Vision," *Fortune,* May 24, 1999, 285–288. Also see Stewart Alsop, "Now I Know How a Real Visionary Sounds," *Fortune,* September 8, 1997, 161–162.

12. This section is based on Burt Nanus, *Visionary Leadership* (San Francisco: Jossey-Bass, 1992), 16–18; and Richard L. Daft and Robert H. Lengel, *Fusion Leadership: Unlocking the Subtle Forces That Change People and Organizations* (San Francisco: Berrett-Koehler, 1998).

13. Oren Harari, "Looking Beyond the Vision Thing," *Management Review,* June 1997, 26–29; and William D. Hitt, *The Leader-Manager: Guidelines for Action* (Columbus, OH: Battelle Press, 1988), 54.

14. Nancy Chambers, "The Really Long View," *Management Review,* January 1998, 11–15, and Arie de Geus, "The Living Company," *Harvard Business Review,* March-April 1997, 51–59.

15. Nanus, *Visionary Leadership,* 16.

16. Collins and Porras, "Building Your Company's Vision," 74.

17. Roger E. Herman and Joyce L. Gioia, "Making Work Meaningful: Secrets of the Future-Focused Corporation," *The Futurist,* December 1998, 24–26.

18. Mark Lipton, "Demystifying the Development of an Organizational Vision," *Sloan Management Review,* Summer 1996, 83–92.

19. James M. Kouzes and Barry Z. Posner, *The Leadership Challenge: How to Get Extraordinary Things Done in Organizations* (San Francisco: Jossey-Bass, 1988), 98.

20. B. Thomas, *Walt Disney: An American Tradition* (New York: Simon & Schuster, 1976), 246–247.

21. Marshall Sashkin, "The Visionary Leader," in Jay Conger and Rabindra N. Kanungo, eds., *Charismatic Leadership: The Elusive Factor in Organizational Effectiveness* (San Francisco: Jossey-Bass, 1988), 122–160.

22. James C. Collins and Jerry I. Porras, "Organizational Vision and Visionary Organizations," *California Management Review* (Fall 1991), 30–52.

23. Nanus, *Visionary Leadership,* 26; John W. Gardner, "Leadership and the Future," *The Futurist,* May-June 1990, 9–12; and Warren Bennis and Burt Nanus, *Leaders: The Strategies for Taking Charge* (New York: Harper & Row, 1985), 93.

24. Gardner, "Leadership and the Future."

25. William F. Powers, segment in Polly LaBarre, ed., "What's New, What's Not," (Unit of One), *Fast Company,* January 1999, 73.

26. Morris, "Can Michael Dell Escape The Box?"

27. Collins and Porras, "Organizational Vision and Visionary Organizations."
28. Daft and Lengel, *Fusion Leadership*.
29. Kate A. Kane, "Vision for All to See," *Fast Company*, April-May 1996, 44–45.
30. Lipton, "Demystifying the Development of an Organizational Vision."
31. Polly LaBarre, "Leadership—Ben Zander," segment in "Who's Fast 99: Unsung Heroes, Rising Stars," *Fast Company*, December 1998, 111–116.
32. Kouzes and Posner, *The Leadership Challenge*, 82.
33. Alan Farnham, "State Your Values, Hold the Hot Air," *Fortune* (April 19, 1993), 117–124.
34. LaBarre, "Leadership—Ben Zander."
35. This section is based on Peter M. Senge, *The Fifth Discipline: The Art and Practice of the Learning Organization* (New York: Doubleday/Currency, 1990), 205–225.
36. Morris, "Can Michael Dell Escape The Box?"
37. Quoted in Senge, *The Fifth Discipline*, 218.
38. Joe Jaworski, quoted in Alan M. Webber, "Destiny and the Job of the Leader," *Fast Company*, June-July 1996, 40, 42.
39. James Collins, "It's Not What You Make, It's What You Stand For," *Inc.*, October 1997, 42–45.
40. Collins and Porras, "Building Your Company's Vision."
41. "Leadership: Building a Mission-Driven, Values-Centered Organization" (speech delivered by Medtronics Chairman and CEO William W. George at the Premier CEO's in Aspen, Colorado, on September 17, 1998), *Vital Speeches*, May 1, 1999, 439.
42. Collins and Porras, "Building Your Company's Vision."
43. John E. Prescott, "Environments as Moderators of the Relationship between Strategy and Performance," *Academy of Management Journal* 29 (1986), 329–346.
44. Steven V. Brull, "Gateway's Big Gamble," *Business Week E.Biz*, June 5, 2000, EB26–EB36.
45. Jill Rosenfeld, "Down-Home Food, Cutting-Edge Business," *Fast Company*, April 2000, 56, 58.
46. Ronald B. Lieber, "Smart Science," *Fortune*, June 23, 1997, 73.
47. Gail Dutton, "What Business Are We In?" *Management Review*, September 1997, 54–57.
48. John A. Byrne, "PepsiCo's New Formula," *Business Week*, April 10, 2000, 172–184.
49. John S. DeMott, "Company Alliances for Market Muscle," *Nation's Business*, February 1994, 52–53.
50. Gregory M. Bounds, Gregory H. Dobbins, and Oscar S. Fowler, *Management: A Total Quality Perspective* (Cincinnati, OH: South-Western College Publishing, 1995), 244.
51. Michael Treacy, "You Need a Value Discipline—But Which One?" *Fortune*, April 17, 1995, 195.
52. Bethany McLean, "Growing Up Gallo," *Fortune*, August 14, 2000, 211–220.
53. L. J. Bourgeois, III and David R. Brodwin, "Strategic Implementation: Five Approaches to an Elusive Phenomenon," *Strategic Management Journal* 5 (1984), 241–264; and Anil K. Gupta and V. Govindarajan, "Business Unit Strategy,

Managerial Characteristics, and Business Unit Effectiveness at Strategy Implementation," *Academy of Management Journal* (1984), 25–41.

54. Greg Burns, "How a New Boss Got ConAgra Cooking Again," *Business Week,* July 25, 1994, 72–73.

55. Rajan Anandan, Mehrdad Baghai, Stephen Coley, and David White, "Seven Paths to Growth," *Management Review,* November 1999, 39–45.

56. Andy Reinhardt, "The New Intel," *Business Week,* March 13, 2000, 110–124.

57. Thanks to Russell Guinn for the story on which this example is based.

58. Based on Gregory A. Patterson, "Land's End Kicks Out Modern New Managers, Rejecting a Makeover," *The Wall Street Journal,* April 3, 1995, A1, A6.

59. Shelly Branch, "What's Eating McDonald's?" *Fortune,* October 13, 1997, 122–125; and Michael Arndt, "Did Somebody Say McBurrito?" *Business Week,* April 10, 2000, 166, 170.

60. Quoted in Pat McHenry Sullivan, "Finding Visions for Work and Life," *Spirit at Work* April 1997, 3.

61. Nanette Byrnes, "Avon: The New Calling," *Business Week,* September 18, 2000, 136–148.

62. Hamel and Prahalad, "Seeing the Future First."

63. Oren Harari, "Catapult Your Strategy Over Conventional Wisdom," *Management Review* October 1997, 21–24.

64. Hamel and Prahalad, "Seeing the Future First."

65. Harari, "Catapult Your Vision."

66. Pat McHenry Sullivan, "Finding Visions for Work and Life," 3.

67. C. Chet Miller and Laura B. Cardinal, "Strategic Planning and Firm Performance: A Synthesis of More than Two Decades of Research, "*Academy of Management Journal* 37, No. 6 (1994), 1649-1665.

68. Sydney Finkelstein and Donald C. Hambrick, *Strategic Leadership: Top Executives and Their Effect on Organizations* (St. Paul, MN: West Publishing, 1996), 23.

69. Gary Hamel, "Killer Strategies That Make Shareholders Rich," *Fortune,* June 23, 1997, 70–84.

70. Stanley Lieberson and James F. O'Connor, "Leadership and Organizational Performance: A Study of Large Corporations," *American Sociological Review* 37 (1972), 119; Nan Weiner and Thomas A. Mahoney, "A Model of Corporate Performance as a Function of Environmental, Organizational, and Leadership Influences," *Academy of Management Journal* 24 (1981), 453–470; Ralph A. Alexander, "Leadership: It Can Make a Difference," *Academy of Management Journal* 27 (1984), 765-776; and Alan Berkeley Thomas, "Does Leadership Make a Difference to Organizational Performance?" *Administrative Science Quarterly* 33 (1988), 388–400.

71. David G. Day and Robert G. Lord, "Executive Leadership and Organizational Performance: Suggestions for a New Theory and Methodology," *Journal of Management* 14 (1988), 453–464.

72. Ken G. Smith, Ken A. Smith, Judy D. Olian, Henry P. Sims, Jr., Douglas P. O'Bannon, and Judith A. Scully, "Top Management Team Demography and Process: The Role of Social Integration and Communication," *Administrative Science Quarterly* 39 (1994), 412–438.

CHAPTER OUTLINE

YOUR LEADERSHIP CHALLENGE

After reading this chapter, you should be able to:

- Understand why shaping culture is a critical function of leadership.

- Recognize the characteristics of an adaptive as opposed to an unadaptive culture.

- Understand and apply how leaders shape culture and values through ceremonies,

stories, symbols, language, selection and socialization, and daily actions.

- Identify the cultural values associated with adaptability, achievement, clan, and bureaucratic cultures and the environmental conditions associated with each.

- Use the concept of values-based leadership.

Shaping Culture and Values

St. Luke's is one of Europe's most unconventional, daring, and experimental companies. And, over the past few years, it has become the advertising agency to beat. Pretax profits have increased eightfold in three years, and in 1999, St. Luke's won 25 percent more new business than any other agency in the United Kingdom. The company has won a string of awards, even though it refuses to enter contests.

When six former employees of the London office of Chiat/Day started St. Luke's, their primary goal was to revolutionize the way business is done. One thing that is so revolutionary about St. Luke's is that the company preaches—and practices—a gospel of total ethics and common ownership. There is no hierarchy at St. Luke's, and employees own the company—all of it. Shares are distributed equally no matter whether you're answering the phone or creating new advertising campaigns.

At St. Luke's, everyone agrees to do the job that other people in the organization think they would do best. It's not unusual to have someone tell you—in front of everyone—that your last three projects have been of poor quality. "It can be a very harsh experience," says Andy Law, a founder. "Individuals who are used to hiding behind power—or talent—have trouble getting used to it." But part of the culture at St. Luke's is to take fear, ego, and greed out of business. Even though an employee's work may be openly and harshly criticized, the *person* is always respected, supported, and nurtured. "Not being afraid that someone is laughing at you helps you take genuine risks," Law says. At St. Luke's, people are expected to constantly push beyond their comfort zones. And if an ad campaign flops? So what, say company leaders. No one has ever been fired from St. Luke's for making mistakes. In fact, in the company's history, only three people have been fired—for refusing to cooperate with the organization's unique way of doing business.

One way St. Luke's maintains its culture is by careful selection of new employees. On average, people go through seven interviews, and all the interviewers have to agree on the person before he or she is hired. The company refuses to take on any new business that can't be handled by people who believe in the St. Luke's way. St. Luke's could easily double its size (it currently has 115 employees) if it took on all the business opportunities it is offered, but the company prefers to turn business away rather than just hire "arms and legs" to do the work.

At St. Luke's, employees have created a distinctive culture that emphasizes self-motivation, risk-taking, personal growth, and integrity in all actions. "We've created this company to live beyond us," says Law. "We're just renting resources. Remember that we're a collective here—everybody is equal. What's disappeared are ego and greed. . . ."[1]

St. Luke's has definite values that make it unique in the advertising industry. In addition, employees go away once a year to "reinvent" the company, applying its basic values and beliefs to their current needs and interests. At St. Luke's, leaders see their job as helping keep the cultural values relevant to today and the people of St. Luke's.

In the previous chapter, we talked about creating a vision that inspires and motivates people to strive for a better future. This chapter will focus on how leaders align people with the vision by influencing organizational culture and shaping the environment that determines employee morale and performance. The nature of the culture is highly important because it impacts a company for better or worse. Southwest Airlines and Starbucks Coffee have often attributed their success to the cultures their leaders helped create. Louis V. Gerstner's cultural overhaul of IBM has revived the company's reputation and profitability. Leaders at other companies, including Kodak and Kellogg, are trying to shift their cultural values to remain competitive in today's environment. A recent *Fortune* magazine survey found that CEOs cite organizational culture as their most important mechanism for attracting, motivating, and retaining talented employees, a capability that may be the single best predictor of overall organizational excellence.[2]

This chapter explores ideas about organizational culture and values, and the role of leaders in shaping them. The first section will describe the nature of corporate culture and its importance to organizations. Then we turn to a consideration of how shared organizational values can help the organization stay competitive and how leaders influence culture. Leaders emphasize specific cultural values depending on the organization's situation. The final section of the chapter will briefly discuss ethical values in organizations and examine how values-based leadership shapes an ethical atmosphere.

ORGANIZATIONAL CULTURE

The concept of organizational culture is fairly recent. It became a topic of significant concern in the United States during the early 1980s, primarily due to an interest in learning why U.S. corporations were not performing as well as their counterparts in Japan. Observers and researchers thought that the national culture and corporate culture could explain differences in performance.[3] Leaders now understand that when a company's culture fits the needs of its external environment and company strategy, employees can create an organization that is tough to beat.[4]

What Is Culture?

Some people think of culture as the character or personality of an organization. How an organization looks and "feels" when you enter it is a manifestation of the organizational culture. For example, you might visit one company where you get a sense of formality the minute you walk in the door. Desks are neat and orderly, employees wear professional business attire, and there are few personal items such as family photos or other decorations on walls and desks. At another company, employees may be wearing jeans and sweaters, have empty pizza boxes and cola cans on their desks, and bring their dogs to work with them. Both companies may be highly successful, but the underlying cultures are very different.

Culture can be defined as the set of key values, assumptions, understandings, and norms that is shared by members of an organization and taught to new members as correct.[5] Recall from Chapter 10's discussion of team norms that norms are shared standards that define what behaviors are acceptable and desirable within a group of people. At its most basic, culture is a pattern of shared assumptions about how things are done in an organization. As organizational members cope with internal and external problems, they develop shared assumptions and norms of behavior that are taught to new members as the correct way to think, feel, and act in relation to those problems.[6]

Culture can be thought of as consisting of three levels, as illustrated in Exhibit 14.1, with each level becoming less obvious.[7] At the surface level are visible artifacts such as manner of dress, patterns of behavior, physical symbols, organizational ceremonies, and office layout—all the things one can see, hear, and observe by watching members of the organization. The open office layout at St. Luke's, with no personal desks or workspaces, is an example of a visible manifestation of culture. At a deeper level are the expressed values and beliefs, which are not observable but can be discerned from how people explain and justify what they do. These are values that members of the organization hold at a conscious level. At 3M, for example, all employees consciously know that innovation is highly valued and rewarded in the company's culture.

Some values become so deeply embedded in a culture that organizational members may not be consciously aware of them. These basic, underlying assumptions are the deepest essence of the culture. At 3M, these assumptions might include (1) that individual employees are the source of all innovation, (2) that each individual must think for himself and do what he thinks is right, even if it means defying supervisors, and (3) that organization members are part of a family and will take care of and support each other in taking risks.[8] Assumptions generally start out as expressed values, but over time they become more deeply embedded and less open to question—organization members take

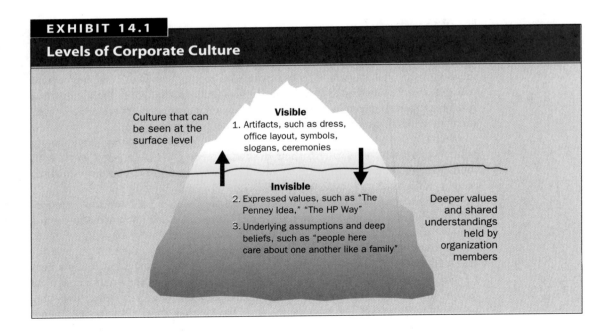

EXHIBIT 14.1

Levels of Corporate Culture

Culture that can be seen at the surface level

Visible
1. Artifacts, such as dress, office layout, symbols, slogans, ceremonies

Invisible
2. Expressed values, such as "The Penney Idea," "The HP Way"

3. Underlying assumptions and deep beliefs, such as "people here care about one another like a family"

Deeper values and shared understandings held by organization members them for granted and often are not even aware of the assumptions that guide their behavior, language, and patterns of social interaction.

Importance of Culture

When people are successful at what they undertake, the ideas and values that led to that success become institutionalized as part of the organization's culture.[9] Culture gives employees a sense of organizational identity and generates a commitment to particular values and ways of doing things. Culture serves two important functions in organizations: (1) it integrates members so that they know how to relate to one another, and (2) it helps the organization adapt to the external environment.

INTERNAL INTEGRATION   Culture helps members develop a collective identity and know how to work together effectively. It is culture that guides day-to-day working relationships and determines how people communicate in the organization, what behavior is acceptable or not acceptable, and how power and status are allocated. Culture can imprint a set of unwritten rules inside employees' minds, which can be very powerful in determining behavior, thus affecting organizational performance.[10]

Organizations are putting increased emphasis on developing strong cultures that encourage teamwork, collaboration, and mutual trust.[11] Recall how St. Luke's has created a culture where people feel validated and supported even when their specific ideas or projects are rejected. In an environment of trust, people are more likely to share ideas, be creative, and be generous with their knowledge and talents. At the Container Store, a chain of retail stores that sells boxes, garbage cans, shelving, and just about anything else you might need to organize your home, office, or car, the culture encourages employees to do whatever needs to be done. Simple maxims like "treat people the way you want to be treated" and "be helpful to others" are granted policy status at the Container Store. Cultural values that promote open communication, cooperation, and equality helped the company win the No. 1 spot two years in a row on *Fortune* magazine's list of the best companies to work for in America.[12]

EXTERNAL ADAPTATION   Culture also determines how the organization meets goals and deals with outsiders. The right cultural values can help the organization respond rapidly to customer needs or the moves of a competitor. Culture can encourage employee commitment to the core purpose of the organization, its specific goals, and the basic means used to accomplish goals.

The culture should embody the values and assumptions needed by the organization to succeed in its environment. If the competitive environment requires extraordinary customer service, for example, the corporate culture should encourage good service. Nordstrom has built one of the strongest customer service cultures in the retail industry. According to one account, the entire employee manual is a five-by-eight-inch card that reads "Rule #1: Use your good judgment in all situations. There will be no additional rules."[13] Nordstrom gives its 40,000 employees the responsibility and the authority to do whatever is needed to best serve the customer. At 3M, the culture has always encouraged experimentation and risk-taking, which gives the company a significant advantage in global as well as domestic markets.

IN THE LEAD   Desi DeSimone, 3M

"3M is uniquely positioned to grow in the global marketplace," says CEO L. D. "Desi" DeSimone. "Innovation remains our engine for growth." The culture of 3M is built on encouraging and rewarding experimentation and risk. Founded as Minnesota Mining and Manufacturing in 1902, the company originally mined an abrasive mineral called corundum. Two years later, when the business was on the brink of failure, the company transformed into a manufacturer of sandpaper and grinding wheels—and change has been a key element of 3M's culture ever since.

The company's first general manager, William McKnight, told his fellow managers: "Encourage experimental doodling. Listen to anyone with an original idea no matter how absurd it might sound at first." Nearly a century later, 3M leaders continue to take "doodling" very seriously. All new 3M employees attend classes on risk-taking where they are encouraged to defy their supervisors if necessary to pursue a promising idea. They hear stories of success won despite opposition from the boss—such as how DeSimone himself five times tried to kill the program that eventually led to the highly successful Thinsulate garment insulation.

Researchers are allowed to use 15 percent of their time to explore ideas outside their assigned projects. Any employee with a new product or technology can always find someone to give advice and moral support. Ideas and knowledge are shared throughout the organization, and a technology that isn't useful in one place may be in another. 3M's emphasis on experimentation, risk-taking, and taking a long-term view keeps the company churning out innovative new products—more than 500 in one recent year alone—and has entrenched the company as a leader in some of today's most dynamic markets.[14]

DeSimone and other leaders at 3M encourage cultural values of experimentation and risk-taking to help the company change and adapt in a fast-paced, global environment. DeSimone points out that 3M is "not a company that relies on charismatic CEOs for success. What's important about the CEO is that he's improved the culture, he's taken away barriers to growth as the future looks different."[15]

Cultures are important for binding employees together, making the organization a community rather than just a collection of individuals. However, to keep an organization healthy and profitable, the culture should also encourage adaptation to the external environment.

CULTURE STRENGTH AND ADAPTATION

A strong organizational culture can have a powerful impact, although not necessarily always a positive one. **Culture strength** refers to the degree of agreement among employees about the importance of specific values and ways of doing things. If widespread consensus exists, the culture is strong and cohesive; if little agreement exists, the culture is weak.[16]

A strong culture can increase employee cohesion and commitment to the values, goals, and strategies of the organization. However, research at Harvard into some 200 corporate cultures found that a strong culture does not ensure success unless it also encourages a healthy adaptation to the external environment.[17] A strong culture that does not encourage adaptation can be more damaging to an organization than a weak culture. For example, Motorola's strong culture based on encouraging internal competition among divisions almost destroyed the company. After many years of success, Motorola's culture had become "set," as if in concrete, and the company failed to adapt as the environment changed. The company that had invented the cellular telephone industry was being pounded by more innovative rivals such as Nokia and was infuriating customers with its arrogant approach. Moreover, leaders viewed the Internet as an oddball curiosity, rather than a trend the company needed to embrace. Fortunately, Motorola CEO Christopher B. Galvin recognized the need for a corporate makeover and began working with other leaders to change the insular and competitive culture. Today employees and executives are focused on collaboration rather than competition to spur development of Internet-based products and improve customer service. The makeover isn't complete, but most observers agree that Motorola is on the right path, toward providing the best lineup of Web phones in the world. Shifting to a more adaptive culture has made Motorola once again a name to fear in the wireless industry.[18]

As illustrated in Exhibit 14.2, adaptive corporate cultures have different values and behavior from unadaptive cultures. In adaptive cultures, leaders are concerned with customers and those internal people, processes, and procedures that bring about useful change. In unadaptive cultures, leaders are concerned

EXHIBIT 14.2

Adaptive versus Unadaptive Cultures

	Adaptive Organizational Culture	Unadaptive Organizational Culture
Visible Behavior:	Leaders pay close attention to all their constituencies, especially customers, and initiate change when needed to serve their legitimate interests, even if it entails taking some risks.	Managers tend to behave somewhat insularly, politically, and bureaucratically. As a result, they do not change their strategies quickly to adjust to or take advantage of changes in their business environments.
Expressed values:	Leaders care deeply about customers, stockholders, and employees. They also strongly value people and processes that can create useful change (e.g., leadership initiatives up and down the management hierarchy)	Managers care mainly about themselves, their immediate work group, or some product (or technology) associated with that work group. They value the orderly and risk-reducing management process much more highly than leadership initiatives.
Underlying Assumption:	Serve whole organization, trust others	Meet own needs, distrust others.

SOURCE: Reprinted with the permission of The Free Press, a division of Simon & Schuster from *Corporate Culture and Performance* by John P. Kotter and James L. Heskett. Copyright © 1992 by Kotter Associates, Inc. and James L. Heskett.

with themselves or their own special projects, and their values tend to discourage risk-taking and change. Thus, a strong culture is not enough, because an unhealthy culture may encourage the organization to march resolutely in the wrong direction. Healthy cultures help companies adapt to the external environment. One issue of concern for many of today's leaders is to help organizations adapt to the growing importance of e-business, as described in this chapter's Leader's Bookshelf.

Culture Gap

An organization's culture may not always be in alignment with the needs of the external environment. The values and ways of doing things may reflect what worked in the past, as they did at Motorola. The difference between desired and actual values and behaviors is called the **culture gap**.[19] Organiza-

Culture.com
Building Corporate Culture
in the Connected Workplace

Peg C. Neuhauser, Ray Bender,
and Kirk L. Stromberg

The transition to a networked economy is the biggest shift in the way the world functions since the Industrial Revolution, and organizations around the globe are busily adjusting their strategies to capitalize on the dot-com revolution. However, Peg Neuhauser, Ray Bender, and Kirk Stromberg, authors of *Culture.com*, argue that the importance of culture in helping organizations deliver on those new strategies has so far received little attention. Their book serves as a practical guide to help leaders shift their organizations' cultures to adapt to the new realities of e-business.

Key Challenges for Shifting to a Dot-Com Culture
The book addresses nine key challenges every organization confronts when moving into the e-business world. They include:

- **Jumping to Warp Speed.** Even for traditional organizations, things are moving ten times faster than they were just a few years ago. Leaders have to create a fast-paced culture to keep pace with the speed of Internet time. This means building trust, valuing risk-taking, loosening control, and sharing power and decision making.

- **Managing People's Brain Power.** Knowledge and information drive today's economy. To succeed, organizations learn to manage people's brain power and the company's collective knowledge. One powerful way to encourage norms of knowledge-sharing and collaboration is by telling stories about company heroes who shared knowledge to help colleagues and the company succeed.

- **Building a Learning Culture.** "Mistake learning, just-in-time learning, stealth learning, and rapid learning become the backbone of the new corporate IQ." A high-IQ culture is one in which people have a collective understanding of the organization's internal competencies and external markets, as well as the ability to rally resources to respond to unexpected challenges. Leaders strive to create a culture in which everyone is responsible for continuous learning and problem-solving.

- **Leading the Journey.** Leaders are the most influential culture carriers in the organization. Many times, leaders have to change themselves to change the organizational culture. The command-and-control mind-set will not work in the e-business world. Leaders learn to use influence more and power less, and they emphasize the importance of leadership at all levels of the organization.

A Road Map for Getting to a Dot-Com Culture
This book is packed with practical tips and strategies for how leaders can help build a culture that supports and is aligned with the needs of an e-business environment. In addition, it includes hundreds of examples and stories from a wide range of businesses, government settings, and not-for-profit organizations, including Ace Hardware Corporation, Amazon.com, Buckman Laboratories, Cisco Systems, Eli Lilly, Fairfax Virginia Public Schools, FedEx, General Services Administration, NASA, Procter & Gamble, the United States Air Force, and the University of Augsburg, Germany.

Culture.com, by Peg C. Neuhauser, Ray Bender, and Kirk L. Stromberg, is published by John Wiley & Sons.

tions can be much more effective when the culture fits the external environment.

Culture gaps can be immense, particularly in the case of mergers. Despite the popularity of mergers and acquisitions as a corporate strategy, many fail. Almost one-half of all acquired companies are sold within five years, and some experts claim that 90 percent of mergers never live up to expectations.[20] One reason for this is the difficulty of integrating cultures.

When Harty Press acquired Pre-Press Graphics to move their company into the digital age, the two cultures clashed from the beginning. Executives initially focused on integrating the acquired firm's financial systems and production technologies, but their failure to pay attention to culture seriously damaged the company. According to general manager Michael Platt, "I thought all that stuff people said about culture when it came to mergers was a bunch of fluff—until it happened."[21] The merger of Citicorp and Travelers has also suffered from culture clash. John Reed, who recently retired as co-CEO of Citigroup, explained the difficulty and frustration of merging two cultures this way: "I will tell you that it is not simple and it is not easy, and it is not clear to me that it will necessarily be successful. . . . As you put two cultures together, you get all sorts of strange, aberrant behavior, and it's not clear whether each side getting to know the other side helps, or whether having common objectives helps, or whether it is just the passage of time."[22] Organizational leaders should remember that the human systems—in particular the norms and values of corporate culture—are what make or break any change initiative. The problem of integrating cultures increases in scope and complexity with global companies and cross-cultural mergers or acquisitions.

SHAPING CULTURE

An organization exists only because of the people who are a part of it, and those people both shape and interpret the character and culture of the organization. That is, an organization is not a slice of objective reality; different people may perceive the organization in different ways and relate to it in different ways. Leaders in particular formulate a viewpoint about the organization and the values that can help people achieve the organization's mission, vision, and goals. Therefore, leaders enact a viewpoint and a set of values that they think are best for helping the organization succeed. An organization's culture is often a reflection of the values advocated by a strong top leader. Consider the culture of Trilogy Software.

IN THE LEAD   ## Joe Liemandt, Trilogy Software

Trilogy Software has been called everything from "the cult on the hill" to "the software sweatshop." But that doesn't bother founder and CEO Joe Liemandt— or his corps of young hardworking, hard-playing employees. The average age at the company is twenty-six (Liemandt himself is barely over thirty), and most of Trilogy's 700 employees are (like Liemandt) overachievers dedicated to accomplishing the vision of being the world's next great software company. Those who aren't don't last long.

Liemandt has strengthened Trilogy's distinctive culture through a rigorous recruitment and training process, designed to find people who are "a good technical and cultural fit" and quickly infuse them with the organization's values. Some of Trilogy's top software developers conduct the first-round interviews. Next, Trilogy flies the top candidates to headquarters in Austin, where they are joined by Trilogians for a night on the town. A morning of highly technical interviews the next day might be followed by an afternoon of mountain biking or roller-blading. The process is time-consuming and expensive—around $13,000 per hire—but Trilogy believes it's worth every minute and every penny. After employees are hired, they spend three months at Trilogy University (TU), where they bond with one another and learn about the company and the software industry. They also get a crash course in Trilogy culture. Trilogy doesn't have a corporate handbook, but there are a number of unwritten cultural rules. Recruits learn quickly that at Trilogy, you work hard, play hard, practice teamwork, and take risks. Liemandt makes it clear to his new employees that he will push them to the limit, give them really hard work and lots of responsibility, and then reward them accordingly.

Trilogy's hard-charging culture isn't for everyone. However, as Jeff Daniel, the company's director of college recruiting, says, ". . . it's definitely an environment where people who are passionate about what they do can thrive."[23]

Liemandt has placed significant emphasis on *selection and socialization* at Trilogy to shape the culture he believes is critical to the company's success. Leaders use a number of techniques to encourage and maintain strong, healthy cultures that provide both smooth internal integration and external adaptation. Leaders can use organizational rites and ceremonies, stories, symbols, and specialized language to enact cultural values. In addition, they can emphasize careful selection and socialization of new employees to keep cultures strong. Perhaps most importantly, leaders signal the cultural values they want to instill in the organization through their day-to-day actions.

Ceremonies

A **ceremony** is a planned activity that makes up a special event and is generally conducted for the benefit of an audience. Leaders can schedule ceremonies to provide dramatic examples of what the company values. Ceremonies reinforce specific values, create a bond among employees by allowing them to share an important event, and anoint and celebrate employees who symbolize important achievements.[24]

A ceremony often includes the presentation of an award. At Mary Kay Cosmetics, one of the most effective companies in the world at using ceremonies, leaders hold elaborate award ceremonies at an annual event called "Seminar," presenting jewelry, furs, and luxury cars to high-achieving sales consultants. The most successful consultants are introduced by film clips like the ones used to present award nominees in the entertainment industry.[25] These ceremonies recognize and celebrate high-performing employees and help bind sales consultants together. Even when they know they will not personally be receiving awards, consultants look forward to Seminar all year because of the emotional bond it creates with others.

Stories

A **story** is a narrative based on true events that is repeated frequently and shared among employees. Stories are told to new employees to illustrate the company's primary values and used by leaders to keep values alive and provide a shared understanding among workers. One frequently told story at UPS concerns an employee who, without authority, ordered an extra Boeing 737 to ensure timely delivery of a load of Christmas packages. As the story goes, rather than punishing the worker, UPS rewarded his initiative. By telling this story, UPS workers communicate that the company stands behind its commitment to worker autonomy and customer service.[26] In some cases, stories may not be supported by facts, but they are consistent with the values and beliefs of the organization. At Nordstrom, for example, leaders do not deny the story about a customer who got his money back on a defective tire, even though Nordstrom does not sell tires. The story reinforces the company's no-questions-asked return policy.[27]

As we discussed in Chapter 9, storytelling is a powerful way to connect with others on an emotional level, helping to convey and transmit important cultural values. Richard Stone runs a company called StoryWork Institute that helps organizations find and circulate stories as a way to strengthen or change cultural values. One client, Nighttime Pediatrics Clinics, which runs after-hours clinics in the Salt Lake City area, hired Stone when CEO Teresa Lever-Pollary became concerned that the organization was losing its values in the face of rapid growth and the strictures of managed care. To solidify values such as individual-centered care, teamwork, and informality, Stone collected stories from patients, doctors, nurses, clerks, and others and put them together in a collection called *Nighttime Stories,* which was given out at the company's fifteenth birthday celebration. "It has helped people remember what is special about us," says Lever-Pollary. One story tells of a doctor who bent the clinic's rules to treat a disoriented elderly woman. Another focuses on a payroll employee who convinced management to scrap an expensive investment in flawed new software.[28]

Symbols

Another tool for conveying cultural values is the symbol. A **symbol** is an object, act, or event that conveys meaning to others. In a sense, stories and ceremonies are symbols, but physical artifacts can also be used by leaders to symbolize particular values. For example, Stephen Quesnelle, head of quality programs at Mitel Corp., placed a nearly life-size wooden heifer outside his office to symbolize the importance of tracking down and destroying sacred cows, "the barriers that everyone knows about but nobody talks about."[29]

At Siebel Systems in San Mateo, California, employees are surrounded by symbolic reminders that the customer always comes first. Every conference room is named after a major Siebel customer. All the artwork on office walls comes from customer ads or annual reports. "The cornerstone of our corporate culture," says Siebel, "is that we are committed to do whatever it takes to make sure that each and every one of our customers succeeds."[30]

Specialized Language

Language can shape and influence organizational values and beliefs. Leaders sometimes use slogans or sayings to express key corporate values. Slogans can easily be picked up and repeated by employees. For example, at Speedy Muffler in Canada, the saying, "At Speedy, you're somebody," applies to customers and employees alike. Leaders at Sequins International, where 80 percent of workers are Hispanic, had W. Edwards Deming's words, "You don't have to please the boss; you have to please the customer," embroidered in Spanish on the pockets of workers' jackets.[31]

Leaders also express and reinforce cultural values through written public statements, such as corporate mission statements or other formal statements that express the core values of the organization. Leaders at Eli Lilly and Company developed a formal statement of corporate values, including respect for all people, honesty and integrity, and striving for continuous improvement.[32] Eaton Corporation's philosophy statement, called "Excellence Through People," includes values such as encouraging employee involvement in all decisions, regular face-to-face communication between executives and employees, emphasizing promotion from within, and always focusing on the positive behavior of workers.[33]

Selection and Socialization

Selection and socialization of new employees helps maintain cultural values. Companies with strong, healthy cultures, such as Southwest Airlines and Nordstrom, often have careful and rigorous hiring practices. At Southwest, prospective employees are subjected to extensive interviewing, sometimes even by Southwest's regular customers, so that only those who fit the culture are hired. Southwest looks first and foremost for a sense of humor. At Nordstrom, "niceness" is an important cultural value. "We can hire nice people and teach them to sell," retired cochairman Bruce Nordstrom likes to say, "but we can't hire salespeople and teach them to be nice."[34]

Starbucks Coffee emphasizes socialization as key to maintaining its strong culture. CEO Howard Schultz compares an employee's first days with the company to the early years of childhood, when you want to instill good values, high self-esteem, and the confidence to begin taking risks and making decisions. Schultz himself welcomes each new employee by video, tells about the company's history and culture, and shares some of his own personal experiences at Starbucks. All employees receive twenty-four hours of training, during which they talk about the Starbucks mission and values and the qualities that make Starbucks a unique company.[35] Even though Schultz believes an employee's first two weeks may be the most important, socialization also continues throughout an employee's tenure with the organization.

Daily Actions

Ceremonies, stories, slogans, and symbols are useless if leaders don't signal and support important cultural values through their daily actions. Employees learn what is valued most in a company by watching what attitudes and behaviors leaders pay attention to and reward, how leaders react to organizational crises, and whether the leader's own behavior matches the espoused values.[36] At Levi Strauss, for example, managers' bonus pay, which can be two-thirds of their total compensation, is tied explicitly to how well they follow the organization's list of "corporate aspirations"—a list of stated core values that includes an emphasis on teamwork, trust, diversity, recognition, ethics, and empowerment.[37] Because leaders at Levi Strauss create linkages between stated values, training, everyday action, and appraisal and reward systems, employees rely on the aspirations as a standard of behavior.

Good leaders recognize how carefully they are watched by employees. The story of Bob Kierlin, chairman, president, and CEO of Fastenal, illustrates clearly that the leader's greatest impact on culture comes from what he or she does on a day-by-day basis.

IN THE LEAD   ## Bob Kierlin, Fastenal Co.

Inc. magazine once referred to Bob Kierlin, the top leader of Fastenal Co. of Winona, Minnesota, as "the cheapest CEO in America." It may sound like a dubious honor, but Kierlin runs a national powerhouse that operates almost 800 branch sites in forty-eight states, Canada, and Puerto Rico. The company sells and custom manufactures nuts and bolts, fasteners, safety supplies, tools, and other industrial and construction products. Despite Kierlin's "cheapness," Fastenal is a growing company because it invests wisely in new equipment and technology. In addition, Fastenal's employees are happy and feel a strong commitment to the company.

Bob Kierlin is the kind of guy who just loves a bargain. He clips coupons from the Sunday paper, eats McDonald's Extra Value Meals, drives an Oldsmobile, and has taken home the same $120,000 yearly paycheck for the last decade. He buys his suits used from the manager of a men's clothing store. Fastenal's culture very much reflects Kierlin's values—scratch pads are made from used paper, annual reports are produced in-house for 40 cents a copy, and the warehouse shelving was bought used for 25 cents on the dollar.

Kierlin sets the example daily. Rather than flying to a conference in Chicago, he and the chief financial officer drove five and a half hours in a van, saving Fastenal hundreds of dollars. They lunched at A&W on burgers and root beer for $5 each and spent the night in a suburb to avoid high city prices—they even shared a room. Top executives have no special privileges. Kierlin fights for a good parking space just like anyone else in the company. Until recently, he shoveled snow at corporate headquarters and sorted the mail himself. That kind of social leveling has created a bond between workers and executives that most companies can only dream of. Workers respect Kierlin—he treats everyone the same, whether you're a janitor or a vice president, and he comes in at 6 A.M. and works as hard as anyone in the company. They also share the cultural values Kierlin models every day—not just the value of a buck, but the importance of being fair and treating everyone as an equal. Because of a profit-sharing plan, they know that cutting costs fattens everyone's paycheck, but the quality of their relationships is just as important.

Kierlin doesn't see anything unusual about his leadership or his company's culture—he thinks it's just good, old-fashioned common sense.[38]

A culture of frugality and fairness is powerful at Fastenal, not just because it saves money. The company's constant obsession with costs promotes a kind of attentiveness to the mundane that inevitably improves quality. In addition, the culture spreads accountability and responsibility everywhere—at Fastenal, you never call somebody else to fix a problem, you fix it yourself. The culture is strong primarily because the company's top leaders live the cultural values every day.

Leaders can also change unadaptive cultures by their actions. On his first day as new chief at IBM, Lou Gerstner called a dozen top executives into his office and asked them to write a five-page report answering such questions as "What business are you in? Who are your customers? What are your strengths and weaknesses?" He asked for the report in two days. In a company known for meetings steeped in ritual, requiring extensive and elaborate preparations and accompanied by massive reports in blue binders, the message was clear: It was no longer business as usual at Big Blue.[39]

Through ceremonies, stories, symbols, language, hiring and training practices, and their own behavior, leaders influence culture. When culture change is needed to adapt to the environment or bring about smoother internal integration, leaders are responsible for instilling new cultural values. Changing cultures is not easy, but through their words, and particularly their actions, leaders let other members know what really counts in the company.

SHAPING VALUES

Today's leaders recognize the importance of shared values and invest time in thinking about and discussing them. **Organizational values** are the enduring beliefs that have worth, merit, and importance for the organization. Changes in the nature of work, as well as the increasing diversity in the workforce, have made the topic of values one of considerable concern to leaders. They are faced with such questions as, "How can I determine what cultural values are important? Are some values 'better' than others? How can the organization's culture help us be more competitive?"

The Competing Values Approach

In considering what values are important for the organization, leaders consider the external environment and the company's vision and strategy. Cultures can vary widely across organizations; however, organizations within the same industry often reveal similar values because they are operating in similar environments.[40] Key values should embody what the organization needs to be effective. For example, if the competitive environment requires flexibility and responsiveness, the culture should value adaptability. Rather than looking at values as either "good" or "bad," leaders look for the right combination. The correct relationship among cultural values, organizational strategy, and the external environment can enhance organizational performance.

Studies of culture and effectiveness have suggested that the fit among environment, strategy, and values is associated with four categories of culture, which are illustrated in Exhibit 14.3. The differences are based on two dimensions: (1) the extent to which the external environment requires flexibility or stability and (2) the extent to which the strategic focus is internal or external. Together the dimensions form four quadrants, each representing a cultural category with emphasis on specific values.[41]

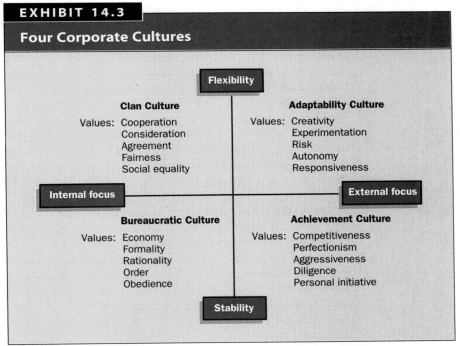

EXHIBIT 14.3

Four Corporate Cultures

Flexibility

Clan Culture

Values: Cooperation
Consideration
Agreement
Fairness
Social equality

Adaptability Culture

Values: Creativity
Experimentation
Risk
Autonomy
Responsiveness

Internal focus   **External focus**

Bureaucratic Culture

Values: Economy
Formality
Rationality
Order
Obedience

Achievement Culture

Values: Competitiveness
Perfectionism
Aggressiveness
Diligence
Personal initiative

Stability

SOURCES: Based on Paul McDonald and Jeffrey Gandz, "Getting Value from Shared Values," *Organizational Dynamics* 21, No. 3 (Winter 1992), 64–76; Deanne N. Den Hartog, Jaap J. VanMuijen, and Paul L. Koopman, "Linking Transformational Leadership and Organizational Culture," *The Journal of Leadership Studies* 3, No. 4 (1996), 68–83; Daniel R. Denison and Aneil K. Mishra, "Toward a Theory of Organizational Culture and Effectiveness," *Organizational Studies* 6, No. 2 (March-April 1995), 204–223; Robert Hooijberg and Frank Petrock, "On Cultural Change: Using the Competing Values Framework to Help Leaders Execute a Transformational Strategy," *Human Resource Management* 32, No. 1 (1993), 29–50; R.E. Quinn, *Beyond Rational Management: Mastering the Paradoxes and Competing Demands of High Performance* (San Francisco: Jossey-Bass, 1998).

The four culture categories are Adaptability, Achievement, Clan, and Bureaucratic. An organization may have cultural values that fall into more than one category, or even into all categories. However, successful organizations with strong cultures will lean more toward one particular cultural category. For example, Fastenal, described in the previous section, clearly values economy, listed in the bureaucratic culture category. However, its overall set of values places it more clearly in the clan culture category because of its strong emphasis on fairness, social equality, and caring for people.

ADAPTABILITY CULTURE   The **adaptability culture** is characterized by strategic leaders encouraging values that support the organization's ability to interpret and translate signals from the environment into new behavior responses. Employees have autonomy to make decisions and act freely to meet new needs, and responsiveness to customers is highly valued. Leaders also actively create change by encouraging and rewarding creativity, experimentation, and risk-taking. 3M is an example of an adaptability culture, where leaders encourage experimentation and taking risks as an everyday way of life. Acxiom Corp., based in Conway, Arkansas, began shifting to an adaptability culture in the early 1990s. After years of rapid growth and an explosion of interest in data management products and services, managers discovered that the company's culture, which emphasized internal efficiency, consistency in following established rules and procedures, and top-down decision making, was no longer suitable to meet the demands of the rapidly changing environment. Acxiom shifted to an external focus emphasizing the importance of employee empowerment, flexibility, and responsiveness.[42] Most e-commerce companies also use this type of culture because they must move quickly to satisfy customers.

ACHIEVEMENT CULTURE   The **achievement culture** is characterized by a clear vision of the organization's goals, and leaders focus on the achievement of specific targets such as sales growth, profitability, or market share. An organization concerned with serving specific customers in the external environment but without the need for flexibility and rapid change is suited to the achievement culture. This is a results-oriented culture that values competitiveness, aggressiveness, personal initiative, and the willingness to work long and hard to achieve results. An emphasis on winning is the glue that holds the organization together.[43]

A good example of an achievement culture is Siebel Systems, which sells complex software systems. Siebel, like its cofounder and CEO Tom Siebel, is intense, competitive, and driven to win. Employees who perform and meet stringent goals are handsomely rewarded; those who don't are fired. Nearly every employee at Siebel is given a ranking within each department, and every six months the bottom five percent are axed. Siebel has procedures and systems for carefully measuring employees on key performance variables such as responsiveness to customers. Succeeding at Siebel Systems means being smart, competitive, aggressive, and thorough. Employees who thrive on the competitive culture have helped Siebel's revenues grow at a rate of 100 percent a year for the past five years.[44]

CLAN CULTURE The **clan culture** has an internal focus on the involvement and participation of employees to rapidly meet changing expectations from the external environment. More than any other, this culture places value on meeting the needs of employees. These organizations are generally friendly places to work and employees may seem almost like a family. Leaders emphasize cooperation, consideration of both employees and customers, and avoiding status differences. Leaders put a premium on fairness and reaching agreement with others.

One company that achieves success with a clan culture is SAS Institute, based in Cary, North Carolina. The most important value is taking care of employees and making sure they have whatever they need to be satisfied and productive. Employees are encouraged to lead a balanced life rather than to work long hours and express a hard-charging, competitive spirit. The company even adopted a seven-hour workday to give employees more personal time. SAS also offers amazing benefits, including two Montessori day-care centers, a 36,000 square foot fitness center, unlimited sick days, an on-site health clinic, elder care advice and referrals, and live music in the cafeteria, where employees may eat with their families. Other key values at SAS are equality, fairness, and cooperation. Employees care about each other and about the company, a focus that has helped SAS adapt to stiff competition and changing markets.[45]

BUREAUCRATIC CULTURE The **bureaucratic culture** has an internal focus and consistency orientation for a stable environment. The culture supports a methodical, rational, orderly way of doing business. Following the rules and being thrifty are valued. The organization succeeds by being highly integrated and efficient.

Safeco Insurance has functioned well with a bureaucratic culture. Employees take their coffee breaks at an assigned time, and a dress code specifies white shirts and suits for men and no beards. However, employees like this culture—reliability is highly valued and extra work isn't required. The bureaucratic culture works for the insurance company, and Safeco succeeds because it can be trusted to deliver on insurance policies as agreed.[46] In today's fast-changing world, very few organizations operate in a stable environment, and most leaders are shifting away from bureaucratic cultures because of a need for greater flexibility.

Each of the four cultures can be successful. The relative emphasis on various cultural values depends on the organization's strategic focus and on the needs of the external environment. It is the responsibility of leaders to ensure that organizations don't get "stuck" in cultural values that worked in the past but are no longer successful. This chapter's Living Leadership highlights the importance of adaptability. As environmental conditions and strategy change, leaders work to instill new cultural values to help the organization meet new needs. For example, when Pitney Bowes Credit Corporation redefined its business to take advantage of new opportunities in the environment, leaders also redefined the culture.

IN THE LEAD — Matthew Kisner, Pitney Bowes Credit Corporation

Pitney Bowes Credit Corporation (PBCC) operated quite successfully with an orderly, predictable bureaucratic culture for many years. The main purpose of the organization was to help Pitney Bowes customers finance their purchases of postage meters, copiers, fax machines, and other office essentials. However, when Matthew Kisner took over as PBCC's president and CEO, he saw an opportunity to be not just a provider of services, but also a *creator* of services. Now, rather than just financing sales and leasing of existing products, PBCC creates new services for customers to buy. One example is Purchase Power, a revolving line of credit that helps companies finance their postage costs. Profitable within nine months, Purchase Power now has more than 400,000 customers.

As PBCC's strategic focus changed, leaders saw a need to redefine the culture, by emphasizing values of teamwork, risk-taking, and creativity. Maintaining the status quo is no longer valued; the emphasis is on breaking new ground. Early in his job, Kisner handed out buttons with the phrase "That's the way we've always done it" crossed out with a red circle and slash. He also changed the company's rituals. Rather than inviting the usual list of high-ranking executives to the annual retreat, Kisner proclaimed that anyone would be eligible to attend. Invitations are now based on individual performance and teamwork rather than on position.

Perhaps the biggest symbolic change was in PBCC's physical environment. The office now looks something like an indoor theme park, featuring cobblestone-patterned carpets, faux gas lamps, and an ornate town-square-style clock. It also has a French-style café, a 1950s-style diner, and the "Cranial Kitchen," where employees sit in cozy booths to surf the Internet or watch training videos. The friendly hallways encourage impromptu conversations, where employees can exchange information and share ideas they wouldn't otherwise share. "We wanted a fun space that would embody our culture," Kisner says. "No straight lines, no linear thinking. Because we're a financial services company, our biggest advantage is the quality of our ideas."[47] Shifting to an adaptability culture has energized employees and helped PBCC become a new-product powerhouse.

ETHICAL VALUES IN ORGANIZATIONS

Of the values that make up an organization's culture, ethical values are considered highly important for leaders. Leaders have made ethical standards part of the formal policies and informal cultures of many organizations. Some companies, such as St. Luke's, described in the opening example, place significant emphasis on ethics. Certified Transmission Rebuilders, a small company based in Omaha, Nebraska, also emphasizes ethics by basing its culture on putting the customer's interests first. Employees receive ongoing training to develop "honest communication" skills. Owner Peter Fink doesn't pay diagnosticians on commission because he doesn't want that to influence their decisions. Customers who have had their transmission repaired at Certified are asked to bring the car back in fifteen days for a free recheck to make sure everything is working right, even though the process is expensive and time-consuming.[48]

Ethics is difficult to define in a precise way. In general, **ethics** is the code of moral principles and values that governs the behavior of a person or group with respect to what is right or wrong. Ethics sets standards as to what is good or bad in conduct and decision making.[49] Many people believe that if you are not breaking the law, then you are behaving in an ethical manner, but ethics often goes far beyond the law.[50] The law arises from a set of codified principles and regulations that are generally accepted in society and are enforceable in the courts. Ethical standards for the most part apply to behavior not covered by law. Although current laws often reflect minimum moral standards, not all moral standards are codified into law. The morality of aiding a drowning person, for example, is not specified by law.

 LIVING LEADERSHIP

Flexible or Rigid

The ability to embrace change is characteristic of growth and vibrancy. This metaphor illustrates that organizations should remain adaptable:

At birth, a person is flexible and flowing. At death, a person becomes rigid and blocked. Consider the lives of plants and trees: during their time of greatest growth, they are relatively tender and pliant. But when they are full grown or begin to die, they become tough and brittle.

The tree which has grown up and become rigid is cut into lumber. . . .

Whatever is flexible and flowing will tend to grow. Whatever is rigid and blocked will atrophy and die.

SOURCE: John Heider, *The Tao of Leadership: Leadership Strategies for a New Age* (New York: Bantam Books, 1985), 151. Copyright © 1985 Humanic Ltd., Atlanta, GA. Used with permission.

The standards for ethical conduct are embodied within each employee as well as within the organization itself. In a recent survey about unethical conduct in the workplace, more than half of the respondents cited poor leadership as a factor.[51] Leaders can create and sustain a climate that emphasizes ethical behavior for all employees.

VALUES-BASED LEADERSHIP

Ethical values in organizations are developed and strengthened primarily through **values-based leadership,** a relationship between leaders and followers that is based on shared, strongly internalized values that are advocated and acted upon by the leader.[52] Leaders influence ethical values through their personal behavior as well as through the organization's systems and policies.

Personal Ethics

Employees learn about values from watching leaders. Values-based leaders generate a high level of trust and respect from employees, based not just on stated values but on the courage, determination, and self-sacrifice they demonstrate in upholding those values. When leaders are willing to make personal sacrifices for the sake of values, employees become more willing to do so.

For organizations to be ethical, leaders need to be openly and strongly committed to ethical conduct. Several factors contribute to an individual leader's ethical stance. Every individual brings a set of personal beliefs, values, personality characteristics, and behavior traits to the job. The family backgrounds and spiritual beliefs of leaders often provide principles by which they conduct business. Personality characteristics such as ego strength, self-confidence, and a strong sense of independence may enable leaders to make ethical decisions even if those decisions might be unpopular.

One important personal factor is the leader's stage of moral development, as described in Chapter 6, which affects an individual's ability to translate values into behavior.[53] For example, some people make decisions and act only to obtain rewards and avoid punishment for themselves. Others learn to conform to expectations of good behavior as defined by society. This means willingly upholding the law and responding to the expectations of others. At the highest level of moral development are people guided by high internal standards. These are self-chosen ethical principles that don't change with reward or punishment. Leaders can strive to develop higher moral principles so that their daily actions reflect important ethical values. When faced with difficult decisions, values-based leaders know what they stand for, and they have the courage to act on their principles.

In a study of ethics policy and practice in successful, ethical companies such as Boeing, Chemical Bank, General Mills, GTE, Xerox, Johnson & Johnson, and Hewlett-Packard, no point emerged more clearly than the crucial role of top leaders.[54] Leaders set the tone for an organization's ethics through their own actions.

Organizational Structure and Systems

Leaders also influence ethical values through formal systems, programs, and policies. Formal systems that have effectively influenced organizational ethics are codes of ethics, ethical structures, training programs, and disclosure mechanisms.

CODE OF ETHICS   A **code of ethics** is a formal statement of the company's ethical values. It communicates to employees what the company stands for. Codes of ethics state the values and behavior that are expected and those that will not be tolerated. A study by the Center for Business Ethics found that 90 percent of *Fortune* 500 companies and almost half of all other companies now have codes of ethics.[55] When leaders support and enforce these codes, they can uplift a company's ethical climate.

Some companies include ethics as a part of broader statements that also define their mission. These statements generally define ethical values as well as corporate culture and contain language about company responsibility, quality of product, and treatment of employees. For example, Northern Telecom's *Code of Business Conduct,* which is provided to all employees and is also available on the Internet, is a set of guidelines and standards that illustrates how the company's mission and core values translate into ethical business practices.

STRUCTURE   Ethical structure represents the various positions or programs an organization uses to encourage ethical behavior. One example is an ethics committee—a group of employees appointed to oversee the company's ethics. The committee provides rulings on questionable ethical issues. An ethics **ombudsperson** is a single person given the responsibility of the corporate conscience who hears and investigates complaints and points out potential ethics failures to top leaders.

Many organizations today are setting up ethics departments with full-time staff. These offices, such as the ethics and business practices office set up by Arthur Martinez at Sears, work more as counseling centers than police departments. They are charged with helping employees deal with day-to-day ethical problems or questions. The offices also provide training based on the organization's code of ethics or business conduct, so that employees can translate the values into daily behavior.[56]

TRAINING   To make sure ethical issues are considered in daily actions, leaders often implement training programs to supplement a written code of ethics. Texas Instruments developed an eight-hour ethics-training course for all employees. In addition, leaders incorporate ethics into every course the company offers.[57]

Companies with a strong commitment to ethical values make ethical issues a part of all training. Starbucks Coffee uses new employee training to begin instilling values such as taking personal responsibility, treating everyone with respect, and doing the right thing even if others disagree with you.[58] At the Holt Companies, all employees attend a two-day training program where they learn about the company's values and talk about values-related cases and dilemmas. In addition, all managers and supervisors attend another two-day session focused specifically on ethics awareness.[59]

DISCLOSURE MECHANISMS   Finally, leaders can support employees who do the right thing and voice their concerns about unethical practices. One important step is to develop policies about **whistle-blowing,** employee disclosure of illegal or immoral practices on the part of the organization. It can be risky for employees to blow the whistle—they can lose their jobs, be transferred to lower-level positions, or be ostracized by coworkers.

Leaders set the standard for how whistle-blowers are treated. If the organization genuinely wants to maintain ethical standards, whistle-blowers are valued and leaders make dedicated efforts to protect them.[60] Leaders can create a climate where people feel free to point out problems without fear of punishment. In addition, they can set up hot lines to give employees a confidential way to report problems, and then make sure action is taken to investigate reported concerns.

In summary, leaders can create an ethical climate for the organization through systems and programs such as codes of ethics, ethics committees or offices, training programs, and mechanisms to protect whistle-blowers. Leaders instill and encourage ethical values most clearly through their own personal actions. Organizations can be ethical only when leaders are ethical.

SUMMARY AND INTERPRETATION

Leaders influence organizational culture and ethical values. Culture is the set of key values, norms, and assumptions that is shared by members of an organization and taught to new members as correct. Culture serves two critically important functions—to integrate organizational members so they know how to relate to one another and to help the organization adapt to the environment. Strong, adaptive cultures have a positive impact on organizational outcomes. A culture gap exists when an organization's culture is not in alignment with the needs of the external environment or company strategy. Leaders use ceremonies, stories, symbols, specialized language, selection, and socialization to influence cultural values. In addition, leaders shape cultural values most strongly through their daily actions.

Leaders consider the external environment and the company's vision and strategy in determining which values are important for the organization. Four types of culture may exist in organizations: Adaptability, Achievement, Clan, and Bureaucratic. Each type emphasizes different values, although organizations may have values that fall into more than one category.

Of the values that make up an organization's culture, ethical values are among the most important. Ethics is the code of moral principles and values that governs the behavior of a person or group with respect to what is right or wrong. Leaders shape ethical values through values-based leadership, including their own personal behavior as well as the organization's systems and policies. Leaders' personal beliefs and level of moral development influence their personal ethics. For organizations to be ethical, leaders have to be openly and strongly committed to ethical conduct in their daily actions. Leaders can also influence ethical values in the organization through codes of ethics, ethics committees or ombudspersons, training programs, and disclosure mechanisms to support employees who voice concerns about ethical practices.

KEY TERMS

culture	organizational values	ethics
culture strength	adaptability culture	values-based leadership
culture gap	achievement culture	code of ethics
ceremony	clan culture	ombudsperson
story	bureaucratic culture	whistle-blowing
symbol		

DISCUSSION QUESTIONS

1. Describe the culture for an organization you are familiar with. Identify the physical artifacts and underlying values and assumptions. What did you learn?

2. Discuss how a strong culture could have either positive or negative consequences for an organization.

3. What is a culture gap? What are some techniques leaders might use to influence and change cultural values when necessary?

4. Compare and contrast the achievement culture with the clan culture. What are some possible *disadvantages* of having a strong clan culture? A strong achievement culture?

5. Which do you think is more important for improving ethical values in an organization: a code of ethics, leader behavior, or employee training? Discuss.

6. In which of the four types of culture (adaptability, achievement, clan, bureaucratic) might you expect to find the greatest emphasis on ethical issues? Why?

7. If a leader directs her health care company to reward hospital managers strictly on hospital profits, is the leader being ethically responsible? Discuss.

8. What is meant by the idea that culture helps a group or organization solve the problem of internal integration?

LEADERSHIP DEVELOPMENT: Personal Feedback

Culture Preference Inventory

The inventory below consists of 14 sets of four responses that relate to typical values or situations facing leaders in organizations. Although each response to a question may appear equally desirable or undesirable, your assignment is to "rank" the four responses in each row according to your preference. Think of yourself as being in charge of a major department or division in an organization. Rank the responses in each row according to how much you would like each one to be a part of your department. There are no correct or incorrect answers; the scores simply reflect your preferences for different responses.

Rank each of the four in each row using the following scale. You must use all four numbers for each set of four responses.

1. Would not prefer at all
2. Would prefer on occasion
4. Would prefer often
8. Would prefer most of all

	I	II	III	IV
1.	_____ Aggressiveness	_____ Cost-efficiency	_____ Experimentation	_____ Fairness
2.	_____ Perfection	_____ Obedience	_____ Risk-taking	_____ Agreement
3.	_____ Pursue future goals	_____ Solve current problems	_____ Be flexible	_____ Develop people's careers

	I	II	III	IV
4.	_____ Apply careful analysis	_____ Rely on proven approaches	_____ Look for creative approaches	_____ Build consensus
5.	_____ Initiative	_____ Rationality	_____ Responsiveness	_____ Collaboration
6.	_____ Highly capable	_____ Productive and accurate	_____ Receptive to brainstorming	_____ Committed to the team
7.	_____ Be the best in our field	_____ Have secure jobs	_____ Recognition for innovations	_____ Equal status
8.	_____ Decide and act quickly	_____ Follow plans and priorities	_____ Refuse to be pressured	_____ Provide guidance and support
9.	_____ Realistic	_____ Systematic	_____ Broad and flexible	_____ Sensitive to the needs of others
10.	_____ Energetic and ambitious	_____ Polite and formal	_____ Open-minded	_____ Agreeable and self-confident
11.	_____ Use key facts	_____ Use accurate and complete data	_____ Use broad coverage of many options	_____ Use limited data and personal opinion
12.	_____ Competitive	_____ Disciplined	_____ Imaginative	_____ Supportive
13.	_____ Challenging assignments	_____ Influence over others	_____ Achieving creativity	_____ Acceptance by the group
14.	_____ Best solution	_____ Good working environment	_____ New approaches or ideas	_____ Personal fulfillment

Scoring

Add the points in each of the four columns—I, II, III, IV. The sum of the point columns should be 210 points. If your sum does not equal 210 points, check your answers and your addition.

Interpretation

The scores represent your preference for I, Achievement culture; II, Bureaucratic culture; III, Adaptability culture; and IV, Clan culture. Your personal values are consistent with the culture for which you achieved the highest score, although all four sets of values exist within you just as they exist within an organization. The specific values you exert as a leader may depend on the group situation, particularly the needs of the external environment. Compare your scores with other students and discuss their meaning. Are you pleased with your preferences? Do you think your scores accurately describe you?

SOURCE: Adapted from Alan J. Rowe and Richard O. Mason, *Managing with Style: A Guide to Understanding, Assessing, and Improving Decision Making* (San Francisco: Jossey-Bass, 1987).

LEADERSHIP DEVELOPMENT: Cases for Analysis

Lisa Benavides, Forest International

Lisa Benavides has just been hired as the vice president of human resources for Forest International. Previously, the company had only a personnel officer and a benefits specialist, who spent most of their time processing applications and benefit forms and tracking vacation and sick days. However, a new CEO came to Forest believing that HR can play a key strategic role in the organization, and he recruited Benavides from a well-known HR consulting firm soon after he took over the top job. The new CEO has lots of ideas about empowerment, shared leadership, and teamwork that he hopes to eventually implement at the company.

Forest International operates in one of the most dangerous industries around. Paper mills, sawmills, and plywood factories are filled with constant noise, giant razor-toothed saw blades, caustic chemicals, and chutes loaded with tons of lumber. Even in this notoriously hazardous industry, Forest's safety record stinks. Within a four-year period, twenty-nine workers have been killed on the job. There are an average of nine serious injuries per 100 employees each year. In addition, productivity has been declining in recent years, and Forest's competitors are gaining market share. As one of her first major projects, the CEO has asked Benavides for her advice on how to improve the company's safety record and increase productivity.

The company, based outside Atlanta, Georgia, has around $11 billion in annual revenues and employs 45,000 people. Many employees' parents and grandparents also worked in Forest's mills and factories. Among many of the workers, missing a finger or two is considered a badge of honor. Taking chances is a way of proving that you're a true "Forest-man" (the term persists even though the company now has a good percentage of female workers). During lunch or break, groups of workers routinely brag about their "close calls" and share stories about parents or grandparents' dangerous encounters with saw blades or lumber chutes.

It is clear to Benavides that worker attitudes are part of the problem, but she suspects that management attitudes may play a role as well. Production managers emphasize the importance of keeping the line moving, getting the product out no matter what. Rather than finding a supervisor and asking that the production line be shut down, most line employees take chances on sticking their hands into moving equipment whenever there is a minor problem. As Benavides talks with workers, she learns that most of them believe managers care more about productivity and profits than they do about the well-being of people in the plant. In fact, most Forest employees don't feel that they're valued at all by the company. One saw operator told Benavides that he has made several suggestions for improving productivity and safety on his line but has been routinely ignored by management. "They never listen to us; they just expect us to do what we're told," he said. This same employee was one of the most vocal in opposing some recent safety-oriented changes requiring that all workers wear safety gear anytime they're on the production floor, not just when they are on the line. "They don't really care about our safety," he boomed. "They just want another way to push us around." Many of the other workers also oppose the new rules, saying that "managers walk around the production floor all the time without goggles and ear plus, so why shouldn't we?"

SOURCE: Based in part on information in Anne Fisher, "Danger Zone," *Fortune*, September 8, 1997, 165–167; and Robert Galford, "Why Doesn't This HR Department Get Any Respect?" *Harvard Business Review*, March-April 1998, 24–26.

Questions

1. How would you describe the culture of Forest International as it relates to internal integration and external adaptation?

2. Would you expect that changing the culture at Forest would be easily accomplished now that a new CEO is committed to change? Why or why not?

3. If you were Lisa Benavides, what suggestions would you make to Forest's new CEO?

Acme and Omega

Acme Electronics and Omega Electronics both manufacture integrated circuits and other electronic parts as subcontractors for large manufacturers. Both Acme and Omega are located in Ohio and often bid on contracts as competitors. As subcontractors, both firms benefited from the electronics boom of the 1980s, and both looked forward to growth and expansion. Acme has annual sales of about $100 million dollars and employs 950 people. Omega has annual sales of $80 million and employs about 800 people. Acme typically reports greater net profits than Omega.

The president of Acme, John Tyler, believed that Acme was the far superior company. Tyler credited his firm's greater effectiveness to his managers' ability to run a "tight ship." Acme had detailed organization charts and job descriptions. Tyler believed that everyone should have clear responsibilities and narrowly defined jobs, which generates efficient performance and high company profits. Employees were generally satisfied with their jobs at Acme, although some managers wished for more empowerment opportunities.

Omega's president, Jim Rawls, did not believe in organization charts. He believed organization charts just put artificial barriers between specialists who should be working together. He encouraged people to communicate face-to-face rather than with written memos. The head of mechanical engineering said, "Jim spends too much time making sure everyone understands what we're doing and listening to suggestions." Rawls was concerned with employee satisfaction and wanted everyone to feel part of the organization. Employees were often rotated among departments so they would be familiar with activities throughout the organization. Although Omega wasn't as profitable as Acme, they were able to bring new products on line more quickly, work bugs out of new designs more accurately, and achieve higher quality because of superb employee commitment and collaboration.

It is the end of May, and John Tyler, president of Acme, has just announced the acquisition of Omega Electronics. Both management teams are proud of their cultures and have unflattering opinions of the other's. Each company's customers are rather loyal, and their technologies are compatible, so Tyler believes a combined company will be even more effective, particularly in a time of rapid change in both technology and products.

The Omega managers resisted the idea of an acquisition, but the Acme president is determined to unify the two companies quickly, increase the new firm's marketing position, and revitalize product lines—all by year end.

SOURCE: Adapted from John F. Veiga, "The Paradoxical Twins: Acme and Omega Electronics," in John F. Veiga and John N. Yanouzas, *The Dynamics of Organization Theory* (St. Paul: West Publishing, 1984), 132–138; and "Alpha and Omega," Harvard Business School Case 9-488-003, published by the President and Fellows of Harvard College, 1988.

Questions

1. Using the competing values model, what type of culture (adaptability, achievement, clan, bureaucratic) would you say is dominant at Acme? At Omega? What is your evidence?

2. Is there a culture gap? Which type of culture do you think is most appropriate for the newly merged company? Why?

3. If you were John Tyler, what techniques would you use to integrate and shape the cultures to overcome the culture gap?

REFERENCES

1. Diane L. Coutu, "Creating the Most Frightening Company on Earth, An Interview with Andy Law of St. Luke's," *Harvard Business Review,* September-October 2000, 143–150; Stevan Alburty, "The Ad Agency to End All Ad Agencies," *Fast Company,* December-January 1997, 116–124; and Jan Burney, "St. Luke's: Making the Irrelevant Relevant," *Graphis* 313 (1998), 84ff.

2. Jeremy Kahn, "What Makes a Company Great?" *Fortune,* October 26, 1998, 218; James C. Collins and Jerry I. Porras, *Built to Last: Successful Habits of Visionary Companies* (New York: HarperBusiness, 1994) ; and James C. Collins, "Change is Good—But First Know What Should Never Change," *Fortune,* May 29, 1995, 141.

3. Edgar H. Schein, "Organizational Culture," *American Psychologist* 45, No. 2 (February 1990), 109–119.

4. Yoash Wiener, "Forms of Value Systems: A Focus on Organizational Effectiveness and Culture Change and Maintenance," *Academy of Management Review* 13 (1988), 534-545; V. Lynne Meek, "Organizational Culture: Origins and Weaknesses," *Organization Studies* 9 (1988), 453–473; and John J. Sherwood, "Creating Work Cultures with Competitive Advantage," *Organizational Dynamics,* Winter 1988, 5–27.

5. W. Jack Duncan, "Organizational Culture: Getting a 'Fix' on an Elusive Concept," *Academy of Management Executive* 3 (1989), 229-236; Linda Smircich, "Concepts of Culture and Organizational Analysis," *Administrative Science Quarterly* 28 (1983), 339–358; and Andrew D. Brown and Ken Starkey, "The Effect of Organizational Culture on Communication and Information," *Journal of Management Studies* 31, No. 6 (November 1994), 807–828.

6. Schein, "Organizational Culture."

7. This discussion of the levels of culture is based on Edgar H. Schein, *Organizational Culture and Leadership,* 2nd ed. (San Francisco: Jossey-Bass, 1992), 3–27.

8. Schein, "Organizational Culture," 113.

9. John P. Kotter and James L. Heskett, *Corporate Culture and Performance* (New York: The Free Press, 1992), 6.

10. Peter B. Scott-Morgan, "Barriers to a High-Performance Business," *Management Review,* July 1993, 37–41.

11. Arthur Ciancutti and Thomas Steding, "Trust Fund," *Business 2.0,* June 13, 2000, 105–117.

12. Daniel Roth, "My Job at the Container Store," *Fortune,* January 10, 2000, 74-78; and Robert Levering and Milton Moskowitz, "The 100 Best Companies to Work For," *Fortune,* January 8, 2001, 148–168.

13. Robert Specter, "The Nordstrom Way," *Corporate University Review,* May/June 1997, 24–25, 66.

14. Joel Hoekstra, "3M's Global Grip," *WorldTraveler,* May 2000, 31–34; and Thomas A. Stewart, "3M Fights Back," *Fortune,* February 5, 1996, 94–99.

15. Ibid.

16. Bernard Arogyaswamy and Charles M. Byles, "Organizational Culture: Internal and External Fits," *Journal of Management* 13 (1987), 647–659.

17. Kotter and Heskett, *Corporate Culture and Performance.*

18. Roger O. Crockett, "A New Company Called Motorola," *Business Week,* April 17, 2000, 86ff.
19. Ralph H. Kilmann, Mary J. Saxton, Roy Serpa, and Associates, *Gaining Control of the Corporate Culture* (San Francisco: Jossey-Bass, 1985).
20. Oren Harari, "Curing the M&A Madness," *Management Review,* July/August 1997, 53–56; Morty Lefkoe, "Why So Many Mergers Fail," *Fortune,* June 20, 1987, 113–114.
21. Edward O. Welles, "Mis-Match," *Inc.,* June 1994, 70–79; Thomas A. Stewart, "Rate Your Readiness to Change," *Fortune,* February 7, 1994, 106–110.
22. "Reed: Reflections on a Culture Clash," box in Patricia Sellers, "Behind the Shootout at Citigroup," *Fortune,* March 20, 2000, 27–32.
23. Chuck Salter, "Insanity Inc.," *Fast Company,* January, 1999, 100–108.
24. Harrison M. Trice and Janice M. Beyer, "Studying Organizational Culture Through Rites and Ceremonials," *Academy of Management Review* 9 (1984), 653–669.
25. Alan Farnham, "Mary Kay's Lessons in Leadership," *Fortune,* September 20, 1993, 68–77.
26. Robert E. Quinn and Gretchen M. Spreitzer, "The Road to Empowerment: Seven Questions Every Leader Should Consider," *Organizational Dynamics,* Autumn 1997, 37–49.
27. Joan O'C. Hamilton, "Why Rivals Are Quaking As Nordstrom Heads East," *Business Week,* June 15, 1987, 99–100.
28. Thomas A. Stewart, "The Cunning Plots of Leadership," *Fortune,* September 7, 1998, 165–166.
29. David Beardsley, "This Company Doesn't Brake for (Sacred) Cows," *Fast Company,* August 1998, 66–68.
30. Melanie Warner, "Confessions of a Control Freak," *Fortune,* September 4, 2000, 130–140.
31. Barbara Ettorre, "Retooling People and Processes," *Management Review,* June 1995, 19–23.
32. "About Lilly: Overview: Our Values," *http://www.lilly.com/about/overview/values. html* accessed on August 9, 2000.
33. Gerald E. Ledford, Jr., Jon R. Wendenhof, and James T. Strahley, "Realizing a Corporate Philosophy," *Organizational Dynamics* 23, No. 3, (Winter 1995), 5–19.
34. Brenda Paik Sunoo, "How Fun Flies at Southwest," *Personnel Journal,* June 1995, 62–73; Specter, "The Nordstrom Way."
35. Stephanie Gruner, "Lasting Impressions," *Inc.,* July 1998, 126.
36. Deanne N. Den Hartog, Jaap J. Van Muijen, and Paul L. Koopman, "Linking Transformational Leadership and Organizational Culture," *The Journal of Leadership Studies* 3, No. 4 (1996), 68–83; and Schein, "Organizational Culture."
37. Stratford Sherman, "Levi's: As Ye Sew, So Shall Ye Reap," *Fortune,* May 12, 1997, 104–116.
38. Marc Ballon, "The Cheapest CEO in America," *Inc.,* October 1997, 53–61; and *www.fastenal.com,* accessed on November 21, 2000.
39. Steve Lohr, "On the Road with Chairman Lou," *The New York Times,* June 26, 1994, Section 3, 1.
40. Jennifer A. Chatman and Karen A. Jehn, "Assessing the Relationship Between Industry Characteristics and Organizational Culture: How Different Can You Be?" *Academy of Management Journal* 37, No. 3 (1994), 522–553.

41. Paul McDonald and Jeffrey Gandz, "Getting Value from Shared Values," *Organizational Dynamics* 21, No. 3 (Winter 1992), 64–76; Daniel R. Denison and Aneil K. Mishra, "Toward a Theory of Organizational Culture and Effectiveness," *Organization Science* 6, No. 2 (March-April 1995), 204–223.
42. Daintry Duffy, "Cultural Evolution," *CIO Enterprise,* Section 2, January 15, 1999, 44–50.
43. Robert Hooijberg and Frank Petrock, "On Cultural Change: Using the Competing Values Framework to Help Leaders Execute a Transformational Strategy," *Human Resource Management* 32, No. 1 (1993), 29–50.
44. Warner, "Confessions of a Control Freak."
45. Charles Fishman, "Sanity Inc.," *Fast Company,* January 1999, 85–96; and Sharon Overton, "And to All a Goodnight," *Sky,* October 1996, 37–40.
46. Carey Quan Jelernter, "Safeco: Success Depends Partly on Fitting the Mold," *Seattle Times,* June 5, 1986, D8.
47. Scott Kirsner, "Designed for Innovation," *Fast Company,* November 1998, 54, 56.
48. Michael Barrier, "Doing the Right Thing," *Nation's Business,* March 1998, 33–38.
49. Gordon F. Shea, *Practical Ethics* (New York: American Management Association, 1988); and Linda Klebe Treviño, "Ethical Decision Making in Organizations: A Person-Situation Interactionist Model," *Academy of Management Review* 11 (1986), 601–617.
50. Dawn-Marie Driscoll, "Don't Confuse Legal and Ethical Standards," *Business Ethics,* July/August 1996, 44.
51. Alison Boyd, "Employee Traps—Corruption in the Workplace," *Management Review,* September 1997, 9.
52. Robert J. House, Andre Delbecq, and Toon W. Taris, "Values-Based Leadership: An Integrated Theory and an Empirical Test" (Working Paper).
53. Lawrence Kohlberg, "Moral Stages and Moralization: The Cognitive-Developmental Approach," in *Moral Development and Behavior: Theory, Research, and Social Issues,* T. Likona, ed. (New York: Holt, Rinehart & Winston, 1976), 31–53; and Jill W. Graham, "Leadership, Moral Development, and Citizenship Behavior," *Business Ethics Quarterly* 5, No. 1, (January 1995), 43–54.
54. "Corporate Ethics: A Prime Business Asset," The Business Roundtable, 200 Park Avenue, Suite 2222, New York, NY 10166, February 1988.
55. Carolyn Wiley, "The ABCs of Business Ethics: Definitions, Philosophies, and Implementation," *IM,* January-February 1995, 2–27.
56. Beverly Geber, "The Right and Wrong of Ethics Offices," *Training,* October 1995, 102–118.
57. Mark Henricks, "Ethics in Action," *Management Review,* January 1995, 53–55.
58. Jennifer Reese, "Starbucks: Inside the Coffee Cult," *Fortune,* December 9, 1996, 190–200.
59. Linda Klebe Treviño and Katherine A. Nelson, *Managing Business Ethics: Straight Talk about How to Do It Right,* 2nd ed. (New York: John Wiley & Sons, Inc., 1999), 274–283.
60. Eugene Garaventa, "*An Enemy of the People* by Henrik Ibsen: The Politics of Whistle-Blowing," *Journal of Management Inquiry* 3, No. 4 (December 1994), 369–374; and Marcia P. Miceli and Janet P. Near, "Whistleblowing: Reaping the Benefits," *Academy of Management Executive* 8, No. 3 (1994), 65–74.

CHAPTER OUTLINE

YOUR LEADERSHIP CHALLENGE

After reading this chapter, you should be able to:

- Trace the evolution of leadership through four eras to the learning leadership required in many organizations today.

- See the basic differences between organizations designed for efficient performance and those designed for learning and adaptability.

- Recognize how leaders build learning organizations through changes in structure, tasks, systems, strategy, and culture.

- Know when and how horizontally organized structures provide advantages over vertical, functionally organized ones.

- Distinguish between tasks and roles and how each impacts employee satisfaction and organizational performance.

- Apply the concept of linked strategy.

Designing and Leading
a Learning Organization

Cementos Mexicanos (Cemex) specializes in developing areas of the world—places where anything can, and usually does, go wrong. To cope with the extreme complexity of their business, CEO Lorenzo Zambrano and other leaders developed a new approach to delivering cement, which they call "living with chaos." Rather than trying to change the customers, the weather, the traffic, or the labor conditions, Cemex designed a company in which last-minute changes and unexpected problems are routine.

A core element of the new approach is the company's complex information technology infrastructure, which includes a global positioning satellite system and on-board computers in all delivery trucks that are continuously fed with streams of day-to-day data on customer orders, production schedules, traffic problems, weather conditions, and so forth. Even more important are changes in how employees think about and do their work. All drivers and dispatchers (many of whom had only a sixth-grade education) attended weekly secondary education classes for two years. Regular training in quality, customer service, and computer skills continues, with Cemex devoting at least 8 percent of total work time to employee training and development. Strict and demanding work rules have been abolished so that workers have more discretion and responsibility for identifying and solving problems. As a result, Cemex trucks now operate as self-organizing business units, run by well-trained employees who think like businesspeople. According to Francisco Perez, operations manager at Cemex in Guadalajara, "They used to think of themselves as drivers. But anyone can deliver concrete. Now our people know that they're delivering a service that the competition cannot deliver." However, far from hoarding its knowledge, Cemex gladly shares it with others. The company's "here's how we do it" learning has been outsourced to a wholly owned subsidiary called Centech, which offers training, service, and consulting to customers, partners, and even competitors.

Cemex has transformed the industry by combining extensive networking technology with a new leadership approach that taps into the mindpower of everyone in the company. People at Cemex are constantly learning—on the job, in training classes, and through visits to other organizations. As a result, the company has a startling capacity to anticipate customer needs, solve problems, and innovate quickly. As a learning organization, Cemex thrives on constant change in a world of complexity.[1]

Organizations, like biological species, must adapt in order to survive. In a stable environment, many companies developed into highly structured systems with strong vertical hierarchies, specialized jobs, and formal information and control systems. However, these organizations do not work in today's fast-shifting environment, and many leaders are struggling to transform their organizations into more flexible systems capable of continuous learning and adaptation. This requires a new approach to leadership. This chapter will first trace the evolution of leadership thought and action, culminating in a discussion of leadership for learning organizations. We will then compare traditional organizations that were designed for efficient production with new organizational forms that emphasize learning, flexibility, and rapid response. We will look at five elements of organization design—structure, tasks, systems, strategy, and culture. The final section of the chapter will explore how e-commerce is driving the need for a new kind of organization and a new way of leading.

THE EVOLUTION OF LEADERSHIP

Many of our concepts of leadership emerged during times of stability, or at least when people believed the world was stable and could be predicted and controlled with logic and rationality. The concepts and organizational forms created during this more stable era still shape the design of many organizations and the training of managers. However, leaders in today's fast-shifting world stand at the threshold of a new era, and they are learning to free themselves from outdated practices and patterns to meet new challenges.

Context of Organizational Leadership

Leadership is directly related to the leader's way of thinking about self, followers, organizations, and the environment. The evolution of leadership thought and action has unfolded in four eras, which we will discuss by looking at two dimensions: whether leadership works on a *micro* level or a *macro* level, and whether environmental conditions are *stable* or *chaotic*.[2]

The micro side of leadership concerns specific situations, specific tasks, and specific individuals. The focus is on one person and one task at a time, and on the processes and behaviors needed to reach certain goals. This is a logical, objective approach to leadership. The macro side of leadership transcends individuals, groups, and specific situations to focus on whole communities, whole organizations, and deeply fundamental ideals, values, and strategies. It is concerned with purpose, strategy, meaning, and culture. Rather than relying on rules, directions, or controls, the leader focuses on building relationships.

The stable versus chaotic dimension refers to whether elements in the environment are dynamic. An environment is stable if it remains the same over a number of months or years. People can expect history to repeat itself—what worked yesterday will work again tomorrow. Under chaotic conditions, though, environmental elements shift abruptly and unpredictably. Leaders learn to support risk and learning. Their work involves creating a vision and strategy, inspiring and empowering others, and keeping everyone focused in the same direction.

Framework

These two dimensions are combined into a framework for examining the evolution of leadership, as illustrated in Exhibit 15.1. Each cell in the model summarizes an era of leadership thinking that may have been correct for its time but may be inappropriate for today's world.

MACRO LEADERSHIP IN A STABLE WORLD   *Era 1* may be conceptualized as pre-industrial and pre-bureaucratic. Most organizations were small and were run by a single individual who many times hired workers because they were friends or relatives, not necessarily because of their skills or qualifications. The size and simplicity of organizations and the stable nature of the environment made it easy for a single person to understand the big picture, coordinate and control all activities, and keep things on track. This is the era of "Great Man" leadership and the emphasis on personal traits of leaders, which we described

EXHIBIT 15.1

Leadership Evolution

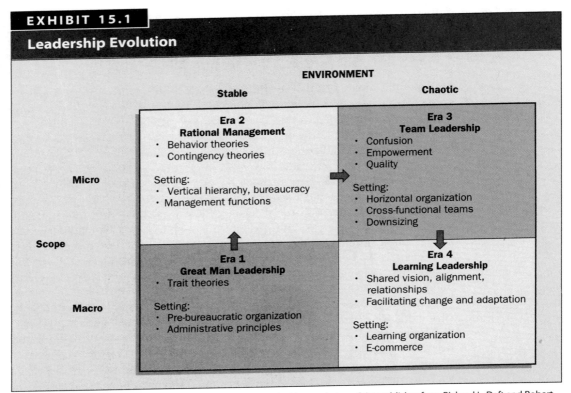

in Chapter 2 of this book. A leader was conceptualized as a single "hero" who saw the big picture and how everything fit into a whole.

MICRO LEADERSHIP IN A STABLE WORLD   In *Era 2,* we have the emergence of hierarchy and bureaucracy. Although the world remains stable, organizations have begun to grow so large that they require rules and standard procedures to ensure that activities are performed efficiently and effectively. Hierarchy of authority provides a sensible mechanism for supervision and control of workers, and decisions once based on rules of thumb or tradition are replaced with precise procedures. This era sees the rise of the "rational manager" who directs and controls others using an impersonal approach. Employees aren't expected to think for themselves; they are expected to do as they're told, follow rules and procedures, and accomplish specific tasks. The focus is on details rather than the big picture.

The rational manager was well-suited to a stable environment. The idea that leaders could analyze their situation, develop careful plans, and control what happened with the organization was quite compelling, but, as we discussed in Chapter 1, rational management is no longer sufficient for leadership in today's chaotic environment.

MICRO LEADERSHIP IN A CHAOTIC WORLD *Era 3* represented a tremendous shock to managers in North America and Europe. Suddenly, the world was no longer stable, and the prized techniques of rational management were no longer successful. Beginning with the OPEC oil embargo of 1972-73 and continuing with the severe global competition of the 1980s and early 1990s, many managers saw that environmental conditions had become chaotic. The Japanese began to dominate world commerce with their ideas of team leadership and superb quality. This became an era of great confusion for leaders. They tried team-based approaches, downsizing, reengineering, quality programs, and empowerment as ways to improve performance and get more motivation and commitment from employees.

This is the era of the team leader. Many of today's leaders have become comfortable with ideas of team leadership, empowerment, diversity, and open communication. However, some are still trapped in old ways of thinking, trying to use rational management for a stable world when their organizations and the environment have already moved on.

MACRO LEADERSHIP IN A CHAOTIC WORLD Enter the digital information age. It seems that everything is changing and changing fast. *Era 4* represents the **learning leader** who has made the leap to giving up control in the traditional sense. Leaders influence others through vision, values, and relationships rather than power and control. They are constantly experimenting, learning, and changing, both in their personal and professional lives, and they encourage the development and growth of others. This chapter's Living Leadership focuses on the importance of individual learning. Era 4 leaders also strive to create *learning organizations,* in which each person is intimately involved in identifying and solving problems so that the organization continues to grow and change to meet new challenges. This requires the full scope of leadership that goes far beyond rational management or even team leadership. Era 3 and Era 4 leadership is what much of this book is about. Specifically in this final section, we focus on the "big picture" skills that leaders need to be successful in this emerging era. Leaders can learn to stop managing details and instead focus on creating a vision and shaping the culture and values that can help achieve it. They develop relationships rather than relying

LIVING LEADERSHIP

Here is Your Assignment . . .

1. You will receive a body.

You may like it or not, but it will be yours for the entire period this time around.

2. You will learn lessons.

You are enrolled in a full-time, informal school called life. Each day in this school you will have the opportunity to learn lessons. You may like the lessons or think them irrelevant and stupid.

3. There are no mistakes, only lessons.

Growth is a process of trial and error, experimentation. The "failed" experiments are as much a part of the process as the experiment that ultimately "works."

4. A lesson is repeated until it is learned.

A lesson will be presented to you in various forms until you have learned it, then you can go on to the next lesson.

5. Learning lessons does not end.

There is no part of life that does not contain its lessons. If you are alive, there are lessons to be learned.

6. "There" is no better than "here."

When your "there" has become a "here," you will simply obtain another "there" that will, again, look better than "here."

7. Others are merely mirrors of you.

You cannot love or hate something about another person unless it reflects to you something you love or hate about yourself.

8. What you make of your life is up to you.

You have all the tools and resources you need; what you do with them is up to you. The choice is yours.

9. The answers lie inside you.

The answers to life's questions lie inside you. All you need to do is look, listen, and trust.

10. Whether you think you can or can't, in either case you'll be right.

Think about it.

Author Unknown

---

on hierarchical control, building whole organizations as communities of shared purpose and information.

Implications

The flow from Great Man leadership to rational management to team leadership to learning leadership illustrates trends in the larger world. The implication is that leadership reflects the era or context of the organization and society. Most of today's organizations and leaders are still struggling with the transition from a stable to a chaotic environment and the new skills and qualities needed in this circumstance. Thus, issues of diversity, team leadership, empowerment, and horizontal relationships are increasingly relevant. In addition, many leaders are rapidly shifting into Era 4 leadership, focusing on change management and facilitating a vision and values to transform their companies into learning organizations. As we will discuss later in this chapter, the burgeoning of e-commerce is making the need for a transition to Era 4 leadership immediate and compelling.

FROM EFFICIENT PERFORMANCE TO THE LEARNING ORGANIZATION

When the environment was stable, leaders could effectively use rational management to maintain control and stability within the organization. They directed and controlled organizational resources toward following plans and achieving specific goals. At a time when the economy was based primarily on mass-production technology, routine specialized jobs and standardized control procedures were quite effective. Today, though, designing organizations strictly for efficient performance is generally not effective. Knowledge and information are more important than production machinery. Many organizations deal almost entirely with "intangibles." As Intuit CEO Bill Harris puts it, "What we do is pure mind. . . . There's nothing physical."[3] Thus, organizations need employees' minds as much as, or more than, their physical labor.

In this new environment, many leaders are redesigning their companies toward something called the **learning organization,** one in which everyone is engaged in identifying and solving problems. The learning organization is skilled at acquiring, transferring, and building knowledge that enables the organization to continuously experiment, improve, and increase its capability. The learning organization is based on equality, open information, little hierarchy, and a shared culture that encourages adaptability and enables the organization to seize opportunities and handle crises. In the learning organization, leaders emphasize employee empowerment and encourage collaboration across departments and with other organizations. The essential value is problem solving, in contrast to the traditional organization designed for efficient performance.

Exhibit 15.2 compares organizations designed for efficient performance with those designed for continuous learning by looking at five elements of organization design: structure, tasks, systems, strategy, and culture. Each of these five elements will be discussed in detail in the following sections.[4] The efficient performance organization is based on a hard, rational model and is characterized by a vertical structure, routine tasks, formalized systems, competitive strategy, and a rigid culture. The learning organization, on the other hand, emerges from a soft, intuitive perspective of organizations. Structures are more horizontal than vertical and employees are empowered to act independently

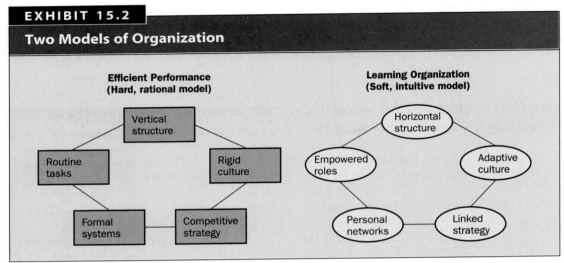

EXHIBIT 15.2

Two Models of Organization

SOURCE: Adapted from David K. Hurst, *Crisis and Renewal: Meeting the Challenge of Organizational Change* (Boston, MA: Harvard Business School Press, 1995).

and creatively rather than performing routine standardized jobs. Systems are fluid, based on networks of shared information. Strategy emerges from collaborative links within and among organizations, and the culture encourages experimentation and adaptability.

ORGANIZATION STRUCTURE

The traditional organization structure, shaped like a pyramid with the CEO at the top and everyone else in layers down below, is a legacy that dates back nearly a century.[5] These vertical structures work well during stable times. However, they become a liability in a fast-changing environment. Hierarchical, vertical structures create distance between managers and workers and build walls between departments; they do not allow for the fast, coordinated response often needed in today's world. Many of today's organizations are shifting toward horizontal structures based on work processes rather than departmental functions. Exhibit 15.3 shows a simple illustration of the change from the vertical to the horizontal organization. Most companies are somewhere in the middle of the evolutionary scale; few companies have shifted to an organization structure based entirely on horizontal processes.[6]

EXHIBIT 15.3

Evolution from Vertical to Horizontal Structure

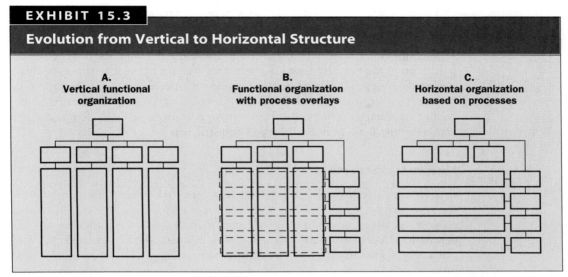

A.
Vertical functional organization

B.
Functional organization with process overlays

C.
Horizontal organization based on processes

SOURCE: George Stalk, Jr. and Jill E. Black, "The Myth of the Horizontal Organization," *Canadian Business Review* (Winter 1994), 26–31.

Vertical Structure

Traditionally, the most common organizational structure has been one in which activities are grouped together by common function from the bottom to the top of the organization, as shown in part A of Exhibit 15.3. For example, all engineers are located in one department, and the vice president of engineering is responsible for all engineering activities. The same is true for manufacturing, accounting, and research and development. Generally little collaboration occurs across departments, and employees are committed to achieving the goals of their own functional units. The whole organization is coordinated and controlled through the vertical hierarchy, with decision-making authority residing with upper-level managers.

The vertical, functionally organized structure can be quite effective. It promotes efficient production and in-depth skill development of employees. Hierarchy of authority provides a sensible mechanism for supervision and control in a large, complex organization. However, in a rapidly changing environment, the vertical hierarchy becomes overloaded. Decisions pile up and top executives cannot respond quickly enough to threats or opportunities. Poor coordination among departments inhibits innovation. Today, the vertical hierarchy and boundaries between departments are beginning to break down in many organizations. At Oticon Holding A/S, a Danish company that introduced the world's first digital hearing aid, leaders did away with departments, titles, and organization charts altogether. Employees are continuously forming and reforming into self-directed teams that work on specific projects.[7]

Other companies maintain elements of a traditional structure but have found ways to increase horizontal communication and collaboration across departments. One popular trend is the use of project managers who coordinate the work of several departments in relation to specific projects, programs, or brands. Organizations are also increasingly using various types of teams, as described in Chapter 10. In the learning organization, self-directed horizontal teams are the basic building block of the structure.

Horizontal Structure

In learning organizations, the vertical structure that created distance between the top and the bottom of the organization is disbanded. Structure is created around workflows or core processes rather than departmental functions. All the people who work on a particular process have access to each other so that they can easily communicate and coordinate their efforts, share knowledge, and provide value directly to customers. Ford Motor Company's Customer Service Division, for example, has core process groups for business development, parts supply and logistics, vehicle service and programs, and technical support. A process owner has responsibility for each core process in its entirety. For Ford's parts supply and logistics process, a number of teams may work on jobs such as parts analysis, purchasing, material flow, and distribution, but a process owner is responsible for coordinating the entire process.[8]

Self-directed teams, as described in Chapter 10, are the fundamental unit of the horizontal structure. Recall that self-directed teams are made up of employees with different skills who share or rotate jobs to produce an entire product or service. Boundaries between departments are reduced or eliminated. In a horizontal structure, the vertical hierarchy is flattened, with perhaps only a few senior executives in traditional support functions such as finance or human resources, as illustrated in part C of Exhibit 15.3. Traditional management tasks are pushed down to lower levels of the organization, with teams and process owners often taking responsibility for training, safety, scheduling, and decisions about work methods, pay and reward systems, and coordination with other teams. People on the team are given the skills, information, tools, motivation, and authority to make decisions central to the team's performance and are empowered to respond creatively and flexibly to new challenges that arise. In a horizontal learning organization, effectiveness is measured by end-of-process performance objectives (based on the goal of bringing value to the customer), as well as customer satisfaction, employee satisfaction, and financial contribution.

Experimentation with teams and horizontal organizing often begins at lower levels of the organization. Today, however, a few companies are structuring practically the entire organization horizontally. Xerox, for example, designed a horizontal structure for everything below the level of executive vice president.

IN THE LEAD   Xerox

Top leaders at Xerox formulated the "Xerox 2005 Strategic Intent" to focus on providing unique value by delivering products and services quickly and reliably, improving customer support, and emphasizing continuous business process improvements. They believed the best way to meet these goals was to reorganize the business into a number of horizontal groups based on work flows rather than functions.

Although the top managerial layers at Xerox remain vertical, responsibility for daily operations, marketing, customer relations, and other activities resides within horizontally aligned groups. Business Groups such as Document Services, Office Document Products, Production Systems, Supplies, and Channels are "mini-businesses." Document Services, for example, is made up of a number of linked, multiskilled teams that are responsible for activities such as business planning, product design and development, manufacturing, marketing, sales, distribution, and customer support. A core process owner has responsibility for the entire Document Services process and for seeing that performance objectives are met. The teams are accountable for taking an idea through all the stages necessary to produce a marketable product or service—that is, employees have the information and skills to perform a major task that would once have been divided among separate departments.

Leaders believe that giving teams greater power to work directly with customers and suppliers has enabled the company to respond faster and more effectively to customer needs as well as improved employee and customer satisfaction.[9]

Learning organizations also strive to break down boundaries with other companies. Companies are collaborating in unprecedented ways to share resources and exploit opportunities. Emerging organizational forms, such as the network organization and virtual organization, are horizontal teams of companies rather than teams of individuals. Much like building blocks, parts can be added or taken away to meet changing needs.[10] In a network structure, a company keeps key activities in-house and then outsources other functions, such as sales, accounting, and manufacturing, to partner organizations or individuals. For example, the computer company Monorail has no factories, no warehouses, no credit department, and no help desks or call centers. The company's core group of employees focus on design and marketing, with all other functions outsourced to partners such as FedEx, Sun Trust Bank, Sykes Enterprises (a call center outsourcing company), and a number of contract manufacturers. Founders Doug Johns, David Hocker, and Nicholas Forlenza concentrate on forming the right partnerships and managing horizontal relationships.[11]

TASKS VERSUS ROLES

Another response to today's rapidly changing environment is the amount of formal structure and control placed on employees in the performance of their work. A **task** is a narrowly defined piece of work assigned to a person. In a stable environment, tasks tend to be rigidly defined and employees generally have little say over how they do their jobs. A **role** is a part in a social system. A role has discretion and responsibility, such as the role of mother in a family or manager in an organization. An organizational role is an opportunity to use one's discretion and ability to achieve an outcome. In chaotic environments, employees need more freedom and responsibility to make decisions and react quickly to changing conditions. One way of considering the distinction between organizations designed for task performance and those designed for learning is through the concept of mechanistic versus organic work processes.

Mechanistic and Organic Processes

Tom Burns and G. M. Stalker use the terms *mechanistic* and *organic* to explain organizational responses to the external environment.[12] When the external environment is stable, the tasks tend to be mechanistic—that is, characterized by rigid rules, formal procedures, and a clear hierarchy of authority with decisions made at the top. Tasks are rigidly defined and are broken down into specialized, separate parts, as in a machine. Knowledge and control of tasks are centralized at the top of the organization, and employees are expected to do as they are told, not to make decisions about how to do it. In rapidly changing environments, on the other hand, tasks tend to be much looser, free flowing, and adaptive. Burns and Stalker use the term *organic* to characterize this type of organization. Leaders push authority and responsibility down to lower-level employees, encouraging them to take care of problems by working with one another and with customers. Teamwork is highly valued and there are few strict rules and procedures for how things should be done. Thus, the organization is more fluid and able to adapt to changes in the environment.[13]

Mechanistic tasks are characteristic of the efficient performance organization. The clearest example is a mass-production assembly line, where jobs are structured by standardization and division of labor into small, specialized tasks that are governed by formal rules and procedures. Workers perform the same small job repetitively, thus little education or experience is needed. Employees are not expected to think for themselves or make any decisions about how they do their jobs. Routine tasks provide little satisfaction for employees, but structuring work into small, specialized tasks made sense in an era of mass-production manufacturing. It was an efficient way of getting the work done, and specialized techniques and procedures ensured reliable performance.

From Routine Tasks to Empowered Roles

Learning organizations use an organic form, an organizational architecture that is fluid and adaptable, with less clear job responsibilities and authority pushed down to the lowest level.[14] Employees play a role in the department or team, and roles are adjusted or redefined through employee interaction within and among teams. There are few rules and procedures, and knowledge and control of tasks are located with workers rather than top executives. Each individual is encouraged to experiment, learn, and solve problems within the team.

The idea of encouraging employees to participate fully in the organization is called empowerment. **Empowerment** means sharing power with everyone in the organization so they can act more freely to accomplish their jobs. For example, Southwest Airlines employees know that within their teams they have the power to do whatever it takes, even if it means breaking the rules, to offer the best service to their customers. The trend today is clearly toward moving power out of the executive suite and into the hands of lower-level workers. Many of today's organizations are knowledge- and information-based rather than machine-based. Knowledge work relies on project teams and cross-functional collaboration that is inherently resistant to formal authority. Employees are also better educated and more willing to question their leaders. In the emerging learning organization, the leader's role is to give workers the information they need and the right to act on it.[15] At Lucent Technologies, plant manager Lynn Mercer has shifted the traditional machine-based assembly line to a system based on teamwork, empowerment, and shared information.

IN THE LEAD   ## Lynn Mercer, Lucent Technologies

Phillip Dailey strings cables inside a steel box the size of a refrigerator—a digital transmitting station for cellular phone systems. Studying a bottleneck along the assembly line one day, Dailey realized a way to increase output by 33 percent. He didn't have to talk to his bosses about his insight; he simply recruited temporary workers from other teams and made it happen.

Lynn Mercer, plant manager at Lucent Technologies' factory in Mount Olive, New Jersey, distributes authority three levels down because she believes those people know the job better than she does. In two years, the factory's self-directed workforce of 480 employees hasn't missed a single delivery deadline, and total labor costs represent an exceedingly low 3 percent of product cost. Teams elect their own leaders to oversee quality, training, scheduling, and coordination with other teams. They all follow a one-page list of "working principles," but teams are continually altering the manufacturing process and even the product design itself. The process is so fluid that none of the manufacturing equipment is bolted to the floor. Engineers and assemblers constantly bat around ideas, and the professional staff cubicles sit right next to the assembly cells to promote constant interaction. According to production manager Steve Sherman, "We solve problems in hallways rather than conference rooms."

The factory is flooded with information because Mercer believes that's how any complex system balances itself. Every single procedure is written down, but procedures are constantly changing—any worker can propose changing any procedure in the plant, subject to ratification by those whose work it affects. Operating statistics are displayed everywhere. Anyone with a few spare minutes consults an "urgents board" listing orders that are behind schedule, so they can jump in where they're most needed. Assemblers also work directly with customers by attending trade shows and installation sites as well as giving tours of the plant.

Yearly bonuses, based equally on individual achievement and team performance, can be equivalent to 15 percent of regular pay. However, for workers, the greatest motivator is that they have a role in shaping the organization. "This business has been handed to us," says technician Tom Guggiari. "This business is ours."[16]

Although many companies, like Lucent Technologies, are implementing empowerment programs, they are empowering workers to varying degrees, as we discussed in Chapter 8 on motivation.[17] When employees are fully empowered, they are given larger roles with decision-making authority and control over how they do their own jobs, as well as the power to influence and change such areas as organizational goals, structures, and reward systems.

SYSTEMS VERSUS NETWORKS

In young, small organizations, communication is generally informal and face-to-face. There are few formal control and information systems because leaders of the company work closely with employees in the day-to-day operation of the business. Because the organization is small, it is easy for everyone to know what is going on. As organizations grow larger, they establish formal systems to manage the growing amount of complex information. In addition, information is increasingly used for control purposes, to detect deviations from established standards and goals.[18] Extensive formal reporting systems allow leaders to monitor operations on an ongoing basis and help them make decisions and maintain steady performance.

The danger is that formal systems become so entrenched that information no longer filters down to the people on the front lines who can use it to do their jobs better and serve customers. The informal grapevine often survives as a remnant of the days when information was freely shared among all employees, but its functioning is hampered by the lack of opportunity for personal interaction.[19] The learning organization strives to return to the condition of a young, entrepreneurial company in which all employees have complete information about the company so that they can identify needs and act quickly. The learning organization is based on personal networks of information. People serve on teams and talk to whoever has the information they need. Learning organizations practice open-book management, which means that data about budgets, profits, expenses, and other financial matters is freely available to anyone. At Whole Foods Market, for example, employees are trained to understand financial and operational information. Even sensitive data such as salaries and bonuses are available to any employee.[20] Leaders at Solectron Corp., the world's largest and fastest-growing contract manufacturer, also believe in widely sharing information to carry out the company's guiding principles: superior customer service and respect for individual workers. "If you really want to respect individuals," says Winston Chen, "you've got to let them know how they're doing—and let them know soon enough so they can do something about it."[21]

Learning organizations encourage open communication, as described in Chapter 9. Knowledge is shared, rather than hoarded, and ideas may be implemented anywhere in the company to improve the organization. At Viant Inc., which helps companies build and maintain Web-based businesses, employees are rewarded not for how much they add to the bottom line, but for their willingness to absorb and share knowledge. In the consulting industry, people have traditionally been rewarded for gaining and keeping specialized knowledge, but at Viant, says leader Bob Gett, "we value you more for how much information you've given to the guy next to you." At least 50 percent of Viant's recruiting and employee selection effort is aimed at determining a person's ability to collaborate, learn, share knowledge, and adapt.[22]

Learning organizations also maintain open lines of communication with customers, suppliers, and competitors. Bringing outside organizations into communication networks enhances learning capability as well as the potential to better serve customers.

New information technology plays a significant role in keeping people in large, complex, global organizations in touch. Networks of computers, Internet technology, and the use of intranets and extranets can change the locus of knowledge by getting information to people who really need it. Buckman Laboratories, which develops and markets more than 1,000 specialty chemicals in eight factories around the world, has a global knowledge-sharing network called K'Netix, which keeps the organization's international workforce connected with one another and brings all of the company's brain power to bear in serving each customer.

IN THE LEAD   ## Bob Buckman, Buckman Laboratories International

Bob Buckman believes the front line and the bottom line have everything to do with each other. "The basic philosophy," he says, "is, 'How do we take this individual and make him bigger, give him power?' How? Connect him to the world."

Buckman Laboratories competes in a variety of businesses, often with companies three to five times its size. Buckman has an edge because any of its employees can tap into a worldwide knowledge resource—a steady stream of information about products, markets, customers, and opportunities, keeping the company so tuned in to customers that it can anticipate their needs. Companies such as AT&T, 3M, International Paper Company, and USWest have made pilgrimages to this small, Memphis, Tennessee-based company to learn how knowledge can be used as a critical corporate asset.

When Bob Buckman took over Buckman Laboratories after the death of his father, he knew he wanted to create a new kind of organization: one in which employees had whatever tools they needed to actively satisfy customer needs. "I realized that if I can give everybody complete access to information about the company, then I don't have to tell them what to do all the time," says Buckman. "The organization starts moving forward of its own initiative."

Today, the knowledge network has become the basis of the organization. Anything is discussable, and anyone can participate. The open sharing of information promotes trust, which in turn promotes wider sharing of information. Buckman admits that getting people to share information in the beginning was difficult because employees had learned to hoard knowledge as a source of power. Now, at Buckman Labs, power comes from being a source of knowledge, sharing whatever you know with others.[23]

COMPETITIVE VERSUS LINKED STRATEGY

In traditional organizations, top executives are responsible for strategy. Strategy is seen as something that is formulated and imposed on the organization. Leaders think about how the organization can best respond to competitors, cope with difficult environmental changes, and effectively use available resources. Research has shown that strategic planning positively affects an organization's performance.[24] Therefore, top executives often engage in formal strategic planning exercises or hire strategic planning experts to help keep the organization performing well.

In learning organizations, however, strategy emerges bottom up as well as top down. Chapter 13 discussed many of the elements of strategy in detail. A strong shared vision is the basis for the emergence of strategy in a learning organization. When all employees are linked with the vision, their accumulated actions contribute to strategy development. Since many employees are in touch with customers, suppliers, and new technologies, they identify needs and solutions and are linked into strategy making.

Strategy can also emerge from partnership linkages with suppliers, customers, and even competitors. Learning organizations have permeable boundaries and are often linked with other companies, giving each organization greater access to information about new strategic needs and directions.[25] Grupo M, the largest private employer in the Dominican Republic, maintains open lines of communication with customers and suppliers, as well as employees, so the organization can stay on the cutting edge in the garment industry. In an industry that's notorious for perpetuating labor abuses, Grupo M takes a different approach. Machine operators are treated like the most important people in the company because they're the ones who intimately understand what makes a style of clothing say "Tommy Hilfiger" or "Liz Claiborne." Employee knowledge and the company's close ties with customers and suppliers helped Grupo M set a new strategic direction that is now spreading throughout the industry. Whereas garment manufacturers typically assemble garments from patterns, cut cloth, and designs provided by manufacturers, Grupo M takes a manufacturer's sketch and does whatever is necessary to transform the sketch into finished products that meet the customer's needs. The next step is "collaborative design." Rather than waiting for customers to provide sketches, a Grupo M team will offer top customers suggestions of styles, colors, and fabric samples for inspiration.[26]

Some learning organizations, like Cemex, described in the opening example, Springfield Remanufacturing, and Andersen Windows, also openly share information with competitors or allow competitors to visit and observe their "best practices." These leading companies believe the best way to keep their organizations competitive is through a mutual sharing of ideas.[27] Other companies go even further in forming strategy together. For example, the CEO of Advanced Circuit Technologies in Nashua, New Hampshire, formed a coalition of ten electronics firms to jointly package and market noncompeting products. Member companies still conduct their own business, but they now can adopt a strategy of bidding on projects larger than they could deliver individually, and ask partners for services they can't do themselves. The coalition landed a job with Compaq Computer Corporation to design and build a specialized computer board that none of the companies could have handled alone.[28]

RIGID VERSUS ADAPTIVE CULTURE

As we discussed in the previous chapter, for an organization to stay healthy, its culture should encourage adaptation to the external environment. When organizations are successful, the values, ideas, and practices that helped attain the success become institutionalized. However, as the environment changes, those values may become detrimental to future performance. Many organizations become victims of their own success, clinging to outdated and even destructive values and behaviors because of rigid cultures that do not encourage adaptability and change.

One of the most important qualities for a learning organization to have is a strong, adaptive organizational culture. The learning organization reflects the values of adaptive cultures discussed in Chapter 14. In addition, a learning organization culture often incorporates the following values.

1. *The whole is more important than the part, and boundaries between parts are minimized.*[29] People in a learning organization are aware of the whole system, how everything fits together, and the relationships among various organizational parts. Therefore, everyone considers how their actions affect other elements of the organization. The emphasis on the whole reduces boundaries both within the organization and with other companies. The free flow of people, ideas, and information allows coordinated action and continuous learning.

2. *Equality is a primary value.* The culture of a learning organization creates a sense of community, compassion, and caring for one another. Each person is valued and the organization becomes a place for creating a web of relationships that allows people to develop to their full potential. Activities that create status differences are discarded. At Viant Inc., no one has an office, interior walls and dividers are practically nonexistent, and every-

one's desk, including chief executive Bob Gett's, is the same size. The learning organization also does away with status symbols such as executive dining rooms and reserved parking places. The emphasis on treating everyone with care and respect creates a climate of safety and trust that allows experimentation, frequent mistakes, and failures that enable learning.

3. *The culture encourages change, risk-taking, and improvement.* A basic value is to question the status quo, the current way of doing things. Constant questioning of assumptions opens the gates to creativity and improvement. The culture rewards and celebrates the creators of new ideas, products, and work processes, as well as sometimes rewarding those who fail in order to symbolize the importance of taking risks.[30]

In a learning organization, the culture encourages openness, boundarylessness, equality, continuous improvement, and change. No company represents a perfect example of a learning organization, but one excellent example of an organization that is built on the concept of a fluid, living system is Cisco Systems, which has been called "the corporation of the future."

IN THE LEAD   Cisco Systems

John Chambers, CEO of Cisco Systems, believes the new rules of business competition demand new organizational forms: ones based on change rather than stability, organized around networks rather than rigid hierarchies, and based on interdependencies with organizational partners.

Not surprisingly, Cisco—the leading maker of routers, switches, and other gear that keeps the Internet running—uses the Internet in virtually every aspect of its business, from sales and marketing to recruiting. In addition, the technology keeps more than 17,000 employees in 50 countries intimately connected and gives them access to whatever information they need. The network also swiftly connects Cisco with its web of partners, making the constellation of suppliers, contract manufacturers, and assemblers look and act like one seamless company.

But it takes more than technology to set Cisco apart from the crowd. Just as important is the company's culture and mind-set. Chambers knows technology can't replace human interaction, and he works hard to encourage open and direct communication among all employees and with Cisco's leaders. He holds quarterly meetings with employees and invites all employees in the month of their birthday to one of his "birthday breakfasts," where they can talk about anything they want. In addition, Chambers spends up to 55 percent of his time with customers. Strategy emerges from Cisco's network of employees, customers, and partners. For example, after both Boeing and Ford Motor Company told Cisco sales reps that their future networking needs were unlikely to be met by Cisco, Cisco found out what the companies needed, then began searching for a company to acquire that would help solve the problem. That first acquisition, of local-area-network switchmaker Crescendo Communications, put Cisco into a new sector of the industry that now accounts for billions in annual revenue.

An egalitarian culture is central to the success of Cisco, because it builds teamwork and employee morale. "You never ask your team to do something you wouldn't do yourself," says Chambers, who always flies coach and has no reserved parking space at headquarters. In addition, Cisco's top leaders work hard to include all employees, making them feel like true partners in the business. The result is an energized, motivated workforce that agrees with Chamber's conviction that his people and his organization are "in the sweet spot"—where technology and the future meet to transform business and everyday life.[31]

THE LEADER'S CHALLENGE

Leaders in learning organizations face a mighty challenge: to maintain efficient performance and become a learning organization at the same time. Companies must maintain an efficient performance remnant of traditional vertical organizations because they have a responsibility to both shareholders and employees to be competitive and profitable. This is achieved by balancing the hard and soft aspects of organizational design. For example, the boundaries in traditional organizations limit learning and change. Thus, leaders can work to replace the sense of concrete walls both vertically and horizontally with permeable boundaries. Also, organizations need mechanisms for controlling and directing resources, but leaders can build mechanisms that are based on shared purpose, common assumptions, and trust. Leaders can support order and change, competition and collaboration.

In the hard, rational view of organizations designed for efficient performance, the leadership model is that of a commander who sets goals, makes decisions, and gives clear, specific instructions for who is to do what and when. David Hurst describes the leadership model in a learning organization as "that of the shepherd, who follows his flock watchfully as it meanders along the natural contours of the land. He carries the weak and collects the strays, for they all have a contribution to make. This style may be inefficient, but it is effective. The whole flock reaches its destination at more or less the same time."[32] To keep learning alive, leaders can build a shared vision, help people see the whole system, design horizontal structures, reduce boundaries, initiate change, and expand the opportunity for employees to shape the future.[33] To promote the change and continuous learning needed in a fast-shifting environment, leaders can challenge assumptions and structures that are no longer appropriate for today's world.[34]

E-COMMERCE AND THE LEARNING ORGANIZATION

Organizations operating in environments characterized by high rates of technological or market change have always faced a greater need for learning and adaptation. However, the world of e-commerce presents a unique challenge to leaders because it moves at an unprecedented pace. Markets and the competitive landscape change not just overnight, but in an instant. As one e-corporation leader put is, "This stuff moves so fast you gotta figure out a way to clone yourself."[35]

E-commerce organizations have to learn and adapt really fast to keep pace with the speed of Internet time. The old ideas about planning, organizing, and controlling things to keep the organization running smoothly no longer apply, as discussed in this chapter's Leader's Bookshelf. The organization is in constant chaos. Leaders—as well as employees throughout the organization—often have to act first and analyze later.[36] There's no time for top leaders to evaluate options, conduct research, develop plans and schedules, tell people what to do and how to do it. E-commerce runs on "real time" rather than "managed time." In traditional organizations, managers can organize and run the organization like a bus route—there are specific routes to follow, schedules to meet, and rules for doing so.[37] E-commerce organizations have to be like taxicabs. They must sense and respond to immediate needs—the wave of a hand in the street, the demand for instant information on the Web. The e-commerce organization operates second-to-second, not year-to-year or even week-to-week.

Thus, e-commerce is making the shift to a learning organization more than a leadership choice. It's becoming a requirement for survival. We're on the threshold of a fundamental shift in how business is done—and how organizations are designed and led. Rational management is too analytical, too slow, too controlling, and too structured for the chaotic, second-to-second e-commerce world. Leaders first have to unlearn old lessons and patterns of behavior from previous eras and adopt new learning organization approaches. "A generational change is underway," says Tim Koogle, Chairman of Yahoo. "We're moving away from command-and-control to distributed decision making."[38]

However, even though e-commerce organizations need to be open, flexible, and free-flowing to allow people the freedom they need to meet

The Cluetrain Manifesto: The End of Business as Usual

Rick Levine, Christopher Locke, Doc Searls, and David Weinberger

Something powerfully new has arrived in the world. As the authors of *The Cluetrain Manifesto* point out, "We don't know what the Web is for, but we've adopted it faster than any technology since fire." The basic premise of *The Cluetrain Manifesto* is that the coming of the Internet is not just another new technology, but a watershed event in human history. Nowhere will its effects be felt more deeply than in how business gets done. The book was born in the form of ninety-five short statements that were posted on the Web *(www.cluetrain. com)* to describe the changing landscape of business communications and marketing.

No Turning Back

In *The Cluetrain Manifesto,* the authors expand on their ideas to argue that the Web is changing business in some fundamental ways.

■ **The pyramid is being replaced by hyperlinks.** Before the Web, computer networks were like organizational hierarchies—carefully planned to determine who got connected to whom and who had central authority and responsibility. But the Web consists of hundreds of millions of hyperlinked pages. Anyone can plug in, and any page can be linked to any other—without asking permission.

■ **Organizations are increasingly decentralized.** Businesses are taking on the structure of the Web—decentralized, messy, and self-organizing. People and teams can hyperlink themselves together as needed to solve problems and make changes. The formal organization chart is becoming a thing of the past.

■ **Boundaries are fading.** On the Web, it's hard to tell where the boundaries are—there's nothing standing between you and the rest of the world of people and pages. The same thing is happening with organizations. Leaders are encouraging open, direct access to information across the organization, with other companies, and especially with customers.

■ **Leaders must learn to get out of the way.** It's not the leader's job to create conversations, but to listen to the conversations that spontaneously occur. Leaders have to understand that they aren't in control any more, and resist the urge to "reassert their authority." The coming generation of leaders will earn respect and influence by being out in the fray, taking risks, and learning to laugh at mistakes—especially their own.

Conclusion

"A powerful global conversation has begun," state the authors. "Through the Internet people are discovering and inventing new ways to share relevant knowledge with blinding speed. As a direct result markets are getting smarter—and getting smarter than most companies." The Internet offers both a threat and a tremendous opportunity to businesses. If companies ignore the networked conversations of the Web, they risk losing touch. However, if leaders can engage their organizations with this global conversation, there is tremendous potential for companies to better understand their markets and leverage the knowledge and energy of their employees.

The Cluetrain Manifesto: The End of Business as Usual, by Rick Levine, Christopher Locke, Doc Searls, and David Weinberger, is published by Perseus Books.

ever-changing demands from the environment, strong leadership may be more important than ever in these new organizations. Providing focus and direction becomes even more critical in an organization where everything is changing all the time. Even though people can't be constrained by rigid tasks and narrow jobs, they do need a context and an understanding of how they can act to serve customers and the organization. We're only beginning to learn what it takes to succeed in this emerging environment, but what we know of effective e-commerce leadership so far offers lessons for leaders as they shape the organization of the future. Exhibit 15.4 compares some skills and qualities of e-commerce leaders with those of traditional organization leaders.[39]

- ■ **Be an evangelist for the vision.** All leaders need to create and communicate a compelling vision, as we discussed in Chapter 13. But for e-commerce leaders, "communicate" doesn't even begin to convey the amount of passion, energy, and time devoted to selling the big picture. Tom Jermoluk of @Home Network says at least 50 percent of his job as CEO is "being an evangelist—with our employees, [Wall] Street, the press, my partners. There's up times and down times, but it's keeping everybody believing that there really is a pot of gold at the end of the rainbow—I don't mean in a money sense, I mean in the accomplishment of the vision."[40] Evangelizing the vision also ensures that it is entrenched in employees' minds and hearts so they can make decisions and take actions that further the vision. Without this focus, the resources of a fast-moving e-commerce organization can quickly become uncoordinated, with employees pursuing radically different activities and strategies.

EXHIBIT 15.4

New Skills for E-Commerce Leaders

Traditional Leader	E-Commerce Leader
Communicates the vision	Evangelizes the vision
Selects information for distribution	Shares information to share power
Manages by pyramid	Manages by web
Analytical and organized	Intuitive and experimental
Loves order and certainty	Loves messiness and ambiguity

- **Share information to share power.** All information, not just some of it. People throughout the organization need to have access to whatever they need, whenever they need it—and they often won't know what they need until the very moment it's needed. If people have been limited to certain areas of information, they are constrained in their thinking and decision making. Onvia.com feeds real-time information to employees on a "wall of data" suspended above the room where they work. In addition, employees have access to any information in the company. In an e-commerce organization, advantage comes from seeing first and moving fastest, which requires extraordinary openness.[41] E-commerce organizations also share astonishing amounts of information with customers, partners, and competitors.

- **Manage by web, not pyramid.** The pyramid is the dominant image of the traditional organization, as described earlier in this chapter. The e-commerce organization, on the other hand, resembles a web, "a flat, intricately woven form that links partners, employees, external contractors, suppliers, and customers in various collaborations."[42] Open, web-like systems are fundamental to the success of e-commerce organizations because new ideas, strategies, and products come not just from employees but from people outside the organization and from around the globe. Sometimes an Internet company's greatest competitor is also its most important collaborator. The business of e-commerce is about companies and people joining together to make something happen—and as they do, they become more and more interdependent. Boundaries are not only blurred but sometimes hard to define. Decisions and changes can arise from anywhere within or outside of the organization. At Onvia.com, for example, which sells to small businesses, customers defined how the company would stock its virtual shelves. An important part of an e-commerce leader's job is coordinating an intricate network of employees, partners, freelancers, spin-offs, contractors, and customers.

- **Embrace intuition and experimentation.** Leaders in e-commerce organizations have to make major decisions incredibly fast. They learn to depend on their intuition because there's no time to analyze and evaluate decisions. In addition, the information and "evidence" to help make a decision in the world of e-commerce often don't even exist. Leaders also encourage employees to develop their intuition and go with their gut feeling when making decisions about how to best serve customers. E-commerce leaders know that every time an employee makes a decision, whether it turns out to have positive or negative consequences, it helps the employee learn and be a better decision maker the next time around. For the same reason, leaders encourage constant experimentation so that people are continuously learning and expanding organizational knowledge.

- **Love messiness.** To give up hierarchical control and manage by web, to embrace intuition and encourage experimentation, and to open the floodgates of information to people both within and outside of the organization means that e-commerce leaders must learn to love messiness, change, and ambiguity. "We're just going to have to be a little more comfortable being uncomfortable," as a Kmart vice-chairman said about the company's independent e-commerce unit, BlueLight.com.[43] E-commerce leaders have to be willing to change direction at the drop of a hat, to take risks, to make mistakes and admit it, and to deal with the constant danger of being blind-sided by competitors or market forces the organization has missed. The best leaders thrive on the ambiguity and volatility that are inherent aspects of business in e-commerce organizations. They are "change-resilient," able to take major disruptions in stride and move on to the next moment.

The Internet and the rise of e-commerce is a significant change in organizations that is bringing about fundamental shifts in how organizations are designed and led. "We're not just witnessing a little change in our economy," says David Ticoll, chief executive of Digital 4Sight Systems and Consulting Ltd., a business think tank and consulting firm. "This is an epochal change in the history of production."[44]

SUMMARY AND INTERPRETATION

This chapter traced the evolution of leadership thought and action, which reflects a shift from stable to chaotic environments. Early leadership perspectives emphasized great men and the traits that enabled them to succeed in government, commerce, the military, or social movements. The next era was rational management that fit the organizational context of vertical hierarchies and bureaucracies. Because of the world's transition to a more chaotic environment in recent years, team leadership became important, with its potential for enabling horizontal organizations and open communication. And finally, the most recent era is about learning leadership, in which leaders use the skills of vision, alignment, and relationships to unlock personal qualities of followers in adaptive, learning organizations.

Leaders can design learning organizations using the five elements of structure, tasks, systems, strategy, and culture. For many of today's companies, these elements developed during a time when environments were stable and organizations were based primarily on mass-production technology. Characteristics such as a strong vertical hierarchy, specialized routine jobs, formal information and control systems, a directed competitive strategy, and a strong internal culture helped organizations perform efficiently and consistently. However, these organizations may no longer work in today's chaotic world.

Many leaders are transforming their organizations into something called the learning organization, a fluid, flexible system almost like a biological entity, capable of continuous learning and adaptability. Vertical structures and functional boundaries are replaced by self-directed teams organized around work processes. Boundaries between organizations are also becoming permeable, as even competitors collaborate to share resources and exploit new opportunities. In a learning organization, responsibility and authority are pushed down to the lowest level. Strategy, rather than being directed top-down as in a traditional organization, can emerge from anywhere in the learning organization. In addition, learning organizations develop cultural values that emphasize adaptation and change.

E-commerce is making the shift to a learning organization a necessity rather than a leadership choice. These companies have to learn and adapt really fast. What is known about successful leadership in e-commerce organizations so far suggests that e-commerce leaders should evangelize the vision, share information to share power, manage by web rather than hierarchy, embrace intuition and experimentation, and learn to love messiness and ambiguity. Effective e-commerce leaders are "change resilient," able to take major disruptions in stride and move on to the next learning moment.

KEY TERMS

learning leader	task
learning organization	role
self-directed team	empowerment

DISCUSSION QUESTIONS

1. Do you agree that the world of organizations and leadership is shifting to a new era? How do you feel about being a leader during this time of transition?

2. Refer to Exhibit 15.1 and compare Era 2 to Era 4. Try to think of two people from your own work or school experience who illustrate these two eras.

3. What are the primary differences between a traditional, functionally organized company and the horizontally organized learning organization?

4. Discuss the primary reasons so many of today's organizations are empowering lower-level workers.

5. Discuss how bringing other organizations into a company's information network might contribute to strategy.

6. Why are cultural values of minimal boundaries and equality important in a learning organization compared to an efficient performance organization?

7. What is the difference between a task and a role? Between formal systems and personal networks? Discuss.

8. If people in e-commerce organizations need almost complete freedom to make decisions and respond to problems immediately, why do they still need leaders?

9. What does it mean to say that e-commerce leaders embrace intuition and experimentation? Do you think this is a good way to make decisions? Discuss.

LEADERSHIP DEVELOPMENT: Personal Feedback

How Resilient Are You?

Rate yourself from 1 to 5 on the following: (1 = very little, 5 = very strong)

_____ Very resilient. Adapt quickly. Good at bouncing back from difficulties.

_____ Optimistic, see difficulties as temporary, expect to overcome them and have things to turn out well.

_____ In a crisis I calm myself and focus on taking useful actions.

_____ Good at solving problems logically.

_____ Can think up creative solutions to challenges. Trust intuition.

_____ Playful, find the humor, laugh at self, chuckle.

_____ Curious, ask questions, want to know how things work, experiment.

_____ Constantly learn from experience and from the experiences of others.

_____ Very flexible. Feel comfortable with inner complexity (trusting and cautious, unselfish and selfish, optimistic and pessimistic, etc.)

_____ Anticipate problems to avoid them and expect the unexpected.

_____ Able to tolerate ambiguity and uncertainty about situations.

_____ Feel self-confident, enjoy healthy self-esteem, and have an attitude of professionalism about work.

_____ Good listener. Good empathy skills. "Read" people well. Can adapt to various personality styles. Non-judgmental (even with difficult people).

_____ Able to recover emotionally from losses and setbacks. Can express feelings to others, let go of anger, overcome discouragement, and ask for help.

_____ Very durable, keep on going during tough times. Independent spirit.

_____ Have been made stronger and better by difficult experiences.

_____ Convert misfortune into good fortune. Discover the unexpected benefit.

_____ Total

Scoring:

Add up your scores from the 17 questions

70 or higher—very resilient!   40–50—you're struggling
60–70—better than most   40 or under—seek help!
50–60—slow, but adequate

Interpretation

In a world that is changing faster than ever, one of the most important qualities a person or organization can have is *resilience*—the ability to bounce back, to thrive in the face of constant chaos and uncertainty. Some companies offer their employees resilience training. Resilience is an important characteristic for leaders in learning organizations, and particularly in e-commerce organizations, because they have to become comfortable with constant questioning and change. You can improve your resilience by practicing the qualities described in this list.

SOURCE: Developed by Al Siebert. Adapted from *The Survivor Personality* by Al Siebert, Ph.D. An explanation of the items can be found at Al Siebert's THRIVEnet web site: http://www.thrivenet.com/

© Copyright 2001, Al Siebert, Ph.D.

LEADERSHIP DEVELOPMENT: CASES FOR ANALYSIS

The Fairfax County Social Welfare Agency

The Fairfax County Social Welfare Agency was created in 1965 to administer services under six federally funded social service grants:

- The Senior Citizens' Development Grant (SCD)
- The Delinquent Juvenile Act Grant (DJA)
- The Abused Children's Support Grant (ACS)
- The Job Development and Vocational Training Grant (JDVT)

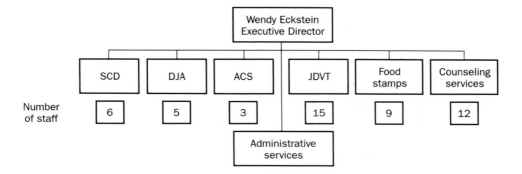

Number of staff

- The Food Stamp Program (Food)
- The Psychological Counseling and Family Therapy Fund (Counseling)

The agency's organizational structure evolved as new grants were received and as new programs were created. Staff members—generally the individuals who had written the original grants—were assigned to coordinate the activities required to implement the programs. All program directors reported to the agency's executive director, Wendy Eckstein, and had a strong commitment to the success and growth of their respective programs. The organizational structure was relatively simple, with a comprehensive administrative department handling client records, financial records, and personnel matters. (See organizational chart above.)

The sense of program "ownership" was intense. Program directors jealously guarded their resources and only reluctantly allowed their subordinates to assist on other projects. Consequently, there was a great deal of conflict among program directors and their subordinates.

The executive director of the agency was concerned about increasing client complaints regarding poor service and inattention. Investigating the matter, Eckstein discovered the following.

1. Staff members tended to "protect" their clients and not refer them to other programs, even if another program could provide better services.
2. There was a total absence of integration and cooperation among program directors.
3. Programs exhibited a great deal of duplication and redundancy; program directors acquired administrative support for their individual programs.

Eckstein concluded that the present client or program-based structure no longer met the agency's needs. A major reorganization of this county social welfare agency is being considered.

SOURCE: "The Fairfax County Social Welfare Agency," in 1998–99 *Annual Editions: Management,* Fred Maidment, ed. (Guilford, CT: Dushkin/McGraw-Hill, 1998), 78. Used with permission.

Questions

1. Refer back to Exhibit 15.2. What elements of the agency could be causing the problems?

2. In what era (Exhibit 15.1) do the program directors seem to be? Explain.

3. If you were Eckstein, how would you lead the agency toward becoming more of a learning organization? Discuss.

Acworth Systems

Richard Acworth feels his company slipping away. "How could something that was going so great suddenly turn into such a mess?" he mused. Acworth Systems helps companies design, install, and implement complex back-office software systems. Richard and his brother Tom started the company on a shoestring and within two years had twenty employees and nearly $5 million in revenues.

The brothers made a conscious choice to run the company with as few formal rules and procedures as possible. Richard and Tom both remembered what it was like to have to ask permission "every time you wanted to go to the bathroom," as Tom put it. They had a strong vision of a collaborative organization in which everyone shared the mission and goals of the company and put the good of the whole above individual interests. They spent long hours talking with one another and with trusted advisors to develop a corporate mission statement that outlined their philosophy of an organization built on mutual trust and respect. One thing they were intent on was that people shouldn't be constrained by rigid boundaries. Thus, Acworth had no formal organization chart, no job titles or descriptions, no close supervision, and very few rules. People were expected to decide for themselves, based on widely-shared company information, how best to contribute to the mission and goals.

In the early days, everyone in the office would work on a project, but after the firm started getting more business, work was handled by shifting teams of employees. Although Richard and Tom participated in the hands-on work, each team made its own decisions about what it needed to get the job done— whether that meant buying more equipment, bringing in other team members, or consulting with another company. Everyone knew what everyone else was working on, so people could easily pitch in to help if a team ran into problems. Acworth employees were a close-knit group. Not only did they spend long hours in the office and working together at customer sites, but many employees also socialized together. Every once in a while, the Acworths would throw a party or cookout to reward everyone for a job well done.

But all that was before the growth explosion. Within eighteen months, sales grew from $5 million to nearly $20 million and the staff grew from twenty to one hundred. Consultants who were constantly on the go began working out of their homes and keeping in touch with headquarters via phone and e-mail. Teams rarely called on one another for help any more. Everyone was so busy handling their own projects that they had little interest in anyone else's problems. The Acworths scheduled a few "all-hands" meetings to try to keep everyone focused on a common goal. The meetings seemed to bring people together for a while, but eventually, communication and collaboration between teams would decline again.

Richard and Tom have discussed the situation several times and both feel they're out of their league now that the company has grown so large. They miss the camaraderie of the early days and being able to pitch in with the hands-on work. Today, it seems like they spend most of their time trying to find out where the teams are and whether projects are on schedule. Richard finally contacted one of his former professors, who now runs a management consulting firm. Dr. Tyler told Richard and Tom that the first thing they needed to do was create some structure for the organization. Richard is confused. He thought all that stuff about organizational structure was for grandpa's company. "Today's organizations are supposed to be open and flexible, just like Acworth," he thought. "So why do I feel like the company is starting to come apart at the seams?"

Questions

1. What do you think is the primary problem at Acworth Systems?

2. What elements of a learning organization are evident at Acworth? What elements seem to be missing?

3. Do you agree that the Acworths need to create "some structure" for the organization? Discuss how they might do so.

REFERENCES

1. Thomas Petzinger Jr., "In Search of the New World (of Work)," *Fast Company*, April 1999, 214–220+; Peter Katel, "Bordering on Chaos," *Wired*, July 1997, 98–107; and Oren Harari, "The Concrete Intangibles," *Management Review*, May 1999, 30–33.

2. The discussion of micro and macro is based on Ed Kur, "Developing Leadership in Organizations: A Continuum of Choices," *Journal of Management Inquiry* 4, No. 2 (June 1995): 198–206.

3. Geoffrey Colvin, "How To Be a Great eCEO," *Fortune*, May 24, 1999, 104–110.

4. Based on David K. Hurst, "Of Boxes, Bubbles, and Effective Management," *Harvard Business Review*, May-June 1984, 78–88; and *Crisis and Renewal:*

Meeting the Challenge of Organizational Change (Boston, MA: Harvard Business School Press, 1995), 32–52.

5. Alan Webber, "The Best Organization Is No Organization," *USA Today,* March 6, 1997, 13A.

6. George Stalk, Jr. and Jill E. Black, "The Myth of the Horizontal Organization," *Canadian Business Review,* Winter 1994, 26–31.

7. Polly LaBarre, "This Organization Is Disorganization," *Fast Company,* June-July 1996, 77.

8. The discussion of the horizontal organization is based on Frank Ostroff, *The Horizontal Organization: What the Organization of the Future Looks Like and How It Delivers Value to Customers* (New York: Oxford University Press, 1999).

9. Based on information in Ostroff, *The Horizontal Organization,* 130–143.

10. Kevin Kelly and Otis Port, with James Treece, Gail DeGeorge, and Zachary Schiller, "Learning from Japan," *Business Week,* January 27, 1992, 52–60; and Gregory G. Dess, Abdul M. A. Rasheed, Kevin J. McLaughlin, and Richard L. Priem, "The New Corporate Architecture," *Academy of Management Executive* 9, No. 3 (1995), 7–20.

11. Heath Row, "This 'Virtual' Company is for Real," *Fast Company,* December-January 1998, 48–50; and Evan Ramstad, "A PC Maker's Low-Tech Formula: Start with the Box," *The Wall Street Journal,* December 29, 1997, B1, B8.

12. Tom Burns and G. M. Stalker, *The Management of Innovation* (London: Tavistock, 1961).

13. John A. Coutright, Gail T. Fairhurst, and L. Edna Rogers, "Interaction Patterns in Organic and Mechanistic Systems," *Academy of Management Journal* 32 (1989), 773–802.

14. Stanley F. Slater, "Learning to Change," *Business Horizons,* November-December 1995, 13–20.

15. Thomas A. Stewart, "Get with the New Power Game," *Fortune,* January 13, 1997, 58–62.

16. Thomas Petzinger, Jr., "How Lynn Mercer Manages a Factory That Manages Itself," *The Wall Street Journal,* March 7, 1997, B11.

17. Robert C. Ford and Myron D. Fottler, "Empowerment: A Matter of Degree," *Academy of Management Executive* 9, No. 3 (1995), 21–31.

18. Hurst, *Crisis and Renewal,* 44.

19. Ibid.

20. Julie Carrick Dalton, "Between the Lines: The Hard Truth about Open Book Management," *CFO,* March 1999, 58–64.

21. Alex Markels, "The Wisdom of Chairman Ko," *Fast Company,* November 1999, 258–276.

22. Edward O. Welles, "Mind Gains," *Inc.* December 1999, 112–124.

23. Glenn Rifkin, "Nothing But Net," *Fast Company,* June-July 1996, 118–127; and "CIO Panel: Knowledge-Sharing Roundtable," *InformationWeek Online,* News in Review, April 26, 1999, downloaded from *InformationWeek* Web site, *www.informationweek.com,* April 30, 1999.

24. C. Chet Miller and Laura B. Cardinal, "Strategic Planning and Firm Performance: A Synthesis of More than Two Decades of Research," *Academy of Management Journal* 37, No. 6 (1994), 1649–1665.

25. Marc S. Gerstein and Robert B. Shaw, "Organizational Architectures for the Twenty-First Century," in David A. Nadler, Marc S. Gerstein, Robert B. Shaw, and Associates, eds., *Organizational Architecture: Designs for Changing Organizations* (San Francisco: Jossey-Bass, 1992), 263–274.
26. Cheryl Dahle, "The New Fabric of Success," *Fast Company,* June 2000, 252–270.
27. Justin Martin, "Are You as Good as You Think You Are?" *Fortune,* September 30, 1996, 142–152.
28. Jessica Lipnack and Jefferey Stamps, "One Plus One Equals Three," *Small Business Reports,* August 1993, 49–58.
29. Mary Anne DeVanna and Noel Tichy, "Creating the Competitive Organization of the Twenty-First Century: The Boundaryless Corporation," *Human Resource Management* 29 (Winter 1990), 455–471; and Fred Kofman and Peter M. Senge, "Communities of Commitment: The Heart of Learning Organizations," *Organizational Dynamics* 22, No. 2 (Autumn 1993), 4–23.
30. Bernard M. Bass, "The Future of Leadership in Learning Organizations," *The Journal of Leadership Studies* 7, No. 3 (2000): 18–40.
31. John A. Byrne, "The Corporation of the Future," *Business Week,* August 31, 1998, 102–106; and "And the Winner Is . . . Cisco Systems," in "In Depth: *Business 2.0* 100," compiled by Walid Mougayar, project head; Michael Mattis, Kate McKinley, and Nissa Crawford, *Business 2.0,* May 1999, 58–94.
32. Hurst, "Of Boxes, Bubbles, and Effective Management."
33. Peter M. Senge, "The Leader's New Work: Building Learning Organizations," *Sloan Management Review,* Fall 1990, 7–22.
34. Slater, "Learning to Change;" and Bass, "The Future of Leadership in Learning Organizations."
35. Colvin, "How To Be a Great eCEO."
36. See Katharine Mieskowski, "Digital Competition," *Fast Company,* December 1999, 155–162; Thomas A. Stewart, "Three Rules for Managing in the Real-Time Economy," *Fortune,* May 1, 2000, 333-334; and Colvin, "How to Be a Great eCEO."
37. This comparison was made by Stephan Haeckel, a strategist at IBM, and reported in Stewart, "Three Rules for Managing in the Real-Time Economy."
38. Mark Gimein, "CEOs Who Manage Too Much," *Fortune,* September 4, 2000, 235–242.
39. This section is based on Colvin, "How To Be a Great eCEO"; Mieszkowski, "Digital Competition"; John A. Byrne, "Management by Web," *Business Week,* August 28, 2000, 84; Stewart, "Three Rules for Managing in the Real-Time Economy"; and Emelie Rutherford, "End Game" (a conversation with David Weinberger), *CIO,* April 1, 2000, 98–104.
40. Quoted in Colvin, "How To Be a Great eCEO."
41. Stewart, "Three Rules for Managing in the Real-Time Economy."
42. Byrne, "Management by Web."
43. Suzanne Koudsi, "Attention Kmart Bashers," *Fortune,* November 13, 2000, 213–222.
44. Quoted in Byrne, "Management by Web."

CHAPTER OUTLINE

YOUR LEADERSHIP CHALLENGE

After reading this chapter, you should be able to:

- Recognize social and economic pressures for change in today's organizations.

- Implement the eight-stage model of planned change.

- Use techniques of communication, training, and participation to overcome resistance to change.

- Effectively and humanely address the negative impact of change.

- Expand your own potential for creativity and encourage creativity in others.

- Understand how to use concepts of organizational development and large-group intervention.

Leading Change

"**D**o you have the Louisiana quarter yet?" "When's the next state quarter coming out?" "My girlfriend got me one of those 'state quarters' maps for my birthday." People across the country have been talking about the hottest new consumer product of the past decade: the U.S. Mint's state quarters. Launched in December 1998, the 50 State Quarters Program puts a new state quarter into circulation every 10 weeks for 10 years. The program has rejuvenated public interest in coins and coin collecting. And it's one small part of a massive change initiative that has also rejuvenated the U.S. Mint, transforming it from a clumsy, inefficient government bureaucracy into a fast-moving, energetic, even passionate enterprise with a customer-satisfaction rating second only to Mercedes-Benz North America.

When Philip Diehl was appointed director of the Mint in 1994, he and his colleagues embarked on a series of strategic, technical, and cultural revolutions that have combined to produce widespread and deepseated change at the Mint. Diehl's first step was to fix the Mint's relationship with customers, particularly collectors. "One of the greatest lessons I've learned," he says, "is that you identify a problem that customers really care about, and then commit yourself publicly to fixing it—taking that risk is absolutely crucial to changing an organization. And if you fix the problem, you build an incredible sense of confidence that the organization can tackle the next problem."

Tackling one problem at a time, building on the successes of the past, Diehl and his leadership team have turned the U.S. Mint into an almost completely different place. Today, rather than being financed by annual government appropriations, the Mint operates from its own profits, which enables the organization to respond quickly and flexibly to the market. Rather than having top executives appointed by Congress, the director now has the authority to put whomever he wants and believes is best-qualified in leadership positions. Employees are thinking and acting more like entrepreneurs than government bureaucrats. The Mint also has a thriving Web business, including selling collectibles and commemoratives online, gathering customer feedback on new coin designs, and providing educational tools through its HIP (History in Your Pocket) Pocket Change site. Even though Diehl's tenure is drawing to a close, he has put in place mechanisms that he believes will keep the Mint changing and thriving. "We've fundamentally changed people's expectations of our performance," he says. "When you change expectations, it's very hard for an organization to relax and slip back into old patterns of behavior."[1]

Leaders in many organizations throughout the United States and Canada have had to reconceptualize almost every aspect of how they do business to meet the needs of increasingly demanding customers, keep employees motivated and satisfied, and remain competitive in a global, information-based economy. Dramatic social, economic, and technological changes in the environment have affected every organization, from small entrepreneurial companies such as natural soap-maker Woodspirits to huge government agencies like the U.S. Mint. As we discussed in the previous chapter, many companies are becoming learning organizations that are poised for constant change and adaptation. The pressing need for change management is reflected in the fact that many companies are hiring "transformation officers" who are charged with radically rethinking and remaking either the entire organization or major parts of it.[2]

Recall from our definition used throughout this book that leadership is about change rather than stability. However, in recent years, the pace of change has increased dramatically, presenting significant challenges for leaders. Many leaders today feel as if "they are flying the airplane at the same time they are building it."[3] The patterns of behavior and attitudes that were once successful no longer work, but new patterns are just emerging—and there are no guarantees that the new ways will succeed. Leaders are responsible for guiding people through the discomfort and dislocation brought about by major change.

This chapter explores how leaders guide change and transformation. We will first look briefly at the need for change in today's organizations and examine a step-by-step model for leading major change. We will also explore why people resist change and how leaders can overcome resistance and help people cope with the potentially negative consequences of change. The chapter will then examine how leaders facilitate change by fostering creative people and organizations. The final sections of the chapter will focus on leading changes in culture. Culture plays a role in all types of organizational change, so leaders must understand how to influence culture to create lasting change.

CHANGE OR PERISH

As we discussed in Chapter 1, the world is changing more rapidly than ever before. Today's most successful organizations are changing fast. Their leaders recognize that internal changes must keep pace with what is happening in the external environment. As Jack Welch of General Electric once stated, "When the rate of change outside exceeds the rate of change inside, the end is in sight."[4] Organizations must poise themselves to change, not only to prosper but to survive in today's world. As illustrated in Exhibit 16.1, rapid technological changes, a globalized economy, changing markets, and the rise of e-commerce are creating more threats as well as more opportunities for organizational leaders.

Many of the changes in today's world are being driven by advances in computer and information technology. Organizations are using new technology to improve productivity, customer service, and competitiveness, but leaders find that because the technology changes so rapidly, they must constantly evaluate and upgrade systems, examine new technological developments, adopt new ways of doing business, and provide employees with new skills. One crucial area of technological change for today's organizations is the Internet and e-commerce, as discussed in the previous chapter. The significance of the Internet and its effect on the rate of change is illustrated by the results of a study by Opinion Research Corporation International. The study found that a handful of Internet companies, including Amazon, Yahoo, and America Online, became "household names" (meaning that more than 50 million Americans recognize them by name) within only a few years, whereas it took powerhouse companies such as Coca-Cola and McDonald's decades longer to achieve the same status.[5]

Organizations also face increased competition, both domestically and internationally. Consider the case of chains such as Camelot Music, Record Giant, Wherehouse Entertainment, and Strawberries, all of which filed for bankruptcy protection. The whole nature of the CD-selling business changed overnight when home electronics behemoth Best Buy started selling CDs for only about half what they cost in traditional music stores. Today, electronics stores like Best Buy and Circuit City sell more CDs than Sam Goody's and other music retail chains.[6] In the insurance industry, large companies such as

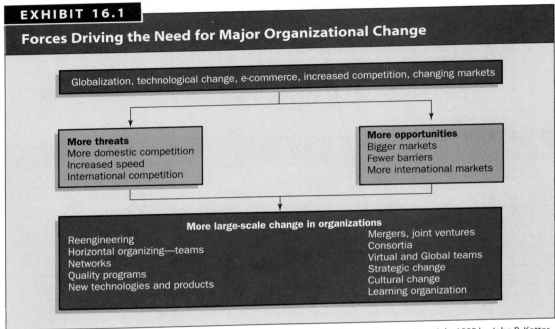

EXHIBIT 16.1

Forces Driving the Need for Major Organizational Change

Globalization, technological change, e-commerce, increased competition, changing markets

More threats
More domestic competition
Increased speed
International competition

More opportunities
Bigger markets
Fewer barriers
More international markets

More large-scale change in organizations

Reengineering
Horizontal organizing—teams
Networks
Quality programs
New technologies and products

Mergers, joint ventures
Consortia
Virtual and Global teams
Strategic change
Cultural change
Learning organization

SOURCE: Based on John P. Kotter, *The New Rules: How to Succeed in Today's Post-Corporate World.* Copyright 1995 by John P. Kotter. Adapted with permission from The Free Press.

Allstate and State Farm are facing threats from smaller, nimble competitors such as Geico and Progressive, which rely on phone solicitation, direct mail, and the Internet to bypass the costs associated with doing business through independent agents. In addition to brutal domestic competition, companies also face global competition on their home turf as well as the need to be competitive in international markets.

The ability to deliver customized goods and services—and deliver them fast—is another challenge for today's organizations.[7] Leaders at Delphi Automotive Systems created a new kind of factory to speed the delivery of customized automotive products.

IN THE LEAD   Peter Wood, Delphi Automotive Systems

The history of Delphi Automotive Systems, a former division of General Motors, goes back almost a century. But the most dramatic changes in the organization have occurred over the past several years. Peter Wood, manufacturing-systems manager for Delphi's Oak Creek, Wisconsin, plant and "change agent" for the company's massive redesign effort, proudly explains that whereas deliveries used to take twenty-one days, now "if you order on Monday, we can deliver on that precise order by Friday."

Delphi's Oak Creek factory makes catalytic converters for some 40 automobile manufacturers. The plant's 2,200 people used to work on a traditional assembly line—workers would sit or stand along the line performing one small, distinct task, such as bending a tab or inserting a filter substrate. The process was slow and inflexible, but it worked just fine until automakers began demanding converters that were customized to their individual needs. At the same time, manufacturers began cutting down the number of suppliers they used, establishing relationships with a few large vendors who could best meet their needs. Delphi leaders knew the organization needed a new way of working—one that would cut costs, increase productivity, allow for flexibility, and most of all, speed things up. Today, the Oak Creek factory uses only half of its 1 million square feet of floor space because 98 percent of the powered conveyor system has been eliminated. The factory floor is now divided into "work cells," each one consisting of a few workers who make an entire converter from beginning to end. Workers in each cell determine their own schedules, inspect for quality, and communicate directly with customers. Because they have responsibility for a complete finished product rather than only a small task, people are constantly coming up with new ideas for improvement.

Wood admits the transformation wasn't easy. At first, many people were frightened, angry, and resistant to the massive changes. But everyone knew the survival of the company was at stake, and with the assistance and support of organizational and union leaders, employees gradually began coming up with ideas for how to make the transformation successful for everyone.[8]

Leaders initiate many dramatic changes in organizations, but change is not always successful. For example, many organizations are responding to global challenges by reengineering business processes, yet by one estimate nearly 70 percent of reengineering projects fail to reach their intended goals.[9] The 1990s saw the greatest wave of mergers in American history, with more than 10,000 mergers taking place and more than $660 billion changing hands in one year alone.[10] Chrysler merged with Germany's Daimler-Benz, Citicorp and Travelers Group combined to form Citigroup Inc., Hewlett-Packard purchased VeriFone, and AOL and Time Warner are involved in the biggest media merger of all time. All of these "marriages" have the potential to be enormously successful, but many will be disappointing failures. One analyst estimates that only 29 percent of mergers and acquisitions in the United States are successes.[11]

As another example of the difficulties of change, the massive downsizing of the 1980s and early 1990s lowered costs and improved profits for many companies, but leaders and employees are still struggling with the aftermath of more work, fewer resources, and diminished trust. And the challenges of leading effective change aren't limited to the U.S. Studies of major change initiatives in France and the United Kingdom found that approximately 70 percent of the projects were deemed failures.[12]

However, leaders may find that they have to change their organizations almost continuously to keep pace with changes in the external environment. Some ways organizations are responding to external changes are by shifting to self-directed work teams or adopting structural innovations such as outsourcing functions to other companies. Some become involved in joint ventures, consortia, or virtual organizations to extend their operations and markets internationally. Leaders face an unending need for dramatic structural and cultural change and for rapid innovations in technology and products. Some are leading their companies to become learning organizations that continually learn and adapt to a chaotic environment. All of these changes provide potential for outright failure. The process of organizational change is complex and messy, and many times leaders stick with the known for fear of the unknown. As the head of one large U.S. corporation said, "The tragedy of top leadership . . . is that it is so much more reassuring to stay as you are, even though you know the result will be certain failure, than to try to make a fundamental change when you cannot be certain that the effort will succeed."[13]

LEADING MAJOR CHANGE

Major change does not happen easily. However, leaders do facilitate change and thereby help organizations adapt to external problems and opportunities. It is important for leaders to recognize that the change process goes through stages, that each stage is important, and that each may require a significant amount of time. Leaders are responsible for guiding employees and the organization through the change process.

Exhibit 16.2 presents an eight-stage model of planned change.[14] To successfully implement change, leaders pay careful attention to each stage. Skipping stages or making critical mistakes at any stage can cause the change process to fail.

1. At Stage 1, leaders *establish a sense of urgency* that change is really needed. Crises or threats will thaw resistance to change. At IBM, for example, dramatically declining profits and stock prices in the early 1990s provided an undoubted sense of urgency. In many cases, however, there is no public

---

EXHIBIT 16.2

The Eight-Stage Model of Planned Organizational Change

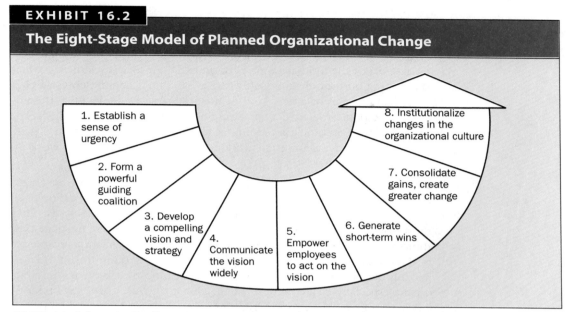

1. Establish a sense of urgency

2. Form a powerful guiding coalition

3. Develop a compelling vision and strategy

4. Communicate the vision widely

5. Empower employees to act on the vision

6. Generate short-term wins

7. Consolidate gains, create greater change

8. Institutionalize changes in the organizational culture

SOURCE: John P. Kotter, *Leading Change* (Boston: Harvard Business School Press, 1996), 21.

crisis and leaders have to make others aware of the need for change. Leaders carefully scan the external and internal environment—looking at competitive conditions; market position; social, technological, and demographic trends; profit and loss; operations; and other factors. After identifying potential crises or problems, they find ways to communicate the information broadly and dramatically.

2. Stage 2 involves *establishing a coalition* with enough power to guide the change process and then developing a sense of teamwork among the group. For the change process to succeed, there must be a shared commitment to the need and possibilities for organizational transformation. Middle management change will seek top leader support in the coalition. It is also essential that lower-level executives become involved. Mechanisms such as off-site retreats can get people together and help them develop a shared assessment of problems and how to approach them. At MasterBrand Industries, transformation began with an off-site meeting of some seventy-five key managers who examined the need for change and discussed ways to remake MasterBrand into a team-based organization.[15]

3. Stage 3 requires *developing a vision and strategy*. Leaders are responsible for formulating and articulating a compelling vision that will guide the change effort, and developing the strategies for achieving that vision. A

"picture" of a highly desirable future motivates people to change. Jeff Campbell, president of Burger King, worked with other leaders to develop a vision to be the best convenience restaurant in America. Linda Wachner, CEO of Warnaco, created a vision to make the company's brands "the Coca-Cola of the intimate apparel business."[16] At SEI Investments, which started as a business making software for bank trust departments, CEO Al West had a vision of a new kind of financial services company that could quickly respond to customers' changing needs with new products and services. His vision included doing away with the old hierarchical organization chart and assigning all work to self-directed teams that work directly with customers.[17]

4. In Stage 4, leaders use every means possible to widely *communicate the vision and strategy*. At this stage, the coalition of change agents should set an example by modeling the new behaviors needed from employees. They must communicate about the change at least ten times more than they think necessary. Transformation is impossible unless a majority of people in the organization are involved and willing to help, often to the point of making personal sacrifices. Widely communicating the vision and strategy can be especially challenging in huge, global organizations like London-based Cadbury Schweppes. CEO John Sunderland personally met with 2,000 top managers to explain his vision of changing to a value-based management system and motivate them to go back and mobilize commitment in their own units.[18]

5. Stage 5 involves *empowering employees throughout the organization to act on the vision*. This means getting rid of obstacles to change, which may require revising systems, structures, or procedures that hinder or undermine the change effort. People are empowered with knowledge, resources, and discretion to make things happen. At Delphi Automotive Systems, described earlier, leaders did away with many strict work rules that limited employee initiative. They also revised reward systems, including offering stock options. Delphi encourages people to contribute ideas for improvement by entering everyone who makes at least one serious suggestion in a raffle for prizes such as big-screen televisions, lawn mowers, and microwaves. At this stage, leaders can also encourage and reward risk-taking and nontraditional ideas and actions.

6. At Stage 6, leaders *generate short-term wins*. Leaders plan for visible performance improvements, enable them to happen, and celebrate employees who were involved in the improvements. Major change takes time, and a transformation effort loses momentum if there are no short-term accomplishments that employees can recognize and celebrate. At the U.S. Mint, Philip Diehl publicly set an early goal of processing 95 percent of orders within six weeks. Even though that sounds agonizingly slow in today's

fast-paced business world, it was a tremendous improvement for the Mint. Achieving the goal energized employees and kept the transformation efforts moving.[19] A highly visible and successful short-term accomplishment boosts the credibility of the change process and renews the commitment and enthusiasm of employees.[20]

7. Stage 7 builds on the credibility achieved by short-term wins to *consolidate improvements, tackle bigger problems, and create greater change.* Leaders change systems, structures, and policies that do not fit the vision but have not yet been confronted. They hire, promote, and develop employees who can implement the vision for change. In addition, leaders revitalize the process with a new round of projects, themes, or change agents. At this stage, Philip Diehl of the U.S. Mint charged his top leadership team with reorganizing the agency to better fit the new vision and strategy. The process resulted in the decision to break the Mint into three strategic business units that can better respond to different sets of customers: one division for circulating coins, one for collectibles, and the third for protection services.

8. Stage 8 involves *institutionalizing the new approaches in the organizational culture.* This is the follow-through stage that makes the changes stick. Old habits, values, traditions, and mind-sets are permanently replaced. New values and beliefs are instilled in the culture so that employees view the changes not as something new but as a normal and integral part of how the organization operates. This stage also requires developing a means to ensure leadership development and succession so that the new values and behaviors are carried forward to the next generation of leadership.

Stages in the change process generally overlap, but each is important for successful change to occur. When dealing with a major change effort, leaders can follow the eight-stage change process as a road map to provide a strong foundation for success. Sometimes, leaders initiate profound changes in all parts of the organization simultaneously, but change may also occur in only specific areas.

THE FOCUS OF CHANGE

The eight-stage model of planned change applies particularly to top-down change initiatives, such as changes in organizational strategy and structure. **Strategy and structure changes** pertain to the administrative domain of an organization. These include changes in policies, reward systems, coordination, control systems, and so forth, in addition to changes in the organization's structure or strategic focus. This is one of four different types of change, as illustrated in Exhibit 16.3. Other types of change are technology changes, changes in products or services, and people and culture changes.

Technology changes are changes in an organization's production processes, including its knowledge and skill base, that enable distinctive competence. Technology changes, including changes in work methods, equipment, and work flow, are designed to make production more efficient or to produce greater volume. **Product and service changes** pertain to product or service outputs. New products are normally designed to increase market share or to develop new markets, customers, or clients. **Culture change** refers to changes in the values, attitudes, expectations, beliefs, and behaviors of employees. In the exhibit, the arrows connecting the types of change indicate that a change in one part may affect other parts of the organization. For example, a new strategic plan may lead to new products, which in turn require changes in technology. In addition, the exhibit shows that changes in culture provide the foundation for all other changes in the organization. Because all change depends on people and culture, we will discuss culture change in detail later in this chapter.

Changes in strategy, structure, and culture are generally top-down, that is, initiated by top leaders, whereas product and technology changes usually come from the bottom up. The *bottom-up approach* means that ideas are initiated at lower levels of the organization and channeled upward for approval.

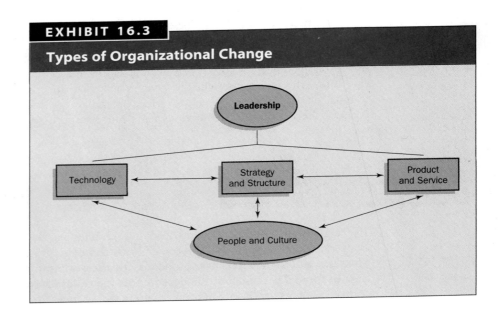

EXHIBIT 16.3

Types of Organizational Change

Leaders know that employees at lower levels understand the technology and have the expertise to propose changes. For example, at Dana Corporation's Elizabethtown, Kentucky plant, two workers came up with an idea for automatically loading steel sheets into a forming press. This technology change saves the auto-parts maker $250,000 a year.[21] The bottom-up approach also applies to product and service changes. However, because products and services also must meet customer needs, these changes generally require expertise from several different departments simultaneously. Ideas originate at lower levels, as they do for technology change, but they also flow horizontally across departments. Leaders ensure horizontal coordination to facilitate success of product and service changes. For example, people in research, marketing, and manufacturing interact frequently to share ideas and solve problems. People in research inform marketing of new developments to learn whether they will be useful to customers. Marketing people pass customer complaints to research to use in the design of new products. Manufacturing informs other departments whether a new product idea can be manufactured within cost limits.

At Kellogg, leaders developed a new approach to product development to improve horizontal coordination. In the past, Kellogg's marketing department came up with new ideas and tossed them to manufacturing, a process that over the past few years has led to more failures than successful new products. Leaders revised the process so that employees now work in cross-functional teams, with market researchers alongside nutritionists, food scientists, production specialists, and engineers. The improved horizontal coordination has dramatically increased Kellogg's new product success rate, such as with the introduction of Rice Krispies Treats and Raisin Bran Crunch cereal.[22]

Companies such as Kellogg, IBM, Dana, and 3M depend on lower-level employees to develop new ideas for technology and product changes. However, all change requires active leadership. Leaders look for ways to encourage the development of new ideas. Some companies, such as Dana and 3M, offer classes to train employees in drumming up better ideas. Companies may also offer rewards to employees whose suggestions or ideas are implemented. A significant way in which leaders can encourage more ideas from lower-level employees is by fostering an environment that promotes creativity. Creativity will be discussed in detail later in this chapter. First, we will examine the problem of resistance to change and how leaders can help to overcome resistance.

OVERCOMING RESISTANCE TO CHANGE

Continuous change has become a way of life for organizations and employees in today's world, and the rate of societal and organizational change is increasing. Whereas change initiatives such as corporate restructurings, introduction of new technologies, or development of new products often took years to accomplish in the past, they now must be done in months. Books and magazine articles are constantly proclaiming the need for change. Change leaders are heeding the call and marching forward to reinvent their organizations for the twenty-first century.

Leaders frequently see change as a way to strengthen the organization, but many people view change only as painful and disruptive. A critical aspect of leading people through change is understanding that resistance to change is natural—and that there are often legitimate reasons for it. This chapter's Living Leadership box takes a lighthearted look at why employees may resist changes in some overly bureaucratic organizations.

One management scholar and consultant, Oren Harari, recommends that leaders accept the chaos of change: "As you lead people through the process of change, it will be like heading into Class V whitewater rapids. You'll confront the myriad realities as they come at you fast and furious."[23] To prepare for the chaos, leaders can understand why people resist change and use mechanisms to smooth the process.

Why Do People Resist Change?

The underlying reason why employees resist change is that it violates the **personal compact** between workers and the organization.[24] Personal compacts are the reciprocal obligations and commitments that define the relationship between employees and organizations. They include such things as job tasks, performance requirements, evaluation procedures, and compensation packages. These aspects of the compact are generally clearly defined and may be in written form. Other aspects are less clear-cut. The personal compact incorporates elements such as mutual trust and dependence as well as shared values. Employees perceive that change violates the personal compact for several reasons.

- **Self-Interest** Employees typically resist a change they believe will take away something of value. Changes in job design, structure, or technology may lead to a perceived loss of power, prestige, pay, company benefits, or even an employee's job. For middle managers and lower-level supervisors, for example, a shift to empowered teams of workers can be quite threatening. Fear of personal loss may be the biggest obstacle to organizational change.[25]

- **Uncertainty** Uncertainty is the lack of information about future events. It represents a fear of the unknown. Employees often do not understand how a proposed change may affect them and may worry about whether they will be able to meet the demands of a new task, procedure, or technology. When leaders at Lands' End embarked on a

LIVING LEADERSHIP

Dealing with a Dead Horse

Ancient wisdom says that when you discover you are astride a dead horse, the best strategy is to dismount. In government and other overly bureaucratic organizations, many different approaches are tried. Here are some of our favorite strategies for dealing with the "dead horse" scenario:

1. Change the rider.

2. Buy a stronger whip.

3. Beat the horse harder.

4. Shout at and threaten the horse.

5. Appoint a committee to study the horse.

6. Arrange a visit to other sites to see how they ride dead horses.

7. Increase the standards for riding dead horses.

8. Appoint a committee to revive the dead horse.

9. Create a training session to improve riding skills.

10. Explore the state of dead horses in today's environment.

11. Change the requirements so that the horse no longer meets the standards of death.

12. Hire an external consultant to show how a dead horse can be ridden.

13. Harness several dead horses together to increase speed.

14. Increase funding to improve the horse's performance.

15. Declare that no horse is too dead to ride.

16. Fund a study to determine if outsourcing will reduce the cost of riding a dead horse.

17. Buy a computer program to enhance the dead horse's performance.

18. Declare a dead horse less costly to maintain than a live one.

19. Form a work group to find uses for dead horses.

    And . . . if all else fails . . .

20. Promote the dead horse to a supervisory position. Or, in a large corporation, make it a Vice President.

SOURCE: Author unknown. Another version of this story may be found at *http://www.abcsmallbiz.com/funny/deadhorse.html*

---

dramatic effort to incorporate some of today's trends such as teams, peer reviews, and the elimination of guards and time clocks, employees balked because they liked the familiar "Lands' End Way" of doing things and were uncertain about how the changes would affect them.[26]

■ **Different Assessments and Goals** Another reason for resistance to change is that people who will be affected by the innovation may assess the situation differently from those who propose the change. Sometimes critics voice legitimate disagreements over the proposed benefits of a change. Employees in different departments pursue different goals, and a change may detract from performance and goal achievement for some departments.

These reasons for resistance are legitimate and real. Leaders cannot ignore resistance to change, but can diagnose the reasons and come up with ways to gain acceptance of the change by employees.

Overcoming Resistance

Leaders can improve the chances for a successful outcome by following the eight-stage model discussed earlier in this chapter. In addition, leaders may use a number of specific implementation techniques to overcome employee resistance.

- **Communication and Training** Communication informs employees about the need for change and about the consequences of a proposed change, preventing false rumors, misunderstandings, and resentment. In one study of change efforts, the most commonly cited reason for failure was that employees learned of the change from outsiders.[27] Top leaders concentrated on communicating with the public and shareholders, but failed to communicate with the people who would be most intimately affected by the changes—their own employees. It is also important that leaders communicate major change efforts face-to-face rather than through videos, memos, or company newsletters. In addition, training is needed to help employees acquire skills for their role in the change process or their new responsibilities. Canadian Airlines International spent a year and a half preparing and training employees before changing its entire reservations, airport, cargo, and financial systems. This intensive training and communication effort, which involved 50,000 tasks, 12,000 people, and twenty-six classrooms around the world, resulted in a smooth implementation.[28]

- **Participation and Involvement** Participation involves employees in helping to design the change. Although this approach is time-consuming, it pays off by giving people a sense of control over the change activity. Employees come to understand the change better and become committed to its successful implementation. A study of the implementation and adoption of new computer technology at two companies, for example, showed a much smoother implementation process at the company that introduced the change using a participatory approach.[29]

■ **Coercion** As a last resort, leaders overcome resistance by threatening employees with the loss of jobs or promotions or by firing or transferring them. Coercion may be necessary in crisis situations when a rapid response is needed. Coercion may also be needed for administrative changes that flow from the top down, such as downsizing the workforce. However, as a general rule, this approach to change is not advisable because it leaves employees angry at leaders, and the change may be sabotaged.

THE NEGATIVE IMPACT OF CHANGE

Leaders can use the techniques just described to overcome resistance in any of the areas of change—strategy and structure, technology, product and service, and culture. Leaders are responsible for smoothly implementing changes that can help the organization survive and prosper. However, it is also essential for leaders to recognize that change can have negative as well as positive consequences.

The Two Faces of Change

Effectively and humanely leading change is one of the greatest challenges for leaders. The nature and pace of change in today's environment can be exhilarating and even fun. But it can also be inconvenient, painful, and downright scary. Even when a change appears to be good for individual employees as well as the organization, it can lead to decreased morale, lower commitment, and diminished trust in the organization if not handled carefully.

In addition, some changes that may be necessary for the good of the organization can cause real, negative consequences for individual employees, who may experience high levels of stress, be compelled to quickly learn entirely new tasks and ways of working, or possibly lose their jobs. Some of the most difficult changes are those related to structure, such as redefining positions and responsibilities, reengineering the company, redesigning jobs, departments, or divisions, or downsizing the organization. In many cases, these types of changes mean that some people will be seriously hurt because they will lose their jobs.

Leadership and Downsizing

When Greg Dyke took over at the BBC, he knew the organization needed to increase expenditures on programming to compete with commercial stations, and that meant cuts would need to be made in other areas. Dyke initiated a complete restructuring and cost-cutting program that had highly positive results for the organization. Unfortunately, the changes led to layoffs for many employees.[30] Dyke and other top managers confronted one of the most difficult situations leaders may face—how to handle downsizing in a way that eases pain and tension for departing employees and maintains the trust and morale of employees who remain with the organization.

Downsizing, which refers to intentionally reducing the size of a company's workforce, is not as widespread today as it was during the 1980s and early 1990s, but it is still a part of many change initiatives.[31] Motorola, DuPont, Sears, and Disney are among the many companies that have recently had significant layoffs. Reengineering projects, which focus on radically redesigning business processes to improve cost, quality, service, and speed, often lead to the elimination of some organizational positions, and those employees may be let go. Mergers and acquisitions frequently mean that some functions and some employees will be "redundant." In addition, some mergers may be followed by a general "housecleaning" or perhaps by the closing of less profitable or outdated facilities, leading to a loss of jobs.[32] Increasing automation of jobs, the trend toward outsourcing, and the transition from an industrial to an information-based economy have all led to job reductions.[33] In addition, the decline in the U.S. economy during early 2001 once again made downsizing a priority for many organizations seeking to cut costs and improve profitability. Consider the case of the Internet-based company Techies.com.

IN THE LEAD   ## Dan Frawley, Techies.com

"I may not like it, but you understand the larger picture why you have to do it," said Dan Frawley, CEO of Techies.com. "It's the defense of a company." Frawley was talking about the layoffs of sixty workers at the online exchange company for technology professionals and businesses hoping to recruit them.

Not long ago, the fast-growing firm was making plans for an initial public offering. Employees had stock options and dreams of getting rich. Now, many of them have lost their jobs. Scott LaFrenz, one of the employees let go, recalls how it was after the announcement was made: "It was just quiet. People just kind of looking around, probably shocked." When the employees went back to their desks, they found cardboard boxes waiting—by the end of the day, they were packed and gone. The company offered severance packages and outplacement services, but the pain was still real and substantial.

The layoffs are but one piece of a difficult change effort that leaders hope will guarantee the survival of the company. By focusing on building sales and market share at the expense of profitability, Techies.com racked up losses of $37.7 million in one year alone. Leaders reorganized to focus on increasing profits and cutting expenditures. They scrapped about half of the projects people were working on and abandoned plans for overseas expansion. As Mark Engelter, director of Techies e-learning business, put it, "We've gone from an environment of endless opportunity and not enough time in the day to do all things you want to do, to really having to rigorously analyze and justify and really look at what we're going to focus on."[34]

Since 1979, more than 43 million American jobs have been lost.[35] Some researchers have found that massive downsizing, like many other change initiatives, has often not achieved the intended benefits and in some cases has significantly harmed the organization.[36] Nevertheless, there are times when downsizing is a necessary part of a thoughtful restructuring of assets or other important change initiatives. Leaders need to understand that downsizing not only hurts those who lose their jobs but can also have many negative consequences on the morale, commitment, and performance of "survivors," those who remain with the organization. For example, although Frawley went to great lengths to assure Techies.com employees that further layoffs would not occur, no one is sure that the changes now underway will really save the organization. Uncertainty about their own job responsibilities, changing work relationships, and the pain of losing coworkers can also spur some key employees to leave the organization. If downsizing is not carefully handled, it can have a detrimental impact on the organization.

When job cuts are necessary, leaders should be prepared for increased conflict and stress, even greater resistance to change, and a decrease in morale, trust, and employee commitment.[37] A number of techniques can help leaders smooth the downsizing process and ease tensions for employees who leave as well as those who remain.[38]

- **Involve employees.** One important way to cut jobs and keep morale high among remaining employees is to let lower-level employees assist with shaping the criteria for which jobs will be cut or which employees will leave the company. Naturally, this requires that employees be trained to understand the goals leaders hope to achieve through the downsizing. Another option is to offer incentive packages for employees to leave voluntarily. One drawback is that there's no way to predict which employees will take the offer, and the company may lose key employees with critical knowledge and skills. Leaders can offer options, such as job-sharing and part-time work, which may suit some employees well, enabling them to remain employed part-time and allowing the company to retain their talents.

- **Communicate more, not less.** Some leaders seem to think the less that's said about a pending layoff, the better. Not so. Leaders should provide advance notice with as much information as possible. Even when they're not certain about exactly what is going to happen, leaders should be as open and honest with employees as possible. When Compaq Computer in Houston had to lay off 15 percent of its workforce, top human resource executives developed a comprehensive communication campaign and trained leaders throughout the organization to help people understand and cope with the impending layoffs.[39] Communication with survivors continued following the layoffs so that the uncertainty and anxiety of workers was reduced. Leaders should remember that it's impossible to "overcommunicate" during turbulent times. Remaining employees need to know what is expected of them, whether future layoffs are a possibility, and what the organization is doing to help coworkers who have lost their jobs.

- **Provide assistance to displaced workers.** Leaders have a responsibility to help displaced workers cope with the loss of their jobs and get reestablished in the job market. The organization can provide training, severance packages, extended benefits, and outplacement assistance. One organization researched the local job market, helped employees fill out applications, and invited agency employment counselors for on-site interviews and job placement assistance. In addition, counseling services for both employees and their families can ease the trauma associated with a job loss.

- **Help the survivors thrive.** Leaders should remember the emotional needs of survivors, as well. Many people experience guilt, anger, confusion, and sadness after the loss of colleagues, and these feelings should be acknowledged. People may also be concerned about their own jobs and have difficulty adapting to the changes in job duties, responsibilities, and so forth. The state of Oregon hired consultant Al Siebert to help employees adapt following the elimination of more than 1,000 jobs. Most people "just aren't emotionally prepared to handle major disruptions," Siebert says. Through a series of workshops, Siebert helped people acknowledge their anger and unhappiness, then helped them become "change-resilient" by developing coping skills such as flexibility, curiosity, and optimism.[40]

Even the best-led organizations may sometimes need to lay off employees in a turbulent environment. Leaders can attain positive results if they handle downsizing in a way that enables remaining organization members to be motivated, productive, and committed to a better future.

MOVING THE ORGANIZATION FORWARD—THE ROLE OF CREATIVITY

Today's organizations frequently need to implement major changes such as restructuring, downsizing, mergers, adoption of new technologies, and so forth. In addition, the most successful organizations are continuously implementing smaller changes as well. As we discussed earlier, successful leaders find ways to encourage the development and sharing of new ideas throughout the organization.

In response to the question, "What must one do to survive in the twenty-first century?" the top answer among 500 CEOs surveyed by the American Management Association was "practice creativity and innovation." However, only 6 percent of the respondents felt that their companies were successfully accomplishing this goal.[41] There's a creativity deficit in many of today's organizations, but leaders are beginning to respond by adopting structures and systems that promote rather than squelch the creation and implementation of new ideas. Effective leaders find ways to promote creativity in the departments where it is most needed. For example, some organizations, such as hospitals, government agencies, and nonprofit organizations, may need frequent changes in policies and procedures, and leaders can promote creativity among administrative workers. For companies that rely on new products, leaders need to promote the generation and sharing of ideas across departments. In learning organizations, leaders want everyone to constantly be coming up with new ideas for solving problems and meeting customer needs. One of the best ways for leaders to facilitate continuous change is to create an environment that nourishes creativity. **Creativity** is the generation of new ideas that result in improved efficiency and effectiveness of the organization.[42] Creative people come up with ideas that may meet perceived needs, solve problems, or respond to opportunities and are therefore adopted by the organization. However, creativity itself is a process rather than an outcome, a journey rather than a destination. One of the most important tasks of leaders today is to harness the creative energy of all employees to further the interests of the organization.

Leading Creativity in Organizations and People

Leaders can create an environment that helps individuals as well as entire organizations or departments be more creative. Six elements of creative organizations are listed in the left-hand column of Exhibit 16.4, and each is described below.[43] These elements correspond to the characteristics of creative individuals, listed in the right-hand column of the exhibit.

EXHIBIT 16.4

Characteristics of Creative People and Organizations

The Creative Organization	The Creative Individual
Alignment	Commitment Focused approach
Self-initiated activity	Interdependence Persistence Energy
Unofficial activity	Self-confidence Nonconformity
Serendipity	Playfulness Curiosity Undisciplined exploration
Diverse stimuli	Open-mindedness Conceptual fluency Enjoy variety
Within-company communication	Social competence Emotionally expressive Loves people

SOURCE: Based on Alan G. Robinson and Sam Stern, *Corporate Creativity: How Innovation and Improvement Actually Happen* (San Francisco: Berrett-Koehler, 1997); Rosabeth Moss Kanter, "The Middle Manager as Innovator," *Harvard Business Review*, July-August 1982, 104–105; and James Brian Quinn, "Managing Innovation: Controlled Chaos," *Harvard Business Review*, May-June 1985, 73–84.

ALIGNMENT   For creative acts that benefit the organization to occur consistently, the interests and actions of all employees should be aligned with the company's purpose, vision, and goals. Leaders make clear what the company stands for, consistently promote the vision, and clarify specific goals. In addition, they make a commitment of time, energy, and resources to activities and initiatives that support the vision, and they hold employees accountable for decisions that affect key goals.

SELF-INITIATED ACTIVITY   Most people have a natural desire to explore and create, which leads them to want to initiate creative activity on their own. Unfortunately, this desire is sometimes squelched early in life by classroom teachers who insist on strict adherence to the rules. It is the responsibility of leaders to unleash deep-seated employee motivation for creative acts. For example, an effective system for responding to employee ideas and suggestions is essential to encouraging self-initiated activity. When employees feel that their ideas are valued, they begin to have more ideas.

UNOFFICIAL ACTIVITY   Employees need to be able to experiment and dream outside of their regular job description. Leaders can give employees free time for activities that are not officially sanctioned. One study of creativity found that in almost every case the essence of the creative act came during the "unofficial" time period.[44] Dream time is what makes it possible for companies to go where they never expected to. The best-known example is 3M's Post-it Notes, one of the five most popular 3M products and one that resulted from an engineer's free-time experiments with another worker's "failure"—a not-very-sticky glue. 3M lets employees spend 15 percent of their time on any project of their own choosing, without management approval.[45]

SERENDIPITY   As originally defined by Horace Walpole in 1754, "serendipity combines a fortunate accident with sagacity."[46]   A good example of serendipity was the naming of Small Dogs Electronics Inc., a computer reseller. Founder Don Mayer decided the name fit the company because he really *was* a small dog—an entrepreneur doing almost everything himself out of his living room. Plus, he actually had a bunch of small dogs. What Mayer didn't expect was the loyal following the name has generated among dog lovers. "Somehow, we've tapped into the idea that dog lovers inherently trust each other," Mayer says.[47] Serendipity often seems like a magical occurrence and, thus, one leaders can do little to promote. However, leaders can encourage "fortunate accidents" by creating a culture that values risk-taking and exploration. They promote sagacity by helping employees develop their potential to think and solve problems so that they are able to recognize the potential value of an accidental discovery. Far from being magic, serendipity is present in every creative act, whether it is readily apparent or not.

DIVERSE STIMULI   It is impossible to know in advance what stimulus will lead any particular person to come up with a creative idea. The seeds of the idea for Post-it Notes were planted when an engineer's bookmarks kept falling out of his church hymnal. Leaders can help provide the sparks that set off creative ideas. Companies such as Hallmark, Nortel Networks' Broad Band, and Bell Labs bring in outside speakers on diverse topics to open people up to different ideas. During a nature talk at Bell Labs several years ago, a scientist jumped up and ran out of the auditorium—something the presenter said about animal communication helped the scientist see a creative solution to a problem with a new technology he'd been working on.[48] Other simple ways leaders can provide employees with diverse stimuli are by rotating people into different jobs, allowing them time off to participate in volunteer activities, and giving them opportunities to mix with people different from themselves. Organizations can give employees opportunities to work with customers, suppliers, and others outside the industry.

INTERNAL COMMUNICATION Creativity flourishes when there is frequent contact with interdisciplinary networks of people at all levels of the organization.[49] Leaders can provide opportunities for employees who don't normally interact with one another to get together. Novartis, a $24 billion life sciences corporation that produces diverse products such as pharmaceuticals, genetically engineered seeds, baby food, contact lenses, and animal health products, holds "knowledge fairs" four times a year to give people a chance to learn about creative activities in other parts of the organization.[50] Leaders can also make collaboration and widespread sharing of information an integral part of the organizational culture.

Leaders can incorporate these six elements to ignite creativity in specific departments or the entire organization. Leaders at Play, a small marketing agency in Richmond, Virginia, have unleashed the creativity of everyone in the organization by creating an environment that encourages people to be themselves, have fun, and take risks.

IN THE LEAD   **Play**

The agency Play's clients include some of the world's most serious companies, such as American Express, Nationwide Insurance, Calvin Klein, and the Weather Channel. So why do employees handle their most important assignments wearing construction paper headdresses and googly eyes?

The name of the company captures this organization's approach to the hard work of creativity: Build an environment of playfulness, give employees heavy doses of fun and freedom, and the good ideas will start flying like the bright red rubber balls that bounce around Play's offices. Play develops creative concepts, marketing and branding campaigns, promotional products, and event strategies. But the company's ultimate creation may be the process of creativity itself. Employees are continuously dreaming, experimenting, and sharing ideas, unconstrained by job titles, permanent assignments, or job descriptions. People who would be dismissed as "mere accountants" or support staff at other agencies join in brainstorming sessions and meet with clients. In addition, it's not unusual to find that a UPS delivery person has been pulled into a brainstorming session or a visiting supplier asked to participate in a role-playing exercise. Play will take ideas wherever it can find them. Exposure to new ideas is encouraged through "radical sabbaticals," which give employees time off to learn to surf, climb mountains, or do anything else that will inspire and help them expand their thinking.

"One person is as creative as the next," says cofounder Andy Stefanovich. "That creativity just needs to be discovered within each person. What we're doing is building a creative *community*—not mystifying creativity as a special talent of the chosen few." Play's approach to building creativity seems to be working. When the Center for Creative Leadership (CCL) evaluated the company using a tool that appraises an organization's ability to foster creativity, Play not only beat CCL's benchmark model, but also beat *all* other companies in the CCL database. Play is now helping other organizations break out of conventional thinking and open the doors to new ideas; in fact, more that 30 percent of its business comes from teaching other companies to be more creative. The company's leaders talk about play as both a process and a movement. In today's environment, where every organization depends on new ideas to survive, it's a movement that's catching on fast.[51]

Naturally, to create this kind of environment, Play's leaders tend toward hiring people who display some of the characteristics of creative individuals, as listed in the right-hand column of Exhibit 16.4, but they emphasize that anyone can develop creative qualities. Creative people are often known for open-mindedness, a focused approach to problem solving, independence, persistence, self-confidence, nonconformity, a relaxed, playful attitude, and good social and interpersonal skills. Clearly, these characteristics are stronger in some people than in others. However, recent research on creativity suggests that everyone has roughly equal creative potential. Leaders can foster environments that encourage both individuals and organizations to be more creative.

Stages in the Personal Creative Process

One important part of becoming more creative is understanding the stages of the creative process. One model of creativity is illustrated in Exhibit 16.5. Stages do not always occur in the same order and may overlap. In addition, if a person encounters a block at one stage, he or she may cycle back to an earlier stage and try again.[52]

- **Stage 1: Recognition of Problem/Opportunity** Creativity often begins with the recognition of a problem that needs to be solved or an opportunity to explore. For example, the idea for Pringles brand potato chips (now owned by Procter & Gamble) began when an employee at a small snack manufacturer started wondering how they could pack a large number of chips into a small package.[53]

- **Stage 2: Information Gathering** The next step is to search for background information and knowledge about the problem or opportunity. This may involve reading in a variety of fields; attending professional meetings and seminars; traveling to new places; talking to anyone and

EXHIBIT 16.5

Stages in the Creative Process

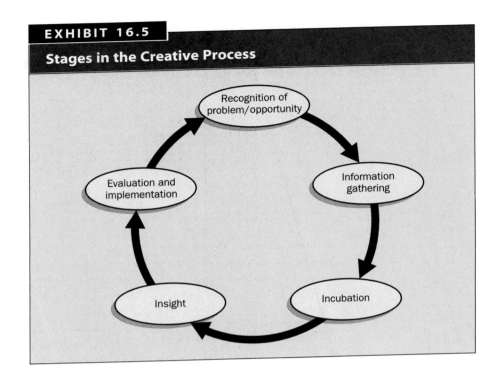

everyone about the subject; scanning magazines, newspapers, and journals; and carrying a notebook to jot down useful information and random thoughts. It is also important to set aside time specifically for pursuing ideas and giving curiosity free rein.

- **Stage 3: Incubation** This is the stage where a person allows the subconscious to mull things over. The incubation stage happens while the person is involved in activities totally unrelated to the subject—even during sleep. This is the period that really allows creativity to spring forth. Some helpful ideas for encouraging the incubation period are: engage in routine, "mindless" activities such as cutting the grass; get regular exercise; play and have fun; meditate; and try to relax on a regular basis.

- **Stage 4: Insight** This is the stage that most people think of as "creativity." It is when the person hits upon an idea. The idea may occur while watching television, taking a shower, or reading the newspaper, or it may occur while one is thinking specifically about the problem. In most cases, the idea doesn't come as a bolt out of the blue, but in gradual increments. Ideas to speed up this stage include: daydream and fantasize about the project; practice your hobbies; keep a notebook by your bedside to record late-night or early-morning ideas; take regular breaks from working.

■ **Stage 5: Evaluation and Implementation** This is the most difficult stage and requires courage, tenacity, and self-discipline. Creative people often fail many times before they succeed and have to cycle back through the information gathering and incubation stages. In addition, others may think the "brilliant" idea is crazy. Creative people don't give up when they run into obstacles. Some suggestions during this phase include: increase your energy level with proper diet, rest, and exercise; take note of your intuitive hunches; seek the advice of others; educate yourself in how to sell your ideas; and remember that you are facing challenges rather than problems.

These stages apply to individual creativity, but a similar creative process occurs in groups, as described in this chapter's Leaders Bookshelf. Leaders of today's organizations have powerful reasons to encourage creativity. As we discussed in Chapter 1, many organizations are undergoing fundamental transformations to respond to new challenges. They need employees throughout the organization to contribute new ideas. In addition, creative people are less resistant to change because they are open-minded, curious, and willing to take risks. The success of change in any part of the organization depends on people's attitudes and culture. Because people are so important for any change effort, the remainder of this chapter is devoted to a detailed discussion of leading culture change.

LEADING CULTURE CHANGE

Organizations are shifting from cherishing stability to valuing change, from control to empowerment, from encouraging competition to supporting collaboration, and from an emphasis on machines and objects to an emphasis on people, ideas, and relationships. Rapid advances in technology are driving many of these changes and creating turbulence and uncertainty. Many companies are striving to become learning organizations, as discussed in the previous chapter, so that they quickly learn and adapt in chaotic environments.

One of the greatest challenges for leading change, and particularly for a major transformation such as the shift to a learning organization, is reshaping organizational culture. To create successful change means changing people's behavior and attitudes, a challenge that has been referred to as "perplexing,

LEADER'S BOOKSHELF

When Sparks Fly: Igniting Creativity in Groups

by Dorothy A. Leonard and Walter C. Swap

When the team designing the Nissan Pathfinder got bogged down and weeks behind schedule, Jerry Hirshberg (then a vice president at Nissan Design International) shut down the whole place and took everybody to the movies. Hirshberg recalls, "The tension began to dissipate. Within days ideas started flowing, knotty problem areas unraveled, and the design began to lead the designers. . . ." The team met its deadline, and the Pathfinder became a huge hit. This is one of many stories told in *When Sparks Fly: Igniting Creativity in Groups*, by Dorothy A. Leonard and Walter C. Swap. The coauthors set out to debunk the idea that organizational creativity cannot be managed, and they show how a knack for innovation can be made to bloom "even in groups of people who don't consider themselves particularly creative, or think they have to be."

Five Steps toward Group Creativity

The authors emphasize that leaders must accept the creativity process as inherently "messy." For clarity, they identify five steps, while pointing out that a physical model of the process would look more like a plate of spaghetti than a set of linear steps.

- **Getting Ready** This is the preparation stage, during which people develop deep knowledge and expertise. Creativity grows out of the combined knowledge and experience of organization members.

- **Identifying Opportunity** The call for creativity often comes as a crisis or a problem to be solved. Other times, it's an opportunity waiting to be exploited.

- **Encouraging Divergent Thinking** Once a problem or opportunity appears, the way to make creative sparks fly is to get "unlike-minded people" together. People who differ in expertise, background, and thinking style generate more and better options.

- **Pausing for Incubation** A period of reflection may seem like a waste of time in today's fast-paced world, but it is crucial for subconscious problem-solving. People need "time out" from thinking to let their subconscious minds work on a solution. This invisible "fermentation period" is one of the most important steps in creativity.

- **Selecting Options** After the group is fired up with loads of ideas and solutions, the tricky part may be choosing the best one. A leader's role is to guide convergence so that the group comes together around a chosen solution.

Creativity Needs the Right Environment

In addition to offering tools and tips for managing the five steps of the creative process, the authors give suggestions for creating both a physical and a psychological environment that is conducive to creativity. Creativity flourishes in an environment of open communication and trust. Leaders encourage risk taking, accept mistakes as keys to learning, and inspire passion among employees for the organization and their role in it. Physical spaces can also be designed to encourage creativity by promoting divergent interactions and creating a stimulating, playful environment.

When Sparks Fly, by Dorothy A. Leonard and Walter C. Swap, is published by Harvard Business School Press.

annoying, distressing, and confusing."[54] Dick Evans, who successfully led a major transformation of British Aerospace, talks about the change process: "By far the greatest difficulties we faced were people difficulties. . . . Anyone who thinks that behavior change can be done fast is wrong."[55]

Despite the difficulties of changing people and culture, leaders in numerous organizations have accomplished highly successful culture change. Changing organizational culture fundamentally shifts how people think about their work and generally leads to renewed commitment and empowerment of employees and a stronger bond among workers and between the organization and its customers.[56] Two traditional ways leaders bring about culture change are through total quality management and organizational development programs.

Total Quality Management

The approach known as **total quality management (TQM)** infuses quality values throughout every activity within an organization. By requiring organization-wide participation in quality control, TQM requires a major shift in mind-set for both leaders and employees. Workers must be trained, involved, and empowered in a way that is new for them and can be frightening. One way to involve workers is through quality circles, groups of six to twelve workers who meet voluntarily to analyze and solve problems. Another technique is benchmarking, a process whereby companies find out how others do something better than they do and then try to imitate or improve on it. Through research and field trips by teams of frontline workers, companies compare their products and service with those of their competitors and other companies. While the focus of total quality programs is on improving quality and productivity, TQM always involves a significant change in organizational culture.

Organizational Development

A more straightforward method of bringing about culture change is known as organizational development. **Organizational development (OD)** is a planned, systematic process of change that uses behavioral science knowledge and techniques to improve an organization's health and effectiveness through its ability to adapt to the environment, improve internal relationships, and increase learning and problem-solving capabilities.[57] Although the field of OD evolved in the 1970s as a way to achieve organizational excellence, the concept has been enlarged to examine how people and groups can change to a learning organization culture in today's turbulent environment. Organizational development is not a step-by-step procedure to solve a specific problem but rather a process of fundamental change in the human and social systems of the organization, including organizational culture.[58]

Although organizational development is directed from the top, there is a strong emphasis on participation and collaboration. OD leaders use knowledge and techniques from the behavioral sciences to create a learning environment through increased trust, open confrontation of problems, employee empowerment and participation, knowledge and information sharing, the design of meaningful work, cooperation and collaboration between groups, and the full use of human potential. One technique is to survey employees about their job satisfaction, attitudes, and quality of work relationships. Change leaders then use the data to stimulate a discussion of organizational problems and plan for changes. Off-site meetings can also be held to give people a chance to talk about problems and the change mission with limited interference and distractions. Another OD technique is team building. Team-building activities bring people together to discuss conflicts, goals, communication, creativity, and leadership, and plan how to overcome problems and improve results.

Changing organizational culture is not easy, but organizational development techniques can help leaders smooth the process by getting people to think in new ways about human relationships.

Large-Group Interventions

Early work in organizational development focused on one or two groups or work teams at a time. In recent years, there has been a growing interest in applications to large-group settings, which are more attuned to accelerating large-scale culture change in today's complex organizations.[59] The **large-group intervention** approach brings together participants from all parts of the organization—often including key stakeholders from outside the organization as well—to discuss problems or opportunities and plan for change. A large-group intervention might involve 50 to 500 people and last several days. The idea is to involve everyone who has a stake in the change, gather perspectives from all parts of the system, and enable people to create a collective future through sustained, guided conversation and dialogue. General Electric's Work Out program, a leadership initiative by CEO Jack Welch, is an excellent example of the large-scale intervention approach. It accelerates the eight steps in Exhibit 16.2 from years to months.

IN THE LEAD   ### General Electric's Work Out

The Work Out program is one of the ways Jack Welch reshaped General Electric's culture for renewed productivity and growth. The program was created out of Welch's desire to reach and motivate 300,000 employees and his insistence that the people on the front lines, where change had to happen, be empowered to create that change.

GE's Work Out began in large-scale off-site meetings facilitated by a combination of top leaders, outside consultants, and human resources specialists. In each business unit, the basic pattern was the same. Hourly and salaried workers came together from many different parts of the organization in an informal three- to five-day meeting to discuss and solve problems. Gradually, the Work Out events began to include external stakeholders such as suppliers and customers as well as employees. Today, Work Out is not an event, but a process of how work is done and problems are solved at GE.

The format for Work Out includes seven steps:

1. Choose a work process or problem for discussion.
2. Select an appropriate cross-functional team (thirty to fifty people), which may also include external stakeholders.
3. Assign a "champion" to follow through on recommendations.
4. Meet for several days and come up with recommendations to improve work processes and solve problems.
5. Meet with leaders, who are required to respond to recommendations on the spot.
6. Hold additional meetings as needed to implement the recommendations.
7. Start the process all over again with a new process or problem.

GE's Work Out process not only solves problems and improves productivity for the company but also gives employees the experience of openly and honestly interacting with one another without regard to vertical or horizontal boundaries. By doing so, Work Out has helped to create what Welch calls a "culture of boundarylessness" that is critical for continuous learning and improvement.[60]

Large-group interventions are a powerful tool for leaders, and are a significant social innovation compared to earlier OD concepts and approaches. Exhibit 16.6 lists the primary differences between the traditional OD model and the large-group intervention model of organizational change.[61] In the newer approach, the focus is on the entire system, which takes the organization's interaction with its environment into account. The source of information is expanded to include shop floor workers, customers, suppliers, community members, even competitors, and this information is discussed widely so that everyone has the same picture of the organization and its environment. The acceleration of change when the entire system is involved in a single retreat can be remarkable. In addition, learning occurs across all parts of the organization simultaneously, rather than in individuals, small groups, or business units. The end result is that the large-group approach offers great possibilities for fundamental, radical transformation of the entire culture, whereas the traditional approach creates incremental change in a few individuals or small groups at a time.

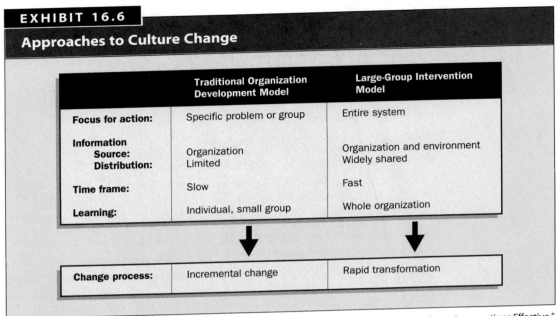

SOURCE: Adapted from Barbara Benedict Bunker and Billie T. Alban, "Conclusion: What Makes Large Group Interventions Effective," *The Journal of Applied Behavioral Science* 28, No. 4 (December 1992), 579–591. Used by permission of Sage Publications, Inc.

Large-group interventions represent a significant shift in the way leaders think about change and reflect an increasing awareness of the importance of including the entire organization in any significant change effort.

SUMMARY AND INTERPRETATION

The important point of this chapter is that tools and approaches are available to help leaders manage and create change. Change is inevitable in organizations, and the increased pace of change in today's global environment has created even greater problems for leaders. Despite the difficulties of major change, leaders can help ensure a successful change effort by following the eight-stage model of planned change—establish a sense of urgency; create a powerful coalition; develop a compelling vision and strategy; communicate the vision; empower employees to act; generate short-term wins; consolidate gains and tackle bigger problems; and institutionalize the change in the organizational culture. There are four types of planned change that can occur in organizations: strategy and structure changes, technology changes, product and service changes, and culture changes.

A critical aspect of leading change is understanding why people resist change and how to overcome resistance. Leaders use communication and training, participation and involvement, and—as a last resort—coercion to overcome resistance. Leaders should recognize that change can have negative as well as positive consequences. One of the most difficult situations leaders may face is downsizing. Leaders can use techniques to help ease the stress and hardship for employees who leave as well as maintain the morale and trust of those who remain.

Leaders are also responsible for moving the organization forward. One way is by creating an environment that nourishes creativity in particular departments or the entire organization. Six elements of creative organizations are alignment, self-initiated activity, unofficial activity, serendipity, diverse stimuli, and within-company communication. These correspond to characteristics of creative individuals. Creative people are less resistant to change. The success of any change depends on people, and all types of change involve organizational culture.

Two traditional ways leaders bring about culture change are total quality management and organizational development programs. TQM focuses on improving quality and productivity, but leads to culture change by getting employees to think about work and human relationships in new ways. Leaders use OD interventions to promote trust, open confrontation of problems, employee empowerment and participation, and the full use of employee potential. A new approach is large-group interventions that hold great promise for rapid transformation even in large organizations.

KEY TERMS

strategy and structure changes
technology changes
product and service changes
culture changes
personal compact

downsizing
creativity
total quality management
organizational development
large-group intervention

DISCUSSION QUESTIONS

1. Of the eight stages of planned change, which one do you think leaders are most likely to skip? Why?

2. What advice would you give a leader who perceives an urgent need for a bottom-up change in work technology versus a leader who perceives a need for new products?

3. Do you think creative individuals and creative organizations have characteristics in common? Discuss.

4. What advice would you give a leader who wants to increase creativity in her department?

5. Why do employees resist change? What are some ways leaders can overcome this resistance?

6. Discuss the primary differences between large-group interventions and the traditional organizational development approach to changing culture. Why is the new approach more applicable in today's world?

7. Planned change is often considered ideal. Do you think unplanned change could be effective? Discuss. Can you think of an example?

8. Is the world really changing faster today, or do people just assume so?

LEADERSHIP DEVELOPMENT: Personal Feedback

Are You a Change Leader?

Complete the following questions based on how you act in a typical leadership situation at work or school. For each item, circle the number that best describes you.

	Disagree				Agree
	1	2	3	4	5

1. I have a clear sense of mission for change, which I repeatedly describe to others.   1 2 3 4 5

2. I signal the value of a change and improvement with various symbols and statements.   1 2 3 4 5

3. One of my strengths is to encourage people to frequently express ideas and opinions that differ from my own.   1 2 3 4 5

4. I always celebrate the "effort" to improve things, even if the final outcome is disappointing.   1 2 3 4 5

5. I see my primary job as "inspiring" others toward improvement in their jobs.   1 2 3 4 5

6. Sometimes I use dramatic flourishes—a brainstorming session, stop work, go to an off-site—to signal an important change to people.   1 2 3 4 5

7. Often I take risks and let others take risks that could be a problem if the idea failed.   1 2 3 4 5

8. I spend time developing new ways of approaching old   1 2 3 4 5
problems.

9. I always believe the "effort" to improve something   1 2 3 4 5
should be rewarded, even if the final improvement is
disappointing.

10. I frequently compliment others on changes they have   1 2 3 4 5
made.

11. I am personally involved in several improvement   1 2 3 4 5
projects at one time.

12. I try to be a good listener and be patient with what   1 2 3 4 5
people suggest, even when it is a "stupid" idea.

13. I like to support change efforts, even when the idea   1 2 3 4 5
may not work.

14. I work at the politics of change to build agreement   1 2 3 4 5
for ideas for improvement.

15. I am able to get higher-ups to support ideas for   1 2 3 4 5
improvement.

Scoring and Interpretation

Add the numbers you circled for your total change leadership score. Your score indicates the extent to which you are a positive leader force for change. The questions represent behaviors associated with successful change leadership.

> 60-75: Great. A dynamo for leading change.
> 45-60: Good. A positive change leader.
> 30-45: Adequate. You have a typical attitude toward change.
> 15-30: Poor. You may be dragging down change efforts.

Go back over the questions on which you scored lowest and develop a plan to improve your approach toward change. Discuss your score and your ideas with other students.

LEADERSHIP DEVELOPMENT: Cases for Analysis

Southern Discomfort

Jim Malesckowski remembers the call of two weeks ago as if he just put down the telephone receiver: "I just read your analysis and I want you to get down to Mexico right away," Jack Ripon, his boss and chief executive officer, had blurted in his ear. "You know we can't make the plant in Oconomo work any more—the costs are just too high. So go down there, check out what our operational costs would be if we move, and report back to me in a week."

At that moment, Jim felt as if a shiv had been stuck in his side, just below the rib cage. As president of the Wisconsin Specialty Products Division of Lamprey, Inc., he knew quite well the challenge of dealing with high-cost labor in a third-generation, unionized U.S. manufacturing plant. And although he had done the analysis that led to his boss's knee-jerk response, the call still stunned him. There were 520 people who made a living at Lamprey's Oconomo facility, and if it closed, most of them wouldn't have a journeyman's prayer of finding another job in the town of 9,900 people.

Instead of the $16-per-hour average wage paid at the Oconomo plant, the wages paid to the Mexican workers—who lived in a town without sanitation and with an unbelievably toxic effluent from industrial pollution—would amount to about $1.60 an hour on average. That's a savings of nearly $15 million a year for Lamprey, to be offset in part by increased costs for training, transportation, and other matters.

After two days of talking with Mexican government representatives and managers of other companies in the town, Jim had enough information to develop a set of comparative figures of production and shipping costs. On the way home, he started to outline the report, knowing full well that unless some miracle occurred, he would be ushering in a blizzard of pink slips for people he had come to appreciate.

The plant in Oconomo had been in operation since 1921, making special apparel for persons suffering injuries and other medical conditions. Jim had often talked with employees who would recount stories about their fathers or grandfathers working in the same Lamprey company plant—the last of the original manufacturing operations in town.

But friendship aside, competitors had already edged past Lamprey in terms of price and were dangerously close to overtaking it in product quality. Although both Jim and the plant manager had tried to convince the union to accept lower wages, union leaders resisted. In fact, on one occasion when Jim and the plant manager tried to discuss a cell manufacturing approach, which would cross-train employees to perform up to three different jobs, local union leaders could barely restrain their anger. Yet probing beyond the fray, Jim sensed the fear that lurked under the union reps' gruff exterior. He sensed their vulnerability, but could not break through the reactionary bark that protected it.

A week has passed and Jim just submitted his report to his boss. Although he didn't specifically bring up the point, it was apparent that Lamprey could put its investment dollars in a bank and receive a better return than what its Oconomo operation is currently producing.

Tomorrow, he'll discuss the report with the CEO. Jim doesn't want to be responsible for the plant's dismantling, an act he personally believes would be wrong as long as there's a chance its costs can be lowered. "But Ripon's right," he says to himself. "The costs are too high, the union's unwilling to cooperate, and the company needs to make a better return on its investment if it's to continue at all. It sounds right but feels wrong. What should I do?"

SOURCE: Doug Wallace, "What Would You Do?" *Business Ethics,* March/April 1996, 52–53. Reprinted with permission from *Business Ethics,* P.O. Box 8439, Minneapolis, MN 55408. 612/879-0695.

Questions

1. If you were Jim Malesckowski, would you fight to save the plant? Why?

2. Assume you want to lead the change to save the plant. Describe how you would enact the eight stages outlined in Exhibit 16.2.

3. How would you overcome union leader resistance?

MediScribe Corporation

MediScribe provides medical transcription, insurance claims, and billing and collection services for doctors, clinics, and hospitals in south Florida. As a production supervisor, Ramona Fossett is responsible for the work of approximately 40 employees, 25 of whom are classified as data entry clerks. Fossett recently agreed to allow a team of outside consultants to come to her production area and make time and systems-analysis studies in an effort to improve efficiency and output. She had little choice but to do so—the president of the company had personally issued instructions that supervisors should cooperate with the consultants.

The consultants spent three days studying job descriptions, observing employees' daily tasks, and recording each detail of the work of the data entry clerks. After this period of observation, they told Fossett that they would begin more detailed studies and interviews on the following day.

The next morning, four data entry clerks were absent. On the following day, ten failed to show up for work. The leader of the systems analysis team explained to Fossett that, if there were as many absences the next day, his team would have to drop the study and move on to another department, as a valid analysis would be impossible with 10 out of 25 workers absent.

Fossett, who had only recently been promoted to the supervisor's position, knew that she'd be held responsible for the failure of the systems analysis. Concerned both for her employees and her own job, she telephoned several of the absent workers to find out what was going on. Each told approximately the same story, saying they were stressed out and exhausted after being treated like "guinea pigs" for three days.

One employee said she was planning to ask for a leave of absence if working conditions didn't improve.

At the end of the day, Fossett sat at her desk considering what could be done to provide the necessary conditions for completion of the study. In addition, she was greatly concerned about implementing the changes that she knew would be mandated after the consultants finished their work and presented their findings to the president. Considering how her employees had reacted to the study, Fosset doubted they would instantly comply with orders issued from the top as a result of the findings—and, again, she would be held responsible for the failure.

Questions

1. Why do you think employees are reacting in this way to the study?
2. How could leaders have handled this situation to get greater cooperation from employees?
3. If you were Ramona Fossett, what would you do now? What would you do to implement any changes recommended by the study?

SOURCE: Adapted from "Resistance to Change" in John M. Champion and John H. James, *Critical Incidents in Management: Decision and Policy Issues,* 6th ed. (Homewood, IL: Irwin, 1989), 230–231.

REFERENCES

1. Anna Muoio, "Mint Condition," *Fast Company,* December 1999, 330-348; and Carol Hildebrand, "The New Realm of the Coin," *CIO Enterprise,* Section 2, April 15, 1999, 54–64.
2. Marlene Piturro, "The Transformation Officer," *Management Review,* February 2000, 21–25.
3. Nicholas Imparato and Oren Harari, "When New Worlds Stir," *Management Review,* October 1994, 22–28.
4. Quoted in *Inc.* (March 1995), 13.
5. Megan Santosus, "The Organic Root System," *CIO,* December 15, 1998-January 1, 1999, 38–45.
6. Tim Carvell, "The Crazy Record Business: These Prices Really Are Insane," *Fortune,* August 4, 1997, 109–115.

7. George Stalk, Jr., "Time and Innovation," *Canadian Business Review,* Autumn 1993, 15–18.

8. David Dorsey, "Change Factory," *Fast Company,* June 2000, 210–224.

9. Eric Brynjolfsson, Amy Austin Renshaw, and Marshall Van Alstyne, "The Matrix of Change," *Sloan Management Review,* Winter 1997, 37–54.

10. David Whitford, "Sale of the Century," *Fortune,* February 17, 1997, 92-100.

11. Jenny C. McCune, "The Change Makers," *Management Review,* May 1999, 16–22.

12. Ibid.

13. Sumantra Ghoshal and Christopher A. Bartlett, "Rebuilding Behavioral Context: A Blueprint for Corporate Renewal," *Sloan Management Review,* Winter 1996, 23–36.

14. The following discussion is based heavily on John P. Kotter, *Leading Change* (Boston: Harvard Business School Press, 1996), 20–25; and "Leading Change: Why Transformation Efforts Fail," *Harvard Business Review,* March-April 1995, 59–67.

15. Patrick Flanagan, "The ABCs of Changing Corporate Culture," *Management Review,* July 1995, 57–61.

16. Noel M. Tichy and Mary Anne Devanna, *The Transformational Leader,* (New York: John Wiley & Sons, 1986), 122, 124; Charles Pappas, "The Top 20 Best-Paid Women in Corporate America," *Working Woman,* February 1998, 26–39.

17. Jeremy Main, "The Shape of the New Corporation," *Working Woman,* October 1998, 60–63.

18. McCune, "The Change Makers."

19. Muoio, "Mint Condition."

20. Kotter, "Leading Change: Why Transformation Efforts Fail," 65.

21. Richard Teitelbaum, "How to Harness Gray Matter," *Fortune,* June 9, 1997, 168.

22. Alex Taylor III, "Kellogg Cranks Up Its Idea Machine," *Fortune,* June 5, 1999, 181–182.

23. Oren Harari, "Leading Change From the Middle," *Management Review,* February 1999, 29–32.

24. Based on Paul Stebel, "Why Do Employees Resist Change?" *Harvard Business Review,* May-June 1996, 86–92.

25. John P. Kotter and Leonard A. Schlesinger, "Choosing Strategies for Change," *Harvard Business Review,* March-April 1979, 106–114.

26. Gregory A. Patterson, "Lands' End Kicks Out Modern New Managers, Rejecting a Makeover," *The Wall Street Journal,* April 3, 1995, A1, A6.

27. Peter Richardson and D. Keith Denton, "Communicating Change," *Human Resource Management* 35, No. 2 (Summer 1996), 203–216.

28. T. J. Larkin and Sandar Larkin, "Reaching and Changing Frontline Employees," *Harvard Business Review,* May-June 1996, 95–104; and Rob Muller, "Training for Change," *Canadian Business Review,* Spring 1995, 16–19.

29. Phillip H. Mirvis, Amy L. Sales, and Edward J. Hackett, "The Implementation and Adoption of New Technology in Organizations: The Impact of Work, People, and Culture," *Human Resource Management* 30 (Spring 1991), 113–139.

30. Robert Goffee and Gareth Jones, "Why Should Anyone Be Led By You?" *Harvard Business Review,* September-October 2000, 63–70.

31. William McKinley, Carol M. Sanchez, and Allen G. Schick, "Organizational Downsizing: Constraining, Cloning, Learning," *Academy of Management Executive* 9, No. 3 (1995), 32–42.

32. Gregory B. Northcraft and Margaret A. Neale, *Organizational Behavior: A Management Challenge*, 2nd ed. (Fort Worth: The Dryden Press, 1994), 626.

33. A. Catherine Higgs, "Executive Commentary" on McKinley, Sanchez, and Schick, "Organizational Downsizing: Constraining, Cloning, Learning," *Academy of Management Executive* 9, No. 3 (1995), 43–44.

34. Hilary Stout, "Techies.Com Changes Its Corporate Culture, Reviving Hope for IPO," *The Wall Street Journal*, September 6, 2000, B1.

35. James R. Morris, Wayne F. Cascio, and Clifford E. Young, "Downsizing After All These Years: Questions and Answers About Who Did It, How Many Did It, and Who Benefitted From It," *Organizational Dynamics*, Winter 1999, 78–86.

36. Morris, Cascio, and Young, "Downsizing After All These Years"; McKinley, Sanchez, and Schick, "Organizational Downsizing"; Stephen Doerflein and James Atsaides, "Corporate Psychology: Making Downsizing Work," *Electrical World* September-October 1999, 41–43; and Brett C. Luthans and Steven M. Sommer, "The Impact of Downsizing on Workplace Attitudes," *Group & Organization Management* 2, No. 1 (1999), 46–70.

37. K. S. Cameron, S. J. Freeman, and A. K. Mishra, "Downsizing and Redesigning Organizations," in G. P. Huber and W. H. Glick, eds., *Organizational Change and Redesign* (New York: Oxford University Press, 1993), 19–63.

38. This section is based on Bob Nelson, "The Care of the Un-downsized," *Training and Development,* April 1997, 40–43; Shari Caudron, "Teach Downsizing Survivors How to Thrive," *Personnel Journal,* January 1996, 38ff; Joel Brockner, "Managing the Effects of Layoffs on Survivors," *California Management Review,* Winter 1992, 9–28; Ronald Henkoff, "Getting Beyond Downsizing," *Fortune,* January 10, 1994, 58–64; Kim S. Cameron, "Strategies for Successful Organizational Downsizing," *Human Resource Management* 33, No. 2 (Summer 1994): 189–211; and Stephen Doerflein and James Atsaides, "Corporate Psychology: Making Downsizing Work."

39. Caudron, "Teach Downsizing Survivors How to Thrive."

40. Ibid.

41. Stanley S. Gryskiewicz, "Cashing In On Creativity at Work," *Psychology Today,* September-October 2000, 63–66.

42. Timothy A. Matherly and Ronald E. Goldsmith, "The Two Faces of Creativity," *Business Horizons,* September/October 1985, 8.

43. The elements of creative organizations come from Alan G. Robinson and Sam Stern, *Corporate Creativity: How Innovation and Improvement Actually Happen* (San Francisco: Berrett-Koehler, 1997).

44. Robinson and Stern, *Corporate Creativity,* 14.

45. Gail Dutton, "Enhancing Creativity," *Management Review,* November 1996, 44–46.

46. Robinson and Stern, *Corporate Creativity,* 192.

47. Erika Germer, "When This Dog Barks, Customers Byte," *Fast Company,* November 2000, 64.

48. Gryskiewicz, "Cashing In On Creativity."

49. Cameron M. Ford, "Creativity Is a Mystery: Clues from the Investigators' Notebooks," in Cameron M. Ford and Dennis A. Gioia, eds., *Creative Action in Organizations: Ivory Tower Visions & Real World Voices* (Thousand Oaks, CA: Sage Publications, 1995), 12–49.

50. Gary Abramson, "Wiring the Corporate Brain," *CIO Enterprise,* Section 2, March 15, 1999, 30–36.

51. Cheryl Dahle, "Mind Games," *Fast Company,* January-February 2000, 169–180.

52. This section is based on Donald F. Kuratko and Richard M. Hodgetts, *Entrepreneurship: A Contemporary Approach* (Fort Worth: The Dryden Press, 1998), 125–127.

53. Magaly Olivero, "Some Wacko Ideas That Worked," *Working Woman,* September 1990, 147–148.

54. Michael Hammer, *The Reengineering Revolution* (quoted in Anne Fisher, "Making Change Stick," *Fortune,* April 17, 1995, 122).

55. Quoted in Gary Abramson, "From the Ashes," *CIO,* December 15, 1998–January 1, 1999, 57–64.

56. Benson L. Porter and Warrington S. Parker, Jr., "Culture Change," *Human Resource Management* 31 (Spring/Summer 1992), 45–67.

57. M. Sashkin and W. W. Burke, "Organizational Development in the 1980s," *General Management* 13 (1987), 393-417; and Richard Beckhard, "What is Organization Development?" in *Organization Development and Transformation: Managing Effective Change,* Wendell L. French, Cecil H. Bell, Jr., and Robert A. Zawacki, eds. (Burr Ridge, Illinois: Irwin McGraw Hill, 2000), 16–19.

58. W. Warner Burke, "The New Agenda for Organization Development," in French, Bell, and Zawacki, eds., *Organization Development and Transformation,* 523-535; and Wendell L. French and Cecil H. Bell, Jr., "A History of Organizational Development," in French, Bell, and Zawacki, eds., *Organization Development and Transformation,* 20–42.

59. This discussion is based on Kathleen D. Dannemiller and Robert W. Jacobs, "Changing the Way Organizations Change: A Revolution of Common Sense," *The Journal of Applied Behavioral Science* 28, No. 4 (December 1992), 480–498; and Barbara Benedict Bunker and Billie T. Alban, "Conclusion: What Makes Large Group Interventions Effective?" *The Journal of Applied Behavioral Science* 28, No. 4 (December 1992), 570–591.

60. Judy Quinn, "What a Work-Out!" *Performance* (November 1994), 58–63; Bunker and Alban, "Conclusion: What Makes Large Group Interventions Effective?"; and Brian R. Strohmeier, "The Leadership Principles Used by Jack Welch as He Re-energized, Revolutionized, and Reshaped General Electric," *The Journal of Leadership Studies* 5, No. 2 (1998), 16–26.

61. Bunker and Alban, "Conclusion: What Makes Large Group Interventions Effective?"

Index

Company Index

Subject Index

P. 263 Leadership Development: Personal Feedback
From *The Power of Fellowship*, by Robert E. Kelley. Copyright © 1992 by Consultants to Executives and Organizations, Ltd. Used by permission of Doubleday, a division of Random House, Inc.

Exhibit 8.2
From *Motivation and Leadership at Work*, 6th edition, by Richard M. Steers, Lyman W. Porter and Gregory A. Bigley, p. 498. Copyright © 1996. Reprinted by permission of The McGraw-Hill Companies.

P. 292 Living Leadership
From "An Academy Classic: On the Folly of Rewarding A, While Hoping for B," and "More on the Folly," *Academy of Management Executive*, 9, No. 1 (1995), 7–16. Reprinted by permission of Copyright Clearance Center, Inc. on behalf of the publisher, Academy of Management Executive.

Exhibit 8.8
Excerpt from "How We Went Digital without a Strategy," by Ricardo Semler. *Harvard Business Review* (September-October 2000), pp. 51–58. Copyright © 2000 by the Harvard Business School Publishing Corporation. Reprinted by permission of Harvard Business Review

P. 304 Leadership Development: Personal Feedback
From *Development Management Skills*, 2/e by D. Whetten and C. Cameron, pp. 336–337. Copyright © 1998. Reprinted by permission of Pearson Education, Inc., Upper Saddle River, NJ 07458.

P. 306 Case for Analysis
"The Parlor," from *Contemporary Incidents in Management*, by Bernard A. Deitzer and Karl A. Schillif, pp. 167–168. Copyright © 1977 Grid, Inc. This material is used by permission of Jossey-Bass, Inc., a subsidiary of John Wiley & Sons, Inc.

P. 329 Living Leadership
From *Zen Lessons: The Art of Leadership*, translated by Thomas Cleary, © 1989 by Thomas Cleary, pp. 83–84. Reprinted by arrangement with Shambhala Publications, Inc., Boston, ww.shambhala.com.

Exhibit 10.6
Adapted from "Conflict and Conflict Management," by Kenneth Thomas, in *Handbook of Industrial and Organizational Behavior*, ed. M.D. Dunnette. New York: John Wiley, 1976, 900. Used by permission of Marvin D. Dunnette.

P. 385 Case for Analysis
"Valena Scientific Corporation," from *Organization Theory and Design*, 5th edition, by Richard L. Daft. Copyright © 1995. Reprinted with permission of South-Western College Publishing, a division of Thomson Learning. Fax 800/730-2215.

Exhibit 11.1
From *Implementing Diversity*, by Marilyn Loden. Copyright © 1996. Reprinted by permission of The McGraw-Hill Companies.

Exhibit 11.4
From *America's Competitive*, Secret by Judy Rosener, p. 142. Copyright © 1995 by Oxford University Press, Inc. Used by permission of Oxford University Press, Inc.

P. 421 Living Leadership
From *Zen Lessons: The Art of Leadership*, translated by Thomas Cleary. Copyright © 1989 by Thomas Cleary, pp. 45–46. Reprinted by arrangement with Shambhala Publications, Inc., Boston, ww.shambhala.com.

P. 426 Leadership Development: Personal Feedback
Adapted *from Proversity: Getting Past Face Values and Finding the Soul of People*, by Lawrence Otis Grahm, John Wiley & Sons, 1997. Used with permission of Lawrence Otis Graham.

P. 429 Case for Analysis
"Trouble with Bangles," from *Effective Behavior in Organizations: Cases, Concepts, and Student Experiences*, 7th edition, by Allan R. Cohen, Stephen L. Fink, Herman Gadon and Robin D. Willits, pp. 413–414. Copyright © 2001. Reprinted by permission of The McGraw-Hill Companies.

P. 446 Leader's Bookshelf
Reprinted from *The Nine Natural Laws of Leadership*. Copyright © 1995 Warren Blank. Published by AMACOM, a division of American Management Association International, New York, NY. Used with permission. All rights reserved. http://www.amacombooks.org.

P. 443 Living Leadership
From *The Tao of Leadership: Leadership Strategies for a New Age*, by John Heider. New York: Bantam Books, 1986, 3. Copyright © 1985 Humanic Ltd., Atlanta, GA. Used with permission.

P. 478 Living Leadership
From *The Book of Qualities*, by J. Ruth Gendler. New York: Harper & Row, 1988. Used with permission.

Exhibit 3.14
From Fast Company, April-May 1996.

Exhibit 14.2
From *Corporate Culture and Performance by*, John P. Kotter and James L. Heskett. Copyright © 1992 by Kotter Associates, Inc. and James L. Heskett. Reprinted with the permission of The Free Press, a Division of Simon & Schuster, Inc.

P. 529 Living Leadership
From *The Tao of Leadership: Leadership Strategies for a New Age*, by John Heider. New York: Bantam Books, 1986, 3. Copyright © 1985 Humanic Ltd., Atlanta, GA. Used with permission.

Exhibit 15.1
From *Fusion Leadership: Unlocking the Subtle Forces That Change People and Organizations*, by Richard L. Daft and Robert H. Lengel. Copyright © 1998 by Richard L. Daft and Robert H. Lengel, Berrett-Koehler Publishers, Inc., San Francisco, CA. Reprinted with permission of the publisher. All rights reserved. www.bkconnection.com.

Exhibit 15.3
From "The Myth of the Horizontal Organization," by George Stalk, Jr. and Jill E. Black, *Canadian Business Review*, Winter 1994, pp. 26–31. Reprinted by permission of the author.

P. 569 Leadership Development: Personal Feedback
"How Resilient Are You?" adapted from *The Survivor Personality*, by Al Siebert, Ph.D. An explanation of the items can be found at Al Siebert's THRIVEnet website: http://www.thrivenet.com. Reprinted by permission.

Exhibit 16.1
From *The New Rules: How to Succeed in Today's Post-Corporate World*, by John P. Kotter. Copyright © 1995 by John P. Kotter. Adapted with the permission of The Free Press, a Division of Simon & Schuster, Inc.

P. 609 Case for Analysis
"Southern Discomfort," from "What Would You Do?" by Doug Wallace from *Business Ethics*, March/April 1996, pp. 52–53. Reprinted with permission from *Business Ethics*, P.O. Box 8439, Minneapolis, MN 55408, 612/879-0695.

P. 611 Case for Analysis
"MediScribe Corporation," From *Critical Incidents in Management: Decision and Policy Issues*, 6th edition, by John M. Champion and John H. James, pp. 230–231. Copyright © 1989. Reprinted by permission of The McGraw-Hill Companies, Inc.